ARMY LINEAGE SERIES

INFANTRY

Part I:

Regular Army

by

John K. Mahon

and

Romana Danysh

MILITARY INSTRVCTION

OFFICE OF THE CHIEF OF MILITARY HISTORY
UNITED STATES ARMY
WASHINGTON, D.C., 1972

Library of Congress Catalog Card Number: 74–610219

First Printing

For sale by the Superintendent of Documents, U.S. Government Printing Office
Washington, D.C. 20402 – Price: $9.75
Stock Number 0829–0082

ARMY LINEAGE SERIES

Maurice Matloff, General Editor

Advisory Committee
(As of 15 April 1971)

Walter C. Langsam
University of Cincinnati

Richard W. Leopold
Northwestern University

Maj. Gen. Edward Bautz, Jr.
U.S. Continental Army Command

Brig. Gen. Wallace C. Magathan, Jr.
U.S. Army War College

Charles B. Burdick
San Jose State College

Louis Morton
Dartmouth College

Brig. Gen. James M. Gibson
U.S. Army Command and General
Staff College

Forrest C. Pogue
George C. Marshall Research
Foundation

Col. Thomas E. Griess
United States Military Academy

Frank E. Vandiver
Rice University

Office of the Chief of Military History

Brig. Gen. James L. Collins, Jr., Chief of Military History

Chief Historian	Maurice Matloff
Chief, Historical Services Division	Col. Robert H. Fechtman
Chief, Histories Division	Col. John E. Jessup, Jr.
Editor in Chief	Joseph R. Friedman

III

Foreword

In all of the major wars of the United States from the American Revolution through the conflict in Southeast Asia the dominant combat arm of the United States Army has been the infantry. It was natural therefore in producing an Army Lineage Series to devote the first published volume to that arm. Appearing in 1953, the first infantry lineage book has long been out of print, and subsequent organizational developments have amply warranted a revised and enlarged edition and its publication in more durable form. As explained in the Preface, *Infantry* is now to appear in two parts, this one with Regular Army and the one to come with Army National Guard and Army Reserve lineages and heraldic data; the historical narrative on the branch is to be included in both. In addition to the second parts of this work and of the *Armor-Cavalry* volume, other volumes on artillery and on divisions and separate brigades are now being prepared.

The Army Lineage Series is designed to foster the *esprit de corps* of United States Army units, and within the Army it is intended for use at all levels of command, in service schools, and in training programs. The short history of the infantry that precedes the lineages in this volume is an illuminating and thoroughly researched survey that should appeal to everyone interested in military history.

Washington, D.C.
15 April 1971

JAMES L. COLLINS, JR.
Brigadier General, USA
Chief of Military History

v

The Authors

John K. Mahon received the B.A. degree from Swarthmore College in 1934 and the Ph.D. degree in history from the University of California, Los Angeles, in 1950. He served with the Army on active duty from 1942 to 1946 and as a civilian historian in the Office of the Chief of Military History from 1951 to 1954. A professor of history at the University of Florida since 1954 and Chairman of the Department of History since 1965, he is author of works on the early militia and of *History of the Second Seminole War, 1835–1842*.

Romana Danysh graduated from Barnard College in 1962 and received the M.A. degree in history from Stanford University in 1963. Since 1964 she has served as a historian in the Organizational History Branch of the Office of the Chief of Military History.

Preface

Infantry are those troops that fight on foot and that rely chiefly upon the small arms carried by individuals. This volume on infantry in the United States Army deals with the organization of foot units at the level of regiments and below. Infantry brigades and divisions will be covered in a subsequent volume in the Army Lineage Series.

Although the narrative portion discusses infantry in the reserve components as well as in the Regular Army, this volume (Part I) includes lineages only for Regular Army parent regiments organized under the Combat Arms Regimental System (CARS) and for those of their elements that have been active since the establishment of CARS. Army National Guard and Army Reserve infantry lineages will be published in the near future in a separate volume (Part II), because infantry units of all three components are far too numerous to be included in one book. Lineages for Army Reserve elements of Regular Army parent regiments which appear in this volume will be reprinted in the second part, so that a complete set of reserve infantry lineages will be available in that volume.

In the first edition of this book, published in 1953, the narrative ended with World War II and most of the lineages were carried only to the outbreak of the Korean War. Since that time several major reorganizations and the adoption of CARS have significantly changed infantry organization, while many infantry units have earned additional honors in Korea and Vietnam. In the present volume, the narrative has been brought up to date through 31 December 1969 and the lineages through 31 December 1970. Only those Vietnam campaign participation credits that have been confirmed in Department of the Army General Orders are listed, but all unit decorations reported up to the time the book went to the printer are included.

The 1953 edition was prepared by Dr. Mahon, and his narrative from the American Revolution through World War II is reprinted in this volume with only minor changes. Miss Danysh wrote the narrative from 1945 to the end and selected the illustrations to accompany the text. The Organizational History Branch (OHB) of the Office of the Chief of Military History (OCMH) is responsible for the determination of official unit lineages and honors. The lineages which appear in this volume are the result of research done by many members of OHB, past and present. Miss Danysh brought all the lineages up to date and added the Vietnam honors.

Descriptions of coats of arms, historic badges, distinctive insignia, and other heraldic items approved for infantry regiments are included with the lineages. These descriptions as well as the color illustrations of the heraldic items were furnished by the Institute of Heraldry, U.S. Army. The authors are particularly grateful to Dr. Opal V. Landrum, Miss Ellen Bantz, and Mr. Charles A. Reynolds.

Miss Janice E. McKenney of OHB compiled the unit bibliographies with the assistance of Mr. Charles E. Dornbusch's comprehensive bibliography entitled *Histories, Personal Narratives, United States Army* (Cornwallville, New York: Hope Farm Press, 1967). Most of the unit histories cited are unofficial works that were prepared outside the Department of the Army. They are, nevertheless, valuable sources of additional information about the units.

The authors want to thank Brig. Gen. Hal C. Pattison, who as Chief of Military History took a personal interest in the publication of this volume and generously shared his broad professional knowledge and experience. All members of the OCMH review panel for the revised edition (Dr. Stetson Conn, then Chief Historian, chairman; Mr. Joseph R. Friedman, Editor in Chief; Col. Robert H. Fechtman, Chief, Historical Services Division; Mr. John W. Wike, Deputy Chief, Historical Services Division; Mrs. Mary Lee Stubbs, Chief, OHB; Mr. Stanley Russell Connor, Deputy Chief, OHB; and Dr. Ernest F. Fisher, Jr., General History Branch) were most helpful, and their constructive criticism of the draft improved the final product considerably.

Special thanks are given to Dr. Conn, who took time from a very busy schedule to make valuable oral and written comments, and to Mrs. Stubbs and Mr. Connor, coauthors of the *Armor-Cavalry* volume, published in 1969 in the Army Lineage Series. In addition to reviewing the narrative, Mrs. Stubbs provided guidance and inspiration for the entire revision project, while Mr. Connor carefully read draft after draft and made numerous excellent suggestions.

Helpful comments and suggestions were also made by Col.

x

Wolfred K. White, formerly Chief, Histories Division; Mr. Charles B. MacDonald, Chief, Current History Branch; Mr. John B. Wilson, OHB; Col. S. B. Sightler, Jr., USA, Retired; and the United States Army Infantry School. The manuscript was edited by Mr. David Jaffé, Chief of the Editorial Branch, assisted by Mr. Bernard F. Halloran and Miss Christine A. Otten. We owe our thanks, too, to Mrs. Corinna L. Swan and Miss Maxine L. Pressley for expertly typing and retyping countless pages without losing their sense of humor.

Many others contributed to the completion of this volume by their knowledge, advice, co-operation, and encouragement—and to all of them we are sincerely grateful. For any and all errors in the narrative and in the lineages the authors alone are responsible.

Washington, D.C.   JOHN K. MAHON
15 April 1971   ROMANA DANYSH

Contents

Chart

Illustrations

All illustrations are from the files of the Department of Defense except the picture on page 46, which was furnished by the National Archives and Records Service.

INFANTRY:

REGULAR ARMY

425-618 O - 72 - 2

History of the Organization
of the Infantry

The Era of Revolution

When Congress, on 14 June 1775, moved to take over the New England Army then besieging Boston as a Continental establishment, it also authorized ten companies of riflemen to be raised in Pennsylvania, Maryland, and Virginia as part of the new Continental Army. The next day, Congress appointed George Washington its Commander in Chief. Before leaving their home state, the six rifle companies from Pennsylvania were combined to form William Thompson's Rifle Battalion. This battalion and the other new rifle units organized rapidly and marched quickly to Boston.

The New England Army around Boston was composed of citizen soldiers. From the earliest times that type of soldier (male members of the community aged 18–45) had been required to associate in military organizations called "militia," and to train to defend his own locality. The militia system amounted to universal military training for men of active ages, but it was for local defense almost entirely. What is more, its enforcement rested altogether with the colonies. At the outbreak of the Revolution, all the colonies had military organizations operating, but their effectiveness was, in many cases, slight. It was the general ineffectiveness of the militia system, coupled with the need for centralized control, that brought about the creation of the Continental Army. Even so, on account of the militia, the colonies were able to utilize the experience of many veterans of England's colonial wars, familiar with the British Army and with the Indian modes of fighting it. These veterans were a very valuable asset.

In addition to the rifle units and the besieging army, Congress later authorized the raising and maintaining of Continental infantry battalions in the southern states. By December 1775 there were forty-nine infantry battalions (or regiments, for the two terms were virtually synonymous) and several unattached companies in the establishment.

The Continental Congress took the bulk of the army besieging Boston in 1775 as it found it. Since most of the units were enlisted only for the calendar year, General Washington had either to attempt to re-enlist the soldiers already in service or to assemble a new army. During the fall of 1775, he strove to retain the Continental troops for the duration of the war, but was only successful in keeping part of them, and those for just one more year. A canvass of the officers of thirty-nine regiments in November showed that 751 officers were willing to continue their service for one year while 406 were not.

The legislators set the size of the army around Boston at 20,372 officers and men, to be organized into twenty-seven regiments and some separate companies. In this scheme New England, which had supplied forty-two in 1775, provided twenty-six Continental regiments in 1776. These twenty-six were numbered from the 2d through the 27th. They were designated Continental infantry in an attempt to transfer the men's loyalty from the states to the Congress.

The 1st Continental did not come from New England, but was built around the nine companies of riflemen then in William Thompson's Pennsylvania Rifle Battalion. Six of those companies were among the original units of the Continental Army, while the other three joined up later. All lost their specialization as rifle companies and the "regiment" became a standard element of the line.

Diverse units entered the Continental service, until by December 1776 there were eighty-two battalions of foot soldiers in all. During the year 1776 the following new units of battalion size were added to the establishment:

> John Haslet's Delaware Regiment
> James Livingston's Regiment, known as the 1st Canadian.
> Moses Hazen's Regiment, known as the 2d Canadian, also as Congress' Own. (The two Canadian regiments contained about equal numbers of Canadians and New Englanders, but in January 1781 all foreigners in the service were transferred to Hazen's.)
> Seth Warner's Regiment, officered by men who had participated in the invasion of Canada in 1775 and filled in part by Green Mountain Boys.
> Samuel Miles' Pennsylvania Rifle Regiment
> 2d–12th Pennsylvania
> 1st–3d Georgia
> 1st–3d New Jersey
> 1st–9th Virginia
> William Smallwood's Maryland Regiment

Charles Burrall's Connecticut Regiment
Samuel Elmore's Connecticut Regiment
Andrew Ward's Connecticut Regiment
The German Battalion

Their officers were appointed by Congress upon the recommendation of the Commander in Chief.

Late in 1776 it was once again necessary to cope with the dissolution of the army, but this time Congress took a new tack. It attempted to create a force to serve "during the present war." The legislators, observing the size of the army in being, set the new establishment at eighty-eight battalions, and apportioned these among all the states, so that Massachusetts had to provide the greatest number, fifteen, and Delaware and Georgia the smallest, one apiece. The eighty-eight battalions thus authorized were raised, equipped, and officered by the states. They were no longer known by Continental numbers, but carried instead numbers in the several state organizations. These state organizations were called "lines," the term used then for the regular infantry or "foot" that made up the line of battle of an army. The state lines together comprised the Continental Line. These should not be confused with the occasional state regiments which were raised on a permanent basis for local service only.

Although the regiments of the several states, arranged in the Continental Line, replaced the numbered regiments of 1776 (for example, the 9th Continental of 1776 became the 1st Regiment of the Rhode Island Line in 1777), the change was mostly one of name. The relationship of regiments to states remained about as it had been, and the appointment of officers continued to be in practice a collaboration between Congress, the Commander in Chief, and the states. Some of the Continental regiments became units in the state lines, while the men and officers of others transferred to the new regiments of 1777 without carrying the lineages of their 1776 outfits with them. The reorganization of the winter of 1776 did not radically alter the way men came into the Continental service or the manner in which regiments were organized, but it did place responsibility for procurement, replacement, and supply more squarely upon the states. This stimulated an increased effort in some states: for example, Massachusetts and Connecticut (although later overruled by Congress) voted to supplement the Continental pay of their lines.

In December 1776, while the reorganization of the American Army was taking place, the British advanced into New Jersey. Faced with this threat, Congress authorized Washington to add sixteen purely Continental battalions to the foot establishment. This action resulted in part from the fact that the states had been unutterably slow in supplying their quotas for the eighty-eight line battalions. The term of service of the new sixteen was the same as that of the state lines, for three years or for the duration, but the similarity ended there. Washington raised them wherever he could, and appointed all their officers himself. The new Continental regiments were usually recruited within one state and, like all other units, had a hard struggle to reach full strength.

The organization established late in 1776 and early in 1777—containing as it did the state lines coupled with the sixteen additional Continental battalions—was a compromise between two needs. The first need was to utilize the powerful authority of the states, without which the conflict could not be prosecuted; the second was to have at least some regiments subject only to the will of the Commander in Chief.

All regiments sent out their own recruiting parties to prescribed areas, but to keep the fighting army up to strength was almost an impossible job. In consequence, during 1780, when the theater of war had moved south, Washington had not enough troops to act against the enemy with the part of the army that he commanded in person. Indeed, Congress found it necessary to consolidate the sixteen additional Continentals with the state lines, and, at the same time, to fuse the separate corps and the German Battalion into them too. More important, the infantry of the entire Continental establishment was reduced to fifty battalions by 1 January 1781. Such a reduction of the infantry was not dictated by strategy. On the contrary, it was the result of a grave failure, the failure to be able to maintain a larger number of regiments.

As in previous years, new units appeared in the roster of the Continental Army during the four years beginning with 1777. They were often the result of the reorganization of earlier outfits. From various sources came the following units:

> 1st–15th Massachusetts
> 5th New York
> 1st–6th Maryland
> 4th New Jersey
> 7th–10th North Carolina
> 10th–15th Virginia
> The Corps of Invalids

These regiments and those in the preceding list made up the spine of the Army after 1776. They were not static; indeed some of the early ones provided elements of the others. Moreover, they supplied companies to special corps such as the legions of Henry Lee and Casimir Pulaski and the Corps of Light Infantry.

An understanding of the internal organization of the Continental

MAJ. GEN. FRIEDRICH WILHELM VON STEUBEN *training American soldiers at Valley Forge.*

infantry regiments and their components requires a short explanation of infantry tactics in the eighteenth century. To begin with, the heart of a battle as fought in western Europe was the line of infantry. It was this line which had to be broken if victory were to be won; hence the heavy fire of the artillery and the maneuvers of the cavalry were chiefly directed against it. It was common in Europe for the battle line to be formed on an open plain just outside of effective artillery range of the enemy. This meant that the two lines took their positions within 500 yards of each other, a distance at which, with modern firearms, few men would be left standing. This is the fact which makes it hardest for moderns to visualize early warfare. The effective range of the musket of the period was not over 100 yards and was often nearer 50. Fighting at such ranges, infantry organization was founded upon the need to form the line, control it in battle, renew it when decimated, and maneuver it so as to place the enemy at a disadvantage. But this was not the beginning and the end of infantry tactics, particularly in the rough, wooded terrain of North America.

In the colonial wars of the eighteenth century, the need had grown for infantrymen to precede the battle line. Their purpose was to screen the advance or retreat of their own main body, to break up the power of the volley from the enemy's line, and otherwise to soften that line for an assault with bayonets. Such an assault commonly began at a distance of fifty yards or less from the foe. As a result, one of two things took place: either a savage hand-to-hand encounter, or a collapse and retreat by one of the lines. In any case, the infantrymen who moved out ahead of the line were trained to aim at individuals, to protect themselves by using cover, and to operate with an interval of several yards between them. They came to be called "light infantry." In contrast to their action, the line fired by volley without taking individual aim, remained standing unless ordered to do otherwise, and advanced with the men in it actually elbow to elbow up to the moment of the assault.

In the American service, as in the British, battalions and regiments were usually one and the same. An English regiment had ten companies in it, eight of them (the "battalion companies") for the line, the other two for special uses. These were the elite or "flank companies." One called the "grenadier company" was composed of men picked for their strength and courage. As often as not (for instance, at Bunker Hill) the grenadier companies were detached from their regiments and used together in provisional grenadier battalions. These were given the most difficult assignments, and the posts of honor (that is, of greatest danger) if used in the battle line.

The tenth company in a British battalion was called the "light company." Light companies were also detached and consolidated into provisional battalions, but as often they were assigned a truly light mission, that is, to advance ahead of the line, screen it, and demoralize the enemy. This mission of light infantry in the American service was usually performed by rifle units, which fanned out in front of the army and, with their accurate fire, galled the enemy severely.

At first there was no counterpart to flank companies in the Continental infantry. Beginning in August 1777, however, General Washington directed that 108 men and 9 officers be drawn from each brigade and formed into a temporary Corps of Light Infantry. When winter came this corps was disbanded, but it had proved so useful that Washington urged Congress to authorize one light company for each battalion to be formed into a separate corps during every campaign thereafter. It was with the Light Corps, which resulted, that Anthony Wayne stormed Stony Point on 16 July 1779 in the most celebrated night attack made by Americans during the Revolution.

Like the British Grenadiers, the American Corps of Light Infantry became the elite body of the Army. Command was eagerly sought in it by the most enterprising officers and places in the ranks by the men. Although the Corps as a whole continued to be disbanded each winter and raised afresh for every campaign, one light company became permanent in each Continental battalion after mid-1780. Prior to that time American battalions had contained only eight companies, those of the line, so that the addition brought the total up to nine, still one short of the British. The Corps of Light Infantry received special training in the use of the bayonet. During July 1780 it was put under the command of Lafayette, and made the chief American assaults the following year upon the enemy's works at Yorktown.

One of the distinctive features about the Revolutionary War was the use of rifles and rifle units in it. The rifle was virtually unknown in the New England Army that opened the war. Indeed, throughout the conflict, muskets were the armament of the troops of the line. At 100 yards, the best musketeers could hit a man-sized target only four shots out of every ten. In contrast, expert riflemen could kill a man with every shot at 100 yards and do good execution at twice that range. The chief limitations on the use of riflemen were the scarcity of expert shots and the fact that the rifle could not carry a bayonet. Although the latter deficiency was somewhat overcome through the use of tomahawks and knives, riflemen remained vulnerable to a determined bayonet attack. Accordingly, riflemen were not useful in the line, but both sides made extensive use of them as sharpshooters ahead of and around the main fighting force.

As already mentioned, the rifle companies from Pennsylvania in William Thompson's Battalion soon lost their specialization and became an element of the line, armed with muskets. Nearly as short-lived as a rifle unit was the Maryland and Virginia Rifle Regiment, composed of the original Continental rifle companies from Maryland and Virginia plus some later ones from the same states. This unit was captured at Fort Washington on 16 November 1776 and was never re-formed. Just at the time of its capture, Daniel Morgan received a commission as Colonel of the 11th Virginia. He recruited 118 riflemen and joined the Continental Army with them at Morristown, New Jersey, early in April 1777. Very soon Washington drew 500 picked riflemen from the regiments of his Army and put them under Morgan's command. Thus began the most famous of the rifle corps which persisted intermittently throughout the Revolution.

Sometimes Washington referred to Morgan's unit as a rifle corps, sometimes as "rangers." The latter term requires a little elaboration. Rangers were a species of infantry that the British had developed to cope with the methods of the French and Indians in North America. They were scouts who ranged the forests spying upon the enemy, gathering intelligence on his strength and intentions, and harassing him when they could. Units of rangers had to be made up of men who understood woodcraft and who could match the Indians in stealth. Also, they had to be trained shots. Actually, corps like Daniel Morgan's were rangers a

INFANTRY OFFICER *(right)* AND
ARTILLERY SERGEANT *with state in-*
fantry lines in background, 1781.

good deal of the time. In addition, there were certain units,
such as Thomas Knowlton's Connecticut Rangers, which regularly
bore the title.

From time to time the size of
Continental units was fixed by
resolve of the Congress. Thus during the reorganization which took
place at the end of 1775, regiments were authorized to contain
728 officers and men, companies
78 enlisted men. These strengths
were much larger than the British
counterparts which were 477 and
38, respectively. Although Continental units always exceeded
equivalent B r i t i s h units in
strength, they varied widely from
authorized size. For example, nine
months after the first directive
appeared, some companies had 67
men in them, others 83. This was,
of course, the result of the unequal
fall of casualties upon different outfits and the variation in the effectiveness
of the recruiting systems of the several states. The Delaware Regiment
illustrates a typical case of shrinkage. It was so decimated after the battle
of Camden in 1780 that it had to be combined with Maryland companies
to form a regiment. Later still, with the Maryland remnants, it was reorganized as a light company, commanded by Robert Kirkwood.

In closing this section on the organization of Continental infantry
during the Revolutionary War, nothing should be stressed more heavily
than the confusion which chronically prevailed in it. At all times Washington and his staff were obliged to improvise new organizations from
the remnants of those that had been cut up in battle or had served out
their short terms and gone home. Moreover, at all times it was also
necessary to assimilate thousands of citizen soldiers for brief periods into
some sort of working team with the Continentals. This had to be repeated
over and over again with new increments because militia terms of service
were very short. The attempt to utilize the militia, and put it into good

enough order to be effective for at least one campaign, was perhaps the hardest of the Commander in Chief's almost insupportable duties.

In spite of its burdensomeness the effort was well placed. Indeed, John W. Fortescue, historian of the British Army, declared that the militia was the decisive factor. Be that as it may, the militia formed around the Continental Army as a nucleus, and would not have turned out had that often ragtag force not been in the field. Most of the estimated 164,000 militiamen who took up arms for terms from a day up to three months were infantry. In addition to them were other infantrymen, raised and maintained on a relatively permanent basis by the several states, who, with the militia, rallied on the Continentals and abetted the cause.

When the British surrendered at Yorktown on 19 October 1781, there were sixty battalions of infantry in the Continental establishment. Afterwards, as time passed and it appeared that the British intended no new attack, that number was steadily reduced. Finally, in November 1783, after a peace had been formally ratified, only one foot regiment remained, commanded by Henry Jackson. Then, on 2 June 1784, the end came even for that unit, leaving as the only authorized vestige of the Continental Army still in service fewer than a hundred men to guard military stores at West Point and at Fort Pitt.

Through the Second War With England

Congress nevertheless realized the need for at least enough infantry to replace Jackson's regiment. Accordingly, the day after the latter was directed to be discharged, the legislators established a regiment which was to be raised and officered by obtaining volunteers from the militia of four of the states. This non-Regular unit, called the First American Regiment and commanded until 1 January 1792 by Josiah Harmar of Pennsylvania, gradually turned into a Regular outfit. It became known as the 1st Infantry in 1791, and in 1815 was redesignated as the 3d Infantry. From 1784 to 1787 Harmar's regiment was a hybrid, containing eight companies of infantry and two of artillery.

Although England was a constant threat to the new nation after the War for Independence, the Indians presented the most immediate menace. Accordingly, the First American Regiment was stationed on the frontier. In October 1790, the Miami Indians and their allies defeated the first field army, commanded by Harmar, to be organized by the government of the United States acting under the Constitution. This defeat caused the raising of another regiment of infantry in 1791, and the numbering of the old one as the 1st and the new one as the 2d. As a result of the radical reorganization after the War of 1812, the latter became the 1st Infantry.

Serious trouble with the Indians of the Northwest continued; indeed, in the very year the 2d Infantry was organized, the Miamis defeated the second force sent by the Federal government against them. The army defeated in 1791, led by Arthur St. Clair, consisted of the Regular establishment augmented by militia and a new species of foot troops known as levies. Goaded by defeats, Congress gradually increased the military establishment from 700 men in 1784 to 5,104 in 1793. As the size of the entire Army increased, so did the strength of the infantry elements. Regiments rose from 560 to 1,140 enlisted men, companies from 70 to 95. Regiment and battalion remained one and the same.

Two beatings inflicted by the Northwest Indians brought about an experiment in organization which had precedents in certain European corps and in some of the Continental Army. The entire military establishment was converted in 1792 into a legion, that is, into a field army in which the three combat branches, infantry, cavalry, and artillery, were combined in the same organization. The legion consisted of four sub-legions. Each sub-legion contained infantry, riflemen, cavalry, and artillery; indeed it was the forerunner of the twentieth century regimental combat team.

Although Congress had authorized a total of five regiments on 5 March 1792, when the Legion of the United States came into being, none but the 1st and 2d Infantry were actually organized. Hence it was necessary to go out and recruit infantry for the 3d and 4th Sub-Legions. Likewise it was necessary to recruit the rifle units for all the sub-legions.

Command of the new Legion fell to Anthony Wayne, who had been a successful leader of light troops during the Revolution. Wayne did not employ the sub-legions as such to any important extent; on the contrary, he combined the infantry from all of them, likewise the artillery, and so forth. However, he instituted so stern a system of discipline that he forged an army which, in 1794, finally beat the Indians of the Northwest and defied the power of England which had fostered Indian unrest.

Once the threat in that quarter was reduced, the need to hold a field army together seemed to diminish. What was needed instead, statesmen believed, was an organization which could easily be split up and parcelled out to guard the frontiers and the seacoast. As long as Henry Knox remained Secretary of War, the legionary form had a stout champion, but he left office at the end of 1794. The Legion persisted for another year and a half, then went out of existence by act of Congress effective 31 October 1796. In the new establishment the infantry of the four sub-legions became the 1st, 2d, 3d, and 4th Infantry.

Peace promised to prevail, so that during 1796 and 1797 the entire Army was reduced, and the size of regiments and companies as well. For scattered use, a large complement of officers and small companies filled the bill.

All too soon the sense of security evaporated as war loomed with France. In consequence, the establishment swelled precipitately, and the strength of units with it. By 1799 a total of forty infantry regiments was authorized, although none but the 1st through the 4th ever attained the required strength. Only 3,400 men were raised for the 5th through the 16th, and none at all for any others. Fortunately, the war with France never took shape; by 1800 the crisis was over and the immediate need for more infantry gone. In addition, a new administration took office in 1801, an administration that almost pathologically feared a standing army. Accordingly, under Thomas Jefferson the infantry was cut back in 1802 to two regiments, the 1st and 2d.

Jefferson's administration had only a brief chance to test its convictions regarding a strong militia and a small standing army, for war clouds were gathering once more. The United States almost began the second war with England when the British warship *Leopard* attacked the American *Chesapeake* in 1807. This aggression caused Congress to add five Regular infantry regiments in 1808, the 3d through the 7th, and also to constitute the Regiment of Riflemen. The latter was a product of the Revolutionary experience and the first rifle unit since the end of the Legion in 1796. Rifle elements re-entered the service through the agency of Brig. Gen. James Wilkinson, commanding the army, and Henry Dearborn, Secretary of War, both of whom had had firsthand experience with them in the last war.

Aside from the augmentation of April 1808 there was no further preparation for a fight until just six months before the second war with England. At that time, that is, in January 1812, Congress constituted ten new regiments of Regular infantry. The act of 11 January 1812 which created them was remarkable in at least two ways: first, it provided for the largest regiments and battalions authorized in the United States before the Civil War and, second, it established an organization that was at variance with the seven existing regiments. As a result, in the first six months of 1812 there were three different-sized infantry regiments, besides one of riflemen. The 1st and 2d regiments made up the infantry of the "military peace establishment," and they had ten companies in them of seventy-six enlisted men. The 3d through the 7th regiments, authorized in 1808, were called the infantry of the "additional force," and comprised ten companies with two more officers and two more enlisted men each than the 1st and 2d had. The 8th through the 17th in no way resembled the others, for they had eighteen companies of 110 enlisted men, arranged in two battalions.

Although some of the bulky eighteen-company regiments were raised, several never acquired their second battalions. Recruiting was so difficult that they lacked the time to raise many men before Congress voted a fresh reorganization. Late in June 1812, the legislators changed the law. According to the new arrangement there were to be twenty-five regiments of infantry, exclusive of the rifle regiment, each containing ten companies of 102 men. Thus all the infantry regiments were made uniform on paper, and a standard of organization was established that persisted throughout the conflict. This standard was more often than not honored in the breach. Once constituted, all the twenty-five regiments organized and recruited actively, but during the first two years of the struggle their efforts brought in less than half of the total number of infantrymen authorized.

Regulars at first could only enlist for five years, but late in 1812 newcomers were given a chance to enroll "during the war." All the while the states competed with the Federal government for soldiers, and the shorter "hitches" they offered drew men into their service. To combat this Congress directed the creation, in January 1813, of twenty new infantry regiments enlisted for just one year. Nineteen of them were raised and designated as the 26th through the 44th Infantry. Later, they were converted into long-term outfits (five years or the duration), but all the units constituted after 1811 had men in them enlisted for different terms. For example, there were in a single regiment one-year regulars, eighteen-month men, three- and five-year men, and some in for "during the war."

Early in 1814 four more infantry regiments and three more regiments of riflemen were constituted. Finally, therefore, forty-eight infantry regiments, numbered from the 1st to the 48th, came into being, plus four rifle regiments, the 1st through the 4th. This was the greatest number of infantry units included in the Regular Army until the world wars of the twentieth century. A mighty effort was made in 1814 to raise the Army to strength, and nearly 27,000 men came in, but in spite of this, four of the regiments had to be consolidated because they were too small. The 17th, 19th, 26th, and 27th were joined to form a new 17th and a new 19th, while the two highest numbered, the 47th and 48th, were redesignated the 27th and 26th, respectively.

No sooner was war over than Congress scrambled to rid itself of its more than 30,000 infantrymen. An act of 3 March 1815 set the peace

BATTLE OF NEW ORLEANS, WAR OF 1812.

establishment at 10,000 men, divided among infantry, rifle, and artillery regiments. Cavalry was eliminated, and eight infantry regiments and one rifle regiment arose from the ruins of the forty-six and four in existence. The rifles were consolidated and the infantry, after many rearrangements, settled as follows:

1st Infantry formed by consolidation of the 2d, 3d, 7th, and 44th

2d Infantry formed by consolidation of the 6th, 16th, 22d, 23d, and 32d

3d Infantry formed by consolidation of the 1st, 5th, 17th, 19th, and 28th

4th Infantry formed by consolidation of the 14th, 18th, 20th, 36th, and 38th

5th Infantry formed by consolidation of the 4th, 9th, 13th, 21st, 40th, and 46th

6th Infantry formed by consolidation of the 11th, 25th, 27th, 29th, and 37th

7th Infantry formed by consolidation of the 8th, 24th, and 39th

8th Infantry formed by consolidation of the 10th and 12th

The eight remaining infantry regiments were smaller than their war predecessors because, although the number of companies in each remained at ten, every company contained 78 men instead of 103. There was no effort to preserve the honors or traditional numbers of any of the prewar regiments. The 1st was merged with other regiments and redesignated the 3d, and the old 2d, 3d, 4th, 5th, 6th, and 7th were likewise lost in the remains of disbanded regiments. The new numbers were founded on the seniority of the colonels, the senior colonel commanding the 1st, and so forth. As a consequence of the reduction, 25,000 infantrymen were separated from the service. Another consequence was that the form of the infantry establishment was set roughly for the next thirty years. Not until the Mexican War, thirty-one years later, was it substantially expanded.

The Germinal Period, 1816–1860

After the reorganization of 1815, the Regular infantry fluctuated in size with the whole military establishment. Prospects of peace appeared to improve, and in 1821 Congress felt safe enough to cut expenses by disbanding the Rifle Regiment and the 8th Infantry. Having reduced the infantry establishment to seven foot regiments, which were thought adequate to meet all contingencies, the legislators next sliced the size of companies to fifty-one enlisted men, the smallest ever. This arrangement endured for fifteen years when, as usual, the Indians forced an enlargement.

At all times there was trouble with the Indians on the frontier, but two affairs assumed the magnitude of war. The first in 1831 and 1832 against the tribes of the Iowa, Illinois, and Wisconsin area, known as the Black Hawk War, was easily won by a force composed mostly of militia. The whole affair had no permanent impact on the Regular infantry. Not so the second of the several scraps against the Seminole Indians in Florida, which began in December 1835 and lasted until 1842. Volunteers and militia bore the brunt of the Florida War at first, but Regulars gradually replaced them. As a result, after more than two years of inconclusive fighting, Congress was obliged to augment the Regular infantry (in 1838) by adding thirty-eight privates and one sergeant to each company, and by raising a new 8th Infantry, the fourth unit to go by that number. At one time or another, every one of the eight regiments of infantry served in the Florida swamps.

As quickly as the war in Florida was over in 1842, although all were retained, regiments and companies were reduced to minimum size. However, by a fluke, the Regular infantry actually increased. This came about because in the spring of 1843, to save money, the 2d Dragoons were converted into a rifle regiment. They thus became the first rifle corps included in the establishment for two decades, that is, since the Rifle Regiment had been disbanded in 1821. The erstwhile horsemen, who felt degraded on foot, clung hard to their dragoon organization, but they received rifles and, as far as is known, trained as riflemen. Agitation to remount them was continuous, and within a year they became the 2d Dragoons again. When they were reconverted, rifle corps disappeared once more from the Army, except that the President received authority from Congress to convert two or more infantry regiments into rifles if he thought it expedient. He never exercised this authority.

In May 1846 a new rifle unit, the Regiment of Mounted Riflemen, was constituted. This regiment had initially been designated for use on the Oregon Trail but was diverted at its origin into Mexican War service. Its animals were lost on the way, so only two companies, mounted on Mexican horses, acted as cavalry. The rest, armed with Model 1841 rifles, bayonets, and flintlock pistols, fought on foot.

At the start of the Mexican War, Congress tried to get along with just eight infantry regiments of Regulars, but in doing so gave the President power to expand their companies to one hundred enlisted men during the war. Ten months after hostilities commenced, it was necessary to change this policy and add nine new regiments—with the same organization as the old ones—to the Regular infantry. Eight of them, as was customary, bore numbers, the 9th through the 16th; but the other got a name. It was called the Regiment of Voltigeurs and Foot Riflemen. Half of this unit was to be mounted, the other half on foot, and each horseman was paired with a foot soldier who was to get up behind him for rapid movements. This arrangement was never executed, and the Voltigeurs became in fact a regiment of foot riflemen, armed with the same rifle (a muzzle-loader) as the Mounted Riflemen. Quite by chance, the regiment included a company of mountain howitzers and war rockets, but it was not linked with the riflemen tactically, nor were the rockets and howitzers ever used together.

Although raised as Regulars, the nine new infantry regiments created during the Mexican War were disbanded when the war was over. Their dissolution left a peace establishment of eight foot regiments. This structure seemed less adequate than it would have before 1846, for "Manifest Destiny" had entered the reckoning of the legislators. The inescapable need to protect, at least partially, the vast area taken from Mexico, and to help settlers across the great plains to California and Oregon, caused Congress to add the 9th and 10th Infantry in 1855, the fourth of both numbers in United States service. The ten regiments in existence after

1855, the 1st through the 10th, made up the foot establishment until after the actual opening of hostilities in 1861. The Regiment of Mounted Riflemen remained active after the Mexican War, but in 1861 it was redesignated as the 3d Cavalry.

The new 9th and 10th Infantry organized in 1855 were the first infantry units to receive rifle muskets instead of smoothbores as their standard arm. The rifle issued to them was built to utilize a new type of ammunition, known as Minié bullets. Because these conoidal bullets expanded when fired, they could be made small enough to be rammed easily down the barrel of a rifle. When the propellant exploded, the ball expanded into the rifling which imparted to it the spin that made rifle fire superior to that of muskets. The principle implicit in the Minié bullet worked a true revolution in the use of small arms by enabling accurate rifles to replace inaccurate muskets as standard firearms for the infantry.

A regiment of teh companies—with regiment and battalion one and the same—was standard throughout the period. For training and for battle purposes, the eight battalion companies were placed in line by a complex arrangement according to the seniority of their captains, which seems to have had its origin in the protocol of medieval armies. It had no functional basis, since once lined up, the companies were renumbered from right to left. For official designation, however, a new system began in 1816. Under this system the companies were known by letters, instead of by numbers or by the names of their commanders. The two flank companies received the letters A and B, and the others C through K. There was no Company J, because *J* was too easily confused with *I* in writing.

At this point it is necessary to remember that there had been only one flank company per battalion during the Revolution. The addition of a second company had occurred in 1798 when war with France seemed certain. Its adoption brought the American battalion into conformity with those of England and France, the potential European foes. But whereas their flank companies received special weapons, those in the United States infantry did not. As a result, the latter had less chance to develop techniques apart from the line. They were simply composed of men picked for their strength and courage.

The truth is that conditions in America did not favor the specialization of particular companies. Indian wars had to be fought by whatever troops were available; there was no time to await the arrival of elite corps, whether called grenadiers or something else. Nor did fights with Indians give much opportunity for infantry to assume the formal line of battle with light units out front. Finally, the scattering of the companies of Regular regiments made specialized training impossible.

Nevertheless, the drill manuals of the United States infantry after 1825 called the two flank units grenadier and light infantry companies. The latter term had some application, the former none at all. The acceptance of European designations resulted from the dominance of French military arrangements throughout the world in the decades after the wars of Napoleon. More specifically, it came from the fact that American drill manuals were in reality translations, only slightly modified, of French regulations.

It was during this epoch that Americans borrowed a verb from the French to describe the operations of light flank companies. That verb was "to skirmish." It grew in use and importance because the extended order of light or skirmishing infantry was very slowly challenging the tighter formations of the line. In the United States the challenge had not proceeded far at the time of the Mexican War. Rather, it was the introduction of the Minié ball, and other advances in firearms, which in the fifties forced infantry all over the world toward wider use of skirmish tactics. The trend was to give all infantrymen training as skirmishers. As a result, the *Tactics* adopted in 1855 discarded the distinction in name among the ten companies of a battalion. All ten took their places in line, and all were prepared, when called on, to move ahead of the line and skirmish with the foe.

In the Mexican War, light battalions of Regulars were often formed for specific missions by temporarily detaching companies—not necessarily the flank ones—from different regiments. Composite battalions of this sort usually did not do as well in battle as established ones, in which men and officers understood each other and regimental pride was an active stimulant. There was, however, more distinction between flank and line in volunteer regiments. Two companies out of ten were specifically organized as light and given a choice between rifles and muskets. The flank rifle companies which resulted were often detached from their regiments and used together for special sharpshooting assignments. This was the case in the fighting on the mountains to the left of the American position at Buena Vista.

Throughout this period there was a growing emphasis on the use of segments within a company. This emphasis resulted from the increase in the power of firearms which followed adoption of the Minié principle and the extensive experiments under way on repeating and breech-loading rifles. In order to offset the mounting vitality of firepower, professional soldiers began to stress dispersion in the official drill manuals. Dispersion, of course, strained the ability of officers to control large bodies of men, and consequently highlighted the need to organize smaller

STORMING OF CHAPULTEPEC DURING MEXICAN WAR. *(From a lithograph by Nathaniel Currier.)*

elements within units. Applied to a company, this meant an increased use of platoons (half companies), sections (half platoons), and the beginning of the fighting squad.

The earliest suggestion of the squad was a file of two men, the two being taught to stick together during a fight. Later, for purposes of training, squads gradually changed from being irregular knots of men, in the drill manual of 1815, to being specified fractions of a company in 1841. The latter were to be quartered and exercised together. There was no expansion of their use in combat until 1855 when the new manual prescribed "Comrades in Battle" (two files, totaling four men) who were to work together in battle.

There is another point about this period which deserves emphasis: the frequency with which the other two combat arms served as infantry.

In the Florida War, artillery fought on foot and dragoons did likewise more often than not. During the Mexican War, the bulk of the Regiment of Mounted Riflemen fought on foot and only ten artillery companies had cannon, while the other thirty-eight served as infantry. They carried musketoons instead of muskets, and swords instead of bayonets; but they were trained for infantry service, and made an impressive record fighting as such.

Under the provisions of the Constitution, the United States received complete control of the Regular Army—the descendant of the Continental Army—but not of the militia. Most of the power over the latter remained with the states, and the extent to which the Federal government could use state militias became a matter of endless controversy. Worse by far, from the standpoint of efficiency, was the fact that militiamen could only be held to serve for three months and that they were not liable to do duty very far from home. What is more, militia training differed widely from state to state, so that it was hard to fuse units from the several states into one army.

When obliged to wage war as a nation, the United States was caught between the fear of a standing army and the inadequacies of a militia controlled by the several states. Some sort of compromise was necessary, and that proved to be an old type, volunteer soldiers organized into provisional wartime regiments. There were also peacetime volunteers— quite distinct from those raised for a war—at hand in the militia.

In the large seaboard cities there were independent or chartered companies of citizen soldiers apart from the common or standing militia. They were composed of men who liked military exercise well enough to buy their own uniforms, drill regularly, and hold together in peace as well as war. These units usually received charters from the states, and they very soon constituted an elite corps. This corps became the parent of the National Guard of the twentieth century. The title "Volunteers" with a capital V was applied to them early in the nineteenth century, and it is used here to distinguish them from individuals or units who volunteered only for the duration of a given war.

Volunteer infantrymen, when associated with the compulsory militia, took the posts of honor and their units were consequently often referred to as flank or light companies. Sometimes they had special weapons and actually trained as light infantry. When war came they sometimes volunteered to go as units or they became a relatively trained cadre around which some provisional regiment was built. By the 1850's, the standing militia had deteriorated so far, and the Volunteers had become so stable, that many of the states abandoned the idea of compulsory service, and accepted the Volunteers as their constitutional militia. This done, they began to organize the scattered companies into battalions and regiments, a grouping that was well advanced in some states in the decade of the 1850's.

Volunteers were supposed to be organized and to train according to the discipline of the Regular infantry, but this was rarely the case. The *Tactics* of the Army were not widely enough disseminated, and were too voluminous for general use by the state militias anyway. As a result, Volunteers and militia used whatever manuals they could come by, which ranged from Steuben's *Regulations* of 1779 to the latest translations of the French system.

In the Mexican War, most volunteers reached the seat of war with little or no training; but some of them, once arrived, were associated with Regular brigades and quickly introduced to the Army drill. Like the training, the organization of citizen soldiers of all types was required by law to conform to the United States' standards, but much latitude existed. The Maryland and District of Columbia Battalion of the Mexican War, for example, reached the combat area with only one field officer of the three required in the Regular service. Also, the size of regiments at that time varied from 923 on the under side of the Federal standard of 1,004 enlisted men, to 1,423, on the upper. In general, the Volunteers of the cities came closest to adhering to U.S. standards, both for training and for organization.

The wide use of militiamen and volunteers carried with it an inevitable flabbiness in discipline. Citizens temporarily turned soldiers had no sense of unquestioning obedience to anyone and were usually not in service long enough to acquire more than a shade of it. Moreover, they almost always elected their own officers, which did not make for stern authority.

Frequently, the lack of training and of discipline resulted in rout in battle, as happened on part of the field at Buena Vista. On the other hand, citizen soldiers often showed remarkable fighting ability, as was true, for example, of the Mississippi Rifles, commanded by Jefferson Davis, on another part of the same battlefield. In all instances, training and leadership were the ingredients that made the difference. Lack of training caused trouble less often in combat than in the intervals between, when life grew very dull. It must be remembered that a hitch in wartime was a lark for many a citizen, during which he left his inhibitions at home. Citizen soldiers made relations with the people of Mexico difficult because, as General Zachary Taylor said, ". . . it is impossible effectually to control these troops [for they lose] in bodies the restraining sense of individual responsibility."

Whatever the quality of U.S. Army foot troops, figures show quite well

THE MISSISSIPPI RIFLES AT BUENA VISTA.

the change that was taking place in their source during wars. Nine out of ten infantrymen in the War of 1812 were militiamen. Only one out of ten foot soldiers was a militiaman in the Mexican War; three were Regulars, and six were war volunteers. This trend continued until the adoption of conscription in the twentieth century. The point to stress is that infantry doctrine and standards were set by the Regulars, but the mass of American infantrymen in wartime were citizen soldiers.

The Civil War

The infantry, both North and South, was far from ready for war in 1861. There were but ten Union foot regiments, and they were largely in the West, scattered by companies over thousands of miles. Until assembled, which would take time, they could be counted on for very little. Many of the Regular officers, the core of any expansion, had served in the Mexican War fifteen years before, but few had commanded any sizable body of troops. Moreover, although a small number had kept abreast of world military developments after their services in Mexico, they were not in a position to dictate policy in Washington.

To add to the problems of the infantry early in the war, virtually no preparations had been made, apparently because statesmen hoped until the last minute that conflict could be averted. They believed that military adjustments would damage the chances of peaceful compromise. Thus, when war began, the foundations of what was to become a huge infantry establishment had to be commenced hastily and without real planning.

Since Congress was not in session, President Lincoln began the war buildup in May 1861 with a proclamation of doubtful constitutionality. On the strength of his executive authority, he summoned thirty-nine regiments of volunteer infantry and one of cavalry to serve for three years. His next step was to authorize an addition of eight infantry regiments to the Regular Army. Somehow a ninth got included. Thereafter, the nineteen regiments in being—the 1st through the 19th—were the whole of the Regular infantry during the war. So neglected a part of the whole establishment were these nineteen that they were never able to attain their full authorized strength.

Prior to issuing his call, the President consulted the War Department as to the best organization for the new Regular units. The Secretary of War, being overburdened, turned the matter over to Salmon P. Chase, Secretary of the Treasury, and loaned him three officers as technical advisors. The result was a recommendation in favor of the French structure. This included regiments of three battalions instead of one. Two battalions were supposed to take the field, the third to maintain a regimental depot for collecting and training recruits. Battalions of 800 men in eight companies were adopted as the most efficient fighting units because they were thought to be small enough to maneuver and to be controlled by the voice of the commanding officer, yet large enough to withstand attack by cavalry.

A battalion in the French system was the fighting unit, a regiment the unit of administration. The French felt that a regimental headquarters could administer more than one battalion, an arrangement which appealed to Americans because it eliminated some field officers and thus saved money. The new three-battalion organization, however, was not extended to the ten old regiments, which continued to comprise ten companies each, with regiment and battalion one and the same. The men in authority felt that there was no time to bother with reorganizing outfits already extant, when so many remained to be organized from scratch. Furthermore, the old, single-battalion regiment was hallowed by age and tradition. This meant that two different regimental organizations were tolerated in the Regular infantry, a dualism that might have caused much confusion had the Regular regiments loomed larger than they did in the whole infantry establishment.

The number of men in all Regular companies was raised at once to the maximum authorized by law, that is, 84 enlisted men in the first ten regiments and 97 in the other nine. Even so, the regiments never reached full strength because they could not compete with the volunteers for enlistments. By December 1861, some 30,000 Regular infantrymen were authorized, but barely 11,000 enlisted, while during the same period 640,000 volunteers entered the service. The third battalions of the 12th, 13th, 14th, 17th, and 19th Infantry were never organized, and not all the companies were raised for the third battalions of the other four new regiments. In fact, the 11th, 12th, and 13th only imperfectly organized their second battalions. Each battalion of the new regiments designated its companies by letters beginning with A, so that, if fully raised, there were three A companies, three B companies, and so on in each regiment.

Since replacements came more slowly than losses to the Regular regiments, all of them grew smaller as the war continued. By July 1864, as an illustration, the 2d Infantry had shrunk to 7 officers and 38 enlisted men, who were thereafter grouped into one company and assigned to guard duty. Moreover, by 1 November 1864 all the Regular outfits of the Army of the Potomac were so reduced that it was necessary to withdraw them from the field. Such shrinkage was, of course, not confined to the Regulars. The average strength of regiments—most of which ought to have contained 1,046 officers and men—was as follows in the battles named:

Shiloh (6–7 April 1862)	560
Fair Oaks (31 May–1 June 1862)	650
Chancellorsville (1–5 May 1863)	530
Gettysburg (1–3 July 1863)	375
Chickamauga (19–20 September 1863)	440
Wilderness (5–7 May 1864)	440

The comments so far have referred mainly to Regulars, but this should not obscure the fact that most infantrymen were volunteers. These volunteers were members of regiments raised and officered by the several states. Initially President Lincoln called for thirty-nine such outfits, but before the war was over more than 1,700 volunteer regiments served. This was not far from one hundred times as many as there were units of Regulars. The three-battalion organization was not extended to the volunteers because the states, which raised them, were thought to be too much accustomed to the old system to change. As a result, the volunteer units, like the first ten Regular regiments, contained ten companies in one battalion.

These regiments were variously numbered and designated by the several states, but in practice came to be called merely the "8th Indiana" or the "45th New York." Although patterned after the old regiments in overall organization, the state regiments borrowed their company structure from the new, that is, they had ninety-seven enlisted men, instead of eighty-four, plus one wagoner whom the Regulars did not have. As matters were arranged, therefore, there were three different regimental organizations in the infantry. The volunteer regiments aggregated 1,046 officers and men; the 1st through the 10th Infantry, 878; and the 11th through the 19th, 2,367. Actually the battalions of the latter ought to be compared with the old regiments, since they were designed to act independently and approximated the size of the others. They contained a few more than 800 enlisted men.

Even though most of the volunteer infantrymen were raised and officered by the states, a few hundred units were not. Several types of volunteers were more directly linked to the United States than to any state, the earliest of these being two regiments of U.S. Sharpshooters (1st and 2d) organized in 1861. These two contained companies from several states, raised by the states. Their origin in more than one state was an uncommon attribute, but their real distinguishing feature was the manner in which they were officered. While the states appointed the company and field officers in ordinary volunteer units, the Federal government appointed them in the Sharpshooters and similar outfits.

The next type appeared when large-scale acceptance of Negro troops began in 1863. A number of battalions had started as state units, but with the exception of two Massachusetts regiments, all Negro outfits were finally mustered directly into Federal service, and were organized and officered under the authority of the United States and not of any particular state. Known at first as the Corps d'Afrique and by other names, these units came to be called U.S. Colored Troops by the spring of 1864. Indian regiments (1st–4th Indian Home Guards) were handled in the same way. In all, there were 138 regiments of Negro infantry and 4 of Indians. Except for these two races, diverse nationalities could and did intermingle in infantry units, although men of German, Irish, and Scandinavian extraction proudly associated together in exclusive regiments.

Yet another type of Federal volunteer emerged because casualties had reached such proportions that provision for the incapacitated, and replacements for them, had become critical problems. To solve these

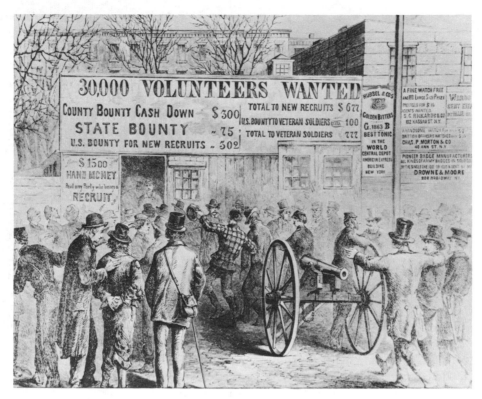

RECRUITING FOR VOLUNTEERS DURING CIVIL WAR. *(From a drawing by Frank Leslie.)*

problems, the Invalid Corps was established in April 1863 and classed as infantry. It was composed of men who in the line of duty had become physically unfit for combat. Those who could handle a gun and make light marches were put in the 1st Battalion and were used for guard duty. The worse crippled formed the 2d Battalion and were used as nurses and cooks around hospitals. Six companies from the 1st Battalion and four from the 2d made up a regiment in the Corps after September 1863. In all, 24 regiments and 188 separate companies of invalids did duty, thus releasing able-bodied soldiers for combat service. In March 1864—because the Corps' abbreviation, "IC," was confused with "Inspected-Condemned"—the name was changed to Veteran Reserve Corps.

Finally, in 1864 six infantry regiments of U.S. Volunteers (1st–6th) were recruited for service on the frontiers (not against the Confederacy) from Confederate prisoners of war. Then in 1865, nine infantry regiments

PICKETT'S CHARGE AT GETTYSBURG.

of U.S. Veteran Volunteers (1st–9th) were raised directly by the United States. Although all types of United States volunteers made up only a small fraction of the foot troops who served for the Union, they merit attention because of the intimate relationship between them and the Federal government, and because of the lack of vital connection between them and any state. This relationship foreshadowed the National Army of the twentieth century.

The Confederate Army arranged infantry units pretty much as the Union did, except that all regiments contained ten companies. Authorized company strength was 64 privates minimum and 125 maximum. Around 642 infantry regiments served at some time or another, along with 9 legions, 163 separate battalions, and 62 unattached companies. Many of the Confederate units were the forbears of Army National Guard elements existing today.

In the heat of the conflict, no changes were made in regimental organization, despite the fact that it was soon recognized as unsuitable. Improved firearms forced regiments and their companies to disperse to such an extent that officers could not effectively exercise control over them. Once a regiment deployed, it was too big for one man and his staff to control. This fact helped to cause a high casualty rate among general officers, since the only way they could influence an assault, or rally a broken line, was to place themselves where everyone in the command could see them. At such times the enemy's sharpshooters saw them equally well.

Years after the Civil War, Maj. Gen. John M. Schofield, who had commanded the Army of the Ohio under Sherman, said that the cumbersome regimental organization had only worked in the course of the war because the replacement system was faulty. What he meant was that the unwieldy regiments at the beginning of the conflict dwindled through casualties until they reached a size which a colonel and his staff could handle. The same attrition, of course, applied to the control of companies.

Companies were also unwieldy yet were not reorganized. On the contrary, the promise of wide use of platoons, sections, and squads—a promise that may be detected in the infantry manuals of the 1850's—was not fulfilled during the war. As a result, notwithstanding the fact that the need was far greater, there were no more officers in an infantry company than there had been forty years before.

The reason why types of organization were retained that had been designed for use under different conditions stemmed from the great haste with which the armies were assembled in 1861. There was no time to make a wide canvass of professional soldiers, and those consulted were deceived by their belief that the conditions of the wars of Napoleon had not been radically modified. Few foresaw, and perhaps could not have foreseen, the full impact of the Minié ball upon warfare.

The keystone of the whole matter was the heightened firepower which the infantry had to face and which it could wield. The foot soldier's rifle musket, although a muzzle-loader, was vastly more effective than the weapons infantrymen had handled before 1855. It was accurate from 200 to 400 yards, and capable of killing at 800 to 1,000. Nor was it the only improved weapon. Scattered among the soldiers were many types of breech-loading repeating rifles which did great execution.

Except for being unwieldy, regiments and their components proved otherwise adaptable to wartime conditions. For example, heightened firepower more than ever before demanded skirmishers in front of the battle line. These the regimental organization was able to supply simply by assigning any of its companies to the duty. Likewise, regimental organization lent itself well to the attack formation which became characteristic of the Civil War. This was a succession of lines. Each line was composed of two ranks with a prescribed distance of thirty-two inches between them. Of course, the lines varied greatly in length and in the distance at which they followed each other. Some were as long as a whole brigade lined up in two ranks, others only as long as a company. If there was a usual length, it was that of a brigade, since attacks by divisions in column of brigades were most frequent. In any case, regiments as organized were easily utilized in that type of attack formation, as they were in others.

New means began to work during the Civil War to knit armies together and to speed their movements. For the first time, railroads were used extensively to move infantrymen to and from battle areas. This employment gave the foot soldier greater speed than he had in the past. In the field of communications, signal flags were first used. These enabled the parts of a force to keep contact with each other and to pass on information about the enemy. Newer still was the use of electricity, in the form of the telegraph, to link the components of a large force and to

UNION INFANTRY ADVANCING TOWARD APPOMATTOX.

connect field elements with the Commander in Chief at Washington. The new modes of communication did not much improve the connection between units of the same army on the battlefield, but their indirect influence on the use of infantry was very great. The Signal Corps was constituted during the conflict to handle the new media of communication. Its service was great, but its relation to the infantry was only a tiny fragment of what it was to become in the future.

In conclusion it must be said that the Civil War occurred in one of those periods, common in history, when weapons outdistanced organization and tactics. It is true that deadly fire brought about modifications in the use of infantry, one of which was the use of a succession of lines in the assault, another the regular employment of temporary field works. But even after taking these into account, it seems clear that the rifle musket was more modern than the organization of the infantry and the resultant formations used in the assault. Otherwise stated, organization and tactics were basically those of the beginning of the nineteenth century, while the weapons were fifty years more modern. This discrepancy between weapons and minor tactics accounts in part for the shocking destructiveness of the Civil War.

A Diverse Half Century, 1866–1915

Four years of war, and the large army built up during them, conditioned the nation in 1866 to the biggest increase in the Regular infantry since the War of 1812. The result was a postwar military peace establishment of twenty-six more Regular regiments of foot soldiers than had served for the Union. The total was forty-five. All regiments were formed on the prewar pattern with ten companies, and with regiment and battalion one and the same. The new companies were strong in noncommissioned officers and specialists, having a total of nineteen, and privates totaled between fifty and one hundred at the discretion of the President.

The expansion of the infantry worked out as follows. The 1st through 10th Infantry retained their numbers. The first battalions of the 11th through the 19th expanded into regiments of the same respective numbers, and the second battalions into the 20th through the 28th Infantry. The first ten regiments needed no expansion, but the converted first and second battalions, being composed of just eight companies, required two more companies apiece. The 29th through the 37th Infantry were supposed to come from the third battalions of the Civil War units, but, since these had never been raised for the 12th, 13th, 14th, 17th, and 19th regiments, and only imperfectly for the other four, the postwar units had to be recruited. The other eight regiments were new. Negro personnel, commanded by white officers, staffed the 38th through the 41st, while men from the Veteran Reserve Corps, wounded but still able to do active duty, filled up the 42d through the 45th.

During 1866, twenty-six of the forty-five regiments remained in the area of the Confederacy, while twelve were sent west into Indian country. To the men who personally fought the Indians, there never seemed to be enough soldiers, but the level of forty-five regiments was altogether too high for the rest of the nation when the stimulus of the great conflict had worn off. In consequence, recruiting was stopped, and in 1867 the companies were directed not to replace their losses until only fifty privates per company remained. Two years later, on 3 March 1869, Congress reduced the infantry to twenty-five regiments. This set off a reorganization which, for disrupting the history and traditions of regiments, almost rivaled the upheaval of 1815. The following consolidations resulted:

    43d consolidated with the 1st to form the new 1st

    16th consolidated with the 2d to form the new 2d

    Half of the 37th consolidated with the 3d to form the new 3d

    30th consolidated with the 4th to form the new 4th

    Half of the 37th consolidated with the 5th to form the new 5th

    42d consolidated with the 6th to form the new 6th

36th consolidated with the 7th to form the new 7th
33d consolidated with the 8th to form the new 8th
27th consolidated with the 9th to form the new 9th
26th consolidated with the 10th to form the new 10th
24th consolidated with the 29th to form the new 11th
12th Infantry not affected
13th Infantry not affected
45th consolidated with the 14th to form the new 14th
35th consolidated with the 15th to form the new 15th
11th consolidated with the 34th to form the new 16th
44th consolidated with the 17th to form the new 17th
25th consolidated with the 18th to form the new 18th
28th consolidated with the 19th to form the new 19th
20th Infantry not affected
32d consolidated with the 21st to form the new 21st
31st consolidated with the 22d to form the new 22d
23d Infantry not affected
38th consolidated with the 41st to form the new 24th
39th consolidated with the 40th to form the new 25th

Twenty-one outfits emerged from the reorganization bearing the same numbers they had borne through the war, but the new 11th, 16th, 24th, and 25th Infantry were not so fortunate. They had no connection with the war units of the same numbers. However, the 24th and 25th—created by consolidation of the 38th through the 41st—carried on the tradition of the Negro regiments begun during the Civil War.

The Regular infantry stood unchanged at twenty-five regiments for thirty-two years, and was at last altered only because of the need to hold the territory outside the continental United States acquired from Spain in 1898. Within the regiments the size of companies fluctuated. In the trough of economic depression the number of men authorized per company dropped in 1876 as low as thirty-seven. Infantry officers pointed out that when sickness and desertion occurred, these little companies were much too small to do their duty in the Indian country where 180 out of 250 of them were stationed in the 1870's. The severe cut that reduced the companies to skeleton strength came about in the following manner. One month after the famous massacre of Custer's troops in June 1876, Congress reduced the enlisted strength of the Army from 30,000 to 25,000. Then in August the legislators allowed existing cavalry units to be augmented by 2,500 men, since cavalry was considered the chief reliance against the Plains Indians. As a result, the reduction of 5,000 fell almost entirely upon the infantry.

By 1890 the long fight against the red man was practically won. This

INFANTRYMEN GUARDING SUPPLY TRAIN AGAINST INDIANS. *(From a painting by Frederic Remington.)*

made it possible to abandon some of the small posts, held by one or two companies, and to concentrate the units under regimental control. The shift, however, was not made easily, and as late as 1912 the Secretary of War complained that dispersion made of the Army nothing but a scattered constabulary. In any case, in 1890 it seemed sensible to make the whole infantry establishment more compact without increasing it. In consequence, Companies I and K of each regiment were stripped of all personnel, and their men and officers used to fill out the remaining companies. Thus, fifty infantry companies existed only in name with their records and trophies preserved by the regiments. The two hundred companies that survived had one sergeant and four corporals fewer than formerly, and a total of forty-six privates each. Within a year, however, the War Department directed that Company I of nineteen of the regiments be filled out with fifty-five Indians, but because it was unsuccessful the project was soon dropped.

While these changes were taking place, observers were pointing out that the ten-company, one-battalion regiment was obsolete. The increased accuracy of firearms, they said, had forced dispersion so that no one man could control ten companies in battle. Accordingly, the Secretary of War in 1890 urged that a regiment of three battalions of four companies each be adopted. Such an arrangement was backed by statistics, for wars in Europe had demonstrated that one-third of a regiment now occupied the same front in battle as an entire regiment once had. This being so, a single leader could hardly be expected to direct more than four companies in action. In the next few years, the Secretary's successors repeated the request, but without success.

Throughout the period under consideration, there was ceaseless experimentation with infantry small arms; but, even so, changes came slowly. The reason for this was that the Army had to practice the strictest economy. Accordingly, Ordnance sought for the last refinement before standardizing any model, since once a rifle was adopted, it could not soon be discarded in favor of a new one costing large sums. As a result, the rifle musket of the Civil War remained in general use for a few years after the return of peace.

When at last the almost hallowed old piece made way for a new one in the early 1870's, the United States infantry took a forward stride as great as when it had adopted the Minié principle in the 1850's. The new gun, the celebrated Springfield Model 1873, embodied several indispensable improvements. It was the first official infantry rifle to load at the breech. Next, it operated without a touch-hole—an essential in all previous American foot soldiers' guns—because the primer was included as part of a brass cartridge which had replaced paper cartridges. Last but not least, it dropped .13 of an inch in caliber, being .45 instead of .58 across the bore.

The Springfield '73 remained the official shoulder arm of the infantry for nineteen years. Actually it served longer than that, for citizen soldiers used it in 1898 and 1899, and the Philippine Scouts even later. When finally it was superseded in 1892, its replacement embodied an advance that had been widely used for decades. Called the Krag-Jörgensen, it was the foot soldier's first standard repeating rifle. In addition, it continued the trend toward smaller bullets, being .30 caliber instead of .45. The Krag lasted nine years before yielding to the Springfield Model 1903. The latter remained standard for almost forty years, that is, to the outbreak of World War II. Although it was not a new departure as the '73 and the Krag had been, it utilized the latest improvements, and was as fine a rifle as infantry had anywhere in the world.

All of a sudden, in the spring of 1898, the United States jumped into a war with Spain. There were then 26,000 enlisted men, in round figures, in the Regular Army, of whom half were infantry. A three-battalion organization was put into effect at once by the following arrangement. The existing eight companies in each regiment were divided into two battalions, while the two skeleton companies were filled out and combined with two new companies to make the third battalion. Also, the size of companies rose from around 50 to 106 enlisted men. The result was a substantial regiment of 1,309 enlisted men. However, it still contained 1,000 men fewer than the authorized strength of the 11th through 19th Infantry in the Civil War and 2,400 less than the 3,700-man units of World War I.

Conflict with Spain did not add even one to the total of twenty-five Regular infantry regiments, for, as in the Civil War, chief reliance was not placed upon Regulars. No sooner was war declared than Congress passed an act putting a second component beside the Regulars. This was called the Volunteer Army of the United States. The regiments of this force were raised and officered by the states, and in the main sprang from existing organized militia units. Officers of the Regular Army were at liberty, without losing Regular status, to accept commissions for field grades in state units, provided there was no more than one Regular in any volunteer regiment. Congress also ruled that state units had to conform to the organization of the Army, and that general and staff officers for corps, divisions, and brigades be appointed by the President.

Before the end of May, President William McKinley made two calls for troops, requesting a total of 141 regiments, 20 separate battalions, and 46 separate companies of infantry, all of which were raised quickly. Most of the regiments came into Federal service with around 950 enlisted men, but three or four contained as few as 650. Nearly all of them recruited up before the war was over, although none reached the 1,309 prescribed. This was not surprising when one considers that, except for the regiments that went to the Philippines, all the volunteer infantry units were released by 8 June 1899, having served in most cases less than a year.

It was decided, in the second month of the war (May 1898), to organize ten regiments of volunteers not related to any state, an action for which there was precedent in the United States volunteers of the Civil War. The latter had been raised from special groups such as sharpshooters or Confederate prisoners of war. The earliest regiments of United States Volunteer Infantry in the War with Spain were also made up from a special group, that is, from men who were immune to tropical disease: five regiments of Negroes and five of whites. They were authorized to contain only 992, instead of 1,309, enlisted men, and all had close to that number when they were mustered in.

As early as March 1899, the use of United States Volunteer Infantry was carried beyond the employment of the 10,000 immunes. By September 1899, twenty-four new regiments, not to remain in service beyond

1 July 1901, had been authorized to be raised from the country at large. Their designating numbers started where the Regular infantry's left off (that is, at 26) and ran through 49. The 36th and 37th were recruited from men already on duty in the Philippines, the 48th and 49th from Negroes. Practically all the officers of field grade for the new outfits came from the Regular Army.

In March 1899, companies went up in size to 112 enlisted men and regiments to 1,378. Three months later, companies in active areas, such as the Philippines, increased to 128. Thus enlarged, twenty-four regiments of United States Volunteers and twenty-five of Regulars made up the infantry which garrisoned the Philippines, Cuba, and Puerto Rico, as well as the United States itself. Soon it was necessary to make new provisions, since after 1 July 1901 the authorization for Volunteers and for the increases in Regulars ran out. The new arrangement, dated 2 February 1901, gave the number of Regular infantry regiments its first boost since 1866. Five new ones were authorized, the 26th through the 30th. These were the fourth units with these numbers to have been in the Regular service, the first having existed during the French crisis in 1798–99, the second during the War of 1812, and the third from 1866 to 1869.

This and other legislation of 1901 set the upper limits of the military establishment, but allowed the President to increase the size of companies by 6 noncommissioned officers and to raise the privates up to a total of 127 if he thought it necessary. Under this discretion, the authorized size of the Army fluctuated by executive order until World War I. Also, two new nationalities joined the infantry establishment, for the law sanctioned up to 12,000 Philippine Scouts and a provisional regiment of Puerto Ricans.

Native Filipinos had been organized into companies as early as September 1899, but having no official sanction, had been paid as civilian employees of the Quartermaster. Their official organization, which took effect on 1 October 1901, provided for fifty companies. The officers were from the Regular Army except for the 1st and 2d lieutenants, who could be selected from qualified natives. A battalion organization was introduced in 1904, and in the following decade thirteen Philippine Scout battalions came into being. After World War I these battalions, most of which had been parts of provisional regiments during the war, were grouped into permanent regiments and given numbers. They became the 43d, 45th, 57th, and 62d Infantry (Philippine Scouts).

As with the Filipinos, there had been an earlier organization in Puerto Rico, a battalion which had begun to operate during March 1899. This was combined with a battalion of mounted infantry, or-

VOLUNTEER INFANTRYMEN DURING PHILIPPINE INSURRECTION.

ganized in 1900, to make a regiment. Its companies were smaller than those of the Regulars and of the Philippine Scouts, and it contained two instead of three battalions. The Puerto Rico Regiment was manned by natives of that island but commanded by officers from the continent. In 1908 this outfit was incorporated into the Regular Army, and in 1920 it was redesignated as the 65th Infantry.

The organization of infantry regiments into three battalions of four companies each—finally brought about by the War with Spain—persisted as a permanent alteration. It is interesting to note, that with this change the Army returned to the regimental organization used from 1790 to 1792. This 100-year reversion, however, did not arise from a study of the earlier period—rather it sprang from the experience of the Civil War, coupled with that of the later wars in Europe. Experience had demonstrated that the old regiments were far too big to be effectively controlled in battle. As long as the system in which battalion and regiment were one and the same was followed, the regiment was a fighting subdivision in the line of battle. On the other hand, in the shift to more modern practice which the infantry was making, the battalion was a fighting subdivision while the regiment exercised administrative control over three battalions. The fault in the shift was that the American battalion was too small to perform its work. This may be illustrated by comparing the new organization with those in Europe. The French and Prussian infantries both used regiments of three battalions, but the battalions were far larger. The Prussians had 1,000 enlisted men in theirs, the French close to 700, while Americans had no more than 425.

One of the major trends in military organization during the second half of the nineteenth century had to do with the organization of infantry below company level. Within two years after the Civil War, a new United States manual on infantry tactics was issued. Prepared by Maj. Gen. Emory Upton, it based all troop evolutions on movement by fours. Since a front of four men in proper line had a rear rank, the basic subdivision of the new system was really a squad, although that term was not used.

Upton's *Infantry Tactics* remained official for twenty-four years. During these years organization within companies took form. Accordingly, the *Infantry Drill Regulations* (the first manual to bear that name), issued in 1891, defined a squad more sharply than before. A squad contained seven privates and one corporal, and was made the basis of drill in extended order. Since extended order was gradually displacing close order, the squad gained new importance. Likewise, as the duties and the organization of a squad became clearer, those of half companies (that is, platoons) also took firmer form. Indeed, the fire of an advancing infantry line was carried out, according to the manuals, by platoon.

Throughout the half century the movement was toward the refinement of organization further and further. This meant giving small knots of men, and combinations of such knots, cohesion and special leadership. The development that launched this movement was the gradual replacement of line tactics by skirmish tactics. Along with it came changes in training and techniques, such as a set of arm signals by which company officers and their subordinates could control their men. All the changes, whether in organization or techniques, stemmed from the growing deadliness of firearms.

A weapon that would change the character of warfare, the machine gun, was being developed during this period. The first important model, the Gatling gun patented in 1862, was purchased by the United States during the Civil War. Tests made in the 1870's showed the Gatling to be equal to seventy Springfield rifles well aimed at 150 to 200 yards. Interest in the weapon increased and the United States bought several lots of it in the years after the Civil War.

As a result of the intercession of 1st Lt. John H. Parker, an inde-

GATLING GUNS SUPPORTING INFANTRY ON SAN JUAN HILL.

pendent battery of four Gatling guns, directly under the corps commander, took an active part in the Santiago campaign. The guns were
directed against entrenched Spanish infantry with telling effect, and even
against artillery. Parker contended they could do anything necessary to
support infantry, but believed they would be more effective if made
lighter (they weighed two hundred pounds). He also recommended that
some sort of mounting, other than the awkward cannon carriage, be
devised for them. Not infected with Parker's enthusiasm, higher commanders were inclined to look at the Gatlings as artillery, and not very
good artillery at that.

The machine gun made its greatest advance when Hiram Maxim,
an American inventor, patented one in 1883 which eliminated the need
for a hand crank by operating on the energy of its own recoil. The United
States experimented with it as early as 1888 but did not adopt it officially
until the first decade of the twentieth century. Tests made in 1910 showed
that one machine gun was equal to sixteen riflemen at ranges up to 600

yards; to twenty-two men from 600 to 1,200; and to thirty-nine men beyond 1,200 yards. Comparing these figures with those given for tests in the 1870's, it is clear that the repeating rifle had reduced the discrepancy between shoulder arms and machine guns a good deal. In any case, on account of the unwieldiness of the weapon and for other reasons, official doctrine on the machine gun remained very conservative.

This did not, however, prevent experiments in organization to utilize it. In 1906, for example, a provisional machine gun platoon of twenty-one men and two Vickers-Maxim guns was added to each regiment. Although the Secretary of War reported three years later that this arrangement had not worked well, the salient fact is that infantry regiments were never again without machine guns. In February 1908, an experimental company was constituted, headed by John H. Parker, now a captain. This company, although it went through several changes in organization, was the forerunner of the machine gun companies of infantry regiments in World War I.

There were other experiments in organization besides those dealing with machine guns. A headquarters detachment of seventeen enlisted men and fifteen mounted scouts was added to each regiment in 1912 for trial. With the machine gun platoon, it made up a regimental detachment the parts of which were trained intensively in their specialized duties. By 1915 the headquarters detachment had grown into a headquarters company "provisionally provided" for each regiment of infantry. (There had never before been headquarters companies in them.) In the same way, the machine gun platoon became a machine gun company, while a third new company, a supply unit, was also under trial.

The size of infantry regiments varied, within the limits imposed by law on the President, according to the duty performed. Regiments in the United States in 1912 had 65 enlisted men per company and a total of 870; those in the Philippines, 150 and 1,836; those in Hawaii and the Canal Zone, 72 and 954; the Puerto Rico Regiment, 65 per company with 591 total. The beginning of World War I in Europe added to the variety, for the possibility of American involvement caused the preparation of alternate tables of organization, one for peace, the other for war. Thus in June 1915, the peace strength of an infantry regiment was set at 959 officers and enlisted men; the war strength at 1,945.

Once the nation had become a colonial power on account of the War with Spain, the study of war grew more important, and Americans turned to a review of what they had to fight with. It was clear that the Regular Army was too small to make up the whole defense and that stimulation of the militia was therefore necessary. As a result, one phase of the reform of 1903 was to replace the Federal militia law which had been on the books since 1792. This reform was particularly significant for the infantry because it comprised the bulk of the militia force. When the revised law went into effect, there were 107,422 enlisted men in the organized militia and 93,314 of them, or 87 percent, were foot soldiers.

The Militia Act of 1903 attempted to draw the National Guard (as the organized militias of the several states were coming to be called) closer into the military force controlled by the Federal government. This implied better training in peace time. When the act was passed, the improved training began to operate, and this, plus the beginning of war in Europe, accelerated the drawing together. Initially, according to the act of 1903, the United States could retain National Guard forces in its service for just nine months, whereas by 1908 Federal power had so enlarged that the President could specify the length of their service. Also, National Guard units volunteering for Federal service in 1903 could keep the officers they had; but by 1914 the power to appoint all officers, when the Guard was on active duty, had fallen to the President with the advice and consent of the Senate.

The great reforms in the Army which took place in 1903 affected the Regular infantry only indirectly. Creation of a General Staff and Army War College brought about co-ordinated thinking which, of course, touched the infantry. Very early, it was seen that, because of the great preponderance of infantry in the National Guard, the forces of the United States were out of balance. The Secretary of War hoped to offset the imbalance by maintaining a high proportion of cavalry and artillery in the Regular Army. Also, some foot units of the National Guard in seaboard states were converted into coast artillery. This does not mean that there was an excess of Regular infantry. On the contrary, in 1909 the Secretary asked that both infantry and artillery be increased. He fixed the proper proportion of infantry at 50 percent of the whole; but in the decade from 1901 to 1911, the ratio actually dropped from 50 to 35 percent.

Finally, it is necessary to mention the growing role of the Signal Corps in support of infantry. During the Civil War, the Corps had provided strategic communication, but by the time of the War with Spain it gave some tactical communication as well. This was accomplished by means of signal flags and, to an ever increasing extent, by telephones. Telephone lines began to follow the infantry very close to the firing line. This was but a beginning, for telephones supplemented by radios were to be the medium which in the twentieth century would link units of the same force on the vast battlefields, and link them better than they had once been linked by close-order formations.

The First World War

A full ten months ahead of the formal entry of the United States into World War I, the National Defense Act of 3 June 1916 erected the framework on which to expand the military establishment if conflict should come. At the time, there were thirty-one regiments of Regular infantry, counting the Puerto Rico Regiment of two battalions, plus thirteen battalions of Philippine Scouts. In addition, the National Guard contained around 110 regiments of infantry.

The National Defense Act raised the authorized size of the Army from 100,000 to 175,000, and provided that the increase be made in five annual increments, beginning 1 July 1916. The first increment included seven new infantry regiments, the 31st through the 37th. The 31st was organized in the Philippines, the 32d in Hawaii, the 33d in the Canal Zone, and the other four were organized in the continental United States. All seven of them expanded from cadres supplied by specified existing regiments. As soon as the United States entered the war, twenty-seven new infantry regiments were constituted and organized by the transfer of cadres from the other thirty-seven. When this process was completed, the Regular infantry comprised sixty-five regiments, seventeen more than ever before in American history.

The National Defense Act recognized four elements in the land forces: the Regular Army, the National Guard, the Reserve Corps, and in wartime the Volunteer Army. Once the nation actually went to war, the character of the latter element changed, for volunteering was scrapped except in the Regular Army and in the National Guard. The Volunteer Army became the National Army, which was raised by conscription. All in all, the wartime Army contained 297 infantry regiments of one kind or another and 165 machine gun battalions classed as infantry.

Infantry regiments and machine gun battalions together totaled 462 in World War I, a figure which is dwarfed by the 1,700-plus infantry units that served in the Civil War. One of the reasons for the contrast was the fact that regiments had increased three times in size; but the chief reason was that the units of the later war remained to the end, while those of the earlier one came and went.

The War Department on 11 July 1917 set up a system by which infantry units were to be designated. The designating numbers for all segments of the Regular Army began with 1. Regiments ran from 1 through 100, but these slots were never all filled. Just sixty-five Regular infantry regiments, in twenty divisions, came into being, and the higher numbers allocated to the Regulars were finally used by National Army units. No 66th was raised, but during July, August, and September 1918,

INFANTRYMEN ADVANCING THROUGH BARBED WIRE IN FRANCE.

the 67th through the 90th were organized around cadres from the first sixty-four. None of them (67th–90th) reached the theater of war. The numbers reserved for infantry regiments of the National Guard began at 101 and ran to 300, those for the National Army began with 301. Actually, the Guard regiments never used the numbers beyond 168, nor the National Army those past 388. The 376th through 378th, 381st, 382d, 385th, and 386th never came into being.

Late in the conflict, on 7 August 1918, the distinction between National Guard, Reserve Corps, Regular Army, and National Army was legally abrogated and all four elements were fused into one organization, the United States Army. This was the first time in American history that career soldiers, citizen soldiers, and drafted men of the infantry found themselves on the same legal basis.

Three years of observation of the war in Europe had convinced the General Staff that American tables of organization were obsolete. Accordingly, a series of changes in them began. The first one altered the existing triangular division, containing elements grouped by threes, to a square one. In this change, the three brigades of a division and the three regiments of a brigade gave way to two of each. The final result was a much larger division and brigade than any used by the nations of Europe. At the time of the armistice on 11 November 1918, an American division contained 28,105 men, nearly twice the number in European units. Firepower in both division and brigade was greatly augmented.

In the transition from triangular to square divisions, and in the consequent alteration of regiments and battalions, the elements of the National Guard were seriously dislocated. Since out of the 367,223 enlisted men of the Guard originally inducted, 242,000 (66 percent) were infantrymen, it was believed necessary to break up many infantry units. As a result, old regiments and other units were consolidated and broken up, thereby losing their identity and their proud state designations.

A typical example of the dislocation took place in the infantry elements of the state of Massachusetts. The old 2d Infantry was fortunate enough to remain intact under a new number as the 104th Infantry. The three other regiments, however, provided men for three infantry regiments (the 101st, 102d, and 103d) as well as for the 101st Engineer Train, the 101st Supply Train, the 101st Train Headquarters and Military Police, and the 3d, 4th, and 5th Pioneer Infantry.

Several of the newly constituted regiments of pioneer infantry drew their personnel from the breakup of National Guard units. Resembling standard infantry regiments only in size (3,551 men), they were in reality a labor force used primarily to repair roads and bridges. Thirty-seven regiments were organized in all, the 1st through the 6th, 51st through 65th, and 801st through 816th. National Guard personnel went into the 1st through the 59th regiments and drafted men into the 60th through the 65th. The outfits in the 800 series were formed of Negro personnel in 1918 to relieve the 1st through the 61st regiments, so that the latter could reorganize for service as combat infantry.

Regimental organization underwent some changes, but the National Defense Act forbade increasing the number of companies in a regiment beyond fifteen. Among the fifteen, a headquarters, a supply, and a machine gun company received permanent status for the first time. In any case, the changes reflected the requirements of trench warfare in Europe. Hence, an infantry regiment jumped from 2,002 to 3,720 enlisted men with an even larger increase in firepower.

The increase in size resulted from the need for deep formations in both attack and defense. In the attack, two battalions abreast might make up the first wave and the companies within them would be arranged also in depth. Behind the attack wave would come a support wave, perhaps the third battalion, and behind it would be elements withdrawn from the three battalions operating as a reserve. Likewise, successive positions in depth were the standard formation in defense. Such formations to be adequate required large regiments. As had been the case since the War with Spain, infantry regiments contained three battalions of four companies each.

At the root of the organizational changes listed, and others that took place, were the demands of weapons. The machine gun led the list. The necessity to develop a proper organizational framework for the best use of that lethal arm raised a thorny problem, a problem which was heightened by the great increase in the number of guns. In May 1917 there was but one machine gun company for each infantry regiment, while by July the number had risen to one per battalion. The ideal arrangement, after July, was to include three machine gun companies in every infantry regiment. Unfortunately, this could not be done because of the way the National Defense Act was worded—without cutting some rifle companies out of the regiment. Accordingly, it was necessary to create machine gun battalions that were elements of brigades and divisions, leaving just one company organic to infantry regiments. In numbering, the machine gun battalions followed the general rule. Battalions of Regular divisions and brigades were given numbers from 1 through 60; those of the National Guard from 101 through 151; and those of the National Army from 301 through 366. Since the 6th, 46th, 352d through 357th, 361st, 362d, 364th, and 365th were not organized, there was a total of 165 active infantry machine gun battalions during World War I. These units had to be put together from diverse segments of others that were broken up, hence their histories have not been passed down to modern outfits except in the National Guard.

The brigade battalions of machine guns contained three companies, while the division battalion was at first organized with four. This made a very awkward arrangement since machine gun companies had to be drawn from three sources—regiment, brigade, and division—in order to work with infantry battalions. Although the arrangement remained awkward throughout the war, and brigade and divisional battalions continued to exist, the division machine gun battalion was finally reduced to two companies. These were motorized and used as a highly mobile element of the divisional reserve.

It was easier to alter organization in order to include machine guns than it was to supply these weapons. Although machine guns had been included in American arms since 1862, World War I expanded their use so much that manufacturers in the United States could not at first supply enough of them. As a result, American doughboys employed Chauchat

2D Lt. Val A. Browning, son of the inventor, *instructing men of 315th Machine Gun Battalion in use of Browning machine gun.*

automatic rifles and Hotchkiss heavy machine guns made in France, as well as some British and American Vickers machine guns. The new American .30-caliber heavy machine guns and automatic rifles invented by John M. Browning were not used against the enemy at all until September 1918, only a few weeks before the armistice.

Of all the weapons an infantryman handled, his rifle changed the least. For supply reasons, the British Enfield became standard. It did not differ very much from the Springfield Model 1903, which the soldier knew. Likewise, the bayonet of the Enfield, a knife seventeen inches long, resembled the one it temporarily replaced.

In short, the standard rifle required no changes in the organization of units, but its power, coupled with that of other weapons, enforced changes in fighting formations.

Trench warfare brought with it a pressing need for weapons that were decisive in close combat. Out of this need came hand grenades, rifle grenades, and more extensive use of pistols and revolvers. Such short-range fireweapons tended to supersede cold steel and rifle butts as the tools of shock action, but American doctrine considered proficiency with the bayonet as still indispensable because it gave confidence and aggressiveness to foot soldiers.

In addition to the weapons that infantrymen handled as individuals, there were two served by crews. One, also a creature of trench warfare, was the Stokes mortar, which could lob projectiles into enemy trenches and shell holes. Another was the one-pounder cannon, an antitank and antimachine gun piece. These two weapons were placed together in a platoon of the headquarters company of every infantry regiment.

The weapons mentioned above, coupled with artillery, gas, tanks, and aircraft, dictated the minor tactics of infantry and slaughtered the troops of commanders who failed to heed their dictates. Indeed, machine guns are credited with having created the war of position and the accompanying stalemates which prevailed during 1915, 1916, and 1917. General

23D INFANTRY ADVANCING NEAR BOURESCHES, FRANCE. *(One-pounder cannon in foreground.)*

John J. Pershing carried this interpretation farther. He said that trench warfare had caused the belligerents in Europe to embrace a faulty doctrine. They placed too great a reliance on artillery and on mechanical aids. Pershing insisted, in contrast, that the basis of a sound army remained, as it had always been, a sturdy infantry. Accordingly, he required that American foot soldiers be trained primarily for open warfare, and only incidentally for duty in the trenches.

As already noted, depth was necessary to infantry formations. In the attack this meant successive waves of men; in defense, numerous positions, staggered irregularly one behind the other. Thus, all units from division down to platoon were organized to give the required depth within their respective sectors. The war confirmed the trend toward refining the organization of infantry units. Squads and platoons proved to be indispensable in twentieth century combat. Frequently the outcome of a fight depended on the integrity of those elements since they, and they alone, could be controlled personally by their leaders when under very heavy fire.

In addition to being organized to give depth, units at all levels were formed to give effect to the new weapons and to avoid losses from them in the hands of the enemy. It has been noted that the expanding use of machine guns required reorganizations which reached from divisions down to companies. The other weapons exacted changes, but they were not quite as widely disseminated. For example, infantry mortars and one-pounder guns found a place in the headquarters companies of regiments. Hand grenades, rifle grenades, and automatic rifles caused many changes in the organization of companies and their components. The question as to their best arrangement was never definitely settled during the war. All were included in a rifle company, but sometimes the automatic riflemen were formed together, as were the grenadiers and rifle grenadiers, other times they were scattered among the squads. As late as November 1918, in the Meuse-Argonne campaign, the specialists stayed together in combat groups, but the trend was toward dispersion so that every squad contained at least one automatic rifleman, one good grenade thrower, and one rifle grenadier.

Whatever the organization, extended order became necessary in combat. Men could not bunch up and live. Therefore, close formations had to break up when they came within artillery range. Approach to the enemy resulted in a progressive extension, and this in turn threw a greater burden on the commanders of platoons and squads. Small units of men inched themselves forward, taking advantage of shell holes and other cover.

It remains to mention briefly two allies of infantrymen that virtually revolutionized their combat methods. The first was the motor truck, which gave foot soldiers greater mobility than they had ever before had. The second was a miscellany of signal equipment. This helped the infantry to operate with some degree of co-ordination on huge battlefields where arm signals could no longer be seen and noise drowned out the human voice. It aided in making foot troops an effective instrument of the will of the commander, and served to rectify, at least a little, the disorganization that resulted from the necessity for soldiers to disperse widely in order to survive.

Between World Wars, 1919–1941

During the two decades between world wars, the infantry underwent startling changes that exceeded any in its previous history. The greatest of these was in speed. In 1919 a prime object had been to secure trucks to replace horses, so that foot soldiers could move toward the battlefield at fifteen to twenty-five miles an hour. In contrast, twenty years later the equivalent object was to use aircraft so that doughboys could hurtle toward fields of battle ten times as fast.

These twenty years were as contradictory as they were revolutionary. In them, the foot establishment declined steadily for the first seventeen years, and then soared to great heights in the last two.

During the first of the two decades, the impact of World War I was naturally dominant. Civilian Americans were determined to retrench from the unheard of costs of world war and, while they were at it, to forget warfare altogether. As a result, the authorized strength of the Regular infantry slid from 110,000 in 1920 to 40,331 in 1932. The proportion of foot soldiers to the whole establishment likewise dropped from near 50 percent to slightly less than 25.

So great a cut in the infantry—it amounted to 63 percent—of course played havoc with the regiments. Of the sixty-five in the Regular service, eighteen were inactivated in 1921 and eight during 1922. None of these were revived until 1940 and after. This heavy pruning left the block of regiments from the 1st through the 31st intact, with scattered numbers thereafter. The 33d, 34th, 35th, 38th, 42d, 45th (Philippine Scouts), 57th (Philippine Scouts), and 65th (Puerto Rico) Infantry survived, but the 42d was inactivated in 1927.

Even after twenty-seven infantry regiments had been inactivated, it was necessary to lop some battalions from those that survived. In consequence, by 1938 there were fourteen regiments out of the thirty-eight with but two battalions apiece. Nor was the whole reduction yet complete. Next, it was necessary to modify the tables of organization so that in peacetime all but two regiments had headquarters detachments instead of companies, while only one had a howitzer company, the rest having howitzer platoons. Also, rifle and machine gun companies contained two instead of three platoons. Thus reduced, they were hard pressed to turn out one war-strength platoon for purposes of training.

It is apparent from the figures just given that the thinking of Congress and of the people was more isolationist than before World War I. This fact, reflected in the emaciation of the Army, enforced a defensive psychology on the officers in the service. Accordingly, during the 1920's strategic planning was based on the assumption that if a major war came, it would be waged against the United States by some first-class power fighting in the Western Hemisphere.

The squeeze was aggravated by the expansion of the Air Corps, whose growth could only proceed at the expense of the other arms. By mid-1931 the infantry had already given 2,656 enlisted men to the growing air arm, and was soon to be drawn on for more. It was necessary to inactivate five battalions in 1930 to meet the quota.

A sharp pinch persisted until 1935, when the government's policy of spending to combat the Great Depression finally reached the Army and resulted, among other things, in an increased appropriation for personnel. This policy was abetted by the troubled state of Europe. At first the growth was slow, so that by 1939 the infantry had risen 17,000 from its 1932 low. That year the overall policy changed. Whereas before 1939 the Army had been recognized as no more than a cadre, afterwards there was official recognition that an army-in-being was needed, and $1,000,000,000 appropriated to implement its creation.

Beginning in 1940, some of the Regular infantry regiments, inactive for eighteen or nineteen years, were reactivated. That same year, forty regiments of National Guard infantry were inducted into Federal service, and the next year, thirty-six more. Hence, by mid-1941, there were 379,845 infantrymen of all types in service, organized in 136 regiments (including 18 armored) , 32 battalions (15 of them tank) , and 34 separate companies.

Even this number did not seem adequate to the Chief of Infantry, whose office was created in 1920. He pointed out that combat infantry-men made up less than 25 percent of the whole Army under the expansion plans, as contrasted with 50 percent in the German establishment. Such a proportion, he said, was not justified. It resulted from the fact that certain elements had been brought into the Army which tended to squeeze the infantry out. One of these was the heavy siege elements introduced during World War I for reducing trenches; the other was the armored element brought in afterward for use in distant maneuver. If the high command shared this view, it did not show the fact by altering the ratio of infantry to the whole Army. However, basic doctrine as late as 1939 restated the old principle that infantry was the prime element in combat, and that rifle and bayonet were still the chief weapons.

The experience of World War I was distilled into one document that cut across every phase of military life. This was the National Defense Act of 1920. It touched the infantry in many ways, but the principal way was in the creation of a Chief of Infantry. For some years agitation to provide the combat arms with chiefs had been growing. As a result of the National Defense Act, the doughboys after 1 July 1920, for the first time in United States history, had a chief who was the peer of the chiefs of the cavalry, coast artillery, field artillery, and of the technical services.

Another consequence of that comprehensive act was the assignment of tank units to the infantry. Thereafter for twenty years, development of tank materiel and doctrine was a responsibility of the Chief of Infantry. Tank units were known as "infantry (tanks)." A Tank Board and a Tank School were transferred in 1920 from the abolished Tank Corps of World War I, along with a number of tank companies. In 1929 some of these companies were formed into two newly constituted regiments, designated the 1st and 2d Tank Regiments. In 1932 they were redesignated as the 66th Infantry (Light Tanks) and 67th Infantry (Medium Tanks), respectively. The next year saw the constitution of two additional light tank regiments, the 68th and 69th, which were kept inactive. In 1940 the 69th was disbanded and the other three regiments, together with the former divisional tank companies, were assigned to the new Armored Force.

Lean as the infantry establishment was between world wars—even with the tanks in it—it nonetheless benefited from more careful planning and study than ever before. A few months prior to the appointment of a Chief, an Infantry Board designed to guide and plan developments in weapons and organization came into being at Fort Benning, Georgia. This body reported to The Adjutant General through the Infantry School. Attached to it was a Department of Experiment whose mission was to subject weapons and equipment to extensive tests. Naturally, when the Chief took office these units became responsible to him.

The Chief of Infantry, the Infantry School, the Infantry Board, the Department of Experiment, the Tank Board, and the Tank School engaged vigorously in the development of infantry. Their earliest contribution was a complete revision of the tables of organization. In this alteration, made during the twenties, the square division survived, but some of its infantry components were considerably modified. The most extreme change took place in infantry battalions, where one rifle company was eliminated and replaced by a machine gun company. This corrected the confusion of World War I in the use of machine guns by placing heavy machine guns under the control of infantry battalion commanders. Almost as extreme was the reduction of the number of platoons in a rifle company from four to three. Both these changes were in the direction of what was later called "triangularization," although it was not yet accepted as a broad principle.

Such changes, of course, reduced the firepower actually carried forward by infantrymen in an assault. No one claimed that the heavy machine guns, now organic to a battalion, could keep pace with the attacking doughboy. The reduction stemmed in part from the experience of the recent war which had shown that the number of rifles in a regiment was close to impossible to control. Also, it stemmed from the shrinking quantity of manpower available to the Army. In any case, two types of tables of organization were prepared, one for war, the other for peace. This dualism persisted to the very eve of the next war.

By the early thirties, improvements in weapons had made it possible for fewer men to deliver the same volume of fire. As an example, experts tinkered with the Browning Automatic Rifle (BAR) in an effort to correct its known weaknesses. By adding a butt plate, a small bipod, and a cyclic rate regulator, they greatly augmented the value of the weapon. The improvements, unfortunately, added five pounds to its weight.

The automatic rifle remained located within the rifle squad where it had come to rest at the close of the war. In 1930, one more was added provisionally to build up infantry firepower, making two to every squad. This arrangement did not last long but gave place to the older order in which one BAR was in every squad. Not until 1 February 1940 was this organization disturbed. Then, at the express request of the Chief of Infantry, who thought the added weight of the gun had put it out of the class of arms to be carried forward by riflemen, the BAR was removed from the rifle squad and put into a separate squad within the rifle platoon.

The BAR was not regarded as the decisive element in infantry firepower. American emphasis remained on the individual doughboy's shoulder arm. Accordingly, in the effort to substitute firepower for manpower there was a continuous search for an efficient self-loading rifle. Experiments by the Infantry Board soon made it clear that a semi-automatic rifle could increase the infantryman's rate of fire from ten or fifteen aimed shots to twenty or thirty per minute. What is more, the rounds could be better aimed because the marksman did not have to unsettle his aim to operate a bolt.

The Garand rifle, designated M1, was selected for development. By 1934 there were eighty M1's on hand, and by the fall of 1938 they were replacing the 1903 Springfield at the rate of 150 per week. Even so, the new rifle did not replace the old until after war had begun. Since the new rifle could deliver twice the fire of its predecessor, it made possible reductions in other weapons. For example, the total of automatic rifles in a regiment dropped from 189 to 81 in 1943. Although the figure subsequently rose, it never again, not even in war, attained the earlier level.

Likewise, the M1 influenced fire tactics. Notwithstanding that arms like it were known and used in Europe, they did not affect doctrine the same way as in this country. On the continent, firepower was increased principally by augmenting the number of light machine guns, while in the United States the increase came principally from the faster shooting shoulder arm of the individual rifleman. Thus in Europe, fire superiority depended on a gun served by a crew; in the United States it depended on the individual doughboy and his weapon.

It is not implied that the American Army slighted light machine guns. On the contrary, the World War I weaknesses of the BAR, together with its limitations, provoked much research to develop a suitable light machine gun. During the twenties and part of the thirties, the BAR was included in infantry armament only as a substitute for a hypothetical light machine gun which experts expected to be developed. Finally, in February 1940, at the suggestion of the Chief of Infantry, a true light machine gun appeared for the first time in the table of equipment. As this weapon was in very short supply, the improved BAR was made the official substitute. As a result, for the time being, BAR's were found in two different portions of an infantry company. They were standard armament in each rifle squad, and in addition, they were substitute armament in what was called the weapons platoon.

This weapons platoon (new in 1939) was part of a trend to integrate all necessary weapons except artillery and tanks into the basic tactical unit, the battalion. That trend made every element of an infantry battalion, even the squad, a more complex organization than before, and at the same time vastly increased its firepower. The heightened complexity, of course, brought with it the need for better communications, better training, and above all better leadership.

The improvements in portable weapons were important, but by no means as sharp a break with the past as the development of the arms that have come to be known as heavy weapons. These were first used during World War I; hence there was much to be done toward improving them and adjusting organization to use them most efficiently.

The first change to accommodate organization to the heavy weapons was the creation in 1920 of a howitzer company in each regiment to utilize the Stokes mortars and one-pounder cannon. Since the Regular infantry had not enough men to maintain the new howitzer companies, they were reduced to platoons. The National Guard, however, continued to support full companies. Into the howitzer unit, whether platoon or company, from time to time went various heavy infantry weapons devised between the wars. Among these were 81-mm. mortars, which were first used in very limited quantities in 1932; the various types of 37-mm. cannon, which replaced the one-pounder cannon; and .50-caliber machine guns.

The howitzer company was always more of an aspiration than a reality. Its name gave no clue to the weapons in it. Rather the name indicated the desire for a howitzer to accompany the infantry, a need which combat in World War I had seemed to reveal. In the years between wars no adequate accompanying cannon was developed. Finally, in the sweeping revision of 1939, the howitzer company was eliminated and its

DISPLAY OF THE VARIETY OF INFANTRY WEAPONS, 1927.

37-mm. cannon put into a new antitank company in each regiment.

In the same broad revision, the old machine gun companies of infantry battalions were reorganized to become heavy weapons companies. They absorbed the .30-caliber heavy machine guns of the older company and, in addition, acquired two 81-mm. mortars and two .50-caliber machine guns. The creation of the battalion heavy weapons company was part of the trend to include all weapons within a battalion that it would need to use whether attacking or defending. The process added greatly to the firepower of a battalion.

All the changes in organization and all the vigorous experiment with arms did not actually produce the weapons that were needed for training. Everything was in very short supply. In consequence, as late as 1941 mortar crews went through maneuvers with stove pipes and the crews of light machine guns set up and aimed broomsticks. These harsh facts caused the Chief of Infantry to state on the eve of war that a consciousness of obsolescence in all their arms had seriously damaged the morale of American infantrymen.

After 1939, battalion heavy weapons companies, regimental antitank companies, and weapons platoons within rifle companies were largely manned by soldiers who required some side arm other than the heavy Garand rifle. The ideal weapon for the crews of mortars, machine guns, and antitank guns had to be light, have a rapid rate of fire, and yet have greater range and accuracy than a pistol. As a result, the number of pistols authorized declined steadily, while new light side arms multiplied. One of the latter was the carbine, which came into general use in 1942. Another was the submachine gun, which had been used experimentally since 1922.

World War I had displayed two very pressing needs in warfare. One was for protection from devastating fires, the other for greater mobility. When applied to infantry, the two were contradictory, for the more protection the infantryman had, the heavier and slower he tended to become. After the war, tanks were made part of the infantry. They offered foot soldiers some added mobility and some protection. Accordingly, infantry doctrine took tanks into account, and the American infantry division included a company of light tanks in its organic structure. Indeed, in the basic theory expressed in the Field Service Regulations of 1939, armor was given the primary mission of helping the infantry advance. This being so, one can understand why the Chief of Infantry strongly protested when in July 1940 armor was removed from infantry control. As of 1939, tanks dropped out of infantry divisions, and never re-entered organically until after World War II.

Mobility was slowly increased in the infantry by the use of trucks. Hardly anyone doubted the value of motor vehicles to speed the movement of foot troops, but lack of funds restricted their use. Beginning in 1922 trucks replaced animals in the field and combat trains of four regiments. Later, other regiments received vehicles for the same purpose. By 1932, twelve were partly motorized. The trucks, however, were mostly worn-out leftovers from World War I.

It was the priming of the economic pump that finally secured some new vehicles for the infantry. In 1936 Congress authorized the purchase of 1,000 trucks and cars. With these, division and regimental headquarters could have autos, and six regiments could motorize their machine gun companies and howitzer and communications platoons.

Experiments with organization, motorization, weapons, and equipment were continuous in the decades between the wars, but the culminating experiments took place in 1937, 1938, and 1939. These were brought about by a growing belief among military leaders that the square divisional organization of World War I was too large and too unwieldy. Experts did not expect the static warfare of 1915–17 to recur; hence they no longer saw the need for the great power of penetration possessed by the square division. On the contrary, mobility was rising in importance, and it was hampered by large numbers. Regimental organization was in such confusion that there were five different types in the United States, while no two regiments serving overseas were alike. This was another consideration which prompted attempts to reorganize.

The object sought was an infantry division that was smaller and faster than the old one but with as much firepower. To obtain it the infantry establishment, from squad up to division, was given the most thorough examination it had ever received. Not everyone engaged in the examination agreed as to the means to the end. Most accepted three infantry regiments to a division, but differed as to their composition. The Chief of Infantry, for example, proposed four instead of three platoons to a rifle company, and a fourth rifle company in each battalion.

In any case, in 1937 the 2d Division was formed into a provisional unit to test the various proposals. For several months it tried out the suggested arrangements in the field. The trials were remarkably thorough, although they were handicapped by shortages of weapons and vehicles. For example, no light mortars were available, while only one regiment could be completely equipped with the M1 rifle. There were not enough .50-caliber machine guns and, of course, no light machine guns at all.

What emerged from the tests was a full new set of tables of organization which became effective during 1939. The new tables were built upon a triangular basis in which elements within an infantry division, from squads up to regiments, were associated by three's. Two levels of organization in the infantry were eliminated altogether, one large and the other small. These were brigades and sections. Triangularization made possible a simple and effective tactical doctrine, but some experts belittled this aspect. They said that the real reform in 1939 did not come from embracing a triangular organization but from the modernization of weapons that accompanied it.

The cornerstone of all infantry organization, the squad, was enlarged for wartime from eight men to twelve. This was done in spite of the evidence produced in the field tests that seven or eight men were all one corporal could hope to control in battle. The Chief of Infantry strongly urged the increase. The command weakness of so large a squad was corrected late in 1940 when the leader was made a sergeant and his assistant a corporal. With two noncoms in charge of it, the infantry squad would remain at twelve throughout the coming war.

One fact that made smaller divisions feasible was the fixed principle

2D BATTALION, 140TH INFANTRY, MISSOURI NATIONAL GUARD, *at Camp Joseph T. Robinson, Arkansas, 1941. (Remainder of regiment in background.)*

that divisions would usually operate as parts of larger units, that is, corps and armies. As parts, they could draw upon pools established in the big elements whenever they needed more men or more equipment than was normal. In other words, they would retain as organic only the units they needed for normal operations. The War Department called this arrangement "pooling," and put it into effect wherever practicable. The new grouping of heavy and crew-served weapons into battalion heavy weapons companies was a practical application of pooling. Also, the antitank weapons of regiments were pooled in antitank companies, and light machine guns and mortars in the weapons platoons of rifle companies.

The regiment adopted in 1939 was much smaller than before, containing but 2,542 men. According to the Chief of Infantry, such a regiment was too small by several hundred for effective combat action, and he vehemently protested. His protests resulted in new tables of organization the next year which raised the strength of a regiment by 907 men, and battalion and company proportionately.

The new triangular organization was put into effect in the Regular Army during 1939. Within the National Guard, however, the square organization, somewhat modified, persisted even after many units had entered Federal service in 1940.

All in all, the Chief of Infantry contended, and rightly, that in the years from 1937 to 1941 American infantry had undergone a real revolution. The foot establishment had been arranged along lines that were more carefully tested than ever before in peacetime. As for weapons, they were turned over completely, except for the .30-caliber heavy machine gun. The 60-mm. mortar (first adopted as standard in 1937, but remaining scarce) had replaced the old Stokes and its successors, while the heavier 81-mm. mortar had been introduced. A light machine gun had actually been adopted, and the BAR was so much improved as to be virtually made over. Finally, the 1903 Springfield shoulder rifle had yielded its place to the semi-automatic M1. In addition, new small arms such as carbines and submachine guns had entered infantry armament, together with a larger machine gun, the .50-caliber.

As a result of the revolution, the Chief of Infantry believed his branch to be organized on sound principles. The battalion, he said, was now a complete combat unit which contained within itself all elements, save armor and artillery, necessary to attack or to defend. Its weapons could be employed in direct or indirect fire and for high angle missions, or, if needed, for those requiring flat trajectories and high muzzle velocity. It was no longer dependent on attachments from regimental units for its firepower, needing to draw on pools only under unusual conditions.

Moreover, the elements of infantry were arranged according to mobility. A squad had the standard mobility of a rifleman; a platoon that of a BAR man. Platoons contained no crew-served weapons, and none requiring continuous resupply of ammunition. No weapon in the platoon served as a focus for hostile fire. At company level, the heaviest weapons (light machine guns and 60-mm. mortars) could be carried by hand; even a battalion contained no guns which could not be manhandled for several hundred yards. All weapons needing prime movers were placed in regimental units.

The Second World War

The coming of war resulted in the largest expansion of the infantry ever undertaken. During the three years, 1941–43, it increased 600 percent. Although this was 100 percent more than the field artillery, it fell far short of some of the newer arms, for example the antiaircraft artillery, which expanded 1,150 percent and later had to be cut back. In any case, before the conflict ended sixty-seven infantry divisions saw overseas service, plus one mountain and five airborne divisions, as well as a cavalry division which fought as infantry. Even the creation of armored divisions expanded the infantry, since they contained substantial foot components.

There were in all, at some time during the war, 317 regiments of infantry of various kinds. Among these were types unknown before the war, such as three mountain, twelve glider, and sixteen parachute infantry regiments. In addition there were 99 separate battalions, some of which were also very highly specialized.

Among the remarkable separate battalions were the 1st–6th Rangers. These were light infantry trained to slash deep into enemy-held territory in order to demoralize the foe in every way they could. Although the ranger battalions were not created by redesignating existing infantry outfits, and so not given any official history before the time of their constitution in 1942, they were nevertheless heirs to a very old and proud tradition. That tradition went further back than the American Revolution; indeed the rules drawn up by Robert Rogers in 1757 for his famous ranger companies that served for England in North America were reprinted for use in training the rangers of World War II.

The rangers were not the only infantry constituted to perform commando missions. A comparable unit was the 1st Special Service Force, established in July 1942. This force was designed to operate behind enemy lines when snow covered Europe. Accordingly, all its men were volunteers whose civilian aptitudes seemed to prepare them for swift operations in snow. Among them were lumberjacks, game wardens, forest rangers, and professional skiers. The 1st Special Service Force was remarkable also in another way; its personnel were drawn about equally from Canada and from the United States. It was an early experiment in international co-operation, and it worked well. After vigorous campaigning—but not much of it in snow—the unit was disbanded in January 1945 and most of its American personnel transferred to a new regiment, the 474th Infantry.

Still another commando-type outfit was the 5307th Composite Unit (Provisional), which was organized in October 1943. Its specialization was operation in Burma along the Ledo Road, and its personnel were drawn from men who knew jungle fighting. This unit was commanded by Brig. Gen. Frank D. Merrill and became very famous under the nickname of "Merrill's Marauders." Like the men of the ranger battalions and of the 1st Special Service Force, the Marauders were volunteers. At length, on 10 August 1944 the unit was reorganized and called the 475th Infantry.

Another type of specialized infantry was that intended to provide the foot elements of the new armored divisions. It was called "armored infantry." The first unit of this type in the United States Army came into being when the old 6th Infantry was reorganized as armored on 15 July 1940. In addition to the 6th, certain regiments which had been on the inactive list since just after World War I were reactivated to become armored infantry. These were the 36th, 41st, 46th, 48th–52d, 54th–56th, 59th, and 62d Infantry. Most of the armored infantry regiments were broken up during World War II to form separate armored infantry battalions, but the 41st and 36th Armored Infantry—assigned to the 2d and 3d Armored Division, respectively—retained the regimental structure throughout the war.

Armored infantry differed very little from standard infantry, and Lt. Gen. Lesley J. McNair, Chief of Staff, General Headquarters, objected to its differing at all. The chief variance was that armored troops had enough organic vehicles to move all of their men at once. They shared this characteristic with motorized infantry (an element of motorized divisions), which came into existence in August 1940 and lasted only until July 1943. Unlike motorized, armored infantry had vehicles that could operate cross-country and that were lightly armored to repel small arms fire.

Several types of light infantry were also extensively tested. One was specialized for jungle action. This type, embodied in the regiments of the 71st Light Division, never had a chance to prove itself in combat. It had not shown to very good advantage in training; hence it was converted to standard infantry in the early summer of 1944. In consequence, it was the ordinary doughboy who, beginning in the fall of 1942, did the jungle fighting in the Southwest Pacific. Another specialized type was organized for use in mountains. It was embodied in the regiments of the 10th Mountain Division, which, unlike the jungle division, enjoyed a brief opportunity to practice its specialty. The 10th Division reached Italy late in 1944 and took part in the fight. Its arrival, however, did not preclude many other infantry outfits from having to fight in the mountains the best way they could.

The last of the nonstandard types of infantry units to be considered here was the most specialized. It included the foot soldiers who were trained and equipped to reach the combat zone by air and to assault from the air. Their primary mission was to land behind the enemy's main line of resistance and there employ commando tactics. This type, new in the United States, like armored infantry, was first organized in 1940. As with

PARATROOPERS OF 503D PARACHUTE INFANTRY *dropping on Corregidor.*

armored, General McNair objected in the beginning to so high a degree of specialization, but by 1942 acknowledged the need for airborne troops.

Some foot troops that assaulted from the air were dropped behind the enemy's line by parachute. Numbers above 500 were reserved for the designation of paratroops. Thus the lowest numbered paratroop infantry regiment was the 501st Parachute Infantry. In addition, there was a second type of airborne foot troops, called "glider infantry." According to the doctrine, these landed by glider in the airheads cleared by the paratroops to reinforce the latter and to widen the assault upon the rear of the foe. The numerical designations for glider units were drawn from the whole range of numbers below 500. This was the result of an effort to perpetuate earlier history, as in the case of the 88th Glider Infantry, which descended from the 88th Infantry of World War I. Likewise, the 325th–328th Glider Infantry were redesignated from the infantry regiments of the same numbers which had made up the 82d Division in World War I. The same was true of the 401st Glider Infantry of the

101st Division. Both the 82d and the 101st Divisions became airborne on 15 August 1942.

The World War II infantry also included a few units that were made up of Americans of different racial or ethnic extraction. There was ample precedent for such outfits. Indian and Negro infantry regiments were the oldest, but Puerto Rican and Filipino units came close behind. Added to these during the war were several separate battalions, the most conspicuous of which was the 100th Infantry Battalion because it contained soldiers of an enemy race. Its men were American-born Japanese. The 100th Battalion was organized in June 1942, and two years later was absorbed as one of the battalions of a Japanese-American regiment designated the 442d Infantry.

Another unit of this type was the 99th Infantry Battalion, which was made up of Norwegian-Americans and marked for use in Scandinavia. Although the 99th did not get to the Scandinavian Peninsula until the Germans there had surrendered, it did distinguish itself in the fighting in Europe. Finally, early in 1945, when its use as a separate battalion seemed to be over, it was made one of the battalions of a newly organized regiment designated the 474th. The latter was a remarkable hybrid. It contained many men from the disbanded 1st Special Service Force, some from the 1st, 3d, and 4th Ranger Battalions, as well as the entire 99th Battalion. Another hybrid was the 473d Infantry. Also created early in 1945, it absorbed no groups of nationals but rather the veterans of four antiaircraft battalions coupled with the headquarters of an armored group.

Early in the war, the organization of scores of new units proceeded along the lines laid down in the reorganization of 1939. The National Guard, however, entered Federal service in square combinations and retained them until directed to triangularize during the first four months of 1942. As in World War I, the reorganization of the National Guard for Federal service wrecked many old outfits and associations. For example, in each of the square divisions one whole regiment of infantry had to be cut away and broken up or associated elsewhere.

In spite of the wrench it gave the National Guard, triangularization brought with it important benefits. Not the least of these was a very simple tactical doctrine which had the advantage of being applicable to the use of units of any size from squad up to division. This doctrine was developed and well established by the time the National Guard was triangularized. Its essence was that one of the three elements of every level, say one regiment, should, in the assault, fix the enemy in position; a second was to maneuver around him, once fixed, in order to strike a decisive blow; while the third element acted as a reserve. This doctrine gave great flexibility to American infantry.

During the five years before Pearl Harbor, the position of the dough-boy's champion, the Chief of Infantry, weakened. The Chief himself felt that his office was being bypassed in important matters, while the Chief of Staff inclined more and more to the opinion that all of the heads of combat arms fostered schisms within the Army. In any case, during the grand revision of the late thirties, the General Staff, more often than not, overruled the recommendations of the Chief of Infantry. Moreover, the latter had less control over his branch than he thought necessary. For example, in the revamping of the infantry division, his responsibility was held to the preparation of tables of organization and equipment for brigades and below. The end came in the spring of 1942 when the top command was completely reorganized. In that great realigning the Chief of Infantry, together with the other chiefs of combat arms, was eliminated. Thereafter, the problems of the infantry were considered by special branches of the newly created Army Ground Forces.

General McNair became Commanding General of the new organization. He had been chief of staff of the provisional division that had tested triangularization in 1937, and he believed in the basic principles of the revision that had resulted. Foremost among these was pooling. Its natural corollary was to keep all units lean, because, when extraordinary needs arose, those units could draw from the pools maintained at the next higher level. Another of the important principles embraced by McNair was that which gave the best of men and equipment to the offensive portions of units, and cut the other segments to a minimum. The application of these austere principles was sharpened by the urgent need to conserve shipping space; McNair, therefore, caused infantry organization to be finely combed for excess personnel and equipment.

A general revision of the tables of organization and equipment (TOE's) took place in the spring of 1942. For the most part, McNair's principles prevailed, but he was unable to prevent two significant changes in a contrary direction. The first of these was the substitution of head-quarters companies for detachments in all battalions. In spite of this alteration the total strength of a battalion dropped by sixteen, the cut occurring in the rifle companies and in heavy weapons. The second change brought a new company, the cannon company, into the regiment. In it were at last to be found the accompanying cannon that officers had been seeking since World War I. As first equipped, the new cannon company contained six self-propelled 75-mm. howitzers and two self-propelled 105's. It added 123 men to each regiment, but since the other regimental companies were cut at the same time, a regiment was actually enlarged by only 23 men. The TOE's of 1 April 1942 moved automatic rifles for the last time. These weapons, which were proving themselves more and more valuable, went back to the rifle squad where they had been placed prior to February 1940. They had gone into a separate squad at the insistence of the Chief of Infantry, and they returned to the rifle squad when that office was eliminated.

The pinch for shipping space continued so great that the War Department requested cuts in the April tables. Accordingly, a Reduction Board was established in November 1942. Before its recommendations were approved, General McNair strove to reduce the infantry regiment by 400 men, a slice which he believed could be made without diminishing the number of front-line riflemen to any great extent. His proposal was made into a new TOE published on 1 March 1943. The chief casualty was the cannon company, which was eliminated altogether; its howitzers were put into headquarters company. This arrangement was shortlived, since the final work of the board resulted in a cut of only 216 which, when finally approved, was embodied in tables dated 15 July 1943. Most of the 216 came from administrative elements and from heavy weapons. The cannon company was back, but this time with towed howitzers. The sharpest reduction in arms that accompanied the drop in personnel fell upon BAR's. These were eliminated from every echelon except the rifle squad, where there was one per squad. This change removed very little automatic rifle fire from the firing line, but it did reduce the number of BAR's in a regiment from 189 to 81 (there being 81 rifle squads in a regiment).

If a regiment lost any firepower by the cut in automatic rifles, it made it up by the addition of twenty-five .50-caliber machine guns plus one hundred and twelve new 2.36-inch rocket launchers, nicknamed "bazookas." The bazookas, which had splendid attributes for antitank and antipillbox use, were extra weapons; that is, no specific men were designated to operate them. In consequence, each regiment made its own organizational modification to use the new arm. Later the orphan situation of rocket launchers was officially corrected.

Bazookas and .50-caliber machine guns fitted into General McNair's theory of antitank and antiaircraft defense for infantry regiments. He held that such defense should center on weapons which individual infantrymen, not crews, could operate. Once again, he did not win out 100 percent, for he failed to eliminate either the towed antitank guns from the armament of regiments or the mine platoon from antitank companies. There were, however, changes in the antitank guns: their caliber was increased from 37-mm. to 57-mm., while the number of guns in the regiment dropped from twenty-four to eighteen. Half of the remaining guns were in the regimental antitank company, the other half divided evenly (three each) among the battalions. Considering the mine platoon as strictly defensive, General McNair strove to eliminate it altogether. Accordingly, it did not find a place in the TOE of 26 May 1943; but was back on 15 July, thirty-one strong.

Removal of tanks from the infantry and the creation of an armored force in 1940 had left unsolved problems in the relationship of foot soldiers to tanks. The principle of pooling took care of the association of tanks with infantry units, for tank elements were simply attached in the quantities needed. This, however, did not help to determine how much infantry ought to be organic to armored divisions. Since these divisions, as first set up, did not include enough foot soldiers, General McNair created pools of separate armored infantry battalions (AIB's) from which the divisions could draw. Later his solution was scrapped, and in the TOE of 15 September 1943 the proportion of organic infantry to armor doubled. In consequence, all but one of the separate AIB's were inactivated.

Each of the studies of infantry organization, made in the first three years of the war, had to take vehicles into account. The number of motors allowed to units was closely related to the shipping space then available. Shortage of shipping was one of the factors which caused the elimination of motorized infantry in the summer of 1943, since the planners felt that more economical means of moving standard infantry by motor were at hand. The first such means was to attach truck outfits to the infantry for specific movements. This method remained standard until divisions developed the field expedient of piling their doughboys onto their tanks, tank destroyers, and howitzers.

All these complications were faced by Army Ground Forces during the year from October 1942 to October 1943, and the organization developed for infantry in that year persisted for the duration of the war in Europe with only minor changes. However, when redeployment to the Pacific area became necessary, Ground Forces once more examined the tables of organization and equipment. This time three factors were decisive in the appraisal. The first one was the wealth of combat experience accumulated in Europe; the second, that the scarcity of shipping space had eased; and the third, the death of General McNair. These new factors resulted in a general enlargement of infantry units.

The new tables were dated 1 June 1945. They carried the implication that the earlier arrangements had been too lean for greatest efficiency. For example, they increased the total strength of an infantry regiment from 3,256 to 3,697, and added weapons and vehicles. Most of the increase took place in rifle companies, which jumped from 193 to 242 men. Indeed,

ADVANCING INFANTRYMEN FROM 29TH INFANTRY DIVISION *enter St. Lô, France.*

two new sections were added to them, both in the weapons platoons. The first one, called an assault section, was based on the 2.36-inch bazooka (the number of which increased to six per rifle company). With this change, rocket launchers ceased to be orphans. They became the principal weapons of the men in the new section. The other, a special weapons section, employed a revolutionary type of new arm, the 57-mm. recoilless rifle.

Further use of the recoilless technique occurred at battalion level. Here a 75-mm. rifle was added to the armament, and a gun platoon was created in the heavy weapons company to operate it. The two new types of recoilless guns, which combined the effect of artillery with the mobility of soldier-carried arms, gave an unheard of weight of fire to the infantry.

Yet another remarkable change related to the infantry regiment's artillery. All towed guns were at last eliminated from the regiment. The 57's of the regimental antitank company gave place to tanks which mounted 90-mm. guns, while those in battalions went out with the anti-

INFANTRYMAN USING WALKIE-TALKIE.

tank platoons. The cannon company became in effect a tank unit equipped with heavy tanks mounting 105-mm. howitzers. The pieces of the antitank and the cannon companies, mounted as they were on tanks, were much more mobile than their predecessors, and they threw much more metal.

The organization established in June 1945, slightly modified from time to time, was the one that governed to the end of the conflict. There was, however, one development which went forward apart from the tables of organization. This was an ever widening use of regimental combat teams (RCT's). An RCT was a grouping of combat units around an infantry regiment in order to accomplish a special mission. A typical combat team contained a regiment of infantry, a battalion of 105-mm. artillery, a company of combat engineers, a medical collecting company, and a signal detachment. But, because its very essence was flexibility, any element needed to accomplish the special mission might be attached. RCT's proved of great value in adapting organization to all types of terrain and conditions of combat. They remained, however, temporary arrangements without official history or lineage, and were discontinued when their special mission had been accomplished.

Before concluding the discussion of infantry organization during World War II, it remains to record a few generalizations relating to the use of infantry in that war. First, it is clear that no earlier conflict had sent American infantrymen into so many different parts of the world. Although specialized units were at first created to fight in extreme zones, mountain, jungle, and arctic foot soldiers carried, in fact, a very small part of the fighting in extreme climates and terrain. As a result, the standard doughboy took over the job.

The doctrine of fixing the enemy, maneuvering to strike him in flank or rear, all the while holding an element in reserve to exploit an ad-

ASSAULT LANDING BY 163D INFANTRY ON WAKDE ISLAND, *18 May 1944.*

INFANTRYMEN LANDING ON OMAHA BEACH ON D-DAY.

vantage or cover a retreat, applied in all terrains. Naturally the details of using it varied with geography. Thus in Normandy the hedgerows obliged the infantry to work out a team play with tanks and engineers. Likewise, in the jungles of the Southwest Pacific, the coral atolls of the Central Pacific, the desert of North Africa, and the mountains of Italy, it was necessary to develop the exact means by which the doctrine was applied. But in all cases it required closer-than-ever co-operation with the other arms.

Furthermore, never before had the doughboys been required to use so bewildering a complex of weapons. Perhaps the most confusing of the latter to adjust to was the greatly enlarged class of defensive weapons, which included land mines and boobytraps. These insidious manglers complicated an infantryman's task and introduced a new type of terror into his campaigning. He dared no longer even trust the ground, which had always been his close ally. As a result, it was necessary to learn not only to detect and disarm the enemy's mines and traps, but to lay some effectively for his own protection. Also, he had to learn to use demolition charges and often to improvise them out of materials at hand.

To add to the confusion, types of grenades (hand and rifle) were multiplied. What is more, their use vastly increased. Whether the enemy lurked in rocks or in dense vegetation, grenades helped to root him out. To supplement them in the business of dislodging the foe from strong positions, new weapons developed. The most notable of these, not already mentioned, was a flame thrower which, carried by foot soldiers or mounted on tanks, did terrible execution.

Tank and air enthusiasts, observing the Nazi *blitzkrieg*, had jumped to the conclusion that infantry could be used only to hold ground taken by armor or by air bombardment. This did not prove to be the case. Although foot soldiers, more than ever before, had to learn to co-operate with tanks and with planes, this did not spare them from having to be in the forefront of almost all important assaults. In short, while they could not advance against the enemy without the aid of tanks, artillery, and air, neither could those arms gain ground or destroy the enemy's will to fight without the aid of the infantry. What was required was not a reshuffling of the importance of the several branches, but the development of better techniques by means of which they could work together. Such techniques were far from perfect when the conflict came to an end.

Battlefield communication continued its trend—which stretched back to the Civil War—toward improvement. For the first time there was radio communication between the elements of a company. By the end of World War II eight radios were included in the rifle company's equipment. Radios and telephones knit companies tighter together, but by no means made them act as one man. Dispersion to avoid the deadly effects of enemy fire threw squads, or fractions of squads, on their own in combat, particularly in dense foliage, in the mountains, and in night operations. This put a heavier-than-ever burden on the ingenuity of squad and platoon leaders, and even on the individual doughboy.

Probably the most important technique to come out of the war had to do with landing an attacking force on hostile shores. The doctrine for such operations had been in the process of development by the U.S. Marine Corps since the 1920's. Marine theory worked well, but it required the assistance of special amphibious equipment which was not developed until war had commenced. Indeed, in the early landings in 1942, landing forces were obliged to use the vessels that were ready at hand. Gradually, however, landing craft were developed, such as LCI's, LST's, LCT's, amphibious tanks, and DUKW's. In the greatest amphibious operations of World War II, these craft were as essential to success as the weapons of the infantry.

Whether in landing actions, in airborne assaults, or in advances of a traditional type, infantry was better prepared than in the past to fight on a circular perimeter. This was true because of the many supporting mortars, machine guns, and rocket launchers, made organic to infantry units, which enabled them to throw fire quickly in all directions. Thus, the tendency was to be less sensitive about the flanks than in earlier wars, and to push forward with slighter concern for the progress of the units to the right and to the left.

During World War II new terrains, new climates, strange weapons, and unfamiliar peoples acted upon American infantrymen. These destroyed thousands of men, put a lifelong mark on others, and changed somewhat the techniques of fighting on foot; nevertheless, in spite of everything, the basic characteristics of the infantry hardly shifted. Foot soldiers continued to be the only carriers of weapons who, in theory, were never exhausted, could always go another mile, and who could be counted upon to move across any terrain in every quarter of the globe.

World War II to Korea

With the end of World War II came the difficult task of demobilizing the huge wartime military establishment and of reorganizing the infantry for its peacetime role. The demobilization was extremely hasty and, as General of the Army George C. Marshall stated before a joint session of Congress, ". . . [it had] no relationship whatsoever to the size of the Army in the future." Furthermore, it was carried out on the basis of an individual point system, not by units. The point system was designed to be fair to the individual soldier and satisfied the insistent demands of Congress, the public, and the press to "bring the boys back home" as soon as possible, but its effects on unit integrity, efficiency, and combat capability were disastrous. There were too few units left to meet all the worldwide responsibilities the United States had acquired with victory, while infantry organizations remaining active were so understrength and suffered such constant personnel turnover that they seemed more like replacement centers than combat units.

By 30 June 1947 demobilization was officially completed. From a peak strength of 8,291,336 on 31 May 1945 the Army had been reduced to 989,664 in only twenty-five months. During the same period the infantry totals dropped at an even faster rate from 1,782,832 to 126,121. The number of infantry regiments decreased from 288 to 41, and only seven separate infantry battalions remained active. More than three-fourths of the active infantry units were assigned to divisions: 8 infantry, 2 airborne, 1 armored, and 1 cavalry. With the exception of the 88th, which was in the process of being inactivated in Italy, each infantry division had three organic infantry regiments. The airborne divisions had one glider and two parachute infantry regiments each, and the armored division had three armored infantry battalions. Only the 1st Cavalry Division still retained the square structure with four organic regiments which, although reorganized in 1945 as infantry, kept their cavalry designations. As of 1 July 1947, all separate infantry battalions and eleven regiments were stationed in the United States. The rest of the infantry regiments were overseas with nineteen in Japan and Korea and the other eleven in Germany, Italy, the Philippines, the Canal Zone, Puerto Rico, and Trinidad.

Although the first problem of the postwar infantry was demobilization, even while that was going on plans were being made for the reorganization of infantry units in the light of the experience gained and the lessons learned during World War II. Since the war had been won and infantry organization, weapons, and tactics had proved to be effective in different theaters of operations and against different enemy forces, there was no motivation for radical innovations. The explosion of the atomic bomb was still too recent to influence infantry organization at this time. Nevertheless, it did have an indirect effect on infantry units, since in the general enthusiasm over this ultimate modern weapon the infantry was sometimes forgotten or, at any rate, overshadowed. Attempts to re-establish the office of the Chief of Infantry failed, because Army leaders believed that chiefs of the combat arms would tend to encourage undesirable branch consciousness and interbranch rivalry. To the infantry this meant that it had no official spokesman, nobody to look out for

PRESENTATION OF PRESIDENTIAL UNIT CITATION (ARMY) STREAMER TO
442D INFANTRY *by Lt. Gen. John C. H. Lee.*

its interests, and no one to take care of its problems.

Responsibility for the development and preparation of infantry tables
of organization and equipment, formerly the function of the Chief of
Infantry, had been passed in 1942 to Headquarters, Army Ground Forces,
which became the Office, Chief of Army Field Forces, in March 1948.
The postwar TOE's for standard and armored infantry units were published between late 1947 and mid-1948 after months of careful study,
evaluation, and review. They reflected various recommendations and
suggestions, particularly those of the General Board, United States
Forces, European Theater, and of the Infantry Conference which was
sponsored by the Infantry School at Fort Benning, Georgia, in June 1946.
Although they did not introduce any significant new organizational con-
cepts, the 1947–48 tables brought some changes to all infantry units from
the squad to the division.

One of the most important changes was made in the rifle squad. The consensus was that the 12-man squad of World War II was too large and unwieldy. As a result, the ammunition bearer and the two scouts were eliminated, and the new unit had only nine men: a squad leader, an assistant squad leader, a BAR team of two men, and five riflemen, one of whom was armed with the sniper version of the M1 rifle. The M1, which had been highly effective and very popular during the war, was retained as the basic individual weapon of the infantryman, and a bayonet was issued with each rifle.

With the reduction of the squad by three men, the rifle platoon lost nine rifles, but its firepower did not decrease. On the contrary, the post-war organization gave the platoon leader greater firepower under his immediate control by adding a new 9-man weapons squad to support the three rifle squads. The final World War II TOE had placed the infantry company's 2.36-inch rocket launchers and .30-caliber light machine guns in one weapons platoon. The postwar table moved both of these weapons to the new squad in the rifle platoon, leaving only 60-mm. mortars and 57-mm. recoilless rifles in the weapons platoon.

The heavy weapons company, organic to each infantry battalion, was also streamlined under the 1947 TOE. One of the machine gun platoons was dropped and the 81-mm. mortars and 75-mm. recoilless rifles authorized in June 1945 were both reduced from six to four per company. Of its nine rocket launchers only six remained, but the new ones were the more powerful 3.5-inch bazookas, whereas the old ones had been 2.36-inch launchers.

Even more changes were made on the regimental level. During World War II, the artillery provided such responsive and effective fire support that the infantry regiment no longer needed its own cannon company. Chemical mortar companies, on the other hand, had been frequently and very successfully attached to infantry units. Combat experience had also shown that the best antitank weapon was the tank itself and that the infantry-tank team was an extremely effective fighting unit. Accordingly, both the cannon and the antitank company were eliminated, while a heavy mortar company (armed with twelve 4.2-inch mortars) and a tank company of 148 men and twenty-two tanks became organic to the postwar infantry regiment. Additional tank support for divisional infantry units was available from a tank battalion, which was made part of the infantry division for the first time in the 1947–48 tables.

There was no special unit for air defense in the infantry regiment, but the number of .50-caliber Browning machine guns, employed primarily as antiaircraft weapons, increased from thirty-three to forty-seven, and a newly created automatic weapons battalion in the division artillery further improved antiaircraft protection. The 1948 regiment also had a larger headquarters and headquarters company, a larger service company, and an organic medical company instead of an attached medical detachment. All of these changes, which made the postwar infantry regiment a much more powerful and sophisticated unit than its World War II predecessor, were accomplished with only a slight gain in overall regimental strength from 3,697 to 3,774.

While three infantry regiments remained the basic combat elements of the infantry division, as they had been throughout the war, the postwar armored division had more organic infantry units than either the "heavy" or "light" armored division of World War II. The General Board, United States Forces, European Theater, had concluded that there were not enough infantrymen in the armored divisions, especially in those organized under the "heavy" 1942 TOE's. The board recommended that three composite tank-infantry regiments, each comprised of one tank battalion and two armored rifle battalions, be assigned to the division. Although this suggestion was not adopted in the postwar organization, the ratio of infantry to tank units was improved by authorizing four armored infantry battalions for each division and four rifle companies for each battalion, thus raising the total number of armored infantry companies in the armored division from nine to sixteen.

The structure of the armored infantry battalion (AIB) differed somewhat from that of the standard infantry battalion. The 917-man infantry battalion consisted of a headquarters and headquarters company, a heavy weapons company, and three rifle companies of 211 men each. The AIB was larger by 152 men and had a headquarters, headquarters and service company, a medical detachment, and four armored infantry companies of 208 men each. The infantry company's weapons platoon and three rifle platoons of three rifle squads and a weapons squad paralleled the armored infantry company's mortar platoon and three rifle platoons of three rifle squads and a light machine gun squad. There were ten men in the 1948 armored infantry rifle squad—one more than in its regular infantry counterpart. The tenth man drove the squad's newly issued full-tracked armored utility vehicle, M44, which replaced the half-track personnel carrier used during World War II.

The basic weapons of the standard infantry and the armored infantry were the same, although the quantity of the weapons varied. Armored infantry units, however, were not authorized any recoilless rifles. On the other hand, they had many more rocket launchers and machine guns. In an armored rifle company, for example, there were ten bazookas and nineteen machine guns, as opposed to only three and four, respectively, in a regular rifle company. As a result, the armored infantry was capable of providing greater automatic fire support than other infantry units.

The first postwar airborne infantry TOE's did not appear until 1 April 1950, but airborne units had been organized earlier under draft tables similar to the final published tables. Perhaps the main reason for this delay was the fact that there were more changes made in airborne organization than in other types of infantry. Despite their unique and highly specialized primary mission of seizing and holding important objectives by attack from the air, airborne units in World War II were frequently called upon to perform normal infantry missions. Both combat experience and tests conducted after the war at Fort Bragg, North Carolina, showed that they needed to be organized more like standard infantry units in order to be self-sustaining in ground operations over extended periods. The new TOE's, therefore, gave the airborne infantry more staying power and organized it along the same lines as the regular infantry, while retaining its special air assault capability.

During World War II there had been two types of airborne regiments—parachute and glider. After the war both of these units were eliminated, and the 1 April 1950 TOE's introduced an airborne infantry regiment, which was capable of landing by parachute, glider, or aircraft. Three of these new units were organic to the postwar airborne division, and provisions were also made for nondivisional regiments. The airborne infantry regiment had a strength of 3,376 men and contained a headquarters and headquarters company, a service company, a support company, a medical company, and three airborne infantry battalions. Its structure was similar to that of the regular infantry regiment, except that instead of a tank company and a heavy mortar company, the airborne unit had a support company. The disadvantages of not having a regimental tank company were somewhat offset in divisional units by the fact that the airborne division was authorized two organic tank battalions, while the infantry division had only one.

The support company consisted of a company headquarters, two heavy mortar platoons armed with four 4.2-inch mortars each, and an antitank platoon with six 3.5-inch rocket launchers, three heavy .50-caliber machine guns, and six 90-mm. antitank guns on airborne carriages. It was a very powerful unit, completely motorized, capable of landing by parachute or aircraft, with its own fire direction center and its own communications system. The organization of the airborne infantry battalion, company, platoon, and squad was almost identical to that of the corresponding standard infantry units. Likewise, the weapons used by both types of infantry were also the same, except for the airborne antitank gun.

There was a considerable time lag between the publication of the postwar TOE's and the actual reorganization of infantry units under the new tables. Even after the reorganization had officially taken place, there were still differences between the paper organizations and the actual units, since most units were understrength and not fully equipped. A separate reduced strength column, to be effective in peacetime, was added to all TOE's in November 1950, but until then special cut sheets or reduction tables were prepared for infantry units by the Office, Chief of Army Field Forces.

On the eve of the Korean War, only one of ten active combat divisions was being maintained at full strength. The others averaged about 70 percent of their authorized strength and had major shortages in equipment. For example, infantry units generally did not have the organic armor provided by the new TOE's or were equipped with lighter and older tank models than those authorized. Nor did they have their full allowances of 57-mm. and 75-mm. recoilless rifles and 4.2-inch mortars, while the 3.5-inch rocket launchers were still in the process of being tested. Many infantry battalions were short one rifle company, and in most infantry regiments only two out of the three battalions were active. Since current infantry tactics were based on triangular organization, such reductions were very serious handicaps.

Shortcomings in infantry personnel and equipment were caused by budget cuts, strength ceilings, and other limitations placed upon the postwar Army by an economy-minded Congress and administration. These actions were supported by a war-weary public traditionally opposed to a large peacetime military establishment and overly dependent on the atomic bomb as a deterrent to future wars. Even after demobilization had been completed and the Air Force had become a separate service, the strength of the Army still continued to decline. The crisis produced by the Soviet blockade of Berlin and the Allied airlift of supplies to the isolated city brought about a temporary increase in Regular Army personnel. By 30 June 1950, however, the actual strength had dropped again to 591,487 out of an authorized total of 630,000. The active infantry at that time numbered 130,554 officers and enlisted men.

In mid-1950 the infantry in the Regular Army consisted of forty-six regiments and thirteen separate battalions. There were seven infantry combat divisions with three organic infantry regiments each, including the 1st Cavalry Division, which had finally been triangularized in 1949. The 2d Armored Division was organized under the 1947–48 TOE's that authorized four armored infantry battalions (AIB's) per division. The 82d Airborne Division had three airborne infantry regiments, while in the 11th Airborne Division only two of the three organic regiments were active. In addition to the ten combat divisions, there were four training divisions (three infantry and one armored), which had nine infantry regiments and four AIB's assigned to them. The eleven separate regiments were all organized as standard infantry; two of the five nondivisional battalions were AIB's and the other three were regular infantry battalions. There were no separate airborne regiments or battalions, neither of the old parachute and glider infantry nor of the new airborne infantry.

Besides having major shortages in both personnel and equipment, the active infantry units were also inadequately trained. At first the disintegration caused by rapid demobilization had made effective unit training virtually impossible, and the numerous administrative chores of occupa-

INFANTRYMAN ON OCCUPATION DUTY IN JAPAN.

tion duty also interfered with training programs. Occupation of the countries defeated in World War II remained by far the single greatest responsibility of the infantry throughout the 1945–50 period and was a heavy drain on the Army's overall effort. Although the duties were gradually reduced everywhere and troops were completely removed from some areas as peace treaties were signed, on the eve of the Korean War about one-third of the infantry was still on occupation duty.

Not until late in the postwar era was more emphasis placed on training and readiness. In January 1950, General Mark W. Clark, Chief of Army Field Forces, announced that the most extensive and diversified peacetime maneuver training program in Army history was then under way. In this program infantry units participated in various joint and combined maneuvers with other Army units and with the U.S. Navy and Air Force. Exercises were also held with the armed forces of Canada, France, and other countries allied with the United States in 1949 under the provisions of the North Atlantic Treaty Organization (NATO).

Infantrymen from the reserve components as well as Regular Army infantry units took part in some of these maneuvers. The National Guard and the Organized Reserve Corps, as reorganized in the 1945–50 period, were considerably larger and somewhat better trained than the reserve components of the 1930's. With many men having World War II combat experience and with better participation in paid drills, the Organized

Reserve Corps' infantry was significantly less of a paper organization than it had been in the prewar period. In the National Guard, all of the twenty-five infantry divisions and twenty regimental combat teams had been Federally recognized by 30 June 1950. Also, the entire National Guard infantry had been reorganized under the postwar TOE's, as modified by special reduction tables. Although all units participated in some form of training, it took place under major handicaps because funds were limited, armory facilities were inadequate, and equipment shortages were estimated at over 50 percent. Even in mobilization planning, the reserve structure was not expected to become effective until one or two years after a general mobilization.

By June 1950 the infantry of all components was better organized and trained than it had been at any time since the hasty post-World War II demobilization had reduced it to near impotence. Nevertheless, infantry units were far from combat ready for the war which broke out suddenly in Korea.

The Korean War

When the North Koreans crossed the 38th parallel and invaded South Korea on 25 June 1950, the only U.S. Army personnel in the country were members of the United States Military Advisory Group to the Republic of Korea. The last of the American occupation forces had been withdrawn almost exactly a year earlier, when on 29 June 1949 the final increment of the 5th Infantry Regimental Combat Team moved from Korea to Hawaii. Thus as the war began, the closest U.S. infantry units were the twelve regiments of the 7th, 24th, and 25th Infantry Divisions and the 1st Cavalry Division (organized as infantry), all of which were still on occupation duty in Japan. The first American ground troops to arrive in Korea were the 406 infantrymen of Task Force Smith from the 1st Battalion, 21st Infantry, organic to the 24th Infantry Division, who were flown in from Japan on 1 July 1950. After being reinforced by 134 artillerymen, they met the enemy four days later at Osan in the first American engagement of the Korean War.

During July nine of the twelve infantry regiments from Japan arrived in Korea, and the other three arrived in September. The 2d and 3d Infantry Divisions, stationed in the continental United States, were also ordered to Korea. Since the 3d was greatly understrength, one of its organic regiments was replaced by the 65th Infantry from Puerto Rico. In addition to the divisional infantry units, the 29th RCT from Okinawa, the 5th RCT from Hawaii, and the 187th Airborne RCT from Fort Campbell, Kentucky, came to Korea in the first few months of the war.

By the end of September 1950, four National Guard infantry divisions had been federalized. The 40th Infantry Division from California, the 45th from Oklahoma, the 28th from Pennsylvania, and the 43d from Connecticut, Rhode Island, and Vermont brought twelve more infantry regiments into the active Army. The 45th and 40th Infantry Divisions later served in Korea, entering combat in December 1951 and January 1952, respectively. The other two divisions were sent to Europe to strengthen NATO forces. Later in the war, four more National Guard infantry divisions with three organic infantry regiments each were called into Federal service. These units were not sent overseas but remained in the United States. Although three separate RCT's were also federalized during the Korean War, none of the nondivisional infantry regiments from the National Guard served in Korea.

As for the Organized Reserve Corps, which was redesignated as the Army Reserve in 1952, its contributions to the Korean War consisted mostly of individuals, not units. An important contribution came from the Reserve Officers' Training Corps (ROTC) program; many of the junior officers who led infantry units in Korea were ROTC graduates. Some small support units were called in, but no Army Reserve infantry regiments were ordered to active duty. They were kept intact and retained as a final reserve in case of an emergency developing elsewhere.

By the time the Korean armistice was signed in July 1953, there were ninety infantry regiments in the active Army, almost double the prewar total of forty-six regiments. Meanwhile, separate infantry battalions had increased from thirteen to thirty-one. The number of infantrymen in the active Army grew during the Korean War from 130,554 in June 1950 to a peak of 344,143 in May 1951. In July 1953 the infantry total was 251,685 officers and enlisted men, of whom 146,052 were overseas. They were assigned to units stationed in Germany, Japan, Alaska, Okinawa, Austria, Trieste, Iceland, Puerto Rico, and the Canal Zone, as well as to twenty-three infantry regiments and two infantry battalions serving in Korea.

In some ways Korea was a new kind of war for the infantry. The limited nature of the conflict contrasted sharply with the total warfare of World Wars I and II. The United States did not use the atomic bomb and settled for a bitterly negotiated armistice instead of complete military victory. The war was fought in a new geographic area, against new enemies, and for the first time the American infantryman acted as a representative not only of his own country but of the United Nations as well.

In spite of these differences, infantry organization during the Korean War was basically the organization adopted after World War II, and infantry weapons used in Korea were by and large World War II weapons.

Several organizational changes were made during the war, but there were no striking innovations. As the war progressed, authorized strengths of infantry units were lowered. The 15 November 1950 TOE strength of the infantry regiment was 3,781, on 15 May 1952 it was 3,662, and by 13 April 1953 it had dropped to 3,531. During that same time period the infantry battalion decreased from 919 to 859 and the rifle company from 211 to 197. These reductions streamlined units by eliminating non-essential personnel in administrative and service positions but kept combat strength high.

The internal organization of the infantry regiment, battalion, and company remained almost entirely the same throughout the war. The only major change took place in the heavy weapons company of the battalion and was the result of a new weapon, the 105-mm. recoilless rifle. Although 57-mm. and 75-mm. recoilless rifles had been first used in combat during the last months of World War II and were authorized for all infantry units by the 1 June 1945 TOE's, it was too late to permit wide use of the new rifles before the end of the war. Korea, therefore, became the first real testing ground for recoilless weapons. "The infantry's personal hand artillery," as the recoilless rifles were often called, proved to be hard-hitting, accurate, and reliable, and the more powerful 105-mm. recoilless rifle, which had been developed since the end of World War II, was adopted as a standard infantry weapon. In September 1952 the organization of the heavy weapons company was modified to include four of the new 105's, thereby significantly augmenting the company's firepower.

Basically, the two new companies added to the infantry regiment in the postwar reorganization remained unchanged during the Korean War. However, several different tank models were used by the tank company, and in the heavy mortar company a new model of the 4.2-inch mortar increased the maximum range from 4,400 to 6,000 yards. The mountainous Korean terrain made employment of tank units difficult, but it was natural mortar country, and infantry mortars of all types (4.2-inch, 81-mm., and 60-mm.) were used extensively. Since the U.N. forces retained control of the air over Korea, there was no special need for improving the infantry's antiaircraft capability. Even the artillery's multiple-fire antiaircraft weapons, the twin-40 and the quad-50, were frequently and successfully employed in ground support of infantry.

The organic firepower of the infantry rifle company also increased during the Korean War; both the automatic rifles and the light machine guns in the company doubled in number and its 2.36-inch bazookas were replaced by 3.5-inch rocket launchers. The small bazooka was simply not powerful enough to stop the Soviet-built T34 tanks used by the North

GUN CREW FROM 31ST RCT FIRING 75-MM. RECOILLESS RIFLE IN KOREA.

Koreans and the Chinese Communists. The 3.5-inch launcher, on the other hand, which was rushed into production when the Korean War began and quickly flown to Korea, was credited with knocking out eight T34's on the first day it was used in combat. Described by one infantry officer as "the answer to a rifleman's prayer for a tank killer," the 3.5 was so effective that it was decided not to limit its use to battalion level but to extend it to the rifle company as well. A new TOE dated 15 May 1952 authorized three of these "superbazookas" and placed them in the rifle platoon headquarters. The same table assigned two machine guns to each weapons squad.

The nine additional BAR's did not become organic to the rifle company until 13 April 1953, but many infantry units fighting in Korea had used two automatic rifles per rifle squad long before the official TOE change. Although the Chief of Army Field Forces recommended that concurrently with the doubling of the BAR's the rifle squad be increased to eleven men, the strength of the squad remained at nine—at least for the time being. However, the suggestion of an 11-man rifle squad was not

MACHINE GUN POSITION IN KOREA.

completely dropped. It was eventually adopted in the Pentomic reorganization subsequent to the Korean War.

The rifle, carbine, submachine gun, and pistol carried by the infantryman in Korea were exact copies of the ones with which he had fought in World War II. Only the carbine was criticized by a majority of the men who used it, since it frequently misfired or jammed both in the extreme cold of the Korean winters and in the dust of the summers. The M1 rifle, on the other hand, was consistently dependable. It remained the basic weapon of the infantry during the Korean War, and contemporary surveys showed that the M1 was regarded by the troops "with a liking amounting to affection."

The bayonet became more important in Korea than it had been during World War II. It was valued as a morale builder and as a last resort weapon, although most infantry units never fought with it. In general, infantrymen preferred the M4 knife bayonet, issued to men armed with carbines and other weapons, to the M1 bayonet, which had been authorized for the M1 rifle by every TOE since 30 January 1945. A knife bayonet, however, was not officially adopted for the rifle until 1 February 1955.

Infantry units in Korea had more firepower than World War II units, and their communication and transportation equipment was also much better. Between 1 June 1945 and 13 April 1953 the number of radios in the rifle company increased from 8 to 14 and telephone wire from 2½ to 4 miles, while the various trucks and trailers organic to the infantry regiment grew from 243 and 159 to 330 and 223, respectively.

A new item of equipment added to the infantry regiment during the Korean War was organic aircraft. Although a November 1945 change to the World War II TOE had given one airplane to the headquarters company of the infantry regiment, it was not included in the April 1948 table. In December 1948 a light aviation section augmentation of five men and two fixed-wing aircraft was provided for nondivisional regiments. Then, in May 1952, a 6-man light aviation section became organic to all infantry regiments and a helicopter, as well as a fixed-wing airplane, was authorized for the first time. In Korea, however, the infantry regiments' aircraft were usually combined with aircraft organic to other elements of the division for centralized operations. Often provisional division aviation companies were organized, although no such units were included in the TOE's. Organic aviation was of great value to the infantry, since it was effectively used for observation, surveillance, and reconnaissance, for quick resupply of weapons and equipment, for transporting commanders, outposts, and patrols over difficult terrain, and—most frequently—for rapid evacuation of the wounded. Successful tactical employment of helicopters was also a big step toward completely airmobile infantry units, which would be capable of moving soldiers quickly into a battle zone and flying them out again after their mission was accomplished.

It has been said that no new infantry lessons were learned in Korea, but many old lessons were relearned. The soundness of U.S. tactical doctrine was once again confirmed and no basic changes in infantry tactics were introduced, although the growth of Army aviation foreshadowed the development of the airmobile concept. The Korean War, however, did highlight certain weaknesses in infantry techniques, particularly in such areas as terrain analysis, night operations, patrols, and defensive warfare over an extended front. As soon as these deficiencies became apparent, the Infantry School adjusted its training to include the neglected subjects. The school's activities in general increased a great deal during the war. In the 1949–50 academic year, only 16 classes received tactical instruction at Fort Benning; in 1951–52 there were 118 classes.

MEN OF COMPANY K, 35TH INFANTRY, PLAN A NIGHT PATROL NEAR KUMHWA, KOREA.

Since Korean combat experience showed that many infantrymen did not fully understand the triangular concept of organization and its relationship to infantry tactics, General J. Lawton Collins, Army Chief of Staff, directed the Infantry School to place more emphasis on these fundamentals in its instruction and publications. In changes dated 2 and 3 December 1952, a paragraph on triangular organization was added to each infantry unit field manual. During the Korean War there was also a renewed emphasis throughout the Army on the basic combat principles of offensive combat, often referred to as "the Four F's of Fighting"— FIND 'EM, FIX 'EM, FIGHT 'EM, and FINISH 'EM!

Not only the regular infantry, but also some of the specialized infantry units that had been organized during World War II fought in Korea. The airborne infantry was represented by the 187th RCT. It participated in two combat jumps, one at Sukch'on and Sunch'on on 20 October 1950 and the other at Munsan-ni on 23 March 1951. Additional combat forces were almost always attached to the RCT for ground operations, and additional transportation had to be attached for any movement required. Artillery support, service units, and particularly antitank defenses were found to be inadequate in airborne operations. Various changes in the composition of the RCT and the organization of the airborne regiment were therefore recommended to correct these shortcomings. In the TOE changes actually adopted during the Korean War, the airborne infantry company's machine guns were doubled, four 105-mm. recoilless rifles were authorized for the battalion's heavy weapons company, and all 2.36-inch bazookas in the regiment were replaced by 3.5-inch rocket launchers. An organic tank company and a larger service company, however, were not added to the airborne infantry regiment until 1954, at which time the number of BAR's was also increased from one to two per rifle squad and from nine to eighteen in each airborne rifle company. Since gliders were not used in Korea and the development of the helicopter made their employment highly unlikely in the future, beginning on 1 January 1953 glider landings were deleted from the capabilities of the airborne infantry.

No armored infantry units served in Korea, because the terrain was unsuitable for their employment and there was an absence of heavy enemy armor after the early stages of the war. Several armored infantry battalions were nevertheless activated during the Korean War; some went to Europe, others remained in the United States. No major changes were made in armored infantry organization during this period, but there were some changes in weapons. For example, the .30-caliber heavy water-cooled machine guns were replaced by lighter air-cooled models, the 2.36-inch rocket launchers by 3.5-inch bazookas, and the 60-mm. mortars by 81-mm. mortars. A new armored personnel carrier was also authorized as the basic vehicle for armored infantry.

Ranger units, which had fought in World War II and had been dropped from the postwar organization, reappeared during the Korean War. Whereas the World War II rangers had been organized in battalions, the Korean War rangers were organized into separate companies that were normally attached to infantry divisions. All rangers were volunteers, airborne qualified, and specially trained for their mission of infiltrating enemy lines and attacking command posts, artillery positions, tank parks, communications centers, and other key facilities. Since their highly specialized capabilities were not utilized in Korea to the extent anticipated, the ranger companies were inactivated by the end of 1951. Ranger techniques were perpetuated by individual training. In the fall of 1951 a Ranger Department was established at the Infantry School with the goal of providing one ranger-qualified officer per rifle company and one noncommissioned officer per platoon. Starting in July 1954, every newly commissioned Regular Army officer assigned to the infantry was required to take either ranger or airborne training.

The elimination of separate Negro units, some of which dated back as far as 1866, was still another change undergone by the infantry during the Korean War. Although both the executive order and the Department of the Army directives on integration had been issued in the late 1940's, the first real application of the new policy came in Korea. On 1 August 1951 the 24th Infantry, the largest Negro unit in Korea, was replaced by the 14th Infantry in the 25th Infantry Division. Personnel of the 24th were transferred to other units, and the regiment was inactivated on 1 October 1951. Other Negro units, including the 3d Battalion, 9th Infantry, from the 2d Infantry Division and the 3d Battalion, 15th Infantry, from the 3d Infantry Division, were integrated by transfer of personnel and subsequent assignment of replacements without regard to race. By the end of 1951, all units stationed in Korea had been integrated. Originally spurred on by serious personnel shortages and an acute need to increase the combat effectiveness of units in Korea, integration eventually spread throughout the military establishment. As of 30 June 1954, no separate Negro units were left on the rolls of the Army, and all schools and training programs were open without racial restrictions.

In addition to Negro units, there had been other infantry organizations in the post-World War II Army made up of different racial and ethnic groups. Several Philippine Scout infantry regiments were among them, but all were inactivated after the Philippines achieved independence and before the Korean War began. There was also the 442d Infantry, the famous Nisei of World War II, composed of Japanese-Americans; this unit remained in Hawaii on reserve status throughout the war and was not called to active duty. As for Puerto Rican units, Army policy at the outbreak of the Korean War authorized their use only in the Caribbean Command. In September 1950, however, the 65th Infantry (organized with Puerto Rican enlisted personnel) was assigned to the 3d Infantry Division and sent to Korea to alleviate the major replacement problem. Starting in October 1951, English-speaking Puerto Ricans were made available for assignment on an Army-wide basis and were no longer limited to separate Puerto Rican units or to service in only one geographic area. The 65th Infantry returned to its home island in November 1954 and in 1959 was allotted to the Puerto Rico Army National Guard.

Another innovation, caused by the drastic personnel shortages and heavy casualties in the early days of the Korean War, was the integration of 100 South Koreans into each U.S. infantry company. This Korean Augmentation to the United States Army (KATUSA) took several different forms. Some units integrated the Koreans according to the "buddy system" with one U.S. soldier for each Korean, others organized separate Korean squads and platoons commanded by Americans, still others combined both of these methods. Instituted as an emergency measure, KATUSA presented major difficulties to infantry units because of the language barrier, cultural differences, the Koreans' lack of training, and their nonfamiliarity with U.S. Army organization, weapons, and tactics. As American replacements became available, the number of KATUSA soldiers declined and the South Koreans were used to rebuild the Republic of Korea Army, but later in the war when U.S. strength was reduced, an increase in KATUSA personnel was again authorized. The longer the Koreans remained with American units, the more effective they became, and many of the original difficulties were overcome. As a rule, however, they were more successfully integrated into service units than into the U.S. infantry.

Although South Koreans and Americans carried the greatest part of the burden, twenty-one other nations also contributed to the U.N. war effort in Korea. Most infantry units from these countries were relatively small, and in combat they were frequently attached to U.S. organizations. As the war progressed, a technique was developed whereby a U.N. battalion was habitually attached to the same American infantry regiment and, in fact, operated as an organic fourth battalion of the U.S. unit.

In spite of all of these special infantry organizations, it was the standard infantry that constituted the great majority of infantry units in Korea. Infantry in general played a most significant role in the Korean War. The first American ground troops to arrive in Korea were infantrymen, and all eight U.S. divisions sent to Korea were organized as infantry. As always, the combined effort of all arms and services was necessary for success in Korea, and the infantry depended heavily on their co-operation, particularly on artillery support in the last two years of comparatively static warfare. But, even then, it was the infantry that had the difficult mission of actually capturing the numerous enemy-held hills and outposts. As Lt. Gen. Maxwell D. Taylor, Commanding General of Eighth Army, put it, "the last 200 yards still had to be taken by a determined man on the ground with his rifle and hand grenade." By far the heaviest casualties were suffered by the infantry (out of an Army total of 109,958 casualties, 92,185 were infantrymen), while among the Army's seventy-eight Korean War Medal of Honor winners, seventy came from infantry units.

The Pentomic Concept and the Combat Arms Regimental System

The armistice in Korea did not bring about the rapid demobilization of infantry units that traditionally followed the cessation of hostilities in American military history. President Dwight D. Eisenhower gave the reason for this departure from the usual pattern when he said: "We have won an armistice on a single battleground—not peace in the world. We may not now relax our guard nor cease our quest." There was, nevertheless, a gradual reduction of both personnel and units throughout the mid-1950's. When the Korean armistice was signed, the active Army had ninety infantry regiments, a year later the total was seventy-four, and by the end of 1956 only fifty-four regiments were active. The number of separate infantry battalions decreased from thirty-one to twenty-six during the same period, while the infantry's personnel strength dropped from 251,685 to 133,931.

By December 1954, all National Guard infantry units that had been federalized during the Korean War reverted to state control and were reorganized at their home stations. Several Regular Army infantry regiments were activated to replace them in the active Army. The number of these organizations, however, never equaled the total of National Guard units released, and some of the Regular regiments were inactivated as the authorized strength of the Army declined. Although the number of units decreased, the responsibilities of the infantry remained worldwide. In December 1956, in addition to those in the continental United States, infantry units were stationed in the Canal Zone, Alaska, Hawaii, Iceland, Italy, Berlin, West Germany, Japan, and Korea. In Korea, two infantry divisions with three organic infantry regiments each were still on duty.

The period immediately following the Korean War was a difficult time for the infantry. The new administration re-evaluated the national military policy, and with this "New Look" the United States entered the so-called "Era of Massive Retaliation." The doctrine of massive retaliation rested on the assumption that the threat of instant and large-scale nuclear reprisals would serve as an effective deterrent to future wars and, therefore, make large conventional forces unnecessary. It emphasized the role of the Air Force in national defense and relegated the Army with its infantry to an inferior position.

Unable to convince the administration of the likelihood of small limited wars in the future and of the need for what he called "a strategy of flexible response," General Maxwell D. Taylor (then Army Chief of Staff) decided that it was necessary to reorganize and modernize the Army to make it readily adaptable to the requirements of the atomic battlefield. As a result, starting in late 1956 Army units were reorganized under the Pentomic system. Two of the most salient characteristics of this concept were reflected in its name—pentagonal structure and atomic capability. Low-yield tactical nuclear weapons became a mainstay of the Army, and an organization based on five major subordinate units replaced the traditional three basic elements of the triangular system.

Many features of the Pentomic organization were dictated by the nature of atomic warfare as well as by a desire to take full advantage of the tremendous technological advances of recent years. For example, the absolute requirement for wide dispersion on the nuclear battlefield to avoid offering the enemy any single lucrative target was an important consideration in adopting an organization with five small basic combat units, while new developments in the field of communications made a broader span of control possible. Since the Soviet Union had acquired an atomic capability in 1949 and from all indications its nuclear arsenal had kept on growing steadily, an enemy with atomic combat power was not entirely theoretical. In order to be successful in a nuclear war, U.S. infantry units had to be small and lean, more powerful and harder hitting, self-sufficient, and geared for long periods of independent action on a wide and fluid battlefield. They had to be capable of rapid and effective concentration in the attack as well as equally rapid dispersal for defense. The Pentomic system attempted to give the infantry all of these capabilities.

The reorganization went through several stages. The Continental Army Command (CONARC), which replaced the Office, Chief of Army Field Forces, on 1 February 1955, began studies of the new concept in the fall of 1955. Test TOE's entitled "Reorganization of the Airborne Division (ROTAD)," "Reorganization of the Current Armored Division (ROCAD)," and "Reorganization of the Current Infantry Division (ROCID)" were published on 10 August, 1 December, and 20 December 1956, respectively. By June 1958, all fifteen active Regular Army divisions and their subordinate units had been reorganized under these tables, and by mid-1959 all but one of the thirty-seven divisions in the reserve components had adopted the new structure. Meanwhile the system was being field tested and evaluated by CONARC, and the Infantry School was revising infantry manuals to cover Pentomic organization and warfare on the nuclear battlefield. In December 1958, a major Infantry Conference, the first such gathering since 1946, met at Fort Benning, Georgia, to discuss the radical changes that were taking place in infantry organization, materiel, and tactics. The ROTAD tables were superseded by the final TOE's for Pentomic airborne units on 31 June 1958, but the final D-series tables for elements of infantry and armored divisions were not published until 1 February and 1 May 1960.

Pentomic was basically a divisional reorganization and as such is beyond the scope of this narrative, but it did introduce major changes in all infantry units. The single most important innovation was the elimination of the regiment from the infantry structure. It was replaced by a new organization called the "battle group." Smaller than a regiment and

U.S. Army Infantry School, Fort Benning, Georgia.

larger than a battalion, the new unit was commanded by a full colonel. Five battle groups were organic to the Pentomic infantry division.

The strength of the ROCID battle group was 1,427, but this was reduced to 1,356 by the D-series TOE. Initially it consisted of a headquarters, headquarters and service company; an artillery battery, equipped with 4.2-inch mortars; and four rifle companies, each having four rifle platoons and a weapons platoon. After reorganization under the D-tables, the battle group had a headquarters and headquarters company, a combat support company, and five rifle companies composed of three rifle platoons and a weapons platoon. All of the tactical support elements (including a radar section and reconnaissance, heavy mortar, and assault weapons platoons) were located in the combat support company. The radar section's two medium-range and five short-range radar sets greatly increased the battle group's ground surveillance capability, while the heavy mortar platoon brought the 4.2-inch mortar back to the infantry. The assault weapons platoon introduced the first operational infantry guided missile, the French-manufactured SS10, a lightweight, long-range, and accurate weapon, employed primarily against tanks.

The weapons platoon in the Pentomic rifle company became a much more powerful unit since it no longer used 60-mm. mortars and 57-mm. recoilless rifles. It now had 81-mm. mortars and 106-mm. recoilless rifles, which prior to ROCID were classified as battalion-level equipment. The 106-mm. rifle had been adopted in October 1954 as a replacement for the 75-mm. and 105-mm. recoilless rifles in the infantry battalion's heavy weapons company. This was the only significant change in infantry weapons between the Korean armistice and the Pentomic reorganization. The ROCID and D-series TOE's made the 106-mm. recoilless rifle a standard rifle company weapon, giving the unit highly effective antitank protection.

The tank company organic to the pre-ROCID infantry regiment was not continued in the Pentomic structure. The divisional tank battalion, however, was reorganized to consist of five tank companies, so that a company of seventeen tanks was available to support each of the five battle groups. Other divisional elements, normally providing direct support for battle groups, were also organized pentagonally.

The Pentomic infantry rifle squad had eleven men, two more than the squad of the Korean War era. This increase represented more than just a gain of two additional rifles. It introduced the concept of two fire teams within a squad and gave the unit not only increased firepower, but also greater maneuverability, the ability to withstand more attrition, a greater capacity for sustained combat, and more effective control over individual riflemen. Under the 1960 TOE, a portable radio set was issued to each of the three rifle squads and to the weapons squad. These radios were part of a newly established platoon net linking together, for the first time, all subordinate elements of the rifle platoon and making them immediately responsive to the platoon leader's orders. Communications were improved on other organizational levels as well, because a rapid and efficient communications system was an essential ingredient of the Pentomic concept.

Since a high degree of mobility was another requirement of Pentomic units, transportation equipment was also improved. In addition to employing its own organic transport, the battle group could depend on the divisional transportation battalion, which was added to the structure under ROCID. This unit's two armored personnel carrier companies were capable of moving an entire infantry battle group. By also using its light truck company, the transportation battalion could move two battle groups simultaneously. As for organic aviation, the battle group did not inherit the regiment's 6-man aviation section. All of the aircraft, both rotary and fixed-wing, authorized for the Pentomic infantry division were centralized in one combat aviation company. The company was organized to give direct support to battle groups when needed as well as to furnish general support for the entire division.

When organized for combat, the infantry battle group often had other units attached. These were usually a tank company, an engineer company, and a field artillery battalion. A battle group, reinforced in this manner, was a balanced combined arms force and, although considerably smaller, greatly resembled the regimental combat teams of World War II and the Korean War. Most infantry battle groups were divisional units. There were, however, some nondivisional groups which were assigned to higher commands or served as school troops. Others were organic to a new organization, the separate infantry brigade. Two such brigades, the 1st and 2d, were activated in the Regular Army in 1958. In the Army National Guard, the 29th, 92d, and 258th Infantry Brigades were organized in 1959 with their respective headquarters in Hawaii, Puerto Rico, and Arizona.

The airborne infantry was also reorganized under the Pentomic system. The units organic to the 101st Airborne Division were the first in the Army to be evaluated and tested under the new concept. In September 1956, the 101st was reorganized in accordance with the ROTAD TOE's, and the following month tests of the new structure began at Fort Campbell, Kentucky, and Fort Bragg, North Carolina, in a series of exercises called JUMP LIGHT. The name given to the exercises reflected one of the most important characteristics of ROTAD units—their relative lightness. The entire division, with the personnel and equipment of all of its elements, including five airborne battle groups, was completely trans-portable by Air Force medium transport aircraft (the C-119, C-123, and C-130). Some of the equipment provided by the TOE's was not yet available and interim items authorized did not meet all of the airlift criteria, but it was understood that these items were only temporary issue and would be replaced as soon as possible.

The airborne battle group was similar to the corresponding unit in the regular infantry. Under ROTAD it contained 1,584 men, organized into a headquarters, headquarters and service company, a heavy mortar battery, and five airborne infantry companies. With the adoption of the D-series TOE, total group strength increased by only one man and its basic structure remained the same. Each of the five rifle companies had four rifle platoons and a weapons platoon, which was equipped with 81-mm. mortars and 106-mm. recoilless rifles. The rifle platoon consisted of a weapons squad and three rifle squads, composed of eleven men and organized into two fire teams. The group's organic fire support was provided by an artillery battery, armed with eight 4.2-inch mortars, while its assault gun platoon was equipped with six 90-mm., self-propelled, full-tracked antitank guns, which could be transported and landed by C-119 or C-123 aircraft or dropped by parachute from the C-119.

In recognition of the importance of communications on the modern battlefield, the signal equipment of the airborne battle group was made greatly superior to that of the former airborne infantry regiment. Although the total strength of the battle group was less than half that of the regiment, the group was authorized the same number of radios and even more telephones than had been organic to the regiment. In addition to its 100 percent air transportability, the Pentomic airborne battle group also had increased ground mobility. The most significant development in this field was the adoption of the infantry light weapons carrier, M274, better known as the mule or mechanical mule. By taking some of the load off the paratrooper's back, the mechanical mule improved the mobility of airborne infantry units in ground operations.

In comparison with the almost complete transformation of standard and airborne infantry units during the Pentomic era, changes in armored infantry structure during the same period were minor. With the battalion as its basic element, the armored infantry was already organized into small, powerful, flexible, and highly mobile units, capable of the rapid concentration and wide dispersion which would be essential in nuclear warfare. The armored division's combat command organization was also well suited to the atomic battlefield. Therefore, although the armored division gained an atomic capability under the ROCAD and D-series TOE's, it did not adopt the pentagonal structure. The division retained both its three combat commands and its four organic armored infantry battalions. Each battalion continued to have four rifle companies consisting of three rifle platoons and an 81-mm. mortar platoon. The total strength of the battalion, however, increased somewhat from 978 to 1,027, and the unit was designated an armored rifle battalion.

Two BAR's had been authorized for each rifle squad in the regular and airborne infantry during 1953 and 1954, but the second automatic rifle was not included in the armored infantry rifle squad until the ROCAD TOE of December 1956. At the same time the squad increased from ten to twelve men and, like its 11-man standard and airborne infantry counterparts, was subdivided into two fire teams. The extra man drove the squad's organic M59 armored personnel carrier (APC), a full-tracked amphibious vehicle with ground mobility equal that of a tank and having great agility in water. Meanwhile, a lighter and less expensive amphibious armored personnel carrier, M113, was being developed. Although designed primarily to give the armored infantry mobility, the M113 could also be employed as a self-propelled heavy weapons carrier, an ambulance, a command vehicle, a cargo carrier, or a fire direction center. Under the 1960 TOE's, there were seventeen APC's in each armored infantry company and a total of seventy-seven in the armored rifle battalion. The battalion had enough organic transportation to make it 100 percent mobile, and its communications system was more extensive and more efficient than ever before.

One very important item, authorized by the D-series TOE's for all types of infantry units, was the new M14 rifle. The result of more than ten years of experimentation and testing, the M14 was almost a pound lighter than its predecessor, the M1 rifle, and held a 20-round magazine instead of the M1's 8-round clip. Since it fired the 7.62-mm. cartridge adopted by the other NATO countries, standard U.S. rifle ammunition became interchangeable with that of major allies. A selector for automatic or semi-automatic fire increased the M14's versatility and enabled it to serve as a replacement not only for the M1, but also for the carbine, the submachine gun and, when used with a bipod, for the much heavier BAR. Because any rifleman could now become an automatic rifleman with little additional training, the rifle squad and other small infantry units acquired greater tactical flexibility. Although the M1 and the BAR had served the infantry well for many years and most soldiers were sorry to see these "old reliables" go, the M14 was adopted as the new standard weapon of the rifleman and began to be issued to infantry units in 1960. Shortly thereafter, TRAINFIRE, the official rifle marksmanship course since 1957, designed to simulate actual combat conditions and featuring a pop-up silhouette target known as "Punchy Pete," was modified for use with the M-14.

PARATROOPERS FROM 101ST AIRBORNE DIVISION TESTING M14 RIFLES.

At about the same time, a new general purpose machine gun, the M60, was adopted as a replacement for both the heavy water-cooled and the light air-cooled Browning .30-caliber machine guns. The M60 fired 7.62-mm. NATO ammunition at a rate of 600 rounds per minute, weighed only twenty-three pounds, and could be fired from the shoulder or hip, from an attached bipod, or from a newly developed aluminum tripod. Other infantry weapons and equipment were meanwhile being developed and tested by the Infantry School and by CONARC's Infantry Board. Among them were a lightweight rifle, a shoulder-fired air defense guided missile, an improved model of the 81-mm. mortar, a new grenade launcher, more powerful and lighter radar sets, the Claymore antipersonnel mine, and better radios, including an experimental combat helmet model. Thus, although the spectacular advances made during the Pentomic era were in the fields of nuclear weapons, giant guided missiles, and huge rockets, there was also solid progress in the development of conventional small arms and equipment for the individual rifleman.

The Pentomic concept brought about the most drastic reorganization of infantry units since triangularization. When the square divisions became triangular, one infantry regiment had to be dropped from each division. Pentomic affected all of the infantry elements organic to the infantry and airborne divisions, leaving only the infantry battalions in the armored division relatively unchanged. Since both regiments and battalions were eliminated in the regular and airborne infantry, the chain of command went directly from the division headquarters to the five new battle groups and from there to the company level. The combined strength of the three regiments under the last triangular TOE was 10,560 in the infantry division and 10,083 in the airborne division. Under ROCID the five infantry battle groups totaled 7,135 men, while the five ROTAD airborne battle groups had a strength of 7,920. In both cases, therefore, the Pentomic reorganization caused a significant reduction in infantry personnel. By eliminating the traditional regiment, it also raised the question of what the new infantry units were to be called, how they were to be numbered, and what their relationship to former organizations was to be.

If some means of perpetuating the history of infantry and other combat regiments had not been combined with the tactical reorganization, hundreds of independent units would have been created with no historical affiliation. The numerical designations of such a multiplicity of separate units would have run into three or possibly four digits. At the same time, the failure to pass regimental lineages and honors to the new Pentomic units would have brought an end to the history and traditions acquired by U.S. Army combat regiments in the past. Such difficulties were avoided by the adoption of the Combat Arms Regimental System (CARS), a plan developed by the Army Staff on the model of the British regimental system and approved by the Secretary of the Army on 24 January 1957. CARS was designed to maintain the continuity of the Army's distinguished combat units and to provide an organizational framework that would remain stable in spite of fluctuations in strength and tactical structure. It also gave every combat soldier the opportunity of being a member of a traditional unit, one of which he could be genuinely proud, thereby improving troop morale and *esprit de corps.*

The system was built around the regiment for two reasons. First, the regiment had always been the principal repository of unit history and tradition in the United States Army. Second, since it was becoming obsolete as a tactical unit, the regiment would no longer be subject to periodic reorganizations and could serve as a permanent vehicle for perpetuating unit lineage, honors, and customs without restricting future organizational trends. Consequently, a number of distinguished infantry,

TYPICAL INFANTRY REGIMENT UNDER COMBAT ARMS REGIMENTAL SYSTEM.

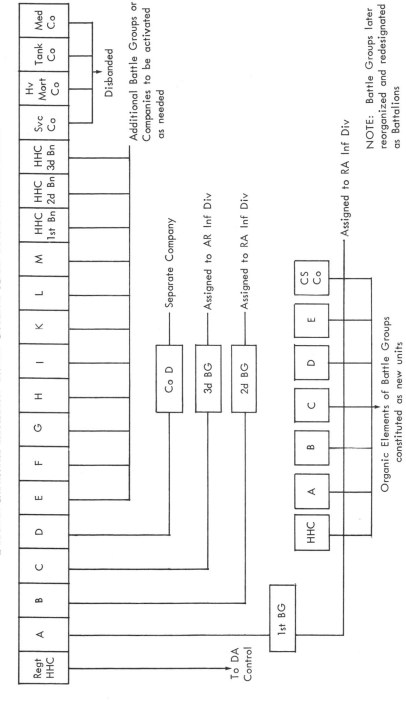

425-618 O - 72 - 8

artillery, armor, and cavalry regiments were selected and designated as so-called parent units. Each infantry parent regiment was capable of providing a base for a variable number of tactical elements, which could be battle groups, battalions, or companies. Their number and size varied according to the needs of the Army, but each element traced its lineage back to one of the organic companies of the parent regiment. When the element was a battle group or battalion, its headquarters was the direct descendant of one of the former regimental companies, while its own organic elements were constituted as new units.

Elements of the same parent regiment could be assigned to different divisions or other commands and could be allotted to either the Regular Army or the Army Reserve. These two components shared their CARS regiments, while the Army National Guard had its own, those traditionally associated with a given geographic area. The Regular Army and Army Reserve parent units were selected on the basis of a point system which credited one point per year since original activation and two points for each campaign credit and American decoration. Initially, fifty-five infantry regiments were chosen: the 1st through 23d, 26th through 32d, 34th, 35th, 36th, 38th, 39th, 41st, 46th, 47th, 48th, 50th, 51st, 52d, 54th, 58th, 60th, 87th, 187th, 325th, 327th, and 501st through 506th. Because of their airborne backgrounds, the last nine designations on this list were reserved for airborne units; the 6th, 36th, 41st, 46th, 48th, 50th, 51st, 52d, 54th, and 58th Infantry became parent regiments for the armored infantry with which they had been associated in the past; the remaining thirty-six were for the regular infantry. The infantry elements of the 1st Cavalry Division were not assigned to infantry parent units but had cavalry parent regiments, which they shared with cavalry reconnaissance units. (Their lineages are included in the *Armor-Cavalry* volume of the Army Lineage Series.)

In 1959 eighteen more infantry regiments, all with Army Reserve backgrounds, were added to the list of parent units, since reservists felt that it was detrimental to the morale of the Army Reserve not to have any parent regiments of its own. The 59th, 305th through 307th, 313th through 315th, 357th through 359th, and 442d Infantry were chosen because of their outstanding records, and the 100th Battle Group, 442d Infantry, from Hawaii was permitted to retain the number under which it had distinguished itself during World War II. The seven other infantry regiments selected (the 322d, 345th, 381st, 383d, 409th, 410th, and 411th) had special ties with certain communities. They were organized with only one element each, their lineages differing somewhat from those of other CARS units.

The reorganization of airborne and standard infantry units under

CARS was a relatively simple procedure because they had retained the regimental structure up to that time. The former armored infantry regiments, however, had been broken up into battalions for many years, and it was necessary to restore them to their original regiments. Many battalion designations made famous in World War II combat were lost in the process, but their honors were perpetuated by the new CARS units. Under CARS there were two kinds of honors, earned and shared. All elements of the parent unit shared the regimental campaign credits and decorations. Color bearing units identified their own contributions to the regiment's honors by special devices on campaign and decoration streamers and by asterisks on their official Lineage and Honors Certificates. Company-sized units, which were authorized guidons, displayed only those honors that they themselves had earned. Provisions were also made for recognition of honors awarded subsequent to the adoption of CARS.

As originally planned, Phase V of the system had provided for the establishment of a regimental headquarters, not as it had existed prior to CARS, but as a home for all members of the regiment. The headquarters would be assigned to a permanent location and would maintain regimental history and traditions, keep records, display colors, trophies, and other properties, and perhaps conduct regimental recruiting and operate regimental training units. A proposal to centralize all infantry regimental headquarters at the Infantry Center at Fort Benning, Georgia, was tentatively approved by the Army Staff in 1959, but it was rejected the following year because of lack of funds, personnel, and appropriate on-post facilities. As of 31 December 1969, Phase V of CARS had not yet been implemented. Headquarters of former infantry regiments remained at zero strength under Department of the Army control and, pending their establishment, the lowest numbered or lettered active element of each regiment was designated as the custodian of the regimental colors. It was also the unit which usually displayed regimental historical properties and co-ordinated the selection of a regimental unit day. Members of all elements of a CARS parent regiment shared the regiment's distinctive insignia, although they could wear different shoulder sleeve insignia, depending upon the division or other command to which their unit was assigned.

In general, redesignation of infantry units to conform to CARS was accomplished simultaneously with their reorganization under the Pentomic concept. Only the elements of the 101st Airborne Division, which became Pentomic in 1956 prior to approval of CARS, had to be reorganized again in April 1957 to include the proper new designations. In June 1956, just before the Pentomic reorganization began, there had been fifty-nine infantry regiments (with three battalions each) and twenty-three separate infantry battalions in the Regular Army. By June 1958 they had been replaced by seventy-six Pentomic battle groups and nineteen armored rifle battalions, all of which were elements of fifty-five infantry and five cavalry CARS parent regiments. CARS and Pentomic were not limited to the Regular Army; all Army National Guard and Army Reserve infantry units were also reorganized according to the new historical and tactical organizational systems. The only exceptions were the training regiments of the thirteen training divisions in the Army Reserve, which were organized under entirely different TOE's and were neither Pentomic nor CARS units.

ROAD and Flexible Response

The Pentomic battle group had a rather brief existence as the basic unit of the infantry. From its inception, the Pentomic system had been considered an interim measure by the Army Staff. It was intended as the first step, not the last, in the Army's adaptation to the nuclear battlefield and to the increasingly complicated military situations that might be expected to arise in the future. Planning for a new combat structure began even before all infantry units had been reorganized under the D-series TOE's. In December 1960, CONARC was directed to re-evaluate the current organization and to make recommendations for necessary changes. The result of this re-evaluation was not another modification of the existing Pentomic system but a major Army-wide reorganization under an entirely new concept called ROAD (Reorganization Objective Army Divisions). ROAD was approved by the Secretary of the Army in April 1961 and was publicly announced by President John F. Kennedy before a joint session of Congress on 25 May 1961. The first ROAD units were organized in February 1962 under draft TOE's. The final tables were published on 15 July and 15 August 1963, and by the end of June 1964 the reorganization was completed both in the Regular Army and in the reserve components.

The fundamental assumption behind the Pentomic organization had been that atomic war was the most likely form of future warfare and that tactical nuclear weapons would definitely be used. The new Kennedy administration questioned this assumption and was seriously concerned about limited conflicts and the ability to handle situations short of nuclear war. General Maxwell D. Taylor, long-time champion of what he called "flexible response," was appointed Military Representative of the President in the Office of the Secretary of Defense and later Chairman of the Joint Chiefs of Staff. Pentomic, a product of the era of massive retaliation, did not fit into the strategy of flexible response, which now became official national policy. ROAD, on the other hand, was specifically designed to carry out such a policy.

The single most important characteristic of the new system was its flexibility. Under ROAD each division had a fixed base, common to all divisions, but the number and type of its infantry and armor elements varied according to its mission, geographic location, and strategic as well as tactical requirements. By different combinations of organic maneuver elements, divisions could be tailored to fit any environment or situation. Without reducing the Pentomic division's tactical nuclear weapons, ROAD increased conventional firepower and personnel strength. As a result, ROAD units had a genuine dual capability and greater staying power on the non-atomic battlefield. The new system had the additional advantage of introducing an organization that was more compatible with that of major NATO allies.

ROAD, like Pentomic, was primarily a divisional reorganization. It did, however, affect the infantry as a whole by changing the structure of infantry units of all sizes down to and including the squad. Among the most serious shortcomings of the Pentomic organization was the fact that the battle group, which had been planned as a lean, highly mobile, scaled-down regiment, was too small and not powerful enough to be an adequate substitute for the regiment; it was much more like an oversized and reinforced battalion. Nor was the combat capability of all five Pentomic battle groups equivalent to that of the three regiments of the triangular division. ROAD, therefore, dropped the battle group from the infantry structure, but it did not bring back the regiment. Instead, it made the battalion the basic tactical and administrative unit of the infantry.

Command and control also posed major problems in the Pentomic system. With the elimination of infantry regiments and battalions and the introduction of the pentagonal, as opposed to the triangular organization, only one echelon of command remained between the division commander (a major general) and the company commander (a captain). As a result, the commanding general was burdened by having five major independent combat elements under his immediate control. Experience showed that even with modern communications this span of control was too wide for efficient operations. Furthermore, infantry majors and lieutenant colonels had extremely limited command opportunities, since only about 5 percent of them could expect to acquire command experience in peacetime under the Pentomic system. ROAD improved both the command and control structure and infantry officer career opportunities by dropping the pentagonal organization and by establishing three brigades in each division to serve as intermediary headquarters between the division commander and the combat battalions. Contrary to the fixed structure of the five Pentomic battle groups and of the old infantry regiments with three identical battalions, the new brigades could control a variable number and type of units. The brigades, which were made organic to all divisions, were similar to the combat commands that the armored division had since World War II, but they provided greater flexibility.

Battalions were attached to brigades according to what was appropriately described as the "building-block" concept. In order to facilitate interchangeability of maneuver elements between and within divisions and to simplify training, a certain degree of standardization of structure was introduced. Thus not only did different types of infantry battalions resemble each other more than ever before, but even tank battalions were organized along similar lines. This similarity was accompanied by a renewed emphasis on the employment of combined arms teams, and new techniques were developed for task force formation of infantry and armor elements on brigade, battalion, and company levels. Under ROAD, divisional brigades with their infantry and armor elements were capable of operating independently when reinforced by support and service units from the division base. In such cases, the brigades were comparable to the infantry RCT's that had been employed with great success during World War II and the Korean War.

The ROAD infantry battalion differed considerably from the Pentomic battle group, but it had several things in common with the infantry battalion of the pre-ROCID period. Like the earlier battalion, it was organized with three organic rifle companies. In both units each rifle company had three rifle platoons and a weapons platoon; the rifle platoon consisted of three rifle squads and a weapons squad, and the weapons platoon had a mortar and an antitank section. Unlike the pre-Pentomic battalion, the ROAD unit had no separate heavy weapons company; all the organic support elements were included in the headquarters company. This company also contained a mess section, which for the first time consolidated company mess teams on the battalion level. Furthermore, the ROAD infantry battalion was tactically self-sufficient and thus had a greater degree of independence than the battalions which had been organic to the infantry regiment.

The new rifle squad contained ten men. It was larger by one man than the squad of the post-World War II and Korean War period but smaller than the 11-man Pentomic squad. It consisted of a squad leader, two 4-man fire teams (team leader, automatic rifleman, rifleman, and grenadier), and an extra rifleman, who could be used to reinforce either fire

ENTAC ANTITANK GUIDED MISSILE.   M29 DAVY CROCKETT.

team or assist the squad leader. Organizationally, the squad reflected
ROAD's characteristic flexibility down to the very last man.

The M14 rifle, introduced in the D-series TOE's, remained the infantryman's basic weapon; with a selector and bipod it also served as an
automatic rifle. The ROAD tables provided a new knife-type bayonet for
the M14 instead of the former carbine bayonet, which had been temporarily issued with the M14. The M79 grenade launcher was also authorized as a new individual weapon. Designed to close the gap between
the maximum range of a hand grenade and the minimum range of a
mortar, the lightweight M79 fired a 40-mm. high-explosive fragmentation
projectile to a range of approximately 400 meters. With two launchers
per rifle squad and a total of eighty-five in the battalion, the M79 helped
to improve the capabilities of small infantry units.

Several new antitank weapons, both close-in and long-range, were
introduced by the ROAD TOE's. The 90-mm. recoilless rifle, M67, replaced the 3.5-inch rocket launcher in the weapons squad of the rifle
platoon, and the ENTAC (ENgin-Téléguidé Anti-Char) became the new
weapon for the battalion's three antitank squads. A French-manufactured
wire-guided missile with a range of 2,000 meters, the ENTAC was a
considerable improvement over the SS10 antitank missile which was being
phased out. Some 3.5-inch rocket launchers were still found in the ROAD
infantry battalion, but the TOE clearly stated that they were to be issued
only until the new 66-mm. high explosive antitank rocket, M72, became
available. Commonly known as the LAW (Light Antitank Weapon),
this weapon was designed to be carried and operated by one man. Although the rocket together with its launcher weighed only about 4.75

pounds and was only 25 inches long and 3 inches in diameter, the LAW had an effective range of 200 meters and was capable of penetrating armor of the heaviest known tank.

For the first time under ROAD, the portable flame thrower was made organic to the infantry battalion. Flame throwers had been used by infantry units before, but they had been considered special purpose weapons and as such had to be requested in advance from ammunition points. Nine of them were included in the ROAD battalion's TOE equipment. With three in each rifle company headquarters, flame throwers were immediately available whenever needed. The ROAD TOE's also returned the .50-caliber heavy machine gun to the infantry battalion. The number of these guns, used primarily as antiaircraft weapons, had been drastically reduced under ROCID, and they were completely eliminated from the battle group by the D-series tables. Under ROAD, thirteen .50-caliber machine guns were again authorized for each infantry battalion. All of the guns were located in the headquarters company, although they were not grouped in any one section within the company. Meanwhile, the new Redeye air defense missile was being developed and tested and its availability for distribution to infantry units was being projected for the near future.

All of these weapons gave ROAD units much more conventional firepower, and thus helped to correct one of the major weaknesses of the Pentomic organization. Although ROAD emphasized conventional capabilities, it did not neglect atomic power. On the contrary, even the infantry had its own nuclear weapons system, the Davy Crockett, which could be employed in either a direct or indirect fire support role against a wide variety of targets—primarily massed enemy personnel. While the weapon was being developed, CONARC had proposed and tested several different organizations for its employment, including separate TOE platoons and sections organic to the heavy mortar platoon in the battle group's combat support company. Selected personnel began special training at the Infantry School in October 1961. In the final ROAD TOE, there was a 12-man Davy Crockett section augmentation in the headquarters company of the infantry battalion. It could be organized only by special authorization from the Department of the Army, but should that authority be given, the battalion commander would have four low-yield nuclear weapons under his direct control and the capability of initiating a nuclear fire mission within minutes.

The ROAD infantry battalion was not only more powerful than the ROCID battle group; its firepower was also much greater than that of the pre-Pentomic infantry battalion. The battalion that had fought in Korea ten years earlier had no M14 rifles, M60 machine guns, M79 grenade launchers, 90-mm. or 106-mm. recoilless rifles, ENTAC's, or Davy Crocketts. Although it could depend on close support from the regimental heavy mortar company, the Korean War unit did not have organic 4.2-inch mortars, whereas the ROAD battalion had heavy mortars in its own headquarters company. The 3.5-inch rocket launcher, .50-caliber machine gun, and 81-mm. mortar used by the earlier infantry battalion were still authorized for the ROAD unit. However, the LAW was being tested as a substitute for the bazooka, the Redeye was being designed to replace the machine gun in the antiaircraft role, while the 81-mm. mortar being issued was a new and improved model.

Only the .45-caliber automatic pistol was the same in both the older and newer battalions. All other weapons organic to the Korean War unit had either been replaced or were scheduled to be replaced in the near future by more sophisticated and powerful weapons. As a result, the ROAD battalion's total firepower was significantly greater than that of its Korean War predecessor, in spite of the fact that its personnel strength was less by fifty-seven men. The communication and transportation equipment of the ROAD infantry battalion was also considerably better. The number of radios and telephones had increased from 66 and 29 to 176 and 149, respectively; trucks had more than doubled from 49 to 115. Neither helicopters nor fixed-wing airplanes were authorized for the infantry battalion, but there was an aviation battalion in the division base of each ROAD division with enough organic aircraft to airlift an entire infantry company at one time.

In keeping with the new trend toward standardization, the ROAD airborne infantry battalion was almost identical in structure to the regular infantry battalion. There was only one significant difference: the airborne unit had six instead of three antitank squads armed with ENTAC's in its headquarters company. ENTAC's were also authorized for the antitank squads of airborne infantry companies, while the standard infantry used the 106-mm. recoilless rifle at company level. More ENTAC's were authorized because the airborne ROAD division usually had only one tank battalion assigned to it and consequently needed a greater antitank capability in its infantry units. The airborne battalion TOE also provided for thirteen infantry light weapons carriers or mechanical mules, which were not included in the standard battalion's equipment. The regular infantry unit, on the other hand, had more heavy trucks and trailers. In general, the airborne battalion was a little lighter than the standard infantry battalion and was 100 percent transportable by medium aircraft. The capabilities of the ROAD airborne battalion were the same as those of the regular infantry battalion, with one important exception: the airborne unit was organized and trained for frequent airborne assault by parachute or assault aircraft.

The third type of infantry battalion under ROAD was called "mechanized infantry." It replaced the former armored infantry battalion (AIB) and armored rifle battalion. Mechanized infantry units were characterized by their high cross-country mobility with light armor protection and multiple communications. In addition to sharing the capabilities of the regular infantry, the mechanized infantry battalion could provide a highly mobile exploitation force when suitably reinforced, exploit the effects of mass destruction weapons, and complement and enhance the inherent capabilities of tank elements when employed in tank-infantry task forces. AIB's and armored rifle battalions had been organic only to armored divisions; mechanized battalions were assigned to armored divisions as well as infantry and mechanized infantry divisions. The mechanized division was a new organization created under ROAD which, although not as heavy in armor as the armored division, was particularly suitable for employment in such terrain as the plains of Europe or against an enemy with highly mechanized forces. All three types of ROAD infantry battalions were also assigned to separate brigades, which became more numerous during the 1960's.

The organization of the mechanized infantry battalion was very similar to that of standard and airborne infantry units. Having a strength of 901, compared to 830 for the regular and 828 for the airborne battalion, the mechanized battalion was the largest unit. Additional drivers and maintenance personnel were required for the extra organic vehicles that made the mechanized unit 100 percent mobile. Signal equipment was also more numerous and, because of the mobility factor, wireless communication was more essential. Although there were fewer telephones in the mechanized battalion, the number of radios was twice that of a regular infantry battalion. Each rifle squad, for example, was authorized a vehicular radio set in addition to its portable radio. In the draft TOE the mechanized infantry rifle squad had only ten men, like the standard and airborne squads; one of the riflemen was expected to double as the driver of the squad's M113 armored personnel carrier (APC). In the final table another rifleman was added, thus permitting the driver to remain with the APC at all times.

In the process of adopting an organization similar to that of the regular infantry, the mechanized infantry battalion lost the fourth rifle company that had been organic to the AIB and to the armored rifle battalion ever since the post-World War II reorganization. However, the battalion did gain an improved antitank capability. The only antitank weapon in the AIB and armored rifle battalion had been the 3.5-inch rocket launcher, while the ROAD mechanized battalion was also authorized 90-mm. and 106-mm. recoilless rifles, the ENTAC guided missile, and finally the LAW. The number of machine guns was reduced by the ROAD TOE's, but in spite of this reduction there were still more 7.62-mm. and .50-caliber machine guns in mechanized infantry units than in other infantry organizations.

With the adoption of ROAD, the designations of different types of infantry units became standardized. The official designation for all infantry battalions consisted of the battalion and the parent regiment, and descriptive terms such as mechanized or airborne were now put in parentheses after the battalion. Also placed in parentheses, following the parent unit, was the traditional or distinctive designation of the regiment, shared by all of its elements. For example, the 1st Battalion (Airborne), 506th Infantry (Currahee), organic to the 101st Airborne Division, and the 3d Battalion (Mechanized), 118th Infantry (Palmetto Regiment), a unit of the South Carolina Army National Guard, were officially designated as the 1st Battalion, 506th Infantry, and the 3d Battalion, 118th Infantry. Thus while official designations were standardized and simplified for efficiency's sake, provisions were made for retention of descriptive terms and historical nicknames.

Although the number and types of infantry battalions assigned to any given division depended on its mission and geographic location, the particular units were selected on the basis of their historical association with the division. The parent regiments of most of the infantry battalions organic to a ROAD division had fought with that division in World War I or II or in the Korean War. Whereas under the Pentomic system each of the organic infantry elements came from a different parent unit, under ROAD two or more battalions from the same parent regiment were usually assigned to each division. This change involved some reassignments and reshuffling of units and was made concurrently with reorganization under the new TOE's.

CARS adapted very well to ROAD, proving its ability to provide a stable historical and traditional background for combat units in spite of major tactical reorganizations. Except for the addition of five more infantry parent regiments—the 61st, 188th, 508th, 509th, and 511th—no changes were made in the system. Separate parent units were not created for the new mechanized infantry battalions. Those that were organized from former armored rifle battalions had parent regiments with armored infantry backgrounds, but since there were far more mechanized units, many of them shared parent regiments with the standard infantry. The airborne parent regiments had only airborne elements. The only exception was the 509th Infantry, whose 1st and 2d Battalions were organized as airborne/mechanized, that is, as mechanized units with parachute-qualified personnel. Two airborne regiments, the 188th and 511th, were

MEN OF 1ST ARMORED RIFLE BATTALION, 144TH INFANTRY, TEXAS ARMY NATIONAL GUARD, *with armored personnel carrier on maneuvers, 1962.*

added to CARS in order to furnish organic elements for the 11th Air Assault Division, newly organized at Fort Benning, Georgia, with the special purpose of testing the airmobile concept.

The greater emphasis on limited war capabilities and flexible response, which had set the stage for the ROAD reorganization, also helped to bring about an increase in Army and infantry strength in the early 1960's. The number of infantrymen had been gradually reduced since the Korean armistice and kept on declining after the adoption of the Pentomic organization. Reaching its lowest point in August and September 1958, infantry strength had dropped to less than 100,000 and to approximately 11 percent of the overall Army strength, which also continued to decrease. At that time there were ninety-three infantry units of battle group or battalion size in the active Army. Three-fourths of them were organic elements of divisions and about half were stationed overseas. After this low point, infantry personnel strength began to grow gradually, but it was the Berlin crisis of mid-1961 that brought about a significant gain in both infantry personnel and units.

The increase was at first mainly the result of federalizing two Army

National Guard divisions. The 32d Infantry Division from Wisconsin with five organic infantry battle groups and the 49th Armored Division from Texas with its four armored rifle battalions were federalized on 15 October 1961. An Army Reserve training division, the 100th, was also ordered into active military service. Thus, the reserve components played an important role during the Berlin crisis. However, in order to be prepared for such crises in the future, a buildup in Regular Army strength was necessary. To satisfy this need, existing units were made more combat ready and two additional divisions were authorized. In February 1962 the 1st Armored Division and the 5th Infantry Division (Mechanized) were activated. These divisions and their organic elements became the first units to be organized under the new ROAD concept.

By the time the ROAD reorganization was officially completed in June 1964, active infantry strength had grown to 130,131, even though infantry units from the reserve components had reverted to reserve status. The Regular Army now had sixteen combat divisions: 5 infantry, 2 airborne, 4 armored, 4 mechanized infantry, and 1 cavalry (organized as infantry), with 107 organic infantry battalions among them. Sixteen infantry battalions were assigned to seven separate brigades: 3 infantry, 1 airborne, 1 armored, and 2 mechanized infantry. There were also three battalions assigned to the 11th Air Assault Division (Test), four separate battalions, and five separate companies. One unit was still designated a battle group; it was the 1st Battle Group, 1st Infantry, active at zero strength at West Point. From this total of 136 infantry units, 67 were stationed in the continental United States and 69 were overseas with 31 in West Germany, 19 in Korea, and the remainder in Okinawa, Hawaii, Alaska, Berlin, and the Canal Zone.

Infantry readiness in the Army Reserve and Army National Guard was also considerably improved during the 1960's, but it was accompanied by a reduction in the total number of organized units. Robert S. McNamara, Secretary of Defense during the Kennedy and Johnson administrations, was instrumental in bringing about several realignments of the reserve components. He recommended drastic cuts in the number of reserve units, which in turn would enable the remaining organizations to be more fully manned and equipped. One of McNamara's original suggestions was to eliminate all infantry and other combat units from the Army Reserve, leaving only service units, and to make the Army National Guard the combat reserve. Congress rejected this proposal and modified many of his other recommendations. Nevertheless, after the reorganization of 1967–68 both the Army Reserve and the Army National Guard were significantly different from the reserve components of a decade earlier.

The twenty-seven Army National Guard divisions of the late 1950's, with sixty-three organic infantry regiments (of three battalions each) and twenty-four organic armored infantry battalions, had been reduced by 1968 to only eight divisions and eighteen separate brigades, having a total of 111 organic ROAD infantry battalions. There were also four separate infantry companies and twelve separate infantry battalions, including two scout battalions organized in Alaska with Eskimo personnel. All of the Army National Guard infantry units were elements of seventy-six CARS parent regiments.

In the 1968 Army Reserve there were no divisional combat infantry units left, since four of the ten combat divisions had been inactivated in 1963 and the other six by the end of 1965. Only three separate brigades, each having three organic infantry battalions, remained active together with one separate infantry battalion. In the course of these realignments twelve of the eighteen CARS infantry parent regiments with Army Reserve backgrounds had been eliminated. The 313th, 314th, 315th, 409th, 410th, and 442d Infantry were retained with one battalion each, while the other four active infantry battalions were elements of Regular Army parent units. The Army Reserve continued to have thirteen training divisions, but these too had undergone a major reorganization. The five training regiments previously organic to each division were replaced by thirteen battalions, with eight for Basic Combat Training (BCT), three for Advanced Individual Training (AIT), and two for Combat Support Training (CST), all of which were attached to four brigades within the division. Although a battalion and brigade structure was introduced, the training divisions were not organized under ROAD and the new battalions did not become elements of designated CARS parent regiments. The former training regiments, however, were reorganized under a modified CARS concept with a variable number of BCT, AIT, or CST battalions and with the regimental headquarters inactive.

One other type of infantry organization, the Special Forces, remained active in the Army Reserve and also had elements in the Regular Army and in the Army National Guard. Although part of CARS, the Special Forces were not like any other CARS units, but had a unique structure. Their basic operational unit was the 12-man "A" detachment, commanded by a captain. Forty-eight of these detachments were organic to a full strength Special Forces group. The parent regiment for all Special Forces units from all three components, designated the 1st Special Forces, was created on 15 April 1960 by consolidation of the six ranger infantry battalions and the 1st Special Service Force of World War II. Since the ranger companies of the Korean War period traced their lineages back to elements of the World War II ranger battalions, their histories were also perpetuated by the new parent unit.

Team from 5th Special Forces Group, 1st Special Forces, *firing 81-mm. mortar in Vietnam.*

The mission of the Special Forces was to fight both as guerrillas and against guerrillas and to organize, train, advise, direct, and assist indigenous forces anywhere in the world in the conduct of guerrilla warfare as well as in counterinsurgency and counterguerrilla operations. Special Forces personnel were therefore among the first Americans to be sent to Vietnam as advisors to the South Vietnamese in their struggle against Communist aggression. As the conflict in Vietnam developed into a major war, the U.S. involvement deepened. Regular infantry and other combat troops were committed, and the war in Vietnam became the first actual battle test of the strategy of flexible response and the ROAD organization.

The War in Vietnam

The first U.S. infantry combat units arrived in Vietnam in May 1965.

They were the 1st and 2d Battalions, 503d Infantry, elements of the 173d Airborne Brigade, previously stationed on Okinawa. These units were joined in July by three battalions from the 1st Infantry Division and three battalions from the 101st Airborne Division, and in September by eight battalions of the 1st Cavalry Division (Airmobile). The infantry battalions organic to the 173d Airborne Brigade and the 101st Airborne Division were airborne, those assigned to the 1st Infantry Division were standard infantry, while the elements of the 1st Cavalry Division were a new type of unit called "airmobile." Although the airmobile infantry battalions had no organic aircraft, the division was authorized 428 helicopters, enough to give all of its elements tactical mobility by air.

Military strategists had long dreamed of airmobile units that would introduce a true third dimension to the battlefield. The first practical application of the airmobile concept, the organization of the 11th Air Assault Division, was made possible by the great strides of recent years in the design, production, and doctrine of employment of the helicopter. Elements of this test division were activated at Fort Benning, Georgia, starting in February 1963 as a result of the recommendations of the U.S. Army Tactical Mobility Requirement Board, more commonly known as the Howze Board after its chairman, Lt. Gen. Hamilton H. Howze. Following more than two years of testing and evaluation, the Secretary of Defense approved the creation of a combat ready airmobile division. The 1st Cavalry Division was selected. It was transferred less personnel and equipment from Korea to Fort Benning and was reorganized as airmobile on 1 July 1965. With the formation of this division the Army acquired a new way of bringing the infantry and other ground troops in contact with the enemy. One of the major goals of the ROAD reorganization had been to furnish appropriate tactical mobility to combat units in different geographical areas. The development of airmobile units was another example of ROAD's continuing flexibility. Since in Vietnam the use of ground vehicles was severely limited by terrain, the new airmobile division was ideally suited for employment there.

Probably the most significant innovation of the war was the large-scale use of helicopters in general and of airmobile combat units in particular. All units in Vietnam depended heavily on the helicopter for aerial reconnaissance, medical evacuation, and resupply, as well as rapid transportation into and out of otherwise inaccessible areas. Helicopters used by the infantry were Army not Air Force aircraft and, as such, were more responsive to the needs of the units. The infantry in turn quickly adjusted to airmobile operations. Although all types of infantry units were regularly transported by helicopter, the airmobile division was the only infantry organization that could move all of its elements with its own organic aircraft.

MEN OF 1ST BATTALION, 2D INFANTRY, *just dropped from helicopter, rush into action near Phuoc Vinh.*

Airmobile units were capable of moving rapidly and directly to their objective regardless of terrain obstacles or enemy troop concentrations. Responding swiftly to changes in the tactical situation, they could break off action at one point and fly quickly in any direction to fight at another point or disperse to widely separated bases. Characterized by speed, surprise, maneuverability, and aggressiveness, the airmobile assault proved to be a highly successful offensive technique. In terrain such as that of Southeast Asia, it was a great improvement over airborne assault techniques developed in World War II. Except for one jump by elements of the 173d Airborne Brigade on 22 February 1967, no combat parachute drops were made by U.S. Army units in Vietnam, whereas literally thousands of helicopter missions took place. On 1 July 1968, therefore, the 101st Airborne Division was reorganized as airmobile. Although the division base was significantly changed in the process of airmobilization, this was not a major reorganization for the ten airborne infantry battalions assigned to the division. By that time their structure had already been standardized under Modification Tables of Organization and Equipment (MTOE's) for light infantry battalions.

When the buildup of U.S. troops in Vietnam began in 1965, infantry units in general were organized under the ROAD tables of 15 July and 15 August 1963. Shortly thereafter a new series of infantry TOE's was published. These tables were prepared under the direction of the U.S. Army Combat Developments Command, which had been created during the 1962 reorganization of the Department of the Army. The new command took over the responsibility for development and processing of TOE's from the Continental Army Command (CONARC), but training of infantry units and supervision of the Infantry School remained CONARC functions. The standard and mechanized infantry tables were dated 31 March 1966, while the airborne infantry had two sets of tables, dated 30 June 1965 and 30 June 1966. These TOE's added an air defense section to the headquarters company of all three types of battalions, which was organized to use the new Redeye guided missile system (a man-portable, shoulder-fired, low altitude, antiaircraft weapon). The Davy Crockett section augmentation was eliminated from the battalions, but in February 1967 a tentative test TOE for a separate infantry Davy Crockett platoon was published. Its primary mission was to provide close-in nuclear fire support for the maneuver battalions of a division or brigade. Since this was a test TOE, units were to be organized under it only when specifically directed.

The number of personnel in airborne units was reduced by the 1965 and 1966 TOE's, and lighter equipment was authorized for them. The battalion's antitank weapon was changed from the ENTAC to the 106-mm. recoilless rifle, which in turn was to be replaced by the TOW (Tube-launched, Optically-tracked, Wire-guided) missile system as soon as it became available. A new individual rifle, the lightweight M16, was also authorized for airborne infantrymen. All three types of infantry battalions—standard, mechanized, and airborne—retained the ROAD structure of a headquarters and headquarters company and three rifle companies.

Meanwhile, test TOE's had been prepared by the Combat Developments Command for two new types of infantry units, the airmobile battalion organic to the airmobile division and a special infantry battalion which was to be assigned to light infantry divisions and separate light infantry brigades. With authorized strengths of 767 and 769, respectively, these units were smaller than the regular infantry battalion of 849 men. Both battalions had a headquarters and headquarters company, three rifle companies, and a combat support company consisting of a mortar platoon equipped with 81-mm. mortars, a reconnaissance platoon, and an antitank platoon armed with 106-mm. recoilless rifles. The rifle companies in both battalions had three rifle platoons supported by an 81-mm. mortar platoon, and the rifle squads consisted of ten men. The basic individual weapon in the light infantry battalion was the M14 rifle, while the airmobile unit was authorized M16 rifles. The new battalions had fewer telephones and radios than other infantry units and the number of vehicles, particularly in the airmobile battalion, was considerably smaller than in the standard infantry battalion.

Regular infantry units serving in Vietnam did not use all of their authorized heavy weapons and equipment. As a rule, most of their vehicles and weapons like ENTAC's, 4.2-inch mortars, and 106-mm. recoilless rifles were left behind either in storage or in base camps while the units were in the field. Although 90-mm. recoilless rifles and 81-mm. mortars were employed much more frequently than their more powerful and heavier counterparts, a rifle company rarely carried its full TOE complement of these weapons on operations and often used the much lighter LAW instead of the 90-mm. recoilless rifle. The resulting loss in firepower was offset by a corresponding gain in mobility and a decrease in fatigue among the soldiers. Transporting heavy equipment in most parts of Vietnam was a very difficult procedure, while excellent air and artillery support was readily available. Infantrymen, therefore, were not reluctant to leave some of their own fire support weapons behind. Since the enemy did not employ heavy armored forces, certain heavy weapons (notably the big antitank missiles and 106-mm. recoilless rifles) were used rarely or not at all, simply because they were not needed.

Personnel who would normally man the heavier infantry weapons were frequently used to make up a small fourth rifle company within the battalion. This unit served as a command post security force and as an emergency reserve, thereby giving the battalion commander three maneuver companies and additional flexibility in the employment of the battalion. Since this provisional extra company was so common, and it increased the capabilities of the battalion significantly, official permission was given to all infantry battalions in Vietnam to organize such units on a permanent basis. Battalions stationed elsewhere were not authorized the additional company. This variation from the basic TOE structure was approved by MTOE's prepared under the direction of the Commander in Chief, United States Army, Pacific. Such tables were published from time to time by the major Army commands to make appropriate changes for particular units necessary to meet certain requirements without altering the basic TOE for other units of the same type. Another change approved by MTOE's was the addition of a separate combat support company to standard and airborne infantry battalions. Only those battalions that were stationed in or scheduled to be deployed to Vietnam were permitted to have this extra company, which was similar to the one in airmobile and light infantry units.

Gradually all infantry battalions in Vietnam, with the exception of mechanized and riverine units, were reorganized under modifications of the light infantry battalion TOE with a headquarters and headquarters company, four rifle companies, a combat support company, and a total authorized strength of 920. Eventually the organizational modifications adopted in Vietnam were also recommended as changes to the basic infantry TOE's. One suggestion was to remove the mortar, reconnaissance, and antitank platoons and the ground surveillance and air defense sections from the headquarters company of the infantry battalion and to organize them into a separate combat support company, leaving only the administrative and service support elements in the new headquarters company. Another suggestion was to authorize a fourth rifle company for the infantry battalion in wartime, but to retain the three-company structure in peacetime. By the end of 1969 this recommendation was still under study by the Army Staff, but TOE's were already being prepared for the new headquarters and combat support companies.

Although few mechanized infantry units were sent to Vietnam, those that served there operated effectively wherever the terrain permitted. They were equipped with M113 and M113A1 armored personnel carriers, which were sometimes employed as fighting vehicles in a tank-like role. The mechanized battalion was modified to include a smaller fourth rifle company, but a separate combat support company was not authorized. Mechanized infantry battalions located outside of Vietnam were organized with three rifle companies, as provided by the basic TOE.

Units from the 9th Infantry Division, together with a Navy task force, created the Mobile Riverine Force which operated in the Mekong Delta— a low and flat region with innumerable canals, rivers, swamps, and inundated rice paddies, almost completely inaccessible to ground troops, especially during the long monsoon season. Riverine infantry units fought as regular infantry but lived on barrack ships and were transported by specially modified landing craft, known as armored troop carriers. They received fire support from Navy gunboats as well as from Army artillery mounted on barges.

Since there were no clearly defined front lines and it was difficult to find and fix the enemy without running the risk of falling into an ambush, reconnaissance, intelligence, and patrolling became particularly important in Vietnam. Although all units took part in such operations, specialized infantry units were also organized to carry out certain types of missions. Among them were scout dog platoons and combat tracker teams—both of which used dogs to detect the presence of enemy troops—and long range reconnaissance patrols (LRRP's), also called long range patrols (LRP's). LRP's were small teams specially trained to penetrate deep into enemy-held territory. From there they reported detailed, accurate, and timely information concerning troop concentrations, installations, and activities needed for planning future operations, or they called in and adjusted artillery fire or air strikes.

Infantry long range patrol companies, having twenty-four patrols of five men each, were first assigned on the basis of one per corps or field force, while within divisions LRRP missions were performed by provisional detachments or platoons. Starting in late 1967, a LRP company was attached to each division in Vietnam and eventually to each separate brigade. The number of companies continued to increase and by the end of 1968 about half of all separate infantry companies in the active Army were long range patrol units. They were elements of various different regiments and had no common numerical designation or historical connection with each other until 1 January 1969. On that day the 75th Infantry, the famous "Merrill's Marauders" of World War II, was reorganized under CARS and became the parent regiment for LRP units. At the same time the parenthetical designation of the companies was changed from LRP to ranger, although their long range patrol mission remained unchanged.

The importance of small units in Vietnam was not limited to such specialized organizations as long range patrols, scout dog platoons, combat tracker teams, or Special Forces detachments. Regular infantry contacts with the enemy were frequently made at the squad and platoon level. Small unit actions were typical and often decisive. As a result, the war in Vietnam has often been called a platoon leader's war. Most major operations were conducted on the brigade level with varying numbers of maneuver elements attached for specific missions in accordance with the ROAD principle of tailored brigades. Vietnam was the first test of the ROAD organization under actual combat conditions, and the system proved its flexibility by adapting quickly to a difficult terrain and an elusive enemy in a war with many unconventional aspects.

The most popular infantry weapons in Vietnam were the lightest ones. Among them were the M79 grenade launcher, the LAW, and the Claymore antipersonnel mine. The mine, which scattered hundreds of steel

INFANTRYMAN WITH M60 MACHINE GUN.

fragments in a fan-shaped pattern, could be deliberately detonated by the operator or concealed and left to be activated by trip wire. As its official field manual stated, the number of ways in which the Claymore might be employed was limited only by the imagination of the user. Another widely used weapon was the M60 machine gun.

There was also the new M16 rifle. The rifle itself weighed 6.5 pounds and its firing weight, including a shoulder sling and a fully loaded 20-round magazine, was only 7.6 pounds. The M16 used 5.56-mm. (.223-caliber) ammunition. A clothespin-type bipod and a 6-inch bayonet were issued with the rifle. Having a muzzle velocity of approximately 3,150 feet per second and an average cyclic rate of fire of 750 rounds per minute, the M16 was particularly effective at short ranges. It was less accurate and less effective than the M14 at long ranges and, unlike the M14, did not fire standard NATO ammunition. However, its light weight and lethal close-in effectiveness made the M16 an ideal weapon in terrain such as Vietnam's. Although originally adopted for limited use by Special Forces and airborne troops, the M16 was soon authorized for all infantry units in Southeast Asia. In mid-1967 it was standardized for general Army distribution in addition to the M14 rifle, which continued to be used by most infantrymen stationed outside of Vietnam.

Meanwhile, the manufacturers of the M16 were developing an entire family of 5.56-mm. weapons to supplement the M16 rifle. These included a carbine, a submachine gun, a very light survival rifle, a heavy assault rifle, and several machine guns, as well as a 40-mm. grenade launcher attachment for the M16. By late 1968, the submachine gun was being authorized for selected infantry units, such as long range patrol companies and combat tracker platoons. A completely new kind of weapon called SPIW (Special Purpose Individual Weapon) was also in the process of development. The new SPIW may combine the capabilities of a rifle, a controlled pattern shotgun, and a light mortar. It could be designed to fire a single medium-sized dart, a cluster of small darts, a microcaliber bullet, or a high explosive round. Many military experts predicted that the SPIW, or something like it, would become the basic infantry weapon of the future. By the end of 1969, however, the SPIW was still purely experimental, and no such weapon was available to the infantryman fighting in Vietnam.

Infantry strength in Vietnam had increased gradually as the war escalated. By mid-1969, when the eleventh official campaign was being fought and just before the first phase in the withdrawal of U.S. troops began, there were seven divisions and four brigades in Vietnam. To make this large scale deployment possible without moving units from Europe and Korea or reducing the strategic reserve to a dangerously low level, the overall strength of the Army and the infantry had been built up. Between June 1964 and June 1969 the number of divisions in the active Army grew from sixteen to eighteen, while brigades increased from seven to eleven.

Two of the brigades were federalized Army National Guard units, the 29th Infantry Brigade from Hawaii and the 69th Infantry Brigade from Kansas. They were ordered into active Federal service on 13 May 1968, as a result of the Pueblo crisis and the Tet offensive earlier that year. Only two of the three organic infantry battalions from the 69th were called up, but the 2d Battalion, 133d Infantry, from Iowa was also federalized and joined the brigade at Fort Carson, Colorado. At the same time the 100th Battalion, 442d Infantry, a Hawaiian Army Reserve unit, was called to active duty and attached to the 29th Infantry Brigade at Schofield Barracks, Hawaii. One other infantry unit was federalized— Company D, 151st Infantry, from Indiana. After training at Fort Benning, Georgia, this long range patrol company served in Vietnam for eleven months. It was the only infantry organization from the reserve components to participate in the war.

In the second half of 1969 the number of infantry units started to decline for the first time since the Vietnam buildup began. President Richard M. Nixon's decision to withdraw U.S. forces gradually from Southeast Asia was accompanied by a plan to reduce the strength of the Army. Among the first units to be redeployed were six infantry battalions organic to the 9th Infantry Division. They left Vietnam in July and August 1969, and were inactivated in August and September at Fort Riley, Kansas, and Schofield Barracks, Hawaii. By mid-December 1969, all infantry units from the reserve components had been released and reorganized at their home stations. Meanwhile, the second increment of organizations scheduled for redeployment was in the process of leaving Vietnam.

INFANTRYMEN SWEEPING THROUGH RICE PADDIES IN VIETNAM. (*M16 rifle in foreground.*)

Although airmobile and light infantry units were most common in Vietnam, other types of infantry were not neglected elsewhere during the late 1960's. Only a handful of mechanized units went to Vietnam, but numerous mechanized infantry battalions were assigned to mechanized and armored divisions in Europe and in the United States. Most airborne personnel in Vietnam lost their jump pay, because their units did not have the opportunity to utilize their unique capabilities, but the airborne battalions in the strategic reserve proved their constant readiness in various emergencies, such as the 1965 Dominican Republic crisis and several domestic civil disturbances. In spite of the heavy infantry commitment in Vietnam, as the decade of the 1960's ended there were still infantry units stationed all over the world—in West Germany, Berlin, Korea, the Canal Zone, Alaska, and Hawaii, as well as in the continental United States. The Regular Army infantry was backed up by Army Reserve and Army National Guard infantry units which, although fewer in number, were better trained and equipped than ever before.

The infantry organizational structure existing in 1969 was well suited to the strategy and tactics of flexible response, but regardless of the great variety of infantry units, many of them highly specialized, the basic mission of the infantry remained unchanged. The infantryman of the future may be armed with the SPIW, may wear a spacesuit-like uniform with a built-in two-way radio, and may be transported by his own individual jet propulsion system. Nevertheless, his job will continue to be essentially the same as it has been since 14 June 1775, the birthday of the United States infantry and of the United States Army—to close with and destroy the enemy.

HERALDIC ITEMS

Heraldic items for Army organizations reflect history, tradition, ideals, and accomplishments. Coats of arms, historic badges, and distinctive insignia have been so designed that each is distinctive to the organization for which approved. They serve as identifying devices, an inspiration, and an incentive for unity of purpose.

A coat of arms or a historic badge and a distinctive insignia are authorized for each regiment. The designs of these items are based on the lineages and battle honors of the organizations.

While the custom of bearing various symbols on shields, helmets, and flags existed in antiquity, heraldry was not introduced until the Middle Ages. The use of heraldic devices became more prevalent with the increased use of armor and the requirements for insignia to assist in distinguishing friend from foe on the battlefield. The symbols selected for use on these devices were commemorative of incidents of valor, mythological beasts, and, later, other symbols to which specific symbolism was ascribed. These heraldic bearings were placed on a surcoat worn over the armor, from which the term *coat of arms* was derived. Gradually a formal system of heraldry evolved, complete with rules for design, use, and display. These rules or principles were for the purpose of facilitating designs that would be distinctive and easily recognized. Present-day heraldic devices stem from this heraldic system which was established during the twelfth and thirteenth centuries.

A complete coat of arms consists of a shield, a crest, and a motto. The shield, the most important portion of the arms, contains the field or ground on which the charges are placed. The crest as originally used was placed upon the top of the helmet of the chief or leader to enable his followers to distinguish him during battle. The crest is placed upon a wreath of six skeins or twists composed of the principal metal and principal color of the shield, alternately, in the order named. This wreath (or torse) represents the piece of cloth which the knight twisted around the top of his helmet, and by means of which the actual crest was attached. Mottoes have been in use longer than coats of arms, many of the older ones having originated from war cries. They usually are of an idealistic nature and sometimes allude to a well-known event in the history of the organization.

Some organizations are authorized historic badges of a symbolic composition in lieu of coats of arms. These badges are not shield-shaped, but they include mottoes.

The elements of the coat of arms or the badge, as applicable, are embroidered on the organizational flag—the central element of which is the American eagle. The shield of the coat of arms is on the eagle's breast; a scroll bearing the motto is held in his beak; and the crest is placed above his head.

On flags of those organizations which have historic badges in lieu of coats of arms, the badge is placed above the eagle's head and the scroll bearing the motto is in his beak.

Distinctive insignia, manufactured in metal and enamel and worn on the uniform by all personnel of the regiment, usually are based on elements of the design of the coat of arms or historic badge. Thus the organizational flag (color) and the distinctive insignia include the same design elements.

Heraldic items today, as in the past, serve to distinguish specific organizations and their members.

1st Infantry

2d Infantry

3d Infantry

4th Infantry

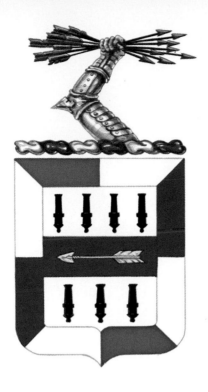

5th Infantry

6th Infantry

7th Infantry

8th Infantry

9th Infantry

10th Infantry

11th Infantry

12th Infantry

13th Infantry

14th Infantry

15th Infantry

16th Infantry

17th Infantry

18th Infantry

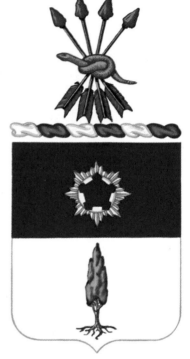

19th Infantry

20th Infantry

21st Infantry

22d Infantry

23d Infantry

26th Infantry

27th Infantry

28th Infantry

29th Infantry

30th Infantry

31st Infantry

32d Infantry

34th Infantry

35th Infantry

36th Infantry

38th Infantry

39th Infantry

41st Infantry

46th Infantry

47th Infantry

48th Infantry

50th Infantry

51st Infantry

52d Infantry

54th Infantry

58th Infantry

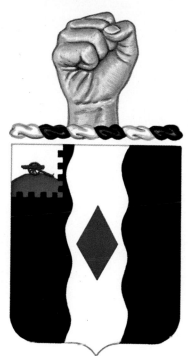

60th Infantry

61st Infantry

75th Infantry

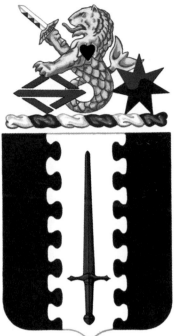

87th Infantry

187th Infantry

188th Infantry

325th Infantry

327th Infantry

501st Infantry

502d Infantry

503d Infantry

504th Infantry

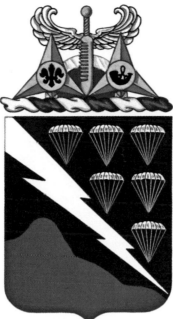

505th Infantry

506th Infantry

508th Infantry

509th Infantry

511th Infantry

1st Special Forces

LINEAGES AND HERALDIC DATA

Honors and Asterisks

Campaigns and decorations for each battalion and battle group under the Combat Arms Regimental System (CARS) include all honors of the parent regiment. Asterisks (*) appearing in the list of honors indicate the honors for which a particular unit is the *earning unit.* This means that either the unit itself, or a unit from which it has directly descended, earned the honor. For company-sized elements (those that have not been used to form battle groups or battalions), only the honors for which the companies are the *earning units* are listed. In these instances, asterisks are unnecessary and are not used, since all of the honors shown are earned.

Authorities for Decorations

General orders announcing decorations are shown parenthetically for parent regiments and for those decorations of their component elements for which the elements are the *earning units.*

Heraldic Text

In some instances, the text relating to the heraldic items approved for the regiments is not as comprehensive as in the original letters of approval, amendment, or redesignation sent to the organizations. Minor changes in heraldic material have been made to meet the need for brevity in this volume.

The Lineages

The unit lineages in this volume are adapted from the official Lineage and Honors Certificates prepared by the Office of the Chief of Military History. To the units, these documents represent their birth certificates, their deeds to organizational properties, and documentation of their war service. The lineage and honors data has been compressed to save space, but the information is the same as that on the certificates, which accounts for the technical language used. The glossary on page 923 will assist the reader who is unfamiliar with lineage terms.

125

1st INFANTRY

HERALDIC ITEMS

COAT OF ARMS

Shield: Per bend gules and azure on a bend or a bendlet argent indented of seven and counter indented of the same fimbriated sable. (And for informal use, the escutcheon encircled with an infantry officer's full dress belt with plate in base proper inscribed on the belt in chief "1791" in dexter "First Infantry" and in sinister the regimental motto; the escutcheon and belt displayed in front of two flintlock muskets with slings and bayonets crossed in saltire all proper.)

Crest: On a wreath of the colors the Arabic numeral "1" azure fimbriated or within a garland of laurel vert.

Motto: *Semper Primus* (Always First).

Symbolism: The regiment's campaigns and wars are represented by the notches on the diagonal band across the shield. The upper part of the shield is red; this was the color of the old 2d Sub-Legion. The lower part is blue, the infantry color.

The crest with the numeral within the laurel wreath of victory and the motto long in use by the regiment are self-explanatory.

DISTINCTIVE INSIGNIA

The distinctive insignia is the shield of the coat of arms surmounting a gold oval belt with three blue stripes parallel to the edges of the oval and surmounted by a plain gold buckle in base and a gold band on each side of the shield bearing the motto, *Semper* on the dexter band and *Primus* on the sinister band, in red letters.

LINEAGE AND HONORS

LINEAGE

Constituted 3 March 1791 in the Regular Army as the 2d Infantry. Organized in March 1791 in New England. Redesignated in 1792 as the

Infantry of the 2d Sub-Legion. Redesignated 31 October 1796 as the 2d Infantry.

Consolidated May–October 1815 with the 3d and 7th Infantry (both constituted 12 April 1808) and the 44th Infantry (constituted 29 January 1813) to form the 1st Infantry. Consolidated in April 1869 with the 43d Infantry, Veteran Reserve Corps (constituted 21 September 1866), and consolidated unit designated as the 1st Infantry.

Assigned 11 September 1918 to the 13th Division. Relieved 8 March 1919 from assignment to the 13th Division. Assigned 27 July 1921 to the 2d Division. Relieved 16 October 1939 from assignment to the 2d Division and assigned to the 6th Division (later redesignated as the 6th Infantry Division). Inactivated 10 January 1949 in Korea. Activated 4 October 1950 at Fort Ord, California. Relieved 3 April 1956 from assignment to the 6th Infantry Division. Assigned 15 May 1956 to the United States Military Academy at West Point, New York.

Relieved 15 May 1958 from assignment to the United States Military Academy and reorganized as a parent regiment under the Combat Arms Regimental System.

Campaign Participation Credit

War of 1812
Canada
Lundy's Lane
New Orleans
Florida 1814
Alabama 1814
Alabama 1815
Louisiana 1815

Mexican War
Monterey
Vera Cruz

Civil War
Mississippi River
Vicksburg
Texas 1861
Missouri 1861
Mississippi 1862

Indian Wars
Miami
Creeks

Seminoles
Black Hawk
Apaches
Pine Ridge
Texas 1850

War With Spain
Santiago

Philippine Insurrection
Samar 1901

World War II
New Guinea (with arrowhead)
Luzon (with arrowhead)

Vietnam
Counteroffensive, Phase II
Counteroffensive, Phase III
Tet Counteroffensive
(other campaigns to be determined)

Decorations

Presidential Unit Citation (Army), Streamer embroidered MAFFIN BAY (3d Battalion, 1st Infantry cited; WD GO 113, 1946)

Philippine Presidential Unit Citation, Streamer embroidered 17 OCTOBER 1944 TO 4 JULY 1945 (6th Infantry Division cited; DA GO 47, 1950)

1st BATTALION, 1st INFANTRY

RA

(United States Military Academy)

LINEAGE

Constituted 3 March 1791 in the Regular Army as a company of the 2d Infantry. Organized in March 1791 in New England. Redesignated in 1792 as a company of the Infantry of the 2d Sub-Legion. Redesignated 31 October 1796 as a company of the 2d Infantry.

Consolidated May–October 1815 with a company each of the 3d and 7th Infantry (both constituted 12 April 1808) and a company of the 44th Infantry (constituted 29 January 1813) to form a company of the 1st Infantry. Designated 21 August 1816 as Company A, 1st Infantry.

Consolidated in April 1869 with Company A, 43d Infantry, Veteran Reserve Corps (constituted 21 September 1866) and consolidated unit designated as Company A, 1st Infantry. (1st Infantry assigned 11 September 1918 to the 13th Division; relieved 8 March 1919 from assignment to the 13th Division; assigned 27 July 1921 to the 2d Division; relieved 16 October 1939 from assignment to the 2d Division and assigned to the 6th Division [later redesignated as the 6th Infantry Division].) Inactivated 10 January 1949 in Korea. Activated 4 October 1950 at Fort Ord, California. (1st Infantry relieved 3 April 1956 from assignment to the 6th Infantry Division; assigned 15 May 1956 to the United States Military Academy at West Point, New York.)

Reorganized and redesignated 15 May 1958 as Headquarters and Headquarters Company, 1st Battle Group, 1st Infantry and remained assigned to the United States Military Academy (organic elements concurrently constituted and activated). Redesignated 31 December 1964 as the 1st Battalion, 1st Infantry.

CAMPAIGN PARTICIPATION CREDIT

War of 1812
Canada
Lundy's Lane
*New Orleans
*Florida 1814
*Alabama 1814
Alabama 1815
*Louisiana 1815

Mexican War
Monterey
Vera Cruz

Civil War
*Mississippi River
*Vicksburg
Texas 1861
Missouri 1861
*Mississippi 1862

Indian Wars
*Miami
Creeks
*Seminoles
*Black Hawk
*Apaches
*Pine Ridge
Texas 1850

War With Spain
*Santiago

Philippine Insurrection
Samar 1901

World War II
*New Guinea (with arrowhead)
*Luzon (with arrowhead)

DECORATIONS

Presidential Unit Citation (Army), Streamer embroidered MAFFIN BAY

*Philippine Presidential Unit Citation, Streamer embroidered 17 OCTOBER 1944 TO 4 JULY 1945 (6th Infantry Division cited; DA GO 47, 1950)

2d BATTALION, 1st INFANTRY

RA

(23d Infantry Division)

LINEAGE

Constituted 3 March 1791 in the Regular Army as a company of the 2d Infantry. Organized in March 1791 in New England. Redesignated in 1792 as a company of the Infantry of the 2d Sub-Legion. Redesignated 31 October 1796 as a company of the 2d Infantry.

Consolidated May–October 1815 with a company each of the 3d and 7th Infantry (both constituted 12 April 1808) and a company of the 44th Infantry (constituted 29 January 1813) to form a company of the 1st Infantry. Designated 21 August 1816 as Company B, 1st Infantry.

Consolidated in April 1869 with Company B, 43d Infantry, Veteran Reserve Corps (constituted 21 September 1866) and consolidated unit designated as Company B, 1st Infantry. (1st Infantry assigned 11 September 1918 to the 13th Division; relieved 8 March 1919 from assignment to the 13th Division; assigned 27 July 1921 to the 2d Division; relieved 16 October 1939 from assignment to the 2d Division and assigned to the 6th Division [later redesignated as the 6th Infantry Division].) Inactivated 10 January 1949 in Korea. Activated 4 October 1950 at Fort Ord, California. (1st Infantry relieved 3 April 1956 from assignment to the 6th Infantry Division; assigned 15 May 1956 to the United States Military Academy at West Point, New York.)

Inactivated 15 May 1958 at West Point, New York, relieved from assignment to the United States Military Academy, and redesignated as Headquarters and Headquarters Company, 2d Battle Group, 1st Infantry (organic elements concurrently constituted). Battle Group activated 14 June 1958 at Fort Benning, Georgia, and assigned to the 2d Infantry Division. Inactivated 10 May 1963 at Fort Benning, Georgia, and relieved from assignment to the 2d Infantry Division.

Redesignated 10 September 1965 as the 2d Battalion, 1st Infantry and assigned to the 196th Infantry Brigade. Activated 15 September 1965 at Fort Devens, Massachusetts. Relieved 15 February 1969 from assignment to the 196th Infantry Brigade and assigned to the 23d Infantry Division.

132

CAMPAIGN PARTICIPATION CREDIT

War of 1812
Canada
Lundy's Lane
*New Orleans
*Florida 1814
*Alabama 1814
Alabama 1815
*Louisiana 1815

Mexican War
Monterey
Vera Cruz

Civil War
*Mississippi River
*Vicksburg
Texas 1861
*Missouri 1861
*Mississippi 1862

Indian Wars
*Miami

Creeks
*Seminoles
*Black Hawk
Apaches
*Pine Ridge
Texas 1850

War With Spain
*Santiago

Philippine Insurrection
*Samar 1901

World War II
*New Guinea (with arrowhead)
*Luzon (with arrowhead)

Vietnam
*Counteroffensive, Phase II
*Counteroffensive, Phase III
*Tet Counteroffensive
(other campaigns to be determined)

DECORATIONS

Presidential Unit Citation (Army), Streamer embroidered MAFFIN BAY

*Philippine Presidential Unit Citation, Streamer embroidered 17 OCTOBER 1944 TO 4 JULY 1945 (6th Infantry Division cited; DA GO 47, 1950)

3d BATTALION, 1st INFANTRY

LINEAGE

Constituted 3 March 1791 in the Regular Army as a company of the 2d Infantry. Organized in March 1791 in New England. Redesignated in 1792 as a company of the Infantry of the 2d Sub-Legion. Redesignated 31 October 1796 as a company of the 2d Infantry.

Consolidated May–October 1815 with a company each of the 3d and 7th Infantry (both constituted 12 April 1808) and a company of the 44th Infantry (constituted 29 January 1813) to form a company of the 1st Infantry. Designated 21 August 1816 as Company C, 1st Infantry.

Consolidated in April 1869 with Company C, 43d Infantry, Veteran Reserve Corps (constituted 21 September 1866) and consolidated unit designated as Company C, 1st Infantry. (1st Infantry assigned 11 September 1918 to the 13th Division; relieved 8 March 1919 from assignment to the 13th Division; assigned 27 July 1921 to the 2d Division; relieved 16 October 1939 from assignment to the 2d Division and assigned to the 6th Division [later redesignated as the 6th Infantry Division].) Inactivated 10 January 1949 in Korea. Activated 4 October 1950 at Fort Ord, California. (1st Infantry relieved 3 April 1956 from assignment to the 6th Infantry Division; assigned 15 May 1956 to the United States Military Academy at West Point, New York.) Inactivated 15 May 1958 at West Point, New York, and relieved from assignment to the United States Military Academy.

Redesignated 7 April 1959 as Headquarters and Headquarters Company, 3d Battle Group, 1st Infantry, withdrawn from the Regular Army, allotted to the Army Reserve, and assigned to the 77th Infantry Division (organic elements concurrently constituted). Battle Group activated 1 May 1959 with Headquarters at New York, New York. Inactivated 26 March 1963 at New York, New York, and relieved from assignment to the 77th Infantry Division.

Redesignated 15 April 1966 as the 3d Battalion, 1st Infantry; concurrently, withdrawn from the Army Reserve and allotted to the Regular Army. Activated 1 July 1966 in Hawaii and assigned to the 11th Infantry Brigade. Relieved 15 February 1969 from assignment to the 11th Infantry Brigade and assigned to the 23d Infantry Division.

134

CAMPAIGN PARTICIPATION CREDIT

War of 1812
Canada
Lundy's Lane
*New Orleans
*Florida 1814
*Alabama 1814
Alabama 1815
*Louisiana 1815

Mexican War
Monterey
Vera Cruz

Civil War
*Mississippi River
*Vicksburg
Texas 1861
*Missouri 1861
*Mississippi 1862

Indian Wars
*Miami

Creeks
*Seminoles
Black Hawk
Apaches
*Pine Ridge
Texas 1850

War With Spain
*Santiago

Philippine Insurrection
*Samar 1901

World War II
*New Guinea (with arrowhead)
*Luzon (with arrowhead)

Vietnam
*Counteroffensive, Phase III
*Tet Counteroffensive
(other campaigns to be determined)

DECORATIONS

Presidential Unit Citation (Army), Streamer embroidered MAFFIN BAY

*Philippine Presidential Unit Citation, Streamer embroidered 17 OCTOBER 1944 TO 4 JULY 1945 (6th Infantry Division cited; DA GO 47, 1950)

*Vietnamese Cross of Gallantry with Palm, Streamer embroidered VIETNAM 1968–1969 (3d Battalion, 1st Infantry cited; DA GO 2, 1971)

Company C additionally entitled to: Valorous Unit Award, Streamer embroidered QUANG NGAI PROVINCE (Company C, 3d Battalion, 1st Infantry cited; DA GO 43, 1970)

4th BATTALION, 1st INFANTRY

RA
(inactive)

LINEAGE

Constituted 3 March 1791 in the Regular Army as a company of the 2d Infantry. Organized in March 1791 in New England. Redesignated in 1792 as a company of the Infantry of the 2d Sub-Legion. Redesignated 31 October 1796 as a company of the 2d Infantry.

Consolidated May–October 1815 with a company each of the 3d and 7th Infantry (both constituted 12 April 1808) and a company of the 44th Infantry (constituted 29 January 1813) to form a company of the 1st Infantry. Designated 21 August 1816 as Company D, 1st Infantry.

Consolidated in April 1869 with Company D, 43d Infantry, Veteran Reserve Corps (constituted 21 September 1866) and consolidated unit designated as Company D, 1st Infantry. (1st Infantry assigned 11 September 1918 to the 13th Division; relieved 8 March 1919 from assignment to the 13th Division; assigned 27 July 1921 to the 2d Division; relieved 16 October 1939 from assignment to the 2d Division and assigned to the 6th Division [later redesignated as the 6th Infantry Division].) Inactivated 10 January 1949 in Korea. Activated 4 October 1950 at Fort Ord, California. (1st Infantry relieved 3 April 1956 from assignment to the 6th Infantry Division; assigned 15 May 1956 to the United States Military Academy at West Point, New York.)

Inactivated 15 May 1958 at West Point, New York, and relieved from assignment to the United States Military Academy; concurrently, redesignated as Headquarters and Headquarters Company, 4th Battle Group, 1st Infantry. Redesignated 24 November 1967 as Headquarters and Headquarters Company, 4th Battalion, 1st Infantry, assigned to the 6th Infantry Division, and activated at Fort Campbell, Kentucky (organic elements concurrently constituted and activated). Relieved 24 July 1968 from assignment to the 6th Infantry Division. Inactivated 21 July 1969 at Fort Campbell, Kentucky.

136

Campaign Participation Credit

War of 1812
Canada
Lundy's Lane
*New Orleans
*Florida 1814
Alabama 1814
Alabama 1815
Louisiana 1815

Mexican War
Monterey
Vera Cruz

Civil War
*Mississippi River
*Vicksburg
Texas 1861
*Missouri 1861
*Mississippi 1862

Indian Wars
*Miami
Creeks
*Seminoles
Black Hawk
*Apaches
*Pine Ridge
Texas 1850

War With Spain
*Santiago

Philippine Insurrection
*Samar 1901

World War II
*New Guinea (with arrowhead)
*Luzon (with arrowhead)

Decorations

Presidential Unit Citation (Army), Streamer embroidered MAFFIN BAY

*Philippine Presidential Unit Citation, Streamer embroidered 17 OCTOBER 1944 TO 4 JULY 1945 (6th Infantry Division cited; DA GO 47, 1950)

5th BATTALION, 1st INFANTRY

RA
(inactive)

LINEAGE

Constituted 3 March 1791 in the Regular Army as a company of the 2d Infantry. Organized in March 1791 in New England. Redesignated in 1792 as a company of the Infantry of the 2d Sub-Legion. Redesignated 31 October 1796 as a company of the 2d Infantry.

Consolidated May–October 1815 with a company each of the 3d and 7th Infantry (both constituted 12 April 1808) and a company of the 44th Infantry (constituted 29 January 1813) to form a company of the 1st Infantry. Designated 21 August 1816 as Company E, 1st Infantry.

Consolidated in April 1869 with Company E, 43d Infantry, Veteran Reserve Corps (constituted 21 September 1866) and consolidated unit designated as Company E, 1st Infantry. (1st Infantry assigned 11 September 1918 to the 13th Division; relieved 8 March 1919 from assignment to the 13th Division; assigned 27 July 1921 to the 2d Division; relieved 16 October 1939 from assignment to the 2d Division and assigned to the 6th Division [later redesignated as the 6th Infantry Division].) Inactivated 10 January 1949 in Korea. Activated 4 October 1950 at Fort Ord, California. (1st Infantry relieved 3 April 1956 from assignment to the 6th Infantry Division; assigned 15 May 1956 to the United States Military Academy at West Point, New York.)

Inactivated 15 May 1958 at West Point, New York, and relieved from assignment to the United States Military Academy; concurrently, redesignated as Headquarters and Headquarters Company, 5th Battle Group, 1st Infantry. Redesignated 24 November 1967 as Headquarters and Headquarters Company, 5th Battalion, 1st Infantry, assigned to the 6th Infantry Division, and activated at Fort Campbell, Kentucky (organic elements concurrently constituted and activated). Relieved 24 July 1968 from assignment to the 6th Infantry Division. Inactivated 21 July 1969 at Fort Campbell, Kentucky.

CAMPAIGN PARTICIPATION CREDIT

War of 1812
  Canada
  Lundy's Lane
  *New Orleans
  *Florida 1814
  Alabama 1814
  Alabama 1815
  Louisiana 1815

Mexican War
  *Monterey
  *Vera Cruz

Civil War
  Mississippi River
  *Vicksburg
  Texas 1861
  *Missouri 1861
  Mississippi 1862

Indian Wars
  *Miami
  Creeks
  *Seminoles
  Black Hawk
  Apaches
  *Pine Ridge
  Texas 1850

War With Spain
  *Santiago

Philippine Insurrection
  Samar 1901

World War II
  *New Guinea (with arrowhead)
  *Luzon (with arrowhead)

DECORATIONS

Presidential Unit Citation (Army), Streamer embroidered MAFFIN BAY

*Philippine Presidential Unit Citation, Streamer embroidered 17 OCTOBER 1944 TO 4 JULY 1945 (6th Infantry Division cited; DA GO 47, 1950)

6th BATTALION, 1st INFANTRY

RA
(inactive)

Constituted 3 March 1791 in the Regular Army as a company of the 2d Infantry. Organized in March 1791 in New England. Redesignated in 1792 as a company of the Infantry of the 2d Sub-Legion. Redesignated 31 October 1796 as a company of the 2d Infantry.

Consolidated May–October 1815 with a company each of the 3d and 7th Infantry (both constituted 12 April 1808) and a company of the 44th Infantry (constituted 29 January 1813) to form a company of the 1st Infantry. Designated 21 August 1816 as Company F, 1st Infantry.

Consolidated in April 1869 with Company F, 43d Infantry, Veteran Reserve Corps (constituted 21 September 1866) and consolidated unit designated as Company F, 1st Infantry. (1st Infantry assigned 11 September 1918 to the 13th Division; relieved 8 March 1919 from assignment to the 13th Division; assigned 27 July 1921 to the 2d Division; relieved 16 October 1939 from assignment to the 2d Division and assigned to the 6th Division [later redesignated as the 6th Infantry Division].) Inactivated 10 January 1949 in Korea. Activated 4 October 1950 at Fort Ord, California. (1st Infantry relieved 3 April 1956 from assignment to the 6th Infantry Division; assigned 15 May 1956 to the United States Military Academy at West Point, New York.)

Inactivated 15 May 1958 at West Point, New York, and relieved from assignment to the United States Military Academy; concurrently, redesignated as Headquarters and Headquarters Company, 6th Battle Group, 1st Infantry. Redesignated 24 November 1967 as Headquarters and Headquarters Company, 6th Battalion, 1st Infantry, assigned to the 6th Infantry Division, and activated at Fort Campbell, Kentucky (organic elements concurrently constituted and activated). Relieved 24 July 1968 from assignment to the 6th Infantry Division. Inactivated 21 July 1969 at Fort Campbell, Kentucky.

140

Campaign Participation Credit

War of 1812
Canada
Lundy's Lane
*New Orleans
*Florida 1814
Alabama 1814
Alabama 1815
Louisiana 1815

Mexican War
Monterey
Vera Cruz

Civil War
Mississippi River
*Vicksburg
Texas 1861
Missouri 1861
Mississippi 1862

Indian Wars
*Miami
Creeks
*Seminoles
Black Hawk
*Apaches
Pine Ridge
Texas 1850

War With Spain
*Santiago

Philippine Insurrection
*Samar 1901

World War II
*New Guinea (with arrowhead)
*Luzon (with arrowhead)

Decorations

Presidential Unit Citation (Army), Streamer embroidered MAFFIN BAY

*Philippine Presidential Unit Citation, Streamer embroidered 17 OCTOBER 1944 TO 4 JULY 1945 (6th Infantry Division cited; DA GO 47, 1950)

1ST INFANTRY, BIBLIOGRAPHY

Buchwald, Donald M. "History of the First United States Infantry Regiment." Master's thesis, Fairleigh Dickinson University, 1966.

Burnet, William E. "Letters; Notes on Removal of Indians from Texas to Indian Territory . . . ," *Chronicles of Oklahoma*, XXXVIII (1960), 274–309; XXXIX (1961), 15–41.

Cheyenne Chamber of Commerce. *Fort Francis E. Warren, Wyoming, 1930*. Cheyenne: Wyoming Labor Journal Publishing Company, 1930, pp. 29–34.

1st Battalion, 1st Infantry. "Always First: A Brief History of the First United States Infantry, 175th Anniversary Edition." Mimeographed pamphlet. West Point: United States Military Academy, n.d.

Lacey, Captain, Adjutant. *History of the First U.S. Infantry*. Fort Wayne, Michigan, 1904.

Lloyd, William, ed. *First U.S. Infantry Year Book, 1925: Containing the History of the Organization, 1784–1925*. San Antonio, 1925. (Erroneously connects this regiment with an earlier one of the same designation.)

Mahon, John K. *History of the Second Seminole War, 1835–1842*. Gainesville: University of Florida Press, 1967.

Marshall, S.L.A. *Ambush*. New York: Cowles Book Company, 1969.

Rodenbough, Theophilus F. and William L. Haskin, eds. *The Army of the United States*. New York: Maynard, Merrill and Company, 1896. "The First Regiment of Infantry," pp. 401–413. (Originally published in the *Journal of the Military Service Institution of the United States*, XVI [1895], 197–209.)

2d Battle Group, 1st Infantry. Baton Rouge: Army and Navy Publishing Company, 1959.

Smith, Robert Ross. *The Approach to the Philippines*. United States Army in World War II. Washington: Government Printing Office, 1953.

———.*Triumph in the Philippines*. United States Army in World War II. Washington: Government Printing Office, 1963.

Sprague, John T. *The Origin, Progress and Conclusion of the Florida War*. New York: D. Appleton and Company, 1848. (Reprint. Gainesville: University of Florida Press, 1964.)

Thomas, Richard G., ed. *First U.S. Infantry Year Book, 1927: Containing History of the Organization, 1784–1927*. San Antonio, 1927. (Erroneously connects this regiment with an earlier one of the same designation.)

Viele, Teresa Griffin. *Following the Drum: A Glimpse of Frontier Life*. New York, 1858. (Later edition in Philadelphia, 1864.)

2d INFANTRY

HERALDIC ITEMS

COAT OF ARMS

Shield: Or on a saltire azure between in fess a cross pattée and a five-bastioned fort gules and in base a giant cactus vert, two arrows in a quiver proper crossed with a bolo argent hilted sable.

Crest: On a wreath of the colors a lion passant guardant or.

Motto: *Noli Me Tangere* (Do Not Touch Me).

Symbolism: Service in the Civil War is shown by the blue cross from the Confederate flag and the red cross pattée, the badge of the 18th Division, V Corps, in which the regiment served during the greater part of that war. Service in the Mexican War is shown by the cactus; in the War with Spain by the five-bastioned fort, the badge of the V Corps in Cuba. The Indian campaigns of the regiment are shown by the arrows and quiver, and the bolo is for service in the Philippine Insurrection.

The lion in the crest represents the Canadian campaigns of the War of 1812.

DISTINCTIVE INSIGNIA

The distinctive insignia is the shield and motto of the coat of arms.

LINEAGE AND HONORS

LINEAGE

Constituted 12 April 1808 in the Regular Army as the 6th Infantry. Organized May–July 1808 in Pennsylvania, New York, and New Jersey. Consolidated May–October 1815 with the 16th Infantry (constituted 11 January 1812), the 22d and 23d Infantry (both constituted 26 June 1812), and the 32d Infantry (constituted 29 January 1813) to form the 2d Infantry. Consolidated 18 April 1869 with the 16th Infantry (see ANNEX) and consolidated unit designated as the 2d Infantry.

Assigned 27 July 1918 to the 19th Division. Relieved 14 February 1919 from assignment to the 19th Division. Assigned 24 March 1923 to the 6th Division. Relieved 16 October 1939 from assignment to the 6th

Division and assigned to the 5th Division (later redesignated as the 5th Infantry Division). Inactivated 20 September 1946 at Camp Campbell, Kentucky. Activated 15 July 1947 at Fort Jackson, South Carolina. Inactivated 30 April 1950 at Fort Jackson, South Carolina. Activated 1 March 1951 at Indiantown Gap Military Reservation, Pennsylvania. Inactivated 1 September 1953 at Indiantown Gap Military Reservation, Pennsylvania. Activated 25 May 1954 at Munich, Germany.

Relieved 1 June 1957 from assignment to the 5th Infantry Division and reorganized as a parent regiment under the Combat Arms Regimental System.

ANNEX

Constituted 3 May 1861 in the Regular Army as the 1st Battalion, 16th Infantry. Organized 21 August 1861 at Camp Slemmer, Illinois. Reorganized and redesignated 21 September 1866 as the 16th Infantry. Consolidated 18 April 1869 with the 2d Infantry and consolidated unit designated as the 2d Infantry.

CAMPAIGN PARTICIPATION CREDIT

War of 1812
  Canada
  Chippewa
  Lundy's Lane
  Alabama 1814

Mexican War
  Vera Cruz
  Cerro Gordo
  Contreras
  Churubusco
  Molino del Rey
  Chapultepec

Civil War
  Bull Run
  Peninsula
  Shiloh
  Manassas
  Antietam
  Fredericksburg
  Murfreesborough
  Chancellorsville
  Gettysburg
  Chickamauga
  Chattanooga
  Wilderness
  Atlanta
  Spotsylvania
  Cold Harbor
  Petersburg
  Missouri 1861
  Mississippi 1862
  Virginia 1862
  Kentucky 1862
  Virginia 1863

  Tennessee 1863
  Georgia 1864

Indian Wars
  Miami
  Seminoles
  Nez Perces
  Bannocks
  Pine Ridge
  California 1850
  California 1851
  California 1852

War With Spain
  Santiago

Philippine Insurrection
  Without inscription

World War II
  Normandy
  Northern France
  Rhineland
  Ardennes-Alsace
  Central Europe

Vietnam
  Defense
  Counteroffensive
  Counteroffensive, Phase II
  Counteroffensive, Phase III
  Tet Counteroffensive
  (other campaigns to be
    determined)

DECORATIONS

Valorous Unit Award, Streamer embroidered BINH DOUNG (2d Battalion, 2d Infantry cited; DA GO 40, 1966)

Valorous Unit Award, Streamer embroidered AP BAU BANG (2d Battalion, 2d Infantry cited; DA GO 20, 1967)

Valorous Unit Award, Streamer embroidered BINH LONG PROVINCE, 1969 (2d Battalion, 2d Infantry cited; DA GO 50, 1971)

1st BATTALION, 2d INFANTRY

RA

(1st Infantry Division)

LINEAGE

Constituted 12 April 1808 in the Regular Army as a company of the 6th Infantry. Organized between May and July 1808 in Pennsylvania, New York, or New Jersey. Consolidated May–October 1815 with a company of the 16th Infantry (constituted 11 January 1812), a company each of the 22d and 23d Infantry (both constituted 26 June 1812), and a company of the 32d Infantry (constituted 29 January 1813) to form a company of the 2d Infantry. Designated 22 May 1816 as Company A, 2d Infantry.

Consolidated 18 April 1869 with Company A, 16th Infantry (see ANNEX) and consolidated unit designated as Company A, 2d Infantry. (2d Infantry assigned 27 July 1918 to the 19th Division; relieved 14 February 1919 from assignment to the 19th Division; assigned 24 March 1923 to the 6th Division; relieved 16 October 1939 from assignment to the 6th Division and assigned to the 5th Division [later redesignated as the 5th Infantry Division].) Inactivated 20 September 1946 at Camp Campbell, Kentucky. Activated 15 July 1947 at Fort Jackson, South Carolina. Inactivated 30 April 1950 at Fort Jackson, South Carolina. Activated 1 March 1951 at Indiantown Gap Military Reservation, Pennsylvania. Inactivated 1 September 1953 at Indiantown Gap Military Reservation, Pennsylvania. Activated 25 May 1954 at Munich, Germany.

Inactivated 1 June 1957 at Fort Ord, California, and relieved from assignment to the 5th Infantry Division; concurrently, redesignated as Headquarters and Headquarters Company, 1st Battle Group, 2d Infantry. Redesignated 19 February 1962 as Headquarters and Headquarters Company, 1st Battalion, 2d Infantry, assigned to the 5th Infantry Division, and activated at Fort Devens, Massachusetts (organic elements concurrently constituted and activated). Relieved 12 July 1965 from assignment to the 5th Infantry Division and assigned to the 1st Infantry Division.

ANNEX

Constituted 3 May 1861 in the Regular Army as Company A, 1st Battalion, 16th Infantry. Organized 21 August 1861 at Camp Slemmer, Illinois. Reorganized and redesignated 21 September 1866 as Company A, 16th Infantry. Consolidated 18 April 1869 with Company A, 2d Infantry and consolidated unit designated as Company A, 2d Infantry.

146

Campaign Participation Credit

War of 1812
  *Canada
  *Chippewa
  *Lundy's Lane
  Alabama 1814

Mexican War
  *Vera Cruz
  *Cerro Gordo
  *Contreras
  *Churubusco
  *Molino del Rey
  *Chapultepec

Civil War
  Bull Run
  *Peninsula
  *Shiloh
  *Manassas
  *Antietam
  *Fredericksburg
  *Murfreesborough
  Chancellorsville
  Gettysburg
  *Chickamauga
  *Chattanooga
  Wilderness
  *Atlanta
  Spotsylvania
  Cold Harbor
  Petersburg
  Missouri 1861
  *Mississippi 1862
  *Virginia 1862
  *Kentucky 1862
  Virginia 1863

*Tennessee 1863
*Georgia 1864

Indian Wars
  Miami
  Seminoles
  Nez Perces
  Bannocks
  *Pine Ridge
  *California 1850
  California 1851
  California 1852

War With Spain
  *Santiago

Philippine Insurrection
  *Without inscription

World War II
  *Normandy
  *Northern France
  *Rhineland
  *Ardennes-Alsace
  *Central Europe

Vietnam
  *Defense
  *Counteroffensive
  *Counteroffensive, Phase II
  *Counteroffensive, Phase III
  *Tet Counteroffensive
  (other campaigns to be
    determined)

Decorations

*Vietnamese Cross of Gallantry with Palm, Streamer embroidered VIETNAM 1965–1968 (1st Battalion, 2d Infantry cited; DA GO 21, 1969)

*Vietnamese Cross of Gallantry with Palm, Streamer embroidered VIETNAM 1969–1970 (1st Battalion, 2d Infantry cited; DA GO 2, 1971)

*Vietnamese Civil Action Honor Medal, First Class, Streamer embroidered VIETNAM 1965–1970 (1st Battalion, 2d Infantry cited; DA GO 53, 1970)

Company A additionally entitled to: Valorous Unit Award, Streamer embroidered AN LOC (Company A, 1st Battalion, 2d Infantry cited; DA GO 53, 1970)

2d BATTALION, 2d INFANTRY

RA
(inactive)

LINEAGE

Constituted 12 April 1808 in the Regular Army as a company of the 6th Infantry. Organized between May and July 1808 in Pennsylvania, New York, or New Jersey. Consolidated May–October 1815 with a company of the 16th Infantry (constituted 11 January 1812), a company each of the 22d and 23d Infantry (both constituted 26 June 1812), and a company of the 32d Infantry (constituted 29 January 1813) to form a company of the 2d Infantry. Designated 22 May 1816 as Company B, 2d Infantry.

Consolidated 18 April 1869 with Company B, 16th Infantry (see ANNEX) and consolidated unit designated as Company B, 2d Infantry. (2d Infantry assigned 27 July 1918 to the 19th Division; relieved 14 February 1919 from assignment to the 19th Division; assigned 24 March 1923 to the 6th Division; relieved 16 October 1939 from assignment to the 6th Division and assigned to the 5th Division [later redesignated as the 5th Infantry Division].) Inactivated 20 September 1946 at Camp Campbell, Kentucky. Activated 15 July 1947 at Fort Jackson, South Carolina. Inactivated 30 April 1950 at Fort Jackson, South Carolina. Activated 1 March 1951 at Indiantown Gap Military Reservation, Pennsylvania. Inactivated 1 September 1953 at Indiantown Gap Military Reservation, Pennsylvania. Activated 25 May 1954 at Munich, Germany.

Reorganized and redesignated 15 February 1957 as Headquarters and Headquarters Company, 2d Battle Group, 2d Infantry, relieved from assignment to the 5th Infantry Division, and assigned to the 1st Infantry Division (organic elements concurrently constituted and activated). Relieved 28 January 1959 from assignment to the 1st Infantry Division and assigned to the 24th Infantry Division.

Reorganized and redesignated 19 February 1962 as the 2d Battalion, 2d Infantry; concurrently, relieved from assignment to the 24th Infantry Division and assigned to the 5th Infantry Division. Relieved 12 July 1965 from assignment to the 5th Infantry Division and assigned to the 1st Infantry Division. Inactivated 15 April 1970 at Fort Riley, Kansas.

ANNEX

Constituted 3 May 1861 in the Regular Army as Company B, 1st

148

Battalion, 16th Infantry. Organized 21 August 1861 at Camp Slemmer, Illinois. Reorganized and redesignated 21 September 1866 as Company B, 16th Infantry. Consolidated 18 April 1869 with Company B, 2d Infantry and consolidated unit designated as Company B, 2d Infantry.

CAMPAIGN PARTICIPATION CREDIT

War of 1812
  *Canada
  *Chippewa
  *Lundy's Lane
  Alabama 1814

Mexican War
  *Vera Cruz
  *Cerro Gordo
  *Contreras
  *Churubusco
  *Molino del Rey
  *Chapultepec

Civil War
  Bull Run
  *Peninsula
  *Shiloh
  *Manassas
  *Antietam
  *Fredericksburg
  *Murfreesborough
  *Chancellorsville
  *Gettysburg
  *Chickamauga
  *Chattanooga
  *Wilderness
  *Atlanta
  *Spotsylvania
  *Cold Harbor
  Petersburg
  *Missouri 1861
  *Mississippi 1862
  *Virginia 1862
  *Kentucky 1862
  *Virginia 1863

*Tennessee 1863
*Georgia 1864

Indian Wars
  Miami
  *Seminoles
  Nez Perces
  Bannocks
  *Pine Ridge
  California 1850
  California 1851
  *California 1852

War With Spain
  *Santiago

Philippine Insurrection
  *Without inscription

World War II
  *Normandy
  *Northern France
  *Rhineland
  *Ardennes-Alsace
  *Central Europe

Vietnam
  *Defense
  *Counteroffensive
  *Counteroffensive, Phase II
  *Counteroffensive, Phase III
  *Tet Counteroffensive
   (other campaigns to be
    determined)

DECORATIONS

*Valorous Unit Award, Streamer embroidered BINH DOUNG (2d Battalion, 2d Infantry cited; DA GO 40, 1966)

*Valorous Unit Award, Streamer embroidered AP BAU BANG (2d Battalion, 2d Infantry cited; DA GO 20, 1967)

*Valorous Unit Award, Streamer embroidered BINH LONG PROVINCE, 1969 (2d Battalion, 2d Infantry cited; DA GO 50, 1971)

*Vietnamese Cross of Gallantry with Palm, Streamer embroidered VIETNAM 1965–1968 (2d Battalion, 2d Infantry cited; DA GO 21, 1969)

*Vietnamese Cross of Gallantry with Palm, Streamer embroidered VIETNAM 1969 (2d Battalion, 2d Infantry cited; DA GO 2, 1971)

*Vietnamese Civil Action Honor Medal, First Class, Streamer embroidered VIETNAM 1965–1970 (2d Battalion, 2d Infantry cited; DA GO 53, 1970)

Company C additionally entitled to: Valorous Unit Award, Streamer embroidered BINH LONG PROVINCE (Company C, 2d Battalion, 2d Infantry cited; DA GO 43, 1970)

3d BATTALION, 2d INFANTRY

AR
(inactive)

LINEAGE

Constituted 12 April 1808 in the Regular Army as a company of the 6th Infantry. Organized between May and July 1808 in Pennsylvania, New York, or New Jersey. Consolidated May–October 1815 with a company of the 16th Infantry (constituted 11 January 1812), a company each of the 22d and 23d Infantry (both constituted 26 June 1812), and a company of the 32d Infantry (constituted 29 January 1813) to form a company of the 2d Infantry. Designated 22 May 1816 as Company C, 2d Infantry.

Consolidated 18 April 1869 with Company C, 16th Infantry (see ANNEX 1) and consolidated unit designated as Company C, 2d Infantry. (2d Infantry assigned 27 July 1918 to the 19th Division; relieved 14 February 1919 from assignment to the 19th Division; assigned 24 March 1923 to the 6th Division; relieved 16 October 1939 from assignment to the 6th Division and assigned to the 5th Division [later redesignated as the 5th Infantry Division].) Inactivated 20 September 1946 at Camp Campbell, Kentucky. Activated 15 July 1947 at Fort Jackson, South Carolina. Inactivated 30 April 1950 at Fort Jackson, South Carolina. Activated 1 March 1951 at Indiantown Gap Military Reservation, Pennsylvania. Inactivated 1 September 1953 at Indiantown Gap Military Reservation, Pennsylvania. Activated 25 May 1954 at Munich, Germany. Inactivated 1 June 1957 at Fort Ord, California, and relieved from assignment to the 5th Infantry Division.

Redesignated 19 March 1959 as Headquarters and Headquarters Company, 3d Battle Group, 2d Infantry, withdrawn from the Regular Army, allotted to the Army Reserve, and assigned to the 83d Infantry Division (organic elements concurrently constituted). Battle Group activated 20 March 1959 with Headquarters at Columbus, Ohio (concurrently, Headquarters and Headquarters Company consolidated with Headquarters and Headquarters Company, 332d Infantry [see ANNEX 2] and consolidated unit designated as Headquarters and Headquarters Company, 3d Battle Group, 2d Infantry). Reorganized and redesignated 15 April 1963 as the 3d Battalion, 2d Infantry. Inactivated 31 December 1965 at Columbus, Ohio.

ANNEX 1

Constituted 3 May 1861 in the Regular Army as Company C, 1st Battalion, 16th Infantry. Organized 21 August 1861 at Camp Slemmer, Illinois. Reorganized and redesignated 21 September 1866 as Company C, 16th Infantry. Consolidated 18 April 1869 with Company C, 2d Infantry and consolidated unit designated as Company C, 2d Infantry.

ANNEX 2

Constituted 5 August 1917 in the National Army as Headquarters and Headquarters Company, 332d Infantry, an element of the 83d Division. Organized 30 August 1917 at Camp Sherman, Ohio. Demobilized 1 July 1919 at Camp Sherman, Ohio. Reconstituted 24 June 1921 in the Organized Reserves as an element of the 83d Division. Organized in November 1921 at Findlay, Ohio. Relieved 30 January 1942 from assignment to the 83d Division; concurrently, allotted to the Army of the United States as an inactive unit. (Organized Reserves redesignated 25 March 1948 as the Organized Reserve Corps; redesignated 9 July 1952 as the Army Reserve.)

Allotted 15 May 1952 to the Organized Reserve Corps as an element of the 83d Infantry Division (formerly, the 83d Division). Activated 22 January 1954 at Youngstown, Ohio. Location changed 15 April 1955 to Warren, Ohio; changed 4 January 1956 to Columbus, Ohio. Consolidated 20 March 1959 with Headquarters and Headquarters Company, 3d Battle Group, 2d Infantry and consolidated unit designated as Headquarters and Headquarters Company, 3d Battle Group, 2d Infantry (remainder of 332d Infantry inactivated).

CAMPAIGN PARTICIPATION CREDIT

War of 1812
*Canada
*Chippewa
*Lundy's Lane
Alabama 1814

Mexican War
Vera Cruz
Cerro Gordo
*Contreras
*Churubusco
*Molino del Rey
*Chapultepec

Civil War
*Bull Run
*Peninsula
*Shiloh
*Manassas
*Antietam
*Fredericksburg
*Murfreesborough
*Chancellorsville
*Gettysburg
Chickamauga
Chattanooga
*Wilderness
Atlanta
*Spotsylvania
*Cold Harbor
*Petersburg
Missouri 1861
*Mississippi 1862

*Virginia 1862
*Kentucky 1862
*Virginia 1863
Tennessee 1863
Georgia 1864

Indian Wars
Miami
*Seminoles
*Nez Perces
*Bannocks
*Pine Ridge
California 1850
*California 1851
California 1852

War With Spain
*Santiago

Philippine Insurrection
*Without inscription

World War I
*Vittorio-Veneto
*Venetia 1918

World War II
*Normandy
*Northern France
*Rhineland
*Ardennes-Alsace
*Central Europe

DECORATIONS

None.

4th BATTALION, 2d INFANTRY

AR
(inactive)

Constituted 12 April 1808 in the Regular Army as a company of the 6th Infantry. Organized between May and July 1808 in Pennsylvania, New York, or New Jersey. Consolidated May–October 1815 with a company of the 16th Infantry (constituted 11 January 1812), a company each of the 22d and 23d Infantry (both constituted 26 June 1812), and a company of the 32d Infantry (constituted 29 January 1813) to form a company of the 2d Infantry. Designated 22 May 1816 as Company D, 2d Infantry.

Consolidated 18 April 1869 with Company D, 16th Infantry (see ANNEX) and consolidated unit designated as Company D, 2d Infantry. (2d Infantry assigned 27 July 1918 to the 19th Division; relieved 14 February 1919 from assignment to the 19th Division; assigned 24 March 1923 to the 6th Division; relieved 16 October 1939 from assignment to the 6th Division and assigned to the 5th Division [later redesignated as the 5th Infantry Division].) Inactivated 20 September 1946 at Camp Campbell, Kentucky. Activated 15 July 1947 at Fort Jackson, South Carolina. Inactivated 30 April 1950 at Fort Jackson, South Carolina. Activated 1 March 1951 at Indiantown Gap Military Reservation, Pennsylvania. Inactivated 1 September 1953 at Indiantown Gap Military Reservation, Pennsylvania. Activated 25 May 1954 at Munich, Germany.

Inactivated 1 June 1957 at Fort Ord, California, and relieved from assignment to the 5th Infantry Division; concurrently, redesignated as Headquarters and Headquarters Company, 4th Battle Group, 2d Infantry. Redesignated 27 March 1963 as Headquarters and Headquarters Company, 4th Battalion, 2d Infantry, withdrawn from the Regular Army, allotted to the Army Reserve, and assigned to the 83d Infantry Division (organic elements concurrently constituted). Battalion activated 15 April 1963 with Headquarters at Newark, Ohio. Inactivated 31 December 1965 at Newark, Ohio.

ANNEX

Constituted 3 May 1861 in the Regular Army as Company D, 1st Battalion, 16th Infantry. Organized 21 August 1861 at Camp Slemmer, Illinois. Reorganized and redesignated 21 September 1866 as Company

154

D, 16th Infantry. Consolidated 18 April 1869 with Company D, 2d Infantry and consolidated unit designated as Company D, 2d Infantry.

CAMPAIGN PARTICIPATION CREDIT

War of 1812
*Canada
*Chippewa
*Lundy's Lane
Alabama 1814

Mexican War
*Vera Cruz
*Cerro Gordo
*Contreras
*Churubusco
*Molino del Rey
*Chapultepec

Civil War
Bull Run
*Peninsula
*Shiloh
*Manassas
*Antietam
*Fredericksburg
*Murfreesborough
*Chancellorsville
Gettysburg
*Chickamauga
*Chattanooga
Wilderness
*Atlanta
Spotsylvania
Cold Harbor
Petersburg

Missouri 1861
*Mississippi 1862
*Virginia 1862
*Kentucky 1862
Virginia 1863
*Tennessee 1863
*Georgia 1864

Indian Wars
Miami
Seminoles
Nez Perces
Bannocks
*Pine Ridge
California 1850
*California 1851
*California 1852

War With Spain
*Santiago

Philippine Insurrection
*Without inscription

World War II
*Normandy
*Northern France
*Rhineland
*Ardennes-Alsace
*Central Europe

DECORATIONS

None.

2D INFANTRY, BIBLIOGRAPHY

Blumenson, Martin. *Breakout and Pursuit*. United States Army in World War II. Washington: Government Printing Office, 1961.

Cole, Hugh M. *The Ardennes: Battle of the Bulge*. United States Army in World War II. Washington: Government Printing Office, 1964.

———. *The Lorraine Campaign*. United States Army in World War II. Washington: Government Printing Office, 1950.

Fix Bayonets: 3d Battalion, 2d Infantry, 5th Infantry Division. Atlanta: Albert Love Enterprises, ca. 1952.

Historical Register of Commissioned Officers of the Second U.S. Infantry, From Its Organization, March 4, 1791. Fort Logan, Colorado: Regimental Press, 1905. (Erroneously connects this regiment with an earlier one of the same designation.)

History of the Second Infantry Regiment, Fifth Infantry Division. Baton Rouge: Army and Navy Publishing Company, 1941.

MacDonald, Charles B. and Sidney T. Mathews. *Three Battles: Arnaville, Altuzzo, and Schmidt*. United States Army in World War II. Washington: Government Printing Office, 1952.

Mahon, John K. *History of the Second Seminole War, 1835–1842*. Gainesville: University of Florida Press, 1967.

Reed, Louis A. *Illustrated Historical Review of the United States Army in Oahu, T. H.* Honolulu: Hawaiian Gazette Company, 1911. (Includes roster of 1st and 2d Battalions, 2d Infantry.)

Roster of Commissioned Officers of the Second Regiment of Infantry, United States Army, Who Participated in the Campaign Against Santiago de Cuba, and Who Were Present With the Army at Anytime Between June 22d and July 17th, 1898. Fort D. A. Russell, Wyoming, 1904.

Roster of Enlisted Men of the Second Regiment of Infantry, U. S. Army, Who Participated in the Campaign Against Santiago de Cuba, and Who Were Present with the Army at Anytime Between June 22d and July 17th, 1898. Fort D. A. Russell, Wyoming, 1904.

2d Infantry: Organization Day, 20 December 1946, Fort Lewis, Washington. Tacoma: Johnson-Cox Company, 1946.

Shaw, Frederick Benjamin. *One Hundred and Forty Years of Service in Peace and War, History of the Second Infantry, United States Army*. Detroit: Strathmore Press, 1930. (Erroneously connects this regiment with an earlier one of the same designation.)

Sprague, John T. *The Origin, Progress and Conclusion of the Florida War*. New York: D. Appleton and Company, 1848. (Reprint. Gainesville: University of Florida Press, 1964.)

Swantek, Joseph M. *Historical and Pictorial Review, 2d Infantry Regiment.* Baton Rouge: Army and Navy Publishing Company, 1946.

Wright, W. M. "The Second Regiment of Infantry," *The Army of the United States,* edited by Theophilus F. Rodenbough and William L. Haskin. New York: Maynard, Merrill and Company, 1896, pp. 414–431. (Originally published in the *Journal of the Military Service Institution of the United States,* XVI [1895], 438–455.)

3d INFANTRY
(The Old Guard)

HERALDIC ITEMS

COAT OF ARMS

Shield: Paly of thirteen argent and gules on a chief azure three crosses pattée of the first, an inescutcheon of the like with a mount vert issuing from base and crowned with battlements of the second. (And for informal use, the shield encircled by an infantry officer's dress belt of 1917 or bar tierced celestial blue edged sable with the buckle plate of the period of the first at top between the designation "3 Infantry" and the date "1784," and inscribed in base the regimental motto, all lettered sable; the arms and belt surmounting a triangular bayonet of the Civil War era and the regiment's drum major's Chapultepec baton in saltire all proper.)

Crest: On a wreath argent and azure an infantry officer's cocked hat sable trimmed white (1784 pattern) with a cockade of the third centered of the fourth and plumed white.

Motto: *Noli Me Tangere.*

Symbolism: Because of its direct descent from the First American Regiment, the 3d Infantry is accorded the singular honor of having the shield of the coat of arms of the United States as the basis for its arms. The thirteen stripes, in this instance, commemorate the unit's service in the campaigns of Resaca de la Palma, Monterey, Cerro Gordo, Churubusco, Chapultepec, Bull Run, Peninsula, Manassas, Fredericksburg, Chancellorsville, Gettysburg, Santiago, and Luzon (1899–1900); the alternating colors of silver and red symbolize a constancy of honor and courage. The chief, blue for valor and loyalty, represents the regiment's outstanding record in the Civil War; the white Maltese cross, the badge of Sykes' Division in which the 3d served, in triple form alludes to the regiment's numerical designation. The inescutcheon, in the national colors of Mexico, symbolizes the unit's distinguished service during the Mexican War.

The cocked hat of the crest commemorates the founding of the First American Regiment in 1784.

The Chapultepec baton is made from the wood of the flagpole which in 1847 stood in front of the cathedral in the Grand Plaza in Mexico City. The head and ferrule are of Mexican silver. The baton was presented to the regiment in 1848 and is still in the possession of the 3d Infantry. The bayonet represents the regiment's outstanding service during the Civil War and also its tradition to "pass in review" with bayonets fixed in commemoration of the gallant charge at Cerro Gordo. The officer's dress belt symbolizes the regiment's additional role as the honor and ceremonial unit in the nation's capital (currently performed by the 1st Battalion, 3d Infantry).

DISTINCTIVE INSIGNIA

On a wreath an infantry officer's cocked hat of 1784 with plume, all brass. (The insignia is the crest of the coat of arms of the regiment, without color.)

DISTINCTIVE TRIMMING

(Authorized for all personnel of the 3d Infantry in addition to the distinctive insignia.)

A black leather strap 1/2 inch wide with buff leather strap 1/4 inch wide "woven" in the middle—a simulation of the old buff and black knapsack strap. (Worn on left shoulder only of coat and overcoat at the junction of the sleeve and shoulder with two buff sections showing in front.)

When this unit was under the command of General Anthony Wayne (1792–96), the special markings on the uniform were buff piping and black hair plumes. From this combination the regimental colors became buff and black, and for many years the unit was nicknamed the "Buff Sticks." It is related that men of the 3d Infantry, proud of their distinctive colors, at one time displayed these colors by weaving a broad strip of rawhide (natural buff color) in the broad black shoulder strap of the knapsack carried at that time. This buff and black knapsack strap effect is perpetuated in the distinctive trimming.

LINEAGE AND HONORS

LINEAGE

Constituted 3 June 1784 as the First American Regiment to consist of companies from Connecticut, New York, New Jersey, and Pennsylvania. Organized August–September 1784 in Pennsylvania and New Jersey. (New York and Connecticut companies organized in 1785.) Redesignated 29 September 1789 as the Regiment of Infantry. Redesignated 3 March 1791 as the 1st Infantry. Redesignated in 1792 as the Infantry of the 1st Sub-Legion. Redesignated 31 October 1796 as the 1st Infantry.

Consolidated May–October 1815 with the 5th Infantry (constituted 12 April 1808), the 17th Infantry (constituted 11 January 1812), the 19th Infantry (constituted 26 June 1812), and the 28th Infantry (constituted 29 January 1813) to form the 3d Infantry. Consolidated August–December 1869 with one half of the 37th Infantry (see ANNEX) and consolidated unit designated as the 3d Infantry. (2d and 3d Battalions inactivated 18 November 1921 at Fort Snelling, Minnesota; activated 8 June 1922 at Fort Snelling, Minnesota.)

Assigned 24 March 1923 to the 7th Division. Relieved 15 August 1927 from assignment to the 7th Division and assigned to the 6th Division. Relieved 1 October 1933 from assignment to the 6th Division and assigned to the 7th Division. Relieved 16 October 1939 from assignment to the 7th Division and assigned to the 6th Division. Relieved 10 May 1941 from assignment to the 6th Division. (1st Battalion inactivated 1 June 1941 at Fort Leonard Wood, Missouri; activated 14 February 1942 in Newfoundland.) (2d Battalion [less Headquarters and Headquarters Company] inactivated 1 September 1942 at Fort Snelling, Minnesota [Headquarters and Headquarters Company concurrently inactivated in Greenland]; battalion activated 22 October 1943 at Camp Butner, North Carolina.) Inactivated 20 November 1946 in Germany. Regiment (less 2d Battalion) activated 6 April 1948 at Fort Myer, Virginia (2d Battalion concurrently activated at Fort Lesley J. McNair, Washington, D.C.).

Reorganized 1 July 1957 as a parent regiment under the Combat Arms Regimental System.

ANNEX

Constituted 3 May 1861 in the Regular Army as the 3d Battalion, 19th Infantry. Organized May 1865–September 1866 at Fort Wayne, Michigan; Newport Barracks, Kentucky; and Fort Columbus, New York. Reorganized and redesignated 23 November 1866 as the 37th Infantry. One half of the 37th Infantry consolidated August–December 1869 with the 3d Infantry and consolidated unit designated as the 3d Infantry (remaining half of the 37th Infantry consolidated in June 1869 with the 5th Infantry and consolidated unit designated as the 5th Infantry) .

CAMPAIGN PARTICIPATION CREDIT

War of 1812
  Canada
  Chippewa
  Lundy's Lane

Mexican War
  Palo Alto
  Resaca de la Palma
  Monterey
  Vera Cruz
  Cerro Gordo
  Contreras
  Churubusco
  Chapultepec

Civil War
  Bull Run
  Peninsula
  Manassas
  Antietam
  Fredericksburg
  Chancellorsville
  Gettysburg
  Appomattox
  Texas 1861
  Florida 1861
  Florida 1862
  Virginia 1863

Indian Wars
  Miami
  Seminoles
  Comanches
  New Mexico 1856
  New Mexico 1857
  New Mexico 1858
  New Mexico 1860
  Montana 1887

War With Spain
  Santiago

Philippine Insurrection
  Malolos
  San Isidro
  Luzon 1899
  Luzon 1900
  Jolo 1911

World War II
  American Theater without inscription
  Northern France

Vietnam
  Counteroffensive, Phase II
  Counteroffensive, Phase III
  Tet Counteroffensive
  (other campaigns to be determined)

DECORATIONS

Valorous Unit Award, Streamer embroidered SAIGON–LONG BINH (2d Battalion, 3d Infantry cited; DA GO 48, 1968)

1st BATTALION, 3d INFANTRY
(The Old Guard)

RA
(nondivisional)

LINEAGE

Constituted 3 June 1784 as a company of the First American Regiment. Organized by September 1784 in Pennsylvania or New Jersey. Redesignated 29 September 1789 as a company of the Regiment of Infantry. Redesignated 3 March 1791 as a company of the 1st Infantry. Redesignated in 1792 as a company of the Infantry of the 1st Sub-Legion. Redesignated 31 October 1796 as a company of the 1st Infantry.

Consolidated May–October 1815 with a company of the 5th Infantry (constituted 12 April 1808), a company of the 17th Infantry (constituted 11 January 1812), a company of the 19th Infantry (constituted 26 June 1812), and a company of the 28th Infantry (constituted 29 January 1813) to form a company of the 3d Infantry. Designated 22 May 1816 as Company A, 3d Infantry.

Consolidated 9 September 1869 with one half of Company C, 37th Infantry (see ANNEX) and consolidated unit designated as Company A, 3d Infantry. (3d Infantry assigned 24 March 1923 to the 7th Division; relieved 15 August 1927 from assignment to the 7th Division and assigned to the 6th Division; relieved 1 October 1933 from assignment to the 6th Division and assigned to the 7th Division; relieved 16 October 1939 from assignment to the 7th Division and assigned to the 6th Division; relieved 10 May 1941 from assignment to the 6th Division.) Inactivated 1 June 1941 at Fort Leonard Wood, Missouri. Activated 14 February 1942 in Newfoundland. Inactivated 20 November 1946 in Germany. Activated 6 April 1948 at Fort Myer, Virginia.

Reorganized and redesignated 1 July 1957 as Headquarters and Headquarters Company, 1st Battle Group, 3d Infantry (organic elements concurrently constituted and activated). Reorganized and redesignated 20 September 1963 as the 1st Battalion, 3d Infantry.

ANNEX

Constituted 3 May 1861 in the Regular Army as Company C, 3d Battalion, 19th Infantry. Organized 19 December 1865 at Newport Barracks, Kentucky. Reorganized and redesignated 23 November 1866 as

Company C, 37th Infantry. Consolidated 9 September 1869 with Company A and Company H, 3d Infantry and consolidated units designated as Company A and Company H, 3d Infantry.

CAMPAIGN PARTICIPATION CREDIT

War of 1812
  *Canada
  *Chippewa
  *Lundy's Lane

Mexican War
  *Palo Alto
  *Resaca de la Palma
  Monterey
  Vera Cruz
  *Cerro Gordo
  *Contreras
  *Churubusco
  *Chapultepec

Civil War
  Bull Run
  Peninsula
  Manassas
  Antietam
  *Fredericksburg
  *Chancellorsville
  Gettysburg
  Appomattox
  *Texas 1861
  Florida 1861

Florida 1862
Virginia 1863

Indian Wars
  *Miami
  *Seminoles
  *Comanches
  New Mexico 1856
  New Mexico 1857
  New Mexico 1858
  New Mexico 1860
  Montana 1887

War With Spain
  *Santiago

Philippine Insurrection
  *Malolos
  *San Isidro
  *Luzon 1899
  Luzon 1900
  *Jolo 1911

World War II
  *American Theater without inscription
  *Northern France

DECORATIONS

None.

2d BATTALION, 3d INFANTRY
(The Old Guard)

RA
(inactive)

LINEAGE

Constituted 3 June 1784 as a company of the First American Regiment. Organized by September 1784 in Pennsylvania or New Jersey. Redesignated 29 September 1789 as a company of the Regiment of Infantry. Redesignated 3 March 1791 as a company of the 1st Infantry. Redesignated in 1792 as a company of the Infantry of the 1st Sub-Legion. Redesignated 31 October 1796 as a company of the 1st Infantry.

Consolidated May–October 1815 with a company of the 5th Infantry (constituted 12 April 1808), a company of the 17th Infantry (constituted 11 January 1812), a company of the 19th Infantry (constituted 26 June 1812), and a company of the 28th Infantry (constituted 29 January 1813) to form a company of the 3d Infantry. Designated 22 May 1816 as Company B, 3d Infantry.

Consolidated 19 November 1869 with one half of Company E, 37th Infantry (see ANNEX) and consolidated unit designated as Company B, 3d Infantry. (3d Infantry assigned 24 March 1923 to the 7th Division; relieved 15 August 1927 from assignment to the 7th Division and assigned to the 6th Division; relieved 1 October 1933 from assignment to the 6th Division and assigned to the 7th Division; relieved 16 October 1939 from assignment to the 7th Division and assigned to the 6th Division; relieved 10 May 1941 from assignment to the 6th Division.) Inactivated 1 June 1941 at Fort Leonard Wood, Missouri. Activated 14 February 1942 in Newfoundland. Inactivated 20 November 1946 in Germany. Activated 6 April 1948 at Fort Myer, Virginia.

Reorganized and redesignated 1 July 1957 as Headquarters and Headquarters Company, 2d Battle Group, 3d Infantry and assigned to the 7th Infantry Division (organic elements concurrently constituted and activated). Inactivated 1 July 1963 in Korea and relieved from assignment to the 7th Infantry Division. Redesignated 23 March 1966 as the 2d Battalion, 3d Infantry and assigned to the 199th Infantry Brigade. Activated 1 June 1966 at Fort Benning, Georgia. Inactivated 15 October 1970 at Fort Benning, Georgia.

165

ANNEX

Constituted 3 May 1861 in the Regular Army as Company E, 3d Battalion, 19th Infantry. Organized 7 February 1866 at Newport Barracks, Kentucky. Reorganized and redesignated 23 November 1866 as Company E, 37th Infantry. Consolidated 19 November 1869 with Company B and Company E, 3d Infantry and consolidated units designated as Company B and Company E, 3d Infantry.

CAMPAIGN PARTICIPATION CREDIT

War of 1812
*Canada
*Chippewa
*Lundy's Lane

Mexican War
*Palo Alto
*Resaca de la Palma
Monterey
Vera Cruz
Cerro Gordo
*Contreras
*Churubusco
*Chapultepec

Civil War
*Bull Run
*Peninsula
*Manassas
*Antietam
*Fredericksburg
*Chancellorsville
*Gettysburg
*Appomattox
Texas 1861
Florida 1861
Florida 1862
*Virginia 1863

Indian Wars
*Miami
*Seminoles
*Comanches
*New Mexico 1856
*New Mexico 1857
*New Mexico 1858
*New Mexico 1860
*Montana 1887

War With Spain
*Santiago

Philippine Insurrection
*Malolos
*San Isidro
*Luzon 1899
Luzon 1900
*Jolo 1911

World War II
*American Theater without inscription
*Northern France

Vietnam
*Counteroffensive, Phase II
*Counteroffensive, Phase III
*Tet Counteroffensive
(other campaigns to be determined)

DECORATIONS

*Valorous Unit Award, Streamer embroidered SAIGON–LONG BINH (2d Battalion, 3d Infantry cited; DA GO 48, 1968)

*Vietnamese Cross of Gallantry with Palm, Streamer embroidered VIETNAM 1968 (2d Battalion, 3d Infantry cited; DA GO 43, 1970)

3d BATTALION, 3d INFANTRY
(The Old Guard)

AR
(205th Infantry Brigade)

LINEAGE

Constituted 3 June 1784 as a company of the First American Regiment. Organized by September 1784 in Pennsylvania or New Jersey. Redesignated 29 September 1789 as a company of the Regiment of Infantry. Redesignated 3 March 1791 as a company of the 1st Infantry. Redesignated in 1792 as a company of the Infantry of the 1st Sub-Legion. Redesignated 31 October 1796 as a company of the 1st Infantry.

Consolidated May–October 1815 with a company of the 5th Infantry (constituted 12 April 1808), a company of the 17th Infantry (constituted 11 January 1812), a company of the 19th Infantry (constituted 26 June 1812), and a company of the 28th Infantry (constituted 29 January 1813) to form a company of the 3d Infantry. Designated 22 May 1816 as Company C, 3d Infantry. (3d Infantry assigned 24 March 1923 to the 7th Division; relieved 15 August 1927 from assignment to the 7th Division and assigned to the 6th Division; relieved 1 October 1933 from assignment to the 6th Division and assigned to the 7th Division; relieved 16 October 1939 from assignment to the 7th Division and assigned to the 6th Division; relieved 10 May 1941 from assignment to the 6th Division.) Inactivated 1 June 1941 at Fort Leonard Wood, Missouri. Activated 14 February 1942 in Newfoundland. Inactivated 20 November 1946 in Germany. Activated 6 April 1948 at Fort Myer, Virginia.

Inactivated 1 July 1957 at Fort Myer, Virginia; concurrently, redesignated as Headquarters and Headquarters Company, 3d Battle Group, 3d Infantry. Withdrawn 20 April 1959 from the Regular Army and allotted to the Army Reserve (organic elements concurrently constituted). Battle Group activated 18 May 1959 with Headquarters at Fort Snelling, Minnesota, and assigned to the 103d Infantry Division. Reorganized and redesignated 15 February 1963 as the 3d Battalion, 3d Infantry. Relieved 15 March 1963 from assignment to the 103d Infantry Division and assigned to the 205th Infantry Brigade.

HOME AREA: Fifth United States Army

Campaign Participation Credit

War of 1812
*Canada
*Chippewa
*Lundy's Lane

Mexican War
*Palo Alto
*Resaca de la Palma
*Monterey
*Vera Cruz
*Cerro Gordo
*Contreras
*Churubusco
*Chapultepec

Civil War
Bull Run
*Peninsula
*Manassas
*Antietam
*Fredericksburg
*Chancellorsville
*Gettysburg
*Appomattox
Texas 1861
*Florida 1861

*Florida 1862
*Virginia 1863

Indian Wars
*Miami
Seminoles
Comanches
New Mexico 1856
*New Mexico 1857
*New Mexico 1858
*New Mexico 1860
Montana 1887

War With Spain
*Santiago

Philippine Insurrection
*Malolos
*San Isidro
*Luzon 1899
Luzon 1900
*Jolo 1911

World War II
*American Theater without inscription
*Northern France

Decorations

None.

4th BATTALION, 3d INFANTRY
(The Old Guard)

RA

(23d Infantry Division)

Constituted 3 June 1784 as a company of the First American Regiment. Organized by September 1784 in Pennsylvania or New Jersey. Redesignated 29 September 1789 as a company of the Regiment of Infantry. Redesignated 3 March 1791 as a company of the 1st Infantry. Redesignated in 1792 as a company of the Infantry of the 1st Sub-Legion. Redesignated 31 October 1796 as a company of the 1st Infantry.

Consolidated May–October 1815 with a company of the 5th Infantry (constituted 12 April 1808), a company of the 17th Infantry (constituted 11 January 1812), a company of 19th Infantry (constituted 26 June 1812), and a company of the 28th Infantry (constituted 29 January 1813) to form a company of the 3d Infantry. Designated 22 May 1816 as Company D, 3d Infantry.

Consolidated 16 December 1869 with one half of Company A, 37th Infantry (see ANNEX) and consolidated unit designated as Company D, 3d Infantry. (3d Infantry assigned 24 March 1923 to the 7th Division; relieved 15 August 1927 from assignment to the 7th Division and assigned to the 6th Division; relieved 1 October 1933 from assignment to the 6th Division and assigned to the 7th Division; relieved 16 October 1939 from assignment to the 7th Division and assigned to the 6th Division; relieved 10 May 1941 from assignment to the 6th Division.) Inactivated 1 June 1941 at Fort Leonard Wood, Missouri. Activated 14 February 1942 in Newfoundland. Inactivated 20 November 1946 in Germany. Activated 6 April 1948 at Fort Myer, Virginia.

Inactivated 1 July 1957 at Fort Myer, Virginia; concurrently, redesignated as Headquarters and Headquarters Company, 4th Battle Group, 3d Infantry. Redesignated 15 April 1966 as Headquarters and Headquarters Company, 4th Battalion, 3d Infantry (organic elements concurrently constituted). Battalion activated 1 July 1966 in Hawaii and assigned to the 11th Infantry Brigade. Relieved 15 February 1969 from assignment to the 11th Infantry Brigade and assigned to the 23d Infantry Division.

ANNEX

Constituted 3 May 1861 in the Regular Army as Company A, 3d Battalion, 19th Infantry. Organized 6 May 1865 at Fort Wayne, Michigan. Reorganized and redesignated 23 November 1866 as Company A, 37th Infantry. Consolidated 16 December 1869 with Company D and Company K, 3d Infantry and consolidated units designated as Company D and Company K, 3d Infantry.

CAMPAIGN PARTICIPATION CREDIT

War of 1812
 *Canada
 *Chippewa
 *Lundy's Lane

Mexican War
 *Palo Alto
 *Resaca de la Palma
 *Monterey
 *Vera Cruz
  Cerro Gordo
 *Contreras
 *Churubusco
 *Chapultepec

Civil War
 *Bull Run
 *Peninsula
 *Manassas
 *Antietam
 *Fredericksburg
 *Chancellorsville
  Gettysburg
  Appomattox
  Texas 1861
  Florida 1861
  Florida 1862
  Virginia 1863

Indian Wars
 *Miami
 *Seminoles
 *Comanches
 *New Mexico 1856
  New Mexico 1857
 *New Mexico 1858
  New Mexico 1860
 *Kansas 1868
  Montana 1887

War With Spain
 *Santiago

Philippine Insurrection
 *Malolos
  San Isidro
  Luzon 1899
  Luzon 1900
 *Jolo 1911

World War II
 *American Theater without inscription
 *Northern France

Vietnam
 *Counteroffensive, Phase III
 *Tet Counteroffensive
  (other campaigns to be determined)

DECORATIONS

*Vietnamese Cross of Gallantry with Palm, Streamer embroidered VIETNAM 1968–1969 (4th Battalion, 3d Infantry cited; DA GO 2, 1971)

5th BATTALION, 3d INFANTRY
(The Old Guard)

RA
(inactive)

LINEAGE

Constituted 3 June 1784 as a company of the First American Regiment. Organized in 1785 in New York or Connecticut. Redesignated 29 September 1789 as a company of the Regiment of Infantry. Redesignated 3 March 1791 as a company of the 1st Infantry. Redesignated in 1792 as a company of the Infantry of the 1st Sub-Legion. Redesignated 31 October 1796 as a company of the 1st Infantry.

Consolidated May–October 1815 with a company of the 5th Infantry (constituted 12 April 1808), a company of the 17th Infantry (constituted 11 January 1812), a company of the 19th Infantry (constituted 26 June 1812), and a company of the 28th Infantry (constituted 29 January 1813) to form a company of the 3d Infantry. Designated 22 May 1816 as Company E, 3d Infantry.

Consolidated 19 November 1869 with one half of Company E, 37th Infantry (see ANNEX) and consolidated unit designated as Company E, 3d Infantry. Inactivated 18 November 1921 at Fort Snelling, Minnesota. Activated 8 June 1922 at Fort Snelling, Minnesota. (3d Infantry assigned 24 March 1923 to the 7th Division; relieved 15 August 1927 from assignment to the 7th Division and assigned to the 6th Division; relieved 1 October 1933 from assignment to the 6th Division and assigned to the 7th Division; relieved 16 October 1939 from assignment to the 7th Division and assigned to the 6th Division; relieved 10 May 1941 from assignment to the 6th Division.) Inactivated 1 September 1942 at Fort Snelling, Minnesota. Activated 22 October 1943 at Camp Butner, North Carolina. Inactivated 20 November 1946 in Germany. Activated 6 April 1948 at Fort Lesley J. McNair, Washington, D.C.

Inactivated 1 July 1957 at Fort Lesley J. McNair, Washington, D.C.; concurrently, redesignated as Headquarters and Headquarters Company, 5th Battle Group, 3d Infantry. Redesignated 24 November 1967 as Headquarters and Headquarters Company, 5th Battalion, 3d Infantry, assigned to the 6th Infantry Division, and activated at Fort Campbell, Kentucky (organic elements concurrently constituted and activated). Relieved 24 July 1968 from assignment to the 6th Infantry Division. Inactivated 21 July 1969 at Fort Campbell, Kentucky.

171

ANNEX

Constituted 3 May 1861 in the Regular Army as Company E, 3d Battalion, 19th Infantry. Organized 7 February 1866 at Newport Barracks, Kentucky. Reorganized and redesignated 23 November 1866 as Company E, 37th Infantry. Consolidated 19 November 1869 with Company B and Company E, 3d Infantry and consolidated units designated as Company B and Company E, 3d Infantry.

CAMPAIGN PARTICIPATION CREDIT

War of 1812
  *Canada
  *Chippewa
  *Lundy's Lane

Mexican War
  *Palo Alto
  *Resaca de la Palma
  Monterey
  Vera Cruz
  Cerro Gordo
  *Contreras
  *Churubusco
  *Chapultepec

Civil War
  Bull Run
  *Peninsula
  *Manassas
  *Antietam
  *Fredericksburg
  *Chancellorsville
  *Gettysburg
  Appomattox
  Texas 1861
  *Florida 1861
  *Florida 1862
  Virginia 1863

Indian Wars
  *Miami
  *Seminoles
  *Comanches
  New Mexico 1856
  New Mexico 1857
  New Mexico 1858
  *New Mexico 1860
  *Montana 1887

War With Spain
  *Santiago

Philippine Insurrection
  *Malolos
  *San Isidro
  *Luzon 1899
  *Luzon 1900
  Jolo 1911

World War II
  *American Theater without inscription
  *Northern France

DECORATIONS

None.

6th BATTALION, 3d INFANTRY
(The Old Guard)

RA
(inactive)

LINEAGE

Constituted 3 June 1784 as a company of the First American Regiment. Organized in 1785 in New York or Connecticut. Redesignated 29 September 1789 as a company of the Regiment of Infantry. Redesignated 3 March 1791 as a company of the 1st Infantry. Redesignated in 1792 as a company of the Infantry of the 1st Sub-Legion. Redesignated 31 October 1796 as a company of the 1st Infantry.

Consolidated May–October 1815 with a company of the 5th Infantry (constituted 12 April 1808), a company of the 17th Infantry (constituted 11 January 1812), a company of the 19th Infantry (constituted 26 June 1812), and a company of the 28th Infantry (constituted 29 January 1813) to form a company of the 3d Infantry. Designated 22 May 1816 as Company F, 3d Infantry.

Consolidated 13 October 1869 with one half of Company F, 37th Infantry (see ANNEX) and consolidated unit designated as Company F, 3d Infantry. Inactivated 18 November 1921 at Fort Snelling, Minnesota. Activated 8 June 1922 at Fort Snelling, Minnesota. (3d Infantry assigned 24 March 1923 to the 7th Division; relieved 15 August 1927 from assignment to the 7th Division and assigned to the 6th Division; relieved 1 October 1933 from assignment to the 6th Division and assigned to the 7th Division; relieved 16 October 1939 from assignment to the 7th Division and assigned to the 6th Division; relieved 10 May 1941 from assignment to the 6th Division.) Inactivated 1 September 1942 at Fort Snelling, Minnesota. Activated 22 October 1943 at Camp Butner, North Carolina. Inactivated 20 November 1946 in Germany. Activated 6 April 1948 at Fort Lesley J. McNair, Washington, D.C.

Inactivated 1 July 1957 at Fort Lesley J. McNair, Washington, D.C.; concurrently, redesignated as Headquarters and Headquarters Company, 6th Battle Group, 3d Infantry. Redesignated 24 November 1967 as Headquarters and Headquarters Company, 6th Battalion, 3d Infantry, assigned to the 6th Infantry Division, and activated at Fort Campbell, Kentucky (organic elements concurrently constituted and activated). Relieved 24 July 1968 from assignment to the 6th Infantry Division. Inactivated 1 February 1969 at Fort Campbell, Kentucky.

173

ANNEX

Constituted 3 May 1861 in the Regular Army as Company F, 3d Battalion, 19th Infantry. Organized in March 1866 at Newport Barracks, Kentucky. Reorganized and redesignated 23 November 1866 as Company F, 37th Infantry. Consolidated 13 October 1869 with Company F and Company H, 3d Infantry and consolidated units designated as Company F and Company H, 3d Infantry.

CAMPAIGN PARTICIPATION CREDIT

War of 1812
  *Canada
  *Chippewa
  *Lundy's Lane

Mexican War
  *Palo Alto
  *Resaca de la Palma
  *Monterey
  *Vera Cruz
  *Cerro Gordo
  *Contreras
  *Churubusco
  *Chapultepec

Civil War
  Bull Run
  *Peninsula
  *Manassas
  *Antietam
  *Fredericksburg
  *Chancellorsville
  *Gettysburg
  *Appomattox
  *Texas 1861
  Florida 1861

  Florida 1862
  *Virginia 1863

Indian Wars
  *Miami
  *Seminoles
  *Comanches
  *New Mexico 1856
  New Mexico 1857
  *New Mexico 1858
  New Mexico 1860
  Montana 1887

War With Spain
  *Santiago

Philippine Insurrection
  *Malolos
  *San Isidro
  *Luzon 1899
  *Luzon 1900
  *Jolo 1911

World War II
  *American Theater without inscription
  *Northern France

DECORATIONS

None.

7th BATTALION, 3d INFANTRY
(The Old Guard)

RA
(inactive)

LINEAGE

Constituted 3 June 1784 as a company of the First American Regiment. Organized in 1785 in New York or Connecticut. Redesignated 29 September 1789 as a company of the Regiment of Infantry. Redesignated 3 March 1791 as a company of the 1st Infantry. Redesignated in 1792 as a company of the Infantry of the 1st Sub-Legion. Redesignated 31 October 1796 as a company of the 1st Infantry.

Consolidated May–October 1815 with a company of the 5th Infantry (constituted 12 April 1808), a company of the 17th Infantry (constituted 11 January 1812), a company of the 19th Infantry (constituted 26 June 1812), and a company of the 28th Infantry (constituted 29 January 1813) to form a company of the 3d Infantry. Designated 22 May 1816 as Company G, 3d Infantry.

Consolidated 18 August 1869 with one half of Company I, 37th Infantry (see ANNEX) and consolidated unit designated as Company G, 3d Infantry. Inactivated 18 November 1921 at Fort Snelling, Minnesota. Activated 8 June 1922 at Fort Snelling, Minnesota. (3d Infantry assigned 24 March 1923 to the 7th Division; relieved 15 August 1927 from assignment to the 7th Division and assigned to the 6th Division; relieved 1 October 1933 from assignment to the 6th Division and assigned to the 7th Division; relieved 16 October 1939 from assignment to the 7th Division and assigned to the 6th Division; relieved 10 May 1941 from assignment to the 6th Division.) Inactivated 1 September 1942 at Fort Snelling, Minnesota. Activated 22 October 1943 at Camp Butner, North Carolina. Inactivated 20 November 1946 in Germany. Activated 6 April 1948 at Fort Lesley J. McNair, Washington, D.C.

Inactivated 1 July 1957 at Fort Lesley J. McNair, Washington, D.C.; concurrently, redesignated as Headquarters and Headquarters Company, 7th Battle Group, 3d Infantry. Redesignated 24 November 1967 as Headquarters and Headquarters Company, 7th Battalion, 3d Infantry, assigned to the 6th Infantry Division, and activated at Fort Campbell, Kentucky (organic elements concurrently constituted and activated). Inactivated 25 July 1968 at Fort Campbell, Kentucky.

ANNEX

Constituted 3 May 1861 in the Regular Army as Company I, 3d Battalion, 19th Infantry. Organized 25 September 1866 at Fort Columbus, New York. Reorganized and redesignated 23 November 1866 as Company I, 37th Infantry. Consolidated 18 August 1869 with Company G and Company I, 3d Infantry and consolidated units designated as Company G and Company I, 3d Infantry.

CAMPAIGN PARTICIPATION CREDIT

War of 1812
  *Canada
  *Chippewa
  *Lundy's Lane

Mexican War
  *Palo Alto
  *Resaca de la Palma
  Monterey
  Vera Cruz
  Cerro Gordo
  Contreras
  Churubusco
  *Chapultepec

Civil War
  *Bull Run
  *Peninsula
  *Manassas
  *Antietam
  *Fredericksburg
  *Chancellorsville
  *Gettysburg
  *Appomattox
  Texas 1861
  Florida 1861

Florida 1862
*Virginia 1863

Indian Wars
  *Miami
  *Seminoles
  Comanches
  New Mexico 1856
  New Mexico 1857
  *New Mexico 1858
  New Mexico 1860
  Montana 1887

War With Spain
  *Santiago

Philippine Insurrection
  *Malolos
  *San Isidro
  *Luzon 1899
  *Luzon 1900
  *Jolo 1911

World War II
  *American Theater without inscription
  *Northern France

DECORATIONS

None.

3D INFANTRY, BIBLIOGRAPHY

Bell, William Hemphill. *Ante Bellum: Or Before the War.* Cincinnati, 1883.

Epstein, Harvey M. "History of the 3d U.S. Infantry Regiment, 1784–1954." n.p., 1954.

Heart, Jonathan. *Journal of Captain Jonathan Heart on the March with His Company from Connecticut to Ft. Pitt in Pittsburgh, Penna. from the 7th of September to the 12th of October 1785.* Albany, 1885.

History of the Regiment for the Year 1908. n.p., 1908.

History of the Regiment for the Year 1909. n.p., 1909.

History of the Third Infantry for the Year 1910. n.p., 1910.

History of the Third Regiment, United States Infantry. 1792–1906. n.p., 1907.

History of the Third Regiment, United States Infantry. 1792–1912. n.p., 1912.

Katzenberger, George Anthony. "Major David Ziegler," *Ohio Archives and Historical Quarterly.* Columbus, 1912.

King, Charles D. "Esprit de Corps," *Journal of the Military Service Institution of the United States,* XI (1890), 85.

McRae, James Henry. "The Third Regiment of Infantry," *The Army of the United States,* edited by Theophilus F. Rodenbough and William L. Haskin. New York: Maynard, Merrill and Company, 1896, pp. 432–451. (Originally published in the *Journal of the Military Service Institution of the United States,* XVI [1895], 674–693.)

Mahon, John K. *History of the Second Seminole War, 1835–1842.* Gainesville: University of Florida Press, 1967.

The Old Guard, A Story of the Third Infantry Regiment. Washington: Government Printing Office, editions published in 1941, 1948, 1955, and 1970.

"Organization Day, 21 September 1949, 1784–1949." Washington, 1949.

Smith, Philip R., Junior. "Fife and Drum at Mount Vernon," *Army Digest,* XXIII (February 1968), 17–19.

Souvenir Program, Third Infantry Day, 1929, Being the Eighty-third Anniversary of the Battle of Monterey. Fort Snelling, Minnesota, 1929.

Sprague, John T. *The Origin, Progress and Conclusion of the Florida War.* New York: D. Appleton and Company, 1848. (Reprint. Gainesville: University of Florida Press, 1964.)

Stations of the Third Infantry in the Philippine Islands, March 23, 1899, to March 17, 1902. n.p., 1902.

Third Infantry Day, Celebration of the Eighty-second Anniversary of the

Battle of Monterey, September 21 to 23, 1846, by the Third United States Infantry. Fort Snelling, Minnesota, 1928.

"The Third Infantry Through the Years," *Winners of the West*, XIV (July 1937).

"Tradition on Parade," *Army Digest*, XXIII (December 1968), 50–53.

4th INFANTRY
(Warriors)

HERALDIC ITEMS

COAT OF ARMS

Shield: Vert a cross pattée argent within a circle of fifteen mullets of the like the upper arm of the cross charged with a castle gules, the lower arm with a fleur-de-lis, the dexter with an arrow and the sinister with a bolo both paleways all of the last. (And for informal use, pendant from the shield a French Croix de Guerre with Gilt Star proper.)

Crest: On a wreath of the colors four plumes vert.

Motto: *Noli Me Tangere* (Don't Tread on Me).

Symbolism: The green shield recalls the Mexican War. The national flag bore fifteen stars during the War of 1812. The white Maltese cross represents the service of the regiment in the Civil War; the arrow, the Indian Wars; the castle, the War with Spain; the bolo, the Philippine Insurrection; and the fleur-de-lis, World War I.

Previous to the approval of the coat of arms, the crest and motto were in use by the regiment for many years.

DISTINCTIVE INSIGNIA

The distinctive insignia is a strip of scarlet cloth or ribbon $1\frac{1}{2}$ inches in width with a green stripe $\frac{1}{2}$ inch in width in the center thereof; to be made into a band to fit the shoulder loop of coat.

Subsequent to the Mexican War and until the blue uniform was abolished, the Band of the 4th Infantry was authorized to wear a scarlet piping on the chevrons and trousers stripes in commemoration of distinguished service in the battle of Monterey in serving a captured battery against the enemy. The scarlet is to perpetuate this distinguished service of an element of the regiment. Green is the predominating color of the regimental coat of arms; it also symbolizes the service of the 4th Infantry in the Mexican War.

Lineage and Honors

Lineage

Constituted 11 January 1812 in the Regular Army as the 14th Infantry. Organized in March 1812 in Virginia, Maryland, Delaware, and Pennsylvania. Consolidated May–October 1815 with the 18th and 20th Infantry (both constituted 11 January 1812) and the 36th and 38th Infantry (both constituted 29 January 1813) to form the 4th Infantry. Consolidated in March 1869 with the 30th Infantry (see ANNEX) and consolidated unit designated as the 4th Infantry.

Assigned 1 October 1917 to the 3d Division. Relieved 15 May 1940 from assignment to the 3d Division. Assigned 1 November 1945 to the 25th Infantry Division. Inactivated 31 January 1947 at Osaka, Japan. Relieved 1 February 1947 from assignment to the 25th Infantry Division. Activated 1 October 1948 at Fort Lewis, Washington. Assigned 10 October 1954 to the 71st Infantry Division. Relieved 15 September 1956 from assignment to the 71st Infantry Division.

Reorganized 15 February 1958 as a parent regiment under the Combat Arms Regimental System.

ANNEX

Constituted 3 May 1861 in the Regular Army as the 3d Battalion, 12th Infantry. Organized 23 December 1865 at Fort Hamilton, New York. Reorganized and redesignated 7 December 1866 as the 30th Infantry. Consolidated in March 1869 with the 4th Infantry and consolidated unit designated as the 4th Infantry.

CAMPAIGN PARTICIPATION CREDIT

War of 1812
Canada
Bladensburg
McHenry

Mexican War
Palo Alto
Resaca de la Palma
Monterey
Vera Cruz
Cerro Gordo
Churubusco
Molino del Rey
Chapultepec
Puebla 1847
Tlaxcala 1847

Civil War
Peninsula
Manassas
Antietam
Fredericksburg
Chancellorsville
Gettysburg
Wilderness
Spotsylvania
Cold Harbor
Petersburg
Appomattox
Virginia 1863

Indian Wars
Tippecanoe
Seminoles
Black Hawk
Little Big Horn
Utes
Washington 1855
Oregon 1855
Washington 1856
Oregon 1856

War With Spain
Santiago

Philippine Insurrection
Manila
Malolos
Cavite
Luzon 1899

World War I
Aisne
Champagne-Marne
Aisne-Marne
St. Mihiel
Meuse-Argonne
Champagne 1918

World War II
Aleutian Islands

DECORATIONS

French Croix de Guerre with Gilt Star, World War I, Streamer embroidered CHAMPAGNE-MARNE AISNE-MARNE (4th Infantry cited; WD GO 11, 1924)

1st BATTALION, 4th INFANTRY

(Warriors)

RA
(3d Infantry Division)

LINEAGE

Constituted 11 January 1812 in the Regular Army as a company of the 14th Infantry. Organized in 1812. Consolidated May–October 1815 with a company each of the 18th and 20th Infantry (both constituted 11 January 1812) and a company each of the 36th and 38th Infantry (both constituted 29 January 1813) to form a company of the 4th Infantry. Designated 21 August 1816 as Company A, 4th Infantry.

Consolidated 31 March 1869 with Company A, 30th Infantry (see ANNEX) and consolidated unit designated as Company A, 4th Infantry. (4th Infantry assigned 1 October 1917 to the 3d Division; relieved 15 May 1940 from assignment to the 3d Division; assigned 1 November 1945 to the 25th Infantry Division.) Inactivated 31 January 1947 at Osaka, Japan. (4th Infantry relieved 1 February 1947 from assignment to the 25th Infantry Division.) Activated 1 October 1948 at Fort Lewis, Washington. (4th Infantry assigned 10 October 1954 to the 71st Infantry Division; relieved 15 September 1956 from assignment to the 71st Infantry Division.)

Reorganized and redesignated 15 February 1958 as Headquarters and Headquarters Company, 1st Battle Group, 4th Infantry and assigned to the 2d Infantry Brigade (organic elements concurrently constituted and activated). Inactivated 2 April 1962 at Fort Devens, Massachusetts. Redesignated 18 April 1963 as the 1st Battalion, 4th Infantry; concurrently, relieved from assignment to the 2d Infantry Brigade and assigned to the 3d Infantry Division. Activated 5 June 1963 in Germany.

ANNEX

Constituted 3 May 1861 in the Regular Army as Company A, 3d Battalion, 12th Infantry. Organized 23 December 1865 at Fort Hamilton, New York. Reorganized and redesignated 7 December 1866 as Company A, 30th Infantry. Consolidated 31 March 1869 with Company A, 4th Infantry and consolidated unit designated as Company A, 4th Infantry.

Campaign Participation Credit

War of 1812
* *Canada
* *Bladensburg
* *McHenry

Mexican War
* *Palo Alto
* *Resaca de la Palma
* *Monterey
* *Vera Cruz
* *Cerro Gordo
* *Churubusco
* *Molino del Rey
* *Chapultepec
* *Puebla 1847
  Tlaxcala 1847

Civil War
* *Peninsula
* *Manassas
* *Antietam
* *Fredericksburg
* *Chancellorsville
* *Gettysburg
  Wilderness
  Spotsylvania
  Cold Harbor
  Petersburg
  Appomattox
* *Virginia 1863

Indian Wars
  Tippecanoe
* *Seminoles
  Black Hawk
  Little Big Horn
  Utes
* *Washington 1855
  Oregon 1855
* *Washington 1856
  Oregon 1856

War With Spain
* *Santiago

Philippine Insurrection
* *Manila
* *Malolos
* *Cavite
* *Luzon 1899

World War I
* *Aisne
* *Champagne-Marne
* *Aisne-Marne
* *St. Mihiel
* *Meuse-Argonne
* *Champagne 1918

World War II
* *Aleutian Islands

Decorations

*Presidential Unit Citation (Army), Streamer embroidered CHICHAGOF VALLEY (Company A, 4th Infantry cited; WD GO 10, 1944)

*French Croix de Guerre with Gilt Star, World War I, Streamer embroidered CHAMPAGNE-MARNE AISNE-MARNE (4th Infantry cited; WD GO 11, 1924)

2d BATTALION, 4th INFANTRY

(Warriors)

RA
(nondivisional)

LINEAGE

Constituted 11 January 1812 in the Regular Army as a company of the 14th Infantry. Organized in 1812. Consolidated May–October 1815 with a company each of the 18th and 20th Infantry (both constituted 11 January 1812) and a company each of the 36th and 38th Infantry (both constituted 29 January 1813) to form a company of the 4th Infantry. Designated 21 August 1816 as Company B, 4th Infantry.

Consolidated 31 March 1869 with Company B, 30th Infantry (see ANNEX) and consolidated unit designated as Company B, 4th Infantry. (4th Infantry assigned 1 October 1917 to the 3d Division; relieved 15 May 1940 from assignment to the 3d Division; assigned 1 November 1945 to the 25th Infantry Division.) Inactivated 31 January 1947 at Osaka, Japan. (4th Infantry relieved 1 February 1947 from assignment to the 25th Infantry Division.) Activated 1 October 1948 at Fort Lewis, Washington. (4th Infantry assigned 10 October 1954 to the 71st Infantry Division; relieved 15 September 1956 from assignment to the 71st Infantry Division.)

Reorganized and redesignated 15 February 1958 as Headquarters and Headquarters Company, 2d Battle Group, 4th Infantry and assigned to the 3d Infantry Division (organic elements concurrently constituted and activated). Relieved 18 April 1963 from assignment to the 3d Infantry Division. Inactivated 3 June 1963 in Germany. Redesignated 21 July 1969 as the 2d Battalion, 4th Infantry and activated at Fort Campbell, Kentucky.

ANNEX

Constituted 3 May 1861 in the Regular Army as Company B, 3d Battalion, 12th Infantry. Organized 23 December 1965 at Fort Hamilton, New York. Reorganized and redesignated 7 December 1866 as Company B, 30th Infantry. Consolidated 31 March 1869 with Company B, 4th Infantry and consolidated unit designated as Company B, 4th Infantry.

184

CAMPAIGN PARTICIPATION CREDIT

War of 1812
*Canada
*Bladensburg
*McHenry

Mexican War
*Palo Alto
*Resaca de la Palma
*Monterey
*Vera Cruz
*Cerro Gordo
*Churubusco
*Molino del Rey
*Chapultepec
*Puebla 1847
 Tlaxcala 1847

Civil War
*Peninsula
*Manassas
*Antietam
*Fredericksburg
*Chancellorsville
 Gettysburg
 Wilderness
 Spotsylvania
 Cold Harbor
 Petersburg
 Appomattox
 Virginia 1863

Indian Wars
 Tippecanoe
*Seminoles
 Black Hawk
 Little Big Horn
*Utes
 Washington 1855
*Oregon 1855
 Washington 1856
*Oregon 1856
*California 1861

War With Spain
*Santiago

Philippine Insurrection
*Manila
*Malolos
 Cavite
*Luzon 1899

World War I
*Aisne
*Champagne-Marne
*Aisne-Marne
*St. Mihiel
*Meuse-Argonne
*Champagne 1918

World War II
*Aleutian Islands

DECORATIONS

*French Croix de Guerre with Gilt Star, World War I, Streamer embroidered CHAMPAGNE-MARNE AISNE-MARNE (4th Infantry cited; WD GO 11, 1924)

3d BATTALION, 4th INFANTRY

(Warriors)

LINEAGE

Constituted 11 January 1812 in the Regular Army as a company of the 14th Infantry. Organized in 1812. Consolidated May–October 1815 with a company each of the 18th and 20th Infantry (both constituted 11 January 1812) and a company each of the 36th and 38th Infantry (both constituted 29 January 1813) to form a company of the 4th Infantry. Designated 21 August 1816 as Company C, 4th Infantry.

Consolidated 31 March 1869 with Company C, 30th Infantry (see ANNEX 1) and consolidated unit designated as Company C, 4th Infantry. (4th Infantry assigned 1 October 1917 to the 3d Division; relieved 15 May 1940 from assignment to the 3d Division; assigned 1 November 1945 to the 25th Infantry Division.) Inactivated 31 January 1947 at Osaka, Japan. (4th Infantry relieved 1 February 1947 from assignment to the 25th Infantry Division.) Activated 1 October 1948 at Fort Lewis, Washington. (4th Infantry assigned 10 October 1954 to the 71st Infantry Division; relieved 15 September 1956 from assignment to the 71st Infantry Division.) Inactivated 15 February 1958 at Fort Devens, Massachusetts.

Redesignated 11 May 1959 as Headquarters and Headquarters Company, 3d Battle Group, 4th Infantry, withdrawn from the Regular Army, allotted to the Army Reserve, and assigned to the 102d Infantry Division (organic elements concurrently constituted). Battle Group activated 1 June 1959 with Headquarters at Fairfield, Illinois (concurrently, Headquarters and Headquarters Company consolidated with Headquarters and Headquarters Company, 3d Battalion, 405th Infantry [see ANNEX 2] and consolidated unit designated as Headquarters and Headquarters Company, 3d Battle Group, 4th Infantry). Reorganized and redesignated 1 April 1963 as the 3d Battalion, 4th Infantry. Inactivated 31 December 1965 at Fairfield, Illinois.

ANNEX 1

Constituted 3 May 1861 in the Regular Army as Company C, 3d Battalion, 12th Infantry. Organized 23 December 1865 at Fort Hamilton,

New York. Reorganized and redesignated 7 December 1866 as Company C, 30th Infantry. Consolidated 31 March 1869 with Company C, 4th Infantry and consolidated unit designated as Company C, 4th Infantry.

ANNEX 2

Constituted 24 June 1921 in the Organized Reserves as Headquarters and Headquarters Company, 3d Battalion, 405th Infantry, an element of the 102d Division (later redesignated as the 102d Infantry Division). Organized in November 1921 at Little Rock, Arkansas. Ordered into active military service 15 September 1942 and reorganized at Camp Maxey, Texas. Inactivated 1 June 1946 in Germany.

Activated 12 November 1946 in the Organized Reserves at Mankato, Minnesota. Inactivated 3 January 1947 at Mankato, Minnesota. Activated 25 April 1947 at St. Louis, Missouri. Inactivated 12 March 1948 at St. Louis, Missouri. (Organized Reserves redesignated 25 March 1948 as the Organized Reserve Corps; redesignated 9 July 1952 as the Army Reserve.) Activated 18 December 1950 at Flora, Illinois. Location changed 15 March 1951 to Fairfield, Illinois. Consolidated 1 June 1959 with Headquarters and Headquarters Company, 3d Battle Group, 4th Infantry and consolidated unit designated as Headquarters and Headquarters Company, 3d Battle Group, 4th Infantry.

Campaign Participation Credit

War of 1812
  *Canada
  *Bladensburg
  *McHenry

Mexican War
  *Palo Alto
  *Resaca de la Palma
  *Monterey
  *Vera Cruz
  *Cerro Gordo
  *Churubusco
  *Molino del Rey
  *Chapultepec
  *Puebla 1847
  Tlaxcala 1847

Civil War
  *Peninsula
  *Manassas
  *Antietam
  *Fredericksburg
  *Chancellorsville
  *Gettysburg
  *Wilderness
  *Spotsylvania
  *Cold Harbor
  *Petersburg
  *Appomattox
  *Virginia 1863

Indian Wars
  Tippecanoe
  *Seminoles
  Black Hawk
  *Little Big Horn
  *Utes
  Washington 1855
  *Oregon 1855
  *Washington 1856
  Oregon 1856

War With Spain
  *Santiago

Philippine Insurrection
  *Manila
  *Malolos
  *Cavite
  *Luzon 1899

World War I
  *Aisne
  *Champagne-Marne
  *Aisne-Marne
  *St. Mihiel
  *Meuse-Argonne
  *Champagne 1918

World War II
  *Aleutian Islands
  *Rhineland
  *Central Europe

Decorations

*Presidential Unit Citation (Army), Streamer embroidered ROER RIVER (405th Infantry cited; WD GO 16, 1947)

*French Croix de Guerre with Gilt Star, World War I, Streamer embroidered CHAMPAGNE-MARNE AISNE-MARNE (4th Infantry cited; WD GO 11, 1924)

4TH INFANTRY, BIBLIOGRAPHY

Bisbee, William Henry. *Through Four American Wars: The Impressions and Experiences of Brigadier General William Henry Bisbee, as Told to his Grandson, William Raymond Bisbee*. Boston: Meador Publishing Company, 1931. (The author served in a number of infantry regiments, but principally with the 4th, 1870–1893.)

The Capture of Attu, as Told by the Men who Fought There. Washington: Infantry Journal Press, 1944.

Conn, Stetson; Rose C. Engelman and Byron Fairchild. *Guarding the United States and Its Outposts*. United States Army in World War II. Washington: Government Printing Office, 1964.

Fourth Infantry Day. Celebration of the One Hundred and Seventeenth Anniversary of the Battle of Tippecanoe, November 7, 1928. Fort George Wright, Washington, 1928.

4th U. S. Infantry, Vera Cruz, Mexico. August 15, 1914. n.p., 1914.

A History of the 4th Infantry. Ladd Air Force Base, Alaska, 1951.

History of the 4th RCT. Fort Devens, Massachusetts, 1956?

"History of the 'Old Fourth Regiment,'" *House Reports 322*, 27th Congress (1841–1843), 2d Session, I.

Hodges, Carroll B. "An Old Regiment of Regulars," *Ohio Illustrated Magazine*, III (1907), 211–218.

Leyden, James Alexander. "The Fourth Regiment of Infantry," *The Army of the United States*, edited by Theophilus F. Rodenbough and William L. Haskin. New York: Maynard, Merrill and Company, 1896, pp. 452–465. (Originally published in the *Journal of the Military Service Institution of the United States*, XV [1894], 219–232.)

————. "A Historical Sketch of the Fourth Infantry, From 1796 to 1891." Fort Sherman, Idaho: Press of the 4th Infantry, 1891. (Erroneously connects this regiment with an earlier one of the same designation.)

————. *Register of Commissioned Officers of the Fourth Infantry, From 1796 to 1894*. n.p., Regimental Press, 1895? (Erroneously connects this regiment with an earlier one of the same designation.)

Mahon, John K. *History of the Second Seminole War, 1835–1842*. Gainesville: University of Florida Press, 1967.

McMurtrie, Douglas C. "The Fourth Infantry Press at Fort Bridger," *Annals of Wyoming*, XIII (1941), 347–351.

Organization Day, Fourth Infantry Regiment, September 27, 1952. n.p., 1952.

Organization Day of the Fourth Infantry, at Fort George Wright, Washington. Fort George Wright, Washington, 1923.

Powell, William Henry. *A History of the Organization and Movements of the Fourth Regiment of Infantry, United States Army, From May 30, 1796, to December 31, 1870.* . . . Washington City: McGill and Witherow, 1871. (Erroneously connects this regiment with an earlier one of the same designation.)

Register of Commissioned Officers of the 4th U. S. Infantry from 1796–1890. Fort Sheridan, Idaho: Press of the 4th Infantry, 1891. (Erroneously connects this regiment with an earlier one of the same designation.)

"Souvenir Program, 4th Infantry Regiment, Organization Day, November 7, 1923." Spokane, 1923.

"Souvenir Program, Organization Day, Fourth United States Infantry, One Hundred and Thirteenth Anniversary of the Battle of Tippecanoe." 3d Battalion, 4th Infantry, Fort Lawton, Washington, 1924.

"Souvenir Program, Organization Day, Fourth Infantry, One Hundred and Fifteenth Anniversary of the Battle of Tippecanoe." Fort George Wright, Washington, 1926.

Sprague, John T. *The Origin, Progress and Conclusion of the Florida War.* New York: D. Appleton and Company, 1848. (Reprint. Gainesville: University of Florida Press, 1964.)

5th INFANTRY

COAT OF ARMS

Shield:　　Argent, on a fess gules between seven muzzle-loading cannon sable an arrow or; all within a bordure gyronny of eight, vert and gules alternating with gyrons of the field.

Crest:　　On a wreath of the colors an arm in armor embowed grasping in a mailed hand proper nine arrows sable armed and flitted gules.

Motto:　　I'll try, Sir.

Symbolism: The shield is white, the color of infantry facings when the regiment was organized. The red fess with arrow commemorates the battle of Tippecanoe; the battle of Lundy's Lane is shown by the seven cannon captured there; and the border of green, white, and red is for the Mexican War.

The crest is a modification of the crest of General Nelson A. Miles, who was for many years Colonel of the 5th Infantry and who led it in several notable Indian engagements. His crest is an arm in armor grasping an anchor; arrows, to symbolize Indian campaigns, are substituted for the anchor in the regimental crest.

DISTINCTIVE INSIGNIA

The distinctive insignia is the shield, crest, and motto of the coat of arms, all superimposed on a silver shield with two concave arcs at top.

LINEAGE AND HONORS

LINEAGE

Constituted 12 April 1808 in the Regular Army as the 4th Infantry. Organized May–June 1808 in New England. Consolidated May–October 1815 with the 9th and 13th Infantry (both constituted 11 January 1812), the 21st Infantry (constituted 26 June 1812), the 40th Infantry (constituted 29 January 1813), and the 46th Infantry (constituted 30 March 1814) to form the 5th Infantry. Consolidated in June

1869 with one half of the 37th Infantry (see ANNEX) and consolidated unit designated as the 5th Infantry.

Assigned 27 July 1918 to the 17th Division. Relieved 10 February 1919 from assignment to the 17th Division. Assigned 24 March 1923 to the 9th Division. Relieved 15 August 1927 from assignment to the 9th Division and assigned to the 5th Division. Relieved 1 October 1933 from assignment to the 5th Division and assigned to the 9th Division. Relieved 15 July 1940 from assignment to the 9th Division. Assigned 10 July 1943 to the 71st Light Division (later redesignated as the 71st Infantry Division). Relieved 1 May 1946 from assignment to the 71st Infantry Division. Inactivated 15 November 1946 at Salzburg, Austria. Activated 1 January 1949 in Korea. Assigned 10 October 1954 to the 71st Infantry Division. Relieved 25 August 1956 from assignment to the 71st Infantry Division. Assigned 1 September 1956 to the 8th Infantry Division.

Relieved 1 August 1957 from assignment to the 8th Infantry Division and reorganized as a parent regiment under the Combat Arms Regimental System.

ANNEX

Constituted 3 May 1861 in the Regular Army as the 3d Battalion, 19th Infantry. Organized May 1865–September 1866 at Fort Wayne, Michigan; Newport Barracks, Kentucky; and Fort Columbus, New York. Reorganized and redesignated 23 November 1866 as the 37th Infantry. One half of the 37th Infantry consolidated in June 1869 with the 5th Infantry and consolidated unit designated as the 5th Infantry (remaining half of the 37th Infantry consolidated August–December 1869 with the 3d Infantry and consolidated unit designated as the 3d Infantry).

CAMPAIGN PARTICIPATION CREDIT

War of 1812
Canada
Chippewa
Lundy's Lane

Mexican War
Palo Alto
Resaca de la Palma
Monterey
Churubusco
Molino del Rey
Chapultepec
Vera Cruz 1847

Civil War
New Mexico 1862

Indian Wars
Tippecanoe
Seminoles
Comanches
Little Big Horn
Nez Perces
Bannocks
New Mexico 1860
Montana 1879
Montana 1880
Montana 1881
Montana 1887

Philippine Insurrection
Without inscription

World War II
American Theater without inscription
Rhineland
Central Europe

Korean War
UN defensive
UN offensive
CCF intervention
First UN counteroffensive
CCF spring offensive
UN summer-fall offensive
Second Korean winter
Korea, summer-fall 1952
Third Korean winter
Korea, summer 1953

Vietnam
Counteroffensive
Counteroffensive, Phase II
Counteroffensive, Phase III
Tet Counteroffensive
(other campaigns to be determined)

DECORATIONS

Presidential Unit Citation (Army), Streamer embroidered CHINJU (3d Battalion, 5th Infantry and attached units cited; DA GO 69, 1952)

Presidential Unit Citation (Army), Streamer embroidered BEN CUI (1st Battalion, 5th Infantry cited; DA GO 82, 1969)

Valorous Unit Award, Streamer embroidered CU CHI DISTRICT (1st Battalion, 5th Infantry cited; DA GO 20, 1967)

Republic of Korea Presidential Unit Citation, Streamer embroidered KOREA 1950–1952 (5th Infantry cited; DA GO 33, 1953, as amended by DA GO 41, 1955)

Republic of Korea Presidential Unit Citation, Streamer embroidered KOREA 1950–1953 (5th Infantry cited; DA GO 49, 1954)

Republic of Korea Presidential Unit Citation, Streamer embroidered KOREA 1952–1954 (5th Infantry cited; DA GO 50, 1954)

1st BATTALION, 5th INFANTRY

RA

(25th Infantry Division)

Constituted 12 April 1808 in the Regular Army as a company of the 4th Infantry. Organized in May or June 1808 in New England. Consolidated May–October 1815 with a company each of the 9th and 13th Infantry (both constituted 11 January 1812), a company of the 21st Infantry (constituted 26 June 1812), a company of the 40th Infantry (constituted 29 January 1813), and a company of the 46th Infantry (constituted 30 March 1814) to form a company of the 5th Infantry. Designated 22 May 1816 as Company A, 5th Infantry.

Consolidated in June 1869 with one half of Company K, 37th Infantry (see ANNEX) and consolidated unit designated as Company A, 5th Infantry. (5th Infantry assigned 27 July 1918 to the 17th Division; relieved 10 February 1919 from assignment to the 17th Division; assigned 24 March 1923 to the 9th Division; relieved 15 August 1927 from assignment to the 9th Division and assigned to the 5th Division; relieved 1 October 1933 from assignment to the 5th Division and assigned to the 9th Division; relieved 15 July 1940 from assignment to the 9th Division; assigned 10 July 1943 to the 71st Light Division [later redesignated as the 71st Infantry Division]; relieved 1 May 1946 from assignment to the 71st Infantry Division.) Inactivated 15 November 1946 at Salzburg, Austria. Activated 1 January 1949 in Korea. (5th Infantry assigned 10 October 1954 to the 71st Infantry Division; relieved 25 August 1956 from assignment to the 71st Infantry Division; assigned 1 September 1956 to the 8th Infantry Division.)

Reorganized and redesignated 1 August 1957 as Headquarters and Headquarters Company, 1st Battle Group, 5th Infantry and remained assigned to the 8th Infantry Division (organic elements concurrently constituted and activated). Relieved 1 February 1959 from assignment to the 8th Infantry Division and assigned to the 1st Infantry Division. Relieved 1 February 1963 from assignment to the 1st Infantry Division and assigned to the 25th Infantry Division. Reorganized and redesignated 12 August 1963 as the 1st Battalion, 5th Infantry.

194

ANNEX

Constituted 3 May 1861 in the Regular Army as Company K, 3d Battalion, 19th Infantry. Organized 25 September 1866 at Fort Columbus, New York. Reorganized and redesignated 23 November 1866 as Company K, 37th Infantry. Consolidated in June 1869 with Company A and Company B, 5th Infantry and consolidated units designated as Company A and Company B, 5th Infantry.

CAMPAIGN PARTICIPATION CREDIT

War of 1812
  *Canada
  *Chippewa
  *Lundy's Lane

Mexican War
  *Palo Alto
  *Resaca de la Palma
  Monterey
  *Churubusco
  *Molino del Rey
  *Chapultepec
  Vera Cruz 1847

Civil War
  New Mexico 1862

Indian Wars
  *Tippecanoe
  *Seminoles
  Comanches
  *Little Big Horn
  Nez Perces
  *Bannocks
  *New Mexico 1860
  *Montana 1879
  Montana 1880
  *Montana 1881
  *Montana 1887

Philippine Insurrection
  *Without inscription

World War II
  *American Theater without inscription
  *Rhineland
  *Central Europe

Korean War
  *UN defensive
  *UN offensive
  *CCF intervention
  *First UN counteroffensive
  *CCF spring offensive
  *UN summer-fall offensive
  *Second Korean winter
  *Korea, summer-fall 1952
  *Third Korean winter
  *Korea, summer 1953

Vietnam
  *Counteroffensive
  *Counteroffensive, Phase II
  *Counteroffensive, Phase III
  *Tet Counteroffensive
  (other campaigns to be determined)

DECORATIONS

*Presidential Unit Citation (Army), Streamer embroidered SONGNAE-DONG (Company A, 5th Infantry cited; DA GO 1, 1954)

Presidential Unit Citation (Army), Streamer embroidered CHINJU

*Presidential Unit Citation (Army), Streamer embroidered BEN CUI (1st Battalion, 5th Infantry cited; DA GO 82, 1969)

*Valorous Unit Award, Streamer embroidered CU CHI DISTRICT (1st Battalion, 5th Infantry cited; DA GO 20, 1967)

*Republic of Korea Presidential Unit Citation, Streamer embroidered

KOREA 1950–1952 (5th Infantry cited; DA GO 33, 1953, as amended by DA GO 41, 1955)

*Republic of Korea Presidential Unit Citation, Streamer embroidered KOREA 1950–1953 (5th Infantry cited; DA GO 49, 1954)

*Republic of Korea Presidential Unit Citation, Streamer embroidered KOREA 1952–1954 (5th Infantry cited; DA GO 50, 1954)

*Vietnamese Cross of Gallantry with Palm, Streamer embroidered VIETNAM 1966–1968 (1st Battalion, 5th Infantry cited; DA GO 48, 1971)

2d BATTALION, 5th INFANTRY

RA

(25th Infantry Division)

Constituted 12 April 1808 in the Regular Army as a company of the 4th Infantry. Organized in May or June 1808 in New England. Consolidated May–October 1815 with a company each of the 9th and 13th Infantry (both constituted 11 January 1812), a company of the 21st Infantry (constituted 26 June 1812), a company of the 40th Infantry (constituted 29 January 1813), and a company of the 46th Infantry (constituted 30 March 1814) to form a company of the 5th Infantry. Designated 22 May 1816 as Company B, 5th Infantry.

Consolidated in June 1869 with one half of Company K, 37th Infantry (see ANNEX) and consolidated unit designated as Company B, 5th Infantry. (5th Infantry assigned 27 July 1918 to the 17th Division; relieved 10 February 1919 from assignment to the 17th Division; assigned 24 March 1923 to the 9th Division; relieved 15 August 1927 from assignment to the 9th Division and assigned to the 5th Division; relieved 1 October 1933 from assignment to the 5th Division and assigned to the 9th Division; relieved 15 July 1940 from assignment to the 9th Division; assigned 10 July 1943 to the 71st Light Division [later redesignated as the 71st Infantry Division]; relieved 1 May 1946 from assignment to the 71st Infantry Division.) Inactivated 15 November 1946 at Salzburg, Austria. Activated 1 January 1949 in Korea. (5th Infantry assigned 10 October 1954 to the 71st Infantry Division; relieved 25 August 1956 from assignment to the 71st Infantry Division; assigned 1 September 1956 to the 8th Infantry Division.) Inactivated 1 August 1957 in Germany and relieved from assignment to the 8th Infantry Division.

Redesignated 19 November 1957 as Headquarters and Headquarters Company, 2d Battle Group, 5th Infantry (organic elements concurrently constituted). Battle Group activated 1 December 1957 and assigned to the 9th Infantry Division. Inactivated 31 January 1962 at Fort Carson, Colorado, and relieved from assignment to the 9th Infantry Division. Redesignated 6 December 1969 as the 2d Battalion, 5th Infantry; concurrently, activated in Hawaii as an element of the 25th Infantry Division.

ANNEX

Constituted 3 May 1861 in the Regular Army as Company K, 3d Battalion, 19th Infantry. Organized 25 September 1866 at Fort Columbus, New York. Reorganized and redesignated 23 November 1866 as Company K, 37th Infantry. Consolidated in June 1869 with Company A and Company B, 5th Infantry and consolidated units designated as Company A and Company B, 5th Infantry.

CAMPAIGN PARTICIPATION CREDIT

War of 1812
  *Canada
  *Chippewa
  *Lundy's Lane

Mexican War
  *Palo Alto
  *Resaca de la Palma
  *Monterey
  *Churubusco
  *Molino del Rey
  *Chapultepec
  Vera Cruz 1847

Civil War
  *New Mexico 1862

Indian Wars
  *Tippecanoe
  *Seminoles
  Comanches
  *Little Big Horn
  *Nez Perces
  Bannocks
  *New Mexico 1860

  *Montana 1879
  Montana 1880
  *Montana 1881
  Montana 1887

Philippine Insurrection
  *Without inscription

World War II
  *American Theater without inscription
  *Rhineland
  *Central Europe

Korean War
  *UN defensive
  *UN offensive
  *CCF intervention
  *First UN counteroffensive
  *CCF spring offensive
  *UN summer-fall offensive
  *Second Korean winter
  *Korea, summer-fall 1952
  *Third Korean winter
  *Korea, summer 1953

DECORATIONS

Presidential Unit Citation (Army), Streamer embroidered CHINJU

*Republic of Korea Presidential Unit Citation, Streamer embroidered KOREA 1950–1952 (5th Infantry cited; DA GO 33, 1953, as amended by DA GO 41, 1955)

*Republic of Korea Presidential Unit Citation, Streamer embroidered KOREA 1950–1953 (5th Infantry cited; DA GO 49, 1954)

*Republic of Korea Presidential Unit Citation, Streamer embroidered KOREA 1952–1954 (5th Infantry cited; DA GO 50, 1954)

3d BATTALION, 5th INFANTRY

RA

(193d Infantry Brigade)

Constituted 12 April 1808 in the Regular Army as a company of the 4th Infantry. Organized in May or June 1808 in New England. Consolidated May–October 1815 with a company each of the 9th and 13th Infantry (both constituted 11 January 1812), a company of the 21st Infantry (constituted 26 June 1812), a company of the 40th Infantry (constituted 29 January 1813), and a company of the 46th Infantry (constituted 30 March 1814) to form a company of the 5th Infantry. Designated 22 May 1816 as Company C, 5th Infantry.

Consolidated in June 1869 with one half of Company G, 37th Infantry (see ANNEX) and consolidated unit designated as Company C, 5th Infantry. (5th Infantry assigned 27 July 1918 to the 17th Division; relieved 10 February 1919 from assignment to the 17th Division; assigned 24 March 1923 to the 9th Division; relieved 15 August 1927 from assignment to the 9th Division and assigned to the 5th Division; relieved 1 October 1933 from assignment to the 5th Division and assigned to the 9th Division; relieved 15 July 1940 from assignment to the 9th Division; assigned 10 July 1943 to the 71st Light Division [later redesignated as the 71st Infantry Division]; relieved 1 May 1946 from assignment to the 71st Infantry Division.) Inactivated 15 November 1946 at Salzburg, Austria. Activated 1 January 1949 in Korea. (5th Infantry assigned 10 October 1954 to the 71st Infantry Division; relieved 25 August 1956 from assignment to the 71st Infantry Division; assigned 1 September 1956 to the 8th Infantry Division.)

Inactivated 1 August 1957 in Germany and relieved from assignment to the 8th Infantry Division; concurrently, redesignated as Headquarters and Headquarters Company, 3d Battle Group, 5th Infantry. Withdrawn 6 April 1959 from the Regular Army, allotted to the Army Reserve, and assigned to the 94th Infantry Division (organic elements concurrently constituted). Battle Group activated 1 May 1959 with Headquarters at Boston, Massachusetts. Inactivated 1 March 1963 at Boston, Massachusetts; concurrently, relieved from assignment to the 94th Infantry Division.

Redesignated 26 June 1968 as the 3d Battalion, 5th Infantry, withdrawn from the Army Reserve, allotted to the Regular Army, and assigned to the 193d Infantry Brigade; concurrently, activated at Fort Kobbe, Canal Zone.

ANNEX

Constituted 3 May 1861 in the Regular Army as Company G, 3d Battalion, 19th Infantry. Organized April–May 1866 at Newport Barracks, Kentucky. Reorganized and redesignated 23 November 1866 as Company G, 37th Infantry. Consolidated in June 1869 with Company C and Company D, 5th Infantry and consolidated units designated as Company C and Company D, 5th Infantry.

CAMPAIGN PARTICIPATION CREDIT

War of 1812
  *Canada
  *Chippewa
  *Lundy's Lane

Mexican War
  *Palo Alto
  *Resaca de la Palma
  Monterey
  Churubusco
  Molino del Rey
  Chapultepec
  *Vera Cruz 1847

Civil War
  New Mexico 1862

Indian Wars
  *Tippecanoe
  Seminoles
  *Comanches
  *Little Big Horn
  Nez Perces
  *Bannocks
  New Mexico 1860

*Montana 1879
Montana 1880
*Montana 1881
Montana 1887

Philippine Insurrection
  *Luzon 1900
  *Luzon 1901

World War II
  *American Theater without inscription
  *Rhineland
  *Central Europe

Korean War
  *UN defensive
  *UN offensive
  *CCF intervention
  *First UN counteroffensive
  *CCF spring offensive
  *UN summer-fall offensive
  *Second Korean winter
  *Korea, summer-fall 1952
  *Third Korean winter
  *Korea, summer 1953

DECORATIONS

Presidential Unit Citation (Army), Streamer embroidered CHINJU
  *Republic of Korea Presidential Unit Citation, Streamer embroidered KOREA 1950–1952 (5th Infantry cited; DA GO 33, 1953, as amended by DA GO 41, 1955)
  *Republic of Korea Presidential Unit Citation, Streamer embroidered KOREA 1950–1953 (5th Infantry cited; DA GO 49, 1954)
  *Republic of Korea Presidential Unit Citation, Streamer embroidered KOREA 1952–1954 (5th Infantry cited; DA GO 50, 1954)

5TH INFANTRY, BIBLIOGRAPHY

Appleman, Roy E. *South to the Naktong, North to the Yalu.* United States Army in the Korean War. Washington: Government Printing Office, 1961.

Bordages, Asa. "On Their Battle Honors; How the 5th Came by its Motto," *New York World Telegram* (25 September 1939), 15.

Costello, Michael. "The Army Thinks He's Earned a Rest," *Reader's Digest,* (January 1952). (Experiences of Lt. C. H. Dodd, who was with the 5th Infantry in Korea.)

5th Infantry Regiment, 1808–1955. n.p., 1955.

Guernsey, Alfred Hudson. "Army Life on the Border," *Harper's Magazine,* XXXIII (1866), 429–442.

Gugeler, Russell A. *Combat Actions in Korea.* Washington: Combat Forces Press, 1954.

Hampton, Celwyn E. *The Twenty-first's Trophy of Niagara.* n.p., 1909. (Relates to the present 5th Infantry.)

History of the Fifth United States Infantry. Fort Riley, Kansas: 1st Battle Group, 5th Infantry, April 1960.

List of Commissioned Officers of the Fifth United States Infantry, Commanded by Colonel George Gibson. Fort Keogh, Montana, 1888.

Rodenbough, Theophilus F. and William L. Haskin, editors. "The Fifth Regiment of Infantry," *The Army of the United States.* New York: Maynard, Merrill and Company, 1896, pp. 466–479. (Originally published in the *Journal of the Military Service Institution of the United States,* XV [1894], 1093–1106.)

Sigerfoos, Edward. *Historical Sketch of the 5th United States Infantry. . .* New York?: Regimental Press, 1902.

Thomasson, Nelson. *Recollections of 12 Years I Have Served in the 5th U. S. Infantry.* Chicago, 1926.

Walker, Adam. *A Journal of Two Campaigns of the Fourth Regiment of U. S. Infantry in the Michigan and Indiana Territories, Under the Command of Colonel John P. Boyd and Lt. Col. James Miller, During the Years 1811 and 1812.* Keene, New Hampshire, 1816. (Relates to the present 5th Infantry.)

6th INFANTRY
(The Regulars)

COAT OF ARMS

Shield: Argent, a scaling ladder vert, in fess an alligator statant proper, on a chief wavy gules a cross of the field.

Crest: On a wreath of the colors a lion's face gules.

Motto: Unity is Strength.

Symbolism: The alligator symbolizes service in several Indian campaigns, notably in the Second Seminole War, when the regiment bore the brunt of the fighting at the battle of Lake Okeechobee on 25 December 1837. Service in the Mexican War with General Scott, especially at Churubusco and at the assault on the citadel of Chapultepec, is commemorated with a scaling ladder (in green, the Mexican color), by means of which the walls of Chapultepec were stormed. The chief, symbolic of the crossing of the Meuse near Dun during World War I, is the arms of the ancient Lords of Dun—a silver cross on a red field. The wavy partition line represents the river. The shield is white, the color of infantry facings when the regiment was organized.

The crest represents service in the Canadian campaigns of 1813 and 1814 during the War of 1812.

DISTINCTIVE INSIGNIA

The distinctive insignia is the shield and motto of the coat of arms.

LINEAGE AND HONORS

LINEAGE

Constituted 11 January 1812 in the Regular Army as the 11th Infantry. Organized March–May 1812 in Vermont, New Hampshire, and Connecticut. Consolidated May–October 1815 with the 25th Infantry (constituted 26 June 1812) and the 27th, 29th, and 37th Infantry (all constituted 29 January 1813) to form the 6th Infantry. Consolidated 1 May 1869 with the 42d Infantry, Veteran Reserve Corps (constituted 21 September 1866) and consolidated unit designated as the 6th Infantry. Assigned 18 November 1917 to the 5th Division. Relieved in August 1921 from assignment to the 5th Division. Assigned 24 March 1923 to the 6th Division. Relieved 16 October 1939 from assignment to the 6th Division.

Reorganized 15 July 1940 as the 6th Infantry (Armored) and assigned to the 1st Armored Division. Redesignated 1 January 1942 as the 6th Armored Infantry. Regiment broken up 20 July 1944 and its elements reorganized and redesignated as elements of the 1st Armored Division as follows: 6th Armored Infantry (less 2d and 3d Battalions) as the 6th Armored Infantry Battalion; 2d Battalion as the 11th Armored Infantry Battalion; 3d Battalion as the 14th Armored Infantry Battalion.

6th Armored Infantry Battalion converted and redesignated 1 May 1946 as the 12th Constabulary Squadron; concurrently, relieved from assignment to the 1st Armored Division and assigned to the 1st Constabulary Regiment. Inactivated 20 September 1947 at Fritzlar, Germany. Converted and redesignated 10 October 1950 as the 6th Infantry (less 2d and 3d Battalions) and relieved from assignment to the 1st Constabulary Regiment.

11th Armored Infantry Battalion converted and redesignated 1 May 1946 as the 11th Constabulary Squadron; concurrently, relieved from assignment to the 1st Armored Division and assigned to the 1st Constabulary Regiment. Inactivated 20 September 1947 at Fritzlar, Germany. Converted and redesignated 7 April 1949 as the 11th Armored Infantry Battalion and relieved from assignment to the 1st Constabulary Regiment. Redesignated 10 October 1950 as the 2d Battalion, 6th Infantry.

14th Armored Infantry Battalion converted and redesignated 1 May 1946 as the 14th Constabulary Squadron; concurrently, relieved from assignment to the 1st Armored Division and assigned to the 15th Constabulary Regiment. Inactivated 20 December 1948 at Blaufeldin, Germany, and relieved from assignment to the 15th Constabulary Regiment; concurrently, converted and redesignated as the 14th Armored Infantry Battalion and assigned to the 1st Armored Division. Redesignated 10 October 1950 as the 3d Battalion, 6th Infantry and relieved from assignment to the 1st Armored Division.

6th Infantry activated 16 October 1950 at Grafenwohr, Germany. Reorganized 1 June 1958 as a parent regiment under the Combat Arms Regimental System.

CAMPAIGN PARTICIPATION CREDIT

War of 1812
Canada
Chippewa
Lundy's Lane

Mexican War
Vera Cruz
Cerro Gordo
Churubusco
Molino del Rey
Chapultepec

Civil War
Peninsula
Manassas
Antietam
Fredericksburg
Chancellorsville
Gettysburg
Virginia 1862

Indian Wars
Seminoles
Black Hawk
Little Big Horn
Cheyennes
Utes
South Dakota 1823
Kansas 1829
Nebraska 1855
Kansas 1857
North Dakota 1872
North Dakota 1873
Montana 1879

War With Spain
Santiago

Philippine Insurrection
Jolo
Negros 1899
Panay 1900

Mexican Expedition
Mexico 1916–1917

World War I
St. Mihiel
Meuse-Argonne
Alsace 1918
Lorraine 1918

World War II
Algeria-French Morocco
(with arrowhead)
Tunisia
Naples-Foggia
Anzio
Rome-Arno
North Apennines
Po Valley

Vietnam
Counteroffensive, Phase III
Tet Counteroffensive
(other campaigns to be
determined)

DECORATIONS

Presidential Unit Citation (Army), Streamer embroidered MT. PORCHIA (6th Armored Infantry cited; WD GO's 57, 65, and 78, all 1947)

Presidential Unit Citation (Army), Streamer embroidered ORAN, ALGERIA (3d Battalion, 6th Armored Infantry cited; WD GO 18, 1943)

Valorous Unit Award, Streamer embroidered LO GIANG (1st Battalion, 6th Infantry cited; DA GO 73, 1968)

1st BATTALION, 6th INFANTRY

(The Regulars)

RA
(23d Infantry Division)

LINEAGE

Constituted 11 January 1812 in the Regular Army as a company of the 11th Infantry. Organized March–May 1812 in Vermont, New Hampshire, or Connecticut. Consolidated May–October 1815 with a company of the 25th Infantry (constituted 26 June 1812) and a company each of the 27th, 29th, and 37th Infantry (all constituted 29 January 1813) to form a company of the 6th Infantry. Designated 22 May 1816 as Company A, 6th Infantry. Consolidated 1 May 1869 with Company A, 42d Infantry, Veteran Reserve Corps (constituted 21 September 1866) and consolidated unit designated as Company A, 6th Infantry. (6th Infantry assigned 18 November 1917 to the 5th Division; relieved in August 1921 from assignment to the 5th Division; assigned 24 March 1923 to the 6th Division; relieved 16 October 1939 from assignment to the 6th Division.)

Reorganized 15 July 1940 as Company A, 6th Infantry (Armored), an element of the 1st Armored Division. Redesignated 1 January 1942 as Company A, 6th Armored Infantry. Reorganized and redesignated 20 July 1944 as Company A, 6th Armored Infantry Battalion, an element of the 1st Armored Division. Converted and redesignated 1 May 1946 as Troop A, 12th Constabulary Squadron, an element of the 1st Constabulary Regiment. Inactivated 20 September 1947 at Fritzlar, Germany. Converted and redesignated 10 October 1950 as Company A, 6th Infantry (concurrently, 12th Constabulary Squadron relieved from assignment to the 1st Constabulary Regiment). Activated 16 October 1950 at Grafenwohr, Germany.

Reorganized and redesignated 15 February 1957 as Headquarters and Headquarters Company, 1st Armored Rifle Battalion, 6th Infantry, an element of the 1st Armored Division (organic elements concurrently constituted and activated). Reorganized and redesignated 3 February 1962 as the 1st Battalion, 6th Infantry. Relieved 12 May 1967 from assignment to the 1st Armored Division and assigned to the 198th Infantry Brigade. Relieved 15 February 1969 from assignment to the 198th Infantry Brigade and assigned to the 23d Infantry Division.

Campaign Participation Credit

War of 1812
  *Canada
  *Chippewa
  *Lundy's Lane

Mexican War
  *Vera Cruz
  *Cerro Gordo
  *Churubusco
  *Molino del Rey
  *Chapultepec

Civil War
  *Peninsula
  *Manassas
  *Antietam
  *Fredericksburg
  Chancellorsville
  Gettysburg
  *Virginia 1862

Indian Wars
  *Seminoles
  *Black Hawk
  *Little Big Horn
  Cheyennes
  Utes
  *South Dakota 1823
  *Kansas 1829
  *Nebraska 1855
  Kansas 1857
  *Nevada 1860
  North Dakota 1872
  North Dakota 1873
  Montana 1879

War With Spain
  *Santiago

Philippine Insurrection
  Jolo
  Negros 1899
  *Panay 1900

Mexican Expedition
  *Mexico 1916–1917

World War I
  *St. Mihiel
  *Meuse-Argonne
  *Alsace 1918
  *Lorraine 1918

World War II
  *Algeria-French Morocco
    (with arrowhead)
  *Tunisia
  *Naples-Foggia
  *Anzio
  *Rome-Arno
  *North Apennines
  *Po Valley

Vietnam
  *Counteroffensive, Phase III
  *Tet Counteroffensive
  (other campaigns to be
    determined)

Decorations

*Presidential Unit Citation (Army), Streamer embroidered MT. PORCHIA (6th Armored Infantry cited; WD GO's 57, 65, and 78, all 1947)

Presidential Unit Citation (Army), Streamer embroidered ORAN, ALGERIA

*Valorous Unit Award, Streamer embroidered LO GIANG (1st Battalion, 6th Infantry cited; DA GO 73, 1968)

2d BATTALION, 6th INFANTRY

(The Regulars)

RA
(United States Army Berlin Brigade)

LINEAGE

Constituted 11 January 1812 in the Regular Army as a company of the 11th Infantry. Organized March–May 1812 in Vermont, New Hampshire or Connecticut. Consolidated May–October 1815 with a company of the 25th Infantry (constituted 26 June 1812) and a company each of the 27th, 29th, and 37th Infantry (all constituted 29 January 1813) to form a company of the 6th Infantry. Designated 22 May 1816 as Company B, 6th Infantry. Consolidated 1 May 1869 with Company B, 42d Infantry, Veteran Reserve Corps (constituted 21 September 1866) and consolidated unit designated as Company B, 6th Infantry. (6th Infantry assigned 18 November 1917 to the 5th Division; relieved in August 1921 from assignment to the 5th Division; assigned 24 March 1923 to the 6th Division; relieved 16 October 1939 from assignment to the 6th Division.)

Reorganized 15 July 1940 as Company B, 6th Infantry (Armored), an element of the 1st Armored Division. Redesignated 1 January 1942 as Company B, 6th Armored Infantry. Reorganized and redesignated 20 July 1944 as Company B, 6th Armored Infantry Battalion, an element of the 1st Armored Division. Converted and redesignated 1 May 1946 as Troop B, 12th Constabulary Squadron, an element of the 1st Constabulary Regiment. Inactivated 20 September 1947 at Fritzlar, Germany. Converted and redesignated 10 October 1950 as Company B, 6th Infantry (concurrently, 12th Constabulary Squadron relieved from assignment to the 1st Constabulary Regiment). Activated 16 October 1950 at Grafenwohr, Germany.

Reorganized and redesignated 1 June 1958 as Headquarters and Headquarters Company, 2d Battle Group, 6th Infantry (concurrently, organic elements [constituted 2 May 1958] activated). Reorganized and redesignated 1 September 1963 as the 2d Battalion, 6th Infantry and assigned to the United States Army Berlin Brigade.

208

CAMPAIGN PARTICIPATION CREDIT

War of 1812
 *Canada
 *Chippewa
 *Lundy's Lane

Mexican War
 Vera Cruz
 Cerro Gordo
 *Churubusco
 *Molino del Rey
 *Chapultepec

Civil War
 *Peninsula
 *Manassas
 *Antietam
 *Fredericksburg
 Chancellorsville
 Gettysburg
 *Virginia 1862

Indian Wars
 *Seminoles
 *Black Hawk
 *Little Big Horn
 Cheyennes
 Utes
 *South Dakota 1823
 *Kansas 1829
 Nebraska 1855
 Kansas 1857

*North Dakota 1872
*North Dakota 1873
 Montana 1879

War With Spain
 *Santiago

Philippine Insurrection
 Jolo
 Negros 1899
 Panay 1900

Mexican Expedition
 *Mexico 1916–1917

World War I
 *St. Mihiel
 *Meuse-Argonne
 *Alsace 1918
 *Lorraine 1918

World War II
 *Algeria-French Morocco
  (with arrowhead)
 *Tunisia
 *Naples-Foggia
 *Anzio
 *Rome-Arno
 *North Apennines
 *Po Valley

DECORATIONS

*Presidential Unit Citation (Army), Streamer embroidered MT. PORCHIA (6th Armored Infantry cited; WD GO's 57, 65, and 78, all 1947)

Presidential Unit Citation (Army), Streamer embroidered ORAN, ALGERIA

3d BATTALION, 6th INFANTRY

(The Regulars)

RA
(United States Army Berlin Brigade)

LINEAGE

Constituted 11 January 1812 in the Regular Army as a company of the 11th Infantry. Organized March–May 1812 in Vermont, New Hampshire, or Connecticut. Consolidated May–October 1815 with a company of the 25th Infantry (constituted 26 June 1812) and a company each of the 27th, 29th, and 37th Infantry (all constituted 29 January 1813) to form a company of the 6th Infantry. Designated 22 May 1816 as Company C, 6th Infantry. Consolidated 1 May 1869 with Company C, 42d Infantry, Veteran Reserve Corps (constituted 21 September 1866) and consolidated unit designated as Company C, 6th Infantry. (6th Infantry assigned 18 November 1917 to the 5th Division; relieved in August 1921 from assignment to the 5th Division; assigned 24 March 1923 to the 6th Division; relieved 16 October 1939 from assignment to the 6th Division.)

Reorganized 15 July 1940 as Company C, 6th Infantry (Armored), an element of the 1st Armored Division. Redesignated 1 January 1942 as Company C, 6th Armored Infantry. Reorganized and redesignated 20 July 1944 as Company C, 6th Armored Infantry Battalion, an element of the 1st Armored Division. Converted and redesignated 1 May 1946 as Troop C, 12th Constabulary Squadron, an element of the 1st Constabulary Regiment. Inactivated 20 September 1947 at Fritzlar, Germany. Converted and redesignated 10 October 1950 as Company C, 6th Infantry (concurrently, 12th Constabulary Squadron relieved from assignment to the 1st Constabulary Regiment). Activated 16 October 1950 at Grafenwohr, Germany.

Reorganized and redesignated 1 June 1958 as Headquarters and Headquarters Company, 3d Battle Group, 6th Infantry (concurrently, organic elements [constituted 2 May 1958] activated). Reorganized and redesignated 1 September 1963 as the 3d Battalion, 6th Infantry and assigned to the United States Army Berlin Brigade.

210

Campaign Participation Credit

War of 1812
  *Canada
  *Chippewa
  *Lundy's Lane

Mexican War
  *Vera Cruz
  *Cerro Gordo
  *Churubusco
  *Molino del Rey
  *Chapultepec

Civil War
  *Peninsula
  *Manassas
  *Antietam
  *Fredericksburg
  Chancellorsville
  Gettysburg
  *Virginia 1862

Indian Wars
  Seminoles
  *Black Hawk
  *Little Big Horn
  *Cheyennes
  *Utes
  South Dakota 1823
  Kansas 1829
  Nebraska 1855
  *Kansas 1857

  *North Dakota 1872
  *North Dakota 1873
  *Montana 1879

War With Spain
  *Santiago

Philippine Insurrection
  Jolo
  Negros 1899
  *Panay 1900

Mexican Expedition
  *Mexico 1916–1917

World War I
  *St. Mihiel
  *Meuse-Argonne
  *Alsace 1918
  *Lorraine 1918

World War II
  *Algeria-French Morocco
    (with arrowhead)
  *Tunisia
  *Naples-Foggia
  *Anzio
  *Rome-Arno
  *North Apennines
  *Po Valley

Decorations

*Presidential Unit Citation (Army), Streamer embroidered MT. PORCHIA (6th Armored Infantry cited; WD GO's 57, 65, and 78, all 1947)

Presidential Unit Citation (Army), Streamer embroidered ORAN, ALGERIA

4th BATTALION, 6th INFANTRY

(The Regulars)

AR
(inactive)

Constituted 11 January 1812 in the Regular Army as a company of the 11th Infantry. Organized March–May 1812 in Vermont, New Hampshire, or Connecticut. Consolidated May–October 1815 with a company of the 25th Infantry (constituted 26 June 1812) and a company each of the 27th, 29th, and 37th Infantry (all constituted 29 January 1813) to form a company of the 6th Infantry. Designated 22 May 1816 as Company D, 6th Infantry. Consolidated 1 May 1869 with Company D, 42d Infantry, Veteran Reserve Corps (constituted 21 September 1866) and consolidated unit designated as Company D, 6th Infantry. (6th Infantry assigned 18 November 1917 to the 5th Division; relieved in August 1921 from assignment to the 5th Division; assigned 24 March 1923 to the 6th Division; relieved 16 October 1939 from assignment to the 6th Division.)

Reorganized 15 July 1940 as Company D, 6th Infantry (Armored), an element of the 1st Armored Division. Redesignated 1 January 1942 as Company D, 6th Armored Infantry. Reorganized and redesignated 20 July 1944 as Company A, 11th Armored Infantry Battalion, an element of the 1st Armored Division. Converted and redesignated 1 May 1946 as Troop A, 11th Constabulary Squadron, an element of the 1st Constabulary Regiment. Inactivated 20 September 1947 at Fritzlar, Germany. Converted and redesignated 7 April 1949 as Company A, 11th Armored Infantry Battalion (concurrently, 11th Constabulary Squadron relieved from assignment to the 1st Constabulary Regiment). Redesignated 10 October 1950 as Company D, 6th Infantry. Activated 16 October 1950 at Grafenwohr, Germany. Inactivated 1 June 1958 in Germany.

Redesignated 11 May 1959 as Headquarters and Headquarters Company, 4th Battle Group, 6th Infantry, withdrawn from the Regular Army, allotted to the Army Reserve, and assigned to the 102d Infantry Division (organic elements concurrently constituted). Battle Group activated 1 June 1959 with Headquarters at St. Louis, Missouri (concurrently, Headquarters and Headquarters Company consolidated with Headquarters and Headquarters Company, 407th Infantry [see ANNEX] and consolidated unit designated as Headquarters and Headquarters Company, 4th Battle

Group, 6th Infantry) . Reorganized and redesignated 1 April 1963 as the
4th Battalion, 6th Infantry. Inactivated 31 December 1965 at St. Louis,
Missouri.

ANNEX

Constituted 24 June 1921 in the Organized Reserves as Headquarters
and Headquarters Company, 407th Infantry, an element of the 102d
Division (later redesignated as the 102d Infantry Division) . Organized in
November 1921 at St. Louis, Missouri. Ordered into active military
service 15 September 1942 and reorganized at Camp Maxey, Texas.
Inactivated 16 March 1946 at Camp Kilmer, New Jersey.

Activated 7 April 1947 in the Organized Reserves at Danville, Illinois.
Location changed 15 March 1948 to St. Louis, Missouri. (Organized
Reserves redesignated 25 March 1948 as the Organized Reserve Corps;
redesignated 9 July 1952 as the Army Reserve.) Consolidated 1 June
1959 with Headquarters and Headquarters Company, 4th Battle Group,
6th Infantry and consolidated unit designated as Headquarters and Headquarters Company, 4th Battle Group, 6th Infantry (remainder of 407th
Infantry inactivated) .

CAMPAIGN PARTICIPATION CREDIT

War of 1812
 *Canada
 *Chippewa
 *Lundy's Lane

Mexican War
 *Vera Cruz
 *Cerro Gordo
 *Churubusco
 *Molino del Rey
 *Chapultepec

Civil War
 *Peninsula
 *Manassas
 *Antietam
 *Fredericksburg
 *Chancellorsville
 *Gettysburg
 *Virginia 1862

Indian Wars
 Seminoles
 *Black Hawk
 *Little Big Horn
 Cheyennes
 Utes
 *South Dakota 1823
 Kansas 1829
 Nebraska 1855
 *Kansas 1857
 North Dakota 1872

North Dakota 1873
Montana 1879

War With Spain
 *Santiago

Philippine Insurrection
 Jolo
 Negros 1899
 Panay 1900

Mexican Expedition
 *Mexico 1916–1917

World War I
 *St. Mihiel
 *Meuse-Argonne
 *Alsace 1918
 *Lorraine 1918

World War II
 *Algeria-French Morocco
  (with arrowhead)
 *Tunisia
 *Naples-Foggia
 *Anzio
 *Rome-Arno
 *North Apennines
 *Po Valley
 *Rhineland
 *Central Europe

DECORATIONS

*Presidential Unit Citation (Army), Streamer embroidered MT. PORCHIA (6th Armored Infantry cited; WD GO's 57, 65, and 78, all 1947)

Presidential Unit Citation (Army), Streamer embroidered ORAN, ALGERIA

5th BATTALION, 6th INFANTRY

(The Regulars)

RA
(1st Armored Division)

LINEAGE

Constituted 11 January 1812 in the Regular Army as a company of the 11th Infantry. Organized March–May 1812 in Vermont, New Hampshire, or Connecticut. Consolidated May–October 1815 with a company of the 25th Infantry (constituted 26 June 1812) and a company each of the 27th, 29th, and 37th Infantry (all constituted 29 January 1813) to form a company of the 6th Infantry. Designated 22 May 1816 as Company E, 6th Infantry. Consolidated 1 May 1869 with Company E, 42d Infantry, Veteran Reserve Corps (constituted 21 September 1866) and consolidated unit designated as Company E, 6th Infantry. (6th Infantry assigned 18 November 1917 to the 5th Division; relieved in August 1921 from assignment to the 5th Division; assigned 24 March 1923 to the 6th Division; relieved 16 October 1939 from assignment to the 6th Division.)

Reorganized 15 July 1940 as Company E, 6th Infantry (Armored), an element of the 1st Armored Division. Redesignated 1 January 1942 as Company E, 6th Armored Infantry. Reorganized and redesignated 20 July 1944 as Company B, 11th Armored Infantry Battalion, an element of the 1st Armored Division. Converted and redesignated 1 May 1946 as Troop B, 11th Constabulary Squadron, an element of the 1st Constabulary Regiment. Inactivated 20 September 1947 at Fritzlar, Germany. Converted and redesignated 7 April 1949 as Company B, 11th Armored Infantry Battalion (concurrently, 11th Constabulary Squadron relieved from assignment to the 1st Constabulary Regiment). Redesignated 10 October 1950 as Company E, 6th Infantry. Activated 16 October 1950 at Grafenwohr, Germany.

Inactivated 1 June 1958 in Germany; concurrently, redesignated as Headquarters and Headquarters Company, 5th Battle Group, 6th Infantry. Redesignated 3 February 1962 as Headquarters and Headquarters Company, 5th Battalion, 6th Infantry, assigned to the 1st Armored Division, and activated at Fort Hood, Texas (organic elements concurrently constituted and activated).

215

Campaign Participation Credit

War of 1812
 *Canada
 *Chippewa
 *Lundy's Lane

Mexican War
 Vera Cruz
 Cerro Gordo
 *Churubusco
 *Molino del Rey
 *Chapultepec

Civil War
 *Peninsula
 *Manassas
 *Antietam
 *Fredericksburg
 *Chancellorsville
 Gettysburg
 *Virginia 1862

Indian Wars
 Seminoles
 *Black Hawk
 Little Big Horn
 Cheyennes
 Utes
 *South Dakota 1823
 Kansas 1829
 *Nebraska 1855
 Kansas 1857

North Dakota 1872
North Dakota 1873
Montana 1879

War With Spain
 *Santiago

Philippine Insurrection
 Jolo
 *Negros 1899
 Panay 1900

Mexican Expedition
 *Mexico 1916–1917

World War I
 *St. Mihiel
 *Meuse-Argonne
 *Alsace 1918
 *Lorraine 1918

World War II
 *Algeria-French Morocco
  (with arrowhead)
 *Tunisia
 *Naples-Foggia
 *Anzio
 *Rome-Arno
 *North Apennines
 *Po Valley

Decorations

*Presidential Unit Citation (Army), Streamer embroidered MT. PORCHIA (6th Armored Infantry cited; WD GO's 57, 65, and 78, all 1947)

Presidential Unit Citation (Army), Streamer embroidered ORAN, ALGERIA

*Presidential Unit Citation (Army), Streamer embroidered PALAZZO (Company B, 11th Armored Infantry Battalion cited; WD GO 64, 1947)

6th BATTALION, 6th INFANTRY

(The Regulars)

AR
(inactive)

LINEAGE

Constituted 11 January 1812 in the Regular Army as a company of the 11th Infantry. Organized March–May 1812 in Vermont, New Hampshire, or Connecticut. Consolidated May–October 1815 with a company of the 25th Infantry (constituted 26 June 1812) and a company each of the 27th, 29th, and 37th Infantry (all constituted 29 January 1813) to form a company of the 6th Infantry. Designated 22 May 1816 as Company F, 6th Infantry. Consolidated 1 May 1869 with Company F, 42d Infantry, Veteran Reserve Corps (constituted 21 September 1866) and consolidated unit designated as Company F, 6th Infantry. (6th Infantry assigned 18 November 1917 to the 5th Division; relieved in August 1921 from assignment to the 5th Division; assigned 24 March 1923 to the 6th Division; relieved 16 October 1939 from assignment to the 6th Division.)

Reorganized 15 July 1940 as Company F, 6th Infantry (Armored), an element of the 1st Armored Division. Redesignated 1 January 1942 as Company F, 6th Armored Infantry. Reorganized and redesignated 20 July 1944 as Company C, 11th Armored Infantry Battalion, an element of the 1st Armored Division. Converted and redesignated 1 May 1946 as Troop C, 11th Constabulary Squadron, an element of the 1st Constabulary Regiment. Inactivated 20 September 1947 at Fritzlar, Germany. Converted and redesignated 7 April 1949 as Company C, 11th Armored Infantry Battalion (concurrently, 11th Constabulary Squadron relieved from assignment to the 1st Constabulary Regiment). Redesignated 10 October 1950 as Company F, 6th Infantry. Activated 16 October 1950 at Grafenwohr, Germany.

Inactivated 1 June 1958 in Germany; concurrently, redesignated as Headquarters and Headquarters Company, 6th Battle Group, 6th Infantry. Redesignated 26 March 1963 as Headquarters and Headquarters Company, 6th Battalion, 6th Infantry, withdrawn from the Regular Army, allotted to the Army Reserve, and assigned to the 102d Infantry Division (organic elements concurrently constituted). Battalion activated 1 April 1963 with Headquarters at St. Louis, Missouri. Inactivated 31 December 1965 at St. Louis, Missouri.

Campaign Participation Credit

War of 1812
 *Canada
 *Chippewa
 *Lundy's Lane

Mexican War
 *Vera Cruz
 *Cerro Gordo
 *Churubusco
 *Molino del Rey
 *Chapultepec

Civil War
 *Peninsula
 *Manassas
 *Antietam
 *Fredericksburg
 *Chancellorsville
 *Gettysburg
 *Virginia 1862

Indian Wars
 *Seminoles
 Black Hawk
 Little Big Horn
 *Cheyennes
 Utes
 *South Dakota 1823
 Kansas 1829
 Nebraska 1855
 Kansas 1857

North Dakota 1872
North Dakota 1873
Montana 1879

War With Spain
 *Santiago

Philippine Insurrection
 Jolo
 *Negros 1899
 Panay 1900

Mexican Expedition
 *Mexico 1916–1917

World War I
 *St. Mihiel
 *Meuse-Argonne
 *Alsace 1918
 *Lorraine 1918

World War II
 *Algeria-French Morocco
  (with arrowhead)
 *Tunisia
 *Naples-Foggia
 *Anzio
 *Rome-Arno
 *North Apennines
 *Po Valley

Decorations

*Presidential Unit Citation (Army), Streamer embroidered MT. PORCHIA (6th Armored Infantry cited; WD GO's 57, 65, and 78, all 1947)

Presidential Unit Citation (Army), Streamer embroidered ORAN, ALGERIA

7th BATTALION, 6th INFANTRY

(The Regulars)

RA
(inactive)

LINEAGE

Constituted 11 January 1812 in the Regular Army as a company of the 11th Infantry. Organized March–May 1812 in Vermont, New Hampshire, or Connecticut. Consolidated May–October 1815 with a company of the 25th Infantry (constituted 26 June 1812) and a company each of the 27th, 29th, and 37th Infantry (all constituted 29 January 1813) to form a company of the 6th Infantry. Designated 22 May 1816 as Company G, 6th Infantry. Consolidated 1 May 1869 with Company G, 42d Infantry, Veteran Reserve Corps (constituted 21 September 1866) and consolidated unit designated as Company G, 6th Infantry. (6th Infantry assigned 18 November 1917 to the 5th Division; relieved in August 1921 from assignment to the 5th Division; assigned 24 March 1923 to the 6th Division; relieved 16 October 1939 from assignment to the 6th Division.)

Reorganized 15 July 1940 as Company G, 6th Infantry (Armored), an element of the 1st Armored Division. Redesignated 1 January 1942 as Company G, 6th Armored Infantry. Reorganized and redesignated 20 July 1944 as Company A, 14th Armored Infantry Battalion, an element of the 1st Armored Division. Converted and redesignated 1 May 1946 as Troop A, 14th Constabulary Squadron, an element of the 15th Constabulary Regiment. Inactivated 20 December 1948 at Blaufeldin, Germany; concurrently, converted and redesignated as Company A, 14th Armored Infantry Battalion, an element of the 1st Armored Division. Redesignated 10 October 1950 as Company G, 6th Infantry (concurrently, 14th Armored Infantry Battalion relieved from assignment to the 1st Armored Division). Activated 16 October 1950 at Grafenwohr, Germany.

Inactivated 1 June 1958 in Germany; concurrently, redesignated as Headquarters and Headquarters Company, 7th Battle Group, 6th Infantry. Redesignated 9 May 1967 as Headquarters and Headquarters Company, 7th Battalion, 6th Infantry and assigned to the 1st Armored Division (organic elements concurrently constituted). Battalion activated 12 May 1967 at Fort Hood, Texas. Relieved 20 October 1967 from assignment to the 1st Armored Division and assigned to the 2d Armored Division. Inactivated 16 December 1970 at Fort Hood, Texas.

Campaign Participation Credit

War of 1812
 *Canada
 *Chippewa
 *Lundy's Lane

Mexican War
 Vera Cruz
 Cerro Gordo
 Churubusco
 Molino del Rey
 Chapultepec

Civil War
 *Peninsula
 *Manassas
 *Antietam
 *Fredericksburg
 *Chancellorsville
 *Gettysburg
 *Virginia 1862

Indian Wars
 *Seminoles
 *Black Hawk
 *Little Big Horn
 Cheyennes
 Utes
 *South Dakota 1823
 Kansas 1829
 Nebraska 1855
 *Kansas 1857

North Dakota 1872
North Dakota 1873
Montana 1879

War With Spain
 *Santiago

Philippine Insurrection
 Jolo
 *Negros 1899
 Panay 1900

Mexican Expedition
 *Mexico 1916–1917

World War I
 *St. Mihiel
 *Meuse-Argonne
 *Alsace 1918
 *Lorraine 1918

World War II
 *Algeria-French Morocco
  (with arrowhead)
 *Tunisia
 *Naples-Foggia
 *Anzio
 *Rome-Arno
 *North Apennines
 *Po Valley

Decorations

*Presidential Unit Citation (Army), Streamer embroidered MT. PORCHIA (6th Armored Infantry cited; WD GO's 57, 65, and 78, all 1947)

*Presidential Unit Citation (Army), Streamer embroidered ORAN, ALGERIA (3d Battalion, 6th Armored Infantry cited; WD GO 18, 1943)

6TH INFANTRY, BIBLIOGRAPHY

Babcock, Elkanah. *A War History of the Sixth U.S. Infantry, From 1798 to 1903, With Rosters and Memorials of the Cuban and Philippine Campaigns.* Kansas City, Missouri: Hudson-Kimberly Publishing Company, 1903. (Erroneously connects this regiment with an earlier one of the same designation.)

Bandel, Eugene. *Frontier Life in the Army.* Translated by Olga Brandel and Richard Gente. Edited by Ralph P. Bieber. Glendale: Arthur H. Clarke Company, 1932. (The Southwest Historical Series, II.)

Byrne, Charles. "The Sixth Regiment of Infantry," *The Army of the United States,* edited by Theophilus F. Rodenbough and William L. Haskin. New York: Maynard, Merrill and Company, 1896, pp. 480–497. (Originally published in the *Journal of the Military Service Institution of the United States,* XV [1894], 642–659.)

————. *The Sixth United States Infantry, An Historical Sketch.* Fort Thomas, Kentucky; Regimental Press, 1893.

Cooke, Philip St. George. *Scenes and Adventures in the Army: Or, Romance of Military Life.* Philadelphia, 1859.

Gardner, Hamilton. "A Young West Pointer [Philip St. George Cooke] Reports for Duty at Jefferson Barracks in 1827," *Missouri Historical Society Bulletin,* IX (1952/53), 124–138.

Historical Section, War Department. *Anzio Beachhead.* American Forces in Action Series. Washington: Government Printing Office, 1947.

————. *Fifth Army at the Winter Line.* American Forces in Action Series. Washington: Government Printing Office, 1945.

————. *To Bizerte with the II Corps.* American Forces in Action Series. Washington: Government Printing Office, 1943.

Howe, George F. *Northwest Africa: Seizing the Initiative in the West.* United States Army in World War II. Washington: Government Printing Office, 1957.

Layton, Ruth. *Jefferson Barracks and the Sixth Infantry.* St. Louis: Layton, Layton and Associates (6th U.S. Infantry Association), 1961.

Mahon, John K. *History of the Second Seminole War, 1835–1842.* Gainesville: University of Florida Press, 1967.

Owens, Oscar Lee. *A Brief Historical Sketch of the Sixth United States Infantry, 1798–1918.* 2d edition. n.p., 1919? (Erroneously connects this regiment with an earlier one of the same designation.)

"Program, Regimental Day Exercises of the Sixth Regiment of Infantry, United States Army, Jefferson Barracks, Missouri, November Fourth, 1925." n.p., 1925.

Register of Commissioned Officers of the Sixth Regiment of Infantry,

U.S. Army. Commanded by Colonel Melville.A. Cochran. From 1808 to 1896. Fort Thomas, Kentucky: Regimental Press, 1896. (Erroneously connects this regiment with an earlier one of the same designation.)

Roster of Commissioned Officers of the Sixth U.S. Infantry, Commanded by Colonel Joseph W. Duncan. Zamboanga, Mindanao, Philippine Islands: Sixth Infantry Press, 1906.

Sheehan, Fred. *Anzio.* Norman: University of Oklahoma Press, 1964.

Simmonds, B. and E. R. Christian. "The Sixth and Sixteenth Regiments of Infantry," *The Santiago Campaign.* Richmond: Williams Printing Company, 1927, pp. 66–89.

Sprague, John T. *The Origin, Progress and Conclusion of the Florida War.* New York: D. Appleton and Company, 1848. (Reprint. Gainesville: University of Florida Press, 1964.)

Todd, John Blair Smith. "The Harney Expedition against the Sioux, The Journal of Captain John S. Todd," edited by Ray H. Mattison, *The Nebraska History,* XLII (1962), 89–130.

7th INFANTRY
(Cottonbalers)

Heraldic Items

Coat of Arms

Shield: Per fess argent and azure, a fess embattled to chief or masoned sable between in chief a field gun gules on a mount vert and in base three bendlets sinister of the first. (And for informal use, pendant from the shield, a French Croix de Guerre with Gilt Star proper.)

Crest: On a wreath of the colors a cotton bale argent banded sable in front of two bayonets in saltire or.

Motto: *Volens et Potens* (Willing and Able).

Symbolism: The shield is white and blue, the old and present infantry colors. The field gun is for the battle of Cerro Gordo, where the 7th participated in the decisive attack by an assault on Telegraph Hill, a strongly fortified point. This portion of the shield is in the Mexican colors—red, white, and green. The wall is for the battle of Fredericksburg in which the regiment held for twelve hours a position only eighty yards in front of a stone wall protecting the enemy. The base alludes to the shoulder sleeve insignia of the 3d Division with which the 7th Infantry served during World War I. The French Croix de Guerre with Gilt Star was awarded to the regiment for action in the Aisne-Marne campaign of that war.

The cotton bale and bayonets in the crest are taken from the arms of the 7th Infantry adopted in 1912.

Distinctive Insignia

The distinctive insignia is the crest of the coat of arms encircled by a ribbon bearing the motto of the coat of arms.

223

Lineage and Honors

LINEAGE

Constituted 11 January 1812 in the Regular Army as the 8th Infantry. Organized in 1812 in Tennessee, Georgia, and the adjacent territories. Consolidated May–October 1815 with the 24th Infantry (constituted 26 June 1812) and the 39th Infantry (constituted 29 January 1813) to form the 7th Infantry. Consolidated May–June 1869 with the 36th Infantry (see ANNEX) and consolidated unit designated as the 7th Infantry. Assigned 21 November 1917 to the 3d Division (later redesignated as the 3d Infantry Division).

Relieved 1 July 1957 from assignment to the 3d Infantry Division and reorganized as a parent regiment under the Combat Arms Regimental System.

ANNEX

Constituted 3 May 1861 in the Regular Army as the 3d Battalion, 18th Infantry. Organized 16 October 1861 at Camp Thomas, Ohio. Reorganized and redesignated 26 December 1866 as the 36th Infantry. Consolidated May–June 1869 with the 7th Infantry and consolidated unit designated as the 7th Infantry.

CAMPAIGN PARTICIPATION CREDIT

War of 1812
Canada
New Orleans
Florida 1814
Louisiana 1815

Mexican War
Monterey
Vera Cruz
Cerro Gordo
Contreras
Churubusco
Molino del Rey
Chapultepec
Texas 1846

Civil War
Fredericksburg
Murfreesborough
Chancellorsville
Gettysburg
Chickamauga
Chattanooga
Atlanta
New Mexico 1861
New Mexico 1862
Tennessee 1862
Mississippi 1862
Kentucky 1862
Tennessee 1863
Georgia 1864

Indian Wars
Creeks
Seminoles
Little Big Horn
Nez Perces
Utes
Pine Ridge
New Mexico 1860
Wyoming 1866
Montana 1872

War With Spain
Santiago

Philippine Insurrection
Samar 1901
Samar 1902

World War I
Aisne
Champagne-Marne
Aisne-Marne
St. Mihiel
Meuse-Argonne
Ile de France 1918
Champagne 1918

World War II
Algeria-French Morocco
(with arrowhead)
Tunisia
Sicily (with arrowhead)
Naples-Foggia
Anzio (with arrowhead)
Rome-Arno
Southern France
(with arrowhead)
Rhineland
Ardennes-Alsace
Central Europe

Korean War
CCF intervention
First UN counteroffensive
CCF spring offensive
UN summer-fall offensive
Second Korean winter
Korea, summer-fall 1952
Third Korean winter
Korea, summer 1953

Vietnam
Counteroffensive, Phase II
Counteroffensive, Phase III
Tet Counteroffensive
(other campaigns to be
determined)

DECORATIONS

Presidential Unit Citation (Army), Streamer embroidered COLMAR
(3d Infantry Division cited; WD GO 44, 1945)

Presidential Unit Citation (Army), Streamer embroidered CHOKSONG
(1st Battalion, 7th Infantry cited; DA GO 79, 1951)

Presidential Unit Citation (Army), Streamer embroidered SEGOK (3d Battalion, 7th Infantry cited; DA GO 33, 1952)

Presidential Unit Citation (Army), Streamer embroidered KOWANG-NI (2d Battalion, 7th Infantry and attached units cited; DA GO 71, 1952)

Valorous Unit Award, Streamer embroidered SAIGON–LONG BINH (3d Battalion, 7th Infantry cited; DA GO 48, 1968)

French Croix de Guerre with Gilt Star, World War I, Streamer embroidered AISNE-MARNE (7th Infantry cited; WD GO 11, 1924)

French Croix de Guerre with Palm, World War II, Streamer embroidered COLMAR (7th Infantry cited; DA GO 43, 1950)

French Croix de Guerre, World War II, Fourragere (7th Infantry cited; DA GO 43, 1950)

Republic of Korea Presidential Unit Citation, Streamer embroidered UIJONGBU CORRIDOR (7th Infantry cited; DA GO 20, 1953)

Republic of Korea Presidential Unit Citation, Streamer embroidered IRON TRIANGLE (7th Infantry cited; DA GO 29, 1954)

Chryssoun Aristion Andrias (Bravery Gold Medal of Greece), Streamer embroidered KOREA (7th Infantry cited; DA GO 2, 1956)

1st BATTALION, 7th INFANTRY

(Cottonbalers)

RA
(3d Infantry Division)

LINEAGE

Constituted 11 January 1812 in the Regular Army as a company of the 8th Infantry. Organized in 1812 in Tennessee, Georgia, or the adjacent territories. Consolidated May–October 1815 with a company of the 24th Infantry (constituted 26 June 1812) and a company of the 39th Infantry (constituted 29 January 1813) to form a company of the 7th Infantry. Designated 21 August 1816 as Company A, 7th Infantry. Consolidated 26 May 1869 with Company A, 36th Infantry (see ANNEX) and consolidated unit designated as Company A, 7th Infantry. (7th Infantry assigned 21 November 1917 to the 3d Division [later redesignated as the 3d Infantry Division].)

Reorganized and redesignated 1 July 1957 as Headquarters and Headquarters Company, 1st Battle Group, 7th Infantry, and remained assigned to the 3d Infantry Division (organic elements concurrently constituted and activated). Reorganized and redesignated 20 June 1963 as the 1st Battalion, 7th Infantry.

ANNEX

Constituted 3 May 1861 in the Regular Army as Company A, 3d Battalion, 18th Infantry. Organized in December 1861 at Camp Thomas, Ohio. Reorganized and redesignated 26 December 1866 as Company A, 36th Infantry. Consolidated 26 May 1869 with Company A, 7th Infantry and consolidated unit designated as Company A, 7th Infantry.

CAMPAIGN PARTICIPATION CREDIT

War of 1812
  *Canada
  New Orleans
  *Florida 1814
  Louisiana 1815

Mexican War
  *Monterey
  Vera Cruz
  Cerro Gordo
  *Contreras
  *Churubusco
  *Molino del Rey
  *Chapultepec
  *Texas 1846

Civil War
  *Fredericksburg
  Murfreesborough
  *Chancellorsville
  *Gettysburg
  Chickamauga
  Chattanooga
  Atlanta
  *New Mexico 1861
  New Mexico 1862
  Tennessee 1862
  *Mississippi 1862
  *Kentucky 1862
  Tennessee 1863
  Georgia 1864

Indian Wars
  *Creeks
  *Seminoles
  *Little Big Horn
  *Nez Perces
  Utes
  Pine Ridge
  *New Mexico 1860
  *Wyoming 1866
  Montana 1872

War With Spain
  *Santiago

Philippine Insurrection
  Samar 1901
  Samar 1902

World War I
  *Aisne
  *Champagne-Marne
  *Aisne-Marne
  *St. Mihiel
  *Meuse-Argonne
  *Ile de France 1918
  *Champagne 1918

World War II
  *Algeria-French Morocco
    (with arrowhead)
  *Tunisia
  *Sicily (with arrowhead)
  *Naples-Foggia
  *Anzio (with arrowhead)
  *Rome-Arno
  *Southern France
    (with arrowhead)
  *Rhineland
  *Ardennes-Alsace
  *Central Europe

Korean War
  *CCF intervention
  *First UN counteroffensive
  *CCF spring offensive
  *UN summer-fall offensive
  *Second Korean winter
  *Korea, summer-fall 1952
  *Third Korean winter
  *Korea, summer 1953

DECORATIONS

*Presidential Unit Citation (Army), Streamer embroidered COLMAR
(3d Infantry Division cited; WD GO 44, 1945)

*Presidential Unit Citation (Army), Streamer embroidered CHOKSONG
(1st Battalion, 7th Infantry cited; DA GO 79, 1951)

Presidential Unit Citation (Army), Streamer embroidered SEGOK

Presidential Unit Citation (Army), Streamer embroidered KOWANG-NI

*French Croix de Guerre with Gilt Star, World War I, Streamer embroidered AISNE-MARNE (7th Infantry cited; WD GO 11, 1924)

*French Croix de Guerre with Palm, World War II, Streamer embroidered COLMAR (7th Infantry cited; DA GO 43, 1950)

*French Croix de Guerre, World War II, Fourragere (7th Infantry cited; DA GO 43, 1950)

*Republic of Korea Presidential Unit Citation, Streamer embroidered UIJONGBU CORRIDOR (7th Infantry cited; DA GO 20, 1953)

*Republic of Korea Presidential Unit Citation, Streamer embroidered IRON TRIANGLE (7th Infantry cited; DA GO 29, 1954)

*Chryssoun Aristion Andrias (Bravery Gold Medal of Greece), Streamer embroidered KOREA (7th Infantry cited; DA GO 2, 1956)

2d BATTALION, 7th INFANTRY

(Cottonbalers)

RA
(inactive)

LINEAGE

Constituted 11 January 1812 in the Regular Army as a company of the 8th Infantry. Organized in 1812 in Tennessee, Georgia, or the adjacent territories. Consolidated May–October 1815 with a company of the 24th Infantry (constituted 26 June 1812) and a company of the 39th Infantry (constituted 29 January 1813) to form a company of the 7th Infantry. Designated 21 August 1816 as Company B, 7th Infantry. Consolidated 4 June 1869 with Company B, 36th Infantry (see ANNEX) and consolidated unit designated as Company B, 7th Infantry. (7th Infantry assigned 21 November 1917 to the 3d Division [later redesignated as the 3d Infantry Division].)

Reorganized and redesignated 1 July 1957 as Headquarters and Headquarters Company, 2d Battle Group, 7th Infantry, relieved from assignment to the 3d Infantry Division, and assigned to the 10th Infantry Division (organic elements concurrently constituted and activated). Inactivated 14 June 1958 at Fort Benning, Georgia. Redesignated 18 April 1963 as the 2d Battalion, 7th Infantry; concurrently, relieved from assignment to the 10th Infantry Division and assigned to the 3d Infantry Division. Activated 20 June 1963 in Germany. Inactivated 1 May 1966 in Germany.

ANNEX

Constituted 3 May 1861 in the Regular Army as Company B, 3d Battalion, 18th Infantry. Organized in December 1861 at Camp Thomas, Ohio. Reorganized and redesignated 26 December 1866 as Company B, 36th Infantry. Consolidated 4 June 1869 with Company B, 7th Infantry and consolidated unit designated as Company B, 7th Infantry.

230

CAMPAIGN PARTICIPATION CREDIT

War of 1812
*Canada
New Orleans
*Florida 1814
Louisiana 1815

Mexican War
Monterey
Vera Cruz
Cerro Gordo
*Contreras
*Churubusco
*Molino del Rey
*Chapultepec
*Texas 1846

Civil War
*Fredericksburg
*Murfreesborough
*Chancellorsville
*Gettysburg
Chickamauga
Chattanooga
Atlanta
*New Mexico 1861
New Mexico 1862
*Tennessee 1862
*Mississippi 1862
*Kentucky 1862
Tennessee 1863
Georgia 1864

Indian Wars
*Creeks
*Seminoles
*Little Big Horn
Nez Perces
*Utes
Pine Ridge
New Mexico 1860
Wyoming 1866
Montana 1872

War With Spain
*Santiago

Philippine Insurrection
Samar 1901
Samar 1902

World War I
*Aisne
*Champagne-Marne
*Aisne-Marne
*St. Mihiel
*Meuse-Argonne
*Ile de France 1918
*Champagne 1918

World War II
*Algeria-French Morocco
   (with arrowhead)
*Tunisia
*Sicily (with arrowhead)
*Naples-Foggia
*Anzio (with arrowhead)
*Rome-Arno
*Southern France
   (with arrowhead)
*Rhineland
*Ardennes-Alsace
*Central Europe

Korean War
*CCF intervention
*First UN counteroffensive
*CCF spring offensive
*UN summer-fall offensive
*Second Korean winter
*Korea, summer-fall 1952
*Third Korean winter
*Korea, summer 1953

DECORATIONS

   *Presidential Unit Citation (Army), Streamer embroidered COLMAR
(3d Infantry Division cited; WD GO 44, 1945)
   *Presidential Unit Citation (Army), Streamer embroidered CHOKSONG
(1st Battalion, 7th Infantry cited; DA GO 79, 1951)
   Presidential Unit Citation (Army), Streamer embroidered SEGOK
   Presidential Unit Citation (Army), Streamer embroidered KOWANG-NI

*French Croix de Guerre with Gilt Star, World War I, Streamer embroidered AISNE-MARNE (7th Infantry cited; WD GO 11, 1924)

*French Croix de Guerre with Palm, World War II, Streamer embroidered COLMAR (7th Infantry cited; DA GO 43, 1950)

*French Croix de Guerre, World War II, Fourragere (7th Infantry cited; DA GO 43, 1950)

*Republic of Korea Presidential Unit Citation, Streamer embroidered UIJONGBU CORRIDOR (7th Infantry cited; DA GO 20, 1953)

*Republic of Korea Presidential Unit Citation, Streamer embroidered IRON TRIANGLE (7th Infantry cited; DA GO 29, 1954)

*Chryssoun Aristion Andrias (Bravery Gold Medal of Greece), Streamer embroidered KOREA (7th Infantry cited; DA GO 2, 1956)

3d BATTALION, 7th INFANTRY

(Cottonbalers)

RA
(inactive)

LINEAGE

Constituted 11 January 1812 in the Regular Army as a company of the 8th Infantry. Organized in 1812 in Tennessee, Georgia, or the adjacent territories. Consolidated May–October 1815 with a company of the 24th Infantry (constituted 26 June 1812) and a company of the 39th Infantry (constituted 29 January 1813) to form a company of the 7th Infantry. Designated 21 August 1816 as Company C, 7th Infantry. Consolidated 26 May 1869 with Company C, 36th Infantry (see ANNEX) and consolidated unit designated as Company C, 7th Infantry. (7th Infantry assigned 21 November 1917 to the 3d Division [later redesignated as the 3d Infantry Division].)

Inactivated 1 July 1957 at Fort Benning, Georgia, and relieved from assignment to the 3d Infantry Division; concurrently, redesignated as Headquarters and Headquarters Company, 3d Battle Group, 7th Infantry. Withdrawn 11 May 1959 from the Regular Army, allotted to the Army Reserve, and assigned to the 102d Infantry Division (organic elements concurrently constituted). Battle Group activated 1 June 1959 with Headquarters at Danville, Illinois. Inactivated 1 April 1963 at Danville, Illinois, and relieved from assignment to the 102d Infantry Division.

Redesignated 23 March 1966 as the 3d Battalion, 7th Infantry; concurrently withdrawn from the Army Reserve, allotted to the Regular Army, and assigned to the 199th Infantry Brigade. Activated 1 June 1966 at Fort Benning, Georgia. Inactivated 15 October 1970 at Fort Benning, Georgia.

ANNEX

Constituted 3 May 1861 in the Regular Army as Company C, 3d Battalion, 18th Infantry. Organized in December 1861 at Camp Thomas, Ohio. Reorganized and redesignated 26 December 1866 as Company C, 36th Infantry. Consolidated 26 May 1869 with Company C, 7th Infantry and consolidated unit designated as Company C, 7th Infantry.

CAMPAIGN PARTICIPATION CREDIT

War of 1812
*Canada
New Orleans
*Florida 1814
Louisiana 1815

Mexican War
*Monterey
*Vera Cruz
*Cerro Gordo
*Contreras
*Churubusco
*Molino del Rey
*Chapultepec
*Texas 1846

Civil War
Fredericksburg
*Murfreesborough
*Chancellorsville
Gettysburg
Chickamauga
Chattanooga
Atlanta
New Mexico 1861
*New Mexico 1862
*Tennessee 1862
Mississippi 1862
*Kentucky 1862
*Tennessee 1863
Georgia 1864

Indian Wars
*Creeks
Seminoles
*Little Big Horn
*Nez Perces
*Utes
*Pine Ridge
New Mexico 1860
Wyoming 1866
*Montana 1872

War With Spain
*Santiago

Philippine Insurrection
Samar 1901
Samar 1902

World War I
*Aisne
*Champagne-Marne
*Aisne-Marne
*St. Mihiel
*Meuse-Argonne
*Ile de France 1918
*Champagne 1918

World War II
*Algeria-French Morocco
(with arrowhead)
*Tunisia
*Sicily (with arrowhead)
*Naples-Foggia
*Anzio (with arrowhead)
*Rome-Arno
*Southern France
(with arrowhead)
*Rhineland
*Ardennes-Alsace
*Central Europe

Korean War
*CCF intervention
*First UN counteroffensive
*CCF spring offensive
*UN summer-fall offensive
*Second Korean winter
*Korea, summer-fall 1952
*Third Korean winter
*Korea, summer 1953

Vietnam
*Counteroffensive, Phase II
*Counteroffensive, Phase III
*Tet Counteroffensive
(other campaigns to be
determined)

DECORATIONS

*Presidential Unit Citation (Army), Streamer embroidered COLMAR
(3d Infantry Division cited; WD GO 44, 1945)

*Presidential Unit Citation (Army), Streamer embroidered CHOKSONG
(1st Battalion, 7th Infantry cited; DA GO 79, 1951)

Presidential Unit Citation (Army), Streamer embroidered SEGOK

Presidential Unit Citation (Army), Streamer embroidered KOWANG-NI

*Valorous Unit Award, Streamer embroidered SAIGON–LONG BINH (3d Battalion, 7th Infantry cited; DA GO 48, 1968)

*French Croix de Guerre with Gilt Star, World War I, Streamer embroidered AISNE-MARNE (7th Infantry cited; WD GO 11, 1924)

*French Croix de Guerre with Palm, World War II, Streamer embroidered COLMAR (7th Infantry cited; DA GO 43, 1950)

*French Croix de Guerre, World War II, Fourragere (7th Infantry cited; DA GO 43, 1950)

*Republic of Korea Presidential Unit Citation, Streamer embroidered UIJONGBU CORRIDOR (7th Infantry cited; DA GO 20, 1953)

*Republic of Korea Presidential Unit Citation, Streamer embroidered IRON TRIANGLE (7th Infantry cited; DA GO 29, 1954)

*Chryssoun Aristion Andrias (Bravery Gold Medal of Greece), Streamer embroidered KOREA (7th Infantry cited; DA GO 2, 1956)

*Vietnamese Cross of Gallantry with Palm, Streamer embroidered VIETNAM 1968 (3d Battalion, 7th Infantry cited; DA GO 43, 1970)

4th BATTLE GROUP, 7th INFANTRY

(Cottonbalers)

RA
(inactive)

LINEAGE

Constituted 11 January 1812 in the Regular Army as a company of the 8th Infantry. Organized in 1812 in Tennessee, Georgia, or the adjacent territories. Consolidated May–October 1815 with a company of the 24th Infantry (constituted 26 June 1812) and a company of the 39th Infantry (constituted 29 January 1813) to form a company of the 7th Infantry. Designated 21 August 1816 as Company D, 7th Infantry. Consolidated 4 June 1869 with Company D, 36th Infantry (see ANNEX) and consolidated unit designated as Company D, 7th Infantry. (7th Infantry assigned 21 November 1917 to the 3d Division [later redesignated as the 3d Infantry Division].)

Inactivated 1 July 1957 at Fort Benning, Georgia, and relieved from assignment to the 3d Infantry Division; concurrently, redesignated as Headquarters and Headquarters Company, 4th Battle Group, 7th Infantry. (Organic elements constituted 18 July 1962.) Battle Group activated 24 September 1962 at Fort Benning, Georgia. Inactivated 15 February 1963 at Fort Benning, Georgia.

ANNEX

Constituted 3 May 1861 in the Regular Army as Company D, 3d Battalion, 18th Infantry. Organized in November 1861 at Camp Thomas, Ohio. Reorganized and redesignated 26 December 1866 as Company D, 36th Infantry. Consolidated 4 June 1869 with Company D, 7th Infantry and consolidated unit designated as Company D, 7th Infantry.

236

CAMPAIGN PARTICIPATION CREDIT

War of 1812
*Canada
New Orleans
*Florida 1814
Louisiana 1815

Mexican War
*Monterey
*Vera Cruz
*Cerro Gordo
*Contreras
*Churubusco
*Molino del Rey
*Chapultepec
*Texas 1846

Civil War
*Fredericksburg
*Murfreesborough
Chancellorsville
Gettysburg
Chickamauga
Chattanooga
Atlanta
*New Mexico 1861
New Mexico 1862
Tennessee 1862
Mississippi 1862
*Kentucky 1862
Tennessee 1863
Georgia 1864

Indian Wars
*Creeks
*Seminoles
Little Big Horn
*Nez Perces
Utes
*Pine Ridge
*New Mexico 1860
Wyoming 1866
Montana 1872

War With Spain
*Santiago

Philippine Insurrection
Samar 1901
*Samar 1902

World War I
*Aisne
*Champagne-Marne
*Aisne-Marne
*St. Mihiel
*Meuse-Argonne
*Ile de France 1918
*Champagne 1918

World War II
*Algeria-French Morocco
  (with arrowhead)
*Tunisia
*Sicily (with arrowhead)
*Naples-Foggia
*Anzio (with arrowhead)
*Rome-Arno
*Southern France
  (with arrowhead)
*Rhineland
*Ardennes-Alsace
*Central Europe

Korean War
*CCF intervention
*First UN counteroffensive
*CCF spring offensive
*UN summer-fall offensive
*Second Korean winter
*Korea, summer-fall 1952
*Third Korean winter
*Korea, summer 1953

DECORATIONS

*Presidential Unit Citation (Army), Streamer embroidered COLMAR (3d Infantry Division cited; WD GO 44, 1945)

*Presidential Unit Citation (Army), Streamer embroidered CHOKSONG (1st Battalion, 7th Infantry cited; DA GO 79, 1951)

Presidential Unit Citation (Army), Streamer embroidered SEGOK

Presidential Unit Citation (Army), Streamer embroidered KOWANG-NI

*French Croix de Guerre with Gilt Star, World War I, Streamer embroidered AISNE-MARNE (7th Infantry cited; WD GO 11, 1924)

*French Croix de Guerre with Palm, World War II, Streamer embroidered COLMAR (7th Infantry cited; DA GO 43, 1950)

*French Croix de Guerre, World War II, Fourragere (7th Infantry cited; DA GO 43, 1950)

*Republic of Korea Presidential Unit Citation, Streamer embroidered UIJONGBU CORRIDOR (7th Infantry cited; DA GO 20, 1953)

*Republic of Korea Presidential Unit Citation, Streamer embroidered IRON TRIANGLE (7th Infantry cited; DA GO 29, 1954)

*Chryssoun Aristion Andrias (Bravery Gold Medal of Greece), Streamer embroidered KOREA (7th Infantry cited; DA GO 2, 1956)

7TH INFANTRY, BIBLIOGRAPHY

Bancroft, William *et al. Seventh Infantry, 3d Division, Seventh Army in the Vosges.* n.p., 1945.

Blumenson, Martin. *Salerno to Cassino.* United States Army in World War II. Washington: Government Printing Office, 1969.

Bradley, James H. *The March of the Montana Column, A Prelude to the Custer Disaster.* Edited by Edgar I. Stewart. Norman: University of Oklahoma Press, c. 1961.

A Brief Outline of the History of the Seventh United States Infantry and Roster of the Commissioned and Non-commissioned Officers, Colonel Daniel Corman, Commanding. Fort Leavenworth, Kansas: Regimental Press, 1912.

Cotton Baler. (Periodical printed in Germany by the 7th Infantry from 8 September 1945 to 4 July 1946.)

Garland, Albert N. and Howard McGaw Smyth. *Sicily and the Surrender of Italy.* United States Army in World War II. Washington: Government Printing Office, 1965.

"Hill 717," *Bluebook* (July 1952), 12ff.

Historical Section, War Department. *From the Volturno to the Winter Line.* American Forces in Action Series. Washington: Government Printing Office, 1944.

Howe, George F. *Northwest Africa: Seizing the Initiative in the West.* United States Army in World War II. Washington: Government Printing Office, 1957.

Johnson, Alfred Bainbridge. "The Seventh Regiment of Infantry," *The Army of the United States,* edited by Theophilus F. Rodenbough and William L. Haskin. New York: Maynard, Merrill and Company, 1896, pp. 498–510. (Originally published in the *Journal of the Military Service Institution of the United States,* XV [1894], 896–908.)

Kohr, Herbert Ornando. *Around the World with Uncle Sam, or, Six Years in the United States Army.* Akron: Commercial Printing Company, 1907.

Mahon, John K. *History of the Second Seminole War, 1835–1842.* Gainesville: University of Florida Press, 1967.

Roster of Commissioned Officers and Non-commissioned Officers of the Seventh U.S. Infantry, Commanded by Daniel Corman. Fort Wayne, Michigan: Regimental Press, 1908.

Roster of Commissioned Officers and Non-commissioned Officers of the Seventh United States Infantry, Colonel Daniel Corman, Commanding. Fort William McKinley, Rizal, Philippine Islands: Regimental Press, 1909.

Seventh U.S. Infantry Year Book. 1929. Vancouver Barracks, Washington, 1929.

Sheehan, Fred. *Anzio.* Norman: University of Oklahoma Press, 1964.

Sprague, John T. *The Origin, Progress and Conclusion of the Florida War.* New York: D. Appleton and Company, 1848. (Reprint. Gainesville: University of Florida Press, 1964.)

Story of the Cottonbalers. Tokyo: Japan News, 1954.

Teammates at Fort Devens, Massachusetts. Philadelphia: Dorville Corporation, 1949.

White, Nathan William. *From Fedala to Berchtesgaden, A History of the Seventh United States Infantry in World War II.* Brockton, Massachusetts: Keystone Printing Company, 1947.

Yearbook Seventh Infantry, January 8, 1939. Vancouver: Fleet and Kreis Printing Company, 1939.

Yearbook Seventh Infantry Regiment, January 8, 1937. Vancouver: Fleet and Kreis Printing Company, 1937.

8th INFANTRY

HERALDIC ITEMS

COAT OF ARMS

Shield: Argent on a bend azure, between in sinister chief a tomahawk gules helved sable and an arrow of the last barbed of the third in saltire and in dexter base an eagle's claw erased proper, three roses of the field seeded of the third.

Crest: On a wreath of the colors out of a mural coronet a dexter arm in armor embowed the hand grasping a flag staff with tassel all proper.

Motto: *Patriae Fidelitas* (Loyalty to Country).

Symbolism: The shield is white with a blue bend, the old and present infantry colors. The three heraldic flowers on the bend are symbolic of: first, the rose, the flower of the state of New York, where the regimental headquarters was first organized; second, the hispida, the flower of the Philippines, where the regiment saw service during the Insurrection; and third, the temple flower, which is the flower of Cuba, where the 8th served during the War with Spain. The arrow and tomahawk represent the Indian campaigns in which the regiment has participated. The claw representing the maimed strength of the Prussian eagle alludes to the regiment's part in the occupation of Germany after World War I.

The crest symbolizes service in the Mexican War; the 8th was the first U.S. regiment to plant its colors on the fort at Churubusco.

DISTINCTIVE INSIGNIA

The distinctive insignia is the shield of the coat of arms surmounted by a mural crown, the shield and crown mounted on a heavy Roman gold boss figured in high relief.

Lineage and Honors

Lineage

Constituted 5 July 1838 in the Regular Army as the 8th Infantry. Organized in July 1838 in New York, Vermont, and Michigan. Consolidated in May 1869 with the 33d Infantry (see ANNEX) and consolidated unit designated as the 8th Infantry.

Assigned 17 December 1917 to the 8th Division. Relieved 24 March 1923 from assignment to the 8th Division and assigned to the 4th Division (later redesignated as the 4th Infantry Division). Inactivated 25 February 1946 at Camp Butner, North Carolina. Activated 15 July 1947 at Fort Ord, California.

Relieved 1 April 1957 from assignment to the 4th Infantry Division and reorganized as a parent regiment under the Combat Arms Regimental System.

ANNEX

Constituted 3 May 1861 in the Regular Army as the 3d Battalion, 15th Infantry. Organized by March 1864 at Fort Adams, Rhode Island. Reorganized and redesignated 21 September 1866 as the 33d Infantry. Consolidated in May 1869 with the 8th Infantry and consolidated unit designated as the 8th Infantry.

CAMPAIGN PARTICIPATION CREDIT

Mexican War
Palo Alto
Resaca de la Palma
Monterey
Vera Cruz
Cerro Gordo
Churubusco
Molino del Rey
Chapultepec

Civil War
Peninsula
Manassas
Antietam
Fredericksburg
Chancellorsville
Gettysburg
Wilderness
Atlanta
Spotsylvania
Cold Harbor
Petersburg
Texas 1861

Indian Wars
Seminoles
Apaches
New Mexico 1858

New Mexico 1860
Montana 1872
Arizona 1876

War With Spain
Santiago

Philippine Insurrection
Luzon 1901

World War I
Without inscription

World War II
Normandy (with arrowhead)
Northern France
Rhineland
Ardennes-Alsace
Central Europe

Vietnam
Counteroffensive, Phase II
Counteroffensive, Phase III
Tet Counteroffensive
(other campaigns to be
determined)

DECORATIONS

Presidential Unit Citation (Army), Streamer embroidered BEACHES OF NORMANDY (8th Infantry cited; WD GO 76, 1944)

Presidential Unit Citation (Army), Streamer embroidered PLEIKU PROVINCE (1st and 3d Battalions, 8th Infantry cited; DA GO 69, 1969)

Belgian Fourragere 1940 (8th Infantry cited; DA GO 43, 1950)

Cited in the Order of the Day of the Belgian Army for action in BELGIUM (8th Infantry cited; DA GO 43, 1950)

Cited in the Order of the Day of the Belgian Army for action in the ARDENNES (8th Infantry cited; DA GO 43, 1950)

1st BATTALION, 8th INFANTRY

RA
(inactive)

LINEAGE

Organized 1 July 1838 as a detachment of recruits at Detroit, Michigan. Designated 5 July 1838 as Company A, 8th Infantry, a newly constituted unit in the Regular Army. Consolidated in May 1869 with Company A, 33d Infantry (see ANNEX) and consolidated unit designated as Company A, 8th Infantry. (8th Infantry assigned 17 December 1917 to the 8th Division; relieved 24 March 1923 from assignment to the 8th Division and assigned to the 4th Division [later redesignated as the 4th Infantry Division].) Inactivated 25 February 1946 at Camp Butner, North Carolina. Activated 15 July 1947 at Fort Ord, California.

Reorganized and redesignated 1 April 1957 as Headquarters and Headquarters Company, 1st Battle Group, 8th Infantry and remained assigned to the 4th Infantry Division (organic elements concurrently constituted and activated). Reorganized and redesignated 1 October 1963 as the 1st Battalion, 8th Infantry. Inactivated 10 April 1970 at Fort Lewis, Washington.

ANNEX

Constituted 3 May 1861 in the Regular Army as Company A, 3d Battalion, 15th Infantry. Organized by March 1864 at Fort Adams, Rhode Island. Reorganized and redesignated 21 September 1866 as Company A, 33d Infantry. Consolidated in May 1869 with Company A, 8th Infantry and consolidated unit designated as Company A, 8th Infantry.

244

CAMPAIGN PARTICIPATION CREDIT

Mexican War
  *Palo Alto
  *Resaca de la Palma
  *Monterey
  *Vera Cruz
  *Cerro Gordo
  *Churubusco
  *Molino del Rey
  *Chapultepec

Civil War
  Peninsula
  *Manassas
  *Antietam
  *Fredericksburg
  *Chancellorsville
  *Gettysburg
  *Wilderness
  *Atlanta
  *Spotsylvania
  *Cold Harbor
  *Petersburg
  *Texas 1861

Indian Wars
  Seminoles
  *Apaches

New Mexico 1858
New Mexico 1860
*Montana 1872
Arizona 1876

War With Spain
  *Santiago

Philippine Insurrection
  Luzon 1901

World War I
  *Without inscription

World War II
  *Normandy (with arrowhead)
  *Northern France
  *Rhineland
  *Ardennes-Alsace
  *Central Europe

Vietnam
  *Counteroffensive, Phase II
  *Counteroffensive, Phase III
  *Tet Counteroffensive
  (other campaigns to be
    determined)

DECORATIONS

*Presidential Unit Citation (Army), Streamer embroidered BEACHES OF NORMANDY (8th Infantry cited; WD GO 76, 1944)

*Presidential Unit Citation (Army), Streamer embroidered PLEIKU PROVINCE (1st Battalion, 8th Infantry cited; DA GO 69, 1969)

*Belgian Fourragere 1940 (8th Infantry cited; DA GO 43, 1950)

*Cited in the Order of the Day of the Belgian Army for action in BELGIUM (8th Infantry cited; DA GO 43, 1950)

*Cited in the Order of the Day of the Belgian Army for action in the ARDENNES (8th Infantry cited; DA GO 43, 1950)

*Vietnamese Cross of Gallantry with Palm, Streamer embroidered VIETNAM 1966–1969 (1st Battalion, 8th Infantry cited; DA GO 3, 1970)

*Vietnamese Civil Action Honor Medal, First Class, Streamer embroidered VIETNAM 1966–1969 (1st Battalion, 8th Infantry cited; DA GO 53, 1970)

Company A and Company C each additionally entitled to: Presidential Unit Citation (Army), Streamer embroidered KONTUM PROVINCE (Company A and Company C, 1st Battalion, 8th Infantry cited; DA GO 75, 1969)

2d BATTALION, 8th INFANTRY

RA
(4th Infantry Division)

Constituted 5 July 1838 in the Regular Army as Company B, 8th Infantry, and organized at Detroit, Michigan. Consolidated in May 1869 with Company B, 33d Infantry (see ANNEX) and consolidated unit designated as Company B, 8th Infantry. (8th Infantry assigned 17 December 1917 to the 8th Division; relieved 24 March 1923 from assignment to the 8th Division and assigned to the 4th Division [later redesignated as the 4th Infantry Division].) Inactivated 25 February 1946 at Camp Butner, North Carolina. Activated 15 July 1947 at Fort Ord, California. Inactivated 1 April 1957 at Fort Lewis, Washington, and relieved from assignment to the 4th Infantry Division.

Redesignated 1 August 1957 as Headquarters and Headquarters Company, 2d Battle Group, 8th Infantry, assigned to the 8th Infantry Division, and activated in Germany (organic elements concurrently constituted and activated). Relieved 1 January 1959 from assignment to the 8th Infantry Division and assigned to the 1st Infantry Division. Reorganized and redesignated 1 October 1963 as the 2d Battalion, 8th Infantry; concurrently, relieved from assignment to the 1st Infantry Division and assigned to the 4th Infantry Division.

ANNEX

Constituted 3 May 1861 in the Regular Army as Company B, 3d Battalion, 15th Infantry. Organized by March 1864 at Fort Adams, Rhode Island. Reorganized and redesignated 21 September 1866 as Company B, 33d Infantry. Consolidated in May 1869 with Company B, 8th Infantry and consolidated unit designated as Company B, 8th Infantry.

Campaign Participation Credit

Mexican War
*Palo Alto
*Resaca de la Palma
*Monterey
*Vera Cruz
*Cerro Gordo
*Churubusco
*Molino del Rey
*Chapultepec

Civil War
Peninsula
Manassas
Antietam
Fredericksburg
*Chancellorsville
*Gettysburg
*Wilderness
*Atlanta
*Spotsylvania
*Cold Harbor
*Petersburg
*Texas 1861

Indian Wars
*Seminoles
Apaches
*New Mexico 1858

New Mexico 1860
*Montana 1872
Arizona 1876

War With Spain
*Santiago

Philippine Insurrection
Luzon 1901

World War I
*Without inscription

World War II
*Normandy (with arrowhead)
*Northern France
*Rhineland
*Ardennes-Alsace
*Central Europe

Vietnam
*Counteroffensive, Phase II
*Counteroffensive, Phase III
*Tet Counteroffensive
(other campaigns to be
determined)

Decorations

*Presidential Unit Citation (Army), Streamer embroidered BEACHES OF NORMANDY (8th Infantry cited; WD GO 76, 1944)

*Belgian Fourragere 1940 (8th Infantry cited; DA GO 43, 1950)

*Cited in the Order of the Day of the Belgian Army for action in BELGIUM (8th Infantry cited; DA GO 43, 1950)

*Cited in the Order of the Day of the Belgian Army for action in the ARDENNES (8th Infantry cited; DA GO 43, 1950)

*Vietnamese Cross of Gallantry with Palm, Streamer embroidered VIETNAM 1966–1969 (2d Battalion, 8th Infantry cited; DA GO 3, 1970)

*Vietnamese Civil Action Honor Medal, First Class, Streamer embroidered VIETNAM 1966–1969 (2d Battalion, 8th Infantry cited; DA GO 53, 1970)

3d BATTALION, 8th INFANTRY

RA
(inactive)

LINEAGE

Constituted 5 July 1838 in the Regular Army as Company C, 8th Infantry. Organized 9 July 1838 at Buffalo, New York. Consolidated in May 1869 with Company C, 33d Infantry (see ANNEX) and consolidated unit designated as Company C, 8th Infantry. (8th Infantry assigned 17 December 1917 to the 8th Division; relieved 24 March 1923 from assignment to the 8th Division and assigned to the 4th Division [later redesignated as the 4th Infantry Division].) Inactivated 25 February 1946 at Camp Butner, North Carolina. Activated 15 July 1947 at Fort Ord, California.

Inactivated 1 April 1957 at Fort Lewis, Washington, and relieved from assignment to the 4th Infantry Division; concurrently, redesignated as Headquarters and Headquarters Company, 3d Battle Group, 8th Infantry. Redesignated 21 August 1963 as Headquarters and Headquarters Company, 3d Battalion, 8th Infantry and assigned to the 4th Infantry Division (organic elements concurrently constituted). Battalion activated 1 October 1963 at Fort Lewis, Washington. Inactivated 15 December 1970 at Fort Carson, Colorado.

ANNEX

Constituted 3 May 1861 in the Regular Army as Company C, 3d Battalion, 15th Infantry. Organized by March 1864 at Fort Adams, Rhode Island. Reorganized and redesignated 21 September 1866 as Company C, 33d Infantry. Consolidated in May 1869 with Company C, 8th Infantry and consolidated unit designated as Company C, 8th Infantry.

248

Campaign Participation Credit

Mexican War
  *Palo Alto
  *Resaca de la Palma
  Monterey
  *Vera Cruz
  *Cerro Gordo
  *Churubusco
  *Molino del Rey
  *Chapultepec

Civil War
  Peninsula
  Manassas
  Antietam
  *Fredericksburg
  *Chancellorsville
  *Gettysburg
  *Wilderness
  *Atlanta
  *Spotsylvania
  *Cold Harbor
  *Petersburg
  *Texas 1861

Indian Wars
  Seminoles
  *Apaches
  New Mexico 1858

  New Mexico 1860
  *Montana 1872
  Arizona 1876

War With Spain
  *Santiago

Philippine Insurrection
  Luzon 1901

World War I
  *Without inscription

World War II
  *Normandy (with arrowhead)
  *Northern France
  *Rhineland
  *Ardennes-Alsace
  *Central Europe

Vietnam
  *Counteroffensive, Phase II
  *Counteroffensive, Phase III
  *Tet Counteroffensive
  (other campaigns to be
    determined)

Decorations

*Presidential Unit Citation (Army), Streamer embroidered BEACHES OF NORMANDY (8th Infantry cited; WD GO 76, 1944)

*Presidential Unit Citation (Army), Streamer embroidered PLEIKU PROVINCE (3d Battalion, 8th Infantry cited; DA GO 69, 1969)

*Belgian Fourragere 1940 (8th Infantry cited; DA GO 43, 1950)

*Cited in the Order of the Day of the Belgian Army for action in BELGIUM (8th Infantry cited; DA GO 43, 1950)

*Cited in the Order of the Day of the Belgian Army for action in the ARDENNES (8th Infantry cited; DA GO 43, 1950)

*Vietnamese Cross of Gallantry with Palm, Streamer embroidered VIETNAM 1966–1969 (3d Battalion, 8th Infantry cited; DA GO 3, 1970)

*Vietnamese Civil Action Honor Medal, First Class, Streamer embroidered VIETNAM 1966–1969 (3d Battalion, 8th Infantry cited; DA GO 53, 1970)

COMPANY E, 8th INFANTRY

AR
(inactive)

LINEAGE

Constituted 5 July 1838 in the Regular Army as Company E, 8th Infantry. Organized in July 1838 at Buffalo, New York. Consolidated in May 1869 with Company E, 33d Infantry (see ANNEX) and consolidated unit designated as Company E, 8th Infantry. (8th Infantry assigned 17 December 1917 to the 8th Division; relieved 24 March 1923 from assignment to the 8th Division and assigned to the 4th Division [later redesignated as the 4th Infantry Division].) Inactivated 25 February 1946 at Camp Butner, North Carolina. Activated 15 July 1947 at Fort Ord, California.

Inactivated 1 April 1957 at Fort Lewis, Washington, and relieved from assignment to the 4th Infantry Division; concurrently, redesignated as Headquarters and Headquarters Company, 5th Battle Group, 8th Infantry. Redesignated 5 November 1962 at Company E, 8th Infantry; concurrently, withdrawn from the Regular Army and allotted to the Army Reserve. Activated 22 March 1963 at Roslindale, Massachusetts. Inactivated 17 December 1965 at Roslindale, Massachusetts.

ANNEX

Constituted 3 May 1861 in the Regular Army as Company E, 3d Battalion, 15th Infantry. Organized by March 1864 at Fort Adams, Rhode Island. Reorganized and redesignated 21 September 1866 as Company E, 33d Infantry. Consolidated in May 1869 with Company E, 8th Infantry and consolidated unit designated as Company E, 8th Infantry.

Campaign Participation Credit

Mexican War
Palo Alto
Resaca de la Palma
Monterey
Vera Cruz
Cerro Gordo
Churubusco
Molino del Rey
Chapultepec

Civil War
Chancellorsville
Gettysburg
Wilderness
Spotsylvania
Cold Harbor
Petersburg
Texas 1861

Indian Wars
Apaches
New Mexico 1858
New Mexico 1860
Arizona 1876

War With Spain
Santiago

World War II-EAME
Normandy (with arrowhead)
Northern France
Rhineland
Ardennes-Alsace
Central Europe

Decorations

Presidential Unit Citation (Army), Streamer embroidered BEACHES OF NORMANDY (8th Infantry cited; WD GO 76, 1944)

Belgian Fourragere 1940 (8th Infantry cited; DA GO 43, 1950)

Cited in the Order of the Day of the Belgian Army for action in BELGIUM (8th Infantry cited; DA GO 43, 1950)

Cited in the Order of the Day of the Belgian Army for action in the ARDENNES (8th Infantry cited; DA GO 43, 1950)

8TH INFANTRY, BIBLIOGRAPHY

Albright, John, John A. Cash, and Allan W. Sandstrum. *Seven Firefights in Vietnam*. Washington: Government Printing Office, 1970.

Blumenson, Martin. *Breakout and Pursuit*. United States Army in World War II. Washington: Government Printing Office, 1961.

————. *The Duel for France*. Boston: Houghton Mifflin Company, 1963.

The Bullet. (8th Infantry Annual.) Bad Nauheim: Sprudel Druck, 1953.

Cole, Hugh M. *The Ardennes: Battle of the Bulge*. United States Army in World War II. Washington: Government Printing Office, 1964.

"Eighth Infantry Regiment," *A Pictorial History of the 4th Infantry Division*. Baton Rouge: Army and Navy Publishing Company, 1945.

Elliott, M.A., ed. *As We See It: Eighth Infantry*. n.p., 1942.

Harrison, Gordon A. *Cross-Channel Attack*. United States Army in World War II. Washington: Government Printing Office, 1951.

Historical Section, War Department. *Utah Beach to Cherbourg*. American Forces in Action Series. Washington: Government Printing Office, 1947.

History of the Eighth United States Infantry, 1798–1954. Darmstadt: Stars and Stripes, 1955. (Erroneously connects this regiment with an earlier one of the same designation.)

History of the 4th Infantry Division and Brief Histories of its Components. Fort Lewis, Washington, 1958.

Lazelle, Henry Martyn. "Puritan and Apache, A Diary," edited by Frank D. Reave, *New Mexico Historical Review*, XXIII (1948), 269–301; XXIV (1949), 12–53.

MacDonald, Charles B. *The Battle of Huertgen Forest*. New York and Philadelphia: J. B. Lippincott Company, 1963.

————. *The Siegfried Line Campaign*. United States Army in World War II. Washington: Government Printing Office, 1963.

Mahon, John K. *History of the Second Seminole War, 1835–1842*. Gainesville: University of Florida Press, 1967.

Marshall, S. L. A. *West to Cambodia*. New York: Cowles Education Corporation, 1968.

Roster of the Eighth U.S. Infantry, Colonel Frederick A. Smith, Commanding. Fort Jay, Governor's Island, New York: Regimental Press, C. C. Church, Printer, 1904.

Roster of the Eighth U.S. Infantry, Colonel Frederick A. Smith, Commanding. Camp Jossman, Guimaras, Philippine Islands: Regimental Press, 1906?

Roster: Eighth United States Infantry, n.p., 1942.

Sprague, John T. *The Origin, Progress and Conclusion of the Florida*

War. New York: D. Appleton and Company, 1848. (Reprint. Gainesville: University of Florida Press, 1964.)

Wilhelm, Thomas. *History of the Eighth U.S. Infantry From Its Organization in 1838*. New York: Headquarters, 8th Infantry, 1873.

————. *History of the Eighth U.S. Infantry*. Fort D. A. Russell, Wyoming, 1874.

————. *Synopsis of the History of the Eighth U.S. Infantry and the Military Record of Officers Assigned to the Regiment from Its Organization, July 1838 to September 1871*. David's Island, New York Harbor: Regimental Headquarters, 8th Infantry, 1871.

Wilson, Richard. "The Eighth Regiment of Infantry," *The Army of the United States*, edited by Theophilus F. Rodenbough and William L. Haskin. New York: Maynard, Merrill and Company, 1896, pp. 511–525. (Originally published in the *Journal of the Military Service Institution of the United States*, XV [1894], 660–674.)

9th INFANTRY
(Manchu)

HERALDIC ITEMS

COAT OF ARMS

Shield: Azure, a chevronel wavy argent between in chief an imperial Chinese five-toed dragon affronté or lined azure and a sun in splendor of the third and in base a wigwam of the like garnished gules.

Crest: On a wreath of the colors a pentagon sable charged with the insignia of the 2d Division proper, and encircled by a Fourragere in the colors of the French Croix de Guerre.

Motto: Keep up the Fire.

Symbolism: The field of the shield is blue, the infantry color. The regiment's Indian campaigns are commemorated by the wigwam. Service in the Philippine Insurrection and China Relief Expedition is shown by the sun in splendor, a device used by the Filipino insurrectos, and by the imperial Chinese dragon, respectively. In 1898 the regiment took part in the battle of Santiago, crossing the San Juan River at the "bloody angle"; this is represented by the wavy chevron.

The crest is the insignia used by the division with which the regiment served in World War I, surrounded by a Fourragere awarded by the French government for distinguished services rendered.

DISTINCTIVE INSIGNIA

The distinctive insignia is an imperial five-toed Chinese dragon, head to chief facing the dexter, encircling a disc bearing the numeral "9" all or; the motto "Keep up the Fire" around edge of disc. The design commemorates the campaigns in China.

255

Lineage and Honors

Lineage

Constituted 3 March 1855 in the Regular Army as the 9th Infantry. Organized 26 March 1855 at Fort Monroe, Virginia. Consolidated in June 1869 with the 27th Infantry (see ANNEX) and consolidated unit designated as the 9th Infantry. Assigned 22 September 1917 to the 2d Division (later redesignated as the 2d Infantry Division).

Relieved 20 June 1957 from assignment to the 2d Infantry Division and reorganized as a parent regiment under the Combat Arms Regimental System.

Annex

Constituted 3 May 1861 in the Regular Army as the 2d Battalion, 18th Infantry. Organized in October 1861 at Camp Thomas, Ohio. Reorganized and redesignated 21 September 1866 as the 27th Infantry. Consolidated in June 1869 with the 9th Infantry and consolidated unit designated as the 9th Infantry.

CAMPAIGN PARTICIPATION CREDIT

Civil War
Murfreesborough
Chickamauga
Chattanooga
Atlanta
Mississippi 1862
Kentucky 1862
Tennessee 1863
Georgia 1864

Indian Wars
Little Big Horn
Washington 1856
Washington 1858
Wyoming 1866
Wyoming 1867

War With Spain
Santiago

China Relief Expedition
Tientsin
Yang-tsun
Peking

Philippine Insurrection
San Isidro
Zapote River
Malolos
Tarlac
Luzon 1899
Luzon 1900
Samar 1901

World War I
Aisne
Aisne-Marne
St. Mihiel
Meuse-Argonne
Lorraine 1918
Ile de France 1918

World War II
Normandy (with arrowhead)
Northern France
Rhineland
Ardennes-Alsace
Central Europe

Korean War
UN defensive
UN offensive
CCF intervention
First UN counteroffensive
CCF spring offensive
UN summer-fall offensive
Second Korean winter
Korea, summer-fall 1952
Third Korean winter
Korea, summer 1953

Vietnam
Counteroffensive
Counteroffensive, Phase II
Counteroffensive, Phase III
Tet Counteroffensive
(other campaigns to be
determined)

DECORATIONS

Presidential Unit Citation (Army), Streamer embroidered BREST, FRANCE (3d Battalion, 9th Infantry cited; WD GO 15, 1945)

Presidential Unit Citation (Army), Streamer embroidered SIEGFRIED LINE (2d Battalion, 9th Infantry cited; WD GO 38, 1945)

Presidential Unit Citation (Army), Streamer embroidered ARDENNES (1st Battalion, 9th Infantry cited; WD GO 42, 1945)

Presidential Unit Citation (Army), Streamer embroidered HONGCHON (2d Infantry Division cited; DA GO 72, 1951)

Presidential Unit Citation (Navy), Streamer embroidered HWACHON RESERVOIR (1st Battalion, 9th Infantry cited; DA GO 38, 1957)

Navy Unit Commendation, Streamer embroidered PANMUNJOM (1st Battalion, 9th Infantry cited; DA GO 38, 1957)

French Croix de Guerre with Palm, World War I, Streamer embroidered AISNE-MARNE (9th Infantry cited; WD GO 11, 1924)

French Croix de Guerre with Palm, World War I, Streamer embroidered MEUSE-ARGONNE (9th Infantry cited; WD GO 11, 1924)

French Croix de Guerre with Palm, World War I, Streamer embroidered CHATEAU THIERRY (9th Infantry cited; WD GO 11, 1924)

French Croix de Guerre, World War I, Fourragere (9th Infantry cited; WD GO 11, 1924)

Republic of Korea Presidential Unit Citation, Streamer embroidered NAKTONG RIVER LINE (9th Infantry cited; DA GO 35, 1951)

Republic of Korea Presidential Unit Citation, Streamer embroidered KOREA (9th Infantry cited; DA GO 10, 1954)

Luxembourg Croix de Guerre, Streamer embroidered LUXEMBOURG (9th Infantry cited; DA GO 43, 1950)

Belgian Fourragere 1940 (9th Infantry cited; DA GO 43, 1950)

Cited in the Order of the Day of the Belgian Army for action in the ARDENNES (9th Infantry cited; DA GO 43, 1950)

Cited in the Order of the Day of the Belgian Army for action at ELSENBORN CREST (9th Infantry cited; DA GO 43, 1950)

1st BATTALION, 9th INFANTRY

(Manchu)

RA

(2d Infantry Division)

LINEAGE

Constituted 3 March 1855 in the Regular Army as Company A, 9th Infantry. Organized 26 March 1855 at Fort Monroe, Virginia. Consolidated in June 1869 with Company A, 27th Infantry (see ANNEX) and consolidated unit designated as Company A, 9th Infantry. (9th Infantry assigned 22 September 1917 to the 2d Division [later redesignated as the 2d Infantry Division].)

Reorganized and redesignated 20 June 1957 as Headquarters and Headquarters Company, 1st Battle Group, 9th Infantry and remained assigned to the 2d Infantry Division (organic elements concurrently constituted and activated). Relieved 16 December 1957 from assignment to the 2d Infantry Division. Reorganized and redesignated 25 January 1963 as the 1st Battalion, 9th Infantry and assigned to the 2d Infantry Division.

ANNEX

Constituted 3 May 1861 in the Regular Army as Company A, 2d Battalion, 18th Infantry. Organized in October 1861 at Camp Thomas, Ohio. Reorganized and redesignated 21 September 1866 as Company A, 27th Infantry. Consolidated in June 1869 with Company A, 9th Infantry and consolidated unit designated as Company A, 9th Infantry.

259

Campaign Participation Credit

Civil War
*Murfreesborough
*Chickamauga
*Chattanooga
*Atlanta
*Mississippi 1862
*Kentucky 1862
*Tennessee 1863
*Georgia 1864

Indian Wars
Little Big Horn
*Washington 1856
Washington 1858
*Wyoming 1866
*Wyoming 1867

War With Spain
*Santiago

China Relief Expedition
*Tientsin
*Yang-tsun
*Peking

Philippine Insurrection
*San Isidro
Zapote River
*Malolos
*Tarlac

*Luzon 1899
*Luzon 1900
Samar 1901

World War I
*Aisne
*Aisne-Marne
*St. Mihiel
*Meuse-Argonne
*Lorraine 1918
*Ile de France 1918

World War II
*Normandy (with arrowhead)
*Northern France
*Rhineland
*Ardennes-Alsace
*Central Europe

Korean War
*UN defensive
*UN offensive
*CCF intervention
*First UN counteroffensive
*CCF spring offensive
*UN summer-fall offensive
*Second Korean winter
*Korea, summer-fall 1952
*Third Korean winter
*Korea, summer 1953

Decorations

Presidential Unit Citation (Army), Streamer embroidered BREST, FRANCE

Presidential Unit Citation (Army), Streamer embroidered SIEGFRIED LINE

*Presidential Unit Citation (Army), Streamer embroidered ARDENNES (1st Battalion, 9th Infantry cited; WD GO 42, 1945)

*Presidential Unit Citation (Army), Streamer embroidered HONG-CHON (2d Infantry Division cited; DA GO 72, 1951)

*Presidential Unit Citation (Navy), Streamer embroidered HWACHON RESERVOIR (1st Battalion, 9th Infantry cited; DA GO 38, 1957)

*Navy Unit Commendation, Streamer embroidered PANMUNJOM (1st Battalion, 9th Infantry cited; DA GO 38, 1957)

*French Croix de Guerre with Palm, World War I, Streamer embroidered AISNE-MARNE (9th Infantry cited; WD GO 11, 1924)

*French Croix de Guerre with Palm, World War I, Streamer

embroidered MEUSE-ARGONNE (9th Infantry cited; WD GO 11, 1924)

*French Croix de Guerre with Palm, World War I, Streamer embroidered CHATEAU THIERRY (9th Infantry cited; WD GO 11, 1924)

*French Croix de Guerre, World War I, Fourragere (9th Infantry cited; WD GO 11, 1924)

*Republic of Korea Presidential Unit Citation, Streamer embroidered NAKTONG RIVER LINE (9th Infantry cited; DA GO 35, 1951)

*Republic of Korea Presidential Unit Citation, Streamer embroidered KOREA (9th Infantry cited; DA GO 10, 1954)

*Luxembourg Croix de Guerre, Streamer embroidered LUXEMBOURG (9th Infantry cited; DA GO 43, 1950)

*Belgian Fourragere 1940 (9th Infantry cited; DA GO 43, 1950)

*Cited in the Order of the Day of the Belgian Army for action in the ARDENNES (9th Infantry cited; DA GO 43, 1950)

*Cited in the Order of the Day of the Belgian Army for action at ELSENBORN CREST (9th Infantry cited; DA GO 43, 1950)

2d BATTALION, 9th INFANTRY

(Manchu)

RA
(2d Infantry Division)

LINEAGE

Constituted 3 March 1855 in the Regular Army as Company B, 9th Infantry. Organized 26 March 1855 at Fort Monroe, Virginia. Consolidated in June 1869 with Company B, 27th Infantry (see ANNEX) and consolidated unit designated as Company B, 9th Infantry. (9th Infantry assigned 22 September 1917 to the 2d Division [later redesignated as the 2d Infantry Division].)

Inactivated 20 June 1957 in Alaska and relieved from assignment to the 2d Infantry Division; concurrently, redesignated as Headquarters and Headquarters Company, 2d Battle Group, 9th Infantry. (Organic elements constituted 4 March 1958.) Assigned 17 March 1958 to the 2d Infantry Division. Battle Group activated 14 June 1958 at Fort Benning, Georgia. Reorganized and redesignated 1 February 1963 as the 2d Battalion, 9th Infantry.

ANNEX

Organized in October 1861 in the Regular Army at Camp Thomas, Ohio, as Company B, 2d Battalion, 18th Infantry. Reorganized and redesignated 21 September 1866 as Company B, 27th Infantry. Consolidated in June 1869 with Company B, 9th Infantry and consolidated unit designated as Company B, 9th Infantry.

CAMPAIGN PARTICIPATION CREDIT

Civil War
*Murfreesborough
*Chickamauga
*Chattanooga
*Atlanta
*Mississippi 1862
*Kentucky 1862
*Tennessee 1863
*Georgia 1864

Indian Wars
Little Big Horn
*Washington 1856
*Washington 1858
Wyoming 1866
*Wyoming 1867

War With Spain
*Santiago

China Relief Expedition
*Tientsin
*Yang-tsun
*Peking

Philippine Insurrection
San Isidro
*Zapote River
*Malolos
*Tarlac

*Luzon 1899
*Luzon 1900
Samar 1901

World War I
*Aisne
*Aisne-Marne
*St. Mihiel
*Meuse-Argonne
*Lorraine 1918
*Ile de France 1918

World War II
*Normandy (with arrowhead)
*Northern France
*Rhineland
*Ardennes-Alsace
*Central Europe

Korean War
*UN defensive
*UN offensive
*CCF intervention
*First UN counteroffensive
*CCF spring offensive
*UN summer-fall offensive
*Second Korean winter
*Korea, summer-fall 1952
*Third Korean winter
*Korea, summer 1953

DECORATIONS

Presidential Unit Citation (Army), Streamer embroidered BREST, FRANCE

Presidential Unit Citation (Army), Streamer embroidered SIEGFRIED LINE

*Presidential Unit Citation (Army), Streamer embroidered ARDENNES (1st Battalion, 9th Infantry cited; WD GO 42, 1945)

*Presidential Unit Citation (Army), Streamer embroidered HONG-CHON (2d Infantry Division cited; DA GO 72, 1951)

*Presidential Unit Citation (Navy), Streamer embroidered HWACHON RESERVOIR (1st Battalion, 9th Infantry cited; DA GO 38, 1957)

*Navy Unit Commendation, Streamer embroidered PANMUNJOM (1st Battalion, 9th Infantry cited; DA GO 38, 1957)

*French Croix de Guerre with Palm, World War I, Streamer embroidered AISNE-MARNE (9th Infantry cited; WD GO 11, 1924)

*French Croix de Guerre with Palm, World War I, Streamer

embroidered MEUSE-ARGONNE (9th Infantry cited; WD GO 11, 1924)

*French Croix de Guerre with Palm, World War I, Streamer embroidered CHATEAU THIERRY (9th Infantry cited; WD GO 11, 1924)

*French Croix de Guerre, World War I, Fourragere (9th Infantry cited; WD GO 11, 1924)

*Republic of Korea Presidential Unit Citation, Streamer embroidered NAKTONG RIVER LINE (9th Infantry cited; DA GO 35, 1951)

*Republic of Korea Presidential Unit Citation, Streamer embroidered KOREA (9th Infantry cited; DA GO 10, 1954)

*Luxembourg Croix de Guerre, Streamer embroidered LUXEMBOURG (9th Infantry cited; DA GO 43, 1950)

*Belgian Fourragere 1940 (9th Infantry cited; DA GO 43, 1950)

*Cited in the Order of the Day of the Belgian Army for action in the ARDENNES (9th Infantry cited; DA GO 43, 1950)

*Cited in the Order of the Day of the Belgian Army for action at ELSENBORN CREST (9th Infantry cited; DA GO 43, 1950)

3d BATTALION, 9th INFANTRY

(Manchu)

AR
(inactive)

Constituted 3 March 1855 in the Regular Army as Company C, 9th Infantry. Organized 26 March 1855 at Fort Monroe, Virginia. Consolidated in June 1869 with Company C, 27th Infantry (see ANNEX 1) and consolidated unit designated as Company C, 9th Infantry. (9th Infantry assigned 22 September 1917 to the 2d Division [later redesignated as the 2d Infantry Division].)

Inactivated 20 June 1957 in Alaska and relieved from assignment to the 2d Infantry Division; concurrently, redesignated as Headquarters and Headquarters Company, 3d Battle Group, 9th Infantry. Withdrawn 11 May 1959 from the Regular Army, allotted to the Army Reserve, and assigned to the 102d Infantry Division (organic elements concurrently constituted). Battle Group activated 1 June 1959 with Headquarters at Quincy, Illinois (concurrently, Headquarters and Headquarters Company consolidated with Headquarters and Headquarters Company, 405th Infantry [see ANNEX 2] and consolidated unit designated as Headquarters and Headquarters Company, 3d Battle Group, 9th Infantry). Reorganized and redesignated 1 April 1963 as the 3d Battalion, 9th Infantry. Inactivated 31 December 1965 at Quincy, Illinois.

ANNEX 1

Constituted 3 May 1861 in the Regular Army as Company C, 2d Battalion, 18th Infantry. Organized in October 1861 at Camp Thomas, Ohio. Reorganized and redesignated 21 September 1866 as Company C, 27th Infantry. Consolidated in June 1869 with Company C, 9th Infantry and consolidated unit designated as Company C, 9th Infantry.

ANNEX 2

Constituted 24 June 1921 in the Organized Reserves as Headquarters and Headquarters Company, 405th Infantry, an element of the 102d Division (later redesignated as the 102d Infantry Division). Organized in November 1921 at Little Rock, Arkansas. Ordered into active military service 15 September 1942 and reorganized at Camp Maxey, Texas. Inactivated 1 June 1946 in Germany.

Activated 31 October 1946 in the Organized Reserves at Minneapolis, Minnesota. Inactivated 3 January 1947 at Minneapolis, Minnesota. Activated 24 January 1947 at St. Louis, Missouri. Location changed 15 March 1948 to Danville, Illinois; 1 February 1950 to Anna, Illinois; 2 January 1956 to Marion, Illinois; and 24 November 1956 to East St. Louis, Illinois. (Organized Reserves redesignated 25 March 1948 as the Organized Reserve Corps; redesignated 9 July 1952 as the Army Reserve.)

Consolidated 1 June 1959 with Headquarters and Headquarters Company, 3d Battle Group, 9th Infantry and consolidated unit designated as Headquarters and Headquarters Company, 3d Battle Group, 9th Infantry (concurrently, Headquarters and Headquarters Company, 3d Battalion, 405th Infantry consolidated with Headquarters and Headquarters Company, 3d Battle Group, 4th Infantry and consolidated unit designated as Headquarters and Headquarters Company, 3d Battle Group, 4th Infantry; remainder of 405th Infantry inactivated).

Campaign Participation Credit

Civil War
* *Murfreesborough
* *Chickamauga
* *Chattanooga
* Atlanta
* *Mississippi 1862
* *Kentucky 1862
* *Tennessee 1863
* *Georgia 1864

Indian Wars
* *Little Big Horn
* Washington 1856
* *Washington 1858
* *Wyoming 1866
* *Wyoming 1867

War With Spain
* *Santiago

China Relief Expedition
* *Tientsin
* *Yang-tsun
* *Peking

Philippine Insurrection
* *San Isidro
* *Zapote River
* *Malolos
* *Tarlac

* *Luzon 1899
* *Luzon 1900
* *Samar 1901

World War I
* *Aisne
* *Aisne-Marne
* *St. Mihiel
* *Meuse-Argonne
* *Lorraine 1918
* *Ile de France 1918

World War II
* *Normandy (with arrowhead)
* *Northern France
* *Rhineland
* *Ardennes-Alsace
* *Central Europe

Korean War
* *UN defensive
* *UN offensive
* *CCF intervention
* *First UN counteroffensive
* *CCF spring offensive
* *UN summer-fall offensive
* *Second Korean winter
* *Korea, summer-fall 1952
* *Third Korean winter
* *Korea, summer 1953

Decorations

Presidential Unit Citation (Army), Streamer embroidered BREST, FRANCE

*Presidential Unit Citation (Army), Streamer embroidered ROER RIVER (405th Infantry cited; WD GO 16, 1947)

Presidential Unit Citation (Army), Streamer embroidered SIEGFRIED LINE

*Presidential Unit Citation (Army), Streamer embroidered ARDENNES (1st Battalion, 9th Infantry cited; WD GO 42, 1945)

*Presidential Unit Citation (Army), Streamer embroidered HONG-CHON (2d Infantry Division cited; DA GO 72, 1951)

*Presidential Unit Citation (Navy), Streamer embroidered HWACHON RESERVOIR (1st Battalion, 9th Infantry cited; DA GO 38, 1957)

*Navy Unit Commendation, Streamer embroidered PANMUNJOM (1st Battalion, 9th Infantry cited; DA GO 38, 1957)

*French Croix de Guerre with Palm, World War I, Streamer em-

broidered AISNE-MARNE (9th Infantry cited; WD GO 11, 1924)

*French Croix de Guerre with Palm, World War I, Streamer embroidered MEUSE-ARGONNE (9th Infantry cited; WD GO 11, 1924)

*French Croix de Guerre with Palm, World War I, Streamer embroidered CHATEAU THIERRY (9th Infantry cited; WD GO 11, 1924)

*French Croix de Guerre, World War I, Fourragere (9th Infantry cited; WD GO 11, 1924)

*Republic of Korea Presidential Unit Citation, Streamer embroidered NAKTONG RIVER LINE (9th Infantry cited; DA GO 35, 1951)

*Republic of Korea Presidential Unit Citation, Streamer embroidered KOREA (9th Infantry cited; DA GO 10, 1954)

*Luxembourg Croix de Guerre, Streamer embroidered LUXEMBOURG (9th Infantry cited; DA GO 43, 1950)

*Belgian Fourragere 1940 (9th Infantry cited; DA GO 43, 1950)

*Cited in the Order of the Day of the Belgian Army for action in the ARDENNES (9th Infantry cited; DA GO 43, 1950)

*Cited in the Order of the Day of the Belgian Army for action at ELSENBORN CREST (9th Infantry cited; DA GO 43, 1950)

4th BATTALION, 9th INFANTRY

(Manchu)

RA
(25th Infantry Division)

LINEAGE

Constituted 3 March 1855 in the Regular Army as Company D, 9th Infantry. Organized 17 March 1855 at Fort Monroe, Virginia. Consolidated in June 1869 with Company D, 27th Infantry (see ANNEX) and consolidated unit designated as Company D, 9th Infantry. (9th Infantry assigned 22 September 1917 to the 2d Division [later redesignated as the 2d Infantry Division].)

Inactivated 20 June 1957 in Alaska and relieved from assignment to the 2d Infantry Division; concurrently, redesignated as Headquarters and Headquarters Company, 4th Battle Group, 9th Infantry. Activated 25 January 1963 in Alaska (organic elements concurrently constituted and activated). Assigned 20 May 1963 to the 171st Infantry Brigade. Reorganized and redesignated 1 July 1963 as the 4th Battalion, 9th Infantry. Relieved 14 January 1966 from assignment to the 171st Infantry Brigade and assigned to the 25th Infantry Division.

ANNEX

Constituted 3 May 1861 in the Regular Army as Company D, 2d Battalion, 18th Infantry. Organized in October 1861 at Camp Thomas, Ohio. Reorganized and redesignated 21 September 1866 as Company D, 27th Infantry. Consolidated in June 1869 with Company D, 9th Infantry and consolidated unit designated as Company D, 9th Infantry.

269

CAMPAIGN PARTICIPATION CREDIT

Civil War
  *Murfreesborough
  *Chickamauga
  *Chattanooga
  *Atlanta
  *Mississippi 1862
  *Kentucky 1862
  *Tennessee 1863
  *Georgia 1864

Indian Wars
  Little Big Horn
  *Washington 1856
  Washington 1858
  Wyoming 1866
  *Wyoming 1867

War With Spain
  *Santiago

China Relief Expedition
  *Tientsin
  *Yang-tsun
  *Peking

Philippine Insurrection
  San Isidro
  *Zapote River
  *Malolos
  *Tarlac
  *Luzon 1899
  *Luzon 1900
  Samar 1901

World War I
  *Aisne
  *Aisne-Marne
  *St. Mihiel
  *Meuse-Argonne
  *Lorraine 1918
  *Ile de France 1918

World War II
  *Normandy (with arrowhead)
  *Northern France
  *Rhineland
  *Ardennes-Alsace
  *Central Europe

Korean War
  *UN defensive
  *UN offensive
  *CCF intervention
  *First UN counteroffensive
  *CCF spring offensive
  *UN summer-fall offensive
  *Second Korean winter
  *Korea, summer-fall 1952
  *Third Korean winter
  *Korea, summer 1953

Vietnam
  *Counteroffensive
  *Counteroffensive, Phase II
  *Counteroffensive, Phase III
  *Tet Counteroffensive
  (other campaigns to be
    determined)

DECORATIONS

Presidential Unit Citation (Army), Streamer embroidered BREST, FRANCE

Presidential Unit Citation (Army), Streamer embroidered SIEGFRIED LINE

*Presidential Unit Citation (Army), Streamer embroidered ARDENNES (1st Battalion, 9th Infantry cited; WD GO 42, 1945)

*Presidential Unit Citation (Army), Streamer embroidered HONG-CHON (2d Infantry Division; DA GO 72, 1951)

*Presidential Unit Citation (Navy), Streamer embroidered HWACHON RESERVOIR (1st Battalion, 9th Infantry cited; DA GO 38, 1957)

*Navy Unit Commendation, Streamer embroidered PANMUNJOM (1st Battalion, 9th Infantry cited; DA GO 38, 1957)

*French Croix de Guerre with Palm, World War I, Streamer embroidered AISNE-MARNE (9th Infantry cited; WD GO 11, 1924)

*French Croix de Guerre with Palm, World War I, Streamer MEUSE-ARGONNE (9th Infantry cited; WD GO 11, 1924)

*French Croix de Guerre with Palm, World War I, Streamer embroidered CHATEAU THIERRY (9th Infantry cited; WD GO 11, 1924)

*French Croix de Guerre, World War I, Fourragere (9th Infantry cited; WD GO 11, 1924)

*Republic of Korea Presidential Unit Citation, Streamer embroidered NAKTONG RIVER LINE (9th Infantry cited; DA GO 35, 1951)

*Republic of Korea Presidential Unit Citation, Streamer embroidered KOREA (9th Infantry cited; DA GO 10, 1954)

*Luxembourg Croix de Guerre, Streamer embroidered LUXEMBOURG (9th Infantry cited; DA GO 43, 1950)

*Belgian Fourragere 1940 (9th Infantry cited; DA GO 43, 1950)

*Cited in the Order of the Day of the Belgian Army for action in the ARDENNES (9th Infantry cited; DA GO 43, 1950)

*Cited in the Order of the Day of the Belgian Army for action at ELSENBORN CREST (9th Infantry cited; DA GO 43, 1950)

*Vietnamese Cross of Gallantry with Palm, Streamer embroidered VIETNAM 1966–1968 (4th Battalion, 9th Infantry cited; DA GO 48, 1971)

5th BATTALION, 9th INFANTRY

(Manchu)

AR
(inactive)

LINEAGE

Constituted 3 March 1855 in the Regular Army as Company E, 9th Infantry. Organized 17 March 1855 at Fort Monroe, Virginia. Consolidated in June 1869 with Company E, 27th Infantry (see ANNEX) and consolidated unit designated as Company E, 9th Infantry. (9th Infantry assigned 22 September 1917 to the 2d Division [later redesignated as the 2d Infantry Division].)

Inactivated 20 June 1957 in Alaska and relieved from assignment to the 2d Infantry Division; concurrently, redesignated as Headquarters and Headquarters Company, 5th Battle Group, 9th Infantry. Redesignated 26 March 1963 as Headquarters and Headquarters Company, 5th Battalion, 9th Infantry, withdrawn from the Regular Army, allotted to the Army Reserve, and assigned to the 102d Infantry Division (organic elements concurrently constituted). Battalion activated 1 April 1963 with Headquarters at Danville, Illinois. Inactivated 31 December 1965 at Danville, Illinois.

ANNEX

Constituted 3 May 1861 in the Regular Army as Company E, 2d Battalion, 18th Infantry. Organized in October 1861 at Camp Thomas, Ohio. Reorganized and redesignated 21 September 1866 as Company E, 27th Infantry. Consolidated in June 1869 with Company E, 9th Infantry and consolidated unit designated as Company E, 9th Infantry.

CAMPAIGN PARTICIPATION CREDIT

Civil War
  *Murfreesborough
  *Chickamauga
  *Chattanooga
  *Atlanta
  *Mississippi 1862
  *Kentucky 1862
  *Tennessee 1863
  *Georgia 1864

Indian Wars
  Little Big Horn
  *Washington 1856
  *Washington 1858
  *Wyoming 1866
  Wyoming 1867

War With Spain
  *Santiago

China Relief Expedition
  *Tientsin
  *Yang-tsun
  *Peking.

Philippine Insurrection
  San Isidro
  *Zapote River
  *Malolos
  *Tarlac

*Luzon 1899
*Luzon 1900
*Samar 1901

World War I
  *Aisne
  *Aisne-Marne
  *St. Mihiel
  *Meuse-Argonne
  *Lorraine 1918
  *Ile de France 1918

World War II
  *Normandy (with arrowhead)
  *Northern France
  *Rhineland
  *Ardennes-Alsace
  *Central Europe

Korean War
  *UN defensive
  *UN offensive
  *CCF intervention
  *First UN counteroffensive
  *CCF spring offensive
  *UN summer-fall offensive
  *Second Korean winter
  *Korea, summer-fall 1952
  *Third Korean winter
  *Korea, summer 1953

DECORATIONS

Presidential Unit Citation (Army), Streamer embroidered BREST, FRANCE

*Presidential Unit Citation (Army), Streamer embroidered SIEGFRIED LINE (2d Battalion, 9th Infantry cited; WD GO 38, 1945)

Presidential Unit Citation (Army), Streamer embroidered ARDENNES

*Presidential Unit Citation (Army), Streamer embroidered HONG-CHON (2d Infantry Division cited; DA GO 72, 1951)

Presidential Unit Citation (Navy), Streamer embroidered HWACHON RESERVOIR

Navy Unit Commendation, Streamer embroidered PANMUNJOM

*French Croix de Guerre with Palm, World War I, Streamer embroidered AISNE-MARNE (9th Infantry cited; WD GO 11, 1924)

*French Croix de Guerre with Palm, World War I, Streamer embroidered MEUSE-ARGONNE (9th Infantry cited; WD GO 11, 1924)

*French Croix de Guerre with Palm, World War I, Streamer em-

broidered CHATEAU THIERRY (9th Infantry cited; WD GO 11, 1924)

*French Croix de Guerre, World War I, Fourragere (9th Infantry cited; WD GO 11, 1924)

*Republic of Korea Presidential Unit Citation, Streamer embroidered NAKTONG RIVER LINE (9th Infantry cited; DA GO 35, 1951)

*Republic of Korea Presidential Unit Citation, Streamer embroidered KOREA (9th Infantry cited; DA GO 10, 1954)

*Luxembourg Croix de Guerre, Streamer embroidered LUXEMBOURG (9th Infantry cited; DA GO 43, 1950)

*Belgian Fourragere 1940 (9th Infantry cited; DA GO 43, 1950)

*Cited in the Order of the Day of the Belgian Army for action in the ARDENNES (9th Infantry cited; DA GO 43, 1950)

*Cited in the Order of the Day of the Belgian Army for action at ELSENBORN CREST (9th Infantry cited; DA GO 43, 1950)

6th BATTALION, 9th INFANTRY

(Manchu)

RA
(171st Infantry Brigade)

LINEAGE

Constituted 3 March 1855 in the Regular Army as Company F, 9th Infantry. Organized 22 May 1855 at Fort Monroe, Virginia. Consolidated in June 1869 with Company F, 27th Infantry (see ANNEX) and consolidated unit designated as Company F, 9th Infantry. (9th Infantry assigned 22 September 1917 to the 2d Division [later redesignated as the 2d Infantry Division].)

Inactivated 20 June 1957 in Alaska and relieved from assignment to the 2d Infantry Division; concurrently, redesignated as Headquarters and Headquarters Company, 6th Battle Group, 9th Infantry. Redesignated 17 December 1965 as Headquarters and Headquarters Company, 6th Battalion, 9th Infantry and assigned to the 171st Infantry Brigade (organic elements concurrently constituted). Battalion activated 20 December 1965 in Alaska.

ANNEX

Constituted 3 May 1861 in the Regular Army as Company F, 2d Battalion, 18th Infantry. Organized in October 1861 at Camp Thomas, Ohio. Reorganized and redesignated 21 September 1866 as Company F, 27th Infantry. Consolidated in June 1869 with Company F, 9th Infantry and consolidated unit designated as Company F, 9th Infantry.

CAMPAIGN PARTICIPATION CREDIT

Civil War
Murfreesborough
*Chickamauga
*Chattanooga
*Atlanta
*Mississippi 1862
*Kentucky 1862
*Tennessee 1863
*Georgia 1864

Indian Wars
Little Big Horn
*Washington 1856
Washington 1858
Wyoming 1866
*Wyoming 1867

War With Spain
*Santiago

China Relief Expedition
*Tientsin
*Yang-tsun
*Peking

Philippine Insurrection
San Isidro
Zapote River
*Malolos
*Tarlac

*Luzon 1899
*Luzon 1900
*Samar 1901

World War I
*Aisne
*Aisne-Marne
*St. Mihiel
*Meuse-Argonne
*Lorraine 1918
*Ile de France 1918

World War II
*Normandy (with arrowhead)
*Northern France
*Rhineland
*Ardennes-Alsace
*Central Europe

Korean War
*UN defensive
*UN offensive
*CCF intervention
*First UN counteroffensive
*CCF spring offensive
*UN summer-fall offensive
*Second Korean winter
*Korea, summer-fall 1952
*Third Korean winter
*Korea, summer 1953

DECORATIONS

Presidential Unit Citation (Army), Streamer embroidered BREST, FRANCE

*Presidential Unit Citation (Army), Streamer embroidered SIEGFRIED LINE (2d Battalion, 9th Infantry cited; WD GO 38, 1945)

Presidential Unit Citation (Army), Streamer embroidered ARDENNES

*Presidential Unit Citation (Army), Streamer embroidered HONG-CHON (2d Infantry Division cited; DA GO 72, 1951)

Presidential Unit Citation (Navy), Streamer embroidered HWACHON RESERVOIR

Navy Unit Commendation, Streamer embroidered PANMUNJOM

*French Croix de Guerre with Gilt Star, World War I, Streamer embroidered ILE DE FRANCE (Company F, 9th Infantry cited; WD GO 11, 1924)

*French Croix de Guerre with Palm, World War I, Streamer embroidered AISNE-MARNE (9th Infantry cited; WD GO 11, 1924)

*French Croix de Guerre with Palm, World War I, Streamer embroidered MEUSE-ARGONNE (9th Infantry cited; WD GO 11, 1924)

*French Croix de Guerre with Palm, World War I, Streamer embroidered CHATEAU THIERRY (9th Infantry cited; WD GO 11, 1924)

*French Croix de Guerre, World War I, Fourragere (9th Infantry cited; WD GO 11, 1924)

*Republic of Korea Presidential Unit Citation, Streamer embroidered NAKTONG RIVER LINE (9th Infantry cited; DA GO 35, 1951)

*Republic of Korea Presidential Unit Citation, Streamer embroidered KOREA (9th Infantry cited; DA GO 10, 1954)

*Luxembourg Croix de Guerre, Streamer embroidered LUXEMBOURG (9th Infantry cited; DA GO 43, 1950)

*Belgian Fourragere 1940 (9th Infantry cited; DA GO 43, 1950)

*Cited in the Order of the Day of the Belgian Army for action in the ARDENNES (9th Infantry cited; DA GO 43, 1950)

*Cited in the Order of the Day of the Belgian Army for action at ELSENBORN CREST (9th Infantry cited; DA GO 43, 1950)

9TH INFANTRY, BIBLIOGRAPHY

Appleman, Roy E. *South to the Naktong, North to the Yalu.* United States Army in the Korean War. Washington: Government Printing Office, 1961.

Blumenson, Martin. *Breakout and Pursuit.* United States Army in World War II. Washington: Government Printing Office, 1961.

Bookmiller, Edwin W. "The Ninth Infantry in the Santiago Campaign," *The Santiago Campaign.* Richmond: Williams Printing Company, 1927, pp. 58–65.

Bumpus, Everett C. *In Memoriam.* Norwood: Norwood Press, 1902.

Brown, Fred Radford. *History of the Ninth U.S. Infantry, 1799–1909.* Chicago: R. R. Donelly and Sons Company, Inc., 1909. (Erroneously connects this regiment with an earlier one of the same designation.)

Brown, William. *The Adventures of an American Doughboy.* Tacoma, 1919.

Carrington, Frances (Courtney). *My Army Life and the Fort Phil Kearney Massacre, with an Account of the Celebration of "Wyoming Opened."* Philadelphia and London, 1910.

Cole, Hugh M. *The Ardennes: Battle of the Bulge.* United States Army in World War II. Washington: Government Printing Office, 1964.

Gugeler, Russell A. *Combat Actions in Korea.* Washington: Combat Forces Press, 1954.

Harrison, Gordon A. *Cross-Channel Attack.* United States Army in World War II. Washington: Government Printing Office, 1951.

Hermes, Walter G. *Truce Tent and Fighting Front.* United States Army in the Korean War. Washington: Government Printing Office, 1966.

Historical Section, War Department. *Omaha Beachhead.* American Forces in Action Series. Washington: Government Printing Office, 1945.

The History of the Ninth United States Infantry. n.p., 1946.

The History of the 9th U.S. Infantry and the Liscum Bowl, 1798–1956. Fort Lewis, Washington, 1956. (Erroneously connects this regiment with an earlier one of the same designation.)

MacDonald, Charles B. *The Siegfried Line Campaign.* United States Army in World War II. Washington: Government Printing Office, 1963.

Marshall, S. L. A. *The River and the Gauntlet.* New York: William Morrow and Company, 1953.

9th Infantry Regiment. Fort Lewis Review. Baton Rouge: Army and Navy Publishing Company, 1947.

The Ninth U.S. Infantry in the World War. Neuwied am Rhein : Louis Heusersche Buchdruckerei (J. Meincke), 1919.

Robertson, Edgar Brooks. "The Ninth Regiment of Infantry," *The Army of the United States,* edited by Theophilus F. Rodenbough and William L. Haskin. New York: Maynard, Merrill and Company, 1896, pp. 526–530. (Originally published in the *Journal of the Military Service Institution of the United States,* XV [1894], 446–450.)

"Unveiling Exercises of Memorial Tablet to Emerson Hamilton Liscum. . . Fletcher Free Library, Burlington, Vermont, 10:30 AM, April 28, 1911." Burlington: Free Press Printing, 1911.

Vail, Glenn H. "Lest We Forget, A Personal Narrative of the Prowess of the 9th Infantry While 'Over There' . . ." n.p., 192?

Wall, Gerald C., Jr. "What's Left of Company C?" *Saga* (November 1953), 35ff.

Wood, Lambert. *His Job, Letters Written by a 22-year-old Lieutenant in the World War to his Parents and Others in Oregon.* Portland, Oregon: Metropolitan Press, 1932.

10th INFANTRY

HERALDIC ITEMS

BADGE (Regimental badge in lieu of coat of arms)

Blazonry: A Roman numeral "X" azure, superimposed on a Roman sword in scabbard palewise point down or, overall a circular band argent, fimbriated of the second, bearing the regimental motto "Courage and Fidelity" in chief and the date in Roman numerals "MDCCCLV" in base, both of the first.

Symbolism: The Roman numeral "X" signifies the numerical designation of the regiment; the sword is representative of the dress sabers carried by the officers of the regiment when it was organized; the circular band is indicative of the knapsack straps and waist belts, like those of the French *chasseurs-à-pied,* worn by the 10th Infantry in the late 1850's. The motto is taken from an address made by Colonel Edmund B. Alexander, first colonel of the regiment, upon the occasion of the presentation of the regimental colors at Carlisle Barracks, Pennsylvania, in September 1855. The Roman numerals "MDCCCLV" signify the year the regiment was constituted and organized.

DISTINCTIVE INSIGNIA

The distinctive insignia is the badge of the regiment.

LINEAGE AND HONORS

LINEAGE

Constituted 3 March 1855 in the Regular Army as the 10th Infantry. Organized in April 1855 at Carlisle Barracks, Pennsylvania. Consolidated June–July 1869 with the 26th Infantry (see ANNEX) and consolidated unit designated as the 10th Infantry.

Assigned 5 July 1918 to the 14th Division. Relieved in February 1919 from assignment to the 14th Division. (2d and 3d Battalions inactivated 16 December 1921 at Camp Sherman, Ohio; activated 7 June

1922 at Camp Knox, Kentucky.) Assigned 24 March 1923 to the 5th Division (later redesignated as the 5th Infantry Division). (1st Battalion inactivated 31 October 1929 at Fort Thomas, Kentucky; activated 1 October 1933 at Fort Hayes, Ohio.) Inactivated 20 September 1946 at Camp Campbell, Kentucky.

Activated 15 July 1947 at Fort Jackson, South Carolina. Inactivated 30 April 1950 at Fort Jackson, South Carolina. Activated 1 March 1951 at Indiantown Gap Military Reservation, Pennsylvania. Inactivated 1 September 1953 at Indiantown Gap Military Reservation, Pennsylvania. Activated 25 May 1954 at Galingen, Germany.

Relieved 1 June 1957 from assignment to the 5th Infantry Division and reorganized as a parent regiment under the Combat Arms Regimental System.

ANNEX

Constituted 3 May 1861 in the Regular Army as the 2d Battalion, 17th Infantry. Organized in June 1862 at Fort Preble, Maine. Reorganized and redesignated 16 December 1866 as the 26th Infantry. Consolidated June–July 1869 with the 10th Infantry and consolidated unit designated as the 10th Infantry.

CAMPAIGN PARTICIPATION CREDIT

Civil War
  Peninsula
  Manassas
  Antietam
  Fredericksburg
  Chancellorsville
  Gettysburg
  Wilderness
  Spotsylvania
  Cold Harbor
  Petersburg
  New Mexico 1862
  Virginia 1862
  Virginia 1863

Indian Wars
  Comanches
  Apaches

War With Spain
  Santiago

Philippine Insurrection
  Without inscription

World War II
  Normandy
  Northern France
  Rhineland
  Ardennes-Alsace
  Central Europe

DECORATIONS

French Croix de Guerre with Palm, World War II, Streamer embroidered MOSELLE RIVER (10th Infantry cited; DA GO 43, 1950)

1st BATTALION, 10th INFANTRY

RA

(4th Infantry Division)

LINEAGE

Constituted 3 March 1855 in the Regular Army as Company A, 10th Infantry. Organized in June 1855 at Carlisle Barracks, Pennsylvania. Consolidated 10 June 1869 with Company A, 26th Infantry (see AN-NEX) and consolidated unit designated as Company A, 10th Infantry. (10th Infantry assigned 5 July 1918 to the 14th Division; relieved in February 1919 from assignment to the 14th Division; assigned 24 March 1923 to the 5th Division [later redesignated as the 5th Infantry Division].) Inactivated 31 October 1929 at Fort Thomas, Kentucky. Activated 1 October 1933 at Fort Hayes, Ohio. Inactivated 20 September 1946 at Camp Campbell, Kentucky.

Activated 15 July 1947 at Fort Jackson, South Carolina. Inactivated 30 April 1950 at Fort Jackson, South Carolina. Activated 1 March 1951 at Indiantown Gap Military Reservation, Pennsylvania. Inactivated 1 September 1953 at Indiantown Gap Military Reservation, Pennsylvania. Activated 25 May 1954 at Galingen, Germany.

Reorganized and redesignated 1 June 1957 as Headquarters and Headquarters Company, 1st Battle Group, 10th Infantry and relieved from assignment to the 5th Infantry Division (organic elements concurrently constituted and activated or organized from existing units). Inactivated 25 April 1961 at Fort Ord, California. Redesignated 3 February 1962 as the 1st Battalion, 10th Infantry and activated at Fort Carson, Colorado. Assigned 19 February 1962 to the 5th Infantry Division. Relieved 15 December 1970 from assignment to the 5th Infantry Division and assigned to the 4th Infantry Division.

ANNEX

Constituted 3 May 1861 in the Regular Army as Company A, 2d Battalion, 17th Infantry. Organized in June 1862 at Fort Preble, Maine. Reorganized and redesignated 16 December 1866 as Company A, 26th Infantry. Consolidated 10 June 1869 with Company A, 10th Infantry and consolidated unit designated as Company A, 10th Infantry.

Campaign Participation Credit

Civil War
Peninsula
Manassas
Antietam
Fredericksburg
*Chancellorsville
*Gettysburg
*Wilderness
*Spotsylvania
*Cold Harbor
*Petersburg
*New Mexico 1862
Virginia 1862
*Virginia 1863

Indian Wars
*Comanches

Apaches
*New Mexico 1860
*New Mexico 1861

War With Spain
*Santiago

Philippine Insurrection
*Mindanao

World War II
*Normandy
*Northern France
*Rhineland
*Ardennes-Alsace
*Central Europe

Decorations

*French Croix de Guerre with Palm, World War II, Streamer embroidered MOSELLE RIVER (10th Infantry cited; DA GO 43, 1950)

2d BATTALION, 10th INFANTRY

RA
(4th Infantry Division)

LINEAGE

Constituted 3 March 1855 in the Regular Army as Company B, 10th Infantry. Organized in June 1855 at Carlisle Barracks, Pennsylvania. Consolidated 23 June 1869 with Company B, 26th Infantry (see ANNEX) and consolidated unit designated as Company B, 10th Infantry. (10th Infantry assigned 5 July 1918 to the 14th Division; relieved in February 1919 from assignment to the 14th Division; assigned 24 March 1923 to the 5th Division [later redesignated as the 5th Infantry Division].) Inactivated 31 October 1929 at Fort Thomas, Kentucky. Activated 1 October 1933 at Fort Hayes, Ohio. Inactivated 20 September 1946 at Camp Campbell, Kentucky.

Activated 15 July 1947 at Fort Jackson, South Carolina. Inactivated 30 April 1950 at Fort Jackson, South Carolina. Activated 1 March 1951 at Indiantown Gap Military Reservation, Pennsylvania. Inactivated 1 September 1953 at Indiantown Gap Military Reservation, Pennsylvania. Activated 25 May 1954 at Galingen, Germany. Inactivated 1 June 1957 at Fort Ord, California, and relieved from assignment to the 5th Infantry Division.

Redesignated 1 July 1957 as Headquarters and Headquarters Company, 2d Battle Group, 10th Infantry, assigned to the 10th Infantry Division, and activated in Germany (organic elements concurrently constituted and activated). Inactivated 14 June 1958 at Fort Benning, Georgia, and relieved from assignment to the 10th Infantry Division. Activated 23 April 1960 at Fort William D. Davis, Canal Zone. Reorganized and redesignated 19 February 1962 as the 2d Battalion, 10th Infantry and assigned to the 5th Infantry Division. Relieved 15 December 1970 from assignment to the 5th Infantry Division and assigned to the 4th Infantry Division.

ANNEX

Constituted 3 May 1861 in the Regular Army as Company B, 2d Battalion, 17th Infantry. Organized in June 1862 at Fort Preble, Maine. Reorganized and redesignated 16 December 1866 as Company B, 26th Infantry. Consolidated 23 June 1869 with Company B, 10th Infantry and consolidated unit designated as Company B, 10th Infantry.

CAMPAIGN PARTICIPATION CREDIT

Civil War
  *Peninsula
  Manassas
  Antietam
  Fredericksburg
  Chancellorsville
  Gettysburg
  *Wilderness
  *Spotsylvania
  *Cold Harbor
  *Petersburg
  New Mexico 1862
  Virginia 1862
  Virginia 1863

Indian Wars
  Comanches
  *Apaches

War With Spain
  *Santiago

Philippine Insurrection
  *Without inscription

World War II
  *Normandy
  *Northern France
  *Rhineland
  *Ardennes-Alsace
  *Central Europe

DECORATIONS

*French Croix de Guerre with Palm, World War II, Streamer embroidered MOSELLE RIVER (10th Infantry cited; DA GO 43, 1950)

3d BATTALION, 10th INFANTRY

RA
(inactive)

Constituted 3 March 1855 in the Regular Army as Company C, 10th Infantry. Organized in June 1855 at Carlisle Barracks, Pennsylvania. Consolidated 25 July 1869 with Company C, 26th Infantry (see ANNEX 1) and consolidated unit designated as Company C, 10th Infantry. (10th Infantry assigned 5 July 1918 to the 14th Division; relieved in February 1919 from assignment to the 14th Division; assigned 24 March 1923 to the 5th Division [later redesignated as the 5th Infantry Division].) Inactivated 31 October 1929 at Fort Thomas, Kentucky. Activated 1 October 1933 at Fort Hayes, Ohio. Inactivated 20 September 1946 at Camp Campbell, Kentucky.

Activated 15 July 1947 at Fort Jackson, South Carolina. Inactivated 30 April 1950 at Fort Jackson, South Carolina. Activated 1 March 1951 at Indiantown Gap Military Reservation, Pennsylvania. Inactivated 1 September 1953 at Indiantown Gap Military Reservation, Pennsylvania. Activated 25 May 1954 at Galingen, Germany. Inactivated 1 June 1957 at Fort Ord, California, and relieved from assignment to the 5th Infantry Division.

Redesignated 19 March 1959 as Headquarters and Headquarters Company, 3d Battle Group, 10th Infantry, withdrawn from the Regular Army, allotted to the Army Reserve, and assigned to the 83d Infantry Division (organic elements concurrently constituted). Battle Group activated 20 March 1959 with Headquarters at Cleveland, Ohio (concurrently, Headquarters and Headquarters Company consolidated with Headquarters and Headquarters Company, 1st Battalion, 331st Infantry [see ANNEX 2] and consolidated unit designated as Headquarters and Headquarters Company, 3d Battle Group, 10th Infantry). Reorganized and redesignated 15 April 1963 as the 3d Battalion, 10th Infantry. Inactivated 31 December 1965 at Cleveland, Ohio.

Withdrawn 10 May 1967 from the Army Reserve and allotted to the Regular Army; concurrently, relieved from assignment to the 83d Infantry Division and assigned to the 5th Infantry Division. Activated 26 May 1967 at Fort Carson, Colorado. Inactivated 15 December 1970 at Fort Carson, Colorado.

ANNEX 1

Constituted 3 May 1861 in the Regular Army as Company C, 2d Battalion, 17th Infantry. Organized in June 1862 at Fort Preble, Maine. Reorganized and redesignated 16 December 1866 as Company C, 26th Infantry. Consolidated 25 July 1869 with Company C, 10th Infantry and consolidated unit designated as Company C, 10th Infantry.

ANNEX 2

Constituted 5 August 1917 in the National Army as Headquarters and Headquarters Company, 1st Battalion, 331st Infantry, an element of the 83d Division. Organized 30 August 1917 at Camp Sherman, Ohio. Demobilized 9 February 1919 at Camp Sherman, Ohio. Reconstituted 24 June 1921 in the Organized Reserves as an element of the 83d Division (later redesignated as the 83d Infantry Division). Organized in November 1921 at Cleveland, Ohio. Ordered into active military service 15 August 1942 and reorganized at Camp Atterbury, Indiana. Inactivated 30 March 1946 at Camp Kilmer, New Jersey.

Activated 26 December 1946 in the Organized Reserves at Columbus, Ohio. (Organized Reserves redesignated 25 March 1948 as the Organized Reserve Corps; redesignated 9 July 1952 as the Army Reserve.) Consolidated 20 March 1959 with Headquarters and Headquarters Company, 3d Battle Group, 10th Infantry and consolidated unit designated as Headquarters and Headquarters Company, 3d Battle Group, 10th Infantry.

CAMPAIGN PARTICIPATION CREDIT

Civil War
  Peninsula
  Manassas
  Antietam
  *Fredericksburg
  Chancellorsville
  Gettysburg
  *Wilderness
  *Spotsylvania
  *Cold Harbor
  *Petersburg
  New Mexico 1862
  Virginia 1862
  *Virginia 1863

Indian Wars
  *Comanches
  *Apaches

War With Spain
  *Santiago

Philippine Insurrection
  *Without inscription

World War I
  *Without inscription

World War II
  *Normandy
  *Northern France
  *Rhineland
  *Ardennes-Alsace
  *Central Europe

DECORATIONS

*French Croix de Guerre with Palm, World War II, Streamer embroidered MOSELLE RIVER (10th Infantry cited; DA GO 43, 1950)

4th BATTALION, 10th INFANTRY

RA

(193d Infantry Brigade)

LINEAGE

Constituted 3 March 1855 in the Regular Army as Company D, 10th Infantry. Organized in June 1855 at Carlisle Barracks, Pennsylvania. Consolidated 25 July 1869 with Company D, 26th Infantry (see AN-NEX) and consolidated unit designated as Company D, 10th Infantry. (10th Infantry assigned 5 July 1918 to the 14th Division; relieved in February 1919 from assignment to the 14th Division; assigned 24 March 1923 to the 5th Division [later redesignated as the 5th Infantry Division].) Inactivated 31 October 1929 at Fort Thomas, Kentucky. Activated 1 October 1933 at Fort Hayes, Ohio. Inactivated 20 September 1946 at Camp Campbell, Kentucky.

Activated 15 July 1947 at Fort Jackson, South Carolina. Inactivated 30 April 1950 at Fort Jackson, South Carolina. Activated 1 March 1951 at Indiantown Gap Military Reservation, Pennsylvania. Inactivated 1 September 1953 at Indiantown Gap Military Reservation, Pennsylvania. Activated 25 May 1954 at Galingen, Germany.

Inactivated 1 June 1957 at Fort Ord, California, and relieved from assignment to the 5th Infantry Division; concurrently, redesignated as Headquarters and Headquarters Company, 4th Battle Group, 10th Infantry. Activated 19 February 1962 at Fort William D. Davis, Canal Zone (organic elements concurrently constituted and activated). Reorganized and redesignated 1 October 1962 as the 4th Battalion, 10th Infantry and assigned to the 193d Infantry Brigade.

ANNEX

Constituted 3 May 1861 in the Regular Army as Company D, 2d Battalion, 17th Infantry. Organized in June 1862 at Fort Preble, Maine. Reorganized and redesignated 16 December 1866 as Company D, 26th Infantry. Consolidated 25 July 1869 with Company D, 10th Infantry and consolidated unit designated as Company D, 10th Infantry.

CAMPAIGN PARTICIPATION CREDIT

Civil War
  Peninsula
  Manassas
  Antietam
  Fredericksburg
  *Chancellorsville
  *Gettysburg
  *Wilderness
  *Spotsylvania
  *Cold Harbor
  *Petersburg
  New Mexico 1862
  Virginia 1862
  *Virginia 1863

Indian Wars
  Comanches
  *Apaches

War With Spain
  *Santiago

Philippine Insurrection
  *Without inscription

World War II
  *Normandy
  *Northern France
  *Rhineland
  *Ardennes-Alsace
  *Central Europe

DECORATIONS

*French Croix de Guerre with Palm, World War II, Streamer embroidered MOSELLE RIVER (10th Infantry cited; DA GO 43, 1950)

5th BATTALION, 10th INFANTRY

RA
(inactive)

LINEAGE

Constituted 3 March 1855 in the Regular Army as Company E, 10th Infantry. Organized in June 1855 at Carlisle Barracks, Pennsylvania. Consolidated in July 1869 with Company E, 26th Infantry (see AN-NEX) and consolidated unit designated as Company E, 10th Infantry. (10th Infantry assigned 5 July 1918 to the 14th Division; relieved in February 1919 from assignment to the 14th Division.) Inactivated 16 December 1921 at Camp Sherman, Ohio. Activated 7 June 1922 at Camp Knox, Kentucky. (10th Infantry assigned 24 March 1923 to the 5th Division [later redesignated as the 5th Infantry Division].) Inactivated 20 September 1946 at Camp Campbell, Kentucky.

Activated 15 July 1947 at Fort Jackson, South Carolina. Inactivated 30 April 1950 at Fort Jackson, South Carolina. Activated 1 March 1951 at Indiantown Gap Military Reservation, Pennsylvania. Inactivated 1 September 1953 at Indiantown Gap Military Reservation, Pennsylvania. Activated 25 May 1954 at Galingen, Germany.

Reorganized and redesignated 1 June 1957 as Company E, 1st Battle Group, 10th Infantry (concurrently, 10th Infantry relieved from assignment to the 5th Infantry Division). Inactivated 25 April 1961 at Fort Ord, California; concurrently, redesignated as Headquarters and Head-quarters Company, 5th Battle Group, 10th Infantry. Redesignated 15 November 1969 as Headquarters and Headquarters Company, 5th Battalion, 10th Infantry and activated at Fort Carson, Colorado, as an element of the 5th Infantry Division (organic elements concurrently constituted and activated). Inactivated 15 October 1970 at Fort Carson, Colorado.

ANNEX

Constituted 3 May 1861 in the Regular Army as Company E, 2d Battalion, 17th Infantry. Organized in June 1862 at Fort Preble, Maine. Reorganized and redesignated 16 December 1866 as Company E, 26th Infantry. Consolidated in July 1869 with Company E, 10th Infantry and consolidated unit designated as Company E, 10th Infantry.

291

CAMPAIGN PARTICIPATION CREDIT

Civil War
  *Peninsula
  *Manassas
  *Antietam
  *Fredericksburg
  Chancellorsville
  Gettysburg
  Wilderness
  Spotsylvania
  Cold Harbor
  Petersburg
  New Mexico 1862
  *Virginia 1862
  Virginia 1863

Indian Wars
  Comanches
  Apaches
  *Nebraska 1855

War With Spain
  *Santiago

Philippine Insurrection
  *Without inscription

World War II
  *Normandy
  *Northern France
  *Rhineland
  *Ardennes-Alsace
  *Central Europe

DECORATIONS

*French Croix de Guerre with Palm, World War II, Streamer embroidered MOSELLE RIVER (10th Infantry cited; DA GO 43, 1950)

10TH INFANTRY, BIBLIOGRAPHY

Blumenson, Martin. *Breakout and Pursuit*. United States Army in World War II. Washington: Government Printing Office, 1961.

Breckinridge, W. E. *10th Infantry Regiment Combat Narrative*. Birmingham, Alabama: Military Service Publication Company, 1947.

Cole, Hugh M. *The Ardennes: Battle of the Bulge*. United States Army in World War II. Washington: Government Printing Office, 1964.

————. *The Lorraine Campaign*. United States Army in World War II. Washington: Government Printing Office, 1950.

History of the Tenth Infantry From 1855 to 1938. Fort Thomas, Kentucky, 1938.

History of Tenth Infantry Regiment, United States Army. Birmingham, Alabama: Military Service Publication Company, 1946.

MacDonald, Charles B. and Sidney T. Mathews. *Three Battles: Arnaville, Altuzzo, and Schmidt*. United States Army in World War II. Washington: Government Printing Office, 1952.

Seyburn, Stephen Young. *History of the Tenth United States Infantry*. Santa Fe, 1890.

————. "The Tenth Regiment of Infantry," *The Army of the United States*, edited by Theophilus F. Rodenbough and William L. Haskin. New York: Maynard, Merrill and Company, 1896, pp. 531–544. (Originally published in the *Journal of the Military Service Institution of the United States*, XIII [1892], 415–428.)

10th Infantry's Centennial. Augsburg, Germany, 1955.

10th United States Infantry. Monterey: W. T. Lee Company, 1957.

11th INFANTRY

HERALDIC ITEMS

COAT OF ARMS

Shield: Azure, Satanta's arrow in fess argent, between in chief a castle or, in base a kampilan and bolo in saltire of the second hilted of the third; on a chief embattled of the second a cross gules.

Crest: On a wreath of the colors a fusil gules bearing a cross pattée argent charged with an acorn of the first.

Motto: *Semper Fidelis* (Always Faithful).

Symbolism: The shield is blue, the infantry color, and carries the castle from the arms of Spain for the War with Spain and Satanta's "arrow" for the regiment's campaign against the Comanches, Cheyennes, and Kiowas in 1874. Satanta was a noted Kiowa Indian chief whose "arrow" was really a spear with feathers on the end and a handle. The crossed kampilan and bolo show engagements against the Moros of Mindanao and the Filipinos of the Visayas, respectively. A chief of honorable augmentation bearing the cross of the ancient Lords of Dun commemorates the crossing of the Meuse River near Dun during World War I. The embattled partition represents the siege of Chattanooga in 1863.

During the Civil War the predecessors of the 11th Infantry served in the 1st Division, XIV Corps and the 2d Division, V Corps, whose badges were a red acorn and a white Maltese cross, respectively. In World War I the regiment was an element of the 5th Division, with a red lozenge as the shoulder sleeve insignia. A combination of these three insignia forms the crest.

DISTINCTIVE INSIGNIA

The distinctive insignia is the shield of the coat of arms.

Lineage and Honors

Lineage

Constituted 3 May 1861 in the Regular Army as the 2d Battalion, 15th Infantry. Organized 6 May 1862 at Newport Barracks, Kentucky. Reorganized and redesignated 1 December 1866 as the 24th Infantry. Consolidated 25 April 1869 with the 29th Infantry (see ANNEX) and consolidated unit designated as the 11th Infantry.

Assigned 17 November 1917 to the 5th Division (later redesignated as the 5th Infantry Division). Inactivated 20 September 1946 at Camp Campbell, Kentucky. Activated 15 July 1947 at Fort Jackson, South Carolina. Inactivated 30 April 1950 at Fort Jackson, South Carolina. Activated 1 March 1951 at Indiantown Gap Military Reservation, Pennsylvania. Inactivated 1 September 1953 at Indiantown Gap Military Reservation, Pennsylvania. Activated 25 May 1954 in Germany.

Relieved 1 June 1957 from assignment to the 5th Infantry Division and reorganized as a parent regiment under the Combat Arms Regimental System.

Annex

Constituted 3 May 1861 in the Regular Army as the 3d Battalion, 11th Infantry. Organized 20 August 1863 at Fort Independence, Massachusetts. Reorganized and redesignated 1 December 1866 as the 29th Infantry. Consolidated 25 April 1869 with the 24th Infantry and consolidated unit designated as the 11th Infantry.

CAMPAIGN PARTICIPATION CREDIT

Civil War
  Shiloh
  Murfreesborough
  Chickamauga
  Chattanooga
  Atlanta
  Mississippi 1862
  Kentucky 1862
  Tennessee 1863
  Georgia 1864

Indian Wars
  Comanches

War With Spain
  Puerto Rico

Philippine Insurrection
  Mindanao

World War I
  St. Mihiel
  Meuse-Argonne
  Alsace 1918
  Lorraine 1918

World War II
  Normandy
  Northern France
  Rhineland
  Ardennes-Alsace
  Central Europe

Vietnam
  (to be determined)

DECORATIONS
None.

1st BATTALION, 11th INFANTRY

RA
(5th Infantry Division)

Constituted 3 May 1861 in the Regular Army as Company A, 2d Battalion, 15th Infantry. Organized 6 May 1862 at Newport Barracks, Kentucky. Reorganized and redesignated 1 December 1866 as Company A, 24th Infantry.

Consolidated 25 April 1869 with Company A, 29th Infantry (see ANNEX) and consolidated unit designated as Company A, 11th Infantry. (11th Infantry assigned 17 November 1917 to the 5th Division [later redesignated as the 5th Infantry Division].) Inactivated 20 September 1946 at Camp Campbell, Kentucky. Activated 15 July 1947 at Fort Jackson, South Carolina. Inactivated 30 April 1950 at Fort Jackson, South Carolina. Activated 1 March 1951 at Indiantown Gap Military Reservation, Pennsylvania. Inactivated 1 September 1953 at Indiantown Gap Military Reservation, Pennsylvania. Activated 25 May 1954 in Germany. Inactivated 1 June 1957 at Fort Ord, California.

Redesignated 4 March 1958 as Headquarters and Headquarters Company, 1st Battle Group, 11th Infantry and relieved from assignment to the 5th Infantry Division. Battle Group activated 14 June 1958 at Fort Benning, Georgia, as an element of the 2d Infantry Division. Reorganized and redesignated 19 February 1962 as the 1st Battalion, 11th Infantry; concurrently, relieved from assignment to the 2d Infantry Division and assigned to the 5th Infantry Division.

ANNEX

Constituted 3 May 1861 in the Regular Army as Company A, 3d Battalion, 11th Infantry. Organized 20 August 1863 at Fort Independence, Massachusetts. Reorganized and redesignated 1 December 1866 as Company A, 29th Infantry. Consolidated 25 April 1869 with Company A, 24th Infantry and consolidated unit designated as Company A, 11th Infantry.

298

Campaign Participation Credit

Civil War
Shiloh
Murfreesborough
Chickamauga
*Chattanooga
*Atlanta
Mississippi 1862
Kentucky 1862
Tennessee 1863
Georgia 1864

Indian Wars
*Comanches

War With Spain
*Puerto Rico

Philippine Insurrection
Mindanao

World War I
*St. Mihiel
*Meuse-Argonne
*Alsace 1918
*Lorraine 1918

World War II
*Normandy
*Northern France
*Rhineland
*Ardennes-Alsace
*Central Europe

Vietnam
(to be determined)

Decorations

*Vietnamese Cross of Gallantry with Palm, Streamer embroidered VIETNAM 1968 (1st Battalion, 11th Infantry cited; DA GO 43, 1970)

2d BATTALION, 11th INFANTRY

RA
(4th Infantry Division)

Constituted 3 May 1861 in the Regular Army as Company B, 2d Battalion, 15th Infantry. Organized in May 1862 at Newport Barracks, Kentucky. Reorganized and redesignated 1 December 1866 as Company B, 24th Infantry.

Consolidated 25 April 1869 with Company B, 29th Infantry (see ANNEX) and consolidated unit designated as Company B, 11th Infantry. (11th Infantry assigned 17 November 1917 to the 5th Division [later redesignated as the 5th Infantry Division].) Inactivated 20 September 1946 at Camp Campbell, Kentucky. Activated 15 July 1947 at Fort Jackson, South Carolina. Inactivated 30 April 1950 at Fort Jackson, South Carolina. Activated 1 March 1951 at Indiantown Gap Military Reservation, Pennsylvania. Inactivated 1 September 1953 at Indiantown Gap Military Reservation, Pennsylvania. Activated 25 May 1954 in Germany.

Inactivated 1 June 1957 at Fort Ord, California, and relieved from assignment to the 5th Infantry Division; concurrently, redesignated as Headquarters and Headquarters Company, 2d Battle Group, 11th Infantry. Redesignated 19 February 1962 as Headquarters and Headquarters Company, 2d Battalion, 11th Infantry, assigned to the 5th Infantry Division, and activated at Fort Carson, Colorado (organic elements concurrently constituted and activated). Relieved 15 December 1970 from assignment to the 5th Infantry Division and assigned to the 4th Infantry Division.

ANNEX

Constituted 3 May 1861 in the Regular Army as Company B, 3d Battalion, 11th Infantry. Organized 20 August 1863 at Fort Independence, Massachusetts. Reorganized and redesignated 1 December 1866 as Company B, 29th Infantry. Consolidated 25 April 1869 with Company B, 24th Infantry and consolidated unit designated as Company B, 11th Infantry.

Campaign Participation Credit

Civil War
- Shiloh
- Murfreesborough
- Chickamauga
- *Chattanooga
- *Atlanta
- Mississippi 1862
- Kentucky 1862
- Tennessee 1863
- Georgia 1864

Indian Wars
- Comanches

War With Spain
- *Puerto Rico

Philippine Insurrection
- Mindanao

World War I
- *St. Mihiel
- *Meuse-Argonne
- *Alsace 1918
- *Lorraine 1918

World War II
- *Normandy
- *Northern France
- *Rhineland
- *Ardennes-Alsace
- *Central Europe

Decorations
None.

3d BATTALION, 11th INFANTRY

RA

(4th Infantry Division)

LINEAGE

Constituted 3 May 1861 in the Regular Army as Company C, 2d Battalion, 15th Infantry. Organized 19 May 1862 at Newport Barracks, Kentucky. Reorganized and redesignated 1 December 1866 as Company C, 24th Infantry.

Consolidated 25 April 1869 with Company C, 29th Infantry (see ANNEX 1) and consolidated unit designated as Company C, 11th Infantry. (11th Infantry assigned 17 November 1917 to the 5th Division [later redesignated as the 5th Infantry Division].) Inactivated 20 September 1946 at Camp Campbell, Kentucky. Activated 15 July 1947 at Fort Jackson, South Carolina. Inactivated 30 April 1950 at Fort Jackson, South Carolina. Activated 1 March 1951 at Indiantown Gap Military Reservation, Pennsylvania. Inactivated 1 September 1953 at Indiantown Gap Military Reservation, Pennsylvania. Activated 25 May 1954 in Germany. Inactivated 1 June 1957 at Fort Ord, California, and relieved from assignment to the 5th Infantry Division.

Redesignated 19 March 1959 as Headquarters and Headquarters Company, 3d Battle Group, 11th Infantry, withdrawn from the Regular Army, allotted to the Army Reserve, and assigned to the 83d Infantry Division (organic elements concurrently constituted). Battle Group activated 20 March 1959 with Headquarters at Cincinnati, Ohio (concurrently, Headquarters and Headquarters Company consolidated with Headquarters and Headquarters Company, 336th Infantry [see ANNEX 2] and consolidated unit designated as Headquarters and Headquarters Company, 3d Battle Group, 11th Infantry). Reorganized and redesignated 15 April 1963 as the 3d Battalion, 11th Infantry. Inactivated 31 December 1965 at Cincinnati, Ohio.

Withdrawn 10 May 1967 from the Army Reserve and allotted to the Regular Army; concurrently, relieved from assignment to the 83d Infantry Division and assigned to the 5th Infantry Division. Activated 26 May 1967 at Fort Carson, Colorado. Relieved 15 December 1970 from assignment to the 5th Infantry Division and assigned to the 4th Infantry Division.

Constituted 3 May 1861 in the Regular Army as Company C, 3d Battalion, 11th Infantry. Organized 20 August 1863 at Fort Independence, Massachusetts. Reorganized and redesignated 1 December 1866 as Company C, 29th Infantry. Consolidated 25 April 1869 with Company C, 24th Infantry and consolidated unit designated as Company C, 11th Infantry.

Constituted 5 August 1917 in the National Army as Headquarters and Headquarters Company, 336th Infantry, an element of the 84th Division. Organized 25 August 1917 at Camp Zachary Taylor, Kentucky. Demobilized 18 February 1919 at Camp Zachary Taylor, Kentucky. Reconstituted 21 June 1921 in the Organized Reserves as an element of the 84th Division. Organized in November 1921 at Culver, Indiana. Inactivated 30 January 1942 at Culver, Indiana (concurrently, 336th Infantry relieved from assignment to the 84th Division). (Organized Reserves redesignated 25 March 1948 as the Organized Reserve Corps; redesignated 9 July 1952 as the Army Reserve.)

Activated 5 December 1955 in the Army Reserve at Fort Thomas, Kentucky, as an element of the 83d Infantry Division. Consolidated 20 March 1959 with Headquarters and Headquarters Company, 3d Battle Group, 11th Infantry and consolidated unit designated as Headquarters and Headquarters Company, 3d Battle Group, 11th Infantry (remainder of 336th Infantry inactivated).

CAMPAIGN PARTICIPATION CREDIT

Civil War
Shiloh
Murfreesborough
Chickamauga
*Chattanooga
*Atlanta
Mississippi 1862
Kentucky 1862
Tennessee 1863
Georgia 1864

Indian Wars
Comanches

War With Spain
*Puerto Rico

Philippine Insurrection
Mindanao

World War I
*St. Mihiel
*Meuse-Argonne
*Alsace 1918
*Lorraine 1918

World War II
*Normandy
*Northern France
*Rhineland
*Ardennes-Alsace
*Central Europe

DECORATIONS

None.

4th BATTALION, 11th INFANTRY

AR
(inactive)

LINEAGE

Constituted 3 May 1861 in the Regular Army as Company D, 2d Battalion, 15th Infantry. Organized in May 1862 at Newport Barracks, Kentucky. Reorganized and redesignated 1 December 1866 as Company D, 24th Infantry.

Consolidated 25 April 1869 with Company D, 29th Infantry (see ANNEX) and consolidated unit designated as Company D, 11th Infantry. (11th Infantry assigned 17 November 1917 to the 5th Division [later redesignated as the 5th Infantry Division].) Inactivated 20 September 1946 at Camp Campbell, Kentucky. Activated 15 July 1947 at Fort Jackson, South Carolina. Inactivated 30 April 1950 at Fort Jackson, South Carolina. Activated 1 March 1951 at Indiantown Gap Military Reservation, Pennsylvania. Inactivated 1 September 1953 at Indiantown Gap Military Reservation, Pennsylvania. Activated 25 May 1954 in Germany.

Inactivated 1 June 1957 at Fort Ord, California, and relieved from assignment to the 5th Infantry Division; concurrently, redesignated as Headquarters and Headquarters Company, 4th Battle Group, 11th Infantry. Redesignated 27 March 1963 as Headquarters and Headquarters Company, 4th Battalion, 11th Infantry, withdrawn from the Regular Army, allotted to the Army Reserve, and assigned to the 83d Infantry Division (organic elements concurrently constituted). Battalion activated 15 April 1963 with Headquarters at South Charleston, West Virginia. Inactivated 31 December 1965 at South Charleston, West Virginia.

ANNEX

Constituted 3 May 1861 in the Regular Army as Company D, 3d Battalion, 11th Infantry. Organized 20 August 1863 at Fort Independence, Massachusetts. Reorganized and redesignated 1 December 1866 as Company D, 29th Infantry. Consolidated 25 April 1869 with Company D, 24th Infantry and consolidated unit designated as Company D, 11th Infantry.

CAMPAIGN PARTICIPATION CREDIT

Civil War
Shiloh
Murfreesborough
Chickamauga
*Chattanooga
*Atlanta
Mississippi 1862
Kentucky 1862
Tennessee 1863
Georgia 1864

Indian Wars
Comanches

War With Spain
*Puerto Rico

Philippine Insurrection
Mindanao
*Samar 1901

World War I
*St. Mihiel
*Meuse-Argonne
*Alsace 1918
*Lorraine 1918

World War II
*Normandy
*Northern France
*Rhineland
*Ardennes-Alsace
*Central Europe

DECORATIONS

None.

5th BATTALION, 11th INFANTRY

RA
(inactive)

LINEAGE

Constituted 3 May 1861 in the Regular Army as Company E, 2d Battalion, 15th Infantry. Organized in May 1862 at Newport Barracks, Kentucky. Reorganized and redesignated 1 December 1866 as Company E, 24th Infantry.

Consolidated 25 April 1869 with Company E, 29th Infantry (see ANNEX) and consolidated unit designated as Company E, 11th Infantry. (11th Infantry assigned 17 November 1917 to the 5th Division [later redesignated as the 5th Infantry Division].) Inactivated 20 September 1946 at Camp Campbell, Kentucky. Activated 15 July 1947 at Fort Jackson, South Carolina. Inactivated 30 April 1950 at Fort Jackson, South Carolina. Activated 1 March 1951 at Indiantown Gap Military Reservation, Pennsylvania. Inactivated 1 September 1953 at Indiantown Gap Military Reservation, Pennsylvania. Activated 25 May 1954 in Germany.

Inactivated 1 June 1957 at Fort Ord, California, and relieved from assignment to the 5th Infantry Division; concurrently, redesignated as Headquarters and Headquarters Company, 5th Battle Group, 11th Infantry. Redesignated 15 November 1969 as Headquarters and Headquarters Company, 5th Battalion, 11th Infantry and activated at Fort Carson, Colorado, as an element of the 5th Infantry Division (organic elements concurrently constituted and activated). Inactivated 15 December 1970 at Fort Carson, Colorado.

ANNEX

Constituted 3 May 1861 in the Regular Army as Company E, 3d Battalion, 11th Infantry. Organized 20 August 1863 at Fort Independence, Massachusetts. Reorganized and redesignated 1 December 1866 as Company E, 29th Infantry. Consolidated 25 April 1869 with Company E, 24th Infantry and consolidated unit designated as Company E, 11th Infantry.

Campaign Participation Credit

Civil War
Shiloh
Murfreesborough
*Chickamauga
*Chattanooga
*Atlanta
Mississippi 1862
Kentucky 1862
Tennessee 1863
Georgia 1864

Indian Wars
*Comanches

War With Spain
*Puerto Rico

Philippine Insurrection
*Mindanao

World War I
*St. Mihiel
*Meuse-Argonne
*Alsace 1918
*Lorraine 1918

World War II
*Normandy
*Northern France
*Rhineland
*Ardennes-Alsace
*Central Europe

Decorations

*French Croix de Guerre with Palm, World War II, Streamer embroidered FONTAINEBLEAU (2d Battalion, 11th Infantry cited; DA GO 43, 1950)

11TH INFANTRY, BIBLIOGRAPHY

Blumenson, Martin. *Breakout and Pursuit.* United States Army in World War II. Washington: Government Printing Office, 1961.

Brief History of the Eleventh United States Infantry, November 5, 1926. Fort Benjamin Harrison, Indiana, 1926.

Cole, Hugh M. *The Ardennes: Battle of the Bulge.* United States Army in World War II. Washington: Government Printing Office, 1964.

————. *The Lorraine Campaign.* United States Army in World War II. Washington: Government Printing Office, 1950.

11th Infantry, 5th Infantry Division, Fort Custer, Michigan, 1941. Baton Rouge: Army and Navy Publishing Company, 1941.

Eleventh Infantry Organization Day, 16 July 1956, Fort Ord, California. San Francisco?: E. F. [Bill] Shannon, 1956.

History of the 11th Infantry Regiment, Fifth Infantry Division. Baton Rouge: Army and Navy Publishing Company, 1946.

MacDonald, Charles B. and Sidney T. Mathews. *Three Battles: Arnaville, Altuzzo, and Schmidt.* United States Army in World War II. Washington: Government Printing Office, 1952.

A Manual for the Men of the Eleventh. Fort Benjamin Harrison, Indiana, 1934.

Patterson, J. H. and R. J. C. Irvine. "The Eleventh Regiment of Infantry," *The Army of the United States,* edited by Theophilus F. Rodenbough and William L. Haskin. New York: Maynard, Merrill and Company, 1896, pp. 545–554. (Originally published in the *Journal of the Military Service Institution of the United States,* XII [1891], 371–380.)

Roster of the 11th U.S. Infantry, From the 14th Day of May 1861, to the 14th Day of May, 1866. Richmond, 1866.

12th INFANTRY

HERALDIC ITEMS

COAT OF ARMS

Shield: Azure, in fess two crosses moline argent, in base a wigwam of the like garnished gules with five poles of the last; on a chief embattled or a sea lion of the third holding in dexter paw a sword of the field.

Crest: On a wreath of the colors an armored arm embowed proper, grasping in the naked hand a broken flag staff gules, to which is attached a pennant or.

Motto: *Ducti Amore Patriae* (Having Been Led by Love of Country).

Symbolism: The field is blue for infantry. This regiment took part in the Civil War; its great achievement was its first engagement at Gaines' Mill, Virginia, on 27 and 28 June 1862, where its losses were almost 50 percent. This is shown by the moline crosses which represent the iron fastening of a millstone and recall the crushing losses sustained. The wigwam stands for the Indian campaigns in which the regiment took part. The chief is for the War with Spain and the Philippine Insurrection, yellow and red being the Spanish colors, red and blue the Katipunan colors; the embattled partition line is for the capture of the blockhouse at El Caney, Cuba, and the sea lion is from the arms of the Philippine Islands.

The crest in the Spanish colors commemorates the capture of a Spanish flag at El Caney.

DISTINCTIVE INSIGNIA

The distinctive insignia is a modified version of the shield of the coat of arms.

311

Lineage and Honors

Lineage

Constituted 3 May 1861 in the Regular Army as the 1st Battalion, 12th Infantry. Organized 20 October 1861 at Fort Hamilton, New York. Reorganized and redesignated 7 December 1866 as the 12th Infantry.

Assigned 17 December 1917 to the 8th Division. Relieved 15 August 1927 from assignment to the 8th Division and assigned to the 4th Division. Relieved 1 October 1933 from assignment to the 4th Division and assigned to the 8th Division. Relieved 10 October 1941 from assignment to the 8th Division and assigned to the 4th Division (later redesignated as the 4th Infantry Division). Inactivated 27 February 1946 at Camp Butner, North Carolina. Activated 15 July 1947 at Fort Ord, California.

Relieved 1 April 1957 from assignment to the 4th Infantry Division and reorganized as a parent regiment under the Combat Arms Regimental System.

Campaign Participation Credit

Civil War
  Peninsula
  Manassas
  Antietam
  Fredericksburg
  Chancellorsville
  Gettysburg
  Wilderness
  Spotsylvania
  Cold Harbor
  Petersburg
  Virginia 1862
  Virginia 1863

Indian Wars
  Modocs
  Bannocks
  Pine Ridge

War With Spain
  Santiago

Philippine Insurrection
  Malolos
  Tarlac
  Luzon 1899

World War II
  Normandy (with arrowhead)
  Northern France
  Rhineland
  Ardennes-Alsace
  Central Europe

Vietnam
  Counteroffensive, Phase II
  Counteroffensive, Phase III
  Tet Counteroffensive
  (other campaigns to be
    determined)

Decorations

Presidential Unit Citation (Army), Streamer embroidered LUXEMBOURG (12th Infantry cited; WD GO 54, 1945)

Presidential Unit Citation (Army), Streamer embroidered SUOI TRE, VIETNAM (2d Battalion, 12th Infantry cited; DA GO 59, 1968)

Presidential Unit Citation (Army), Streamer embroidered PLEIKU

PROVINCE (3d Battalion, 12th Infantry cited; DA GO 69, 1969)

Valorous Unit Award, Streamer embroidered PLEIKU PROVINCE (1st Battalion, 12th Infantry cited; DA GO 17, 1968)

Valorous Unit Award, Streamer embroidered SAIGON–LONG BINH (4th Battalion, 12th Infantry cited; DA GO 48, 1968)

Valorous Unit Award, Streamer embroidered CENTRAL HIGHLANDS (1st Battalion, 12th Infantry cited; DA GO 43, 1970)

Belgian Fourragere 1940 (12th Infantry cited; DA GO 43, 1950)

Cited in the Order of the Day of the Belgian Army for action in BELGIUM (12th Infantry cited; DA GO 43, 1950)

Cited in the Order of the Day of the Belgian Army for action in the ARDENNES (12th Infantry cited; DA GO 43, 1950)

1st BATTALION, 12th INFANTRY

RA
(4th Infantry Division)

LINEAGE

Constituted 3 May 1861 in the Regular Army as Company A, 1st Battalion, 12th Infantry. Organized 20 October 1861 at Fort Hamilton, New York. Reorganized and redesignated 7 December 1866 as Company A, 12th Infantry. (12th Infantry assigned 17 December 1917 to the 8th Division; relieved 15 August 1927 from assignment to the 8th Division and assigned to the 4th Division; relieved 1 October 1933 from assignment to the 4th Division and assigned to the 8th Division; relieved 10 October 1941 from assignment to the 8th Division and assigned to the 4th Division [later redesignated as the 4th Infantry Division].) Inactivated 27 February 1946 at Camp Butner, North Carolina. Activated 15 July 1947 at Fort Ord, California.

Reorganized and redesignated 1 April 1957 as Headquarters and Headquarters Company, 1st Battle Group, 12th Infantry and remained assigned to the 4th Infantry Division (organic elements concurrently constituted and activated). Reorganized and redesignated 1 October 1963 as the 1st Battalion, 12th Infantry.

314

CAMPAIGN PARTICIPATION CREDIT

Civil War
*Peninsula
*Manassas
*Antietam
*Fredericksburg
*Chancellorsville
*Gettysburg
*Wilderness
*Spotsylvania
*Cold Harbor
*Petersburg
Virginia 1862
*Virginia 1863

Indian Wars
Modocs
Bannocks
*Pine Ridge

War With Spain
*Santiago

Philippine Insurrection
*Malolos
*Tarlac
*Luzon 1899

World War II
*Normandy (with arrowhead)
*Northern France
*Rhineland
*Ardennes-Alsace
*Central Europe

Vietnam
*Counteroffensive, Phase II
*Counteroffensive, Phase III
*Tet Counteroffensive
(other campaigns to be determined)

DECORATIONS

*Presidential Unit Citation (Army), Streamer embroidered LUXEMBOURG (12th Infantry cited; WD GO 54, 1945)

*Valorous Unit Award, Streamer embroidered PLEIKU PROVINCE (1st Battalion, 12th Infantry cited; DA GO 17, 1968)

*Valorous Unit Award, Streamer embroidered CENTRAL HIGHLANDS (1st Battalion, 12th Infantry cited; DA GO 43, 1970)

*Belgian Fourragere 1940 (12th Infantry cited; DA GO 43, 1950)

*Cited in the Order of the Day of the Belgian Army for action in BELGIUM (12th Infantry cited; DA GO 43, 1950)

*Cited in the Order of the Day of the Belgian Army for action in the ARDENNES (12th Infantry cited; DA GO 43, 1950)

*Vietnamese Cross of Gallantry with Palm, Streamer embroidered VIETNAM 1966–1969 (1st Battalion, 12th Infantry cited; DA GO 3, 1970)

*Vietnamese Civil Action Honor Medal, First Class, Streamer embroidered VIETNAM 1966–1969 (1st Battalion, 12th Infantry cited; DA GO 53, 1970)

Company B and Company C each additionally entitled to: Valorous Unit Award, Streamer embroidered KONTUM (Company B and Company C, 1st Battalion, 12th Infantry cited; DA GO 43, 1970)

2d BATTALION, 12th INFANTRY

RA

(25th Infantry Division)

LINEAGE

Constituted 3 May 1861 in the Regular Army as Company B, 1st Battalion, 12th Infantry. Organized 20 October 1861 at Fort Hamilton, New York. Reorganized and redesignated 7 December 1866 as Company B, 12th Infantry. (12th Infantry assigned 17 December 1917 to the 8th Division; relieved 15 August 1927 from assignment to the 8th Division and assigned to the 4th Division; relieved 1 October 1933 from assignment to the 4th Division and assigned to the 8th Division; relieved 10 October 1941 from assignment to the 8th Division and assigned to the 4th Division [later redesignated as the 4th Infantry Division].) Inactivated 27 February 1946 at Camp Butner, North Carolina. Activated 15 July 1947 at Fort Ord, California. Inactivated 1 April 1957 at Fort Lewis, Washington, and relieved from assignment to the 4th Infantry Division.

Redesignated 1 August 1957 as Headquarters and Headquarters Company, 2d Battle Group, 12th Infantry, assigned to the 8th Infantry Division, and activated in Germany (organic elements concurrently constituted and activated). Relieved 24 March 1959 from assignment to the 8th Infantry Division and assigned to the 1st Infantry Division. Reorganized and redesignated 1 October 1963 as the 2d Battalion, 12th Infantry; concurrently, relieved from assignment to the 1st Infantry Division and assigned to the 4th Infantry Division. Relieved 1 August 1967 from assignment to the 4th Infantry Division and assigned to the 25th Infantry Division.

316

Campaign Participation Credit

Civil War
  *Peninsula
  *Manassas
  *Antietam
  *Fredericksburg
  *Chancellorsville
  *Gettysburg
  *Wilderness
  *Spotsylvania
  *Cold Harbor
  *Petersburg
  *Virginia 1862
  *Virginia 1863

Indian Wars
  Modocs
  Bannocks
  Pine Ridge

War With Spain
  *Santiago

Philippine Insurrection
  *Malolos
  *Tarlac
  *Luzon 1899

World War II
  *Normandy (with arrowhead)
  *Northern France
  *Rhineland
  *Ardennes-Alsace
  *Central Europe

Vietnam
  *Counteroffensive, Phase II
  *Counteroffensive, Phase III
  *Tet Counteroffensive
  (other campaigns to be
  determined)

Decorations

*Presidential Unit Citation (Army), Streamer embroidered LUXEM-BOURG (12th Infantry cited; WD GO 54, 1945)

*Presidential Unit Citation (Army), Streamer embroidered SUOI TRE, VIETNAM (2d Battalion, 12th Infantry cited; DA GO 59, 1968)

*Belgian Fourragere 1940 (12th Infantry cited; DA GO 43, 1950)

*Cited in the Order of the Day of the Belgian Army for action in BELGIUM (12th Infantry cited; DA GO 43, 1950)

*Cited in the Order of the Day of the Belgian Army for action in the ARDENNES (12th Infantry cited; DA GO 43, 1950)

*Vietnamese Cross of Gallantry with Palm, Streamer embroidered VIETNAM 1966–1967 (2d Battalion, 12th Infantry cited; DA GO 3, 1970, as amended by DA GO 48, 1971)

*Vietnamese Cross of Gallantry with Palm; Streamer embroidered VIETNAM 1967–1968 (2d Battalion, 12th Infantry cited; DA GO 48, 1971)

3d BATTALION, 12th INFANTRY

RA
(inactive)

LINEAGE

Constituted 3 May 1861 in the Regular Army as Company C, 1st Battalion, 12th Infantry. Organized 20 October 1861 at Fort Hamilton, New York. Reorganized and redesignated 7 December 1866 as Company C, 12th Infantry. (12th Infantry assigned 17 December 1917 to the 8th Division; relieved 15 August 1927 from assignment to the 8th Division and assigned to the 4th Division; relieved 1 October 1933 from assignment to the 4th Division and assigned to the 8th Division; relieved 10 October 1941 from assignment to the 8th Division and assigned to the 4th Division [later redesignated as the 4th Infantry Division].) Inactivated 27 February 1946 at Camp Butner, North Carolina. Activated 15 July 1947 at Fort Ord, California.

Inactivated 1 April 1957 at Fort Lewis, Washington, and relieved from assignment to the 4th Infantry Division; concurrently, redesignated as Headquarters and Headquarters Company, 3d Battle Group, 12th Infantry. Withdrawn 17 March 1959 from the Regular Army, allotted to the Army Reserve, and assigned to the 79th Infantry Division (organic elements concurrently constituted). Battle Group activated 23 March 1959 with Headquarters at Baltimore, Maryland. Inactivated 28 February 1963 at Baltimore, Maryland. Relieved 28 March 1963 from assignment to the 79th Infantry Division.

Redesignated 16 September 1965 as the 3d Battalion, 12th Infantry; concurrently, withdrawn from the Army Reserve, allotted to the Regular Army, and assigned to the 4th Infantry Division. Activated 1 November 1965 at Fort Lewis, Washington. Inactivated 15 December 1970 at Fort Carson, Colorado.

318

Campaign Participation Credit

Civil War
 *Peninsula
 *Manassas
 *Antietam
 *Fredericksburg
 *Chancellorsville
 *Gettysburg
 *Wilderness
 *Spotsylvania
 *Cold Harbor
 *Petersburg
 *Virginia 1862
 *Virginia 1863

Indian Wars
 Modocs
 *Bannocks
 Pine Ridge

War With Spain
 *Santiago

Philippine Insurrection
 *Malolos
 *Tarlac
 *Luzon 1899

World War II
 *Normandy (with arrowhead)
 *Northern France
 *Rhineland
 *Ardennes-Alsace
 *Central Europe

Vietnam
 *Counteroffensive, Phase II
 *Counteroffensive, Phase III
 *Tet Counteroffensive
 (other campaigns to be
 determined)

Decorations

*Presidential Unit Citation (Army), Streamer embroidered LUXEM-BOURG (12th Infantry cited; WD GO 54, 1945)

*Presidential Unit Citation (Army), Streamer embroidered PLEIKU PROVINCE (3d Battalion, 12th Infantry cited; DA GO 69, 1969)

*Belgian Fourragere 1940 (12th Infantry cited; DA GO 43, 1950)

*Cited in the Order of the Day of the Belgian Army for action in BELGIUM (12th Infantry cited; DA GO 43, 1950)

*Cited in the Order of the Day of the Belgian Army for action in the ARDENNES (12th Infantry cited; DA GO 43, 1950)

*Vietnamese Cross of Gallantry with Palm, Streamer embroidered VIETNAM 1966–1969 (3d Battalion, 12th Infantry cited; DA GO 3, 1970)

*Vietnamese Civil Action Honor Medal, First Class, Streamer embroidered VIETNAM 1966–1969 (3d Battalion, 12th Infantry cited; DA GO 53, 1970)

4th BATTALION, 12th INFANTRY

RA
(inactive)

Constituted 3 May 1861 in the Regular Army as Company D, 1st Battalion, 12th Infantry. Organized in October 1861 at Fort Hamilton, New York. Reorganized and redesignated 7 December 1866 as Company D, 12th Infantry. (12th Infantry assigned 17 December 1917 to the 8th Division; relieved 15 August 1927 from assignment to the 8th Division and assigned to the 4th Division; relieved 1 October 1933 from assignment to the 4th Division and assigned to the 8th Division; relieved 10 October 1941 from assignment to the 8th Division and assigned to the 4th Division [later redesignated as the 4th Infantry Division].) Inactivated 27 February 1946 at Camp Butner, North Carolina. Activated 15 July 1947 at Fort Ord, California.

Inactivated 1 April 1957 at Fort Lewis, Washington, and relieved from assignment to the 4th Infantry Division; concurrently, redesignated as Headquarters and Headquarters Company, 4th Battle Group, 12th Infantry. Redesignated 23 March 1966 as Headquarters and Headquarters Company, 4th Battalion, 12th Infantry and assigned to the 199th Infantry Brigade (organic elements concurrently constituted). Battalion activated 1 June 1966 at Fort Benning, Georgia. Inactivated 15 October 1970 at Fort Benning, Georgia.

CAMPAIGN PARTICIPATION CREDIT

Civil War
  *Peninsula
  *Manassas
  *Antietam
  *Fredericksburg
  *Chancellorsville
  *Gettysburg
  *Wilderness
  *Spotsylvania
  *Cold Harbor
  *Petersburg
  Virginia 1862
  *Virginia 1863

Indian Wars
  Modocs
  *Bannocks
  Pine Ridge
  *Arizona 1881

War With Spain
  *Santiago

Philippine Insurrection
  *Malolos
  *Tarlac
  *Luzon 1899

World War II
  *Normandy (with arrowhead)
  *Northern France
  *Rhineland
  *Ardennes-Alsace
  *Central Europe

Vietnam
  *Counteroffensive, Phase II
  *Counteroffensive, Phase III
  *Tet Counteroffensive
  (other campaigns to be
  determined)

DECORATIONS

*Presidential Unit Citation (Army), Streamer embroidered LUXEM-BOURG (12th Infantry cited; WD GO 54, 1945)

*Valorous Unit Award, Streamer embroidered SAIGON–LONG BINH (4th Battalion, 12th Infantry cited; DA GO 48, 1968)

*Belgian Fourragere 1940 (12th Infantry cited; DA GO 43, 1950)

*Cited in the Order of the Day of the Belgian Army for action in BELGIUM (12th Infantry cited; DA GO 43, 1950)

*Cited in the Order of the Day of the Belgian Army for action in the ARDENNES (12th Infantry cited; DA GO 43, 1950)

*Vietnamese Cross of Gallantry with Palm, Streamer embroidered VIETNAM 1968 (4th Battalion, 12th Infantry cited; DA GO 43, 1970)

Company D additionally entitled to: Presidential Unit Citation (Army), Streamer embroidered SAIGON (Company D, 4th Battalion, 12th Infantry cited; DA GO 60, 1969)

5th BATTALION, 12th INFANTRY

RA
(inactive)

LINEAGE

Constituted 3 May 1861 in the Regular Army as Company E, 1st Battalion, 12th Infantry. Organized 20 October 1861 at Fort Hamilton, New York. Reorganized and redesignated 7 December 1866 as Company E, 12th Infantry. (12th Infantry assigned 17 December 1917 to the 8th Division; relieved 15 August 1927 from assignment to the 8th Division and assigned to the 4th Division; relieved 1 October 1933 from assignment to the 4th Division and assigned to the 8th Division; relieved 10 October 1941 from assignment to the 8th Division and assigned to the 4th Division [later redesignated as the 4th Infantry Division].) Inactivated 27 February 1946 at Camp Butner, North Carolina. Activated 15 July 1947 at Fort Ord, California.

Inactivated 1 April 1957 at Fort Lewis, Washington, and relieved from assignment to the 4th Infantry Division; concurrently, redesignated as Headquarters and Headquarters Company, 5th Battle Group, 12th Infantry. Redesignated 1 November 1967 as Headquarters and Headquarters Company, 5th Battalion, 12th Infantry and activated at Fort Lewis, Washington (organic elements concurrently constituted and activated). Assigned 7 April 1968 to the 199th Infantry Brigade. Inactivated 15 October 1970 at Fort Benning, Georgia.

322

Campaign Participation Credit

Civil War
*Peninsula
*Manassas
*Antietam
*Fredericksburg
Chancellorsville
Gettysburg
Wilderness
Spotsylvania
Cold Harbor
*Petersburg
Virginia 1862
Virginia 1863

Indian Wars
*Modocs
Bannocks
Pine Ridge

War With Spain
*Santiago

Philippine Insurrection
*Malolos
*Tarlac
*Luzon 1899

World War II
*Normandy (with arrowhead)
*Northern France
*Rhineland
*Ardennes-Alsace
*Central Europe

Vietnam
(to be determined)

Decorations

*Presidential Unit Citation (Army), Streamer embroidered LUXEM-BOURG (12th Infantry cited; WD GO 54, 1945)

*Belgian Fourragere 1940 (12th Infantry cited; DA GO 43, 1950)

*Cited in the Order of the Day of the Belgian Army for action in BELGIUM (12th Infantry cited; DA GO 43, 1950)

*Cited in the Order of the Day of the Belgian Army for action in the ARDENNES (12th Infantry cited; DA GO 43, 1950)

12TH INFANTRY, BIBLIOGRAPHY

Abbott, Charles W. "The Twelfth Regiment of Infantry," *The Army of the United States,* edited by Theophilus F. Rodenbough and William L. Haskin. New York: Maynard, Merrill and Company, 1896, pp. 555–574. (Originally published in the *Journal of the Military Service Institution of the United States,* XIV [1893], 1125–1144.)

Albright, John, John A. Cash, and Allan W. Sandstrum. *Seven Firefights in Vietnam.* Washington: Government Printing Office, 1970.

Anderson, T. M. "Civil War Recollections of the Twelfth Infantry," *Journal of the Military Service Institution of the United States,* XLI (November–December 1907) , 379–393.

Blumenson, Martin. *Breakout and Pursuit.* United States Army in World War II. Washington: Government Printing Office, 1961.

"Brief History: 2d Battle Group, 12th Infantry." n.p., 1957.

Cole, Hugh M. *The Ardennes: Battle of the Bulge.* United States Army in World War II. Washington: Government Printing Office, 1964.

Harbeson, James F. and J. G. Knabenshue. *History of the 12th Infantry Regiment.* n.p., 1909.

Harrison, Gordon A. *Cross-Channel Attack.* United States Army in World War II. Washington: Government Printing Office, 1951.

Historical Section, War Department. *Utah Beach to Cherbourg.* American Forces in Action Series. Washington: Government Printing Office, 1947.

History of the 4th Infantry Division and Brief Histories of Its Components. Fort Lewis, Washington, 1958.

Johnson, Gerden F. *History of the Twelfth Infantry Regiment in World War II.* Boston: National Fourth (Ivy) Division Association, 1947.

MacDonald, Charles B. *The Battle of Huertgen Forest.* Philadelphia and New York: J. B. Lippincott Company, 1963.

———. *The Siegfried Line Campaign.* United States Army in World War II. Washington: Government Printing Office, 1963.

Marshall, S. L. A. *West to Cambodia.* New York: Cowles Education Corporation, 1968.

Roster of Commissioned Officers of the 12th U.S. Infantry Since Organization May 4, 1861. Fort Niagara, New York: B. L. Cowley, Printer, 1897.

"Twelfth Infantry Regiment," *A Pictorial History of the 4th Infantry Division.* Baton Rouge: Army and Navy Publishing Company, 1945.

Twelfth U.S. Infantry, 1798–1919, Its Story, By Its Men, Published by the Members of the Twelfth U.S. Infantry. New York: Knickerbocker Press, 1919. (Erroneously connects this regiment with an earlier one of the same designation.)

Wister, Francis. *Recollections of the 12th U.S. Infantry and Regular Division, 1861–1865*. Philadelphia, 1887.

13th INFANTRY

(First at Vicksburg)

COAT OF ARMS

Shield: Barry of four azure and argent, a saltire gules, and in fess two billets paleways sable fimbriated or each bearing four mullets of the second (the shoulder strap of a general of 1870).

Crest: On a wreath of the colors two palm branches saltirewise proper and thereon a McKeever cartridge box sable bearing the legend "Forty Rounds" "U.S." or.

Motto: First at Vicksburg.

Symbolism: The four blue and white bars of the shield are in the present and old infantry colors and indicate service in the Civil War, the War with Spain, the Indian Wars, and the Philippine Insurrection. The saltire cross is from the Confederate battle flag with the color changed from blue to red. The billets are the shoulder straps of the two generals which this regiment has produced, Generals Sherman and Sheridan. (When the 13th Infantry was organized in 1861–62, Sherman was its first colonel and Sheridan was one of its original captains.)

The crest is the badge of the XV Corps of the Civil War and the motto is the proud designation given the regiment by General Grant.

DISTINCTIVE INSIGNIA

The distinctive insignia is the shield, crest, and motto of the coat of arms.

327

Lineage and Honors

Lineage

Constituted 3 May 1861 in the Regular Army as the 1st Battalion, 13th Infantry. Organized 27 July 1861–1 April 1862 at Jefferson Barracks, Missouri, and Alton, Illinois. Reorganized and redesignated 21 September 1866 as the 13th Infantry.

Assigned 17 December 1917 to the 8th Division. (2d and 3d Battalions inactivated 15 September 1921 at Camp Devens, Massachusetts; activated 10 June 1922 at Camp Devens, Massachusetts.) Relieved 24 March 1923 from assignment to the 8th Division and assigned to the 9th Division. Relieved 15 August 1927 from assignment to the 9th Division and assigned to the 5th Division. (1st Battalion inactivated 31 October 1929 at Fort Strong, Massachusetts.) Relieved 1 October 1933 from assignment to the 5th Division and assigned to the 9th Division. Regiment (less 1st Battalion) inactivated 14 June 1940 in the Canal Zone. Relieved 22 June 1940 from assignment to the 9th Division and assigned to the 8th Division (later redesignated as the 8th Infantry Division). Activated 14 July 1940 at Camp Jackson, South Carolina. Inactivated 18 November 1945 at Fort Leonard Wood, Missouri. Activated 17 August 1950 at Fort Jackson, South Carolina.

Relieved 1 August 1957 from assignment to the 8th Infantry Division and reorganized as a parent regiment under the Combat Arms Regimental System.

CAMPAIGN PARTICIPATION CREDIT

Civil War
Mississippi River
Vicksburg
Chattanooga
Mississippi 1863
Tennessee 1863

Indian Wars
North Dakota 1866
Montana 1868

War With Spain
Santiago

Philippine Insurrection
Cavite
San Fabian
Luzon 1899
Luzon 1900

World War II
Normandy
Northern France
Rhineland
Central Europe

DECORATIONS

Presidential Unit Citation (Army), Streamer embroidered HURTGEN FOREST (1st Battalion, 13th Infantry cited; WD GO 21, 1947)

French Croix de Guerre with Palm, World War II, Streamer embroidered NORMANDY (13th Infantry cited; DA GO 43, 1950)

Luxembourg Croix de Guerre, Streamer embroidered LUXEMBOURG (8th Infantry Division cited; DA GO 59, 1969)

1st BATTALION, 13th INFANTRY

(First at Vicksburg)

LINEAGE

Constituted 3 May 1861 in the Regular Army as Company A, 1st Battalion, 13th Infantry. Organized 8 October 1861 at Jefferson Barracks, Missouri. Reorganized and redesignated 21 September 1866 as Company A, 13th Infantry. (13th Infantry assigned 17 December 1917 to the 8th Division; relieved 24 March 1923 from assignment to the 8th Division and assigned to the 9th Division; relieved 15 August 1927 from assignment to the 9th Division and assigned to the 5th Division.) Inactivated 31 October 1929 at Fort Strong, Massachusetts. (13th Infantry relieved 1 October 1933 from assignment to the 5th Division and assigned to the 9th Division; relieved 22 June 1940 from assignment to the 9th Division and assigned to the 8th Division [later redesignated as the 8th Infantry Division].) Activated 14 July 1940 at Camp Jackson, South Carolina. Inactivated 18 November 1945 at Fort Leonard Wood, Missouri. Activated 17 August 1950 at Fort Jackson, South Carolina.

Reorganized and redesignated 1 August 1957 as Headquarters and Headquarters Company, 1st Battle Group, 13th Infantry and remained assigned to the 8th Infantry Division (organic elements concurrently constituted and activated). Relieved 28 February 1959 from assignment to the 8th Infantry Division and assigned to the 1st Infantry Division. Reorganized and redesignated 25 April 1963 as the 1st Battalion, 13th Infantry; concurrently, relieved from assignment to the 1st Infantry Division and assigned to the 8th Infantry Division.

330

CAMPAIGN PARTICIPATION CREDIT

Civil War
- *Mississippi River
- *Vicksburg
- *Chattanooga
- *Mississippi 1863
- *Tennessee 1863

Indian Wars
- North Dakota 1866
- Montana 1868

War With Spain
- *Santiago

Philippine Insurrection
- *Cavite
- *San Fabian
- *Luzon 1899
- Luzon 1900

World War II
- *Normandy
- *Northern France
- *Rhineland
- *Central Europe

DECORATIONS

*Presidential Unit Citation (Army), Streamer embroidered HURTGEN FOREST (1st Battalion, 13th Infantry cited; WD GO 21, 1947)

*French Croix de Guerre with Palm, World War II, Streamer embroidered NORMANDY (13th Infantry cited; DA GO 43, 1950)

*Luxembourg Croix de Guerre, Streamer embroidered LUXEMBOURG (8th Infantry Division cited; DA GO 59, 1969)

2d BATTALION, 13th INFANTRY

(First at Vicksburg)

RA
(8th Infantry Division)

LINEAGE

Constituted 3 May 1861 in the Regular Army as Company B, 1st Battalion, 13th Infantry. Organized 13 November 1861 at Jefferson Barracks, Missouri. Reorganized and redesignated 21 September 1866 as Company B, 13th Infantry. (13th Infantry assigned 17 December 1917 to the 8th Division; relieved 24 March 1923 from assignment to the 8th Division and assigned to the 9th Division; relieved 15 August 1927 from assignment to the 9th Division and assigned to the 5th Division.) Inactivated 31 October 1929 at Fort Strong, Massachusetts. (13th Infantry relieved 1 October 1933 from assignment to the 5th Division and assigned to the 9th Division; relieved 22 June 1940 from assignment to the 9th Division and assigned to the 8th Division [later redesignated as the 8th Infantry Division].) Activated 14 July 1940 at Camp Jackson, South Carolina. Inactivated 18 November 1945 at Fort Leonard Wood, Missouri. Activated 17 August 1950 at Fort Jackson, South Carolina. Inactivated 1 August 1957 in Germany and relieved from assignment to the 8th Infantry Division.

Redesignated 1 December 1957 as Headquarters and Headquarters Company, 2d Battle Group, 13th Infantry, assigned to the 9th Infantry Division, and activated at Fort Carson, Colorado (organic elements concurrently constituted and activated). Inactivated 31 January 1962 at Fort Carson, Colorado. Redesignated 27 March 1963 as the 2d Battalion, 13th Infantry; concurrently, relieved from assignment to the 9th Infantry Division and assigned to the 8th Infantry Division. Activated 1 April 1963 in Germany.

CAMPAIGN PARTICIPATION CREDIT

Civil War
*Mississippi River
*Vicksburg
*Chattanooga
*Mississippi 1863
*Tennessee 1863

Indian Wars
*North Dakota 1866
*Montana 1868

War With Spain
*Santiago

Philippine Insurrection
*Cavite
*San Fabian
*Luzon 1899
Luzon 1900

World War II
*Normandy
*Northern France
*Rhineland
*Central Europe

DECORATIONS

*Presidential Unit Citation (Army), Streamer embroidered HURTGEN FOREST (1st Battalion, 13th Infantry cited; WD GO 21, 1947)

*French Croix de Guerre with Palm, World War II, Streamer embroidered NORMANDY (13th Infantry cited; DA GO 43, 1950)

*French Croix de Guerre with Silver Star, World War II, Streamer embroidered VESLEY, FRANCE (Company B, 13th Infantry cited; DA GO 43, 1950)

*Luxembourg Croix de Guerre, Streamer embroidered LUXEMBOURG (8th Infantry Division cited; DA GO 59, 1969)

3d BATTLE GROUP, 13th INFANTRY

(First at Vicksburg)

AR
(inactive)

LINEAGE

Constituted 3 May 1861 in the Regular Army as Company C, 1st Battalion, 13th Infantry. Organized 13 November 1861 at Jefferson Barracks, Missouri. Reorganized and redesignated 21 September 1866 as Company C, 13th Infantry. (13th Infantry assigned 17 December 1917 to the 8th Division; relieved 24 March 1923 from assignment to the 8th Division and assigned to the 9th Division; relieved 15 August 1927 from assignment to the 9th Division and assigned to the 5th Division.) Inactivated 31 October 1929 at Fort Strong, Massachusetts. (13th Infantry relieved 1 October 1933 from assignment to the 5th Division and assigned to the 9th Division; relieved 22 June 1940 from assignment to the 9th Division and assigned to the 8th Division [later redesignated as the 8th Infantry Division].) Activated 14 July 1940 at Camp Jackson, South Carolina. Inactivated 18 November 1945 at Fort Leonard Wood, Missouri. Activated 17 August 1950 at Fort Jackson, South Carolina.

Inactivated 1 August 1957 in Germany and relieved from assignment to the 8th Infantry Division; concurrently, redesignated as Headquarters and Headquarters Company, 3d Battle Group, 13th Infantry. Withdrawn 6 April 1959 from the Regular Army, allotted to the Army Reserve, and assigned to the 94th Infantry Division (organic elements concurrently constituted). Battle Group activated 1 May 1959 with Headquarters at Roslindale, Massachusetts. Inactivated 1 March 1963 at Roslindale, Massachusetts; concurrently, relieved from assignment to the 94th Infantry Division.

CAMPAIGN PARTICIPATION CREDIT

Civil War
*Mississippi River
*Vicksburg
*Chattanooga
*Mississippi 1863
*Tennessee 1863

Indian Wars
North Dakota 1866
Montana 1868

War With Spain
*Santiago

Philippine Insurrection
*Cavite
*San Fabian
*Luzon 1899
*Luzon 1900

World War II
*Normandy
*Northern France
*Rhineland
*Central Europe

DECORATIONS

*Presidential Unit Citation (Army), Streamer embroidered HURTGEN FOREST (1st Battalion, 13th Infantry cited; WD GO 21, 1947)

*French Croix de Guerre with Palm, World War II, Streamer embroidered NORMANDY (13th Infantry cited; DA GO 43, 1950)

*Luxembourg Croix de Guerre, Streamer embroidered LUXEMBOURG (8th Infantry Division cited; DA GO 59, 1969)

4th BATTALION, 13th INFANTRY

(First at Vicksburg)

RA
(inactive)

LINEAGE

Constituted 3 May 1861 in the Regular Army as Company D, 1st Battalion, 13th Infantry. Organized 1 April 1862 at Alton, Illinois. Reorganized and redesignated 21 September 1866 as Company D, 13th Infantry. (13th Infantry assigned 17 December 1917 to the 8th Division; relieved 24 March 1923 from assignment to the 8th Division and assigned to the 9th Division; relieved 15 August 1927 from assignment to the 9th Division and assigned to the 5th Division.) Inactivated 31 October 1929 at Fort Strong, Massachusetts. (13th Infantry relieved 1 October 1933 from assignment to the 5th Division and assigned to the 9th Division; relieved 22 June 1940 from assignment to the 9th Division and assigned to the 8th Division [later redesignated as the 8th Infantry Division].) Activated 14 July 1940 at Camp Jackson, South Carolina. Inactivated 18 November 1945 at Fort Leonard Wood, Missouri. Activated 17 August 1950 at Fort Jackson, South Carolina.

Inactivated 1 August 1957 in Germany and relieved from assignment to the 8th Infantry Division; concurrently, redesignated as Headquarters and Headquarters Company, 4th Battle Group, 13th Infantry. Redesignated 10 May 1967 as Headquarters and Headquarters Company, 4th Battalion, 13th Infantry, assigned to the 198th Infantry Brigade, and activated at Fort Hood, Texas (organic elements concurrently constituted and activated). Inactivated 12 May 1967 at Fort Hood, Texas; concurrently, relieved from assignment to the 198th Infantry Brigade.

336

Campaign Participation Credit

Civil War
  *Mississippi River
  *Vicksburg
  *Chattanooga
  *Mississippi 1863
  *Tennessee 1863

Indian Wars
  North Dakota 1866
  Montana 1868

War With Spain
  *Santiago

Philippine Insurrection
  *Cavite
  *San Fabian
  *Luzon 1899
  *Luzon 1900

World War II
  *Normandy
  *Northern France
  *Rhineland
  *Central Europe

Decorations

*Presidential Unit Citation (Army), Streamer embroidered HURTGEN FOREST (1st Battalion, 13th Infantry cited; WD GO 21, 1947)

*French Croix de Guerre with Palm, World War II, Streamer embroidered NORMANDY (13th Infantry cited; DA GO 43, 1950)

*Luxembourg Croix de Guerre, Streamer embroidered LUXEMBOURG (8th Infantry Division cited; DA GO 59, 1969)

13TH INFANTRY, BIBLIOGRAPHY

Blumenson, Martin. *Breakout and Pursuit*. United States Army in World War II. Washington: Government Printing Office, 1961.

Carmody, P. J. "The Battle of Collierville," *Journal of the American-Irish Historical Society*, IX (1910), 466–470.

Goe, James B. "The Thirteenth Regiment of Infantry," *The Army of the United States*, edited by Theophilus F. Rodenbough and William L. Haskin. New York: Maynard, Merrill and Company, 1896, pp. 575–585. (Originally published in the *Journal of the Military Service Institution of the United States*, XV [1894], 1107–1117.)

Historical and Pictorial Review. 13th Infantry. Fort Jackson, South Carolina. 1942. Baton Rouge: Army and Navy Publishing Company, 1942.

MacDonald, Charles B. *The Battle of Huertgen Forest*. Philadelphia and New York: J. B. Lippincott Company, 1963.

――――. *The Siegfried Line Campaign*. United States Army in World War II. Washington: Government Printing Office, 1963.

Malone, Paul B. "The Thirteenth Infantry in the Santiago Campaign," *The Santiago Campaign*. Richmond: Williams Printing Company, 1927, pp. 90–101.

McAlexander, Ulysses Grant. *History of the Thirteenth Regiment, United States Infantry*. Fort McDowell, California: Regimental Press, 1905.

"Thirteenth Infantry Regiment," *Eighth Infantry Division: A Combat History by Regiments and Special Units*. Baton Rouge: Army and Navy Publishing Company, 1946.

Wherry, William M. "With the Thirteenth Infantry in Dakota," *Journal of the Military Service Institution of the United States*, XXXVII (November–December 1905), 519–526.

14th INFANTRY

(Golden Dragons)

HERALDIC ITEMS

COAT OF ARMS

Shield: Per fess azure and argent, two arrows chevronwise point to point counterchanged between in chief a cross pattée of the last and in base a spreading palm vert debruised by a castle or.

Crest: On a wreath of the colors an imperial Chinese dragon affronté or scaled and finned azure incensed and armed gules.

Motto: The Right of the Line.

Symbolism: Service in the Civil War is shown by the white cross pattée, the badge of Sykes' Regular Division of the V Corps of the Army of the Potomac. Indian campaigns are indicated by the arrows. The 14th Infantry was at the capture of Manila during the War with Spain, symbolized by the castle, and in the fighting around the same city in 1899 during the Philippine Insurrection, indicated by the palm.

The dragon in the crest symbolizes service in the China Relief Expedition. The motto is the much prized remark made by General Meade directing the station of the regiment in the review just after the Civil War.

DISTINCTIVE INSIGNIA

The distinctive insignia is a gold imperial Chinese dragon placed against a red conventionalized Spanish castle with the motto "The Right of the Line" in gold letters on a blue ribbon scroll. The dragon is the crest of the coat of arms and the castle is one of the charges on the regimental shield.

LINEAGE AND HONORS

LINEAGE

Constituted 3 May 1861 in the Regular Army as the 2d Battalion, 14th Infantry. Organized 1 July 1861 at Fort Trumbull, Connecticut. Reorganized and redesignated 30 April 1862 as the 1st Battalion, 14th Infantry. Reorganized and redesignated 21 September 1866 as the 14th Infantry. Consolidated 26 July 1869 with the 45th Infantry, Veteran Reserve Corps (constituted 21 September 1866) and consolidated unit designated as the 14th Infantry.

Assigned 27 July 1918 to the 19th Division. Relieved 14 February 1919 from assignment to the 19th Division. Assigned 10 July 1943 to the 71st Light Division (later redesignated as the 71st Infantry Division). Relieved 1 May 1946 from assignment to the 71st Infantry Division. Inactivated 1 September 1946 in Germany. Activated 1 October 1948 at Camp Carson, Colorado. Assigned 1 August 1951 to the 25th Infantry Division.

Relieved 1 February 1957 from assignment to the 25th Infantry Division and reorganized as a parent regiment under the Combat Arms Regimental System.

Campaign Participation Credit

Civil War
Peninsula
Manassas
Antietam
Fredericksburg
Chancellorsville
Gettysburg
Wilderness
Spotsylvania
Cold Harbor
Petersburg
Virginia 1862
Virginia 1863

Indian Wars
Little Big Horn
Bannocks
Arizona 1866
Wyoming 1874

War With Spain
Manila

China Relief Expedition
Yang-tsun
Peking

Philippine Insurrection
Manila
Laguna de Bay
Zapote River
Cavite
Luzon 1899

World War II
Rhineland
Central Europe

Korean War
UN summer-fall offensive
Second Korean winter
Korea, summer fall 1952
Third Korean winter
Korea, summer 1953

Vietnam
Counteroffensive
Counteroffensive, Phase II
Counteroffensive, Phase III
Tet Counteroffensive
(other campaigns to be
determined)

Decorations

Presidential Unit Citation (Navy), Streamer embroidered CHU LAI (1st Battalion, 14th Infantry cited; DA GO 59, 1969)

Republic of Korea Presidential Unit Citation, Streamer embroidered MUNSAN-NI (14th Infantry cited; DA GO 19, 1955)

1st BATTALION, 14th INFANTRY

(Golden Dragons)

RA
(25th Infantry Division)

LINEAGE

Constituted 3 May 1861 in the Regular Army as Company A, 2d Battalion, 14th Infantry. Organized 8 July 1861 at Fort Trumbull, Connecticut. Reorganized and redesignated 30 April 1862 as Company A, 1st Battalion, 14th Infantry. Reorganized and redesignated 21 September 1866 as Company A, 14th Infantry.

Consolidated 26 July 1869 with Company G, 45th Infantry, Veteran Reserve Corps (constituted 21 September 1866) and consolidated unit designated as Company A, 14th Infantry. (14th Infantry assigned 27 July 1918 to the 19th Division; relieved 14 February 1919 from assignment to the 19th Division; assigned 10 July 1943 to the 71st Light Division [later redesignated as the 71st Infantry Division]; relieved 1 May 1946 from assignment to the 71st Infantry Division.) Inactivated 1 September 1946 in Germany. Activated 1 October 1948 at Camp Carson, Colorado. (14th Infantry assigned 1 August 1951 to the 25th Infantry Division.)

Reorganized and redesignated 1 February 1957 as Headquarters and Headquarters Company, 1st Battle Group, 14th Infantry and remained assigned to the 25th Infantry Division (organic elements concurrently constituted and activated). Reorganized and redesignated 26 August 1963 as the 1st Battalion, 14th Infantry. Relieved 1 August 1967 from assignment to the 25th Infantry Division and assigned to the 4th Infantry Division. Relieved 15 December 1970 from assignment to the 4th Infantry Division and assigned to the 25th Infantry Division.

CAMPAIGN PARTICIPATION CREDIT

Civil War
- *Peninsula
- *Manassas
- *Antietam
- *Fredericksburg
- *Chancellorsville
- *Gettysburg
- *Wilderness
- *Spotsylvania
- *Cold Harbor
- *Petersburg
- *Virginia 1862
- *Virginia 1863

Indian Wars
- Little Big Horn
- Bannocks
- Arizona 1866
- Wyoming 1874

War With Spain
- *Manila

China Relief Expedition
- Yang-tsun
- Peking

Philippine Insurrection
- *Manila
- *Laguna de Bay
- *Zapote River
- Cavite
- *Luzon 1899

World War II
- *Rhineland
- *Central Europe

Korean War
- *UN summer-fall offensive
- *Second Korean winter
- *Korea, summer-fall 1952
- *Third Korean winter
- *Korea, summer 1953

Vietnam
- *Counteroffensive
- *Counteroffensive, Phase II
- *Counteroffensive, Phase III
- *Tet Counteroffensive
  (other campaigns to be determined)

DECORATIONS

*Presidential Unit Citation (Navy), Streamer embroidered CHU LAI (1st Battalion, 14th Infantry cited; DA GO 59, 1969)

*Republic of Korea Presidential Unit Citation, Streamer embroidered MUNSAN-NI (14th Infantry cited; DA GO 19, 1955)

*Vietnamese Cross of Gallantry with Palm, Streamer embroidered VIETNAM 1966–1967 (1st Battalion, 14th Infantry cited; DA GO 48, 1971)

*Vietnamese Cross of Gallantry with Palm, Streamer embroidered VIETNAM 1967–1969 (1st Battalion, 14th Infantry cited; DA GO 3, 1970, as amended by DA GO 38, 1970)

*Vietnamese Civil Action Honor Medal, First Class, Streamer embroidered VIETNAM 1967–1969 (1st Battalion, 14th Infantry cited; DA GO 53, 1970)

2d BATTALION, 14th INFANTRY

(Golden Dragons)

RA
(25th Infantry Division)

LINEAGE

Constituted 3 May 1861 in the Regular Army as Company B, 2d Battalion, 14th Infantry. Organized 8 July 1861 at Fort Trumbull, Connecticut. Reorganized and redesignated 30 April 1862 as Company B, 1st Battalion, 14th Infantry. Reorganized and redesignated 21 September 1866 as Company B, 14th Infantry.

Consolidated 15 August 1869 with Company A, 45th Infantry, Veteran Reserve Corps (constituted 21 September 1866) and consolidated unit designated as Company B, 14th Infantry. (14th Infantry assigned 27 July 1918 to the 19th Division; relieved 14 February 1919 from assignment to the 19th Division; assigned 10 July 1943 to the 71st Light Division [later redesignated as the 71st Infantry Division]; relieved 1 May 1946 from assignment to the 71st Infantry Division.) Inactivated 1 September 1946 in Germany. Activated 1 October 1948 at Camp Carson, Colorado. (14th Infantry assigned 1 August 1951 to the 25th Infantry Division.) Inactivated 1 February 1957 in Hawaii and relieved from assignment to the 25th Infantry Division.

Redesignated 17 May 1957 as Headquarters and Headquarters Company, 2d Battle Group, 14th Infantry (organic elements concurrently constituted). Battle Group activated 25 May 1957 at Fort Benning, Georgia. Assigned 1 July 1958 to the 1st Infantry Brigade. Inactivated 16 May 1960 at Fort Benning, Georgia. Relieved 25 June 1960 from assignment to the 1st Infantry Brigade. Redesignated 21 June 1963 as the 2d Battalion, 14th Infantry and assigned to the 25th Infantry Division. Activated 26 August 1963 in Hawaii.

344

Campaign Participation Credit

Civil War
- *Peninsula
- *Manassas
- *Antietam
- *Fredericksburg
- *Chancellorsville
- *Gettysburg
- *Wilderness
- *Spotsylvania
- *Cold Harbor
- *Petersburg
- *Virginia 1862
- *Virginia 1863

Indian Wars
- *Little Big Horn
- Bannocks
- *Arizona 1866
- Wyoming 1874

War With Spain
- *Manila

China Relief Expedition
- Yang-tsun
- Peking

Philippine Insurrection
- Manila
- *Laguna de Bay
- *Zapote River
- Cavite
- *Luzon 1899

World War II
- *Rhineland
- *Central Europe

Korean War
- *UN summer-fall offensive
- *Second Korean winter
- *Korea, summer-fall 1952
- *Third Korean winter
- *Korea, summer 1953

Vietnam
- *Counteroffensive
- *Counteroffensive, Phase II
- *Counteroffensive, Phase III
- *Tet Counteroffensive
- (other campaigns to be determined)

Decorations

*Republic of Korea Presidential Unit Citation, Streamer embroidered MUNSAN-NI (14th Infantry cited; DA GO 19, 1955)

*Vietnamese Cross of Gallantry with Palm, Streamer embroidered VIETNAM 1966–1968 (2d Battalion, 14th Infantry cited; DA GO 48, 1971)

3d BATTALION, 14th INFANTRY

(Golden Dragons)

RA
(inactive)

Constituted 3 May 1861 in the Regular Army as Company F, 2d Battalion, 14th Infantry. Organized 8 July 1861 at Fort Trumbull, Connecticut. Reorganized and redesignated 30 April 1862 as Company F, 1st Battalion, 14th Infantry. Reorganized and redesignated 21 September 1866 as Company F, 14th Infantry.

Consolidated 26 July 1869 with Company C, 45th Infantry, Veteran Reserve Corps (constituted 21 September 1866) and consolidated unit designated as Company C, 14th Infantry. (14th Infantry assigned 27 July 1918 to the 19th Division; relieved 14 February 1919 from assignment to the 19th Division; assigned 10 July 1943 to the 71st Light Division [later redesignated as the 71st Infantry Division]; relieved 1 May 1946 from assignment to the 71st Infantry Division.) Inactivated 1 September 1946 in Germany. Activated 1 October 1948 at Camp Carson, Colorado. (14th Infantry assigned 1 August 1951 to the 25th Infantry Division.)

Inactivated 1 February 1957 in Hawaii and relieved from assignment to the 25th Infantry Division; concurrently, redesignated as Headquarters and Headquarters Company, 3d Battle Group, 14th Infantry. Withdrawn 11 May 1959 from the Regular Army, allotted to the Army Reserve, and assigned to the 102d Infantry Division (organic elements concurrently constituted). Battle Group activated 1 June 1959 with Headquarters at Kansas City, Missouri (concurrently, Headquarters and Headquarters Company consolidated with Headquarters and Headquarters Company, 406th Infantry [see ANNEX] and consolidated unit designated as Headquarters and Headquarters Company, 3d Battle Group, 14th Infantry).

Reorganized and redesignated 1 April 1963 as the 3d Battalion, 14th Infantry. Inactivated 31 December 1965 as Kansas City, Missouri, and relieved from assignment to the 102d Infantry Division. Withdrawn 6 December 1969 from the Army Reserve and allotted to the Regular Army; concurrently, activated in Hawaii as an element of the 25th Infantry Division. Inactivated 15 December 1970 in Hawaii.

ANNEX

Constituted 24 June 1921 in the Organized Reserves as Headquarters and Headquarters Company, 406th Infantry, an element of the 102d Division (later redesignated as the 102d Infantry Division). Organized in October 1921 at Springfield, Missouri. Ordered into active military service 15 September 1942 and reorganized at Camp Maxey, Texas. Inactivated 16 March 1946 at Camp Kilmer, New Jersey.

Activated 3 January 1947 in the Organized Reserves at Kansas City, Missouri. (Organized Reserves redesignated 25 March 1948 as the Organized Reserve Corps; redesignated 9 July 1952 as the Army Reserve.) Consolidated 1 June 1959 with Headquarters and Headquarters Company, 3d Battle Group, 14th Infantry and consolidated unit designated as Headquarters and Headquarters Company, 3d Battle Group, 14th Infantry (remainder of 406th Infantry inactivated).

CAMPAIGN PARTICIPATION CREDIT

Civil War
  *Peninsula
  *Manassas
  *Antietam
  *Fredericksburg
  *Chancellorsville
  *Gettysburg
  *Wilderness
  *Spotsylvania
  *Cold Harbor
  *Petersburg
  *Virginia 1862
  *Virginia 1863

Indian Wars
  *Little Big Horn
  *Bannocks
  Arizona 1866
  Wyoming 1874

War With Spain
  *Manila

China Relief Expedition
  Yang-tsun
  Peking

Philippine Insurrection
  *Manila
  *Laguna de Bay
  *Zapote River
  Cavite
  *Luzon 1899

World War II
  *Rhineland
  *Central Europe

Korean War
  *UN summer-fall offensive
  *Second Korean winter
  *Korea, summer-fall 1952
  *Third Korean winter
  *Korea, summer 1953

DECORATIONS

*Republic of Korea Presidential Unit Citation, Streamer embroidered MUNSAN-NI (14th Infantry cited; DA GO 19, 1955)

COMPANY D, 14th INFANTRY

(Golden Dragons)

AR
(inactive)

LINEAGE

Constituted 3 May 1861 in the Regular Army as Company D, 2d Battalion, 14th Infantry. Organized 8 July 1861 at Fort Trumbull, Connecticut. Reorganized and redesignated 30 April 1862 as Company D, 1st Battalion, 14th Infantry. Reorganized and redesignated 21 September 1866 as Company D, 14th Infantry. (14th Infantry assigned 27 July 1918 to the 19th Division; relieved 14 February 1919 from assignment to the 19th Division; assigned 10 July 1943 to the 71st Light Division [later redesignated as the 71st Infantry Division]; relieved 1 May 1946 from assignment to the 71st Infantry Division.) Inactivated 1 September 1946 in Germany. Activated 1 October 1948 at Camp Carson, Colorado. (14th Infantry assigned 1 August 1951 to the 25th Infantry Division.) Inactivated 1 February 1957 in Hawaii and relieved from assignment to the 25th Infantry Division.

Withdrawn 3 June 1959 from the Regular Army and allotted to the Army Reserve. Activated 17 August 1959 at St. Thomas, Virgin Islands. Inactivated 31 March 1968 at St. Thomas, Virgin Islands.

348

CAMPAIGN PARTICIPATION CREDIT

Civil War
Peninsula
Manassas
Antietam
Fredericksburg
Chancellorsville
Gettysburg
Wilderness
Spotsylvania
Cold Harbor
Petersburg
Virginia 1862
Virginia 1863

Indian Wars
Bannocks

War With Spain
Manila

China Relief Expedition
Yang-tsun
Peking

Philippine Insurrection
Manila
Laguna de Bay
Zapote River
Luzon 1899

World War II-EAME
Rhineland
Central Europe

Korean War
UN summer-fall offensive
Second Korean winter
Korea, summer-fall 1952
Third Korean winter
Korea, summer 1953

DECORATIONS

Republic of Korea Presidential Unit Citation, Streamer embroidered MUNSAN-NI (14th Infantry cited; DA GO 19, 1955)

COMPANY E, 14th INFANTRY

(Golden Dragons)

RA
(inactive)

LINEAGE

Constituted 3 May 1861 in the Regular Army as Company E, 2d Battalion, 14th Infantry. Organized 8 July 1861 at Fort Trumbull, Connecticut. Reorganized and redesignated 30 April 1862 as Company E, 1st Battalion, 14th Infantry. Reorganized and redesignated 21 September 1866 as Company E, 14th Infantry.

Consolidated 26 July 1869 with Company D, 45th Infantry, Veteran Reserve Corps (constituted 21 September 1866) and consolidated unit designated as Company E, 14th Infantry. (14th Infantry assigned 27 July 1918 to the 19th Division; relieved 14 February 1919 from assignment to the 19th Division; assigned 10 July 1943 to the 71st Light Division [later redesignated as the 71st Infantry Division]; relieved 1 May 1946 from assignment to the 71st Infantry Division.) Inactivated 1 September 1946 in Germany. Activated 1 October 1948 at Camp Carson, Colorado. (14th Infantry assigned 1 August 1951 to the 25th Infantry Division.)

Inactivated 1 February 1957 in Hawaii and relieved from assignment to the 25th Infantry Division; concurrently, redesignated as Headquarters and Headquarters Company, 5th Battle Group, 14th Infantry. Redesignated 21 December 1960 as Company E, 14th Infantry. Activated 24 December 1960 in Korea. Inactivated 1 January 1966 in Korea.

CAMPAIGN PARTICIPATION CREDIT

Civil War
Peninsula
Manassas
Antietam
Fredericksburg
Chancellorsville
Gettysburg
Wilderness
Spotsylvania
Cold Harbor
Petersburg
Virginia 1862
Virginia 1863

Indian Wars
Bannocks

War With Spain
Manila

China Relief Expedition
Yang-tsun
Peking

Philippine Insurrection
Manila
Laguna de Bay
Zapote River
Cavite
Luzon 1899

World War II-EAME
Rhineland
Central Europe

Korean War
UN summer-fall offensive
Second Korean winter
Korea, summer-fall 1952
Third Korean winter
Korea, summer 1953

DECORATIONS

Republic of Korea Presidential Unit Citation, Streamer embroidered
MUNSAN-NI (14th Infantry cited; DA GO 19, 1955)

14th Infantry, Bibliography

Anderson, Thomas M. "Fourteenth Regiment of Infantry," *The Army of the United States,* edited by Theophilus F. Rodenbough and William L. Haskin. New York: Maynard, Merrill and Company, 1896, pp. 586–609. (Originally published in the *Journal of the Military Service Institution of the United States,* XI [1890], 673–696.)

"84th Organization Day, Fourteenth U.S. Infantry, Gunzberg, Germany, August 14, 1945." n.p., 1945.

"Golden Dragons, 1st Battalion, 14th Infantry." Hawaii, 1965.

Hager, John. "Manuscript Journal, 14th U.S. Infantry, March 1862– December 1863, in original notebook."

History of the 14th U.S. Infantry. Panama: Star and Herald Company, 1933.

Marshall, S. L. A. *West to Cambodia.* New York: Cowles Education Corporation, 1968.

Null, Jack G. *Operations of the 3d Battalion, 14th Infantry (71st Infantry Division) in a River Crossing Near Regensburg, Germany, 26–27 April 1945 (Central European Campaign).* Fort Riley, Kansas: Ground General School, 1949.

The Odyssey of the Fourteenth Infantry Regiment from 9 February 1945 to 8 May 1945. Augsburg: P. Haas and Co., 1945.

"Organization Day, 17 August 1956, 14th United States Infantry." Schofield Barracks, 1956.

Register of Officers of the Fourteenth Infantry, From Date of Organization, May 14, 1861. Camp on White River, Colorado: Regimental Press, 1882.

Sorley, Lewis Stone. *History of the Fourteenth United States Infantry From January 1890 to December 1908.* Chicago: Lakeside Press, 1909.

15th INFANTRY

HERALDIC ITEMS

COAT OF ARMS

Shield: Azure an imperial Chinese dragon affronté or, issuant in chief argent a rock proper between four acorns stem up in fess gules.

Crest: On a wreath of the colors a sun with eight points of rays or in front of a triangle resting on one point gules, in the angles of the triangle and in front of the sun three five-pointed mullets argent.

Motto: Can Do.

Symbolism: The shield is blue and white, the present and former infantry colors. On the lower part is the Chinese dragon, and in the white chief the badge of the XIV Corps in the Civil War is repeated four times for four major campaigns: Murfreesboro, Chickamauga, Chattanooga, and Atlanta. Chickamauga, where the regiment fought and held so gallantly, is further emphasized by the rock.

The crest is the triangle and devices from the Katipunan flag of the Philippine Insurrection. The motto is the watchword of the regiment in "pidgin English," in recollection of the regiment's long service in China.

DISTINCTIVE INSIGNIA

The distinctive insignia is the shield and motto of the coat of arms.

LINEAGE AND HONORS

LINEAGE

Constituted 3 May 1861 in the Regular Army as the 1st Battalion, 15th Infantry. Organized September–October 1861 at Newport Barracks, Kentucky. Reorganized and redesignated 21 September 1866 as the 15th Infantry. Consolidated 12 August 1869 with the 35th Infantry (see ANNEX) and consolidated unit designated as the 15th Infantry.

Assigned 17 July 1922 to the Philippine Division. Regiment (less

353

1st Battalion) relieved 1 April 1923 from assignment to the Philippine Division and assigned to the American Forces in China (later redesignated as the United States Army Troops in China). (1st Battalion inactivated 1 April 1929 at Fort William McKinley, Philippine Islands; relieved 26 June 1931 from assignment to the Philippine Division.) Regiment (less 1st Battalion) relieved 2 March 1938 from assignment to the United States Army Troops in China. Regiment assigned 12 January 1940 to the 3d Division (later redesignated as the 3d Infantry Division). (1st Battalion activated 23 May 1940 at Fort Lewis, Washington.)

Relieved 1 July 1957 from assignment to the 3d Infantry Division and reorganized as a parent regiment under the Combat Arms Regimental System.

ANNEX

Constituted 3 May 1861 in the Regular Army as the 3d Battalion, 17th Infantry. Organized 29 October 1865 at Hart Island, New York. Reorganized and redesignated 21 September 1866 as the 35th Infantry. Consolidated 12 August 1869 with the 15th Infantry and consolidated unit designated as the 15th Infantry.

CAMPAIGN PARTICIPATION CREDIT

Civil War
Shiloh
Murfreesborough
Chickamauga
Chattanooga
Atlanta
Mississippi 1862
Alabama 1862
Tennessee 1862
Kentucky 1862
Tennessee 1863
Georgia 1864

Indian Wars
Utes
New Mexico 1880

China Relief Expedition
Without inscription

Philippine Insurrection
Luzon 1900
Luzon 1901

World War II
Algeria-French Morocco
(with arrowhead)
Tunisia
Sicily (with arrowhead)
Naples-Foggia
Anzio (with arrowhead)
Rome-Arno
Southern France (with arrowhead)
Rhineland
Ardennes-Alsace
Central Europe

Korean War
CCF intervention
First UN counteroffensive
CCF spring offensive
UN summer-fall offensive
Second Korean winter
Korea, summer-fall 1952
Third Korean winter
Korea, summer 1953

DECORATIONS

Presidential Unit Citation (Army), Streamer embroidered COLMAR (3d Infantry Division cited; WD GO 44, 1945)

Presidential Unit Citation (Army), Streamer embroidered MONTELI-MAR (1st Battalion, 15th Infantry cited; WD GO 21, 1945)

Presidential Unit Citation (Army), Streamer embroidered SAN FRATELLO (3d Battalion, 15th Infantry cited; WD GO 15, 1946)

Presidential Unit Citation (Army), Streamer embroidered KOWANG-NI (2d Battalion, 15th Infantry and attached units cited; DA GO 71, 1952)

Presidential Unit Citation (Navy), Streamer embroidered HWACHON RESERVOIR (1st Battalion, 15th Infantry cited; DA GO 38, 1957)

Navy Unit Commendation, Streamer embroidered PANMUNJOM (1st Battalion, 15th Infantry cited; DA GO 38, 1957)

French Croix de Guerre with Palm, World War II, Streamer embroidered COLMAR (15th Infantry cited; DA GO 43, 1950)

French Croix de Guerre, World War II, Fourragere (15th Infantry cited; DA GO 43, 1950)

Republic of Korea Presidential Unit Citation, Streamer embroidered UIJONGBU CORRIDOR (15th Infantry cited; DA GO 20, 1953)

Republic of Korea Presidential Unit Citation, Streamer embroidered IRON TRIANGLE (15th Infantry cited; DA GO 29, 1954)

Chryssoun Aristion Andrias (Bravery Gold Medal of Greece), Streamer embroidered KOREA (15th Infantry cited; DA GO 2, 1956)

1st BATTALION, 15th INFANTRY

RA
(3d Infantry Division)

LINEAGE

Constituted 3 May 1861 in the Regular Army as Company A, 1st Battalion, 15th Infantry. Organized 13 October 1861 at Newport Barracks, Kentucky. Reorganized and redesignated 21 September 1866 as Company A, 15th Infantry.

Consolidated 12 August 1869 with Company A, 35th Infantry (see ANNEX) and consolidated unit designated as Company A, 15th Infantry. (15th Infantry assigned 17 July 1922 to the Philippine Division.) Inactivated 1 April 1929 at Fort William McKinley, Philippine Islands. (1st Battalion, 15th Infantry relieved 26 June 1931 from assignment to the Philippine Division; assigned 12 January 1940 to the 3d Division [later redesignated as the 3d Infantry Division].) Activated 23 May 1940 at Fort Lewis, Washington.

Reorganized and redesignated 1 July 1957 as Headquarters and Headquarters Company, 1st Battle Group, 15th Infantry and remained assigned to the 3d Infantry Division (organic elements concurrently constituted and activated). Reorganized and redesignated 15 July 1963 as the 1st Battalion, 15th Infantry.

ANNEX

Constituted 3 May 1861 in the Regular Army as Company A, 3d Battalion, 17th Infantry. Organized 29 October 1865 at Hart Island, New York. Reorganized and redesignated 21 September 1866 as Company A, 35th Infantry. Consolidated 12 August 1869 with Company A, 15th Infantry and consolidated unit designated as Company A, 15th Infantry.

356

CAMPAIGN PARTICIPATION CREDIT

Civil War
*Shiloh
*Murfreesborough
*Chickamauga
*Chattanooga
*Atlanta
*Mississippi 1862
*Alabama 1862
*Tennessee 1862
*Kentucky 1862
*Tennessee 1863
*Georgia 1864

Indian Wars
Utes
New Mexico 1880

China Relief Expedition
*Without inscription

Philippine Insurrection
Luzon 1900
Luzon 1901

World War II
*Algeria-French Morocco
 (with arrowhead)
*Tunisia
*Sicily (with arrowhead)
*Naples-Foggia
*Anzio (with arrowhead)
*Rome-Arno
*Southern France (with arrowhead)
*Rhineland
*Ardennes-Alsace
*Central Europe

Korean War
*CCF intervention
*First UN counteroffensive
*CCF spring offensive
*UN summer-fall offensive
*Second Korean winter
*Korea, summer-fall 1952
*Third Korean winter
*Korea, summer 1953

DECORATIONS

*Presidential Unit Citation (Army), Streamer embroidered COLMAR (3d Infantry Division cited; WD GO 44, 1945)

*Presidential Unit Citation (Army), Streamer embroidered MONTELIMAR (1st Battalion, 15th Infantry cited; WD GO 21, 1945)

Presidential Unit Citation (Army), Streamer embroidered SAN FRATELLO

Presidential Unit Citation (Army), Streamer embroidered KOWANG-NI

*Presidential Unit Citation (Navy), Streamer embroidered HWACHON RESERVOIR (1st Battalion, 15th Infantry cited; DA GO 38, 1957)

*Navy Unit Commendation, Streamer embroidered PANMUNJOM (1st Battalion, 15th Infantry cited; DA GO 38, 1957)

*French Croix de Guerre with Palm, World War II, Streamer embroidered COLMAR (15th Infantry cited; DA GO 43, 1950)

*French Croix de Guerre, World War II, Fourragere (15th Infantry cited; DA GO 43, 1950)

*Republic of Korea Presidential Unit Citation, Streamer embroidered UIJONGBU CORRIDOR (15th Infantry cited; DA GO 20, 1953)

*Republic of Korea Presidential Unit Citation, Streamer embroidered IRON TRIANGLE (15th Infantry cited; DA GO 29, 1954)

*Republic of Korea Presidential Unit Citation, Streamer embroidered

KOREA (1st Battalion, 15th Infantry cited; DA GO 33, 1953, as amended by DA GO 41, 1955)

*Chryssoun Aristion Andrias (Bravery Gold Medal of Greece), Streamer embroidered KOREA (15th Infantry cited; DA GO 2, 1956)

2d BATTALION, 15th INFANTRY

RA

(3d Infantry Division)

LINEAGE

Constituted 3 May 1861 in the Regular Army as Company B, 1st Battalion, 15th Infantry. Organized in September 1861 at Newport Barracks, Kentucky. Reorganized and redesignated 21 September 1866 as Company B, 15th Infantry.

Consolidated 12 August 1869 with Company B, 35th Infantry (see ANNEX) and consolidated unit designated as Company B, 15th Infantry. (15th Infantry assigned 17 July 1922 to the Philippine Division.) Inactivated 1 April 1929 at Fort William McKinley, Philippine Islands. (1st Battalion, 15th Infantry relieved 26 June 1931 from assignment to the Philippine Division; assigned 12 January 1940 to the 3d Division [later redesignated as the 3d Infantry Division].) Activated 23 May 1940 at Fort Lewis, Washington.

Reorganized and redesignated 1 July 1957 as Headquarters and Headquarters Company, 2d Battle Group, 15th Infantry, relieved from assignment to the 3d Infantry Division, and assigned to the 10th Infantry Division (organic elements concurrently constituted and activated). Inactivated 19 June 1958 at Fort Benning, Georgia. Redesignated 23 May 1963 as the 2d Battalion, 15th Infantry; concurrently, relieved from assignment to the 10th Infantry Division and assigned to the 3d Infantry Division. Activated 3 June 1963 in Germany.

ANNEX

Constituted 3 May 1861 in the Regular Army as Company B, 3d Battalion, 17th Infantry. Organized 29 October 1865 at Hart Island, New York. Reorganized and redesignated 21 September 1866 as Company B, 35th Infantry. Consolidated 12 August 1869 with Company B, 15th Infantry and consolidated unit designated as Company B, 15th Infantry.

359

CAMPAIGN PARTICIPATION CREDIT

Civil War
  *Shiloh
  *Murfreesborough
  Chickamauga
  Chattanooga
  Atlanta
  *Mississippi 1862
  *Alabama 1862
  *Tennessee 1862
  *Kentucky 1862
  Tennessee 1863
  Georgia 1864

Indian Wars
  Utes
  New Mexico 1880

China Relief Expedition
  *Without inscription

Philippine Insurrection
  Luzon 1900
  Luzon 1901

World War II
  *Algeria-French Morocco
    (with arrowhead)
  *Tunisia
  *Sicily (with arrowhead)
  *Naples-Foggia
  *Anzio (with arrowhead)
  *Rome-Arno
  *Southern France (with arrowhead)
  *Rhineland
  *Ardennes-Alsace
  *Central Europe

Korean War
  *CCF intervention
  *First UN counteroffensive
  *CCF spring offensive
  *UN summer-fall offensive
  *Second Korean winter
  *Korea, summer-fall 1952
  *Third Korean winter
  *Korea, summer 1953

DECORATIONS

*Presidential Unit Citation (Army), Streamer embroidered COLMAR (3d Infantry Division cited; WD GO 44, 1945)

*Presidential Unit Citation (Army), Streamer embroidered MONTELIMAR (1st Battalion, 15th Infantry cited; WD GO 21, 1945)

*Presidential Unit Citation (Army), Streamer embroidered SURANG-NI (Company B, 15th Infantry cited; DA GO 18, 1955)

Presidential Unit Citation (Army), Streamer embroidered SAN FRATELLO

Presidential Unit Citation (Army), Streamer embroidered KOWANG-NI

*Presidential Unit Citation (Navy), Streamer embroidered HWACHON RESERVOIR (1st Battalion, 15th Infantry cited; DA GO 38, 1957)

*Navy Unit Commendation, Streamer embroidered PANMUNJOM (1st Battalion, 15th Infantry cited; DA GO 38, 1957)

*French Croix de Guerre with Palm, World War II, Streamer embroidered COLMAR (15th Infantry cited; DA GO 43, 1950)

*French Croix de Guerre, World War II, Fourragere (15th Infantry cited; DA GO 43, 1950)

*Republic of Korea Presidential Unit Citation, Streamer embroidered UIJONGBU CORRIDOR (15th Infantry cited; DA GO 20, 1953)

*Republic of Korea Presidential Unit Citation, Streamer embroidered

IRON TRIANGLE (15th Infantry cited; DA GO 29, 1954)

*Republic of Korea Presidential Unit Citation, Streamer embroidered KOREA (1st Battalion, 15th Infantry cited; DA GO 33, 1953, as amended by DA GO 41, 1955)

*Chryssoun Aristion Andrias (Bravery Gold Medal of Greece), Streamer embroidered KOREA (15th Infantry cited; DA GO 2, 1956)

3d BATTALION, 15th INFANTRY

AR
(inactive)

LINEAGE

Constituted 3 May 1861 in the Regular Army as Company C, 1st Battalion, 15th Infantry. Organized 17 October 1861 at Newport Barracks, Kentucky. Reorganized and redesignated 21 September 1866 as Company C, 15th Infantry.

Consolidated 12 August 1869 with Company C, 35th Infantry (see ANNEX 1) and consolidated unit designated as Company C, 15th Infantry. (15th Infantry assigned 17 July 1922 to the Philippine Division.) Inactivated 1 April 1929 at Fort William McKinley, Philippine Islands. (1st Battalion, 15th Infantry relieved 26 June 1931 from assignment to the Philippine Division; assigned 12 January 1940 to the 3d Division [later redesignated as the 3d Infantry Division].) Activated 23 May 1940 at Fort Lewis, Washington.

Inactivated 1 July 1957 at Fort Benning, Georgia, and relieved from assignment to the 3d Infantry Division; concurrently, redesignated as Headquarters and Headquarters Company, 3d Battle Group, 15th Infantry. Withdrawn 31 March 1959 from the Regular Army, allotted to the Army Reserve, and assigned to the 63d Infantry Division (organic elements concurrently constituted). Battle Group activated 1 May 1959 with Headquarters at Santa Ana, California (concurrently, Headquarters and Headquarters Company consolidated with Headquarters and Headquarters Company, 2d Battalion, 254th Infantry [see ANNEX 2] and consolidated unit designated as Headquarters and Headquarters Company, 3d Battle Group, 15th Infantry). Reorganized and redesignated 1 April 1963 as the 3d Battalion, 15th Infantry. Inactivated 31 December 1965 at Santa Ana, California.

ANNEX 1

Constituted 3 May 1861 in the Regular Army as Company C, 3d Battalion, 17th Infantry. Organized 29 October 1865 at Hart Island, New York. Reorganized and redesignated 21 September 1866 as Company C, 35th Infantry. Consolidated 12 August 1869 with Company C, 15th Infantry and consolidated unit designated as Company C, 15th Infantry.

ANNEX 2

Constituted 18 January 1943 in the Army of the United States as Headquarters and Headquarters Company, 2d Battalion, 254th Infantry, an element of the 63d Infantry Division. Activated 15 June 1943 at Camp Blanding, Florida. Inactivated 29 September 1945 at Camp Kilmer, New Jersey. (63d Infantry Division allotted 22 February 1952 to the Organized Reserve Corps.)

Activated 1 March 1952 at Santa Ana, California. (Organized Reserve Corps redesignated 9 July 1952 as the Army Reserve.) Consolidated 1 May 1959 with Headquarters and Headquarters Company, 3d Battle Group, 15th Infantry and consolidated unit designated as Headquarters and Headquarters Company, 3d Battle Group, 15th Infantry.

CAMPAIGN PARTICIPATION CREDIT

Civil War
  *Shiloh
  *Murfreesborough
  *Chickamauga
  *Chattanooga
  *Atlanta
  *Mississippi 1862
  *Alabama 1862
  *Tennessee 1862
  *Kentucky 1862
  *Tennessee 1863
  *Georgia 1864

Indian Wars
  Utes
  *New Mexico 1880

China Relief Expedition
  *Without inscription

Philippine Insurrection
  Luzon 1900
  Luzon 1901

World War II
  *Algeria-French Morocco
    (with arrowhead)
  *Tunisia
  *Sicily (with arrowhead)
  *Naples-Foggia
  *Anzio (with arrowhead)
  *Rome-Arno
  *Southern France (with arrowhead)
  *Rhineland
  *Ardennes Alsace
  *Central Europe

Korean War
  *CCF intervention
  *First UN counteroffensive
  *CCF spring offensive
  *UN summer-fall offensive
  *Second Korean winter
  *Korea, summer-fall 1952
  *Third Korean winter
  *Korea, summer 1953

DECORATIONS

*Presidential Unit Citation (Army), Streamer embroidered COLMAR (3d Infantry Division and 254th Infantry cited, WD GO 44, 1945)

*Presidential Unit Citation (Army), Streamer embroidered MONTELIMAR (1st Battalion, 15th Infantry cited; WD GO 21, 1945)

*Presidential Unit Citation (Army), Streamer embroidered JEBSHEIM, FRANCE (2d Battalion, 254th Infantry cited; WD GO 42, 1946)

Presidential Unit Citation (Army), Streamer embroidered SAN

FRATELLO

Presidential Unit Citation (Army), Streamer embroidered KOWANG-NI

*Presidential Unit Citation (Navy), Streamer embroidered HWACHON RESERVOIR (1st Battalion, 15th Infantry cited; DA GO 38, 1957)

*Navy Unit Commendation, Streamer embroidered PANMUNJOM (1st Battalion, 15th Infantry cited; DA GO 38, 1957)

*French Croix de Guerre with Palm, World War II, Streamer embroidered COLMAR (15th Infantry cited; DA GO 43, 1950)

*French Croix de Guerre, World War II, Fourragere (15th Infantry cited; DA GO 43, 1950)

*Republic of Korea Presidential Unit Citation, Streamer embroidered UIJONGBU CORRIDOR (15th Infantry cited; DA GO 20, 1953)

*Republic of Korea Presidential Unit Citation, Streamer embroidered IRON TRIANGLE (15th Infantry cited; DA GO 29, 1954)

*Republic of Korea Presidential Unit Citation, Streamer embroidered KOREA (1st Battalion, 15th Infantry cited; DA GO 33, 1953, as amended by DA GO 41, 1955)

*Chryssoun Aristion Andrias (Bravery Gold Medal of Greece), Streamer embroidered KOREA (15th Infantry cited; DA GO 2, 1956)

4th BATTALION, 15th INFANTRY

AR
(inactive)

LINEAGE

Constituted 3 May 1861 in the Regular Army as Company D, 1st Battalion, 15th Infantry. Organized 17 October 1861 at Newport Barracks, Kentucky. Reorganized and redesignated 21 September 1866 as Company D, 15th Infantry.

Consolidated 12 August 1869 with Company D, 35th Infantry (see ANNEX) and consolidated unit designated as Company D, 15th Infantry. (15th Infantry assigned 17 July 1922 to the Philippine Division.) Inactivated 1 April 1929 at Fort William McKinley, Philippine Islands. (1st Battalion, 15th Infantry relieved 26 June 1931 from assignment to the Philippine Division; assigned 12 January 1940 to the 3d Division [later redesignated as the 3d Infantry Division].) Activated 23 May 1940 at Fort Lewis, Washington.

Inactivated 1 July 1957 at Fort Benning, Georgia, and relieved from assignment to the 3d Infantry Division; concurrently, redesignated as Headquarters and Headquarters Company, 4th Battle Group, 15th Infantry. Redesignated 27 March 1963 as Headquarters and Headquarters Company, 4th Battalion, 15th Infantry, withdrawn from the Regular Army, allotted to the Army Reserve, and assigned to the 63d Infantry Division (organic elements concurrently constituted). Battalion activated 1 April 1963 with Headquarters at Santa Barbara, California. Inactivated 31 December 1965 at Santa Barbara, California.

ANNEX

Constituted 3 May 1861 in the Regular Army as Company D, 3d Battalion, 17th Infantry. Organized 29 October 1865 at Hart Island, New York. Reorganized and redesignated 21 September 1866 as Company D, 35th Infantry. Consolidated 12 August 1869 with Company D, 15th Infantry and consolidated unit designated as Company D, 15th Infantry.

365

CAMPAIGN PARTICIPATION CREDIT

Civil War
*Shiloh
*Murfreesborough
Chickamauga
Chattanooga
Atlanta
*Mississippi 1862
*Alabama 1862
*Tennessee 1862
*Kentucky 1862
Tennessee 1863
Georgia 1864

Indian Wars
*Utes
New Mexico 1880

China Relief Expedition
*Without inscription

Philippine Insurrection
Luzon 1900
*Luzon 1901

World War II
*Algeria-French Morocco
(with arrowhead)
*Tunisia
*Sicily (with arrowhead)
*Naples-Foggia
*Anzio (with arrowhead)
*Rome-Arno
*Southern France (with arrowhead)
*Rhineland
*Ardennes-Alsace
*Central Europe

Korean War
*CCF intervention
*First UN counteroffensive
*CCF spring offensive
*UN summer-fall offensive
*Second Korean winter
*Korea, summer-fall 1952
*Third Korean winter
*Korea, summer 1953

DECORATIONS

*Presidential Unit Citation (Army), Streamer embroidered COLMAR (3d Infantry Division cited; WD GO 44, 1945)

*Presidential Unit Citation (Army), Streamer embroidered MONTELIMAR (1st Battalion, 15th Infantry cited; WD GO 21, 1945)

Presidential Unit Citation (Army), Streamer embroidered SAN FRATELLO

Presidential Unit Citation (Army), Streamer embroidered KOWANG-NI

*Presidential Unit Citation (Navy), Streamer embroidered HWACHON RESERVOIR (1st Battalion, 15th Infantry cited; DA GO 38, 1957)

*Navy Unit Commendation, Streamer embroidered PANMUNJOM (1st Battalion, 15th Infantry cited; DA GO 38, 1957)

*French Croix de Guerre with Palm, World War II, Streamer embroidered COLMAR (15th Infantry cited; DA GO 43, 1950)

*French Croix de Guerre, World War II, Fourragere (15th Infantry cited; DA GO 43, 1950)

*Republic of Korea Presidential Unit Citation, Streamer embroidered UIJONGBU CORRIDOR (15th Infantry cited; DA GO 20, 1953)

*Republic of Korea Presidential Unit Citation, Streamer embroidered IRON TRIANGLE (15th Infantry cited; DA GO 29, 1954)

*Republic of Korea Presidential Unit Citation, Streamer embroidered

KOREA (1st Battalion, 15th Infantry cited; DA GO 33, 1953, as amended by DA GO 41, 1955)

*Chryssoun Aristion Andrias (Bravery Gold Medal of Greece), Streamer embroidered KOREA (15th Infantry cited; DA GO 2, 1956)

15TH INFANTRY, BIBLIOGRAPHY

Blumenson, Martin. *Salerno to Cassino*. United States Army in World War II. Washington: Government Printing Office, 1969.

"A Brief History of the 15th Infantry Regiment." n.p., 1950.

Brinkerhoff, H. R. "The Fifteenth Regiment of Infantry," *The Army of the United States,* edited by Theophilus F. Rodenbough and William L. Haskin. New York: Maynard, Merrill and Company, 1896, pp. 610–628. (Originally published in the *Journal of the Military Service Institution of the United States,* XIII [1892], 1256–1274.)

Customs of the 15th Infantry. Tientsin-Peiping, China: Peiyong Press, 192?

Customs of the Fifteenth U.S. Infantry, A Facsimile Reproduction, With An Historical Essay by Edmund Sprague Jones. Cornwallville, New York: Hope Farm Press, 1959.

The Fifteenth Infantry Regiment, 1861–1953. n.p., 1953.

Finney, Charles G. *The Old China Hands*. New York: Doubleday, 1961.

Garland, Albert N. and Howard McGaw Smyth. *Sicily and the Surrender of Italy*. United States Army in World War II. Washington: Government Printing Office, 1965.

Hermes, Walter G. *Truce Tent and Fighting Front*. United States Army in the Korean War. Washington: Government Printing Office, 1966.

Historical Section, War Department. *Anzio Beachhead*. American Forces in Action Series. Washington: Government Printing Office, 1947.

————. *From the Volturno to the Winter Line*. American Forces in Action Series. Washington: Government Printing Office, 1944.

Howe, George F. *Northwest Africa: Seizing the Initiative in the West*. United States Army in World War II. Washington: Government Printing Office, 1957.

"One Hundred Twenty-Sixth Organization Day. 1813–1939. 15th U.S. Infantry, Fort Lewis, Washington, May 4, 1939." (Erroneously connects this regiment with an earlier one of the same designation.)

"The Record, A Brief History of the U.S. 15th Infantry, From 1813 to 1945. . ." n.p., 1945. (Erroneously connects this regiment with an earlier one of the same designation.)

Roster of Commissioned Officers of the 15th Regiment, U.S. Infantry, 1861–1903. Ord Barracks, California: Regimental Press, 1903.

Thomas, Charles W., III. "The United States Army Troops in China 1912–1937." Monograph for Stanford University, June 1937.

Williams, L. L., ed. *15th Infantry Annual, May 4, 1924–May 4, 1925*. Tientsin, China: Tientsin Press, Ltd., 1925.

16th INFANTRY

Heraldic Items

Coat of Arms

Shield: Vair argent and azure, in chief an Indian arrow and a Philippine bolo in saltire or and in base a five-bastioned fort gules fimbriated of the third.

Crest: On a wreath of the colors on a cross pattée argent a garb proper pierced by a devil's trident in pale sable armed gules.

Motto: *Semper Paratus* (Always Prepared).

Symbolism: The shield is the fur vair, white and blue, from the arms of Fléville, France. This town was captured by the 16th Infantry on 4 October 1918 after very heavy fighting in the Meuse-Argonne campaign of World War I. The crossed arrow and bolo recall the Indian and Philippine fighting and the five-bastioned fort was the badge of the V Corps in Cuba.

The crest is the white Maltese cross of the V Corps in the Civil War and represents the desperate fighting in the Wheatfield and Devil's Den at Gettysburg where the regiment lost approximately 50 percent of its effective strength. The motto, "Always Prepared," has been used by the regiment since 1907.

Distinctive Insignia

The distinctive insignia is the shield of the coat of arms.

Lineage and Honors

Lineage

Constituted 3 May 1861 in the Regular Army as the 1st Battalion, 11th Infantry. Organized July 1861–February 1862 at Fort Independence, Massachusetts, and Perryville, Maryland. Reorganized and redesignated 5 December 1866 as the 11th Infantry. Consolidated 28 March–6 April 1869 with the 34th Infantry (see ANNEX) and consolidated unit desig-

369

nated as the 16th Infantry. Assigned 8 June 1917 to the 1st Expeditionary Division (later redesignated as the 1st Infantry Division).

Relieved 15 February 1957 from assignment to the 1st Infantry Division and reorganized as a parent regiment under the Combat Arms Regimental System.

ANNEX

Constituted 3 May 1861 in the Regular Army as the 3d Battalion, 16th Infantry. Organized in April 1864 at Madison Barracks, New York. Reorganized and redesignated 21 September 1866 as the 34th Infantry. Consolidated 28 March–6 April 1869 with the 11th Infantry and consolidated unit designated as the 16th Infantry.

CAMPAIGN PARTICIPATION CREDIT

Civil War
Peninsula
Manassas
Antietam
Fredericksburg
Chancellorsville
Gettysburg
Wilderness
Spotsylvania
Cold Harbor
Petersburg
Virginia 1862
Virginia 1863

Indian Wars
Cheyennes
Utes
Pine Ridge

War With Spain
Santiago

Philippine Insurrection
Luzon 1899

Mexican Expedition
Mexico 1916–1917

World War I
Montdidier-Noyon
Aisne-Marne
St. Mihiel
Meuse-Argonne
Lorraine 1917
Lorraine 1918
Picardy 1918

World War II
Algeria-French Morocco
(with arrowhead)
Tunisia
Sicily (with arrowhead)
Normandy (with arrowhead)
Northern France
Rhineland
Ardennes-Alsace
Central Europe

Vietnam
Defense
Counteroffensive
Counteroffensive, Phase II
Counteroffensive, Phase III
Tet Counteroffensive
(other campaigns to be determined)

DECORATIONS

Presidential Unit Citation (Army), Streamer embroidered NORMANDY (16th Infantry cited; WD GO 73, 1944)

Presidential Unit Citation (Army), Streamer embroidered MATEUR, TUNISIA (1st Battalion, 16th Infantry cited; WD GO 60, 1944)

Presidential Unit Citation (Army), Streamer embroidered SICILY (1st and 2d Battalions, 16th Infantry cited; WD GO 60, 1944)

Presidential Unit Citation (Army), Streamer embroidered HURTGEN FOREST (1st and 2d Battalions, 16th Infantry cited; WD GO 120, 1946)

Presidential Unit Citation (Army), Streamer embroidered HAMICH, GERMANY (3d Battalion, 16th Infantry cited; WD GO 120, 1946)

French Croix de Guerre with Palm, World War I, Streamer embroidered AISNE-MARNE (16th Infantry cited; WD GO 11, 1924)

French Croix de Guerre with Palm, World War I, Streamer embroidered MEUSE-ARGONNE (16th Infantry cited; WD GO 11, 1924)

French Croix de Guerre with Palm, World War II, Streamer embroidered KASSERINE (16th Infantry cited; DA GO 43, 1950)

French Croix de Guerre with Palm, World War II, Streamer embroidered NORMANDY (16th Infantry cited; DA GO 43, 1950)

French Medaille Militaire, Streamer embroidered FRANCE (16th Infantry cited; DA GO 43, 1950)

French Medaille Militaire, Fourragere (16th Infantry cited; DA GO 43, 1950)

Belgian Fourragere 1940 (16th Infantry cited; DA GO 43, 1950)

Cited in the Order of the Day of the Belgian Army for action at EUPEN-MALMEDY (16th Infantry cited; DA GO 43, 1950)

Cited in the Order of the Day of the Belgian Army for action at MONS (16th Infantry cited; DA GO 43, 1950)

1st BATTALION, 16th INFANTRY

RA
(1st Infantry Division)

LINEAGE

Constituted 3 May 1861 in the Regular Army as Company A, 1st Battalion, 11th Infantry. Organized in September 1861 at Fort Independence, Massachusetts. Reorganized and redesignated 5 December 1866 as Company A, 11th Infantry. Consolidated 6 April 1869 with Company A, 34th Infantry (see ANNEX) and consolidated unit designated as Company A, 16th Infantry. (16th Infantry assigned 8 June 1917 to the 1st Expeditionary Division [later redesignated as the 1st Infantry Division].)

Reorganized and redesignated 15 February 1957 as Headquarters and Headquarters Company, 1st Battle Group, 16th Infantry and remained assigned to the 1st Infantry Division (organic elements concurrently constituted and activated). Relieved 13 March 1959 from assignment to the 1st Infantry Division and assigned to the 8th Infantry Division. Reorganized and redesignated 1 April 1963 as the 1st Battalion, 16th Infantry. Relieved 25 April 1963 from assignment to the 8th Infantry Division and assigned to the 1st Infantry Division.

ANNEX

Constituted 3 May 1861 in the Regular Army as Company A, 3d Battalion, 16th Infantry. Organized in April 1864 at Madison Barracks, New York. Reorganized and redesignated 21 September 1866 as Company A, 34th Infantry. Consolidated 6 April 1869 with Company A, 11th Infantry and consolidated unit designated as Company A, 16th Infantry.

372

Campaign Participation Credit

Civil War
*Peninsula
*Manassas
*Antietam
*Fredericksburg
*Chancellorsville
Gettysburg
Wilderness
Spotsylvania
Cold Harbor
Petersburg
*Virginia 1862
Virginia 1863

Indian Wars
*Cheyennes
Utes
Pine Ridge

War With Spain
*Santiago

Philippine Insurrection
*Luzon 1899

Mexican Expedition
*Mexico 1916–1917

World War I
*Montdidier-Noyon
*Aisne-Marne
*St. Mihiel
*Meuse-Argonne
*Lorraine 1917
*Lorraine 1918
*Picardy 1918

World War II
*Algeria-French Morocco
   (with arrowhead)
*Tunisia
*Sicily (with arrowhead)
*Normandy (with arrowhead)
*Northen France
*Rhineland
*Ardennes-Alsace
*Central Europe

Vietnam
*Defense
*Counteroffensive
*Counteroffensive, Phase II
*Counteroffensive, Phase III
*Tet Counteroffensive
   (other campaigns to be determined)

Decorations

*Presidential Unit Citation (Army), Streamer embroidered NORMANDY (16th Infantry cited; WD GO 73, 1944)

*Presidential Unit Citation (Army), Streamer embroidered MATEUR, TUNISIA (1st Battalion, 16th Infantry cited; WD GO 60, 1944)

*Presidential Unit Citation (Army), Streamer embroidered SICILY (1st Battalion, 16th Infantry cited; WD GO 60, 1944)

*Presidential Unit Citation (Army), Streamer embroidered HURTGEN FOREST (1st Battalion, 16th Infantry cited; WD GO 120, 1946)

Presidential Unit Citation (Army), Streamer embroidered HAMICH, GERMANY

*French Croix de Guerre with Palm, World War I, Streamer embroidered AISNE-MARNE (16th Infantry cited; WD GO 11, 1924)

*French Croix de Guerre with Palm, World War I, Streamer embroidered MEUSE-ARGONNE (16th Infantry cited; WD GO 11, 1924)

*French Croix de Guerre with Palm, World War II, Streamer embroidered KASSERINE (16th Infantry cited; DA GO 43, 1950)

*French Croix de Guerre with Palm, World War II, Streamer embroidered NORMANDY (16th Infantry cited; DA GO 43, 1950)

*French Medaille Militaire, Streamer embroidered FRANCE (16th Infantry cited; DA GO 43, 1950)

*French Medaille Militaire, Fourragere (16th Infantry cited; DA GO 43, 1950)

*Belgian Fourragere 1940 (16th Infantry cited; DA GO 43, 1950)

*Cited in the Order of the Day of the Belgian Army for action at EUPEN-MALMEDY (16th Infantry cited; DA GO 43, 1950)

*Cited in the Order of the Day of the Belgian Army for action at MONS (16th Infantry cited; DA GO 43, 1950)

*Vietnamese Cross of Gallantry with Palm, Streamer embroidered VIETNAM 1965–1968 (1st Battalion, 16th Infantry cited; DA GO 21, 1969)

*Vietnamese Cross of Gallantry with Palm, Streamer embroidered VIETNAM 1965–1968 (1st Battalion, 16th Infantry cited; DA GO 21,

*Vietnamese Civil Action Honor Medal, First Class, Streamer embroidered VIETNAM 1965–1970 (1st Battalion, 16th Infantry cited; DA GO 53, 1970)

2d BATTALION, 16th INFANTRY

RA
(1st Infantry Division)

LINEAGE

Constituted 3 May 1861 in the Regular Army as Company B, 1st Battalion, 11th Infantry. Organized in September 1861 at Fort Independence, Massachusetts. Reorganized and redesignated 5 December 1866 as Company B, 11th Infantry. Consolidated 31 March 1869 with Company B, 34th Infantry (see ANNEX) and consolidated unit designated as Company B, 16th Infantry. (16th Infantry assigned 8 June 1917 to the 1st Expeditionary Division [later redesignated as the 1st Infantry Division].)

Inactivated 15 February 1957 at Fort Riley, Kansas, and relieved from assignment to the 1st Infantry Division; concurrently, redesignated as Headquarters and Headquarters Company, 2d Battle Group, 16th Infantry. Activated 1 October 1963 at Fort Riley, Kansas, and assigned to the 1st Infantry Division (organic elements concurrently constituted and activated). Reorganized and redesignated 2 March 1964 as the 2d Battalion, 16th Infantry.

ANNEX

Constituted 3 May 1861 in the Regular Army as Company B, 3d Battalion, 16th Infantry. Organized in April 1864 at Madison Barracks, New York. Reorganized and redesignated 21 September 1866 as Company B, 34th Infantry. Consolidated 31 March 1869 with Company B, 11th Infantry and consolidated unit designated as Company B, 16th Infantry.

375

CAMPAIGN PARTICIPATION CREDIT

Civil War
*Peninsula
*Manassas
*Antietam
*Fredericksburg
*Chancellorsville
*Gettysburg
*Wilderness
*Spotsylvania
*Cold Harbor
*Petersburg
*Virginia 1862
*Virginia 1863

Indian Wars
Cheyennes
Utes
Pine Ridge

War With Spain
*Santiago

Philippine Insurrection
Luzon 1899

Mexican Expedition
*Mexico 1916–1917

World War I
*Montdidier-Noyon
*Aisne-Marne
*St. Mihiel
*Meuse-Argonne
*Lorraine 1917
*Lorraine 1918
*Picardy 1918

World War II
*Algeria-French Morocco
  (with arrowhead)
*Tunisia
*Sicily (with arrowhead)
*Normandy (with arrowhead)
*Northern France
*Rhineland
*Ardennes-Alsace
*Central Europe

Vietnam
*Defense
*Counteroffensive
*Counteroffensive, Phase II
*Counteroffensive, Phase III
*Tet Counteroffensive
  (other campaigns to be determined)

DECORATIONS

*Presidential Unit Citation (Army), Streamer embroidered NOR-MANDY (16th Infantry cited; WD GO 73, 1944)

*Presidential Unit Citation (Army), Streamer embroidered MATEUR, TUNISIA (1st Battalion, 16th Infantry cited; WD GO 60, 1944)

*Presidential Unit Citation (Army), Streamer embroidered SICILY (1st Battalion, 16th Infantry cited; WD GO 60, 1944)

*Presidential Unit Citation (Army), Streamer embroidered HURTGEN FOREST (1st Battalion, 16th Infantry cited; WD GO 120, 1946)

Presidential Unit Citation (Army), Streamer embroidered HAMICH, GERMANY

*French Croix de Guerre with Palm, World War I, Streamer embroidered AISNE-MARNE (16th Infantry cited; WD GO 11, 1924)

*French Croix de Guerre with Palm, World War I, Streamer embroidered MEUSE-ARGONNE (16th Infantry cited; WD GO 11, 1924)

*French Croix de Guerre with Palm, World War II, Streamer embroidered KASSERINE (16th Infantry cited; DA GO 43, 1950)

*French Croix de Guerre with Palm, World War II, Streamer em-

broidered NORMANDY (16th Infantry cited; DA GO 43, 1950)

*French Medaille Militaire, Streamer embroidered FRANCE (16th Infantry cited; DA GO 43, 1950)

*French Medaille Militaire, Fourragere (16th Infantry cited; DA GO 43, 1950)

*Belgian Fourragere 1940 (16th Infantry cited; DA GO 43, 1950)

*Cited in the Order of the Day of the Belgian Army for action at EUPEN-MALMEDY (16th Infantry cited; DA GO 43, 1950)

*Cited in the Order of the Day of the Belgian Army for action at MONS (16th Infantry cited; DA GO 43, 1950)

*Vietnamese Cross of Gallantry with Palm, Streamer embroidered VIETNAM 1965–1968 (2d Battalion, 16th Infantry cited; DA GO 21, 1969)

*Vietnamese Civil Action Honor Medal, First Class, Streamer embroidered VIETNAM 1965–1970 (2d Battalion, 16th Infantry cited; DA GO 53, 1970)

Company C additionally entitled to: Valorous Unit Award, Streamer embroidered COURTENAY PLANTATION (Company C, 2d Battalion, 16th Infantry cited; DA GO 17, 1968)

3d BATTALION, 16th INFANTRY

AR
(187th Infantry Brigade)

Lineage

Constituted 3 May 1861 in the Regular Army as Company C, 1st Battalion, 11th Infantry. Organized 15 February 1862 at Perryville, Maryland. Reorganized and redesignated 5 December 1866 as Company C, 11th Infantry. Consolidated 4 April 1869 with Company C, 34th Infantry (see ANNEX) and consolidated unit designated as Company C, 16th Infantry. (16th Infantry assigned 8 June 1917 to the 1st Expeditionary Division [later redesignated as the 1st Infantry Division].)

Inactivated 15 February 1957 at Fort Riley, Kansas, and relieved from assignment to the 1st Infantry Division; concurrently, redesignated as Headquarters and Headquarters Company, 3d Battle Group, 16th Infantry. Withdrawn 6 April 1959 from the Regular Army, allotted to the Army Reserve, and assigned to the 94th Infantry Division (organic elements concurrently constituted). Battle Group activated 1 May 1959 with Headquarters at Worcester, Massachusetts. Reorganized and redesignated 7 January 1963 as the 3d Battalion, 16th Infantry; concurrently, relieved from assignment to the 94th Infantry Division and assigned to the 187th Infantry Brigade.

ANNEX

Constituted 3 May 1861 in the Regular Army as Company C, 3d Battalion, 16th Infantry. Organized in April 1864 at Madison Barracks, New York. Reorganized and redesignated 21 September 1866 as Company C, 34th Infantry. Consolidated 4 April 1869 with Company C, 11th Infantry and consolidated unit designated as Company C, 16th Infantry.

Home Area: First United States Army

378

CAMPAIGN PARTICIPATION CREDIT

Civil War
  *Peninsula
  *Manassas
  *Antietam
  *Fredericksburg
  *Chancellorsville
  *Gettysburg
  *Wilderness
  *Spotsylvania
  *Cold Harbor
  *Petersburg
  *Virginia 1862
  *Virginia 1863

Indian Wars
  Cheyennes
  *Utes
  Pine Ridge

War With Spain
  *Santiago

Philippine Insurrection
  Luzon 1899

Mexican Expedition
  *Mexico 1916–1917

World War I
  *Montdidier-Noyon
  *Aisne-Marne
  *St. Mihiel
  *Meuse-Argonne
  *Lorraine 1917
  *Lorraine 1918
  *Picardy 1918

World War II
  *Algeria-French Morocco
    (with arrowhead)
  *Tunisia
  *Sicily (with arrowhead)
  *Normandy (with arrowhead)
  *Northern France
  *Rhineland
  *Ardennes-Alsace
  *Central Europe

DECORATIONS

*Presidential Unit Citation (Army), Streamer embroidered NOR-MANDY (16th Infantry cited; WD GO 73, 1944)

*Presidential Unit Citation (Army), Streamer embroidered MATEUR, TUNISIA (1st Battalion, 16th Infantry cited; WD GO 60, 1944)

*Presidential Unit Citation (Army), Streamer embroidered SICILY (1st Battalion, 16th Infantry cited; WD GO 60, 1944)

*Presidential Unit Citation (Army), Streamer embroidered HURTGEN FOREST (1st Battalion, 16th Infantry cited; WD GO 120, 1946)

Presidential Unit Citation (Army), Streamer embroidered HAMICH, GERMANY

*French Croix de Guerre with Palm, World War I, Streamer embroidered AISNE-MARNE (16th Infantry cited; WD GO 11, 1924)

*French Croix de Guerre with Palm, World War I, Streamer embroidered MEUSE-ARGONNE (16th Infantry cited; WD GO 11, 1924)

*French Croix de Guerre with Palm, World War II, Streamer embroidered KASSERINE (16th Infantry cited; DA GO 43, 1950)

*French Croix de Guerre with Palm, World War II, Streamer embroidered NORMANDY (16th Infantry cited; DA GO 43, 1950)

*French Medaille Militaire, Streamer embroidered FRANCE (16th Infantry cited; DA GO 43, 1950)

*French Medaille Militaire, Fourragere (16th Infantry cited; DA GO 43, 1950)

*Belgian Fourragere 1940 (16th Infantry cited; DA GO 43, 1950)

*Cited in the Order of the Day of the Belgian Army for action at EUPEN-MALMEDY (16th Infantry cited; DA GO 43, 1950)

*Cited in the Order of the Day of the Belgian Army for action at MONS (16th Infantry cited; DA GO 43, 1950)

16TH INFANTRY, BIBLIOGRAPHY

Baumgartner, John W. *The 16th Infantry, 1798–1946.* Bamberg: Sebaldus Verlag, 1946. (Erroneously connects this regiment with an earlier one of the same designation.)

Blumenson, Martin. *Breakout and Pursuit.* United States Army in World War II. Washington: Government Printing Office, 1961.

First Battle Group, Sixteenth Infantry, 1861–1961; Centennial. n.p., 1961.

Garland, Albert N. and Howard McGaw Smyth. *Sicily and the Surrender of Italy.* United States Army in World War II. Washington: Government Printing Office, 1965.

Harrison, Gordon A. *Cross-Channel Attack.* United States Army in World War II. Washington: Government Printing Office, 1951.

Historical Section, War Department. *Omaha Beachhead.* American Forces in Action Series. Washington: Government Printing Office, 1945.

————. *To Bizerte with the II Corps.* American Forces in Action Series. Washington: Government Printing Office, 1943.

A History of the 16th Infantry Regiment, 1898–1904. Fort McPherson, Georgia, 1904.

Hoehling, Adolph. *The Fierce Lambs.* Boston: Little, Brown and Company, 1960.

Howe, George F. *Northwest Africa: Seizing the Initiative in the West.* United States Army in World War II. Washington: Government Printing Office, 1957 .

MacDonald, Charles B. *The Battle of Huertgen Forest.* Philadelphia and New York: J. B. Lippincott Company, 1963.

————. *The Siegfried Line Campaign.* United States Army in World War II. Washington: Government Printing Office, 1963.

Marshall, S. L. A. *Ambush.* New York: Cowles Book Company, 1969.

Parr, Frank S. and Ralph J. Crawford, compilers. *Redesignation Day, 16th Infantry Regiment, 1st Infantry Division, Grafenwohr, Germany, 7 July 1948.* Frankfurt am Main: Otto Lembeck, 1948.

Regimental Chaplain. *The Story of the 16th Infantry in France.* Montabaur-Frankfurt: Martin Flock, 1919.

Richards, William V. "The Sixteenth Regiment of Infantry," *The Army of the United States,* edited by Theophilus F. Rodenbough and William L. Haskin. New York: Maynard, Merrill and Company, 1896, pp. 629–633. (Originally published in the *Journal of the Military Service Institution of the United States,* XIV [1893], 1320–1333.)

Roster of Commissioned Officers of the Sixteenth United States Infantry, Commanded by Colonel Hugh A. Theaker. Fort Sherman, Idaho: Regimental Press, 1898.

Roster of Commissioned and Non-commissioned Officers of the Sixteenth U.S. Infantry, Colonel Omar Bundy, Commanding. El Paso, Texas, 1915.

Roster of the 11th Regiment of the U.S. Infantry, from the 14th Day of May, 1861, to the 14th Day of May, 1866. Richmond, 1866. (Relates to the present 16th Infantry.)

Simmonds, B. and E. R. Christia. "The Sixth and Sixteenth Regiments of Infantry," *The Santiago Campaign.* Richmond: Williams Printing Company, 1927, pp. 66–89.

Sixteenth Infantry Organization Day, October Fourth, Nineteen Hundred Forty-one, Commemorating the Twenty-third Anniversary at Fleville, France. Fort Devens, Massachusetts, 1941.

17th INFANTRY

HERALDIC ITEMS

COAT OF ARMS

Shield: Azure, a wall embattled argent, maconné de sable, between in chief a cross pattée and a five-bastioned fort voided, and in base a buffalo statant of the second.

Crest: On a wreath of the colors a sea lion erect or grasping in its dexter claw two arrows sable armed and flitted gules.

Motto: Truth and Courage.

Symbolism: The shield is blue for infantry. Service in the Civil War is shown by the white cross pattée, the badge of the V Corps in the Army of the Potomac, and by the wall which symbolizes the famous stone wall at Fredericksburg. The five-bastioned fort was the badge of the V Corps in Cuba. The buffalo represents service in Korea.

The crest is a sea lion taken from the Spanish arms of Manila, and the arrows represent Indian campaigns.

DISTINCTIVE INSIGNIA

The distinctive insignia is the shield of the coat of arms.

LINEAGE AND HONORS

LINEAGE

Constituted 3 May 1861 in the Regular Army as the 1st Battalion, 17th Infantry. Organized 6 July 1861 at Fort Preble, Maine. Reorganized and redesignated 13 December 1866 as the 17th Infantry. Consolidated 1 June 1869 with the 44th Infantry, Veteran Reserve Corps (constituted 21 September 1866) and consolidated unit designated as the 17th Infantry.

Assigned 5 July 1918 to the 11th Division. (2d and 3d Battalions inactivated 1 October 1921 at Fort McIntosh, Texas; activated 24 June 1922 at Fort Crook, Nebraska.) Relieved 24 March 1923 from assignment to the 11th Division and assigned to the 7th Division. Relieved 15 August

1927 from assignment to the 7th Division and assigned to the 6th Division. (2d Battalion inactivated 31 October 1929 at Fort Des Moines, Iowa.) Relieved 1 October 1933 from assignment to the 6th Division and assigned to the 7th Division (later redesignated as the 7th Infantry Division). (2d Battalion activated 1 July 1940 at Camp Ord, California.)

Relieved 1 July 1957 from assignment to the 7th Infantry Division and reorganized as a parent regiment under the Combat Arms Regimental System.

CAMPAIGN PARTICIPATION CREDIT

Civil War
  Peninsula
  Manassas
  Antietam
  Fredericksburg
  Chancellorsville
  Gettysburg
  Wilderness
  Spotsylvania
  Cold Harbor
  Petersburg
  Virginia 1862
  Virginia 1863

Indian Wars
  Little Big Horn
  Pine Ridge
  North Dakota 1872

War With Spain
  Santiago

Philippine Insurrection
  Manila
  Malolos
  San Isidro

Tarlac
Mindanao
Luzon 1899
Luzon 1900

Mexican Expedition
  Mexico 1916–1917

World War II
  Aleutian Islands (with arrowhead)
  Eastern Mandates (with arrowhead)
  Leyte
  Ryukyus (with arrowhead)

Korean War
  UN defensive
  UN offensive
  CCF intervention
  First UN counteroffensive
  CCF spring offensive
  UN summer-fall offensive
  Second Korean winter
  Korea, summer-fall 1952
  Third Korean winter
  Korea, summer 1953

DECORATIONS

Presidential Unit Citation (Army), Streamer embroidered LEYTE (17th Infantry cited; DA GO 32, 1949)

Philippine Presidential Unit Citation, Streamer embroidered 17 OCTOBER 1944 TO 4 JULY 1945 (17th Infantry cited; DA GO 47, 1950)

Republic of Korea Presidential Unit Citation, Streamer embroidered INCHON (17th Infantry cited; DA GO 35, 1951)

Republic of Korea Presidential Unit Citation, Streamer embroidered KOREA 1952–1953 (17th Infantry cited; DA GO 24, 1954)

Republic of Korea Presidential Unit Citation, Streamer embroidered KOREA 1950–1953 (17th Infantry cited; DA GO 22, 1956)

1st BATTALION, 17th INFANTRY

RA

(7th Infantry Division)

LINEAGE

Constituted 3 May 1861 in the Regular Army as Company A, 1st Battalion, 17th Infantry. Organized 6 July 1861 at Fort Preble, Maine. Reorganized and redesignated 13 December 1866 as Company A, 17th Infantry.

Consolidated 1 June 1869 with Company A, 44th Infantry, Veteran Reserve Corps (constituted 21 September 1866) and consolidated unit designated as Company A, 17th Infantry. (17th Infantry assigned 5 July 1918 to the 11th Division; relieved 24 March 1923 from assignment to the 11th Division and assigned to the 7th Division; relieved 15 August 1927 from assignment to the 7th Division and assigned to the 6th Division; relieved 1 October 1933 from assignment to the 6th Division and assigned to the 7th Division [later redesignated as the 7th Infantry Division].)

Reorganized and redesignated 1 July 1957 as Headquarters and Headquarters Company, 1st Battle Group, 17th Infantry and remained assigned to the 7th Infantry Division (organic elements concurrently constituted and activated). Reorganized and redesignated 1 July 1963 as the 1st Battalion, 17th Infantry.

385

CAMPAIGN PARTICIPATION CREDIT

Civil War
*Peninsula
*Manassas
*Antietam
*Fredericksburg
*Chancellorsville
*Gettysburg
*Wilderness
*Spotsylvania
*Cold Harbor
*Petersburg
*Virginia 1862
*Virginia 1863

Indian Wars
Little Big Horn
*Pine Ridge
*North Dakota 1872

War With Spain
*Santiago

Philippine Insurrection
Manila
*Malolos
*San Isidro

*Tarlac
Mindanao
*Luzon 1899
*Luzon 1900

Mexican Expedition
*Mexico 1916–1917

World War II
*Aleutian Islands (with arrowhead)
*Eastern Mandates (with arrowhead)
*Leyte
*Ryukyus (with arrowhead)

Korean War
*UN defensive
*UN offensive
*CCF intervention
*First UN counteroffensive
*CCF spring offensive
*UN summer-fall offensive
*Second Korean winter
*Korea, summer-fall 1952
*Third Korean winter
*Korea, summer 1953

DECORATIONS

*Presidential Unit Citation (Army), Streamer embroidered LEYTE (17th Infantry cited; DA GO 32, 1949)

*Philippine Presidential Unit Citation, Streamer embroidered 17 OCTOBER 1944 TO 4 JULY 1945 (17th Infantry cited; DA GO 47, 1950)

*Republic of Korea Presidential Unit Citation, Streamer embroidered INCHON (17th Infantry cited; DA GO 35, 1951)

*Republic of Korea Presidential Unit Citation, Streamer embroidered KOREA 1952–1953 (17th Infantry cited; DA GO 24, 1954)

*Republic of Korea Presidential Unit Citation, Streamer embroidered KOREA 1950–1953 (17th Infantry cited; DA GO 22, 1956)

2d BATTALION, 17th INFANTRY

RA
(7th Infantry Division)

LINEAGE

Constituted 3 May 1861 in the Regular Army as Company B, 1st Battalion, 17th Infantry. Organized 6 July 1861 at Fort Preble, Maine. Reorganized and redesignated 13 December 1866 as Company B, 17th Infantry.

Consolidated 1 June 1869 with Company B, 44th Infantry, Veteran Reserve Corps (constituted 21 September 1866) and consolidated unit designated as Company B, 17th Infantry. (17th Infantry assigned 5 July 1918 to the 11th Division; relieved 24 March 1923 from assignment to the 11th Division and assigned to the 7th Division; relieved 15 August 1927 from assignment to the 7th Division and assigned to the 6th Division; relieved 1 October 1933 from assignment to the 6th Division and assigned to the 7th Division [later redesignated as the 7th Infantry Division].)

Inactivated 1 July 1957 in Korea and relieved from assignment to the 7th Infantry Division, concurrently, redesignated as Headquarters and Headquarters Company, 2d Battle Group, 17th Infantry. Assigned 1 February 1963 to the 7th Infantry Division and activated in Korea (organic elements concurrently constituted and activated). Reorganized and redesignated 1 July 1963 as the 2d Battalion, 17th Infantry.

387

Campaign Participation Credit

Civil War
  *Peninsula
  *Manassas
  *Antietam
  *Fredericksburg
  Chancellorsville
  Gettysburg
  Wilderness
  Spotsylvania
  Cold Harbor
  Petersburg
  *Virginia 1862
  Virginia 1863

Indian Wars
  Little Big Horn
  Pine Ridge
  North Dakota 1872

War With Spain
  *Santiago

Philippine Insurrection
  *Manila
  *Malolos
  *San Isidro

  *Tarlac
  Mindanao
  *Luzon 1899
  *Luzon 1900

Mexican Expedition
  *Mexico 1916–1917

World War II
  *Aleutian Islands (with arrowhead)
  *Eastern Mandates (with arrowhead)
  *Leyte
  *Ryukyus (with arrowhead)

Korean War
  *UN defensive
  *UN offensive
  *CCF intervention
  *First UN counteroffensive
  *CCF spring offensive
  *UN summer-fall offensive
  *Second Korean winter
  *Korea, summer-fall 1952
  *Third Korean winter
  *Korea, summer 1953

Decorations

*Presidential Unit Citation (Army), Streamer embroidered ATTU (Company B, 17th Infantry, cited; WD GO 10, 1944)

*Presidential Unit Citation (Army), Streamer embroidered LEYTE (17th Infantry cited; DA GO 32, 1949)

*Philippine Presidential Unit Citation, Streamer embroidered 17 OCTOBER 1944 TO 4 JULY 1945 (17th Infantry cited; DA GO 47, 1950)

*Republic of Korea Presidential Unit Citation, Streamer embroidered INCHON (17th Infantry cited; DA GO 35, 1951)

*Republic of Korea Presidential Unit Citation, Streamer embroidered KOREA 1952–1953 (17th Infantry cited; DA GO 24, 1954)

*Republic of Korea Presidential Unit Citation, Streamer embroidered KOREA 1950–1953 (17th Infantry cited; DA GO 22, 1956)

3d BATTALION, 17th INFANTRY

AR
(inactive)

LINEAGE

Constituted 3 May 1861 in the Regular Army as Company C, 1st Battalion, 17th Infantry. Organized 6 July 1861 at Fort Preble, Maine. Reorganized and redesignated 13 December 1866 as Company C, 17th Infantry.

Consolidated 1 June 1869 with Company C, 44th Infantry, Veteran Reserve Corps (constituted 21 September 1866) and consolidated unit designated as Company C, 17th Infantry. (17th Infantry assigned 5 July 1918 to the 11th Division; relieved 24 March 1923 from assignment to the 11th Division and assigned to the 7th Division; relieved 15 August 1927 from assignment to the 7th Division and assigned to the 6th Division; relieved 1 October 1933 from assignment to the 6th Division and assigned to the 7th Division [later redesignated as the 7th Infantry Division].)

Inactivated 1 July 1957 in Korea and relieved from assignment to the 7th Infantry Division; concurrently, redesignated as Headquarters and Headquarters Company, 3d Battle Group, 17th Infantry. Withdrawn 20 April 1959 from the Regular Army and allotted to the Army Reserve (organic elements concurrently constituted). Battle Group activated 18 May 1959 with Headquarters at Council Bluffs, Iowa, and assigned to the 103d Infantry Division. Reorganized and redesignated 15 February 1963 as the 3d Battalion, 17th Infantry. Relieved 15 March 1963 from assignment to the 103d Infantry Division and assigned to the 205th Infantry Brigade. Inactivated 31 January 1968 at Council Bluffs, Iowa.

389

Campaign Participation Credit

Civil War
*Peninsula
*Manassas
*Antietam
*Fredericksburg
*Chancellorsville
*Gettysburg
*Wilderness
*Spotsylvania
*Cold Harbor
*Petersburg
*Virginia 1862
*Virginia 1863

Indian Wars
*Little Big Horn
Pine Ridge
*North Dakota 1872

War With Spain
*Santiago

Philippine Insurrection
Manila
*Malolos
*San Isidro

*Tarlac
Mindanao
*Luzon 1899
Luzon 1900

Mexican Expedition
*Mexico 1916–1917

World War II
*Aleutian Islands (with arrowhead)
*Eastern Mandates (with arrowhead)
*Leyte
*Ryukyus (with arrowhead)

Korean War
*UN defensive
*UN offensive
*CCF intervention
*First UN counteroffensive
*CCF spring offensive
*UN summer-fall offensive
*Second Korean winter
*Korea, summer-fall 1952
*Third Korean winter
*Korea, summer 1953

Decorations

*Presidential Unit Citation (Army), Streamer embroidered LEYTE (17th Infantry cited; DA GO 32, 1949)

*Philippine Presidential Unit Citation, Streamer embroidered 17 OCTOBER 1944 TO 4 JULY 1945 (17th Infantry cited; DA GO 47, 1950)

*Republic of Korea Presidential Unit Citation, Streamer embroidered INCHON (17th Infantry cited; DA GO 35, 1951)

*Republic of Korea Presidential Unit Citation, Streamer embroidered KOREA 1952–1953 (17th Infantry cited; DA GO 24, 1954)

*Republic of Korea Presidential Unit Citation, Streamer embroidered KOREA 1950–1953 (17th Infantry cited; DA GO 22, 1956)

COMPANY D, 17th INFANTRY

RA
(inactive)

Constituted 3 May 1861 in the Regular Army as Company D, 1st Battalion, 17th Infantry. Organized 6 July 1861 at Fort Preble, Maine. Reorganized and redesignated 13 December 1866 as Company D, 17th Infantry.

Consolidated 1 June 1869 with Company D, 44th Infantry, Veteran Reserve Corps (constituted 21 September 1866) and consolidated unit designated as Company D, 17th Infantry. (17th Infantry assigned 5 July 1918 to the 11th Division; relieved 24 March 1923 from assignment to the 11th Division and assigned to the 7th Division; relieved 15 August 1927 from assignment to the 7th Division and assigned to the 6th Division; relieved 1 October 1933 from assignment to the 6th Division and assigned to the 7th Division [later redesignated as the 7th Infantry Division].)

Inactivated 1 July 1957 in Korea and relieved from assignment to the 7th Infantry Division; concurrently, redesignated as Headquarters and Headquarters Company, 4th Battle Group, 17th Infantry. Redesignated 22 June 1960 as Company D, 17th Infantry. Activated 24 June 1960 in Korea. Inactivated 26 December 1964 in Korea. Activated 15 May 1965 in Germany. Inactivated 21 February 1969 at Fort Benning, Georgia.

Campaign Participation Credit

Civil War
Peninsula
Manassas
Antietam
Fredericksburg
Chancellorsville
Gettysburg
Wilderness
Spotsylvania
Cold Harbor
Petersburg
Virginia 1862
Virginia 1863

War With Spain
Santiago

Philippine Insurrection
Malolos
San Isidro
Tarlac
Luzon 1899
Luzon 1900

Mexican Expedition
Mexico 1916–1917

World War II-AP
Aleutian Islands (with arrowhead)
Eastern Mandates (with arrowhead)
Leyte
Ryukyus (with arrowhead)

Korean War
UN defensive
UN offensive
CCF intervention
First UN counteroffensive
CCF spring offensive
UN summer-fall offensive
Second Korean winter
Korea, summer-fall 1952
Third Korean winter
Korea, summer 1953

Decorations

Presidential Unit Citation (Army), Streamer embroidered LEYTE (17th Infantry cited; DA GO 32, 1949)

Philippine Presidential Unit Citation, Streamer embroidered 17 OCTOBER 1944 TO 4 JULY 1945 (17th Infantry cited; DA GO 47, 1950)

Republic of Korea Presidential Unit Citation, Streamer embroidered INCHON (17th Infantry cited; DA GO 35, 1951)

Republic of Korea Presidential Unit Citation, Streamer embroidered KOREA 1952–1953 (17th Infantry cited; DA GO 24, 1954)

Republic of Korea Presidential Unit Citation, Streamer embroidered KOREA 1950–1953 (17th Infantry cited; DA GO 22, 1956)

17TH INFANTRY, BIBLIOGRAPHY

Appleman, Roy E. *South to the Naktong, North to the Yalu*. United States Army in the Korean War. Washington: Government Printing Office, 1961.

Appleman, Roy E., *et al*. *Okinawa: The Last Battle*. United States Army in World War II. Washington: Government Printing Office, 1948.

Baylis, Charles D., ed. *Historical and Pictorial Review of the Seventeenth Infantry, Seventh Division, United States Army, Fort Ord, California*. Baton Rouge: Army and Navy Publishing Company, 1941.

Cannon, M. Hamlin. *Leyte: The Return to the Philippines*. United States Army in World War II. Washington: Government Printing Office, 1954.

The Capture of Attu, as Told by the Men who Fought There. Washington: Infantry Journal Press, 1944.

Chubb, Charles St. John. "The Seventeenth Regiment of Infantry," *The Army of the United States*, edited by Theophilus F. Rodenbough and William L. Haskin. New York: Maynard, Merrill and Company, 1896, pp. 634–642. (Originally published in the *Journal of the Military Service Institution of the United States*, XV [1894], 1332–1340.)

Conn, Stetson, Rose C. Engelman, and Byron Fairchild. *Guarding the United States and Its Outposts*. United States Army in World War II. Washington: Government Printing Office, 1964.

Crowl, Philip A. and Edmund G. Love. *Seizing the Gilberts and Marshalls*. United States Army in World War II. Washington: Government Printing Office, 1960.

Falk, Stanley L. *Decision at Leyte*. New York: W. W. Norton and Company, Inc., 1966.

Gugeler, Russell A. *Combat Actions in Korea*. Washington: Combat Forces Press, 1954.

Hermes, Walter G. *Truce Tent and Fighting Front*. United States Army in the Korean War. Washington: Government Printing Office, 1966.

Marshall, S. L. A. "Action at the Pigpen," *Infantry Journal*, LV (November 1944), 39–47.

———. *Pork Chop Hill*. New York: William Morrow, 1956.

17th Infantry Regiment, 1812–1951, "The Buffaloes." Korea, 1951. (Erroneously connects this regiment with an earlier one of the same designation.)

18th INFANTRY

HERALDIC ITEMS

COAT OF ARMS

Shield: Azure, a saltire argent, between in chief two arrows in saltire of the second armed and flighted or, in fess the badge of the VIII Corps (2d Division, 2d Brigade [solid white]) in the War with Spain proper and a bolo paleways of the second hilted of the third, on a chief indented of the second a bend gules between two fleurs-de-lis of the field.

Crest: On a wreath of the colors an acorn gules.

(And for informal use, the crest or shield encircled by a Fourragere in the colors of the French Croix de Guerre.)

Motto: *In Omnia Paratus* (In All Things Prepared).

Symbolism: Civil War service is shown by the saltire cross from the Confederate flag. The crossed arrows represent the regiment's Indian campaigns; the VIII Corps badge recalls service in the 2d Brigade, 2d Division of that corps in the War with Spain; and the bolo stands for operations in the Visayas during the Philippine Insurrection. In World War I the regiment was awarded two French Croix de Guerre with Palm and the French Fourragere for its part in the Soissons offensive on 18 July 1918 and the operations of early October 1918 around Exermont and Hill 240 in the old province of Lorraine. The chief bears the bend of the arms of Lorraine between the fleurs-de-lis of the arms of Soissons.

The crest is the badge of the 1st Division of the XIV Corps of the Army of the Cumberland, with which the regiment served during most of its operations in the Civil War.

DISTINCTIVE INSIGNIA

The distinctive insignia is the shield and motto of the coat of arms.

Lineage and Honors

Lineage

Constituted 3 May 1861 in the Regular Army as the 1st Battalion, 18th Infantry. Organized 22 July 1861 at Camp Thomas, Ohio. Reorganized and redesignated 31 December 1866 as the 18th Infantry. Consolidated 28 April 1869 with the 25th Infantry (see ANNEX) and consolidated unit designated as the 18th Infantry. Assigned 8 June 1917 to the 1st Expeditionary Division (later redesignated as the 1st Infantry Division).

Relieved 15 February 1957 from assignment to the 1st Infantry Division and reorganized as a parent regiment under the Combat Arms Regimental System.

Annex

Constituted 3 May 1861 in the Regular Army as the 2d Battalion, 16th Infantry. Organized 12 May 1862 at Camp Thomas, Ohio. Reorganized and redesignated 21 September 1866 as the 25th Infantry. Consolidated 28 April 1869 with the 18th Infantry and consolidated unit designated as the 18th Infantry.

Campaign Participation Credit

Civil War
Murfreesborough
Chickamauga
Chattanooga
Atlanta
Mississippi 1862
Kentucky 1862
Tennessee 1863
Georgia 1864

Indian Wars
Wyoming 1867
Dakota 1867
Montana 1881
Montana 1882

War With Spain
Manila

Philippine Insurrection
Iloilo
Panay 1899
Panay 1900

World War I
Montdidier-Noyon

Aisne-Marne
St. Mihiel
Meuse-Argonne
Lorraine 1917
Lorraine 1918
Picardy 1918

World War II
Algeria-French Morocco
(with arrowhead)
Tunisia
Sicily (with arrowhead)
Normandy (with arrowhead)
Northern France
Rhineland
Ardennes-Alsace
Central Europe

Vietnam
Defense
Counteroffensive
Counteroffensive, Phase II
Counteroffensive, Phase III
Tet Counteroffensive
(other campaigns to be
determined)

Decorations

Presidential Unit Citation (Army), Streamer embroidered NORMANDY (18th Infantry cited; WD GO 14, 1945)

Presidential Unit Citation (Army), Streamer embroidered AACHEN, GERMANY (1st and 3d Battalions, 18th Infantry cited; WD GO's 42 and 30, 1945)

Presidential Unit Citation (Army), Streamer embroidered BEJA, TUNISIA (2d Battalion, 18th Infantry cited; WD GO 4, 1945)

French Croix de Guerre with Palm, World War I, Streamer embroidered AISNE-MARNE (18th Infantry cited; WD GO 11, 1924)

French Croix de Guerre with Palm, World War I, Streamer embroidered MEUSE-ARGONNE (18th Infantry cited; WD GO 11, 1924)

French Croix de Guerre with Palm, World War II, Streamer embroidered KASSERINE (18th Infantry cited; DA GO 43, 1950)

French Croix de Guerre with Palm, World War II, Streamer embroidered NORMANDY (18th Infantry cited; DA GO 43, 1950)

French Medaille Militaire, Streamer embroidered FRANCE (18th Infantry cited; DA GO 43, 1950)

French Medaille Militaire, Fourragere (18th Infantry cited; DA GO

43, 1950)

Belgian Fourragere 1940 (18th Infantry cited; DA GO 43, 1950)

Cited in the Order of the Day of the Belgian Army for action at MONS (18th Infantry cited; DA GO 43, 1950)

Cited in the Order of the Day of the Belgian Army for action at EUPEN-MALMEDY (18th Infantry cited; DA GO 43, 1950)

1st BATTALION, 18th INFANTRY

RA
(1st Infantry Division)

LINEAGE

Organized 17 September 1861 in the Regular Army at Camp Thomas, Ohio, as Company B, 2d Battalion, 18th Infantry. Redesignated 20 September 1861 as Company H, 1st Battalion, 18th Infantry. Redesignated 19 October 1861 as Company A, 1st Battalion, 18th Infantry. Reorganized and redesignated 31 December 1866 as Company A, 18th Infantry. Consolidated 28 April 1869 with Company A, 25th Infantry (see ANNEX) and consolidated unit designated as Company A, 18th Infantry. (18th Infantry assigned 8 June 1917 to the 1st Expeditionary Division [later redesignated as the 1st Infantry Division].)

Reorganized and redesignated 15 February 1957 as Headquarters and Headquarters Company, 1st Battle Group, 18th Infantry and remained assigned to the 1st Infantry Division (organic elements concurrently constituted and activated). Relieved 14 April 1959 from assignment to the 1st Infantry Division and assigned to the 8th Infantry Division. Relieved 1 April 1963 from assignment to the 8th Infantry Division and assigned to the 1st Infantry Division. Reorganized and redesignated 2 January 1964 as the 1st Battalion, 18th Infantry.

ANNEX

Organized 12 May 1862 in the Regular Army at Camp Thomas, Ohio, as Company A, 2d Battalion, 16th Infantry. Reorganized and redesignated 21 September 1866 as Company A, 25th Infantry. Consolidated 28 April 1869 with Company A, 18th Infantry and consolidated unit designated as Company A, 18th Infantry.

CAMPAIGN PARTICIPATION CREDIT

Civil War
  *Murfreesborough
  *Chickamauga
  *Chattanooga
  *Atlanta
  *Mississippi 1862
  *Kentucky 1862
  *Tennessee 1863
  *Georgia 1864

Indian Wars
  Wyoming 1867
  Dakota 1867
  *Montana 1881
  *Montana 1882

War With Spain
  *Manila

Philippine Insurrection
  *Iloilo
  *Panay 1899
  Panay 1900

World War I
  *Montdidier-Noyon
  *Aisne-Marne

*St. Mihiel
*Meuse-Argonne
*Lorraine 1917
*Lorraine 1918
*Picardy 1918

World War II
  *Algeria-French Morocco
    (with arrowhead)
  *Tunisia
  *Sicily (with arrowhead)
  *Normandy (with arrowhead)
  *Northern France
  *Rhineland
  *Ardennes-Alsace
  *Central Europe

Vietnam
  *Defense
  *Counteroffensive
  *Counteroffensive, Phase II
  *Counteroffensive, Phase III
  *Tet Counteroffensive
    (other campaigns to be
    determined)

DECORATIONS

*Presidential Unit Citation (Army), Streamer embroidered NOR-MANDY (18th Infantry cited; WD GO 14, 1945)

*Presidential Unit Citation (Army), Streamer embroidered AACHEN, GERMANY (1st Battalion, 18th Infantry cited; WD GO 42, 1945)

Presidential Unit Citation (Army), Streamer embroidered BEJA, TUNISIA

*French Croix de Guerre with Palm, World War I, Streamer embroidered AISNE-MARNE (18th Infantry cited; WD GO 11, 1924)

*French Croix de Guerre with Palm, World War I, Streamer embroidered MEUSE-ARGONNE (18th Infantry cited; WD GO 11, 1924)

*French Croix de Guerre with Palm, World War II, Streamer embroidered KASSERINE (18th Infantry cited; DA GO 43, 1950)

*French Croix de Guerre with Palm, World War II, Streamer embroidered NORMANDY (18th Infantry cited; DA GO 43, 1950)

*French Medaille Militaire, Streamer embroidered FRANCE (18th Infantry cited; DA GO 43, 1950)

*French Medaille Militaire, Fourragere (18th Infantry cited; DA GO

43, 1950)

*Belgian Fourragere 1940 (18th Infantry cited; DA GO 43, 1950)

*Cited in the Order of the Day of the Belgian Army for action at MONS (18th Infantry cited; DA GO 43, 1950)

*Cited in the Order of the Day of the Belgian Army for action at EUPEN-MALMEDY (18th Infantry cited; DA GO 43, 1950)

*Vietnamese Cross of Gallantry with Palm, Streamer embroidered VIETNAM 1965–1968 (1st Battalion, 18th Infantry cited; DA GO 21, 1969)

*Vietnamese Cross of Gallantry with Palm, Streamer embroidered VIETNAM 1969–1970 (1st Battalion, 18th Infantry cited; DA GO 2, 1971)

*Vietnamese Civil Action Honor Medal, First Class, Streamer embroidered VIETNAM 1965–1970 (1st Battalion, 18th Infantry cited; DA GO 53, 1970)

2d BATTALION, 18th INFANTRY

RA
(inactive)

LINEAGE

Organized 9 September 1861 in the Regular Army at Camp Thomas, Ohio, as Company B, 1st Battalion, 18th Infantry. Reorganized and redesignated 31 December 1866 as Company B, 18th Infantry. Consolidated 28 April 1869 with Company B, 25th Infantry (see ANNEX) and consolidated unit designated as Company B, 18th Infantry. (18th Infantry assigned 8 June 1917 to the 1st Expeditionary Division [later redesignated as the 1st Infantry Division].)

Inactivated 15 February 1957 at Fort Riley, Kansas, and relieved from assignment to the 1st Infantry Division; concurrently, redesignated as Headquarters and Headquarters Company, 2d Battle Group, 18th Infantry. Activated 1 October 1963 at Fort Riley, Kansas, and assigned to the 1st Infantry Division (organic elements concurrently constituted and activated). Reorganized and redesignated 2 March 1964 as the 2d Battalion, 18th Infantry. Inactivated 15 April 1970 at Fort Riley, Kansas.

ANNEX

Organized 12 May 1862 in the Regular Army at Camp Thomas, Ohio, as Company B, 2d Battalion, 16th Infantry. Reorganized and redesignated 21 September 1866 as Company B, 25th Infantry. Consolidated 28 April 1869 with Company B, 18th Infantry and consolidated unit designated as Company B, 18th Infantry.

402

CAMPAIGN PARTICIPATION CREDIT

Civil War
  *Murfreesborough
  *Chickamauga
  *Chattanooga
  *Atlanta
  *Mississippi 1862
  *Kentucky 1862
  *Tennessee 1863
  *Georgia 1864

Indian Wars
  Wyoming 1867
  *Dakota 1867
  *Montana 1881
  *Montana 1882

War With Spain
  *Manila

Philippine Insurrection
  *Iloilo
  *Panay 1899
  Panay 1900

World War I
  *Montdidier-Noyon
  *Aisne-Marne

  *St. Mihiel
  *Meuse-Argonne
  *Lorraine 1917
  *Lorraine 1918
  *Picardy 1918

World War II
  *Algeria-French Morocco
    (with arrowhead)
  *Tunisia
  *Sicily (with arrowhead)
  *Normandy (with arrowhead)
  *Northern France
  *Rhineland
  *Ardennes-Alsace
  *Central Europe

Vietnam
  *Defense
  *Counteroffensive
  *Counteroffensive, Phase II
  *Counteroffensive, Phase III
  *Tet Counteroffensive
    (other campaigns to be
    determined)

DECORATIONS

*Presidential Unit Citation (Army), Streamer embroidered NORMANDY (18th Infantry cited; WD GO 14, 1945)

*Presidential Unit Citation (Army), Streamer embroidered AACHEN, GERMANY (1st Battalion, 18th Infantry cited; WD GO 42, 1945)

Presidential Unit Citation (Army), Streamer embroidered BEJA, TUNISIA

*French Croix de Guerre with Palm, World War I, Streamer embroidered AISNE-MARNE (18th Infantry cited; WD GO 11, 1924)

*French Croix de Guerre with Palm, World War I, Streamer embroidered MEUSE-ARGONNE (18th Infantry cited; WD GO 11, 1924)

*French Croix de Guerre with Palm, World War II, Streamer embroidered KASSERINE (18th Infantry cited; DA GO 43, 1950)

*French Croix de Guerre with Palm, World War II, Streamer embroidered NORMANDY (18th Infantry cited; DA GO 43, 1950)

*French Medaille Militaire, Streamer embroidered FRANCE (18th Infantry cited; DA GO 43, 1950)

*French Medaille Militaire, Fourragere (18th Infantry cited; DA GO

43, 1950)

*Belgian Fourragere 1940 (18th Infantry cited; DA GO 43, 1950)

*Cited in the Order of the Day of the Belgian Army for action at MONS (18th Infantry cited; DA GO 43, 1950)

*Cited in the Order of the Day of the Belgian Army for action at EUPEN-MALMEDY (18th Infantry cited; DA GO 43, 1950)

*Vietnamese Cross of Gallantry with Palm, Streamer embroidered VIETNAM 1965–1968 (2d Battalion, 18th Infantry cited; DA GO 21, 1969)

*Vietnamese Civil Action Honor Medal, First Class, Streamer embroidered VIETNAM 1965–1970 (2d Battalion, 18th Infantry cited; DA GO 53, 1970)

3d BATTALION, 18th INFANTRY

AR
(187th Infantry Brigade)

LINEAGE

Organized 15 August 1861 in the Regular Army at Camp Thomas, Ohio, as Company B, 1st Battalion, 18th Infantry. Redesignated 9 September 1861 as Company C, 1st Battalion, 18th Infantry. Reorganized and redesignated 31 December 1866 as Company C, 18th Infantry. Consolidated 28 April 1869 with Company C, 25th Infantry (see ANNEX 1) and consolidated unit designated as Company C, 18th Infantry. (18th Infantry assigned 8 June 1917 to the 1st Expeditionary Division [later redesignated as the 1st Infantry Division].)

Inactivated 15 February 1957 at Fort Riley, Kansas, and relieved from assignment to the 1st Infantry Division; concurrently, redesignated as Headquarters and Headquarters Company, 3d Battle Group, 18th Infantry. Withdrawn 6 April 1959 from the Regular Army, allotted to the Army Reserve, and assigned to the 94th Infantry Division (organic elements concurrently constituted). Battle Group activated 1 May 1959 with Headquarters at Lawrence, Massachusetts (concurrently, Headquarters and Headquarters Company consolidated with Headquarters and Headquarters Company, 3d Battalion, 301st Infantry [see ANNEX 2] and consolidated unit designated as Headquarters and Headquarters Company, 3d Battle Group, 18th Infantry).

Reorganized and redesignated 7 January 1963 as the 3d Battalion, 18th Infantry, relieved from assignment to the 94th Infantry Division, and assigned to the 187th Infantry Brigade (location of Headquarters concurrently changed from Lawrence, Massachusetts, to Lowell, Massachusetts).

ANNEX 1

Organized 12 May 1862 in the Regular Army at Camp Thomas, Ohio, as Company C, 2d Battalion, 16th Infantry. Reorganized and redesignated 21 September 1866 as Company C, 25th Infantry. Consolidated 28 April 1869 with Company C, 18th Infantry and consolidated unit designated as Company C, 18th Infantry.

ANNEX 2

Constituted 5 August 1917 in the National Army as Headquarters and

Headquarters Company, 3d Battalion, 301st Infantry, an element of the 76th Division. Organized in August 1917 at Camp Devens, Massachusetts. Demobilized in January 1919 at Camp Devens, Massachusetts. Reconstituted 24 June 1921 in the Organized Reserves as an element of the 94th Division (later redesignated as the 94th Infantry Division). Organized in November 1921. Ordered into active military service 15 September 1942 and reorganized at Fort Custer, Michigan. Inactivated 29 January 1946 at Camp Kilmer, New Jersey.

Activated 13 February 1947 in the Organized Reserves at Lawrence, Massachusetts. (Organized Reserves redesignated 25 March 1948 as the Organized Reserve Corps; redesignated 9 July 1952 as the Army Reserve.) Consolidated 1 May 1959 with Headquarters and Headquarters Company, 3d Battle Group, 18th Infantry and consolidated unit designated as Headquarters and Headquarters Company, 3d Battle Group, 18th Infantry.

HOME AREA: First United States Army

CAMPAIGN PARTICIPATION CREDIT

Civil War
  *Murfreesborough
  *Chickamauga
  *Chattanooga
  *Atlanta
  *Mississippi 1862
  *Kentucky 1862
  *Tennessee 1863
  *Georgia 1864

Indian Wars
  *Wyoming 1867
  *Dakota 1867
  *Montana 1881
  Montana 1882

War With Spain
  *Manila

Philippine Insurrection
  Iloilo
  *Panay 1899
  Panay 1900

World War I
  *Montdidier-Noyon
  *Aisne-Marne
  *St. Mihiel
  *Meuse-Argonne
  *Lorraine 1917
  *Lorraine 1918
  *Picardy 1918

World War II
  *Algeria-French Morocco
    (with arrowhead)
  *Tunisia
  *Sicily (with arrowhead)
  *Normandy (with arrowhead)
  *Northern France
  *Rhineland
  *Ardennes-Alsace
  *Central Europe

DECORATIONS

*Presidential Unit Citation (Army), Streamer embroidered NOR-MANDY (18th Infantry cited; WD GO 14, 1945)
    *Presidential Unit Citation (Army), Streamer embroidered AACHEN,

GERMANY (1st Battalion, 18th Infantry cited; WD GO 42, 1945)

Presidential Unit Citation (Army), Streamer embroidered BEJA, TUNISIA

*French Croix de Guerre with Palm, World War I, Streamer embroidered AISNE-MARNE (18th Infantry cited; WD GO 11, 1924)

*French Croix de Guerre with Palm, World War I, Streamer embroidered MEUSE-ARGONNE (18th Infantry cited; WD GO 11, 1924)

*French Croix de Guerre with Palm, World War II, Streamer embroidered KASSERINE (18th Infantry cited; DA GO 43, 1950)

*French Croix de Guerre with Palm, World War II, Streamer embroidered NORMANDY (18th Infantry cited; DA GO 43, 1950)

*French Medaille Militaire, Streamer embroidered FRANCE (18th Infantry cited; DA GO 43, 1950)

*French Medaille Militaire, Fourragere (18th Infantry cited; DA GO 43, 1950)

*Belgian Fourragere 1940 (18th Infantry cited; DA GO 43, 1950)

*Cited in the Order of the Day of the Belgian Army for action at MONS (18th Infantry cited; DA GO 43, 1950)

*Cited in the Order of the Day of the Belgian Army for action at EUPEN-MALMEDY (18th Infantry cited; DA GO 43, 1950)

4th BATTALION, 18th INFANTRY

RA
(United States Army Berlin Brigade)

LINEAGE

Organized 19 September 1861 in the Regular Army at Camp Thomas, Ohio, as Company D, 1st Battalion, 18th Infantry. Reorganized and redesignated 31 December 1866 as Company D, 18th Infantry. Consolidated in April 1869 with Company D, 25th Infantry (see ANNEX) and consolidated unit designated as Company D, 18th Infantry. (18th Infantry assigned 8 June 1917 to the 1st Expeditionary Division [later redesignated as the 1st Infantry Division].)

Inactivated 15 February 1957 at Fort Riley, Kansas, and relieved from assignment to the 1st Infantry Division; concurrently, redesignated as Headquarters and Headquarters Company, 4th Battle Group, 18th Infantry. Redesignated 23 August 1963 as Headquarters and Headquarters Company, 4th Battalion, 18th Infantry (organic elements concurrently constituted). Battalion activated 1 September 1963 in Germany and assigned to the United States Army Berlin Brigade.

ANNEX

Organized 12 May 1862 in the Regular Army at Camp Thomas, Ohio, as Company D, 2d Battalion, 16th Infantry. Reorganized and redesignated 21 September 1866 as Company D, 25th Infantry. Consolidated in April 1869 with Company D, 18th Infantry and consolidated unit designated as Company D, 18th Infantry.

CAMPAIGN PARTICIPATION CREDIT

Civil War
 *Murfreesborough
 *Chickamauga
 *Chattanooga
 *Atlanta
 *Mississippi 1862
 *Kentucky 1862
 *Tennessee 1863
 *Georgia 1864

Indian Wars
 Wyoming 1867
 Dakota 1867
 *Montana 1881
 *Montana 1882

War With Spain
 *Manila

Philippine Insurrection
 *Iloilo
 *Panay 1899
 Panay 1900

World War I
 *Montdidier-Noyon
 *Aisne-Marne
 *St. Mihiel
 *Meuse-Argonne
 *Lorraine 1917
 *Lorraine 1918
 *Picardy 1918

World War II
 *Algeria-French Morocco
  (with arrowhead)
 *Tunisia
 *Sicily (with arrowhead)
 *Normandy (with arrowhead)
 *Northern France
 *Rhineland
 *Ardennes-Alsace
 *Central Europe

DECORATIONS

*Presidential Unit Citation (Army), Streamer embroidered NOR-MANDY (18th Infantry cited; WD GO 14, 1945)

*Presidential Unit Citation (Army), Streamer embroidered AACHEN, GERMANY (1st Battalion, 18th Infantry cited; WD GO 42, 1945)

Presidential Unit Citation (Army), Streamer embroidered BEJA, TUNISIA

*French Croix de Guerre with Palm, World War I, Streamer embroidered AISNE-MARNE (18th Infantry cited; WD GO 11, 1924)

*French Croix de Guerre with Palm, World War I, Streamer embroidered MEUSE-ARGONNE (18th Infantry cited; WD GO 11, 1924)

*French Croix de Guerre with Palm, World War II, Streamer embroidered KASSERINE (18th Infantry cited; DA GO 43, 1950)

*French Croix de Guerre with Palm, World War II, Streamer embroidered NORMANDY (18th Infantry cited; DA GO 43, 1950)

*French Medaille Militaire, Streamer embroidered FRANCE (18th Infantry cited; DA GO 43, 1950)

*French Medaille Militaire, Fourragere (18th Infantry cited; DA GO 43, 1950)

*Belgian Fourragere 1940 (18th Infantry cited; DA GO 43, 1950)

*Cited in the Order of the Day of the Belgian Army for action at

MONS (18th Infantry cited; DA GO 43, 1950)

*Cited in the Order of the Day of the Belgian Army for action at EUPEN-MALMEDY (18th Infantry cited; DA GO 43, 1950)

18TH INFANTRY, BIBLIOGRAPHY

Blumenson, Martin. *Breakout and Pursuit.* United States Army in World War II. Washington: Government Printing Office, 1961.

Cabaniss, Charles H. "The Eighteenth Regiment of Infantry," *The Army of the United States,* edited by Theophilus F. Rodenbough and William L. Haskin. New York: Maynard, Merrill and Company, 1896, pp. 643–656. (Originally published in the *Journal of the Military Service Institution of the United States,* XII [1891], 1111–1124.)

Carrington, Frances (Courtney). *My Army Life and the Fort Phil Kearney Massacre, with an Account of the Celebration of "Wyoming Opened."* Philadelphia and London, 1910.

Carrington, Margaret Irvin (Sullivant). *Absaraka (Ab-sa-ra-ka): Home of the Crows.* Philadelphia: J. B. Lippincott, 1868. (Later edition edited by Milo Milton Quaife. Chicago: Lakeside Press, 1950.)

Chastine, Ben H. *History of the 18th U.S. Infantry, First Division, 1812–1919.* New York: Hymans Publishing Company, 1920. (Erroneously connects this regiment with an earlier one of the same designation.)

Cleary, James W. and Walther K. German. *History and Pictorial Record of the 18th Infantry Regiment on Occupation Duty in Germany.* Frankfurt am Main: Otto Lembeck, 1947.

Cole, Hugh M. *The Ardennes: Battle of the Bulge.* United States Army in World War II. Washington: Government Printing Office, 1964.

Cushing, A. B. "History of the 18th Infantry," *The Veteran* (May–December 1937).

The 18th Infantry, Vanguards. Aschaffenburg: Main-Echo Kirsch Druck, 1953.

Evarts, Jeremiah Maxwell. *Cantigny: A Corner of the War.* New York: Scribner Press, 1938.

Garland, Albert N. and Howard McGaw Smyth. *Sicily and the Surrender of Italy.* United States Army in World War II. Washington: Government Printing Office, 1965.

Harrison, Gordon A. *Cross-Channel Attack.* United States Army in World War II. Washington: Government Printing Office, 1951.

Heidenheimer, Arnold *et al. Vanguard to Victory, History of the 18th Infantry.* Aschaffenburg: Main-Echo Verlag, 1954.

Historical Section, War Department. *Omaha Beachhead.* American Forces in Action Series. Washington: Government Printing Office, 1945.

————. *To Bizerte with the II Corps.* American Forces in Action Series. Washington: Government Printing Office, 1943.

Howe, George F. *Northwest Africa: Seizing the Initiative in the West.*

United States Army in World War II. Washington: Government Printing Office, 1957.

Johnson, Franklyn A. *One More Hill*. New York: Funk and Wagnalls Company, 1949.

MacDonald, Charles B. *The Battle of Huertgen Forest*. Philadelphia and New York: J. B. Lippincott, 1963.

————. *The Siegfried Line Campaign*. United States Army in World War II. Washington: Government Printing Office, 1963.

Marshall, S. L. A. *Ambush*. New York: Cowles Book Company, 1969.

McFarland, Munroe. *Historical Sketch of the 18th Infantry During its Tour Abroad, 1898–1901*. n.p., 1902.

Murphy, William. "The Forgotten Battalion, Being a Short Chronicle of the Hardships and Conditions Endured by the Indian War Veterans in the Phil Kearney Massacre of December 21st, 1866, and the Wagon Box Fight of August 2, 1867. . .," *Annals of Wyoming*, VII (1930–31), 383–401; 441–442.

Organization Day, Eighteenth Infantry Regiment, First Division, Grafenwohr, Germany, 4 May 1949. Frankfurt am Main-Eschersheim: Otto Mingram, 1949.

Organization Day, Eighteenth Regiment of United States Infantry, Fort Devens, Massachusetts, May 3, 1941. Fitchburg, Massachusetts: Blanchard and Brown Printing Company, 1941.

Register of Commissioned Officers, Eighteenth Infantry. Colonel Thomas H. Ruger. From May 4th, 1861, to January 1st, 1883, with Roster of Regiment. Fort Assinaboine, Montana: Regimental Press, 1883.

Roster of Non-commissioned Officers, Eighteenth U.S. Infantry, Commanded by Lieutenant Colonel H. M. Black, Headquarters, McPherson Barracks, Atlanta, Georgia, June 1, 1878. McPherson Barracks, Georgia: Regimental Press, 1878.

19th INFANTRY
(The Rock of Chickamauga)

HERALDIC ITEMS

COAT OF ARMS

Shield: Azure, an infantry bugle of 1861 or enclosing the Arabic numerals "19" argent, in chief three mullets of the last.

Crest: On a wreath of the colors a rock charged with the shoulder strap of a second lieutenant of infantry of 1863 proper.

Motto: The Rock of Chickamauga.

Symbolism: The 19th Infantry was organized in 1861 and the principal charge on the shield is a reproduction of the regimental insignia of that period. The three stars commemorate service in the Civil War, the War with Spain, and the Philippine Insurrection.

The crest symbolizes the great achievement of the regiment at the battle of Chickamauga on 19–20 September 1863, when it formed part of General Thomas' command and earned its nickname and motto, "The Rock of Chickamauga." At the end of the second day, there were only four officers and fifty-one enlisted men on duty and the regiment was commanded by a second lieutenant. The strap of a second lieutenant is shown on the rock.

DISTINCTIVE INSIGNIA

The distinctive insignia is the shield and motto of the coat of arms.

LINEAGE AND HONORS

LINEAGE

Constituted 3 May 1861 in the Regular Army as the 1st Battalion, 19th Infantry. Organized 9 July 1861 at Indianapolis, Indiana. Reorganized and redesignated 1 October 1866 as the 19th Infantry. Con-

425-618 O - 72 - 28

solidated 15 March 1869 with the 28th Infantry (see ANNEX) and consolidated unit designated as the 19th Infantry.

Assigned 29 July 1918 to the 18th Division. Relieved 14 February 1919 from assignment to the 18th Division. Assigned 17 October 1922 to the Hawaiian Division. Relieved 26 August 1941 from assignment to the Hawaiian Division and assigned to the 24th Division (later redesignated as the 24th Infantry Division).

Relieved 5 June 1958 from assignment to the 24th Infantry Division and reorganized as a parent regiment under the Combat Arms Regimental System.

ANNEX

Constituted 3 May 1861 in the Regular Army as the 2d Battalion, 19th Infantry. Organized 31 March 1863 at Fort Wayne, Michigan. Reorganized and redesignated 1 October 1866 as the 28th Infantry. Consolidated 15 March 1869 with the 19th Infantry and consolidated unit designated as the 19th Infantry.

CAMPAIGN PARTICIPATION CREDIT

Civil War
Shiloh
Murfreesborough
Chickamauga
Chattanooga
Atlanta
Mississippi 1862
Kentucky 1862
Tennessee 1863
Georgia 1864

Indian Wars
Utes

War With Spain
Puerto Rico

Philippine Insurrection
Panay 1899
Cebu 1899
Panay 1900

Cebu 1900
Cebu 1901
Bohol 1901

World War II
Central Pacific
New Guinea (with arrowhead)
Leyte (with arrowhead)
Luzon (with arrowhead)
Southern Philippines
(with arrowhead)

Korean War
UN defensive
UN offensive
CCF intervention
First UN counteroffensive
CCF spring offensive
UN summer-fall offensive
Second Korean winter
Korea, summer 1953

DECORATIONS

Presidential Unit Citation (Army), Streamer embroidered DAVAO (19th Infantry cited; DA GO 41, 1949)

Presidential Unit Citation (Army), Streamer embroidered LEYTE (2d Battalion, 19th Infantry cited; WD GO 21, 1945)

Presidential Unit Citation (Army), Streamer embroidered DEFENSE OF KOREA (24th Infantry Division cited; DA GO 45, 1950)

Philippine Presidential Unit Citation, Streamer embroidered 17 OCTOBER 1944 TO 4 JULY 1945 (19th Infantry cited; DA GO 47, 1950)

Republic of Korea Presidential Unit Citation, Streamer embroidered PYONGTAEK (19th Infantry cited; DA GO 35, 1951)

Republic of Korea Presidential Unit Citation, Streamer embroidered KOREA (24th Infantry Division cited; DA GO 24, 1954)

1st BATTALION, 19th INFANTRY

(The Rock of Chickamauga)

RA
(inactive)

LINEAGE

Constituted 3 May 1861 in the Regular Army as Company A, 1st Battalion, 19th Infantry. Organized 24 August 1861 at Indianapolis, Indiana. Reorganized and redesignated 1 October 1866 as Company A, 19th Infantry.

Consolidated 17 April 1869 with Company A, 28th Infantry (see ANNEX) and consolidated unit designated as Company A, 19th Infantry. (19th Infantry assigned 29 July 1918 to the 18th Division; relieved 14 February 1919 from assignment to the 18th Division; assigned 17 October 1922 to the Hawaiian Division; relieved 26 August 1941 from assignment to the Hawaiian Division and assigned to the 24th Division [later redesignated as the 24th Infantry Division].)

Redesignated 5 June 1958 as Headquarters and Headquarters Company, 1st Battle Group, 19th Infantry and remained assigned to the 24th Infantry Division (organic elements concurrently constituted and activated 1 July 1958 in Germany). Reorganized and redesignated 1 February 1963 as the 1st Battalion, 19th Infantry. Inactivated 15 April 1970 at Fort Riley, Kansas.

ANNEX

Constituted 3 May 1861 in the Regular Army as Company A, 2d Battalion, 19th Infantry. Organized 31 March 1863 at Fort Wayne, Michigan. Reorganized and redesignated 1 October 1866 as Company A, 28th Infantry. Consolidated 17 April 1869 with Company A, 19th Infantry and consolidated unit designated as Company A, 19th Infantry.

416

Campaign Participation Credit

Civil War
  *Shiloh
  *Murfreesborough
  *Chickamauga
  *Chattanooga
  *Atlanta
  *Mississippi 1862
  *Kentucky 1862
  *Tennessee 1863
  *Georgia 1864

Indian Wars
  Utes

War With Spain
  *Puerto Rico

Philippine Insurrection
  *Jolo
  *Panay 1899
  Cebu 1899
  *Panay 1900

*Cebu 1900
Cebu 1901
Bohol 1901

World War II
  *Central Pacific
  *New Guinea (with arrowhead)
  *Leyte (with arrowhead)
  *Luzon (with arrowhead)
  *Southern Philippines
    (with arrowhead)

Korean War
  *UN defensive
  *UN offensive
  *CCF intervention
  *First UN counteroffensive
  *CCF spring offensive
  *UN summer-fall offensive
  *Second Korean winter
  *Korea, summer 1953

Decorations

*Presidential Unit Citation (Army), Streamer embroidered DAVAO (19th Infantry cited; DA GO 41, 1949)

Presidential Unit Citation (Army), Streamer embroidered LEYTE

*Presidential Unit Citation (Army), Streamer embroidered DEFENSE OF KOREA (24th Infantry Division cited; DA GO 45, 1950)

*Philippine Presidential Unit Citation, Streamer embroidered 17 OCTOBER 1944 TO 4 JULY 1945 (19th Infantry cited; DA GO 47, 1950)

*Republic of Korea Presidential Unit Citation, Streamer embroidered PYONGTAEK (19th Infantry cited; DA GO 35, 1951)

*Republic of Korea Presidential Unit Citation, Streamer embroidered KOREA (24th Infantry Division cited; DA GO 24, 1954)

2d BATTALION, 19th INFANTRY

(The Rock of Chickamauga)

RA
(inactive)

LINEAGE

Constituted 3 May 1861 in the Regular Army as Company B, 1st Battalion, 19th Infantry. Organized 30 September 1861 at Indianapolis, Indiana. Reorganized and redesignated 1 October 1866 as Company B, 19th Infantry.

Consolidated 15 April 1869 with Company B, 28th Infantry (see ANNEX) and consolidated unit designated as Company B, 19th Infantry. (19th Infantry assigned 29 July 1918 to the 18th Division; relieved 14 February 1919 from assignment to the 18th Division; assigned 17 October 1922 to the Hawaiian Division; relieved 26 August 1941 from assignment to the Hawaiian Division and assigned to the 24th Division [later redesignated as the 24th Infantry Division].)

Reorganized and redesignated 1 February 1957 as Headquarters and Headquarters Company, 2d Battle Group, 19th Infantry, relieved from assignment to the 24th Infantry Division, and assigned to the 25th Infantry Division (organic elements concurrently constituted and activated). Inactivated 25 March 1958 in Hawaii. Activated 1 July 1961 in Hawaii. Relieved 19 February 1962 from assignment to the 25th Infantry Division and assigned to the 24th Infantry Division. Reorganized and redesignated 1 February 1963 as the 2d Battalion, 19th Infantry. Inactivated 1 May 1966 in Germany.

ANNEX

Constituted 3 May 1861 in the Regular Army as Company B, 2d Battalion, 19th Infantry. Organized 2 February 1865 at Fort Wayne, Michigan. Reorganized and redesignated 1 October 1866 as Company B, 28th Infantry. Consolidated 15 April 1869 with Company B, 19th Infantry and consolidated unit designated as Company B, 19th Infantry.

418

CAMPAIGN PARTICIPATION CREDIT

Civil War
  *Shiloh
  *Murfreesborough
  *Chickamauga
  *Chattanooga
  *Atlanta
  *Mississippi 1862
  *Kentucky 1862
  *Tennessee 1863
  *Georgia 1864

Indian Wars
  Utes

War With Spain
  *Puerto Rico

Philippine Insurrection
  *Jolo
  *Panay 1899
  Cebu 1899
  Panay 1900

*Cebu 1900
*Cebu 1901
*Bohol 1901

World War II
  *Central Pacific
  *New Guinea (with arrowhead)
  *Leyte (with arrowhead)
  *Luzon (with arrowhead)
  *Southern Philippines
    (with arrowhead)

Korean War
  *UN defensive
  *UN offensive
  *CCF Intervention
  *First UN counteroffensive
  *CCF spring offensive
  *UN summer-fall offensive
  *Second Korean winter
  *Korea, summer 1953

DECORATIONS

*Presidential Unit Citation (Army), Streamer embroidered DAVAO (19th Infantry cited; DA GO 41, 1949)

Presidential Unit Citation (Army), Streamer embroidered LEYTE

*Presidential Unit Citation (Army), Streamer embroidered DEFENSE OF KOREA (24th Infantry Division cited; DA GO 45, 1950)

*Philippine Presidential Unit Citation, Streamer embroidered 17 OCTOBER 1944 TO 4 JULY 1945 (19th Infantry cited; DA GO 47, 1950)

*Republic of Korea Presidential Unit Citation, Streamer embroidered PYONGTAEK (19th Infantry cited; DA GO 35, 1951)

*Republic of Korea Presidential Unit Citation, Streamer embroidered KOREA (24th Infantry Division cited; DA GO 24, 1954)

3d BATTALION, 19th INFANTRY

(The Rock of Chickamauga)

RA
(inactive)

LINEAGE

Constituted 3 May 1861 in the Regular Army as Company C, 1st Battalion, 19th Infantry. Organized 25 November 1861 at Indianapolis, Indiana. Reorganized and redesignated 1 October 1866 as Company C, 19th Infantry.

Consolidated 15 April 1869 with Company I, 28th Infantry (see ANNEX) and consolidated unit designated as Company C, 19th Infantry. (19th Infantry assigned 29 July 1918 to the 18th Division; relieved 14 February 1919 from assignment to the 18th Division; assigned 17 October 1922 to the Hawaiian Division; relieved 26 August 1941 from assignment to the Hawaiian Division and assigned to the 24th Division [later redesignated as the 24th Infantry Division].) Company C, 19th Infantry relieved 9 April 1958 from assignment to the 24th Infantry Division.

Reorganized and redesignated 1 February 1963 as Headquarters and Headquarters Company, 3d Battalion, 19th Infantry and assigned to the 24th Infantry Division (organic elements [constituted 21 January 1963] concurrently activated). Inactivated 15 April 1970 in Germany.

ANNEX

Constituted 3 May 1861 in the Regular Army as Company I, 2d Battalion, 19th Infantry. Organized in June 1866. Reorganized and redesignated 1 October 1866 as Company I, 28th Infantry. Consolidated 15 April 1869 with Company C, 19th Infantry and consolidated unit designated Company C, 19th Infantry.

420

CAMPAIGN PARTICIPATION CREDIT

Civil War
* *Shiloh
* *Murfreesborough
* *Chickamauga
* *Chattanooga
* *Atlanta
* *Mississippi 1862
* *Kentucky 1862
* *Tennessee 1863
* *Georgia 1864

Indian Wars
* *Utes

War With Spain
* *Puerto Rico

Philippine Insurrection
* *Panay 1899
* Cebu 1899
* *Panay 1900

* *Cebu 1900
* *Cebu 1901
* Bohol 1901

World War II
* *Central Pacific
* *New Guinea (with arrowhead)
* *Leyte (with arrowhead)
* *Luzon (with arrowhead)
* *Southern Philippines
  (with arrowhead)

Korean War
* *UN defensive
* *UN offensive
* *CCF intervention
* *First UN counteroffensive
* *CCF spring offensive
* *UN summer-fall offensive
* *Second Korean winter
* *Korea, summer 1953

DECORATIONS

*Presidential Unit Citation (Army), Streamer embroidered DAVAO (19th Infantry cited; DA GO 41, 1949)

Presidential Unit Citation (Army), Streamer embroidered LEYTE

*Presidential Unit Citation (Army), Streamer embroidered DEFENSE OF KOREA (24th Infantry Division cited; DA GO 45, 1950)

*Philippine Presidential Unit Citation, Streamer embroidered 17 OCTOBER 1944 TO 4 JULY 1945 (19th Infantry cited; DA GO 47, 1950)

*Republic of Korea Presidential Unit Citation, Streamer embroidered PYONGTAEK (19th Infantry cited; DA GO 35, 1951)

*Republic of Korea Presidential Unit Citation, Streamer embroidered KOREA (24th Infantry Division cited; DA GO 24, 1954)

4th BATTLE GROUP, 19th INFANTRY

(The Rock of Chickamauga)

AR
(inactive)

LINEAGE

Constituted 3 May 1861 in the Regular Army as Company D, 1st Battalion, 19th Infantry. Organized 25 December 1861 at Indianapolis, Indiana. Reorganized and redesignated 1 October 1866 as Company D, 19th Infantry.

Consolidated 29 April 1869 with Company H, 28th Infantry (see ANNEX) and consolidated unit designated as Company D, 19th Infantry. (19th Infantry assigned 29 July 1918 to the 18th Division; relieved 14 February 1919 from assignment to the 18th Division; assigned 17 October 1922 to the Hawaiian Division; relieved 26 August 1941 from assignment to the Hawaiian Division and assigned to the 24th Division [later redesignated as the 24th Infantry Division].) Inactivated 5 June 1958 and relieved from assignment to the 24th Infantry Division.

Redesignated 19 March 1959 as Headquarters and Headquarters Company, 4th Battle Group, 19th Infantry, withdrawn from the Regular Army, allotted to the Army Reserve, and assigned to the 83d Infantry Division (organic elements concurrently constituted). Battle Group activated 20 March 1959 with Headquarters at South Charleston, West Virginia. Inactivated 15 April 1963 at South Charleston, West Virginia, and relieved from assignment to the 83d Infantry Division.

ANNEX

Constituted 3 May 1861 in the Regular Army as Company H, 2d Battalion, 19th Infantry. Organized in June 1866. Reorganized and redesignated 1 October 1866 as Company H, 28th Infantry. Consolidated 29 April 1869 with Company D, 19th Infantry and consolidated unit designated as Company D, 19th Infantry.

422

Campaign Participation Credit

Civil War
- *Shiloh
- *Murfreesborough
- *Chickamauga
- *Chattanooga
- *Atlanta
- *Mississippi 1862
- *Kentucky 1862
- *Tennessee 1863
- *Georgia 1864

Indian Wars
- *Utes

War With Spain
- *Puerto Rico

Philippine Insurrection
- *Jolo
- *Panay 1899
- Cebu 1899
- Panay 1900
- *Cebu 1900
- Cebu 1901
- *Bohol 1901

World War II
- *Central Pacific
- *New Guinea (with arrowhead)
- *Leyte (with arrowhead)
- *Luzon (with arrowhead)
- *Southern Philippines (with arrowhead)

Korean War
- *UN defensive
- *UN offensive
- *CCF intervention
- *First UN counteroffensive
- *CCF spring offensive
- *UN summer-fall offensive
- *Second Korean winter
- *Korea, summer 1953

Decorations

*Presidential Unit Citation (Army), Streamer embroidered DAVAO (19th Infantry cited; DA GO 41, 1949)

Presidential Unit Citation (Army), Streamer embroidered LEYTE

*Presidential Unit Citation (Army), Streamer embroidered DEFENSE OF KOREA (24th Infantry Division cited; DA GO 45, 1950)

*Philippine Presidential Unit Citation, Streamer embroidered 17 OCTOBER 1944 TO 4 JULY 1945 (19th Infantry cited; DA GO 47, 1950)

*Republic of Korea Presidential Unit Citation, Streamer embroidered PYONGTAEK (19th Infantry cited; DA GO 35, 1951)

*Republic of Korea Presidential Unit Citation, Streamer embroidered KOREA (24th Infantry Division cited; DA GO 24, 1954)

COMPANY E, 19th INFANTRY

(The Rock of Chickamauga)

RA
(inactive)

LINEAGE

Constituted 3 May 1861 in the Regular Army as Company E, 1st Battalion, 19th Infantry. Organized 15 March 1862 at Indianapolis, Indiana. Reorganized and redesignated 1 October 1866 as Company E, 19th Infantry.

Consolidated in April 1869 with Company E, 28th Infantry (see ANNEX) and consolidated unit designated as Company E, 19th Infantry. (19th Infantry assigned 29 July 1918 to the 18th Division; relieved 14 February 1919 from assignment to the 18th Division; assigned 17 October 1922 to the Hawaiian Division; relieved 26 August 1941 from assignment to the Hawaiian Division and assigned to the 24th Division [later redesignated as the 24th Infantry Division].)

Inactivated 5 June 1958 and relieved from assignment to the 24th Infantry Division; concurrently, redesignated as Headquarters and Headquarters Company, 5th Battle Group, 19th Infantry. Redesignated 1 February 1963 as Company E, 19th Infantry and activated in Korea. Inactivated 1 December 1967 in Korea.

ANNEX

Constituted 3 May 1861 in the Regular Army as Company E, 2d Battalion, 19th Infantry. Organized in October 1865 at Fort Wayne, Michigan. Reorganized and redesignated 1 October 1866 as Company E, 28th Infantry. Consolidated in April 1869 with Company E, 19th Infantry and consolidated unit designated as Company E, 19th Infantry.

Campaign Participation Credit

Civil War
Shiloh
Murfreesborough
Chickamauga
Chattanooga
Atlanta
Mississippi 1862
Kentucky 1862
Tennessee 1863
Georgia 1864

Indian Wars
Utes

War With Spain
Puerto Rico

Philippine Insurrection
Panay 1899
Panay 1900
Cebu 1901

World War II-AP
Central Pacific
New Guinea (with arrowhead)
Leyte (with arrowhead)
Luzon (with arrowhead)
Southern Philippines
(with arrowhead)

Korean War
UN defensive
UN offensive
CCF intervention
First UN counteroffensive
CCF spring offensive
UN summer-fall offensive
Second Korean winter
Korea, summer 1953

Decorations

Presidential Unit Citation (Army), Streamer embroidered DAVAO (19th Infantry cited; DA GO 41, 1949)

Presidential Unit Citation (Army), Streamer embroidered LEYTE (2d Battalion, 19th Infantry cited; WD GO 21, 1945)

Presidential Unit Citation (Army), Streamer embroidered DEFENSE OF KOREA (24th Infantry Division cited; DA GO 45, 1950)

Philippine Presidential Unit Citation, Streamer embroidered 17 OCTOBER 1944 TO 4 JULY 1945 (19th Infantry cited; DA GO 47, 1950)

Republic of Korea Presidential Unit Citation, Streamer embroidered PYONGTAEK (19th Infantry cited; DA GO 35, 1951)

Republic of Korea Presidential Unit Citation, Streamer embroidered KOREA (24th Infantry Division cited; DA GO 24, 1954)

19TH INFANTRY, BIBLIOGRAPHY

A Brief History of the 19th Infantry Regiment (The Rock of Chickamauga). Military History Section, Headquarters, United States Army Forces, Far East, 1954.

Cannon, M. Hamlin. *Leyte: The Return to the Philippines*. United States Army in World War II. Washington: Government Printing Office, 1954.

Dowdall, H. G., ed. *63d Anniversary, 19th Infantry*. Honolulu: Honolulu Star Bulletin, 1924.

Falk, Stanley L. *Decision at Leyte*. New York: W. W. Norton and Company, Inc., 1966.

Hewitt, Christian C. "The Nineteenth Regiment of Infantry," *The Army of the United States,* edited by Theophilus F. Rodenbough and William L. Haskin. New York: Maynard, Merrill and Company, 1896, pp. 657–665. (Originally published in the *Journal of the Military Service Institution of the United States,* XIII [1892], 835–843.)

Hymans, H. I., compiler. *A History and Photographic Record of the 19th Infantry, U. S. A. 1918*. San Antonio: San Antonio Printing Company, 1919.

Ivins, Charles F., ed. *The Rock, Annual Publication of the Nineteenth United States Infantry, "The Rock of Chickamauga Regiment."* Schofield Barracks, Hawaii, 1939.

19th Infantry Regiment, 96th Anniversary. Tokyo: Tosho Printing Company, 1959.

Organization Yearbook of the Nineteenth United States Infantry Regiment, "The Rock of Chickamauga" 1861–1949. Beppu, Kyushu, Japan, 1949.

Register of Commissioned Officers of the 19th Regiment of U.S. Infantry, From May 4, 1861, to July 1, 1883. Fort Clark, Texas: Regimental Press, 1883.

Reports of General MacArthur. Washington: Government Printing Office, 1966.

The Rock of Chickamauga, Nineteenth Infantry Regiment 1861–1944. Reproduced by the 67th Engineer Topographic Company, 1944.

Smith, Robert Ross. *The Approach to the Philippines*. United States Army in World War II. Washington: Government Printing Office, 1953.

———. *Triumph in the Philippines*. United States Army in World War II. Washington: Government Printing Office, 1963.

20th INFANTRY
(Sykes' Regulars)

Heraldic Items

Coat of Arms

Shield: Per bend azure and gules, on a bend or between in chief a cross pattée argent and in base a triangle of the first fimbriated of the third charged with a sun in splendor of the same, a five-bastioned fort of the fourth fimbriated sable.

Crest: On a wreath or and azure four muskets two and two saltirewise conjoined forming the Roman notation "XX" or.

Motto: *Tant Que Je Puis* (To the Limit of Our Ability).

Symbolism: During the Civil War this unit served in the 2d Division of the V Corps, the badge of which was a white cross pattée. The regiment saw service in Cuba in the War with Spain as a portion of the V Corps at El Caney and San Juan. The badge of the V Corps was a five-bastioned fort. During the Philippine Insurrection it took part in the Pasig expedition of 1899, which is signified by the Katipunan device in the base.

The muskets in the crest form the Roman numeral "XX," the numerical designation of the regiment.

Distinctive Insignia

The distinctive insignia is the crest of the coat of arms.

Lineage and Honors

Lineage

Constituted 3 May 1861 in the Regular Army as the 2d Battalion, 11th Infantry. Organized 6 June 1862 at Fort Independence, Massachusetts. Reorganized and redesignated 6 December 1866 as the 20th Infantry.

Assigned 9 July 1918 to the 10th Division. Relieved 14 February 1919 from assignment to the 10th Division. Assigned 18 September 1920 to the 2d Division. Relieved 16 October 1939 from assignment to the 2d Division and assigned to the 6th Division (later redesignated as the 6th Infantry Division). Inactivated 10 January 1949 in Korea. Activated 4 October 1950 at Fort Ord, California. Relieved 3 April 1956 from assignment to the 6th Infantry Division.

Reorganized 15 November 1957 as a parent regiment under the Combat Arms Regimental System.

CAMPAIGN PARTICIPATION CREDIT

Civil War
Peninsula
Manassas
Antietam
Fredericksburg
Chancellorsville
Gettysburg
Wilderness
Spotsylvania
Cold Harbor
Petersburg
Virginia 1862
Virginia 1863

Indian Wars
Little Big Horn
Pine Ridge

War With Spain
Santiago

Philippine Insurrection
Manila
Luzon 1901

World War II
New Guinea
Luzon (with arrowhead)

Vietnam
Counteroffensive, Phase III
Tet Counteroffensive
(other campaigns to be
determined)

DECORATIONS

Presidential Unit Citation (Army), Streamer embroidered CABARUAN HILLS (2d Battalion, 20th Infantry cited; WD GO 31, 1946)

Presidential Unit Citation (Army), Streamer embroidered MAFFIN BAY (3d Battalion, 20th Infantry cited; WD GO 43, 1946)

Presidential Unit Citation (Army), Streamer embroidered MUNOZ (3d Battalion, 20th Infantry cited; WD GO 90, 1945)

Philippine Presidential Unit Citation, Streamer embroidered 17 OCTOBER 1944 TO 4 JULY 1945 (6th Infantry Division cited; DA GO 47, 1950)

1st BATTALION, 20th INFANTRY

(Sykes' Regulars)

RA
(23d Infantry Division)

LINEAGE

Constituted 3 May 1861 in the Regular Army as Company A, 2d Battalion, 11th Infantry. Organized 26 July 1862 at Fort Independence, Massachusetts. Reorganized and redesignated 6 December 1866 as Company A, 20th Infantry. (20th Infantry assigned 9 July 1918 to the 10th Division; relieved 14 February 1919 from assignment to the 10th Division; assigned 18 September 1920 to the 2d Division; relieved 16 October 1939 from assignment to the 2d Division and assigned to the 6th Division [later redesignated as the 6th Infantry Division].) Inactivated 10 January 1949 in Korea. Activated 4 October 1950 at Fort Ord, California. (20th Infantry relieved 3 April 1956 from assignment to the 6th Infantry Division.)

Reorganized and redesignated 15 November 1957 as Headquarters and Headquarters Company, 1st Battle Group, 20th Infantry (organic elements [constituted 8 November 1957] concurrently activated). Inactivated 8 August 1962 at Fort Kobbe, Canal Zone. Redesignated 23 May 1966 as the 1st Battalion, 20th Infantry. Activated 1 July 1966 in Hawaii and assigned to the 11th Infantry Brigade. Relieved 15 February 1969 from assignment to the 11th Infantry Brigade and assigned to the 23d Infantry Division.

429

CAMPAIGN PARTICIPATION CREDIT

Civil War
Peninsula
Manassas
Antietam
*Fredericksburg
Chancellorsville
Gettysburg
Wilderness
Spotsylvania
Cold Harbor
Petersburg
*Virginia 1862
Virginia 1863

Indian Wars
Little Big Horn
Pine Ridge

War With Spain
*Santiago

Philippine Insurrection
*Manila
Luzon 1901

World War II
*New Guinea
*Luzon (with arrowhead)

Vietnam
*Counteroffensive, Phase III
*Tet Counteroffensive
(other campaigns to be
determined)

DECORATIONS

Presidential Unit Citation (Army), Streamer embroidered CABARUAN HILLS

Presidential Unit Citation (Army), Streamer embroidered MAFFIN BAY

Presidential Unit Citation (Army), Streamer embroidered MUNOZ

*Philippine Presidential Unit Citation, Streamer embroidered 17 OCTOBER 1944 TO 4 JULY 1945 (6th Infantry Division cited; DA GO 47, 1950)

*Vietnamese Cross of Gallantry with Palm, Streamer embroidered VIETNAM 1968–1969 (1st Battalion, 20th Infantry cited; DA GO 2, 1971)

2d BATTALION, 20th INFANTRY

(Sykes' Regulars)

RA
(inactive)

LINEAGE

Constituted 3 May 1861 in the Regular Army as Company B, 2d Battalion, 11th Infantry. Organized 8 September 1862 at Fort Independence, Massachusetts. Reorganized and redesignated 6 December 1866 as Company B, 20th Infantry. (20th Infantry assigned 9 July 1918 to the 10th Division; relieved 14 February 1919 from assignment to the 10th Division; assigned 18 September 1920 to the 2d Division; relieved 16 October 1939 from assignment to the 2d Division and assigned to the 6th Division [later redesignated as the 6th Infantry Division].) Inactivated 10 January 1949 in Korea. Activated 4 October 1950 at Fort Ord, California. (20th Infantry relieved 3 April 1956 from assignment to the 6th Infantry Division.)

Inactivated 15 November 1957 at Fort Kobbe, Canal Zone; concurrently, redesignated as Headquarters and Headquarters Company, 2d Battle Group, 20th Infantry. Redesignated 24 November 1967 as Headquarters and Headquarters Company, 2d Battalion, 20th Infantry, assigned to the 6th Infantry Division, and activated at Fort Campbell, Kentucky (organic elements concurrently constituted and activated). Inactivated 25 July 1968 at Schofield Barracks, Hawaii.

CAMPAIGN PARTICIPATION CREDIT

Civil War
Peninsula
Manassas
Antietam
Fredericksburg
Chancellorsville
Gettysburg
Wilderness
Spotsylvania
Cold Harbor
Petersburg
Virginia 1862
Virginia 1863

Indian Wars
Little Big Horn
Pine Ridge

War With Spain
*Santiago

Philippine Insurrection
*Manila
*Luzon 1901

World War II
*New Guinea
*Luzon (with arrowhead)

431

DECORATIONS

Presidential Unit Citation (Army), Streamer embroidered CABARUAN HILLS

Presidential Unit Citation (Army), Streamer embroidered MAFFIN BAY

Presidential Unit Citation (Army), Streamer embroidered MUNOZ

*Philippine Presidential Unit Citation, Streamer embroidered 17 OCTOBER 1944 TO 4 JULY 1945 (6th Infantry Division cited; DA GO 47, 1950)

3d BATTALION, 20th INFANTRY

(Sykes' Regulars)

RA
(inactive)

LINEAGE

Constituted 3 May 1861 in the Regular Army as Company C, 2d Battalion, 11th Infantry. Organized 13 November 1862 at Fort Independence, Massachusetts. Reorganized and redesignated 6 December 1866 as Company C, 20th Infantry. (20th Infantry assigned 9 July 1918 to the 10th Division; relieved 14 February 1919 from assignment to the 10th Division; assigned 18 September 1920 to the 2d Division; relieved 16 October 1939 from assignment to the 2d Division and assigned to the 6th Division [later redesignated as the 6th Infantry Division].) Inactivated 10 January 1949 in Korea. Activated 4 October 1950 at Fort Ord, California. (20th Infantry relieved 3 April 1956 from assignment to the 6th Infantry Division.)

Inactivated 15 November 1957 at Fort Kobbe, Canal Zone; concurrently, redesignated as Headquarters and Headquarters Company, 3d Battle Group, 20th Infantry. Withdrawn 19 March 1959 from the Regular Army, allotted to the Army Reserve, and assigned to the 90th Infantry Division (organic elements concurrently constituted). Battle Group activated 1 April 1959 with Headquarters at Houston, Texas. Inactivated 27 March 1963 at Houston, Texas; concurrently, relieved from assignment to the 90th Infantry Division.

Redesignated 10 May 1967 as the 3d Battalion, 20th Infantry; concurrently, withdrawn from the Army Reserve, allotted to the Regular Army, assigned to the 198th Infantry Brigade, and activated at Fort Hood, Texas. Inactivated 12 May 1967 at Fort Hood, Texas; concurrently, relieved from assignment to the 198th Infantry Brigade. Activated 24 November 1967 at Fort Campbell, Kentucky; concurrently assigned to the 6th Infantry Division. Inactivated 25 July 1968 at Schofield Barracks, Hawaii.

CAMPAIGN PARTICIPATION CREDIT

Civil War
  Peninsula
  Manassas
  Antietam
  Fredericksburg
  *Chancellorsville
  Gettysburg
  Wilderness
  Spotsylvania
  Cold Harbor
  Petersburg
  Virginia 1862
  Virginia 1863

Indian Wars
  Little Big Horn
  Pine Ridge

War With Spain
  *Santiago

Philippine Insurrection
  *Manila
  Luzon 1901

World War II
  *New Guinea
  *Luzon (with arrowhead)

DECORATIONS

Presidential Unit Citation (Army), Streamer embroidered CABARUAN HILLS

Presidential Unit Citation (Army), Streamer embroidered MAFFIN BAY

Presidential Unit Citation (Army), Streamer embroidered MUNOZ

*Philippine Presidential Unit Citation, Streamer embroidered 17 OCTOBER 1944 TO 4 JULY 1945 (6th Infantry Division cited; DA GO 47, 1950)

4th BATTALION, 20th INFANTRY

(Sykes' Regulars)

RA
(193d Infantry Brigade)

LINEAGE

Constituted 3 May 1861 in the Regular Army as Company D, 2d Battalion, 11th Infantry. Organized 26 January 1863 at Fort Independence, Massachusetts. Reorganized and redesignated 6 December 1866 as Company D, 20th Infantry. (20th Infantry assigned 9 July 1918 to the 10th Division; relieved 14 February 1919 from assignment to the 10th Division; assigned 18 September 1920 to the 2d Division; relieved 16 October 1939 from assignment to the 2d Division and assigned to the 6th Division [later redesignated as the 6th Infantry Division].) Inactivated 10 January 1949 in Korea. Activated 4 October 1950 at Fort Ord, California. (20th Infantry relieved 3 April 1956 from assignment to the 6th Infantry Division.)

Inactivated 15 November 1957 at Fort Kobbe, Canal Zone; concurrently, redesignated as Headquarters and Headquarters Company, 4th Battle Group, 20th Infantry. Redesignated 3 August 1962 as Headquarters and Headquarters Company, 4th Battalion, 20th Infantry and assigned to the 193d Infantry Brigade (organic elements concurrently constituted). Battalion activated 8 August 1962 at Fort Clayton, Canal Zone.

CAMPAIGN PARTICIPATION CREDIT

Civil War
  Peninsula
  Manassas
  Antietam
  Fredericksburg
  *Chancellorsville
  Gettysburg
  Wilderness
  Spotsylvania
  Cold Harbor
  Petersburg
  Virginia 1862
  Virginia 1863

Indian Wars
  Little Big Horn
  Pine Ridge

War With Spain
  *Santiago

Philippine Insurrection
  *Manila
  Luzon 1901

World War II
  *New Guinea
  *Luzon (with arrowhead)

435

DECORATIONS

Presidential Unit Citation (Army), Streamer embroidered CABARUAN HILLS

Presidential Unit Citation (Army), Streamer embroidered MAFFIN BAY

Presidential Unit Citation (Army), Streamer embroidered MUNOZ

*Philippine Presidential Unit Citation, Streamer embroidered 17 OCTOBER 1944 TO 4 JULY 1945 (6th Infantry Division cited; DA GO 47, 1950)

COMPANY E, 20th INFANTRY

(Sykes' Regulars)

RA
(inactive)

LINEAGE

Constituted 3 May 1861 in the Regular Army as Company E, 2d Battalion, 11th Infantry. Organized 8 September 1865 at camp near Richmond, Virginia. Reorganized and redesignated 6 December 1866 as Company E, 20th Infantry. (20th Infantry assigned 9 July 1918 to the 10th Division; relieved 14 February 1919 from assignment to the 10th Division; assigned 18 September 1920 to the 2d Division; relieved 16 October 1939 from assignment to the 2d Division and assigned to the 6th Division [later redesignated as the 6th Infantry Division].) Inactivated 10 January 1949 in Korea. Activated 4 October 1950 at Fort Ord, California. (20th Infantry relieved 3 April 1956 from assignment to the 6th Infantry Division.)

Inactivated 15 November 1957 at Fort Kobbe, Canal Zone; concurrently, redesignated as Headquarters and Headquarters Company, 5th Battle Group, 20th Infantry. Redesignated 22 June 1960 as Company E, 20th Infantry. Activated 24 June 1960 in Korea. Inactivated 1 January 1966 in Korea. Activated 25 September 1967 in Vietnam. Inactivated 1 February 1969 in Vietnam.

CAMPAIGN PARTICIPATION CREDIT

War With Spain
  Santiago

Philippine Insurrection
  Manila
  Luzon 1901

World War II-AP
  New Guinea
  Luzon (with arrowhead)

Vietnam
  Counteroffensive, Phase III
  Tet Counteroffensive
  (other campaigns to be
    determined)

437

DECORATIONS

Presidential Unit Citation (Army), Streamer embroidered CABARUAN HILLS (2d Battalion, 20th Infantry cited; WD GO 31, 1946)

Philippine Presidential Unit Citation, Streamer embroidered 17 OCTOBER 1944 TO 4 JULY 1945 (6th Infantry Division cited; DA GO 47, 1950)

Vietnamese Cross of Gallantry with Palm, Streamer embroidered VIETNAM 1967–1968 (Company E, 20th Infantry cited; DA GO 3, 1970)

Vietnamese Civil Action Honor Medal, First Class, Streamer embroidered VIETNAM 1967–1968 (Company E, 20th Infantry cited; DA GO 53, 1970)

6th BATTALION, 20th INFANTRY

(Sykes' Regulars)

RA
(inactive)

LINEAGE

Constituted 3 May 1861 in the Regular Army as Company F, 2d Battalion, 11th Infantry. Organized in September 1865 at camp near Richmond, Virginia. Reorganized and redesignated 6 December 1866 as Company F, 20th Infantry. (20th Infantry assigned 9 July 1918 to the 10th Division; relieved 14 February 1919 from assignment to the 10th Division; assigned 18 September 1920 to the 2d Division; relieved 16 October 1939 from assignment to the 2d Division and assigned to the 6th Division [later redesignated as the 6th Infantry Division].) Inactivated 10 January 1949 in Korea. Activated 4 October 1950 at Fort Ord, California. (20th Infantry relieved 3 April 1956 from assignment to the 6th Infantry Division.)

Inactivated 15 November 1957 at Fort Kobbe, Canal Zone; concurrently, redesignated as Headquarters and Headquarters Company, 6th Battle Group, 20th Infantry. Redesignated 24 November 1967 as Headquarters and Headquarters Company, 6th Battalion, 20th Infantry, assigned to the 6th Infantry Division, and activated at Fort Campbell, Kentucky (organic elements concurrently constituted and activated). Inactivated 25 July 1968 at Schofield Barracks, Hawaii.

CAMPAIGN PARTICIPATION CREDIT

Civil War
- Peninsula
- Manassas
- Antietam
- Fredericksburg
- Chancellorsville
- Gettysburg
- Wilderness
- Spotsylvania
- Cold Harbor
- Petersburg
- Virginia 1862
- Virginia 1863

Indian Wars
- Little Big Horn
- Pine Ridge

War With Spain
- *Santiago

Philippine Insurrection
- *Manila
- *Luzon 1901

World War II
- *New Guinea
- *Luzon (with arrowhead)

DECORATIONS

*Presidential Unit Citation (Army), Streamer embroidered CABARUAN HILLS (2d Battalion, 20th Infantry cited; WD GO 31, 1946)

Presidential Unit Citation (Army), Streamer embroidered MAFFIN BAY

Presidential Unit Citation (Army), Streamer embroidered MUNOZ

*Philippine Presidential Unit Citation, Streamer embroidered 17 OCTOBER 1944 TO 4 JULY 1945 (6th Infantry Division cited; DA GO 47, 1950)

Bibliography, 20th Infantry

Cheyenne Chamber of Commerce. *Fort Francis E. Warren, Wyoming, 1930.* Cheyenne: Wyoming Labor Journal Publishing Company, 1930, pp. 36–41.

Coe, John Nichols. "The Twentieth Regiment of Infantry," *The Army of the United States,* edited by Theophilus F. Rodenbough and William L. Haskin. New York: Maynard, Merrill and Company, 1896, pp. 666–672. (Originally published in the *Journal of the Military Service Institution of the United States,* XIV [1893], 1334–1340.)

Coe, John Nichols and W. P. Burnham. *Historical Sketch, Twentieth U.S. Infantry, July 1861 to October 1902.* n.p., 1902.

Historical Sketch of the Twentieth United States Infantry, 1861–1919. n.p., 1920?

Lewis, Edward Mann. *Historical Register of Commissioned Officers of the Twentieth U.S. Infantry, From its Organization, December 21, 1866.* Presidio of Monterey, 1907.

————. *Historical Sketch of the Twentieth U.S. Infantry, From October 10th, 1902, to December 31st, 1905.* Regimental Press, 1906.

————. *Historical Sketch of the Twentieth U.S. Infantry, From December 31, 1905, to January 1, 1907.* Regimental Press, 1907.

Reed, Louis A. *Illustrated Historical Review of the United States Army in Oahu, T. H.* Honolulu: Hawaiian Gazette Company, 1911.

Smith, Robert Ross. *Approach to the Philippines.* United States Army in World War II. Washington: Government Printing Office, 1953.

————. *Triumph in the Philippines.* United States Army in World War II. Washington: Government Printing Office, 1963.

Sykes' Regulars, Twentieth Infantry Regiment Organization Day, 21 September 1955. Los Angeles?: Myra G. Shannon, 1955.

21st INFANTRY
(Gimlet)

HERALDIC ITEMS

COAT OF ARMS

Shield: Party per fess azure and argent, in chief a sun in splendor or charged with a five-bastioned fort of the first, in base a cedar tree eradicated proper.

Crest: On a wreath of the colors four arrows sable armed and feathered gules, tied with a rattlesnake skin proper.

Motto: Duty.

Symbolism: This unit's baptism of fire was at Cedar Mountain on 9 August 1862, where it performed its mission with such success as to bring forth special mention from General Prince, the brigade commander. This incident is shown by the cedar tree. At Santiago the 21st Infantry was in the V Corps, the badge of which was a five-bastioned fort, and its Philippine Insurrection service is shown by the Katipunan sun. The colors of the shield, blue and white, have been the infantry colors during the existence of the regiment.

The arrows in the crest stand for Indian campaigns. The rattlesnake skin was an Indian emblem of war.

DISTINCTIVE INSIGNIA

The distinctive insignia is the shield, crest, and motto of the coat of arms.

LINEAGE AND HONORS

LINEAGE

Constituted 3 May 1861 in the Regular Army as the 2d Battalion, 12th Infantry. Organized 20 May 1862 at Fort Hamilton, New York. Reorganized and redesignated 7 December 1866 as the 21st Infantry.

Consolidated 9–31 August 1869 with the 32d Infantry (see ANNEX) and consolidated unit designated as the 21st Infantry.

Assigned 29 July 1918 to the 16th Division. Relieved 8 March 1919 from assignment to the 16th Division. Assigned 22 October 1921 to the Hawaiian Division. Relieved 26 August 1941 from assignment to the Hawaiian Division and assigned to the 24th Division (later redesignated as the 24th Infantry Division).

Relieved 5 June 1958 from assignment to the 24th Infantry Division and reorganized as a parent regiment under the Combat Arms Regimental System.

ANNEX

Constituted 3 May 1861 in the Regular Army as the 3d Battalion, 14th Infantry. Organized 27 July 1865 at Fort Trumbull, Connecticut. Reorganized and redesignated 21 September 1866 as the 32d Infantry. Consolidated 9–31 August 1869 with the 21st Infantry and consolidated unit designated as the 21st Infantry.

CAMPAIGN PARTICIPATION CREDIT

Civil War
Peninsula
Manassas
Antietam
Fredericksburg
Chancellorsville
Gettysburg
Wilderness
Spotsylvania
Cold Harbor
Petersburg
Virginia 1862
Virginia 1863

Indian Wars
Modocs
Nez Perces
Bannocks
Arizona 1866
Arizona 1867
Arizona 1868
Arizona 1869
Arizona 1870

War With Spain
Santiago

Philippine Insurrection
Zapote River

Luzon 1899
Luzon 1901
Luzon 1902

World War II
Central Pacific
New Guinea (with arrowhead)
Leyte
Luzon
Southern Philippines
(with arrowhead)

Korean War
UN defensive
UN offensive
CCF intervention
First UN counteroffensive
CCF spring offensive
UN summer-fall offensive
Second Korean winter
Korea, summer 1953

Vietnam
Counteroffensive, Phase II
Counteroffensive, Phase III
Tet Counteroffensive
(other campaigns to be determined)

DECORATIONS

Presidential Unit Citation (Army), Streamer embroidered DEFENSE OF KOREA (24th Infantry Division cited; DA GO 45, 1950)

Presidential Unit Citation (Army), Streamer embroidered SANGHONGJONG-NI (Headquarters and Headquarters Company and Medical Company, 21st Infantry cited; DA GO 77, 1951)

Philippine Presidential Unit Citation, Streamer embroidered 17 OCTOBER 1944 TO 4 JULY 1945 (21st Infantry cited; DA GO 47, 1950)

Republic of Korea Presidential Unit Citation, Streamer embroidered PYONGTAEK (21st Infantry cited; DA GO 35, 1951)

Republic of Korea Presidential Unit Citation, Streamer embroidered KOREA (24th Infantry Division cited; DA GO 24, 1954)

1st BATTALION, 21st INFANTRY

(Gimlet)

RA
(inactive)

LINEAGE

Constituted 3 May 1861 in the Regular Army as Company A, 2d Battalion, 12th Infantry. Organized 20 May 1862 at Fort Hamilton, New York. Reorganized and redesignated 7 December 1866 as Company A, 21st Infantry.

Consolidated 20 August 1869 with Company A, 32d Infantry (see ANNEX) and consolidated unit designated as Company A, 21st Infantry. (21st Infantry assigned 29 July 1918 to the 16th Division; relieved 8 March 1919 from assignment to the 16th Division; assigned 22 October 1921 to the Hawaiian Division; relieved 26 August 1941 from assignment to the Hawaiian Division and assigned to the 24th Division [later redesignated as the 24th Infantry Division].)

Redesignated 5 June 1958 as Headquarters and Headquarters Company, 1st Battle Group, 21st Infantry and remained assigned to the 24th Infantry Division (organic elements concurrently constituted and activated 1 July 1958 in Germany). Reorganized and redesignated 1 February 1963 as the 1st Battalion, 21st Infantry. Inactivated 15 April 1970 in Germany.

ANNEX

Constituted 3 May 1861 in the Regular Army as Company A, 3d Battalion, 14th Infantry. Organized in August 1865 at Fort Trumbull, Connecticut. Reorganized and redesignated 21 September 1866 as Company A, 32d Infantry. Consolidated 20 August 1869 with Company A, 21st Infantry and consolidated unit designated as Company A, 21st Infantry.

446

CAMPAIGN PARTICIPATION CREDIT

Civil War
Peninsula
*Manassas
*Antietam
*Fredericksburg
*Chancellorsville
*Gettysburg
*Wilderness
*Spotsylvania
*Cold Harbor
*Petersburg
Virginia 1862
*Virginia 1863

Indian Wars
Modocs
Nez Perces
Bannocks
Arizona 1866
Arizona 1867
*Arizona 1868
Arizona 1869
*Arizona 1870

War With Spain
*Santiago

Philippine Insurrection
*Zapote River
*Luzon 1899
*Luzon 1900
*Luzon 1901
Luzon 1902

World War II
*Central Pacific
*New Guinea (with arrowhead)
*Leyte
*Luzon
*Southern Philippines
(with arrowhead)

Korean War
*UN defensive
*UN offensive
*CCF intervention
*First UN counteroffensive
*CCF spring offensive
*UN summer-fall offensive
*Second Korean winter
*Korea, summer 1953

DECORATIONS

*Presidential Unit Citation (Army), Streamer embroidered DEFENSE OF KOREA (24th Infantry Division cited; DA GO 45, 1950)

Presidential Unit Citation (Army), Streamer embroidered SANGHONGJONG-NI

*Philippine Presidential Unit Citation, Streamer embroidered 17 OCTOBER 1944 TO 4 JULY 1945 (21st Infantry cited; DA GO 47, 1950)

*Republic of Korea Presidential Unit Citation, Streamer embroidered PYONGTAEK (21st Infantry cited; DA GO 35, 1951)

*Republic of Korea Presidential Unit Citation, Streamer embroidered KOREA (24th Infantry Division cited; DA GO 24, 1954)

2d BATTALION, 21st INFANTRY

(Gimlet)

RA
(inactive)

LINEAGE

Constituted 3 May 1861 in the Regular Army as Company B, 2d Battalion, 12th Infantry. Organized 20 May 1862 at Fort Hamilton, New York. Reorganized and redesignated 7 December 1866 as Company B, 21st Infantry.

Consolidated 26 August 1869 with Company B, 32d Infantry (see ANNEX) and consolidated unit designated as Company B, 21st Infantry. (21st Infantry assigned 29 July 1918 to the 16th Division; relieved 8 March 1919 from assignment to the 16th Division; assigned 22 October 1921 to the Hawaiian Division; relieved 26 August 1941 from assignment to the Hawaiian Division and assigned to the 24th Division [later redesignated as the 24th Infantry Division].)

Reorganized and redesignated 1 February 1957 as Headquarters and Headquarters Company, 2d Battle Group, 21st Infantry, relieved from assignment to the 24th Infantry Division, and assigned to the 25th Infantry Division (organic elements concurrently constituted and activated). Reorganized and redesignated 1 February 1963 as the 2d Battalion, 21st Infantry; concurrently relieved from assignment to the 25th Infantry Division and assigned to the 24th Infantry Division. Inactivated 15 April 1970 at Fort Riley, Kansas.

ANNEX

Constituted 3 May 1861 in the Regular Army as Company B, 3d Battalion, 14th Infantry. Organized in August 1865 at Fort Trumbull, Connecticut. Reorganized and redesignated 21 September 1866 as Company B, 32d Infantry. Consolidated 26 August 1869 with Company B, 21st Infantry and consolidated unit designated as Company B, 21st Infantry.

448

Campaign Participation Credit

Civil War
  Peninsula
  *Manassas
  *Antietam
  *Fredericksburg
  Chancellorsville
  Gettysburg
  Wilderness
  Spotsylvania
  Cold Harbor
  Petersburg
  Virginia 1862
  Virginia 1863

Indian Wars
  *Modocs
  *Nez Perces
  *Bannocks
  *Arizona 1866
  Arizona 1867
  Arizona 1868
  Arizona 1869
  Arizona 1870

War With Spain
  *Santiago

Philippine Insurrection
  *Zapote River
  *Luzon 1899
  *Luzon 1901
  Luzon 1902

World War II
  *Central Pacific
  *New Guinea (with arrowhead)
  *Leyte
  *Luzon
  *Southern Philippines
    (with arrowhead)

Korean War
  *UN defensive
  *UN offensive
  *CCF intervention
  *First UN counteroffensive
  *CCF spring offensive
  *UN summer-fall offensive
  *Second Korean winter
  *Korea, summer 1953

Decorations

*Presidential Unit Citation (Army), Streamer embroidered DEFENSE OF KOREA (24th Infantry Division cited; DA GO 45, 1950)

Presidential Unit Citation (Army), Streamer embroidered SANGHONG JONG-NI

*Philippine Presidential Unit Citation, Streamer embroidered 17 OCTOBER 1944 TO 4 JULY 1945 (21st Infantry cited; DA GO 47, 1950)

*Republic of Korea Presidential Unit Citation, Streamer embroidered PYONGTAEK (21st Infantry cited; DA GO 35, 1951)

*Republic of Korea Presidential Unit Citation, Streamer embroidered KOREA (24th Infantry Division cited; DA GO 24, 1954)

3d BATTALION, 21st INFANTRY

(Gimlet)

RA
(23d Infantry Division)

LINEAGE

Constituted 3 May 1861 in the Regular Army as Company C, 2d Battalion, 12th Infantry. Organized 28 May 1862 at Fort Hamilton, New York. Reorganized and redesignated 7 December 1866 as Company C, 21st Infantry.

Consolidated 27 August 1869 with Company C, 32d Infantry (see ANNEX) and consolidated unit designated as Company C, 21st Infantry. (21st Infantry assigned 29 July 1918 to the 16th Division; relieved 8 March 1919 from assignment to the 16th Division; assigned 22 October 1921 to the Hawaiian Division; relieved 26 August 1941 from assignment to the Hawaiian Division and assigned to the 24th Division [later redesignated as the 24th Infantry Division].) Inactivated 5 June 1958 and relieved from assignment to the 24th Infantry Division.

Redesignated 31 March 1959 as Headquarters and Headquarters Company, 3d Battle Group, 21st Infantry, withdrawn from the Regular Army, allotted to the Army Reserve, and assigned to the 63d Infantry Division (organic elements concurrently constituted). Battle Group activated 1 May 1959 with Headquarters at Santa Barbara, California. Inactivated 1 April 1963 at Santa Barbara, California, and relieved from assignment to the 63d Infantry Division.

Redesignated 10 September 1965 as the 3d Battalion, 21st Infantry; concurrently, withdrawn from the Army Reserve, allotted to the Regular Army, and assigned to the 196th Infantry Brigade. Activated 15 September 1965 at Fort Devens, Massachusetts. Relieved 15 February 1969 from assignment to the 196th Infantry Brigade and assigned to the 23d Infantry Division.

ANNEX

Constituted 3 May 1861 in the Regular Army as Company C, 3d Battalion, 14th Infantry. Organized in September 1865 at Hart Island, New York. Reorganized and redesignated 21 September 1866 as Company C, 32d Infantry. Consolidated 27 August 1869 with Company C, 21st Infantry and consolidated unit designated as Company C, 21st Infantry.

450

CAMPAIGN PARTICIPATION CREDIT

Civil War
 Peninsula
 Manassas
 *Antietam
 *Fredericksburg
 *Chancellorsville
 *Gettysburg
 *Wilderness
 *Spotsylvania
 *Cold Harbor
 *Petersburg
 Virginia 1862
 *Virginia 1863

Indian Wars
 *Modocs
 *Nez Perces
 Bannocks
 Arizona 1866
 Arizona 1867
 *Arizona 1868
 Arizona 1869
 Arizona 1870

War With Spain
 *Santiago

Philippine Insurrection
 *Zapote River

*Luzon 1899
*Luzon 1900
*Luzon 1901
*Luzon 1902

World War II
 *Central Pacific
 *New Guinea (with arrowhead)
 *Leyte
 *Luzon
 *Southern Philippines
  (with arrowhead)

Korean War
 *UN defensive
 *UN offensive
 *CCF intervention
 *First UN counteroffensive
 *CCF spring offensive
 *UN summer-fall offensive
 *Second Korean winter
 *Korea, summer 1953

Vietnam
 *Counteroffensive, Phase II
 *Counteroffensive, Phase III
 *Tet Counteroffensive
 (other campaigns to be determined)

DECORATIONS

*Presidential Unit Citation (Army), Streamer embroidered DEFENSE OF KOREA (24th Infantry Division cited; DA GO 45, 1950)

Presidential Unit Citation (Army), Streamer embroidered SANGHONG JONG-NI

*Philippine Presidential Unit Citation, Streamer embroidered 17 OCTOBER 1944 TO 4 JULY 1945 (21st Infantry cited; DA GO 47, 1950)

*Republic of Korea Presidential Unit Citation, Streamer embroidered PYONGTAEK (21st Infantry cited; DA GO 35, 1951)

*Republic of Korea Presidential Unit Citation, Streamer embroidered KOREA (24th Infantry Division cited; DA GO 24, 1954)

4th BATTALION, 21st INFANTRY

(Gimlet)

RA
(23d Infantry Division)

Constituted 3 May 1861 in the Regular Army as Company D, 2d Battalion, 12th Infantry. Organized 20 August 1862 at Fort Hamilton, New York. Reorganized and redesignated 7 December 1866 as Company D, 21st Infantry.

Consolidated 21 August 1869 with Company D, 32d Infantry (see ANNEX) and consolidated unit designated as Company D, 21st Infantry. (21st Infantry assigned 29 July 1918 to the 16th Division; relieved 8 March 1919 from assignment to the 16th Division; assigned 22 October 1921 to the Hawaiian Division; relieved 26 August 1941 from assignment to the Hawaiian Division and assigned to the 24th Division [later redesignated as the 24th Infantry Division].)

Inactivated 5 June 1958 and relieved from assignment to the 24th Infantry Division; concurrently, redesignated as Headquarters and Headquarters Company, 4th Battle Group, 21st Infantry. Redesignated 11 October 1965 as Headquarters and Headquarters Company, 4th Battalion, 21st Infantry and assigned to the 25th Infantry Division (organic elements concurrently constituted). Battalion activated 6 December 1965 in Hawaii. Inactivated 3 January 1966 in Hawaii; concurrently, relieved from assignment to the 25th Infantry Division. Activated 1 November 1967 in Hawaii; concurrently, assigned to the 11th Infantry Brigade. Relieved 15 February 1969 from assignment to the 11th Infantry Brigade and assigned to the 23d Infantry Division.

ANNEX

Constituted 3 May 1861 in the Regular Army as Company D, 3d Battalion, 14th Infantry. Organized in September 1865 at Hart Island, New York. Reorganized and redesignated 21 September 1866 as Company D, 32d Infantry. Consolidated 21 August 1869 with Company D, 21st Infantry and consolidated unit designated as Company D, 21st Infantry.

CAMPAIGN PARTICIPATION CREDIT

Civil War
Peninsula
Manassas
*Antietam
*Fredericksburg
*Chancellorsville
*Gettysburg
*Wilderness
*Spotsylvania
*Cold Harbor
*Petersburg
Virginia 1862
*Virginia 1863

Indian Wars
Modocs
*Nez Perces
*Bannocks
Arizona 1866
Arizona 1867
Arizona 1868
Arizona 1869
Arizona 1870

War With Spain
*Santiago

Philippine Insurrection
*Zapote River
*Luzon 1899
*Luzon 1901
Luzon 1902

World War II
*Central Pacific
*New Guinea (with arrowhead)
*Leyte
*Luzon
*Southern Philippines
(with arrowhead)

Korean War
*UN defensive
*UN offensive
*CCF intervention
*First UN counteroffensive
*CCF spring offensive
*UN summer-fall offensive
*Second Korean winter
*Korea, summer 1953

Vietnam
(to be determined)

DECORATIONS

*Presidential Unit Citation (Army), Streamer embroidered DEFENSE OF KOREA (24th Infantry Division cited; DA GO 45, 1950)

Presidential Unit Citation (Army), Streamer embroidered SANGHONG JONG-NI

*Philippine Presidential Unit Citation, Streamer embroidered 17 OCTOBER 1944 TO 4 JULY 1945 (21st Infantry cited; DA GO 47, 1950)

*Republic of Korea Presidential Unit Citation, Streamer embroidered PYONGTAEK (21st Infantry cited; DA GO 35, 1951)

*Republic of Korea Presidential Unit Citation, Streamer embroidered KOREA (24th Infantry Division cited; DA GO 24, 1954)

*Vietnamese Cross of Gallantry with Palm, Streamer embroidered VIETNAM 1968–1969 (4th Battalion, 21st Infantry cited; DA GO 2, 1971)

5th BATTALION, 21st INFANTRY

(Gimlet)

RA
(inactive)

LINEAGE

Constituted 3 May 1861 in the Regular Army as Company E, 2d Battalion, 12th Infantry. Organized 20 May 1862 at Fort Hamilton, New York. Reorganized and redesignated 7 December 1866 as Company E, 21st Infantry.

Consolidated 19 August 1869 with Company E, 32d Infantry (see ANNEX) and consolidated unit designated as Company E, 21st Infantry. (21st Infantry assigned 29 July 1918 to the 16th Division; relieved 8 March 1919 from assignment to the 16th Division; assigned 22 October 1921 to the Hawaiian Division; relieved 26 August 1941 from assignment to the Hawaiian Division and assigned to the 24th Division [later redesignated as the 24th Infantry Division].)

Inactivated 5 June 1958 and relieved from assignment to the 24th Infantry Division; concurrently, redesignated as Headquarters and Headquarters Company, 5th Battle Group, 21st Infantry. Redesignated 11 October 1965 as Headquarters and Headquarters Company, 5th Battalion, 21st Infantry and assigned to the 25th Infantry Division (organic elements concurrently constituted). Battalion activated 6 December 1965 in Hawaii. Inactivated 3 January 1966 in Hawaii; concurrently, relieved from assignment to the 25th Infantry Division.

ANNEX

Constituted 3 May 1861 in the Regular Army as Company E, 3d Battalion, 14th Infantry. Organized in September 1865 at Hart Island, New York. Reorganized and redesignated 21 September 1866 as Company E, 32d Infantry. Consolidated 19 August 1869 with Company E, 21st Infantry and consolidated unit designated as Company E, 21st Infantry.

454

Campaign Participation Credit

Civil War
Peninsula
*Manassas
*Antietam
*Fredericksburg
Chancellorsville
Gettysburg
Wilderness
Spotsylvania
Cold Harbor
Petersburg
Virginia 1862
Virginia 1863

Indian Wars
Modocs
*Nez Perces
*Bannocks
Arizona 1866
Arizona 1867
Arizona 1868
Arizona 1869
Arizona 1870

War With Spain
*Santiago

Philippine Insurrection
*Zapote River
*Luzon 1899
*Luzon 1901
Luzon 1902

World War II
*Central Pacific
*New Guinea (with arrowhead)
*Leyte
*Luzon
*Southern Philippines
(with arrowhead)

Korean War
*UN defensive
*UN offensive
*CCF intervention
*First UN counteroffensive
*CCF spring offensive
*UN summer-fall offensive
*Second Korean winter
*Korea, summer 1953

Decorations

*Presidential Unit Citation (Army), Streamer embroidered DEFENSE OF KOREA (24th Infantry Division cited; DA GO 45, 1950)

Presidential Unit Citation (Army), Streamer embroidered SANGHONG JONG-NI

*Philippine Presidential Unit Citation, Streamer embroidered 17 OCTOBER 1944 TO 4 JULY 1945 (21st Infantry Division cited; DA GO 47, 1950)

*Republic of Korea Presidential Unit Citation, Streamer embroidered PYONGTAEK (21st Infantry cited; DA GO 35, 1951)

*Republic of Korea Presidential Unit Citation, Streamer embroidered KOREA (24th Infantry Division cited; DA GO 24, 1954)

21st Infantry, Bibliography

Albright, John, John A. Cash, and Allan W. Sandstrum. *Seven Firefights in Vietnam*. Washington: Government Printing Office, 1970.

Appleman, Roy E. *South to the Naktong, North to the Yalu*. United States Army in the Korean War. Washington: Government Printing Office, 1961.

Busch, George B. *Duty, The Story of the 21st Infantry Regiment*. Sendai, Japan: Hyappan Printing Company, 1953.

Cannon, M. Hamlin. *Leyte: The Return to the Philippines*. United States Army in World War II. Washington: Government Printing Office, 1954.

Ebstein, Frederick Ernst. "Twenty-first Regiment of Infantry," *The Army of the United States*, edited by Theophilus F. Rodenbough and William L. Haskin. New York: Maynard, Merrill and Company, 1896, pp. 673–679. (Originally published in the *Journal of the Military Service Institution of the United States*, XIII [1892], 844–850.)

Falk, Stanley L. *Decision at Leyte*. New York: W. W. Norton and Company, Inc., 1966.

1st Battle Group, 21st Infantry, Gimlets, Pass in Review, 1958–1959. Munich: Leopold-Druckerei, 1959.

Gimlet, 2d Battle Group, 21st Infantry, Hawaii, 1959. Honolulu: Star-Bulletin Printing Company, 1959.

The Gimlet Heritage, 1862–1953. n.p., 1953.

Gugeler, Russell A. *Combat Actions in Korea*. Washington: Combat Forces Press, 1954.

Hampton, Celwyn E. "History of the Twenty-first United States Infantry," *Journal of the United States Infantry Association*, V (1908/1909), 644–686, 854–892; VI (1909/1910), 89–99, 257–265. (Erroneously connects this regiment with an earlier one of the same designation.)

————. *History of the Twenty-first U.S. Infantry from 1812 to 1863*. Columbus, Ohio: Edward T. Miller Company, 1911. (Erroneously connects this regiment with an earlier one of the same designation.)

Historical Sketch of the Operations, etc. of the Twenty-first U.S. Infantry while in the Philippine Islands from May 11, 1899, to May 6, 1902. St. Paul: Randall Printing Company, 1903.

Marshall, S. L. A. *Ambush*. New York: Cowles Book Company, 1969.

Military History Section, Headquarters, United States Army Forces, Far East. *A Brief History of the 21st Infantry Regiment*. n.p., 1954.

Public Information Office, 21st Infantry. *Ninety Years of Duty; the Twenty-first Infantry Regiment, 1862–1952*. Sendai, Japan, 1952.

Reports of General MacArthur. Washington: Government Printing Office, 1966.

Russell, Martin B. *Illustrated Review Twenty-first Infantry, United States Army, Fort Logan, Colorado.* . . . Denver: Medley and Russell, c. 1909.

Smith, Judson MacIver. *The Story of a Regiment, the Twenty-first United States Infantry.* Honolulu: Advertising Publishing Company, Ltd., 1940.

Smith, Robert Ross. *The Approach to the Philippines.* United States Army in World War II. Washington: Government Printing Office, 1953.

————. *Triumph in the Philippines.* United States Army in World War II. Washington: Government Printing Office, 1963.

Verbeck, William Jordan. *A Regiment in Action.* Washington, 1948.

22d INFANTRY

HERALDIC ITEMS

COAT OF ARMS

Shield: Per fess embattled argent and azure, in chief a bundle of five arrows sable armed and flitted gules, in base a sun in splendor or. (And for informal use, supporters: The escutcheon displayed in front of two Springfield rifles proper crossed in saltire and encircled by a belt azure fimbriated argent, bearing the regimental motto of the last, and with a buckle of the same in base charged with the numeral "22" of the first.)

Crest: On a wreath of the colors a five-bastioned fort divided fesswise or and gules, fimbriated gules and or, charged with a royal palm proper.

Motto: Deeds Not Words.

Symbolism: The shield is white and blue, the old and present infantry colors. The embattled partition line is for the wars in which the regiment has taken part. The arrows stand for five Indian campaigns; the sun in splendor was the old Katipunan device in the Philippine Insurrection.

The crest is for the War with Spain, being the badge of the V Corps in the Spanish colors, and charged with a royal palm to commemorate the fact that the 22d Infantry was the first regiment to land on Cuban soil in that war.

DISTINCTIVE INSIGNIA

The distinctive insignia is the shield of the coat of arms.

LINEAGE AND HONORS

LINEAGE

Constituted 3 May 1861 in the Regular Army as the 2d Battalion, 13th Infantry. Organized 15 May 1865 at Camp Dennison, Ohio. Reorganized and redesignated 21 September 1866 as the 22d Infantry. Consolidated 1–31 May 1869 with the 31st Infantry (see ANNEX) and

459

consolidated unit designated as the 22d Infantry.

Assigned 24 March 1923 to the 4th Division (later redesignated as the 4th Infantry Division). (1st Battalion inactivated 30 June 1927 at Fort McPherson, Georgia; activated 1 June 1940 at Fort McClellan, Alabama.) Inactivated 1 March 1946 at Camp Butner, North Carolina. Activated 15 July 1947 at Fort Ord, California.

Relieved 1 April 1957 from assignment to the 4th Infantry Division and reorganized as a parent regiment under the Combat Arms Regimental System.

ANNEX

Constituted 3 May 1861 in the Regular Army as the 3d Battalion, 13th Infantry. Organized in December 1865 at Jefferson Barracks, Missouri. Reorganized and redesignated 21 September 1866 as the 31st Infantry. Consolidated 1–31 May 1869 with the 22d Infantry and consolidated unit designated as the 22d Infantry.

CAMPAIGN PARTICIPATION CREDIT

Indian Wars
   Little Big Horn
   Pine Ridge
   North Dakota 1868
   North Dakota 1869
   Montana 1872

War With Spain
   Santiago

Philippine Insurrection
   Manila
   Malolos
   San Isidro
   Mindanao

   Jolo
   Luzon 1900

World War II
   Normandy (with arrowhead)
   Northern France
   Rhineland
   Ardennes-Alsace
   Central Europe

Vietnam
   Counteroffensive, Phase II
   Counteroffensive, Phase III
   Tet Counteroffensive
   (other campaigns to be determined)

DECORATIONS

Presidential Unit Citation (Army), Streamer embroidered HURTGEN FOREST (22d Infantry cited; WD GO 37, 1946)

Presidential Unit Citation (Army), Streamer embroidered ST. GILLIS-MARIGNY (22d Infantry cited; WD GO 14, 1945)

Presidential Unit Citation (Army), Streamer embroidered CARENTAN (3d Battalion, 22d Infantry cited; WD GO 85, 1944)

Presidential Unit Citation (Army), Streamer embroidered SUOI TRE, VIETNAM (2d Battalion and 3d Battalion [less Company C], 22d Infantry cited; DA GO 59, 1968)

Valorous Unit Award, Streamer embroidered TAY NINH PROVINCE (3d

Battalion, 22d Infantry cited; DA GO 42, 1969)

Valorous Unit Award, Streamer embroidered KONTUM (1st Battalion, 22d Infantry cited; DA GO 43, 1970)

Belgian Fourragere 1940 (22d Infantry cited; DA GO 43, 1950)

Cited in the Order of the Day of the Belgian Army for action in BELGIUM (22d Infantry cited; DA GO 43, 1950)

Cited in the Order of the Day of the Belgian Army for action in the ARDENNES (22d Infantry cited; DA GO 43, 1950)

1st BATTALION, 22d INFANTRY

RA
(4th Infantry Division)

Constituted 3 May 1861 in the Regular Army as Companies A and I, 2d Battalion, 13th Infantry. Organized in May 1865 at Camp Dennison, Ohio. Reorganized and redesignated 21 September 1866 as Companies A and I, 22d Infantry.

Companies A and I, 22d Infantry consolidated 4 May 1869 and consolidated unit designated as Company A, 22d Infantry. (22d Infantry assigned 24 March 1923 to the 4th Division [later redesignated as the 4th Infantry Division].) Inactivated 30 June 1927 at Fort McPherson, Georgia. Activated 1 June 1940 at Fort McClellan, Alabama. Inactivated 1 March 1946 at Camp Butner, North Carolina. Activated 15 July 1947 at Fort Ord, California.

Reorganized and redesignated 1 April 1957 as Headquarters and Headquarters Company, 1st Battle Group, 22d Infantry and remained assigned to the 4th Infantry Division (organic elements concurrently constituted and activated). Reorganized and redesignated 1 October 1963 as the 1st Battalion, 22d Infantry.

CAMPAIGN PARTICIPATION CREDIT

Indian Wars
Little Big Horn
*Pine Ridge
North Dakota 1868
North Dakota 1869
Montana 1872

War With Spain
*Santiago

Philippine Insurrection
*Manila
*Malolos
*San Isidro
*Mindanao

*Jolo
*Luzon 1900

World War II
*Normandy (with arrowhead)
*Northern France
*Rhineland
*Ardennes-Alsace
*Central Europe

Vietnam
*Counteroffensive, Phase II
*Counteroffensive, Phase III
*Tet Counteroffensive
(other campaigns to be determined)

DECORATIONS

*Presidential Unit Citation (Army), Streamer embroidered HURTGEN FOREST (22d Infantry cited; WD GO 37, 1946)

*Presidential Unit Citation (Army), Streamer embroidered ST. GILLIS-MARIGNY (22d Infantry cited; WD GO 14, 1945)

Presidential Unit Citation (Army), Streamer embroidered CARENTAN

*Valorous Unit Award, Streamer embroidered KONTUM (1st Battalion, 22d Infantry cited; DA GO 43, 1970)

*Belgian Fourragere 1940 (22d Infantry cited; DA GO 43, 1950)

*Cited in the Order of the Day of the Belgian Army for action in BELGIUM (22d Infantry cited; DA GO 43, 1950)

*Cited in the Order of the Day of the Belgian Army for action in the ARDENNES (22d Infantry cited; DA GO 43, 1950)

*Vietnamese Cross of Gallantry with Palm, Streamer embroidered VIETNAM 1966–1969 (1st Battalion, 22d Infantry cited; DA GO 3, 1970)

*Vietnamese Civil Action Honor Medal, First Class, Streamer embroidered VIETNAM 1966–1969 (1st Battalion, 22d Infantry cited; DA GO 53, 1970)

2d BATTALION, 22d INFANTRY

RA

(4th Infantry Division)

Constituted 3 May 1861 in the Regular Army as Companies B and K, 2d Battalion, 13th Infantry. Organized in May 1865 at Camp Dennison, Ohio. Reorganized and redesignated 21 September 1866 as Companies B and K, 22d Infantry.

Companies B and K, 22d Infantry consolidated 4 May 1869 and consolidated unit designated as Company B, 22d Infantry. (22d Infantry assigned 24 March 1923 to the 4th Division [later redesignated as the 4th Infantry Division].) Inactivated 30 June 1927 at Fort McPherson, Georgia. Activated 1 June 1940 at Fort McClellan, Alabama. Inactivated 1 March 1946 at Camp Butner, North Carolina. Activated 15 July 1947 at Fort Ord, California.

Inactivated 1 April 1957 at Fort Lewis, Washington, and relieved from assignment to the 4th Infantry Division; concurrently, redesignated as Headquarters and Headquarters Company, 2d Battle Group, 22d Infantry. Redesignated 21 August 1963 as Headquarters and Headquarters Company, 2d Battalion, 22d Infantry and assigned to the 4th Infantry Division (organic elements concurrently constituted). Battalion activated 1 October 1963 at Fort Lewis, Washington. Relieved 1 August 1967 from assignment to the 4th Infantry Division and assigned to the 25th Infantry Division. Relieved 15 December 1970 from assignment to the 25th Infantry Division and assigned to the 4th Infantry Division.

464

CAMPAIGN PARTICIPATION CREDIT

Indian Wars
  Little Big Horn
  Pine Ridge
  *North Dakota 1868
  North Dakota 1869
  Montana 1872

War With Spain
  *Santiago

Philippine Insurrection
  *Manila
  *Malolos
  *San Isidro
  *Mindanao

Jolo
*Luzon 1900

World War II
  *Normandy (with arrowhead)
  *Northern France
  *Rhineland
  *Ardennes-Alsace
  *Central Europe

Vietnam
  *Counteroffensive, Phase II
  *Counteroffensive, Phase III
  *Tet Counteroffensive
  (other campaigns to be determined)

DECORATIONS

*Presidential Unit Citation (Army), Streamer embroidered HURTGEN FOREST (22d Infantry cited; WD GO 37, 1946)

*Presidential Unit Citation (Army), Streamer embroidered ST. GILLIS-MARIGNY (22d Infantry cited; WD GO 14, 1945)

Presidential Unit Citation (Army), Streamer embroidered CARENTAN

*Presidential Unit Citation (Army), Streamer embroidered SUOI TRE, VIETNAM (2d Battalion, 22d Infantry cited; DA GO 59, 1968)

*Belgian Fourragere 1940 (22d Infantry cited; DA GO 43, 1950)

*Cited in the Order of the Day of the Belgian Army for action in BELGIUM (22d Infantry cited; DA GO 43, 1950)

*Cited in the Order of the Day of the Belgian Army for action in the ARDENNES (22d Infantry cited; DA GO 43, 1950)

*Vietnamese Cross of Gallantry with Palm, Streamer embroidered VIETNAM 1966–1967 (2d Battalion, 22d Infantry cited; DA GO 3, 1970, as amended by DA GO 48, 1971)

*Vietnamese Cross of Gallantry with Palm, Streamer embroidered VIETNAM 1967–1968 (2d Battalion, 22d Infantry cited; DA GO 48, 1971)

3d BATTALION, 22d INFANTRY

RA

(25th Infantry Division)

LINEAGE

Constituted 3 May 1861 in the Regular Army as Companies C and F, 2d Battalion, 13th Infantry. Organized in July 1865 at Camp Dennison, Ohio. Reorganized and redesignated 21 September 1866 as Companies C and F, 22d Infantry.

Companies C and F, 22d Infantry consolidated 1 May 1869 and consolidated unit designated as Company C, 22d Infantry. (22d Infantry assigned 24 March 1923 to the 4th Division [later redesignated as the 4th Infantry Division].) Inactivated 30 June 1927 at Fort McPherson, Georgia. Inactivated 1 June 1940 at Fort McClellan, Alabama. Inactivated 1 March 1946 at Camp Butner, North Carolina. Activated 15 July 1947 at Fort Ord, California.

Inactivated 1 April 1957 at Fort Lewis, Washington, and relieved from assignment to the 4th Infantry Division; concurrently, reorganized and redesignated as Headquarters and Headquarters Company, 3d Battle Group, 22d Infantry. Withdrawn 29 April 1959 from the Regular Army, allotted to the Army Reserve, and assigned to the 96th Infantry Division (organic elements concurrently constituted). Battle Group activated 1 June 1959 with Headquarters at Boise, Idaho. Inactivated 15 March 1963 at Boise, Idaho, and relieved from assignment to the 96th Infantry Division.

Redesignated 16 September 1965 as the 3d Battalion, 22d Infantry; concurrently, withdrawn from the Army Reserve, allotted to the Regular Army, and assigned to the 4th Infantry Division. Activated 1 November 1965 at Fort Lewis, Washington. Relieved 1 August 1967 from assignment to the 4th Infantry Division and assigned to the 25th Infantry Division.

466

CAMPAIGN PARTICIPATION CREDIT

Indian Wars
  Little Big Horn
  Pine Ridge
  *North Dakota 1867
  *North Dakota 1868
  North Dakota 1869
  Montana 1872

War With Spain
  *Santiago

Philippine Insurrection
  *Manila
  *Malolos
  *San Isidro
  *Mindanao

  Jolo
  *Luzon 1900

World War II
  *Normandy (with arrowhead)
  *Northern France
  *Rhineland
  *Ardennes-Alsace
  *Central Europe

Vietnam
  *Counteroffensive, Phase II
  *Counteroffensive, Phase III
  *Tet Counteroffensive
  (other campaigns to be determined)

DECORATIONS

*Presidential Unit Citation (Army), Streamer embroidered HURTGEN FOREST (22d Infantry cited; WD GO 37, 1946)

*Presidential Unit Citation (Army), Streamer embroidered ST. GILLIS-MARIGNY (22d Infantry cited; WD GO 14, 1945)

Presidential Unit Citation (Army), Streamer embroidered CARENTAN

*Presidential Unit Citation (Army), Streamer embroidered SUOI TRE, VIETNAM (3d Battalion [less Company C], 22d Infantry cited; DA GO 59, 1968)

*Valorous Unit Award, Streamer embroidered TAY NINH PROVINCE (3d Battalion, 22d Infantry cited; DA GO 42, 1969)

*Belgian Fourragere 1940 (22d Infantry cited; DA GO 43, 1950)

*Cited in the Order of the Day of the Belgian Army for action in BELGIUM (22d Infantry cited; DA GO 43, 1950)

*Cited in the Order of the Day of the Belgian Army for action in the ARDENNES (22d Infantry cited; DA GO 43, 1950)

*Vietnamese Cross of Gallantry with Palm, Streamer embroidered VIETNAM 1966–1967 (3d Battalion, 22d Infantry cited; DA GO 3, 1970, as amended by DA GO 48, 1971)

*Vietnamese Cross of Gallantry with Palm, Streamer embroidered VIETNAM 1967–1968 (3d Battalion, 22d Infantry cited; DA GO 48, 1971)

22D INFANTRY, BIBLIOGRAPHY

Blumenson, Martin. *Breakout and Pursuit*. United States Army in World War II. Washington: Government Printing Office, 1961.

Boice, William S. *History of the Twenty-second United States Infantry in World War II*. Phoenix, 1959?

Cole, Hugh M. *The Ardennes: Battle of the Bulge*. United States Army in World War II. Washington: Government Printing Office, 1964.

Harrison, Gordon A. *Cross-Channel Attack*. United States Army in World War II. Washington: Government Printing Office, 1951.

Historical Section, War Department. *Utah Beach to Cherbourg*. American Forces in Action Series. Washington: Government Printing Office, 1947.

History of the 4th Infantry Division and Brief Histories of Its Components. Fort Lewis, Washington, 1958.

MacDonald, Charles B. *The Battle of Huertgen Forest*. Philadelphia and New York: J. B. Lippincott Company, 1963.

————. *The Siegfried Line Campaign*. United States Army in World War II. Washington: Government Printing Office, 1963.

Palmer, John M. and William R. Smith. *History of the Twenty-second United States Infantry, 1866–1922*. New York?, 1922.

Skehan, William Francis. *Military Life of Private William Francis Skehan, Late of the United States Army*. Boston: Frank J. McQueeney, 1885. (Author served with the 22d Infantry from 1869 to 1879.)

Smith, Oskaloosa M. "The Twenty-second Regiment of Infantry," *The Army of the United States*, edited by Theophilus F. Rodenbough and William L. Haskin. New York: Maynard, Merrill and Company, 1896, pp. 680–691. (Originally published in the *Journal of the Military Service Institution of the United States*, XIII [1892], 1043–1054.)

Smith, Oskaloosa M. and R. L. Hamilton. *A History of the Twenty-second United States Infantry. Compiled from Official Sources*. Manila: E. C. McCullough and Company, Inc., 1904.

Trobriand, Philippe Regis Denis de Keredern de. *Army Life in Dakota, Selections from the Journal of Philippe Regis Denis de Keredern de Trobriand*. Translated by George Francis Will. Edited by Milo Milton Quaife. Chicago: Lakeside Press, 1941. (Originally published as *Vie Militaire dans le Dakota, Notes et Souvenirs*. Paris, 1926.)

"Twenty-second Infantry Regiment," *A Pictorial Record of the 4th Infantry Division*. Baton Rouge: Army and Navy Publishing Company, 1945.

23d INFANTRY

HERALDIC ITEMS

COAT OF ARMS

Shield: Party per chevron wavy azure and argent in dexter chief a cross pattée of the second in sinister chief a sea lion with sword in dexter paw of the like langued gules in base a northern hemisphere with a transport in each ocean both sailing from east to west, all proper.

Crest: On a wreath of the colors an Alaskan totem pole consisting of an eagle, a plate, and a bear, all proper. (And for informal use, encircled by a Fourragere in the colors of the French Croix de Guerre.)

Motto: We Serve.

Symbolism: The shield is blue and white, the present and old infantry colors. Civil War service is indicated by the white cross of the V Corps, and Philippine Insurrection service by the sea lion taken from the seal of Manila. The Mont Blanc operation of October 1918 in World War I is commemorated by the outline of the lower half of the shield. The 23d Infantry has the unique distinction of being the first American regiment to circumnavigate the globe and this is indicated in the base of the shield.

The 23d Infantry went to Alaska in 1867 to take over possession of the territory from the Russians. This is shown in the crest in true Alaskan Indian symbolism. The totem pole is composed of the bear, the old owner, and the eagle, the new owner, and between them is a plate. The bear gave a feast to the eagle when the new owner moved in. The French Fourragere authorized for informal use was awarded to the regiment for service in World War I.

DISTINCTIVE INSIGNIA

The distinctive insignia is the shield and motto of the coat of arms.

469

Lineage and Honors

Lineage

Constituted 3 May 1861 in the Regular Army as the 1st Battalion, 14th Infantry. Organized 8 July 1861 at Fort Trumbull, Connecticut. Redesignated 30 April 1862 as the 2d Battalion, 14th Infantry. Reorganized and redesignated 21 September 1866 as the 23d Infantry. Assigned 22 September 1917 to the 2d Division (later redesignated as the 2d Infantry Division).

Relieved 20 June 1957 from assignment to the 2d Infantry Division and reorganized as a parent regiment under the Combat Arms Regimental System.

Campaign Participation Credit

Civil War
  Peninsula
  Manassas
  Antietam
  Fredericksburg
  Chancellorsville
  Gettysburg
  Wilderness
  Spotsylvania
  Cold Harbor
  Petersburg
  Virginia 1862
  Virginia 1863

Indian Wars
  Little Big Horn
  Arizona 1866
  Idaho 1868

War With Spain
  Manila

Philippine Insurrection
  Manila
  Malolos
  Mindanao
  Jolo
  Jolo 1903

World War I
  Aisne
  Aisne-Marne

  St. Mihiel
  Meuse-Argonne
  Lorraine 1918
  Ile de France 1918

World War II
  Normandy
  Northern France
  Rhineland
  Ardennes-Alsace
  Central Europe

Korean War
  UN defensive
  UN offensive
  CCF intervention
  First UN counteroffensive
  CCF spring offensive
  UN summer-fall offensive
  Second Korean winter
  Korea, summer-fall 1952
  Third Korean winter
  Korea, summer 1953

Vietnam
  Counteroffensive
  Counteroffensive, Phase II
  Counteroffensive, Phase III
  Tet Counteroffensive
  (other campaigns to be determined)

DECORATIONS

Presidential Unit Citation (Army), Streamer embroidered WIRTZ-FELD, BELGIUM (1st Battalion, 23d Infantry cited; WD GO 109, 1945)

Presidential Unit Citation (Army), Streamer embroidered ST. VITH (2d Battalion, 23d Infantry cited; WD GO 109, 1945)

Presidential Unit Citation (Army), Streamer embroidered KRINKEL-TER WALD, BELGIUM (3d Battalion, 23d Infantry cited; WD GO 58, 1945)

Presidential Unit Citation (Army), Streamer embroidered BREST, FRANCE (3d Battalion, 23d Infantry cited; WD GO 15, 1945)

Presidential Unit Citation (Army), Streamer embroidered TWIN TUNNELS (3d Battalion, 23d Infantry cited; DA GO 36, 1951)

Presidential Unit Citation (Army), Streamer embroidered CHIPYONG-NI (23d Infantry cited; DA GO 49, 1951)

Presidential Unit Citation (Army), Streamer embroidered HONGCHON (2d Infantry Division cited; DA GO 72, 1951)

Valorous Unit Award, Streamer embroidered TAY NINH PROVINCE (4th Battalion, 23d Infantry cited; DA GO 42, 1969)

Valorous Unit Award, Streamer embroidered SAIGON (4th Battalion, 23d Infantry cited; DA GO 43, 1970)

French Croix de Guerre with Palm, World War I, Streamer embroidered AISNE-MARNE (23d Infantry cited; WD GO 11, 1924)

French Croix de Guerre with Palm, World War I, Streamer embroidered MEUSE-ARGONNE (23d Infantry cited; WD GO 11, 1924)

French Croix de Guerre with Palm, World War I, Streamer embroidered CHATEAU THIERRY (23d Infantry cited; WD GO 11, 1924)

French Croix de Guerre, World War I, Fourragere (23d Infantry cited; WD GO 11, 1924)

Republic of Korea Presidential Unit Citation, Streamer embroidered NAKTONG RIVER LINE (23d Infantry cited; DA GO 35, 1951)

Republic of Korea Presidential Unit Citation, Streamer embroidered KOREA 1950–1953 (23d Infantry cited; DA GO 10, 1954)

Republic of Korea Presidential Unit Citation, Streamer embroidered KOREA 1952–1953 (23d Infantry cited; DA GO 24, 1954)

Belgian Fourragere 1940 (23d Infantry cited; DA GO 43, 1950)

Cited in the Order of the Day of the Belgian Army for action in the ARDENNES (23d Infantry cited; DA GO 43, 1950)

Cited in the Order of the Day of the Belgian Army for action at ELSENBORN CREST (23d Infantry cited; DA GO 43, 1950)

1st BATTALION, 23d INFANTRY

RA

(2d Infantry Division)

LINEAGE

Constituted 3 May 1861 in the Regular Army as Company A, 1st Battalion, 14th Infantry. Organized 8 July 1861 at Fort Trumbull, Connecticut. Redesignated 30 April 1862 as Company A, 2d Battalion, 14th Infantry. Reorganized and redesignated 21 September 1866 as Company A, 23d Infantry. (23d Infantry assigned 22 September 1917 to the 2d Division [later redesignated as the 2d Infantry Division].)

Reorganized and redesignated 20 June 1957 as Headquarters and Headquarters Company, 1st Battle Group, 23d Infantry and remained assigned to the 2d Infantry Division (organic elements concurrently constituted and activated). Relieved 16 December 1957 from assignment to the 2d Infantry Division. Reorganized and redesignated 25 January 1963 as the 1st Battalion, 23d Infantry; concurrently, assigned to the 2d Infantry Division.

472

CAMPAIGN PARTICIPATION CREDIT

Civil War
- *Peninsula
- *Manassas
- *Antietam
- *Fredericksburg
- Chancellorsville
- Gettysburg
- Wilderness
- Spotsylvania
- Cold Harbor
- Petersburg
- *Virginia 1862
- Virginia 1863

Indian Wars
- Little Big Horn
- Arizona 1866
- *Idaho 1868

War With Spain
- Manila

Philippine Insurrection
- Manila
- *Malolos
- *Mindanao
- Jolo
- Jolo 1903

World War I
- *Aisne
- *Aisne-Marne
- *St. Mihiel
- *Meuse-Argonne
- *Lorraine 1918
- *Ile de France 1918

World War II
- *Normandy
- *Northern France
- *Rhineland
- *Ardennes-Alsace
- *Central Europe

Korean War
- *UN defensive
- *UN offensive
- *CCF intervention
- *First UN counteroffensive
- *CCF spring offensive
- *UN summer-fall offensive
- *Second Korean winter
- *Korea, summer-fall 1952
- *Third Korean winter
- *Korea, summer 1953

DECORATIONS

*Presidential Unit Citation (Army), Streamer embroidered WIRTZ-FELD, BELGIUM (1st Battalion, 23d Infantry cited; WD GO 109, 1945)

Presidential Unit Citation (Army), Streamer embroidered ST. VITH

Presidential Unit Citation (Army), Streamer embroidered KRINKEL-TER WALD, BELGIUM

Presidential Unit Citation (Army), Streamer embroidered BREST, FRANCE

Presidential Unit Citation (Army), Streamer embroidered TWIN TUNNELS

*Presidential Unit Citation (Army), Streamer embroidered CHIPYONG-NI (23d Infantry cited; DA GO 49, 1951)

*Presidential Unit Citation (Army), Streamer embroidered HONG-CHON (2d Infantry Division cited; DA GO 72, 1951)

*French Croix de Guerre with Palm, World War I, Streamer embroidered AISNE-MARNE (23d Infantry cited; WD GO 11, 1924)

*French Croix de Guerre with Palm, World War I, Streamer embroidered MEUSE-ARGONNE (23d Infantry cited; WD GO 11, 1924)

*French Croix de Guerre with Palm, World War I, Streamer embroidered CHATEAU THIERRY (23d Infantry cited; WD GO 11, 1924)

*French Croix de Guerre, World War I, Fourragere (23d Infantry cited; WD GO 11, 1924)

*Republic of Korea Presidential Unit Citation, Streamer embroidered NAKTONG RIVER LINE (23d Infantry cited; DA GO 35, 1951)

*Republic of Korea Presidential Unit Citation, Streamer embroidered KOREA 1950–1952 (1st Battalion, 23d Infantry cited; DA GO 33, 1953, as amended by DA GO 41, 1955)

*Republic of Korea Presidential Unit Citation, Streamer embroidered KOREA 1950–1953 (23d Infantry cited; DA GO 10, 1954)

*Republic of Korea Presidential Unit Citation, Streamer embroidered KOREA 1952–1953 (23d Infantry cited; DA GO 24, 1954)

*Belgian Fourragere 1940 (23d Infantry cited; DA GO 43, 1950)

*Cited in the Order of the Day of the Belgian Army for action in the ARDENNES (23d Infantry cited; DA GO 43, 1950)

*Cited in the Order of the Day of the Belgian Army for action at ELSENBORN CREST (23d Infantry cited; DA GO 43, 1950)

2d BATTALION, 23d INFANTRY

RA

(2d Infantry Division)

LINEAGE

Constituted 3 May 1861 in the Regular Army as Company B, 1st Battalion, 14th Infantry. Organized 8 July 1861 at Fort Trumbull, Connecticut. Redesignated 30 April 1862 as Company B, 2d Battalion, 14th Infantry. Reorganized and redesignated 21 September 1866 as Company B, 23d Infantry. (23d Infantry assigned 22 September 1917 to the 2d Division [later redesignated as the 2d Infantry Division].)

Inactivated 20 June 1957 in Alaska and relieved from assignment to the 2d Infantry Division; concurrently, redesignated as Headquarters and Headquarters Company, 2d Battle Group, 23d Infantry. (Organic elements constituted 4 March 1958.) Assigned 17 March 1958 to the 2d Infantry Division. Battle Group activated 14 June 1958 at Fort Benning, Georgia. Reorganized and redesignated 1 February 1963 as the 2d Battalion, 23d Infantry.

475

Campaign Participation Credit

Civil War
  *Peninsula
  *Manassas
  *Antietam
  *Fredericksburg
  Chancellorsville
  Gettysburg
  Wilderness
  Spotsylvania
  Cold Harbor
  Petersburg
  *Virginia 1862
  Virginia 1863

Indian Wars
  Little Big Horn
  Arizona 1866
  Idaho 1868

War With Spain
  *Manila

Philippine Insurrection
  *Manila
  *Malolos
  Mindanao
  Jolo
  *Jolo 1903

World War I
  *Aisne
  *Aisne-Marne
  *St. Mihiel
  *Meuse-Argonne
  *Lorraine 1918
  *Ile de France 1918

World War II
  *Normandy
  *Northern France
  *Rhineland
  *Ardennes-Alsace
  *Central Europe

Korean War
  *UN defensive
  *UN offensive
  *CCF intervention
  *First UN counteroffensive
  *CCF spring offensive
  *UN summer-fall offensive
  *Second Korean winter
  *Korea, summer-fall 1952
  *Third Korean winter
  *Korea, summer 1953

Decorations

*Presidential Unit Citation (Army), Streamer embroidered WIRTZ-FELD, BELGIUM (1st Battalion, 23d Infantry cited; WD GO 109, 1945)

Presidential Unit Citation (Army), Streamer embroidered ST. VITH

Presidential Unit Citation (Army), Streamer embroidered KRINKEL-TER WALD, BELGIUM

Presidential Unit Citation (Army), Streamer embroidered BREST, FRANCE

Presidential Unit Citation (Army), Streamer embroidered TWIN TUNNELS

*Presidential Unit Citation (Army), Streamer embroidered CHIPYONG-NI (23d Infantry cited; DA GO 49, 1951)

*Presidential Unit Citation (Army), Streamer embroidered HONG-CHON (2d Infantry Division cited; DA GO 72, 1951)

*French Croix de Guerre with Palm, World War I, Streamer embroidered AISNE-MARNE (23d Infantry cited; WD GO 11, 1924)

*French Croix de Guerre with Palm, World War I, Streamer embroidered MEUSE-ARGONNE (23d Infantry cited; WD GO 11, 1924)

*French Croix de Guerre with Palm, World War I, Streamer embroidered CHATEAU THIERRY (23d Infantry cited; WD GO 11, 1924)

*French Croix de Guerre, World War I, Fourragere (23d Infantry cited; WD GO 11, 1924)

*Republic of Korea Presidential Unit Citation, Streamer embroidered NAKTONG RIVER LINE (23d Infantry cited; DA GO 35, 1951)

*Republic of Korea Presidential Unit Citation, Streamer embroidered KOREA 1950–1952 (1st Battalion, 23d Infantry cited; DA GO 33, 1953, as amended by DA GO 41, 1955)

*Republic of Korea Presidential Unit Citation, Streamer embroidered KOREA 1950–1953 (23d Infantry cited; DA GO 10, 1954)

*Republic of Korea Presidential Unit Citation, Streamer embroidered KOREA 1952–1953 (23d Infantry cited; DA GO 24, 1954)

*Belgian Fourragere 1940 (23d Infantry cited; DA GO 43, 1950)

*Cited in the Order of the Day of the Belgian Army for action in the ARDENNES (23d Infantry cited; DA GO 43, 1950)

*Cited in the Order of the Day of the Belgian Army for action at ELSENBORN CREST (23d Infantry cited; DA GO 43, 1950)

3d BATTALION, 23d INFANTRY

RA

(2d Infantry Division)

LINEAGE

Constituted 3 May 1861 in the Regular Army as Company C, 1st Battalion, 14th Infantry. Organized 8 July 1861 at Fort Trumbull, Connecticut. Redesignated 30 April 1862 as Company C, 2d Battalion, 14th Infantry. Reorganized and redesignated 21 September 1866 as Company C, 23d Infantry. (23d Infantry assigned 22 September 1917 to the 2d Division [later redesignated as the 2d Infantry Division].)

Inactivated 20 June 1957 in Alaska and relieved from assignment to the 2d Infantry Division; concurrently, redesignated as Headquarters and Headquarters Company, 3d Battle Group, 23d Infantry. Withdrawn 19 March 1959 from the Regular Army, allotted to the Army Reserve, and assigned to the 90th Infantry Division (organic elements concurrently constituted). Battle Group activated 1 April 1959 with Headquarters at Harlingen, Texas. Inactivated 27 March 1963 at Harlingen, Texas; concurrently, relieved from assignment to the 90th Infantry Division.

Redesignated 1 July 1965 as the 3d Battalion, 23d Infantry; concurrently, withdrawn from the Army Reserve, allotted to the Regular Army, assigned to the 2d Infantry Division, and activated in Korea.

478

CAMPAIGN PARTICIPATION CREDIT

Civil War
  *Peninsula
  *Manassas
  *Antietam
  *Fredericksburg
  Chancellorsville
  Gettysburg
  Wilderness
  Spotsylvania
  Cold Harbor
  Petersburg
  *Virginia 1862
  Virginia 1863

Indian Wars
  *Little Big Horn
  *Arizona 1866
  *Oregon 1866
  Idaho 1868

War With Spain
  *Manila

Philippine Insurrection
  *Manila
  *Malolos
  *Mindanao
  Jolo
  Jolo 1903

World War I
  *Aisne
  *Aisne-Marne
  *St. Mihiel
  *Meuse-Argonne
  *Lorraine 1918
  *Ile de France 1918

World War II
  *Normandy
  *Northern France
  *Rhineland
  *Ardennes-Alsace
  *Central Europe

Korean War
  *UN defensive
  *UN offensive
  *CCF intervention
  *First UN counteroffensive
  *CCF spring offensive
  *UN summer-fall offensive
  *Second Korean winter
  *Korea, summer-fall 1952
  *Third Korean winter
  *Korea, summer 1953

DECORATIONS

*Presidential Unit Citation (Army), Streamer embroidered WIRTZ-FELD, BELGIUM (1st Battalion, 23d Infantry cited; WD GO 109, 1945)

Presidential Unit Citation (Army), Streamer embroidered ST. VITH

Presidential Unit Citation (Army), Streamer embroidered KRINKEL-TER WALD, BELGIUM

Presidential Unit Citation (Army), Streamer embroidered BREST, FRANCE

Presidential Unit Citation (Army), Streamer embroidered TWIN TUNNELS

*Presidential Unit Citation (Army), Streamer embroidered CHIPYONG-NI (23d Infantry cited; DA GO 49, 1951)

*Presidential Unit Citation (Army), Streamer embroidered HONG-CHON (2d Infantry Division cited; DA GO 72, 1951)

*French Croix de Guerre with Palm, World War I, Streamer embroidered AISNE-MARNE (23d Infantry cited; WD GO 11, 1924)

*French Croix de Guerre with Palm, World War I, Streamer em-

broidered MEUSE-ARGONNE (23d Infantry cited; WD GO 11, 1924)

*French Croix de Guerre with Palm, World War I, Streamer embroidered CHATEAU THIERRY (23d Infantry cited; WD GO 11, 1924)

*French Croix de Guerre, World War I, Fourragere (23d Infantry cited; WD GO 11, 1924)

*Republic of Korea Presidential Unit Citation, Streamer embroidered NAKTONG RIVER LINE (23d Infantry cited; DA GO 35, 1951)

*Republic of Korea Presidential Unit Citation, Streamer embroidered KOREA 1950–1952 (1st Battalion, 23d Infantry cited; DA GO 33, 1953, as amended by DA GO 41, 1955)

*Republic of Korea Presidential Unit Citation, Streamer embroidered KOREA 1950–1953 (23d Infantry cited; DA GO 10, 1954)

*Republic of Korea Presidential Unit Citation, Streamer embroidered KOREA 1952–1953 (23d Infantry cited; DA GO 24, 1954)

*Belgian Fourragere 1940 (23d Infantry cited; DA GO 43, 1950)

*Cited in the Order of the Day of the Belgian Army for action in the ARDENNES (23d Infantry cited; DA GO 43, 1950)

*Cited in the Order of the Day of the Belgian Army for action at ELSENBORN CREST (23d Infantry cited; DA GO 43, 1950)

4th BATTALION, 23d INFANTRY

RA
(25th Infantry Division)

LINEAGE

Constituted 3 May 1861 in the Regular Army as Company D, 1st Battalion, 14th Infantry. Organized 8 July 1861 at Fort Trumbull, Connecticut. Redesignated 30 April 1862 as Company D, 2d Battalion, 14th Infantry. Reorganized and redesignated 21 September 1866 as Company D, 23d Infantry. (23d Infantry assigned 22 September 1917 to the 2d Division [later redesignated as the 2d Infantry Division].)

Inactivated 20 June 1957 in Alaska and relieved from assignment to the 2d Infantry Division; concurrently, redesignated as Headquarters and Headquarters Company, 4th Battle Group, 23d Infantry. Activated 25 January 1963 in Alaska (organic elements concurrently constituted and activated). Assigned 20 May 1963 to the 172d Infantry Brigade. Reorganized and redesignated 1 July 1963 as the 4th Battalion, 23d Infantry. Relieved 14 January 1966 from assignment to the 172d Infantry Brigade and assigned to the 25th Infantry Division.

481

Campaign Participation Credit

Civil War
  *Peninsula
  *Manassas
  *Antietam
  *Fredericksburg
  Chancellorsville
  Gettysburg
  Wilderness
  Spotsylvania
  Cold Harbor
  Petersburg
  *Virginia 1862
  Virginia 1863

Indian Wars
  Little Big Horn
  *Arizona 1866
  *Idaho 1868

War With Spain
  *Manila

Philippine Insurrection
  Manila
  *Malolos
  Mindanao
  Jolo
  *Jolo 1903

World War I
  *Aisne
  *Aisne-Marne

*St. Mihiel
*Meuse-Argonne
*Lorraine 1918
*Ile de France 1918

World War II
  *Normandy
  *Northern France
  *Rhineland
  *Ardennes-Alsace
  *Central Europe

Korean War
  *UN defensive
  *UN offensive
  *CCF intervention
  *First UN counteroffensive
  *CCF spring offensive
  *UN summer-fall offensive
  *Second Korean winter
  *Korea, summer-fall 1952
  *Third Korean winter
  *Korea, summer 1953

Vietnam
  *Counteroffensive
  *Counteroffensive, Phase II
  *Counteroffensive, Phase III
  *Tet Counteroffensive
    (other campaigns to be determined)

Decorations

*Presidential Unit Citation (Army), Streamer embroidered WIRTZ-FELD, BELGIUM (1st Battalion, 23d Infantry cited; WD GO 109, 1945)

Presidential Unit Citation (Army), Streamer embroidered ST. VITH

Presidential Unit Citation (Army), Streamer embroidered KRINKEL-TER WALD, BELGIUM

Presidential Unit Citation (Army), Streamer embroidered BREST, FRANCE

Presidential Unit Citation (Army), Streamer embroidered TWIN TUNNELS

*Presidential Unit Citation (Army), Streamer embroidered CHIPYONG-NI (23d Infantry cited; DA GO 49, 1951)

*Presidential Unit Citation (Army), Streamer embroidered HONG-CHON (2d Infantry Division cited; DA GO 72, 1951)

*Valorous Unit Award, Streamer embroidered TAY NINH PROVINCE (4th Battalion, 23d Infantry cited; DA GO 42, 1969)

*Valorous Unit Award, Streamer embroidered SAIGON (4th Battalion, 23d Infantry cited; DA GO 43, 1970)

*French Croix de Guerre with Palm, World War I, Streamer embroidered AISNE-MARNE (23d Infantry cited; WD GO 11, 1924)

*French Croix de Guerre with Palm, World War I, Streamer embroidered MEUSE-ARGONNE (23d Infantry cited; WD GO 11, 1924)

*French Croix de Guerre with Palm, World War I, Streamer embroidered CHATEAU THIERRY (23d Infantry cited; WD GO 11, 1924)

*French Croix de Guerre, World War I, Fourragere (23d Infantry cited; WD GO 11, 1924)

*Republic of Korea Presidential Unit Citation, Streamer embroidered NAKTONG RIVER LINE (23d Infantry cited; DA GO 35, 1951)

*Republic of Korea Presidential Unit Citation, Streamer embroidered KOREA 1950–1952 (1st Battalion, 23d Infantry cited; DA GO 33, 1953, as amended by DA GO 41, 1955)

*Republic of Korea Presidential Unit Citation, Streamer embroidered KOREA 1950–1953 (23d Infantry cited; DA GO 10, 1954)

*Republic of Korea Presidential Unit Citation, Streamer embroidered KOREA 1952–1953 (23d Infantry cited; DA GO 24, 1954)

*Belgian Fourragere 1940 (23d Infantry cited; DA GO 43, 1950)

*Cited in the Order of the Day of the Belgian Army for action in the ARDENNES (23d Infantry cited; DA GO 43, 1950)

*Cited in the Order of the Day of the Belgian Army for action at ELSENBORN CREST (23d Infantry cited; DA GO 43, 1950)

*Vietnamese Cross of Gallantry with Palm, Streamer embroidered VIETNAM 1966–1968 (4th Battalion, 23d Infantry cited; DA GO 48, 1971)

5th BATTALION, 23d INFANTRY

RA
(172d Infantry Brigade)

LINEAGE

Constituted 3 May 1861 in the Regular Army as Company E, 1st Battalion, 14th Infantry. Organized 8 July 1861 at Fort Trumbull, Connecticut. Redesignated 30 April 1862 as Company E, 2d Battalion, 14th Infantry. Reorganized and redesignated 21 September 1866 as Company E, 23d Infantry. (23d Infantry assigned 22 September 1917 to the 2d Division [later redesignated as the 2d Infantry Division].)

Inactivated 20 June 1957 in Alaska and relieved from assignment to the 2d Infantry Division; concurrently, redesignated as Headquarters and Headquarters Company, 5th Battle Group, 23d Infantry. Redesignated 17 December 1965 as Headquarters and Headquarters Company, 5th Battalion, 23d Infantry and assigned to the 172d Infantry Brigade (organic elements concurrently constituted). Battalion activated 20 December 1965 in Alaska.

484

CAMPAIGN PARTICIPATION CREDIT

Civil War
  *Peninsula
  *Manassas
  *Antietam
  *Fredericksburg
  Chancellorsville
  Gettysburg
  Wilderness
  Spotsylvania
  Cold Harbor
  Petersburg
  *Virginia 1862
  Virginia 1863

Indian Wars
  Little Big Horn
  Arizona 1866
  *Idaho 1868

War With Spain
  *Manila

Philippine Insurrection
  *Manila
  *Malolos
  Mindanao
  Jolo
  Jolo 1903

World War I
  *Aisne
  *Aisne-Marne
  *St. Mihiel
  *Meuse-Argonne
  *Lorraine 1918
  *Ile de France 1918

World War II
  *Normandy
  *Northern France
  *Rhineland
  *Ardennes-Alsace
  *Central Europe

Korean War
  *UN defensive
  *UN offensive
  *CCF intervention
  *First UN counteroffensive
  *CCF spring offensive
  *UN summer-fall offensive
  *Second Korean winter
  *Korea, summer-fall 1952
  *Third Korean winter
  *Korea, summer 1953

DECORATIONS

Presidential Unit Citation (Army), Streamer embroidered WIRTZ-FELD, BELGIUM

*Presidential Unit Citation (Army), Streamer embroidered ST. VITH (2d Battalion, 23d Infantry cited; WD GO 109, 1945)

Presidential Unit Citation (Army), Streamer embroidered KRINKEL-TER WALD, BELGIUM

Presidential Unit Citation (Army), Streamer embroidered BREST, FRANCE

Presidential Unit Citation (Army), Streamer embroidered TWIN TUNNELS

*Presidential Unit Citation (Army), Streamer embroidered CHIPYONG-NI (23d Infantry cited; DA GO 49, 1951)

*Presidential Unit Citation (Army), Streamer embroidered HONG-CHON (2d Infantry Division cited; DA GO 72, 1951)

*French Croix de Guerre with Palm, World War I, Streamer embroidered AISNE-MARNE (23d Infantry cited; WD GO 11, 1924)

*French Croix de Guerre with Palm, World War I, Streamer em-

broidered MEUSE-ARGONNE (23d Infantry cited; WD GO 11, 1924)

*French Croix de Guerre with Palm, World War I, Streamer embroidered CHATEAU THIERRY (23d Infantry cited; WD GO 11, 1924)

*French Croix de Guerre, World War I, Fourragere (23d Infantry cited; WD GO 11, 1924)

*Republic of Korea Presidential Unit Citation, Streamer embroidered NAKTONG RIVER LINE (23d Infantry cited; DA GO 35, 1951)

*Republic of Korea Presidential Unit Citation, Streamer embroidered KOREA 1950–1953 (23d Infantry cited; DA GO 10, 1954)

*Republic of Korea Presidential Unit Citation, Streamer embroidered KOREA 1952–1953 (23d Infantry cited; DA GO 24, 1954)

*Belgian Fourragere 1940 (23d Infantry cited; DA GO 43, 1950)

*Cited in the Order of the Day of the Belgian Army for action in the ARDENNES (23d Infantry cited; DA GO 43, 1950)

*Cited in the Order of the Day of the Belgian Army for action at ELSENBORN CREST (23d Infantry cited; DA GO 43, 1950)

COMPANY F, 23d INFANTRY

RA
(inactive)

LINEAGE

Constituted 3 May 1861 in the Regular Army as Company F, 1st Battalion, 14th Infantry. Organized 8 July 1861 at Fort Trumbull, Connecticut. Redesignated 30 April 1862 as Company F, 2d Battalion, 14th Infantry. Reorganized and redesignated 21 September 1866 as Company F, 23d Infantry. (23d Infantry assigned 22 September 1917 to the 2d Division [later redesignated as the 2d Infantry Division].)

Inactivated 20 June 1957 in Alaska and relieved from assignment to the 2d Infantry Division; concurrently, redesignated as Headquarters and Headquarters Company, 6th Battle Group, 23d Infantry. Redesignated 23 September 1963 as Company F, 23d Infantry. Activated 24 September 1963 in Korea. Inactivated 1 January 1966 in Korea.

CAMPAIGN PARTICIPATION CREDIT

Civil War
Peninsula
Manassas
Antietam
Fredericksburg
Chancellorsville
Gettysburg
Virginia 1862

War With Spain
Manila

Philippine Insurrection
Malolos

World War I
Aisne
Aisne-Marne
St. Mihiel
Meuse-Argonne

Lorraine 1918
Ile de France 1918

World War II-EAME
Normandy
Northern France
Rhineland
Ardennes-Alsace
Central Europe

Korean War
UN defensive
UN offensive
CCF intervention
First UN counteroffensive
CCF spring offensive
UN summer-fall offensive
Second Korean winter
Korea, summer-fall 1952
Third Korean winter
Korea, summer 1953

DECORATIONS

Presidential Unit Citation (Army), Streamer embroidered ST. VITH (2d Battalion, 23d Infantry cited; WD GO 109, 1945)

487

Presidential Unit Citation (Army), Streamer embroidered CHIPYONG-NI (23d Infantry cited; DA GO 49, 1951)

Presidential Unit Citation (Army), Streamer embroidered HONGCHON (2d Infantry Division cited; DA GO 72, 1951)

French Croix de Guerre with Palm, World War I, Streamer embroidered AISNE-MARNE (23d Infantry cited; WD GO 11, 1924)

French Croix de Guerre with Palm, World War I, Streamer embroidered MEUSE-ARGONNE (23d Infantry cited; WD GO 11, 1924)

French Croix de Guerre with Palm, World War I, Streamer embroidered CHATEAU THIERRY (23d Infantry cited; WD GO 11, 1924)

French Croix de Guerre, World War I, Fourragere (23d Infantry cited; WD GO 11, 1924)

Republic of Korea Presidential Unit Citation, Streamer embroidered NAKTONG RIVER LINE (23d Infantry cited; DA GO 35, 1951)

Republic of Korea Presidential Unit Citation, Streamer embroidered KOREA 1950–1953 (23d Infantry cited; DA GO 10, 1954)

Republic of Korea Presidential Unit Citation, Streamer embroidered KOREA 1952–1953 (23d Infantry cited; DA GO 24, 1954)

Belgian Fourragere 1940 (23d Infantry cited; DA GO 43, 1950)

Cited in the Order of the Day of the Belgian Army for action in the ARDENNES (23d Infantry cited; DA GO 43, 1950)

Cited in the Order of the Day of the Belgian Army for action at ELSENBORN CREST (23d Infantry cited; DA GO 43, 1950)

23d Infantry, Bibliography

"B" Company in Action—23d Infantry Regiment. Germany, 1919.

Blumenson, Martin. *Breakout and Pursuit.* United States Army in World War II. Washington: Government Printing Office, 1961.

Casson, Melvin H. *The Twenty-third United States Infantry, 1812–1945.* Czechoslovakia, 1947. (Erroneously connects this regiment with an earlier one of the same designation.)

Cole, Hugh M. *The Ardennes: Battle of the Bulge.* United States Army in World War II. Washington: Government Printing Office, 1964.

Harrison, Gordon A. *Cross-Channel Attack.* United States Army in World War II. Washington: Government Printing Office, 1951.

Historical Section, War Department. *Omaha Beachhead.* American Forces in Action Series. Washington: Government Printing Office, 1945.

————. *St. Lô.* American Forces in Action Series. Washington: Government Printing Office, 1946.

————. *To Bizerte with the II Corps.* American Forces in Action Series. Washington: Government Printing Office, 1943.

Hunt, George Alfred. *Over and Back.* Battle Creek, Michigan, 1919.

————. *"With the Twenty-third in France."* Menasha, Wisconsin, 1919.

MacDonald, Charles B. *Company Commander.* Washington: Infantry Journal Press, 1947.

Marshall, S. L. A. *The River and the Gauntlet.* New York: William Morrow and Company, 1953.

Martin, Harold H. "The Two Terrible Nights of the 23rd," *Saturday Evening Post* (19 May 1951), 22ff.

McCrossen, Bernard J. *Diary of the Machine Gun Company, 23d Infantry, Second Division, 1917–1919.* Vallendar-Rhine: Hartmann Brothers, 1919.

Reade, Philip. "Chronicle of the Twenty-third Regiment of Infantry, USA," *Journal of the Military Service Institution of the United States,* XXXV (1904), 419–427.

Thompson, James Kaster. "The Twenty-third Regiment of Infantry," *The Army of the United States,* edited by Theophilus F. Rodenbough and William L. Haskin. New York: Maynard, Merrill and Company, 1896, pp. 692–694. (Originally published in the *Journal of the Military Service Institution of the United States,* XV [1894], 1118–1120.)

The Twenty-third, 1812–1945, United States Infantry. Pilsen, 1945. (Erroneously connects this regiment with an earlier one of the same designation.)

23d Infantry Regiment, Fort Lewis, Washington. Baton Rouge: Army

and Navy Publishing Company, 1947.
Wilkinson, Allen Byron. *Up Front Korea*. New York: Vantage Press, 1967.

26th INFANTRY

HERALDIC ITEMS

COAT OF ARMS

Shield: Argent, a royal palm branch paleways proper, on a chief embattled azure five Mohawk arrowheads of the first. (And for informal use, the shield encircled by a Fourragere in the colors of the French Croix de Guerre.)

Crest: On a wreath of the colors a sun in splendor charged with a Mohawk arrowhead azure.

Motto: *Palmam Qui Meruit Ferat* (Let Him Bear the Palm Who Has Won It).

Symbolism: The shield is white with a blue chief, the old and the present infantry colors. The dividing line embattled stands for the entrenchments which the regiment has so many times assaulted. The Mohawk arrowhead was the regimental insignia during World War I. It was selected by Colonel Hamilton A. Smith as indicating the American virtues and the regimental spirit of courage, resourceful daring, and relentless pursuit of an enemy. Colonel Smith was killed while leading the regiment in the first great offensive in which it took part. The arrow is repeated five times because in five major offensives the regiment exhibited these qualities indicated by the badge which it had adopted and by which it was designated during these engagements. The palm of victory displayed on the shield and the motto refer to the only award the regiment seeks.

The arrowhead is repeated in the crest to indicate the same regimental spirit under all conditions. The sun, taken from the Katipunan flag, symbolizes service in the Philippine Insurrection.

DISTINCTIVE INSIGNIA

The distinctive insignia is the characteristic device of the regiment, an Indian arrowhead, in blue, displayed on a white shield.

Lineage and Honors

Lineage

Constituted 2 February 1901 in the Regular Army as the 26th Infantry. Organized 22 February 1901 with Headquarters at Fort McPherson, Georgia. (1st Battalion organized in December 1900 at the Presidio of San Francisco, California, as the 1st Provisional Battalion of Infantry; redesignated 7 February 1901 as the 1st Battalion, 26th Infantry. 2d Battalion organized March–April 1901 at Fort McPherson, Georgia; redesignated 29 May 1901 as the 1st Battalion, 27th Infantry—hereafter separate lineage; new 2d Battalion, 26th Infantry organized 1 July 1901 in the Philippine Islands. 3d Battalion organized in January 1901 at the Presidio of San Francisco, California, as the 2d Provisional Battalion of Infantry; redesignated 8 February 1901 as the 1st Battalion, 27th Infantry; redesignated 29 May 1901 as the 3d Battalion, 26th Infantry.) Regiment assigned 8 June 1917 to the 1st Expeditionary Division (later redesignated as the 1st Infantry Division).

Relieved 15 February 1957 from assignment to the 1st Infantry Division and reorganized as a parent regiment under the Combat Arms Regimental System.

Campaign Participation Credit

Philippine Insurrection
Without inscription

World War I
Montdidier-Noyon
Aisne-Marne
St. Mihiel
Meuse-Argonne
Lorraine 1917
Lorraine 1918
Picardy 1918

World War II
Algeria-French Morocco
(with arrowhead)

Tunisia
Sicily (with arrowhead)
Normandy (with arrowhead)
Northern France
Rhineland
Ardennes-Alsace
Central Europe

Vietnam
Defense
Counteroffensive
Counteroffensive, Phase II
Counteroffensive, Phase III
Tet Counteroffensive
(other campaigns to be determined)

Decorations

Presidential Unit Citation (Army), Streamer embroidered STOLBERG (1st Battalion, 26th Infantry cited; WD GO 42, 1945)

Valorous Unit Award, Streamer embroidered AP GU (1st Battalion, 26th Infantry cited; DA GO 36, 1970)

French Croix de Guerre with Palm, World War I, Streamer embroidered AISNE-MARNE (26th Infantry cited; WD GO 11, 1924)

French Croix de Guerre with Palm, World War I, Streamer embroidered MEUSE-ARGONNE (26th Infantry cited; WD GO 11, 1924)

French Croix de Guerre with Palm, World War II, Streamer embroidered KASSERINE (26th Infantry cited; DA GO 43, 1950)

French Croix de Guerre with Palm, World War II, Streamer embroidered NORMANDY (26th Infantry cited; DA GO 43, 1950)

French Medaille Militaire, Streamer embroidered FRANCE (26th Infantry cited; DA GO 43, 1950)

French Medaille Militaire, Fourragere (26th Infantry cited; DA GO 43, 1950)

Belgian Fourragere 1940 (26th Infantry cited; DA GO 43, 1950)

Cited in the Order of the Day of the Belgian Army for action at MONS (26th Infantry cited; DA GO 43, 1950)

Cited in the Order of the Day of the Belgian Army for action at EUPEN-MALMEDY (26th Infantry cited; DA GO 43, 1950)

1st BATTALION, 26th INFANTRY

RA
(1st Infantry Division)

LINEAGE

Organized 25 December 1900 in the Regular Army at Model Camp, Presidio of San Francisco, California, as Company A, 1st Provisional Battalion of Infantry. Redesignated 7 February 1901 as Company A, 26th Infantry. (26th Infantry assigned 8 June 1917 to the 1st Expeditionary Division [later redesignated as the 1st Infantry Division].)

Reorganized and redesignated 15 February 1957 as Headquarters and Headquarters Company, 1st Battle Group, 26th Infantry and remained assigned to the 1st Infantry Division (organic elements concurrently constituted and activated). Relieved 14 April 1959 from assignment to the 1st Infantry Division and assigned to the 8th Infantry Division. Relieved 24 October 1962 from assignment to the 8th Infantry Division and assigned to the 2d Infantry Division. Relieved 15 February 1963 from assignment to the 2d Infantry Division and assigned to the 1st Infantry Division. Reorganized and redesignated 13 January 1964 as the 1st Battalion, 26th Infantry.

CAMPAIGN PARTICIPATION CREDIT

Philippine Insurrection
  *Without inscription

World War I
  *Montdidier-Noyon
  *Aisne-Marne
  *St. Mihiel
  *Meuse-Argonne
  *Lorraine 1917
  *Lorraine 1918
  *Picardy 1918

World War II
  *Algeria-French Morocco
    (with arrowhead)
  *Tunisia

*Sicily (with arrowhead)
*Normandy (with arrowhead)
*Northern France
*Rhineland
*Ardennes-Alsace
*Central Europe

Vietnam
  *Defense
  *Counteroffensive
  *Counteroffensive, Phase II
  *Counteroffensive, Phase III
  *Tet Counteroffensive
    (other campaigns to be determined)

DECORATIONS

*Presidential Unit Citation (Army), Streamer embroidered STOLBERG (1st Battalion, 26th Infantry cited; WD GO 42, 1945)

*Valorous Unit Award, Streamer embroidered AP GU (1st Battalion, 26th Infantry cited; DA GO 36, 1970)

*French Croix de Guerre with Palm, World War I, Streamer embroidered AISNE-MARNE (26th Infantry cited; WD GO 11, 1924)

*French Croix de Guerre with Palm, World War I, Streamer embroidered MEUSE-ARGONNE (26th Infantry cited; WD GO 11, 1924)

*French Croix de Guerre with Palm, World War II, Streamer embroidered KASSERINE (26th Infantry cited; DA GO 43, 1950)

*French Croix de Guerre with Palm, World War II, Streamer embroidered NORMANDY (26th Infantry cited; DA GO 43, 1950)

*French Medaille Militaire, Streamer embroidered FRANCE (26th Infantry cited; DA GO 43, 1950)

*French Medaille Militaire, Fourragere (26th Infantry cited; DA GO 43, 1950)

*Belgian Fourragere 1940 (26th Infantry cited; DA GO 43, 1950)

*Cited in the Order of the Day of the Belgian Army for action at MONS (26th Infantry cited; DA GO 43, 1950)

*Cited in the Order of the Day of the Belgian Army for action at EUPEN-MALMEDY (26th Infantry cited; DA GO 43, 1950)

*Vietnamese Cross of Gallantry with Palm, Streamer embroidered VIETNAM 1965–1968 (1st Battalion, 26th Infantry cited; DA GO 21, 1969)

*Vietnamese Civil Action Honor Medal, First Class, Streamer embroidered VIETNAM 1965–1970 (1st Battalion, 26th Infantry cited; DA GO 53, 1970)

2d BATTLE GROUP, 26th INFANTRY

RA
(inactive)

LINEAGE

Organized 28 December 1900 in the Regular Army at Model Camp, Presidio of San Francisco, California, as Company B, 1st Provisional Battalion of Infantry. Redesignated 7 February 1901 as Company B, 26th Infantry. (26th Infantry assigned 8 June 1917 to the 1st Expeditionary Division [later redesignated as the 1st Infantry Division].)

Inactivated 15 February 1957 at Fort Riley, Kansas, and relieved from assignment to the 1st Infantry Division; concurrently, redesignated as Headquarters and Headquarters Company, 2d Battle Group, 26th Infantry. Activated 1 February 1963 at Fort Riley, Kansas, and assigned to the 1st Infantry Division (organic elements concurrently constituted and activated). Inactivated 13 January 1964 at Fort Riley, Kansas, and relieved from assignment to the 1st Infantry Division.

CAMPAIGN PARTICIPATION CREDIT

Philippine Insurrection
*Without inscription

World War I
*Montdidier-Noyon
*Aisne-Marne
*St. Mihiel
*Meuse-Argonne
*Lorraine 1917
*Lorraine 1918
*Picardy 1918

World War II
*Algeria-French Morocco (with arrowhead)
*Tunisia
*Sicily (with arrowhead)
*Normandy (with arrowhead)
*Northern France
*Rhineland
*Ardennes-Alsace
*Central Europe

DECORATIONS

*Presidential Unit Citation (Army), Streamer embroidered STOLBERG (1st Battalion, 26th Infantry cited; WD GO 42, 1945)

*French Croix de Guerre with Palm, World War I, Streamer embroidered AISNE-MARNE (26th Infantry cited; WD GO 11, 1924)

*French Croix de Guerre with Palm, World War I, Streamer embroidered MEUSE-ARGONNE (26th Infantry cited; WD GO 11, 1924)

*French Croix de Guerre with Palm, World War II, Streamer embroidered KASSERINE (26th Infantry cited; DA GO 43, 1950)

*French Croix de Guerre with Palm, World War II, Streamer

embroidered NORMANDY (26th Infantry cited; DA GO 43, 1950)

*French Medaille Militaire, Streamer embroidered FRANCE (26th Infantry cited; DA GO 43, 1950)

*French Medaille Militaire, Fourragere (26th Infantry cited; DA GO 43, 1950)

*Belgian Fourragere 1940 (26th Infantry cited; DA GO 43, 1950)

*Cited in the Order of the Day of the Belgian Army for action at MONS (26th Infantry cited; DA GO 43, 1950)

*Cited in the Order of the Day of the Belgian Army for action at EUPEN-MALMEDY (26th Infantry cited; DA GO 43, 1950)

3d BATTALION, 26th INFANTRY

RA
(inactive)

LINEAGE

Organized 25 December 1900 in the Regular Army at Model Camp, Presidio of San Francisco, California, as Company C, 1st Provisional Battalion of Infantry. Redesignated 7 February 1901 as Company C, 26th Infantry. (26th Infantry assigned 8 June 1917 to the 1st Expeditionary Division [later redesignated as the 1st Infantry Division].)

Inactivated 15 February 1957 at Fort Riley, Kansas, and relieved from assignment to the 1st Infantry Division; concurrently, redesignated as Headquarters and Headquarters Company, 3d Battle Group, 26th Infantry. Withdrawn 7 April 1959 from the Regular Army, allotted to the Army Reserve, and assigned to the 77th Infantry Division (organic elements concurrently constituted) Battle Group activated 1 May 1959 with Headquarters at New York, New York. Inactivated 26 March 1963 at New York, New York; concurrently, relieved from assignment to the 77th Infantry Division.

Redesignated 10 May 1967 as the 3d Battalion, 26th Infantry; concurrently, withdrawn from the Army Reserve, allotted to the Regular Army, assigned to the 198th Infantry Brigade, and activated at Fort Hood, Texas. Inactivated 12 May 1967 at Fort Hood, Texas; concurrently, relieved from assignment to the 198th Infantry Brigade.

CAMPAIGN PARTICIPATION CREDIT

Philippine Insurrection
 *Without inscription

World War I
 *Montdidier-Noyon
 *Aisne-Marne
 *St. Mihiel
 *Meuse-Argonne
 *Lorraine 1917
 *Lorraine 1918
 *Picardy 1918

World War II
 *Algeria-French Morocco
  (with arrowhead)
 *Tunisia
 *Sicily (with arrowhead)
 *Normandy (with arrowhead)
 *Northern France
 *Rhineland
 *Ardennes-Alsace
 *Central Europe

DECORATIONS

*Presidential Unit Citation (Army), Streamer embroidered STOLBERG (1st Battalion, 26th Infantry cited; WD GO 42, 1945)

*French Croix de Guerre with Palm, World War I, Streamer embroidered AISNE-MARNE (26th Infantry cited; WD GO 11, 1924)

*French Croix de Guerre with Palm, World War I, Streamer embroidered MEUSE-ARGONNE (26th Infantry cited; WD GO 11, 1924)

*French Croix de Guerre with Palm, World War II, Streamer embroidered KASSERINE (26th Infantry cited; DA GO 43, 1950)

*French Croix de Guerre with Palm, World War II, Streamer embroidered NORMANDY (26th Infantry cited; DA GO 43, 1950)

*French Medaille Militaire, Streamer embroidered FRANCE (26th Infantry cited; DA GO 43, 1950)

*French Medaille Militaire, Fourragere (26th Infantry cited; DA GO 43, 1950)

*Belgian Fourragere 1940 (26th Infantry cited; DA GO 43, 1950)

*Cited in the Order of the Day of the Belgian Army for action at MONS (26th Infantry cited; DA GO 43, 1950)

*Cited in the Order of the Day of the Belgian Army for action at EUPEN-MALMEDY (26th Infantry cited; DA GO 43, 1950)

26TH INFANTRY, BIBLIOGRAPHY

Blumenson, Martin. *Breakout and Pursuit.* United States Army in World
    War II. Washington: Government Printing Office, 1961.
Carvey, James B. "Faid Pass," *Infantry Journal,* LV (September 1944),
    8–13.
Cole, Hugh M. *The Ardennes: Battle of the Bulge.* United States Army
    in World War II. Washington: Government Printing Office, 1964.
*52d Anniversary Day, 26th Infantry, Blue Spaders, Warner Barracks,
    Bamberg, Germany, October 9–10, 1953.* n.p., 1953.
48 Years of Duty, 26th Infantry Regiment, 1901–February 21st, 1949.
    Bamberg: Frankischer Tag, 1949.
Garland, Albert N. and Howard McGaw Smyth. *Sicily and the Surrender
    of Italy.* United States Army in World War II. Washington: Govern-
    ment Printing Office, 1965.
Harrison, Gordon A. *Cross-Channel Attack.* United States Army in World
    War II. Washington: Government Printing Office, 1951.
Historical Section, War Department. *To Bizerte with the II Corps.*
    American Forces in Action Series. Washington: Government Printing
    Office, 1943.
————. *Omaha Beachhead.* American Forces in Action Series. Washing-
    ton: Government Printing Office, 1945.
Howe, George F. *Northwest Africa: Seizing the Initiative in the West.*
    United States Army in World War II. Washington: Government
    Printing Office, 1957.
MacDonald, Charles B. *The Battle of Huertgen Forest.* Philadelphia and
    New York: J. B. Lippincott Company, 1963.
————. *The Siegfried Line Campaign.* United States Army in World
    War II. Washington: Government Printing Office, 1963.
Marshall, S. L. A. *Ambush.* New York: Cowles Book Company, 1969.
O'Donnell, James P. "They May Have to Fight the Whole Red Army,"
    Saturday Evening Post, CXXIII (11 August 1951), 26–27ff.
Regimental Adjutant. *The Twenty-sixth Infantry in France.* Montabauer-
    Frankfurt: Martin Flock and Company, 1919.

27th INFANTRY
(The Wolfhounds)

HERALDIC ITEMS

COAT OF ARMS

Shield: Argent the insignia of the Siberian American Expeditionary Force proper.

Crest: On a wreath of the colors two krises saltirewise gules, hilted or, in the upper angle a crescent argent.

Motto: *Nec Aspera Terrent* (Frightened by No Difficulties).

Symbolism: Service with the Siberian American Expeditionary Force is indicated by the charge on the shield, the shrapnel casc in blue outline with the blue polar bear seated. Fighting in the Philippine Insurrection, particularly in the Lake Lanao Expedition, is represented by the crest. The motto, "Frightened by No Difficulties," has been used by the regiment for many years.

DISTINCTIVE INSIGNIA

Badge: On a black oblong a wolf's head erased in gold above the motto, *Nec Aspera Terrent,* in gold letters. The wolf's head is a design developed as a result of the regiment's traditional designation, "The Wolfhounds." This designation was adopted by the 27th Infantry in commemoration of its service in Siberia.

LINEAGE AND HONORS

LINEAGE

Constituted 2 February 1901 in the Regular Army as the 27th Infantry. Organized 19 February 1901 with Headquarters at Plattsburg Barracks, New York. (1st Battalion organized in January 1901 at the Presidio of San Francisco, California, as the 2d Provisional Battalion of Infantry; redesignated 8 February 1901 as the 1st Battalion, 27th Infantry; redesignated 29 May 1901 as the 3d Battalion, 26th Infantry—hereafter separate lineage; concurrently, 2d Battalion, 26th Infantry [organized

March–April 1901 at Fort McPherson, Georgia] redesignated as new 1st Battalion, 27th Infantry. 2d and 3d Battalions organized April–July 1901 at Plattsburg Barracks, New York, and Fort McPherson, Georgia.) Regiment assigned 1 March 1921 to the Hawaiian Division. Relieved 26 August 1941 from assignment to the Hawaiian Division and assigned to the 25th Infantry Division.

Relieved 1 February 1957 from assignment to the 25th Infantry Division and reorganized as a parent regiment under the Combat Arms Regimental System.

CAMPAIGN PARTICIPATION CREDIT

Philippine Insurrection
  Mindanao

World War I
  Siberia 1918
  Siberia 1919

World War II
  Central Pacific
  Guadalcanal
  Northern Solomons (with arrowhead)
  Luzon

Korean War
  UN defensive
  UN offensive

CCF intervention
First UN counteroffensive
CCF spring offensive
UN summer-fall offensive
Second Korean winter
Korea, summer-fall 1952
Third Korean winter
Korea, summer 1953

Vietnam
  Counteroffensive
  Counteroffensive, Phase II
  Counteroffensive, Phase III
  Tet Counteroffensive
  (other campaigns to be determined)

DECORATIONS

Presidential Unit Citation (Army), Streamer embroidered TAEGU (27th Infantry [less Heavy Tank Company] cited; DA GO 49, 1951)

Presidential Unit Citation (Army), Streamer embroidered SANGNYONG-NI (27th Infantry [less Heavy Tank Company and 3d Battalion] cited; DA GO 72, 1951)

Presidential Unit Citation (Army), Streamer embroidered HAN RIVER (3d Battalion, 27th Infantry cited; DA GO 87, 1951)

Valorous Unit Award, Streamer embroidered CU CHI DISTRICT (1st and 2d Battalions, 27th Infantry cited; DA GO 20, 1967)

Valorous Unit Award, Streamer embroidered SAIGON (2d Battalion, 27th Infantry cited; DA GO 36, 1970)

Philippine Presidential Unit Citation, Streamer embroidered 17 OCTOBER 1944 TO 4 JULY 1945 (25th Infantry Division cited; DA GO 47, 1950)

Republic of Korea Presidential Unit Citation, Streamer embroidered MASAN-CHINJU (27th Infantry cited; DA GO 35, 1951)

Republic of Korea Presidential Unit Citation, Streamer embroidered MUNSAN-NI (27th Infantry cited; DA GO 19, 1955)

Republic of Korea Presidential Unit Citation, Streamer embroidered KOREA (27th Infantry cited; DA GO 33, 1953, as amended by DA GO 41, 1955)

1st BATTALION, 27th INFANTRY

(The Wolfhounds)

RA
(25th Infantry Division)

LINEAGE

Organized 6 March 1901 in the Regular Army at Fort McPherson, Georgia, as Company E, 26th Infantry. Redesignated 29 May 1901 as Company A, 27th Infantry. (27th Infantry assigned 1 March 1921 to the Hawaiian Division; relieved 26 August 1941 from assignment to the Hawaiian Division and assigned to the 25th Infantry Division.)

Reorganized and redesignated 1 February 1957 as Headquarters and Headquarters Company, 1st Battle Group, 27th Infantry and remained assigned to the 25th Infantry Division (organic elements concurrently constituted and activated). Reorganized and redesignated 26 August 1963 as the 1st Battalion, 27th Infantry.

CAMPAIGN PARTICIPATION CREDIT

Philippine Insurrection
  *Mindanao

World War I
  *Siberia 1918
  *Siberia 1919

World War II
  *Central Pacific
  *Guadalcanal
  *Northern Solomons (with arrowhead)
  *Luzon

Korean War
  *UN defensive
  *UN offensive

*CCF intervention
*First UN counteroffensive
*CCF spring offensive
*UN summer-fall offensive
*Second Korean winter
*Korea, summer-fall 1952
*Third Korean winter
*Korea, summer 1953

Vietnam
  *Counteroffensive
  *Counteroffensive, Phase II
  *Counteroffensive, Phase III
  *Tet Counteroffensive
    (other campaigns to be determined)

DECORATIONS

*Presidential Unit Citation (Army), Streamer embroidered TAEGU (27th Infantry [less Heavy Tank Company] cited; DA GO 49, 1951)

*Presidential Unit Citation (Army), Streamer embroidered SANGNYONG-NI (27th Infantry [less Heavy Tank Company and 3d Battalion] cited; **DA GO 72, 1951)**

Presidential Unit Citation (Army), Streamer embroidered HAN RIVER

*Valorous Unit Award, Streamer embroidered CU CHI DISTRICT (1st Battalion, 27th Infantry cited; DA GO 20, 1967)

*Philippine Presidential Unit Citation, Streamer embroidered 17 OCTOBER 1944 TO 4 JULY 1945 (25th Infantry Division cited; DA GO 47, 1950)

*Republic of Korea Presidential Unit Citation, Streamer embroidered MASAN-CHINJU (27th Infantry cited; DA GO 35, 1951)

*Republic of Korea Presidential Unit Citation, Streamer embroidered MUNSAN-NI (27th Infantry cited; DA GO 19, 1955)

*Republic of Korea Presidential Unit Citation, Streamer embroidered KOREA (27th Infantry cited; DA GO 33, 1953, as amended by DA GO 41, 1955)

*Vietnamese Cross of Gallantry with Palm, Streamer embroidered VIETNAM 1966–1968 (1st Battalion, 27th Infantry cited; DA GO 48, 1971)

2d BATTALION, 27th INFANTRY

(The Wolfhounds)

RA

(25th Infantry Division)

LINEAGE

Organized 18 March 1901 in the Regular Army at Fort McPherson, Georgia, as Company F, 26th Infantry. Redesignated 29 May 1901 as Company B, 27th Infantry. (27th Infantry assigned 1 March 1921 to the Hawaiian Division; relieved 26 August 1941 from assignment to the Hawaiian Division and assigned to the 25th Infantry Division.)

Inactivated 1 February 1957 in Hawaii and relieved from assignment to the 25th Infantry Division; concurrently, redesignated as Headquarters and Headquarters Company, 2d Battle Group, 27th Infantry. Redesignated 22 June 1960 as Company B, 27th Infantry. Activated 24 June 1960 in Korea. Inactivated 26 March 1962 in Korea. Redesignated 21 June 1963 as Headquarters and Headquarters Company, 2d Battalion, 27th Infantry and assigned to the 25th Infantry Division (organic elements concurrently constituted). Battalion activated 26 August 1963 in Hawaii.

CAMPAIGN PARTICIPATION CREDIT

Philippine Insurrection
*Mindanao

World War I
*Siberia 1918
*Siberia 1919

World War II
*Central Pacific
*Guadalcanal
*Northern Solomons (with arrowhead)
*Luzon

Korean War
*UN defensive
*UN offensive

*CCF intervention
*First UN counteroffensive
*CCF spring offensive
*UN summer-fall offensive
*Second Korean winter
*Korea, summer-fall 1952
*Third Korean winter
*Korea, summer 1953

Vietnam
*Counteroffensive
*Counteroffensive, Phase II
*Counteroffensive, Phase III
*Tet Counteroffensive
(other campaigns to be determined)

DECORATIONS

*Presidential Unit Citation (Army), Streamer embroidered TAEGU

506

(27th Infantry [less Heavy Tank Company] cited; DA GO 49, 1951)

*Presidential Unit Citation (Army), Streamer embroidered SANGNYONG-NI (27th Infantry [less Heavy Tank Company and 3d Battalion] cited; DA GO 72, 1951)

Presidential Unit Citation (Army), Streamer embroidered HAN RIVER

*Valorous Unit Award, Streamer embroidered CU CHI DISTRICT (2d Battalion, 27th Infantry cited; DA GO 20, 1967)

*Valorous Unit Award, Streamer embroidered SAIGON (2d Battalion, 27th Infantry cited; DA GO 36, 1970)

*Philippine Presidential Unit Citation, Streamer embroidered 17 OCTOBER 1944 TO 4 JULY 1945 (25th Infantry Division cited; DA GO 47, 1950)

*Republic of Korea Presidential Unit Citation, Streamer embroidered MASAN-CHINJU (27th Infantry cited; DA GO 35, 1951)

*Republic of Korea Presidential Unit Citation, Streamer embroidered MUNSAN-NI (27th Infantry cited; DA GO 19, 1955)

*Republic of Korea Presidential Unit Citation, Streamer embroidered KOREA (27th Infantry cited; DA GO 33, 1953, as amended by DA GO 41, 1955)

*Vietnamese Cross of Gallantry with Palm, Streamer embroidered VIETNAM 1966–1968 (2d Battalion, 27th Infantry cited; DA GO 48, 1971)

3d BATTALION, 27th INFANTRY

(The Wolfhounds)

RA
(inactive)

LINEAGE

Organized 26 March 1901 in the Regular Army at Fort McPherson, Georgia, as Company G, 26th Infantry. Redesignated 29 May 1901 as Company C, 27th Infantry. (27th Infantry assigned 1 March 1921 to the Hawaiian Division; relieved 26 August 1941 from assignment to the Hawaiian Division and assigned to the 25th Infantry Division.)

Inactivated 1 February 1957 in Hawaii and relieved from assignment to the 25th Infantry Division; concurrently, redesignated as Headquarters and Headquarters Company, 3d Battle Group, 27th Infantry. Withdrawn 31 March 1959 from the Regular Army, allotted to the Army Reserve, and assigned to the 63d Infantry Division (organic elements concurrently constituted). Battle Group activated 1 May 1959 with Headquarters at Los Angeles, California (concurrently, Headquarters and Headquarters Company consolidated with Headquarters and Headquarters Company, 255th Infantry [see ANNEX] and consolidated unit designated as Headquarters and Headquarters Company, 3d Battle Group, 27th Infantry).

Reorganized and redesignated 1 April 1963 as the 3d Battalion, 27th Infantry. Inactivated 31 December 1965 at Los Angeles, California, and relieved from assignment to the 63d Infantry Division. Withdrawn 6 December 1969 from the Army Reserve and allotted to the Regular Army; concurrently, activated in Hawaii as an element of the 25th Infantry Division. Inactivated 15 December 1970 in Hawaii.

ANNEX

Constituted 18 January 1943 in the Army of the United States as Headquarters and Headquarters Company, 255th Infantry, an element of the 63d Infantry Division. Activated 15 June 1943 at Camp Blanding, Florida. Inactivated 29 September 1945 at Camp Kilmer, New Jersey. (63d Infantry Division allotted 22 February 1952 to the Organized Reserve Corps.)

Activated 1 March 1952 at Los Angeles, California. (Organized Reserve Corps redesignated 9 July 1952 as the Army Reserve.) Consolidated 1 May 1959 with Headquarters and Headquarters Company, 3d Battle

Group, 27th Infantry and consolidated unit designated as Headquarters and Headquarters Company, 3d Battle Group, 27th Infantry (remainder of 255th Infantry inactivated) .

Campaign Participation Credit

Philippine Insurrection
  Mindanao

World War I
  *Siberia 1918
  *Siberia 1919

World War II
  *Central Pacific
  *Guadalcanal
  *Northern Solomons (with arrowhead)
  *Luzon
  *Rhineland

*Ardennes-Alsace
*Central Europe

Korean War
  *UN defensive
  *UN offensive
  *CCF intervention
  *First UN counteroffensive
  *CCF spring offensive
  *UN summer-fall offensive
  *Second Korean winter
  *Korea, summer-fall 1952
  *Third Korean winter
  *Korea, summer 1953

Decorations

*Presidential Unit Citation (Army), Streamer embroidered TAEGU (27th Infantry [less Heavy Tank Company] cited; DA GO 49, 1951)

*Presidential Unit Citation (Army), Streamer embroidered SANGNYONG-NI (27th Infantry [less Heavy Tank Company and 3d Battalion] cited; DA GO 72, 1951)

Presidential Unit Citation (Army), Streamer embroidered HAN RIVER

*Philippine Presidential Unit Citation, Streamer embroidered 17 OCTOBER 1944 TO 4 JULY 1945 (25th Infantry Division cited; DA GO 47, 1950)

*Republic of Korea Presidential Unit Citation, Streamer embroidered MASAN-CHINJU (27th Infantry cited; DA GO 35, 1951)

*Republic of Korea Presidential Unit Citation, Streamer embroidered MUNSAN-NI (27th Infantry cited; DA GO 19, 1955)

*Republic of Korea Presidential Unit Citation, Streamer embroidered KOREA (27th Infantry cited; DA GO 33, 1953, as amended by DA GO 41, 1955)

Headquarters Company additionally entitled to: Meritorious Unit Commendation, Streamer embroidered EUROPEAN THEATER (Headquarters Company, 255th Infantry cited; GO 423, 63d Infantry Division, 24 July 1945)

4th BATTALION, 27th INFANTRY

(The Wolfhounds)

AR
(inactive)

LINEAGE

Organized 16 April 1901 in the Regular Army at Fort McPherson, Georgia, as Company H, 26th Infantry. Redesignated 29 May 1901 as Company D, 27th Infantry. (27th Infantry assigned 1 March 1921 to the Hawaiian Division; relieved 26 August 1941 from assignment to the Hawaiian Division and assigned to the 25th Infantry Division.)

Inactivated 1 February 1957 in Hawaii and relieved from assignment to the 25th Infantry Division; concurrently, redesignated as Headquarters and Headquarters Company, 4th Battle Group, 27th Infantry. Redesignated 27 March 1963 as Headquarters and Headquarters Company, 4th Battalion, 27th Infantry, withdrawn from the Regular Army, allotted to the Army Reserve, and assigned to the 63d Infantry Division (organic elements concurrently constituted). Battalion activated 1 April 1963 with Headquarters at Long Beach, California. Inactivated 31 December 1965 at Long Beach, California.

CAMPAIGN PARTICIPATION CREDIT

Philippine Insurrection
  *Mindanao

World War I
  *Siberia 1918
  *Siberia 1919

World War II
  *Central Pacific
  *Guadalcanal
  *Northern Solomons (with arrowhead)
  *Luzon

Korean War
  *UN defensive
  *UN offensive
  *CCF intervention
  *First UN counteroffensive
  *CCF spring offensive
  *UN summer-fall offensive
  *Second Korean winter
  *Korea, summer-fall 1952
  *Third Korean winter
  *Korea, summer 1953

DECORATIONS

*Presidential Unit Citation (Army), Streamer embroidered TAEGU (27th Infantry [less Heavy Tank Company] cited; DA GO 49, 1951)

*Presidential Unit Citation (Army), Streamer embroidered SANGNYONG-NI (27th Infantry [less Heavy Tank Company and 3d Battalion]

510

cited; DA GO 72, 1951)

Presidential Unit Citation (Army), Streamer embroidered HAN RIVER

*Philippine Presidential Unit Citation, Streamer embroidered 17 OCTOBER 1944 TO 4 JULY 1945 (25th Infantry Division cited; DA GO 47, 1950)

*Republic of Korea Presidential Unit Citation, Streamer embroidered MASAN-CHINJU (27th Infantry cited; DA GO 35, 1951)

*Republic of Korea Presidential Unit Citation, Streamer embroidered MUNSAN-NI (27th Infantry cited; DA GO 19, 1955)

*Republic of Korea Presidential Unit Citation, Streamer embroidered KOREA (27th Infantry cited; DA GO 33, 1953, as amended by DA GO 41, 1955)

27TH INFANTRY, BIBLIOGRAPHY

Appleman, Roy E. "The Bowling Alley Fights," *Army,* XI (April 1961), 44–49.

————. *South to the Naktong, North to the Yalu.* United States Army in the Korean War. Washington: Government Printing Office, 1961.

The Bark of the Wolfhounds, 27th Inf Regt, Osaka, Organization Day, 2 May 1950. Osaka: Nippon Seihan Company, 1950.

Detzer, Karl. "No Push Buttons for Cap'n Easy," *V. F. W. Magazine* (April 1952). (Condensed in *Reader's Digest,* LX [May 1952], 61–62.)

Graves, William S. *America's Siberian Adventure, 1918–1920.* New York: Cape and H. Smith, 1931.

Hunt, George Alfred, compiler. *The History of the Twenty-seventh Infantry.* Honolulu: Honolulu Star-Bulletin Ltd., 1931.

Kahn, E. J., Jr. "A Reporter at Large: The Gentle Wolfhound," *New Yorker,* XXIX (9 May 1953), 69–82.

Luery, Rodney. *The Story of the Wolfhounds, 27th Infantry Regiment.* Tokyo: Japan News, 1953.

Marshall, S. L. A. *Ambush.* New York: Cowles Book Company, 1969.

————. *The River and the Gauntlet.* New York: William Morrow and Company, 1953.

Michaelis, "Mike" and Bill Davidson. "This We Learned in Korea," *Collier's,* CXXVIII (18 August 1951), 13ff.

Miller, John, jr. *CARTWHEEL: The Reduction of Rabaul.* United States Army in World War II. Washington: Government Printing Office, 1959 .

————. *Guadalcanal: The First Offensive.* United States Army in World War II. Washington: Government Printing Office, 1949.

O'Flaherty, A. E., ed. *The Bark of the 27th U.S. Infantry Wolfhounds.* Schofield Barracks, Hawaii, 1941.

"The Peripatetic 27th," *Life,* XXIX (11 September 1950), 43ff.

Smith, Robert Ross. *Triumph in the Philippines.* United States Army in World War II. Washington: Government Printing Office, 1963.

The Story of the Wolfhounds, 27th Infantry Regiment. n.p., 1953.

Twenty-seventh Infantry Organization Day, 1930. Celebration of the Twenty-eighth Anniversary of the Battle of Bavan and Twenty-ninth Anniversary of the Birth of the Regiment, May 2d, 1930. Schofield Barracks, Hawaii, 1930.

Wolverton, Robert L., ed. *The Bark, Published by the Twenty-seventh Infantry.* Honolulu, 1939.

————. *The Bark of the Twenty-seventh United States Infantry, Wolfhounds, Schofield Barracks, Oahu, T.H.* Honolulu, 1940.

28th INFANTRY

(Lions of Cantigny)

HERALDIC ITEMS

COAT OF ARMS

Shield: Argent, a lion rampant sable.

Crest: On a wreath of the colors a kris and kampilan in saltire argent hilted sable, encircled by a Fourragere in the colors of the French Croix de Guerre.

Motto: *Vincit Amor Patriae* (Love of Country Conquers) .

Symbolism: When this regiment was organized in 1901, the color of infantry facings was white, which has been taken for the color of the shield. As soon as organized, the regiment went to the Philippines, seeing active service against the Moros in Mindanao. The kris and kampilan, the Moro weapons, commemorate such service. During World War I the 28th Infantry was in the 1st Division and was the attacking regiment at Cantigny. Cantigny is in the ancient province of Picardy, whose arms carried three black rampant lions. The regiment received two French Croix de Guerre with Palm for distinguished services rendered during World War I and was also awarded the French Fourragere, which is incorporated in the crest.

DISTINCTIVE INSIGNIA

The distinctive insignia is the shield of the coat of arms.

LINEAGE AND HONORS

LINEAGE

Constituted 2 February 1901 in the Regular Army as the 28th Infantry. Organized March–June 1901 at Vancouver Barracks, Washington. Assigned 8 June 1917 to the 1st Expeditionary Division (later redesignated as the 1st Division) . (1st Battalion inactivated 30 September 1933 at Fort Hayes, Ohio.) Relieved 16 October 1939 from assignment to the

1st Division. Assigned 22 June 1940 to the 8th Division (later redesignated as the 8th Infantry Division). (1st Battalion activated 10 October 1940 at Fort Niagara, New York.) Inactivated 1 November 1945 at Fort Leonard Wood, Missouri. Activated 17 August 1950 at Fort Jackson, South Carolina.

Relieved 1 August 1957 from assignment to the 8th Infantry Division and reorganized as a parent regiment under the Combat Arms Regimental System.

CAMPAIGN PARTICIPATION CREDIT

Philippine Insurrection
  Mindanao

World War I
  Montdidier-Noyon
  Aisne-Marne
  St. Mihiel
  Meuse-Argonne
  Lorraine 1917
  Lorraine 1918
  Picardy 1918·

World War II
  Normandy
  Northern France
  Rhineland
  Central Europe

Vietnam
  Defense
  Counteroffensive
  Counteroffensive, Phase II
  Counteroffensive, Phase III
  Tet Counteroffensive
  (other campaigns to be determined)

DECORATIONS

Presidential Unit Citation (Army), Streamer embroidered STOCKHEIM (3d Battalion, 28th Infantry cited; DA GO 23, 1947)

Presidential Unit Citation (Army), Streamer embroidered NORMANDY (1st Battalion, 28th Infantry cited; WD GO 80, 1947)

Presidential Unit Citation (Army), Streamer embroidered BERGSTEIN (3d Battalion, 28th Infantry cited; WD GO 32, 1947)

Presidential Unit Citation (Army), Streamer embroidered TAY NINH PROVINCE (1st Battalion, 28th Infantry cited; DA GO 23, 1969)

Valorous Unit Award, Streamer embroidered LO KE RUBBER PLANTATION (2d Battalion, 28th Infantry cited; DA GO 20, 1967)

French Croix de Guerre with Palm, World War I, Streamer embroidered PICARDY (28th Infantry cited; WD GO 11, 1924)

French Croix de Guerre with Palm, World War I, Streamer embroidered AISNE-MARNE (28th Infantry cited; WD GO 11, 1924)

French Croix de Guerre, World War I, Fourragere (28th Infantry cited; WD GO 11, 1924)

Luxembourg Croix de Guerre, Streamer embroidered LUXEMBOURG (8th Infantry Division cited; DA GO 59, 1969)

1st BATTALION, 28th INFANTRY

(Lions of Cantigny)

RA

(1st Infantry Division)

LINEAGE

Constituted 2 February 1901 in the Regular Army as Company A, 28th Infantry. Organized 10 June 1901 at Vancouver Barracks, Washington. (28th Infantry assigned 8 June 1917 to the 1st Expeditionary Division [later redesignated as the 1st Division].) Inactivated 30 September 1933 at Fort Hayes, Ohio. (28th Infantry relieved 16 October 1939 from assignment to the 1st Division; assigned 22 June 1940 to the 8th Division [later redesignated as the 8th Infantry Division].) Activated 10 October 1940 at Fort Niagara, New York. Inactivated 1 November 1945 at Fort Leonard Wood, Missouri. Activated 17 August 1950 at Fort Jackson, South Carolina.

Reorganized and redesignated 1 August 1957 as Headquarters and Headquarters Company, 1st Battle Group, 28th Infantry and remained assigned to the 8th Infantry Division (organic elements concurrently constituted and activated). Relieved 1 May 1959 from assignment to the 8th Infantry Division and assigned to the 1st Infantry Division. Reorganized and redesignated 13 January 1964 as the 1st Battalion, 28th Infantry.

CAMPAIGN PARTICIPATION CREDIT

Philippine Insurrection
  Mindanao

World War I
  *Montdidier-Noyon
  *Aisne-Marne
  *St. Mihiel
  *Meuse-Argonne
  *Lorraine 1917
  *Lorraine 1918
  *Picardy 1918

World War II
  *Normandy
  *Northern France
  *Rhineland
  *Central Europe

Vietnam
  *Defense
  *Counteroffensive
  *Counteroffensive, Phase II
  *Counteroffensive, Phase III
  *Tet Counteroffensive
    (other campaigns to be determined)

DECORATIONS

Presidential Unit Citation (Army), Streamer embroidered STOCK-HEIM

*Presidential Unit Citation (Army), Streamer embroidered NORMANDY (1st Battalion, 28th Infantry cited; WD GO 80, 1947)

Presidential Unit Citation (Army), Streamer embroidered BERGSTEIN

*Presidential Unit Citation (Army), Streamer embroidered TAY NINH PROVINCE (1st Battalion, 28th Infantry cited; DA GO 23, 1969)

*French Croix de Guerre with Palm, World War I, Streamer embroidered PICARDY (28th Infantry cited; WD GO 11, 1924)

*French Croix de Guerre with Palm, World War I, Streamer embroidered AISNE-MARNE (28th Infantry cited; WD GO 11, 1924)

*French Croix de Guerre, World War I, Fourragere (28th Infantry cited; WD GO 11, 1924)

*Luxembourg Croix de Guerre, Streamer embroidered LUXEMBOURG (8th Infantry Division cited; DA GO 59, 1969)

*Vietnamese Cross of Gallantry with Palm, Streamer embroidered VIETNAM 1965–1968 (1st Battalion, 28th Infantry cited; DA GO 21, 1969)

*Vietnamese Cross of Gallantry with Palm, Streamer embroidered VIETNAM 1969–1970 (1st Battalion, 28th Infantry cited; DA GO 2, 1971)

*Vietnamese Civil Action Honor Medal, First Class, Streamer embroidered VIETNAM 1965–1970 (1st Battalion, 28th Infantry cited; DA GO 53, 1970)

2d BATTALION, 28th INFANTRY

(Lions of Cantigny)

RA
(inactive)

LINEAGE

Constituted 2 February 1901 in the Regular Army as Company B, 28th Infantry. Organized 17 June 1901 at Vancouver Barracks, Washington. (28th Infantry assigned 8 June 1917 to the 1st Expeditionary Division [later redesignated as the 1st Division].) Inactivated 30 September 1933 at Fort Hayes, Ohio. (28th Infantry relieved 16 October 1939 from assignment to the 1st Division; assigned 22 June 1940 to the 8th Division [later redesignated as the 8th Infantry Division].) Activated 10 October 1940 at Fort Niagara, New York. Inactivated 1 November 1945 at Fort Leonard Wood, Missouri. Activated 17 August 1950 at Fort Jackson, South Carolina.

Reorganized and redesignated 15 February 1957 as Headquarters and Headquarters Company, 2d Battle Group, 28th Infantry, relieved from assignment to the 8th Infantry Division, and assigned to the 1st Infantry Division (organic elements concurrently constituted and activated). Relieved 26 December 1958 from assignment to the 1st Infantry Division and assigned to the 24th Infantry Division. Inactivated 1 February 1963 in Germany and relieved from assignment to the 24th Infantry Division. Redesignated 23 October 1963 as the 2d Battalion, 28th Infantry and assigned to the 1st Infantry Division. Activated 13 January 1964 at Fort Riley, Kansas. Inactivated 15 April 1970 at Fort Riley, Kansas.

517

CAMPAIGN PARTICIPATION CREDIT

Philippine Insurrection
 *Mindanao

World War I
 *Montdidier-Noyon
 *Aisne-Marne
 *St. Mihiel
 *Meuse-Argonne
 *Lorraine 1917
 *Lorraine 1918
 *Picardy 1918

World War II
 *Normandy
 *Northern France
 *Rhineland
 *Central Europe

Vietnam
 *Defense
 *Counteroffensive
 *Counteroffensive, Phase II
 *Counteroffensive, Phase III
 *Tet Counteroffensive
 (other campaigns to be determined)

DECORATIONS

Presidential Unit Citation (Army), Streamer embroidered STOCK-HEIM

*Presidential Unit Citation (Army), Streamer embroidered NORMANDY (1st Battalion, 28th Infantry cited; WD GO 80, 1947)

Presidential Unit Citation (Army), Streamer embroidered BERGSTEIN

*Valorous Unit Award, Streamer embroidered LO KE RUBBER PLANTATION (2d Battalion, 28th Infantry cited; DA GO 20, 1967)

*French Croix de Guerre with Palm, World War I, Streamer embroidered PICARDY (28th Infantry cited; WD GO 11, 1924)

*French Croix de Guerre with Palm, World War I, Streamer embroidered AISNE-MARNE (28th Infantry cited; WD GO 11, 1924)

*French Croix de Guerre, World War I, Fourragere (28th Infantry cited; WD GO 11, 1924)

*Luxembourg Croix de Guerre, Streamer embroidered LUXEMBOURG (8th Infantry Division cited; DA GO 59, 1969)

*Vietnamese Cross of Gallantry with Palm, Streamer embroidered VIETNAM 1965–1968 (2d Battalion, 28th Infantry cited; DA GO 21, 1969)

*Vietnamese Cross of Gallantry with Palm, Streamer embroidered VIETNAM 1969–1970 (2d Battalion, 28th Infantry cited; DA GO 2, 1971)

*Vietnamese Civil Action Honor Medal, First Class, Streamer embroidered VIETNAM 1965–1970 (2d Battalion, 28th Infantry cited; DA GO 53, 1970)

3d BATTALION, 28th INFANTRY

(Lions of Cantigny)

AR
(inactive)

LINEAGE

Constituted 2 February 1901 in the Regular Army as Company C, 28th Infantry. Organized 20 June 1901 at Vancouver Barracks, Washington. (28th Infantry assigned 8 June 1917 to the 1st Expeditionary Division [later redesignated as the 1st Division].) Inactivated 30 September 1933 at Fort Hayes, Ohio. (28th Infantry relieved 16 October 1939 from assignment to the 1st Division; assigned 22 June 1940 to the 8th Division [later redesignated as the 8th Infantry Division].) Activated 10 October 1940 at Fort Niagara, New York. Inactivated 1 November 1945 at Fort Leonard Wood, Missouri. Activated 17 August 1950 at Fort Jackson, South Carolina.

Inactivated 1 August 1957 in Germany and relieved from assignment to the 8th Infantry Division; concurrently, redesignated as Headquarters and Headquarters Company, 3d Battle Group, 28th Infantry. Withdrawn 19 March 1959 from the Regular Army, allotted to the Army Reserve, and assigned to the 83d Infantry Division (organic elements concurrently constituted). Battle Group activated 20 March 1959 with Headquarters at Akron, Ohio (concurrently, Headquarters and Headquarters Company consolidated with Headquarters and Headquarters Company, 331st Infantry [see ANNEX] and consolidated unit designated as Headquarters and Headquarters Company, 3d Battle Group, 28th Infantry). Reorganized and redesignated 15 April 1963 as the 3d Battalion, 28th Infantry. Inactivated 31 December 1965 at Akron, Ohio.

ANNEX

Constituted 5 August 1917 in the National Army as Headquarters and Headquarters Company, 331st Infantry, an element of the 83d Division. Organized 30 August 1917 at Camp Sherman, Ohio. Demobilized 9 February 1919 at Camp Sherman, Ohio. Reconstituted 24 June 1921 in the Organized Reserves as an element of the 83d Division (later redesignated as the 83d Infantry Division). Organized in November 1921 at Cleveland, Ohio. Ordered into active military service 15 August 1942 and reorganized at Camp Atterbury, Indiana. Inactivated 30 March 1946 at Camp Kilmer, New Jersey.

Activated 1 October 1946 in the Organized Reserves at Cleveland, Ohio. (Organized Reserves redesignated 25 March 1948 as the Organized Reserve Corps; redesignated 9 July 1952 as the Army Reserve.) Location changed 31 October 1949 to Akron, Ohio. Consolidated 20 March 1959 with Headquarters and Headquarters Company, 3d Battle Group, 28th Infantry and consolidated unit designated as Headquarters and Headquarters Company, 3d Battle Group, 28th Infantry (concurrently, Headquarters and Headquarters Company, 1st Battalion, 331st Infantry consolidated with Headquarters and Headquarters Company, 3d Battle Group, 10th Infantry and consolidated unit designated as Headquarters and Headquarters Company, 3d Battle Group, 10th Infantry; remainder of 331st Infantry inactivated).

CAMPAIGN PARTICIPATION CREDIT

Philippine Insurrection
  Mindanao

  *Lorraine 1918
  *Picardy 1918

World War I
  *Montdidier-Noyon
  *Aisne-Marne
  *St. Mihiel
  *Meuse-Argonne
  *Lorraine 1917

World War II
  *Normandy
  *Northern France
  *Rhineland
  *Ardennes-Alsace
  *Central Europe

DECORATIONS

Presidential Unit Citation (Army), Streamer embroidered STOCKHEIM

*Presidential Unit Citation (Army), Streamer embroidered NORMANDY (1st Battalion, 28th Infantry cited; WD GO 20, 1947)

Presidential Unit Citation (Army), Streamer embroidered BERGSTEIN

*French Croix de Guerre with Palm, World War I, Streamer embroidered PICARDY (28th Infantry cited; WD GO 11, 1924)

*French Croix de Guerre with Palm, World War I, Streamer embroidered AISNE-MARNE (28th Infantry cited; WD GO 11, 1924)

*French Croix de Guerre, World War I, Fourragere (28th Infantry cited; WD GO 11, 1924)

*Luxembourg Croix de Guerre, Streamer embroidered LUXEMBOURG (8th Infantry Division cited; DA GO 59, 1969)

28th Infantry, Bibliography

History of the 1st Battle Group, 28th Infantry, 1901–1962. "*Lions of Cantigny: First in the Fighting First.*" Fort Riley, Kansas, 1962.

MacDonald, Charles B. *The Siegfried Line Campaign.* United States Army in World War II. Washington: Government Printing Office, 1963.

MacGregor, Harold E. *The Story of the 28th Infantry Regiment.* Washington: Infantry Journal Press, 1947.

——————. *28th Infantry Regiment Review.* Baton Rouge: Army and Navy Publishing Company, 1947 .

Marshall, S. L. A. *Ambush.* New York: Cowles Book Company, 1969.

The Story of the Twenty-eighth Infantry in the Great War: American Expeditionary Forces. Coblenz, 1919.

28th Infantry Regiment. Baton Rouge: Army and Navy Publishing Company, 1946. (Volume II of 8th Infantry Division yearbook.)

The 28th Infantry Regiment History. Dallas: Miller Publishing Company, 1956.

Twenty-eight U.S. Infantry Celebration of "Organization Day," May 28, 1920, Camp Zachary Taylor, Kentucky. Camp Zachary Taylor: Press of the Field Artillery School, 1920.

29th INFANTRY

COAT OF ARMS

Shield: Per fess argent and azure in chief on a mount issuant a mango tree proper in base saltirewise a bayonet and a bolo of the first hilted or.

Crest: On a wreath of the colors a lamp of knowledge or flamed gules.

Motto: We Lead the Way.

Symbolism: White and blue are the old and present infantry colors. The mango tree, the crossed bolo of the Filipino, and the bayonet of the regiment represent service in the Philippine Insurrection. The regiment's long association with the Infantry School at Fort Benning, Georgia, is indicated by the classic lamp of knowledge in the crest.

DISTINCTIVE INSIGNIA

The distinctive insignia is the shield, crest, and motto of the coat of arms.

LINEAGE AND HONORS

LINEAGE

Constituted 2 February 1901 in the Regular Army as the 29th Infantry. Organized 5 March 1901 at Fort Sheridan, Illinois. Assigned 29 July 1918 to the 17th Division. Relieved 10 February 1919 from assignment to the 17th Division. Assigned 1 October 1933 to the 4th Division. Relieved 16 October 1939 from assignment to the 4th Division. Inactivated 31 October 1946 in Germany. Activated 1 May 1949 on Okinawa. Assigned 2 December 1954 to the 23d Infantry Division. Relieved 1 March 1956 from assignment to the 23d Infantry Division.

Reorganized 25 May 1957 as a parent regiment under the Combat Arms Regimental System.

523

Campaign Participation Credit

Philippine Insurrection
  Without inscription

Ardennes-Alsace
Central Europe

World War II
  Northern France
  Rhineland

Korean War
  UN defensive

Decorations

Presidential Unit Citation (Army), Streamer embroidered NAM RIVER (1st Battalion, 29th Infantry cited; DA GO 49, 1951, as amended by DA GO 103, 1952)

1st BATTALION, 29th INFANTRY

LINEAGE

Constituted 2 February 1901 in the Regular Army as Company A, 29th Infantry. Organized 5 March 1901 at Fort Sheridan, Illinois. (29th Infantry assigned 29 July 1918 to the 17th Division; relieved 10 February 1919 from assignment to the 17th Division; assigned 1 October 1933 to the 4th Division; relieved 16 October 1939 from assignment to the 4th Division.) Inactivated 31 October 1946 in Germany. Activated 1 May 1949 on Okinawa. (29th Infantry assigned 2 December 1954 to the 23d Infantry Division; relieved 1 March 1956 from assignment to the 23d Infantry Division.)

Reorganized and redesignated 25 May 1957 as Headquarters and Headquarters Company, 1st Battle Group, 29th Infantry (organic elements concurrently constituted and activated). Assigned 25 July 1958 to the 1st Infantry Brigade. Relieved 20 September 1962 from assignment to the 1st Infantry Brigade. Inactivated 24 September 1962 at Fort Benning, Georgia. Redesignated 4 January 1963 as the 1st Battalion, 29th Infantry and assigned to the 197th Infantry Brigade. Activated 1 February 1963 at Fort Benning, Georgia.

CAMPAIGN PARTICIPATION CREDIT

Philippine Insurrection
*Without inscription

World War II
*Northern France
*Rhineland

*Ardennes-Alsace
*Central Europe

Korean War
*UN defensive

DECORATIONS

*Presidential Unit Citation (Army), Streamer embroidered NAM RIVER (1st Battalion, 29th Infantry cited; DA GO 49, 1951, as amended by DA GO 103, 1952)

525

2d BATTALION, 29th INFANTRY

RA
(inactive)

Constituted 2 February 1901 in the Regular Army as Company B, 29th Infantry. Organized 5 March 1901 at Fort Sheridan, Illinois. (29th Infantry assigned 29 July 1918 to the 17th Division; relieved 10 February 1919 from assignment to the 17th Division; assigned 1 October 1933 to the 4th Division; relieved 16 October 1939 from assignment to the 4th Division.) Inactivated 31 October 1946 in Germany. Activated 1 May 1949 on Okinawa. (29th Infantry assigned 2 December 1954 to the 23d Infantry Division; relieved 1 March 1956 from assignment to the 23d Infantry Division.) Inactivated 25 May 1957 at Fort Benning, Georgia.

Redesignated 1 July 1957 as Headquarters and Headquarters Company, 2d Battle Group, 29th Infantry, assigned to the 10th Infantry Division, and activated in Germany (organic elements concurrently constituted and activated). Inactivated 14 June 1958 in Germany and relieved from assignment to the 10th Infantry Division. Redesignated 4 January 1963 as the 2d Battalion, 29th Infantry and assigned to the 197th Infantry Brigade. Activated 1 February 1963 at Fort Benning, Georgia. Inactivated 14 November 1965 at Fort Benning, Georgia.

CAMPAIGN PARTICIPATION CREDIT

Philippine Insurrection
  *Without inscription

World War II
  *Northern France
  *Rhineland

*Ardennes-Alsace
*Central Europe

Korean War
  *UN defensive

DECORATIONS

*Presidential Unit Citation (Army), Streamer embroidered NAM RIVER (1st Battalion, 29th Infantry cited; DA GO 49, 1951, as amended by DA GO 103, 1952)

526

3d BATTALION, 29th INFANTRY

AR
(inactive)

LINEAGE

Constituted 2 February 1901 in the Regular Army as Company C, 29th Infantry. Organized 5 March 1901 at Fort Sheridan, Illinois. (29th Infantry assigned 29 July 1918 to the 17th Division; relieved 10 February 1919 from assignment to the 17th Division; assigned 1 October 1933 to the 4th Division; relieved 16 October 1939 from assignment to the 4th Division.) Inactivated 31 October 1946 in Germany. Activated 1 May 1949 on Okinawa. (29th Infantry assigned 2 December 1954 to the 23d Infantry Division; relieved 1 March 1956 from assignment to the 23d Infantry Division.)

Inactivated 25 May 1957 at Fort Benning, Georgia; concurrently, redesignated as Headquarters and Headquarters Company, 3d Battle Group, 29th Infantry. Withdrawn 10 April 1959 from the Regular Army, allotted to the Army Reserve, and assigned to the 81st Infantry Division (organic elements concurrently constituted). Battle Group activated 1 May 1959 with Headquarters at Columbus, Georgia (concurrently, Headquarters and Headquarters Company consolidated with Headquarters and Headquarters Company, 519th Infantry [see ANNEX] and consolidated unit designated as Headquarters and Headquarters Company, 3d Battle Group, 29th Infantry). Reorganized and redesignated 1 April 1963 as the 3d Battalion, 29th Infantry. Inactivated 31 December 1965 at Columbus, Georgia.

ANNEX

Constituted 15 July 1946 in the Organized Reserves as Headquarters and Headquarters Company, 519th Parachute Infantry, an element of the 108th Airborne Division. Activated 6 August 1946 at Atlanta, Georgia. (Organized Reserves redesignated 25 March 1948 as the Organized Reserve Corps; redesignated 9 July 1952 as the Army Reserve.) Reorganized and redesignated 1 February 1951 as Headquarters and Headquarters Company, 519th Airborne Infantry. Reorganized and redesignated 1 March 1952 as Headquarters and Headquarters Company, 519th Infantry (concurrently, 519th Infantry relieved from assignment to the 108th Airborne Division and assigned to the 81st Infantry Division).

Consolidated 1 May 1959 with Headquarters and Headquarters Company, 3d Battle Group, 29th Infantry and consolidated unit designated as Headquarters and Headquarters Company, 3d Battle Group, 29th Infantry (remainder of 519th Infantry disbanded) .

CAMPAIGN PARTICIPATION CREDIT

Philippine Insurrection
  *Without inscription

World War II
  *Northern France
  *Rhineland

*Ardennes-Alsace
*Central Europe

Korean War
  *UN defensive

DECORATIONS

*Presidential Unit Citation (Army) , Streamer embroidered NAM RIVER (1st Battalion, 29th Infantry cited; DA GO 49, 1951, as amended by DA GO 103, 1952)

4th BATTALION, 29th INFANTRY

AR
(inactive)

LINEAGE

Constituted 2 February 1901 in the Regular Army as Company D, 29th Infantry. Organized 5 March 1901 at Fort Sheridan, Illinois. (29th Infantry assigned 29 July 1918 to the 17th Division; relieved 10 February 1919 from assignment to the 17th Division; assigned 1 October 1933 to the 4th Division; relieved 16 October 1939 from assignment to the 4th Division.) Inactivated 31 October 1946 in Germany. Activated 1 May 1949 on Okinawa. (29th Infantry assigned 2 December 1954 to the 23d Infantry Division; relieved 1 March 1956 from assignment to the 23d Infantry Division.)

Inactivated 25 May 1957 at Fort Benning, Georgia; concurrently, redesignated as Headquarters and Headquarters Company, 4th Battle Group, 29th Infantry. Redesignated 24 September 1962 as Headquarters and Headquarters Company, 4th Battalion, 29th Infantry, assigned to the 197th Infantry Brigade, and activated at Fort Benning, Georgia (organic elements [constituted 20 September 1962] concurrently activated). Relieved 4 January 1963 from assignment to the 197th Infantry Brigade. Inactivated 1 February 1963 at Fort Benning, Georgia.

Withdrawn 26 March 1963 from the Regular Army, allotted to the Army Reserve, and assigned to the 81st Infantry Division. Activated 1 April 1963 with Headquarters at Tifton, Georgia. Inactivated 31 December 1965 at Tifton, Georgia.

CAMPAIGN PARTICIPATION CREDIT

Philippine Insurrection
*Without inscription

World War II
*Northern France
*Rhineland

*Ardennes-Alsace
*Central Europe

Korean War
*UN defensive

DECORATIONS

*Presidential Unit Citation (Army), Streamer embroidered NAM RIVER (1st Battalion, 29th Infantry cited; DA GO 49, 1951, as amended by DA GO 103, 1952)

529

29TH INFANTRY, BIBLIOGRAPHY

Bush, Byron, O., Jr., ed. *We Lead the Way, The Twenty-ninth Infantry Regiment in World War H, 1941–1946*. Frankfurt am Main: Hauserpresse, 1946.

Dudley, George E. and Byron O. Bush. *The Two-Niner: The 29th Infantry in World War II, 1941–1946*. Germany, 1946.

"53d Anniversary of the Twenty-ninth Infantry Regiment." Okinawa, 1954.

Nichols, A. J., ed. *The Sand-Burr*. Fort Benning, Georgia, 1928.

"Thirty-fifth Organization Day, 1901–1936." Fort Benning, Georgia, 1936.

"26th Organization Day, 1901–1927. Program. Twenty-ninth U.S. Infantry." Fort Benning, Georgia, 1927.

30th INFANTRY

HERALDIC ITEMS

COAT OF ARMS

Shield: Argent, a chevron rompu point debased azure; on a canton of the last three bendlets sinister of the field. (And for informal use, pendant from the escutcheon a French Croix de Guerre with Palm proper.)

Crest: On a wreath of the colors a boar's head erased sable armed and langued gules.

Motto: Our Country, Not Ourselves.

Symbolism: This regiment's assignment to the 3d Division during World War I is shown by the simulation of the divisional shoulder sleeve insignia on the canton. The broken chevron represents the part taken by the 30th Infantry in pushing back the point of the German drive at the Marne in July 1918, for which services the regiment was awarded the French Croix de Guerre with Palm. The boar's head represents the subsequent passage through the German lines and occupation of German territory by this regiment.

DISTINCTIVE INSIGNIA

The distinctive insignia is the shield and crest of the coat of arms within a circlet bearing the motto of the coat of arms and "Rock of the Marne, July 14–18, 1918."

LINEAGE AND HONORS

LINEAGE

Constituted 2 February 1901 in the Regular Army as the 30th Infantry. Organized 12 February–19 August 1901 at Fort Logan, Colorado, at the Presidio of San Francisco, California, and in the Philippine Islands. Assigned 21 November 1917 to the 3d Division. Relieved 12 January 1940 from assignment to the 3d Division. Assigned 15 May 1940 to the 3d Division (later redesignated as the 3d Infantry Division). Relieved

531

6 April 1951 from assignment to the 3d Infantry Division. Assigned 2 December 1954 to the 3d Infantry Division.

Relieved 1 July 1957 from assignment to the 3d Infantry Division and reorganized as a parent regiment under the Combat Arms Regimental System.

CAMPAIGN PARTICIPATION CREDIT

Philippine Insurrection
Mindoro 1901

World War I
Aisne
Champagne-Marne
Aisne-Marne
St. Mihiel
Meuse-Argonne
Champagne 1918

World War II
Algeria-French Morocco
(with arrowhead)
Tunisia
Sicily (with arrowhead)
Naples-Foggia
Anzio (with arrowhead)
Rome-Arno
Southern France (with arrowhead)
Rhineland
Ardennes-Alsace
Central Europe

DECORATIONS

Presidential Unit Citation (Army), Streamer embroidered COLMAR (3d Infantry Division cited; WD GO 44, 1945)

Presidential Unit Citation (Army), Streamer embroidered BESANCON, FRANCE (1st Battalion, 30th Infantry cited; WD GO 18, 1945)

Presidential Unit Citation (Army), Streamer embroidered SICILY (2d Battalion, 30th Infantry cited; WD GO 44, 1944)

Presidential Unit Citation (Army), Streamer embroidered MOUNT ROTUNDO (3d Battalion, 30th Infantry cited; WD GO 79, 1944)

French Croix de Guerre with Palm, World War I, Streamer embroidered CHAMPAGNE-MARNE (30th Infantry cited; WD GO 11, 1924)

French Croix de Guerre with Palm, World War II, Streamer embroidered COLMAR (30th Infantry cited; DA GO 43, 1950)

French Croix de Guerre, World War II, Fourragere (30th Infantry cited; DA GO 43, 1950)

1st BATTALION, 30th INFANTRY

RA

(3d Infantry Division)

LINEAGE

Constituted 2 February 1901 in the Regular Army as Company A, 30th Infantry. Organized 16 March 1901 at the Presidio of San Francisco, California. (30th Infantry assigned 21 November 1917 to the 3d Division; relieved 12 January 1940 from assignment to the 3d Division; assigned 15 May 1940 to the 3d Division [later redesignated as the 3d Infantry Division]; relieved 6 April 1951 from assignment to the 3d Infantry Division; assigned 2 December 1954 to the 3d Infantry Division.)

Reorganized and redesignated 1 July 1957 as Headquarters and Headquarters Company, 1st Battle Group, 30th Infantry and remained assigned to the 3d Infantry Division (organic elements concurrently constituted and activated). Reorganized and redesignated 10 July 1963 as the 1st Battalion, 30th Infantry.

CAMPAIGN PARTICIPATION CREDIT

Philippine Insurrection
Mindoro 1901

World War I
* *Aisne
* *Champagne-Marne
* *Aisne-Marne
* *St. Mihiel
* *Meuse-Argonne
* *Champagne 1918

World War II
* *Algeria-French Morocco
  (with arrowhead)
* *Tunisia
* *Sicily (with arrowhead)
* *Naples-Foggia
* *Anzio (with arrowhead)
* *Rome-Arno
* *Southern France (with arrowhead)
* *Rhineland
* *Ardennes-Alsace
* *Central Europe

DECORATIONS

*Presidential Unit Citation (Army), Streamer embroidered COLMAR (3d Infantry Division cited; WD GO 44, 1945)

*Presidential Unit Citation (Army), Streamer embroidered BESANCON, FRANCE (1st Battalion, 30th Infantry cited; WD GO 18, 1945)

Presidential Unit Citation (Army), Streamer embroidered SICILY

Presidential Unit Citation (Army), Streamer embroidered MOUNT ROTUNDO

*French Croix de Guerre with Palm, World War I, Streamer em-

533

broidered CHAMPAGNE-MARNE (30th Infantry cited; WD GO 11, 1924)

*French Croix de Guerre with Palm, World War II, Streamer embroidered COLMAR (30th Infantry cited; DA GO 43, 1950)

*French Croix de Guerre, World War II, Fourragere (30th Infantry cited; DA GO 43, 1950)

2d BATTALION, 30th INFANTRY

RA
(3d Infantry Division)

LINEAGE

Constituted 2 February 1901 in the Regular Army as Company B, 30th Infantry. Organized 16 March 1901 at the Presidio of San Francisco, California. (30th Infantry assigned 21 November 1917 to the 3d Division; relieved 12 January 1940 from assignment to the 3d Division; assigned 15 May 1940 to the 3d Division [later redesignated as the 3d Infantry Division]; relieved 6 April 1951 from assignment to the 3d Infantry Division; assigned 2 December 1954 to the 3d Infantry Division.) Inactivated 1 July 1957 at Fort Benning, Georgia, and relieved from assignment to the 3d Infantry Division.

Redesignated 3 January 1958 as Headquarters and Headquarters Company, 2d Battle Group, 30th Infantry (organic elements concurrently constituted). Battle Group activated 22 January 1958 at Fort Sill, Oklahoma. Reorganized and redesignated 1 April 1963 as the 2d Battalion, 30th Infantry and assigned to the 3d Infantry Division.

CAMPAIGN PARTICIPATION CREDIT

Philippine Insurrection
  Mindoro 1901

World War I
  *Aisne
  *Champagne-Marne
  *Aisne-Marne
  *St. Mihiel
  *Meuse-Argonne
  *Champagne 1918

World War II
  *Algeria-French Morocco
    (with arrowhead)
  *Tunisia
  *Sicily (with arrowhead)
  *Naples-Foggia
  *Anzio (with arrowhead)
  *Rome-Arno
  *Southern France (with arrowhead)
  *Rhineland
  *Ardennes-Alsace
  *Central Europe

DECORATIONS

*Presidential Unit Citation (Army), Streamer embroidered COLMAR (3d Infantry Division cited; WD GO 44, 1945)

*Presidential Unit Citation (Army), Streamer embroidered BESANCON, FRANCE (1st Battalion, 30th Infantry cited; WD GO 18, 1945)

Presidential Unit Citation (Army), Streamer embroidered SICILY

Presidential Unit Citation (Army), Streamer embroidered MOUNT ROTUNDO

535

*French Croix de Guerre with Palm, World War I, Streamer embroidered CHAMPAGNE-MARNE (30th Infantry cited; WD GO 11, 1924)

*French Croix de Guerre with Palm, World War II, Streamer embroidered COLMAR (30th Infantry cited; DA GO 43, 1950)

*French Croix de Guerre, World War II, Fourragere (30th Infantry cited; DA GO 43, 1950)

3d BATTALION, 30th INFANTRY

AR
(inactive)

LINEAGE

Constituted 2 February 1901 in the Regular Army as Company C, 30th Infantry. Organized 16 March 1901 at the Presidio of San Francisco, California. (30th Infantry assigned 21 November 1917 to the 3d Division; relieved 12 January 1940 from assignment to the 3d Division; assigned 15 May 1940 to the 3d Division [later redesignated as the 3d Infantry Division]; relieved 6 April 1951 from assignment to the 3d Infantry Division; assigned 2 December 1954 to the 3d Infantry Division) .

Inactivated 1 July 1957 at Fort Benning, Georgia, and relieved from assignment to the 3d Infantry Division; concurrently, redesignated as Headquarters and Headquarters Company, 3d Battle Group, 30th Infantry. Withdrawn 31 March 1959 from the Regular Army, allotted to the Army Reserve, and assigned to the 63d Infantry Division (organic elements concurrently constituted) . Battle Group activated 1 May 1959 with Headquarters at Pasadena, California (concurrently, Headquarters and Headquarters Company consolidated with Headquarters and Headquarters Company, 254th Infantry [see ANNEX] and consolidated unit designated as Headquarters and Headquarters Company, 3d Battle Group, 30th Infantry) . Reorganized and redesignated 1 April 1963 as the 3d Battalion, 30th Infantry. Inactivated 31 December 1965 at Pasadena, California.

ANNEX

Constituted 18 January 1943 in the Army of the United States as Headquarters and Headquarters Company, 254th Infantry, an element of the 63d Infantry Division. Activated 15 June 1943 at Camp Blanding, Florida. Inactivated 29 September 1945 at Camp Kilmer, New Jersey. (63d Infantry Division allotted 22 February 1952 to the Organized Reserve Corps.) Activated 1 March 1952 at Pasadena, California. (Organized Reserve Corps redesignated 9 July 1952 as the Army Reserve.)

Consolidated 1 May 1959 with Headquarters and Headquarters Company, 3d Battle Group, 30th Infantry and consolidated unit designated as Headquarters and Headquarters Company, 3d Battle Group, 30th Infantry (concurrently, Headquarters and Headquarters Company, 2d Battalion, 254th Infantry consolidated with Headquarters and Headquarters

Company, 3d Battle Group, 15th Infantry and consolidated unit designated as Headquarters and Headquarters Company, 3d Battle Group, 15th Infantry; remainder of 254th Infantry inactivated).

CAMPAIGN PARTICIPATION CREDIT

Philippine Insurrection
  Mindoro 1901

World War I
  *Aisne
  *Champagne-Marne
  *Aisne-Marne
  *St. Mihiel
  *Meuse-Argonne
  *Champagne 1918

World War II
  *Algeria-French Morocco
    (with arrowhead)
  *Tunisia
  *Sicily (with arrowhead)
  *Naples-Foggia
  *Anzio (with arrowhead)
  *Rome-Arno
  *Southern France
    (with arrowhead)
  *Rhineland
  *Ardennes-Alsace
  *Central Europe

DECORATIONS

*Presidential Unit Citation (Army), Streamer embroidered COLMAR (3d Infantry Division and 254th Infantry cited; WD GO 44, 1945)

*Presidential Unit Citation (Army), Streamer embroidered BESANCON, FRANCE (1st Battalion, 30th Infantry cited; WD GO 18, 1945)

Presidential Unit Citation (Army), Streamer embroidered SICILY

Presidential Unit Citation (Army), Streamer embroidered MOUNT ROTUNDO

*French Croix de Guerre with Palm, World War I, Streamer embroidered CHAMPAGNE-MARNE (30th Infantry cited; WD GO 11, 1924)

*French Croix de Guerre with Palm, World War II, Streamer embroidered COLMAR (30th Infantry cited; DA GO 43, 1950)

*French Croix de Guerre, World War II, Fourragere (30th Infantry cited; DA GO 43, 1950)

4th BATTALION, 30th INFANTRY

RA
(nondivisional)

LINEAGE

Constituted 2 February 1901 in the Regular Army as Company D, 30th Infantry. Organized 16 March 1901 at the Presidio of San Francisco, California. (30th Infantry assigned 21 November 1917 to the 3d Division; relieved 12 January 1940 from assignment to the 3d Division; assigned 15 May 1940 to the 3d Division [later redesignated as the 3d Infantry Division]; relieved 6 April 1951 from assignment to the 3d Infantry Division; assigned 2 December 1954 to the 3d Infantry Division.)

Inactivated 1 July 1957 at Fort Benning, Georgia, and relieved from assignment to the 3d Infantry Division; concurrently, redesignated as Headquarters and Headquarters Company, 4th Battle Group, 30th Infantry. (Organic elements constituted 15 March 1963.) Battle Group activated 1 April 1963 at Fort Sill, Oklahoma. Reorganized and redesignated 24 October 1963 as the 4th Battalion, 30th Infantry.

CAMPAIGN PARTICIPATION CREDIT

Philippine Insurrection
Mindoro 1901

World War I
*Aisne
*Champagne-Marne
*Aisne-Marne
*St. Mihiel
*Meuse-Argonne
*Champagne 1918

World War II
*Algeria-French Morocco (with arrowhead)
*Tunisia
*Sicily (with arrowhead)
*Naples-Foggia
*Anzio (with arrowhead)
*Rome-Arno
*Southern France (with arrowhead)
*Rhineland
*Ardennes-Alsace
*Central Europe

DECORATIONS

*Presidential Unit Citation (Army), Streamer embroidered COLMAR (3d Infantry Division cited; WD GO 44, 1945)

*Presidential Unit Citation (Army), Streamer embroidered BESANCON, FRANCE (1st Battalion, 30th Infantry cited; WD GO 18, 1945)

Presidential Unit Citation (Army), Streamer embroidered SICILY

Presidential Unit Citation (Army), Streamer embroidered MOUNT ROTUNDO

539

*French Croix de Guerre with Palm, World War I, Streamer embroidered CHAMPAGNE-MARNE (30th Infantry cited; WD GO 11, 1924)

*French Croix de Guerre with Palm, World War II, Streamer embroidered COLMAR (30th Infantry cited; DA GO 43, 1950)

*French Croix de Guerre, World War II, Fourragere (30th Infantry cited; DA GO 43, 1950)

COMPANY E, 30th INFANTRY

RA
(nondivisional)

LINEAGE

Constituted 2 February 1901 in the Regular Army as Company E, 30th Infantry. Organized 29 May 1901 at Palte, Laguna, Philippine Islands. (30th Infantry assigned 21 November 1917 to the 3d Division; relieved 12 January 1940 from assignment to the 3d Division; assigned 15 May 1940 to the 3d Division [later redesignated as the 3d Infantry Division]; relieved 6 April 1951 from assignment to the 3d Infantry Division; assigned 2 December 1954 to the 3d Infantry Division.)

Inactivated 1 July 1957 at Fort Benning, Georgia, and relieved from assignment to the 3d Infantry Division; concurrently, redesignated as Headquarters and Headquarters Company, 5th Battle Group, 30th Infantry. Redesignated 25 August 1966 as Company E, 30th Infantry and activated at Fort Rucker, Alabama.

CAMPAIGN PARTICIPATION CREDIT

Philippine Insurrection
Mindoro 1901

World War I
Aisne
Champagne-Marne
Aisne-Marne
St. Mihiel
Meuse-Argonne
Champagne 1918

World War II-EAME
Algeria-French Morocco
(with arrowhead)
Tunisia
Sicily (with arrowhead)
Naples-Foggia
Anzio (with arrowhead)
Rome-Arno
Southern France (with arrowhead)
Rhineland
Ardennes-Alsace
Central Europe

541

DECORATIONS

Presidential Unit Citation (Army), Streamer embroidered COLMAR (3d Infantry Division cited; WD GO 44, 1945)

Presidential Unit Citation (Army), Streamer embroidered SICILY (2d Battalion, 30th Infantry cited; WD GO 44, 1944)

French Croix de Guerre with Palm, World War I, Streamer embroidered CHAMPAGNE-MARNE (30th Infantry cited; WD GO 11, 1924)

French Croix de Guerre with Palm, World War II, Streamer embroidered COLMAR (30th Infantry cited; DA GO 43, 1950)

French Croix de Guerre, World War II, Fourragere (30th Infantry cited; DA GO 43, 1950)

COMPANY F, 30th INFANTRY

RA
(inactive)

LINEAGE

Constituted 2 February 1901 in the Regular Army as Company F, 30th Infantry. Organized 29 May 1901 at Palte, Laguna, Philippine Islands. (30th Infantry assigned 21 November 1917 to the 3d Division; relieved 12 January 1940 from assignment to the 3d Division; assigned 15 May 1940 to the 3d Division [later redesignated as the 3d Infantry Division]; relieved 6 April 1951 from assignment to the 3d Infantry Division; assigned 2 December 1954 to the 3d Infantry Division.)

Inactivated 1 July 1957 at Fort Benning, Georgia, and relieved from assignment to the 3d Infantry Division; concurrently, redesignated as Headquarters and Headquarters Company, 6th Battle Group, 30th Infantry. Redesignated 1 February 1967 as Company F, 30th Infantry and activated at Fort Riley, Kansas. Inactivated 25 March 1967 at Fort Riley, Kansas.

CAMPAIGN PARTICIPATION CREDIT

Philippine Insurrection
Mindoro 1901

World War I
Aisne
Champagne-Marne
Aisne-Marne
St. Mihiel
Meuse-Argonne
Champagne 1918

World War II-EAME
Algeria-French Morocco
(with arrowhead)
Tunisia
Sicily (with arrowhead)
Naples-Foggia
Anzio (with arrowhead)
Rome-Arno
Southern France (with arrowhead)
Rhineland
Ardennes-Alsace
Central Europe

DECORATIONS

Presidential Unit Citation (Army), Streamer embroidered COLMAR (3d Infantry Division cited; WD GO 44, 1945)

Presidential Unit Citation (Army), Streamer embroidered SICILY (2d Battalion, 30th Infantry cited; WD GO 44, 1944)

French Croix de Guerre with Palm, World War I, Streamer embroidered CHAMPAGNE-MARNE (30th Infantry cited; WD GO 11, 1924)

French Croix de Guerre with Palm, World War II, Streamer embroidered COLMAR (30th Infantry cited; DA GO 43, 1950)

French Croix de Guerre, World War II, Fourragere (30th Infantry cited; DA GO 43, 1950)

30TH INFANTRY, BIBLIOGRAPHY

Blumenson, Martin. *Salerno to Cassino.* United States Army in World War II. Washington: Government Printing Office, 1969.

Butts, Edmund Luther. *The Keypoint of the Marne and Its Defense by the 30th Infantry.* Menasha, Wisconsin: G. Banta Publishing Company, 1930.

Garland, Albert N. and Howard McGaw Smyth. *Sicily and the Surrender of Italy.* United States Army in World War II. Washington: Government Printing Office, 1965.

"The German Offensive of July 15, 1918." (Marne Source Book.) General Service School, Fort Leavenworth, Kansas, 1923.

Historical Section, War Department. *Anzio Beachhead.* American Forces in Action Series. Washington: Government Printing Office, 1947.

————. *From the Volturno to the Winter Line.* American Forces in Action Series. Washington: Government Printing Office, 1944.

————. *Salerno: American Operations From the Beaches to the Volturno.* American Forces in Action Series. Washington: Government Printing Office, 1944.

Howe, George F. *Northwest Africa: Seizing the Initiative in the West.* United States Army in World War II. Washington: Government Printing Office, 1957.

Mann, Walter M. "The 30th Infantry in the Hawaiian Maneuvers," *Infantry Journal,* XXXII (1932), 85–92.

Morton, John Nece. *"Re-union Booklet," Original Company "F" of the 30th United States Infantry, 1901–1904. History, Letters and Stories Depicting Army Days in the Philippines.* Springfield, Missouri, 1934.

Prohme, Rupert. *History of the 30th Infantry Regiment, World War II.* Washington: Infantry Journal Press, 1947.

Sheehan, Fred. *Anzio.* Norman: University of Oklahoma Press, 1964.

Thirtieth Infantry Day Celebrated on the Twenty-ninth Anniversary of the Birth of the Regiment, February 3d, 1930. San Francisco: H. S. Crocker Company, 1930.

31st INFANTRY

(The Polar Bears)

HERALDIC ITEMS

COAT OF ARMS

Shield: Azure, a sea lion or grasping in dexter paw a rifle with fixed bayonet proper.

Crest: On a wreath of the colors a polar bear affronté sejant head to sinister, proper.

Motto: *Pro Patria* (For Country).

Symbolism: The shield is blue for infantry. The unit's original organization in the Philippine Islands is indicated by the sea lion taken from the coat of arms of the Philippines. The regiment's service in Siberia in 1918–19 is symbolized by the polar bear crest. The motto is indicative of the spirit of the regiment, although for many years it did not set foot in the United States.

DISTINCTIVE INSIGNIA

The distinctive insignia is the crest and motto of the coat of arms.

LINEAGE AND HONORS

LINEAGE

Constituted 1 July 1916 in the Regular Army as the 31st Infantry. Organized 1 August 1916 at Fort William McKinley, Philippine Islands. Assigned 22 October 1921 to the Philippine Division. Relieved 26 June 1931 from assignment to the Philippine Division. Assigned in 1941 to the Philippine Division. Surrendered 9 April 1942 to the Japanese *14th Army*. Reorganized 19 January 1946 in Korea as an element of the 7th Infantry Division.

Relieved 1 July 1957 from assignment to the 7th Infantry Division and reorganized as a parent regiment under the Combat Arms Regimental System.

Campaign Participation Credit

World War I
  Siberia 1918
  Siberia 1919

World War II
  Philippine Islands

Korean War
  UN defensive
  UN offensive
  CCF intervention
  First UN counteroffensive

CCF spring offensive
UN summer-fall offensive
Second Korean winter
Korea, summer-fall 1952
Third Korean winter
Korea, summer 1953

Vietnam
  Counteroffensive, Phase II
  Counteroffensive, Phase III
  Tet Counteroffensive
  (other campaigns to be determined)

Decorations

Presidential Unit Citation (Army), Streamer embroidered LUZON 1941–1942 (31st Infantry cited; WD GO 14, 1942)

Presidential Unit Citation (Army), Streamer embroidered BATAAN (31st Infantry cited; WD GO 32, 1942)

Presidential Unit Citation (Army), Streamer embroidered DEFENSE OF THE PHILIPPINES (31st Infantry cited; WD GO 22, 1942, as amended by DA GO 46, 1948)

Presidential Unit Citation (Navy), Streamer embroidered CHOSIN RESERVOIR (2d Battalion [less Company E], 31st Infantry and attached units cited; DA GO 86, 1953)

Presidential Unit Citation (Navy), Streamer embroidered HWACHON RESERVOIR (31st Infantry cited; DA GO 38, 1957, as amended by DA GO 42, 1959)

Valorous Unit Award, Streamer embroidered QUE SON–HIEP DUC (4th Battalion, 31st Infantry cited; DA GO 5, 1969)

Valorous Unit Award, Streamer embroidered SAIGON (6th Battalion, 31st Infantry cited; DA GO 43, 1970)

Valorous Unit Award, Streamer embroidered PARROT'S BEAK (6th Battalion, 31st Infantry cited; DA GO 48, 1971)

Navy Unit Commendation, Streamer embroidered PANMUNJOM (31st Infantry cited; DA GO 38, 1957, as amended by DA GO 42, 1959)

Philippine Presidential Unit Citation, Streamer embroidered 7 DECEMBER 1941 TO 10 MAY 1942 (31st Infantry cited; DA GO 47, 1950)

Republic of Korea Presidential Unit Citation, Streamer embroidered INCHON (31st Infantry cited; DA GO 35, 1951)

Republic of Korea Presidential Unit Citation, Streamer embroidered KOREA (31st Infantry cited; DA GO 22, 1956)

1st BATTALION, 31st INFANTRY

(The Polar Bears)

RA

(7th Infantry Division)

LINEAGE

Constituted 1 July 1916 in the Regular Army as Company A, 31st Infantry. Organized 1 August 1916 at Regan Barracks, Philippine Islands. (31st Infantry assigned 22 October 1921 to the Philippine Division; relieved 26 June 1931 from assignment to the Philippine Division; assigned in 1941 to the Philippine Division.) Surrendered 9 April 1942 to the Japanese *14th Army*. Reorganized 19 January 1946 in Korea as an element of the 7th Infantry Division.

Reorganized and redesignated 1 July 1957 as Headquarters and Headquarters Company, 1st Battle Group, 31st Infantry and remained assigned to the 7th Infantry Division (organic elements concurrently constituted and activated). Reorganized and redesignated 1 July 1963 as the 1st Battalion, 31st Infantry.

CAMPAIGN PARTICIPATION CREDIT

World War I
  *Siberia 1918
  *Siberia 1919

World War II
  *Philippine Islands

Korean War
  *UN defensive
  *UN offensive

*CCF intervention
*First UN counteroffensive
*CCF spring offensive
*UN summer-fall offensive
*Second Korean winter
*Korea, summer-fall 1952
*Third Korean winter
*Korea, summer 1953

DECORATIONS

*Presidential Unit Citation (Army), Streamer embroidered LUZON 1941–1942 (31st Infantry cited; WD GO 14, 1942)

*Presidential Unit Citation (Army), Streamer embroidered BATAAN (31st Infantry cited; WD GO 32, 1942)

*Presidential Unit Citation (Army), Streamer embroidered DEFENSE OF THE PHILIPPINES (31st Infantry cited; WD GO 22, 1942, as amended by DA GO 46, 1948)

Presidential Unit Citation (Navy), Streamer embroidered CHOSIN RESERVOIR

*Presidential Unit Citation (Navy), Streamer embroidered HWACHON RESERVOIR (31st Infantry cited; DA GO 38, 1957, as amended by DA GO 42, 1959)

*Navy Unit Commendation, Streamer embroidered PANMUNJOM (31st Infantry cited; DA GO 38, 1957, as amended by DA GO 42, 1959)

*Philippine Presidential Unit Citation, Streamer embroidered 7 DECEMBER 1941 TO 10 MAY 1942 (31st Infantry cited; DA GO 47, 1950)

*Republic of Korea Presidential Unit Citation, Streamer embroidered INCHON (31st Infantry cited; DA GO 35, 1951)

*Republic of Korea Presidential Unit Citation, Streamer embroidered KOREA (31st Infantry cited; DA GO 22, 1956)

2d BATTALION, 31st INFANTRY

(The Polar Bears)

RA
(7th Infantry Division)

LINEAGE

Constituted 1 July 1916 in the Regular Army as Company B, 31st Infantry. Organized 1 August 1916 at Regan Barracks, Philippine Islands. (31st Infantry assigned 22 October 1921 to the Philippine Division; relieved 26 June 1931 from assignment to the Philippine Division; assigned in 1941 to the Philippine Division.) Surrendered 9 April 1942 to the Japanese *14th Army*. Reorganized 19 January 1946 in Korea as an element of the 7th Infantry Division.

Inactivated 1 July 1957 in Korea and relieved from assignment to the 7th Infantry Division; concurrently, redesignated as Headquarters and Headquarters Company, 2d Battle Group, 31st Infantry. (Organic elements constituted 27 February 1958.) Battle Group activated 24 March 1958 at Fort Rucker, Alabama. Reorganized and redesignated 1 July 1963 as the 2d Battalion, 31st Infantry and assigned to the 7th Infantry Division.

CAMPAIGN PARTICIPATION CREDIT

World War I
  *Siberia 1918
  *Siberia 1919

World War II
  *Philippine Islands

Korean War
  *UN defensive
  *UN offensive

*CCF intervention
*First UN counteroffensive
*CCF spring offensive
*UN summer-fall offensive
*Second Korean winter
*Korea, summer-fall 1952
*Third Korean winter
*Korea, summer 1953

DECORATIONS

*Presidential Unit Citation (Army), Streamer embroidered LUZON 1941–1942 (31st Infantry cited; WD GO 14, 1942)

*Presidential Unit Citation (Army), Streamer embroidered BATAAN (31st Infantry cited; WD GO 32, 1942)

*Presidential Unit Citation (Army), Streamer embroidered DEFENSE

OF THE PHILIPPINES (31st Infantry cited; WD GO 22, 1942, as amended by DA GO 46, 1948)

*Presidential Unit Citation (Navy), Streamer embroidered CHOSIN RESERVOIR (Company B, 31st Infantry cited; DA GO 86, 1953)

*Presidential Unit Citation (Navy), Streamer embroidered HWACHON RESERVOIR (31st Infantry cited; DA GO 38, 1957, as amended by DA GO 42, 1959)

*Navy Unit Commendation, Streamer embroidered PANMUNJOM (31st Infantry cited; DA GO 38, 1957, as amended by DA GO 42, 1959)

*Philippine Presidential Unit Citation, Streamer embroidered 7 DECEMBER 1941 TO 10 MAY 1942 (31st Infantry cited; DA GO 47, 1950)

*Republic of Korea Presidential Unit Citation, Streamer embroidered INCHON (31st Infantry cited; DA GO 35, 1951)

*Republic of Korea Presidential Unit Citation, Streamer embroidered KOREA (31st Infantry cited; DA GO 22, 1956)

3d BATTALION, 31st INFANTRY

(The Polar Bears)

AR
(inactive)

LINEAGE

Constituted 1 July 1916 in the Regular Army as Company C, 31st Infantry. Organized 1 August 1916 at Regan Barracks, Philippine Islands. (31st Infantry assigned 22 October 1921 to the Philippine Division; relieved 26 June 1931 from assignment to the Philippine Division; assigned in 1941 to the Philippine Division.) Surrendered 9 April 1942 to the Japanese *14th Army*. Reorganized 19 January 1946 in Korea as an element of the 7th Infantry Division.

Inactivated 1 July 1957 in Korea and relieved from assignment to the 7th Infantry Division; concurrently redesignated as Headquarters and Headquarters Company, 3d Battle Group, 31st Infantry. Withdrawn 31 March 1959 from the Regular Army, allotted to the Army Reserve, and assigned to the 63d Infantry Division (organic elements concurrently constituted). Battle Group activated 1 May 1959 with Headquarters at Los Angeles, California (concurrently, Headquarters and Headquarters Company consolidated with Headquarters and Headquarters Company, 253d Infantry [see ANNEX] and consolidated unit designated as Headquarters and Headquarters Company, 3d Battle Group, 31st Infantry).

Reorganized and redesignated 1 October 1963 as the 3d Battalion, 31st Infantry. (Location of Headquarters changed 16 March 1964 to Playa del Rey, California.) Inactivated 31 December 1965 at Playa del Rey, California.

ANNEX

Constituted 18 January 1943 in the Army of the United States as Headquarters and Headquarters Company, 253d Infantry, an element of the 63d Infantry Division. Activated 15 June 1943 at Camp Blanding, Florida. Inactivated 28 September 1945 at Camp Myles Standish, Massachusetts. (63d Infantry Division allotted 22 February 1952 to the Organized Reserve Corps.) Activated 1 March 1952 at Los Angeles, California. (Organized Reserve Corps redesignated 9 July 1952 as the Army Reserve.)

Consolidated 1 May 1959 with Headquarters and Headquarters Company, 3d Battle Group, 31st Infantry and consolidated unit designated as Headquarters and Headquarters Company, 3d Battle Group, 31st Infantry (remainder of 253d Infantry inactivated).

CAMPAIGN PARTICIPATION CREDIT

World War I
  *Siberia 1918
  *Siberia 1919

World War II
  *Philippine Islands
  *Rhineland
  *Ardennes-Alsace
  *Central Europe

Korean War
  *UN defensive
  *UN offensive
  *CCF intervention
  *First UN counteroffensive
  *CCF spring offensive
  *UN summer-fall offensive
  *Second Korean winter
  *Korea, summer-fall 1952
  *Third Korean winter
  *Korea, summer 1953

DECORATIONS

*Presidential Unit Citation (Army), Streamer embroidered LUZON 1941–1942 (31st Infantry cited; WD GO 14, 1942)

*Presidential Unit Citation (Army), Streamer embroidered BATAAN (31st Infantry cited; WD GO 32, 1942)

*Presidential Unit Citation (Army), Streamer embroidered DEFENSE OF THE PHILIPPINES (31st Infantry cited; WD GO 22, 1942, as amended by DA GO 46, 1948)

Presidential Unit Citation (Navy), Streamer embroidered CHOSIN RESERVOIR

*Presidential Unit Citation (Navy), Streamer embroidered HWACHON RESERVOIR (31st Infantry cited; DA GO 38, 1957, as amended by DA GO 42, 1959)

*Navy Unit Commendation, Streamer embroidered PANMUNJOM (31st Infantry cited; DA GO 38, 1957, as amended by DA GO 42, 1959)

*Philippine Presidential Unit Citation, Streamer embroidered 7 DECEMBER 1941 TO 10 MAY 1942 (31st Infantry cited; DA GO 47, 1950)

*Republic of Korea Presidential Unit Citation, Streamer embroidered INCHON (31st Infantry cited; DA GO 35, 1951)

*Republic of Korea Presidential Unit Citation, Streamer embroidered KOREA (31st Infantry cited; DA GO 22, 1956)

4th BATTALION, 31st INFANTRY

(The Polar Bears)

RA

(23d Infantry Division)

LINEAGE

Constituted 1 July 1916 in the Regular Army as Company D, 31st Infantry. Organized 1 August 1916 at Regan Barracks, Philippine Islands. (31st Infantry assigned 22 October 1921 to the Philippine Division; relieved 26 June 1931 from assignment to the Philippine Division; assigned in 1941 to the Philippine Division.) Surrendered 9 April 1942 to the Japanese *14th Army*. Reorganized 19 January 1946 in Korea as an element of the 7th Infantry Division.

Inactivated 1 July 1957 in Korea and relieved from assignment to the 7th Infantry Division; concurrently, redesignated as Headquarters and Headquarters Company, 4th Battle Group, 31st Infantry. Redesignated 10 September 1965 as Headquarters and Headquarters Company, 4th Battalion, 31st Infantry, assigned to the 196th Infantry Brigade, and activated at Fort Devens, Massachusetts (organic elements concurrently constituted and activated). Relieved 15 February 1969 from assignment to the 196th Infantry Brigade and assigned to the 23d Infantry Division.

CAMPAIGN PARTICIPATION CREDIT

World War I
  *Siberia 1918
  *Siberia 1919

World War II
  *Philippine Islands

Korean War
  *UN defensive
  *UN offensive
  *CCF intervention
  *First UN counteroffensive

  *CCF spring offensive
  *UN summer-fall offensive
  *Second Korean winter
  *Korea, summer-fall 1952
  *Third Korean winter
  *Korea, summer 1953

Vietnam
  *Counteroffensive, Phase II
  *Counteroffensive, Phase III
  *Tet Counteroffensive
    (other campaigns to be determined)

DECORATIONS

*Presidential Unit Citation (Army), Streamer embroidered LUZON 1941–1942 (31st Infantry cited; DA GO 14, 1942)

*Presidential Unit Citation (Army), Streamer embroidered BATAAN (31st Infantry cited; DA GO 32, 1942)

*Presidential Unit Citation (Army), Streamer embroidered DEFENSE OF THE PHILIPPINES (31st Infantry cited; DA GO 22, 1942, as amended by DA GO 46, 1948)

Presidential Unit Citation (Navy), Streamer embroidered CHOSIN RESERVOIR

*Presidential Unit Citation (Navy), Streamer embroidered HWACHON RESERVOIR (31st Infantry cited; DA GO 38, 1957, as amended by DA GO 42, 1959)

*Valorous Unit Award, Streamer embroidered QUE SON–HIEP DUC (4th Battalion, 31st Infantry cited; DA GO 5, 1969)

*Navy Unit Commendation, Streamer embroidered PANMUNJOM (31st Infantry cited; DA GO 38, 1957, as amended by DA GO 42, 1959)

*Philippine Presidential Unit Citation, Streamer embroidered 7 DECEMBER 1941 TO 10 MAY 1942 (31st Infantry cited; DA GO 47, 1950)

*Republic of Korea Presidential Unit Citation, Streamer embroidered INCHON (31st Infantry cited; DA GO 35, 1951)

*Republic of Korea Presidential Unit Citation, Streamer embroidered KOREA (31st Infantry cited; DA GO 22, 1956)

5th BATTALION, 31st INFANTRY

(The Polar Bears)

RA
(197th Infantry Brigade)

LINEAGE

Constituted 1 July 1916 in the Regular Army as Company E, 31st Infantry. Organized 1 August 1916 at Fort William McKinley, Philippine Islands. (31st Infantry assigned 22 October 1921 to the Philippine Division; relieved 26 June 1931 from assignment to the Philippine Division; assigned in 1941 to the Philippine Division.) Surrendered 9 April 1942 to the Japanese *14th Army*. Reorganized 19 January 1946 in Korea as an element of the 7th Infantry Division.

Inactivated 1 July 1957 in Korea and relieved from assignment to the 7th Infantry Division; concurrently, redesignated as Headquarters and Headquarters Company, 5th Battle Group, 31st Infantry. (Organic elements constituted 7 June 1963.) Battle Group activated 1 July 1963 at Fort Rucker, Alabama. Reorganized and redesignated 25 May 1964 as the 5th Battalion, 31st Infantry. Assigned 23 June 1967 to the 197th Infantry Brigade.

CAMPAIGN PARTICIPATION CREDIT

World War I
  *Siberia 1918
  *Siberia 1919

World War II
  *Philippine Islands

Korean War
  *UN defensive

*UN offensive
*CCF intervention
*First UN counteroffensive
*CCF spring offensive
*UN summer-fall offensive
*Second Korean winter
*Korea, summer-fall 1952
*Third Korean winter
*Korea, summer 1953

DECORATIONS

*Presidential Unit Citation (Army), Streamer embroidered LUZON 1941–1942 (31st Infantry cited; DA GO 14, 1942)
  *Presidential Unit Citation (Army), Streamer embroidered BATAAN (31st Infantry cited; DA GO 32, 1942)
  *Presidential Unit Citation (Army), Streamer embroidered DEFENSE

557

OF THE PHILIPPINES (31st Infantry cited; DA GO 22, 1942, as amended by DA GO 46, 1948)

Presidential Unit Citation (Navy), Streamer embroidered CHOSIN RESERVOIR

*Presidential Unit Citation (Navy), Streamer embroidered HWACHON RESERVOIR (31st Infantry cited; DA GO 38, 1957, as amended by DA GO 42, 1959)

*Navy Unit Commendation, Streamer embroidered PANMUNJOM (31st Infantry cited; DA GO 38, 1957, as amended by DA GO 42, 1959)

*Philippine Presidential Unit Citation, Streamer embroidered 7 DECEMBER 1941 TO 10 MAY 1942 (31st Infantry cited; DA GO 47, 1950)

*Republic of Korea Presidential Unit Citation, Streamer embroidered INCHON (31st Infantry cited; DA GO 35, 1951)

*Republic of Korea Presidential Unit Citation, Streamer embroidered KOREA (31st Infantry cited; DA GO 22, 1956)

6th BATTALION, 31st INFANTRY

(The Polar Bears)

RA
(inactive)

LINEAGE

Constituted 1 July 1916 in the Regular Army as Company F, 31st Infantry. Organized 1 August 1916 at Camp McGrath, Philippine Islands. (31st Infantry assigned 22 October 1921 to the Philippine Division; relieved 26 June 1931 from assignment to the Philippine Division; assigned in 1941 to the Philippine Division.) Surrendered 9 April 1942 to the Japanese *14th Army*. Reorganized 19 January 1946 in Korea as an element of the 7th Infantry Division.

Inactivated 1 July 1957 in Korea and relieved from assignment to the 7th Infantry Division; concurrently, redesignated as Headquarters and Headquarters Company, 6th Battle Group, 31st Infantry. Redesignated 1 November 1967 as Headquarters and Headquarters Company, 6th Battalion, 31st Infantry and activated at Fort Lewis, Washington (organic elements concurrently constituted and activated). Assigned 15 February 1969 to the 9th Infantry Division. Inactivated 13 October 1970 at Fort Lewis, Washington.

CAMPAIGN PARTICIPATION CREDIT

World War I
  *Siberia 1918
  *Siberia 1919

World War II
  *Philippine Islands

Korean War
  *UN defensive
  *UN offensive
  *CCF intervention

*First UN counteroffensive
*CCF spring offensive
*UN summer-fall offensive
*Second Korean winter
*Korea, summer-fall 1952
*Third Korean winter
*Korea, summer 1953

Vietnam
  (to be determined)

DECORATIONS

*Presidential Unit Citation (Army), Streamer embroidered LUZON 1941–1942 (31st Infantry cited; WD GO 14, 1942)

*Presidential Unit Citation (Army), Streamer embroidered BATAAN (31st Infantry cited; WD GO 32, 1942)

559

*Presidential Unit Citation (Army), Streamer embroidered DEFENSE OF THE PHILIPPINES (31st Infantry cited; WD GO 22, 1942, as amended by DA GO 46, 1948)

*Presidential Unit Citation (Navy), Streamer embroidered CHOSIN RESERVOIR (2d Battalion [less Company E], 31st Infantry and attached units cited; DA GO 86, 1953)

*Presidential Unit Citation (Navy), Streamer embroidered HWACHON RESERVOIR (31st Infantry cited; DA GO 38, 1957, as amended by DA GO 42, 1959)

*Valorous Unit Award, Streamer embroidered SAIGON (6th Battalion, 31st Infantry cited; DA GO 43, 1970)

*Valorous Unit Award, Streamer embroidered PARROT'S BEAK (6th Battalion, 31st Infantry cited; DA GO 48, 1971)

*Navy Unit Commendation, Streamer embroidered PANMUNJOM (31st Infantry cited; DA GO 38, 1957, as amended by DA GO 42, 1959)

*Philippine Presidential Unit Citation, Streamer embroidered 7 DECEMBER 1941 TO MAY 1942 (31st Infantry cited; DA GO 47, 1950)

*Republic of Korea Presidential Unit Citation, Streamer embroidered INCHON (31st Infantry cited; DA GO 35, 1951)

*Republic of Korea Presidential Unit Citation, Streamer embroidered KOREA (31st Infantry cited; DA GO 22, 1956)

*Vietnamese Cross of Gallantry with Palm, Streamer embroidered VIETNAM, APRIL–JUNE 1968 (6th Battalion, 31st Infantry cited; DA GO 31, 1969)

*Vietnamese Cross of Gallantry with Palm, Streamer embroidered VIETNAM, JULY–NOVEMBER 1968 (6th Battalion, 31st Infantry cited; DA GO 31, 1969)

*Vietnamese Cross of Gallantry with Palm, Streamer embroidered VIETNAM 1969 (6th Battalion, 31st Infantry cited; DA GO 59, 1969)

*Vietnamese Civil Action Honor Medal, First Class, Streamer embroidered VIETNAM 1968–1969 (6th Battalion, 31st Infantry cited; DA GO 59, 1969)

31st Infantry, Bibliography

Appleman, Roy E. *South to the Naktong, North to the Yalu.* United States Army in the Korean War. Washington: Government Printing Office, 1961.

Belote, James H. and William M. *Corregidor, The Saga of a Fortress.* New York: Harper and Row, Publishers, 1967.

Cahill, Howard F. K. "The Thirty-first Infantry in Shanghai," *Infantry Journal,* XXXII (1932), 165–175.

Graves, William S. *America's Siberian Adventure, 1918–1920.* New York: Cape and H. Smith, 1931.

Gugeler, Russell A. *Combat Actions in Korea.* Washington: Combat Forces Press, 1954.

"Here and There with the 31st." Published at intervals between 1919 and 1922 in Vladivostok and the Philippine Islands.

Hermes, Walter G. *Truce Tent and Fighting Front.* United States Army in the Korean War. Washington: Government Printing Office, 1966.

Legionnaired Facts, 31st U.S. Infantry Regiment, "America's Foreign Legion." n.p., 1954.

Marshall, S. L. A. *Ambush.* New York: Cowles Book Company, 1969.

———. *Pork Chop Hill.* New York: William Morrow, 1956.

Morton, Louis. *The Fall of the Philippines.* United States Army in World War II. Washington: Government Printing Office, 1953.

"Seventeenth Anniversary Organization Day, 1916–1933, Thirty-first U.S. Infantry. August 13, 1933." Manila, 1933.

"Twenty-first Anniversary Organization Day, 1916–1937, Thirty-first U.S. Infantry. August 13, 1937." Manila, 1937.

"Twenty-third Anniversary Organization Day, 1916–1939, Thirty-first U.S. Infantry. August 13, 1939." Manila, 1939.

Untenberger, Betty M. *America's Siberian Expedition, 1918–1920.* Durham, North Carolina: Duke University Press, 1956.

32d INFANTRY

HERALDIC ITEMS

COAT OF ARMS

Shield: Azure, a saltire couped argent, overall a puela in pale or; on a canton of the second a lion passant guardant gules.

Crest: On a wreath of the colors a mahiole or garnished gules.

Motto: None.

Symbolism: This regiment was originally organized on the island of Oahu in Hawaii, with personnel from the 1st and 2d Infantry. These organizations are shown on the canton, the lion indicating that both regiments took part in the War of 1812. The central device is taken from the royal Hawaiian arms to symbolize the regiment's birthplace. The puela was an ancient Hawaiian banner with many uses, one of which was in front of the king's tent leaning against two crossed spears (called alia) to indicate both tabu and protection; a saltire cross replaced the spears on the Hawaiian arms.

The colors of the crest are the royal Hawaiian colors. The crest is an ancient Hawaiian war bonnet known as a mahiole.

DISTINCTIVE INSIGNIA

The distinctive insignia is the shield and crest of the coat of arms.

LINEAGE AND HONORS

LINEAGE

Constituted 1 July 1916 in the Regular Army as the 32d Infantry. Organized 7 August 1916 at Schofield Barracks, Hawaii. Assigned 31 July 1918 to the 16th Division. Relieved 8 March 1919 from assignment to the 16th Division. Inactivated 1 November 1921 at the Presidio of San Francisco, California. Activated 1 July 1940 at Camp Ord, California, and assigned to the 7th Division (later redesignated as the 7th Infantry Division).

Relieved 1 July 1957 from assignment to the 7th Infantry Division and reorganized as a parent regiment under the Combat Arms Regimental System.

CAMPAIGN PARTICIPATION CREDIT

World War II
Aleutian Islands (with arrowhead)
Eastern Mandates
Leyte (with arrowhead)
Ryukyus (with arrowhead)

Korean War
UN defensive
UN offensive

CCF intervention
First UN counteroffensive
CCF spring offensive
UN summer-fall offensive
Second Korean winter
Korea, summer-fall 1952
Third Korean winter
Korea, summer 1953

DECORATIONS

Presidential Unit Citation (Army), Streamer embroidered KUMHWA (1st Battalion, 32d Infantry cited; DA GO 42, 1953)

Presidential Unit Citation (Army), Streamer embroidered CENTRAL KOREA (3d Battalion, 32d Infantry and attached units cited; DA GO 81, 1951, as amended by DA GO 54, 1952)

Presidential Unit Citation (Navy), Streamer embroidered INCHON (32d Regimental Combat Team cited; DA GO 63, 1952)

Presidential Unit Citation (Navy), Streamer embroidered HWACHON RESERVOIR (32d Infantry cited; DA GO 38, 1957, as amended by DA GO 42, 1959)

Navy Unit Commendation, Streamer embroidered PANMUNJOM (32d Infantry cited; DA GO 38, 1957, as amended by DA GO 42, 1959)

Philippine Presidential Unit Citation, Streamer embroidered 17 OCTOBER 1944 TO 4 JULY 1945 (32d Infantry cited; DA GO 47, 1950)

Republic of Korea Presidential Unit Citation, Streamer embroidered INCHON (32d Infantry cited; DA GO 35, 1951)

Republic of Korea Presidential Unit Citation, Streamer embroidered KOREA (32d Infantry cited; DA GO 22, 1956)

1st BATTALION, 32d INFANTRY

RA
(7th Infantry Division)

LINEAGE

Constituted 1 July 1916 in the Regular Army as Company A, 32d Infantry. Organized 7 August 1916 at Schofield Barracks, Hawaii. (32d Infantry assigned 31 July 1918 to the 16th Division; relieved 8 March 1919 from assignment to the 16th Division.) Inactivated 13 September 1921 at Vancouver Barracks, Washington. Activated 1 July 1940 at Camp Ord, California (concurrently, 32d Infantry assigned to the 7th Division [later redesignated as the 7th Infantry Division]).

Reorganized and redesignated 1 July 1957 as Headquarters and Headquarters Company, 1st Battle Group, 32d Infantry and remained assigned to the 7th Infantry Division (organic elements concurrently constituted and activated). Reorganized and redesignated 1 July 1963 as the 1st Battalion, 32d Infantry.

CAMPAIGN PARTICIPATION CREDIT

World War II
  *Aleutian Islands (with arrowhead)
  *Eastern Mandates
  *Leyte (with arrowhead)
  *Ryukyus (with arrowhead)

Korean War
  *UN defensive
  *UN offensive

*CCF intervention
*First UN counteroffensive
*CCF spring offensive
*UN summer-fall offensive
*Second Korean winter
*Korea, summer-fall 1952
*Third Korean winter
*Korea, summer 1953

DECORATIONS

*Presidential Unit Citation (Army), Streamer embroidered KUMHWA (1st Battalion, 32d Infantry cited; DA GO 42, 1953)

Presidential Unit Citation (Army), Streamer embroidered CENTRAL KOREA

*Presidential Unit Citation (Navy), Streamer embroidered INCHON (32d Regimental Combat Team cited; DA GO 63, 1952)

*Presidential Unit Citation (Navy), Streamer embroidered HWACHON RESERVOIR (32d Infantry cited; DA GO 38, 1957, as amended by DA GO 42, 1959)

*Navy Unit Commendation, Streamer embroidered PANMUNJOM

(32d Infantry cited; DA GO 38, 1957, as amended by DA GO 42, 1959)

*Philippine Presidential Unit Citation, Streamer embroidered 17 OCTOBER 1944 TO 4 JULY 1945 (32d Infantry cited; DA GO 47, 1950)

*Republic of Korea Presidential Unit Citation, Streamer embroidered INCHON (32d Infantry cited; DA GO 35, 1951)

*Republic of Korea Presidential Unit Citation, Streamer embroidered KOREA (32d Infantry cited; DA GO 22, 1956)

2d BATTALION, 32d INFANTRY

RA
(7th Infantry Division)

LINEAGE

Constituted 1 July 1916 in the Regular Army as Company B, 32d Infantry. Organized 7 August 1916 at Schofield Barracks, Hawaii. (32d Infantry assigned 31 July 1918 to the 16th Division; relieved 8 March 1919 from assignment to the 16th Division.) Inactivated 2 September 1921 at Fort Lawton, Washington. Activated 1 July 1940 at Camp Ord, California (concurrently, 32d Infantry assigned to the 7th Division [later redesignated as the 7th Infantry Division]).

Inactivated 1 July 1957 in Korea and relieved from assignment to the 7th Infantry Division; concurrently, redesignated as Headquarters and Headquarters Company, 2d Battle Group, 32d Infantry. Redesignated 7 June 1963 as Headquarters and Headquarters Company, 2d Battalion, 32d Infantry (organic elements concurrently constituted). Battalion activated 1 July 1963 in Korea and assigned to the 7th Infantry Division.

CAMPAIGN PARTICIPATION CREDIT

World War II
  *Aleutian Islands (with arrowhead)
  *Eastern Mandates
  *Leyte (with arrowhead)
  *Ryukyus (with arrowhead)

Korean War
  *UN defensive
  *UN offensive

*CCF intervention
*First UN counteroffensive
*CCF spring offensive
*UN summer-fall offensive
*Second Korean winter
*Korea, summer-fall 1952
*Third Korean winter
*Korea, summer 1953

DECORATIONS

*Presidential Unit Citation (Army), Streamer embroidered KUMHWA (1st Battalion, 32d Infantry cited; DA GO 42, 1953)

Presidential Unit Citation (Army), Streamer embroidered CENTRAL KOREA

*Presidential Unit Citation (Navy), Streamer embroidered INCHON (32d Regimental Combat Team cited; DA GO 63, 1952)

*Presidential Unit Citation (Navy), Streamer embroidered HWACHON RESERVOIR (32d Infantry cited; DA GO 38, 1957, as amended by DA GO 42, 1959)

*Navy Unit Commendation, Streamer embroidered PANMUNJOM (32d Infantry cited; DA GO 38, 1957, as amended by DA GO 42, 1959)

*Philippine Presidential Unit Citation, Streamer embroidered 17 OCTOBER 1944 TO 4 JULY 1945 (32d Infantry cited; DA GO 47, 1950)

*Republic of Korea Presidential Unit Citation, Streamer embroidered INCHON (32d Infantry cited; DA GO 35, 1951)

*Republic of Korea Presidential Unit Citation, Streamer embroidered KOREA (32d Infantry cited; DA GO 22, 1956)

3d BATTALION, 32d INFANTRY

LINEAGE

Constituted 1 July 1916 in the Regular Army as Company C, 32d Infantry. Organized 7 August 1916 at Schofield Barracks, Hawaii. (32d Infantry assigned 31 July 1918 to the 16th Division; relieved 8 March 1919 from assignment to the 16th Division.) Inactivated 2 September 1921 at Fort Lawton, Washington. Activated 1 July 1940 at Camp Ord, California (concurrently, 32d Infantry assigned to the 7th Division [later redesignated as the 7th Infantry Division]).

Inactivated 1 July 1957 in Korea and relieved from assignment to the 7th Infantry Division; concurrently, redesignated as Headquarters and Headquarters Company, 3d Battle Group, 32d Infantry. Redesignated 8 May 1958 as Company C, 32d Infantry. Activated 25 June 1958 at Fort Bragg, North Carolina. Inactivated 7 February 1963 at Fort Bragg, North Carolina. Reorganized and redesignated 7 June 1963 as Headquarters and Headquarters Company, 3d Battalion, 32d Infantry (organic elements concurrently constituted). Battalion activated 1 July 1963 in Korea and assigned to the 7th Infantry Division.

CAMPAIGN PARTICIPATION CREDIT

World War II
* *Aleutian Islands (with arrowhead)
* *Eastern Mandates
* *Leyte (with arrowhead)
* *Ryukyus (with arrowhead)

Korean War
* *UN defensive
* *UN offensive

* *CCF intervention
* *First UN counteroffensive
* *CCF spring offensive
* *UN summer-fall offensive
* *Second Korean winter
* *Korea, summer-fall 1952
* *Third Korean winter
* *Korea, summer 1953

DECORATIONS

*Presidential Unit Citation (Army), Streamer embroidered KUMHWA (1st Battalion, 32d Infantry cited; DA GO 42, 1953)

Presidential Unit Citation (Army), Streamer embroidered CENTRAL KOREA

*Presidential Unit Citation (Navy), Streamer embroidered INCHON (32d Regimental Combat Team cited; DA GO 63, 1952)

*Presidential Unit Citation (Navy) , Streamer embroidered HWACHON RESERVOIR (32d Infantry cited; DA GO 38, 1957, as amended by DA GO 42, 1959)

*Navy Unit Commendation, Streamer embroidered PANMUNJOM (32d Infantry cited; DA GO 38, 1957, as amended by DA GO 42, 1959)

*Philippine Presidential Unit Citation, Streamer embroidered 17 OCTOBER 1944 TO 4 JULY 1945 (32d Infantry cited; DA GO 47, 1950)

*Republic of Korea Presidential Unit Citation, Streamer embroidered INCHON (32d Infantry cited; DA GO 35, 1951)

*Republic of Korea Presidential Unit Citation, Streamer embroidered KOREA (32d Infantry cited; DA GO 22, 1956)

4th BATTLE GROUP, 32d INFANTRY

AR
(inactive)

LINEAGE

Constituted 1 July 1916 in the Regular Army as Company D, 32d Infantry. Organized 7 August 1916 at Schofield Barracks, Hawaii. (32d Infantry assigned 31 July 1918 to the 16th Division; relieved 8 March 1919 from assignment to the 16th Division.) Inactivated 3 September 1921 at Fort Lawton, Washington. Activated 1 July 1940 at Camp Ord, California (concurrently, 32d Infantry assigned to the 7th Division [later redesignated as the 7th Infantry Division]).

Inactivated July 1957 in Korea and relieved from assignment to the 7th Infantry Division; concurrently, redesignated as Headquarters and Headquarters Company, 4th Battle Group, 32d Infantry. Withdrawn 10 April 1959 from the Regular Army, allotted to the Army Reserve, and assigned to the 81st Infantry Division (organic elements concurrently constituted). Battle Group activated 1 May 1959 with Headquarters at Knoxville, Tennessee. Inactivated 1 April 1963 at Knoxville, Tennessee, and relieved from assignment to the 81st Infantry Division.

CAMPAIGN PARTICIPATION CREDIT

World War II
  *Aleutian Islands (with arrowhead)
  *Eastern Mandates
  *Leyte (with arrowhead)
  *Ryukyus (with arrowhead)

Korean War
  *UN defensive
  *UN offensive

*CCF intervention
*First UN counteroffensive
*CCF spring offensive
*UN summer-fall offensive
*Second Korean winter
*Korea, summer-fall 1952
*Third Korean winter
*Korea, summer 1953

DECORATIONS

*Presidential Unit Citation (Army), Streamer embroidered KUMHWA (1st Battalion, 32d Infantry cited; DA GO 42, 1953)

Presidential Unit Citation (Army), Streamer embroidered CENTRAL KOREA

*Presidential Unit Citation (Navy), Streamer embroidered INCHON (32d Regimental Combat Team cited; DA GO 63, 1952)

*Presidential Unit Citation (Navy), Streamer embroidered HWACHON

RESERVOIR (32d Infantry cited; DA GO 38, 1957, as amended by DA GO 42, 1959)

*Navy Unit Commendation, Streamer embroidered PANMUNJOM (32d Infantry cited; DA GO 38, 1957, as amended by DA GO 42, 1959)

*Philippine Presidential Unit Citation, Streamer embroidered 17 OCTOBER 1944 TO 4 JULY 1945 (32d Infantry cited; DA GO 47, 1950)

*Republic of Korea Presidential Unit Citation, Streamer embroidered INCHON (32d Infantry cited; DA GO 35, 1951)

*Republic of Korea Presidential Unit Citation, Streamer embroidered KOREA (32d Infantry cited; DA GO 22, 1956)

32D INFANTRY, BIBLIOGRAPHY

Appleman, Roy E. *South to the Naktong, North to the Yalu.* United States Army in the Korean War. Washington: Government Printing Office, 1961.

Appleman, Roy E. *et al. Okinawa: The Last Battle.* United States Army in World War II. Washington: Government Printing Office, 1948.

Cannon, M. Hamlin. *Leyte: The Return to the Philippines.* United States Army in World War II. Washington: Government Printing Office, 1954.

The Capture of Attu, as Told by the Men Who Fought There. Washington: Infantry Journal Press, 1944.

Conn, Stetson, Rose C. Engelman, and Byron Fairchild. *Guarding the United States and Its Outposts.* United States Army in World War II. Washington: Government Printing Office, 1964.

Crowl, Philip A. and Edmund G. Love. *Seizure of the Gilberts and Marshalls.* United States Army in World War II. Washington: Government Printing Office, 1955.

Falk, Stanley L. *Decision at Leyte.* New York: W. W. Norton and Company, Inc., 1966.

Gugeler, Russell A. *Combat Actions in Korea.* Washington: Combat Forces Press, 1954.

History of the Queen's Own 32d Infantry, Buccaneers. n.p., 1953.

History: Queen's Own 32d Infantry. n.p., 1956.

"Kwajalein Day-By-Day," *Infantry Journal,* LV (August 1944), 12–13.

Marshall, S. L. A. "Fight to a Finish," *Infantry Journal,* LVI (January 1945), 43–52.

————. *Island Victory.* Washington: Infantry Journal Press, 1944.

————. "Men Against Darkness," *Infantry Journal,* LV (December 1944), 43–51.

————. "One Day on Kwajalein," *Infantry Journal,* LV (August 1944), 14–25.

————. "Ordeal by Fire," *Infantry Journal,* LV (October 1944), 35–44.

————. *Pork Chop Hill.* New York: William Morrow, 1956.

Thirty-second United States Infantry Organization Day Exercises, August 4, 1921. San Francisco?, 1921.

34th INFANTRY

Heraldic Items

Coat of Arms

Shield: Azure, crusilly fitche or; on a canton of the last masoned sable a cross pattée argent fimbriated of the first.

Crest: On a wreath of the colors a cactus (prickly pear) vert.

Motto: *Toujours en Avant* (Always Forward).

Symbolism: The regiment was originally organized at El Paso, Texas, by transfer of personnel from the 7th, 20th, and 23d Infantry. These units are symbolized on the canton; the masoned wall is from the arms of the 7th Infantry and the white Maltese cross is from the arms of the 20th and 23d Infantry. The blue background with gold cross crosslets sharpened at the foot reflects World War I service. The 34th Infantry served in that part of the province of Lorraine which was anciently the Barony of Commercy. The arms of those Barons were blue, scattered with gold cross crosslets sharpened at the foot.

The crest commemorates Texas, the birthplace of the regiment.

Distinctive Insignia

The distinctive insignia is the shield of the coat of arms.

Lineage and Honors

Lineage

Constituted 1 July 1916 in the Regular Army as the 34th Infantry. Organized 15 July 1916 at El Paso, Texas. Assigned 6 December 1917 to the 7th Division. Relieved 24 March 1923 from assignment to the 7th Division and assigned to the 8th Division. Relieved 15 August 1927 from assignment to the 8th Division and assigned to the 4th Division. Relieved 1 October 1933 from assignment to the 4th Division and assigned to the 8th Division (later redesignated as the 8th Infantry Division). Inactivated 5 June 1940 at Fort Benning, Georgia. Activated 1 July 1940 at

Camp Jackson, South Carolina. Relieved 12 June 1943 from assignment to the 8th Infantry Division and assigned to the 24th Infantry Division.

Relieved 5 June 1958 from assignment to the 24th Infantry Division and reorganized as a parent regiment under the Combat Arms Regimental System.

CAMPAIGN PARTICIPATION CREDIT

World War I
   Lorraine 1918

Luzon
Southern Philippines

World War II
   New Guinea
   Leyte (with arrowhead)

Korean War
   UN defensive
   UN summer-fall offensive
   Korea, summer 1953

DECORATIONS

Presidential Unit Citation (Army), Streamer embroidered KILAY RIDGE (1st Battalion, 34th Infantry cited; WD GO 30, 1945)

Presidential Unit Citation (Army), Streamer embroidered CORREGIDOR (Company A and 3d Battalion, 34th Infantry cited; WD GO 53, 1945)

Presidential Unit Citation (Army), Streamer embroidered DEFENSE OF KOREA (24th Infantry Division cited; DA GO 45, 1950)

Philippine Presidential Unit Citation, Streamer embroidered 17 OCTOBER 1944 TO 4 JULY 1945 (34th Infantry cited; DA GO 47, 1950)

Republic of Korea Presidential Unit Citation, Streamer embroidered PYONGTAEK (34th Infantry cited; DA GO 35, 1951)

Republic of Korea Presidential Unit Citation, Streamer embroidered KOREA (34th Infantry cited; DA GO 33, 1953, as amended by DA GO 41, 1955)

1st BATTALION, 34th INFANTRY

RA
(inactive)

LINEAGE

Constituted 1 July 1916 in the Regular Army as Company A, 34th Infantry. Organized 15 July 1916 at El Paso, Texas. (34th Infantry assigned 6 December 1917 to the 7th Division; relieved 24 March 1923 from assignment to the 7th Division and assigned to the 8th Division; relieved 15 August 1927 from assignment to the 8th Division and assigned to the 4th Division; relieved 1 October 1933 from assignment to the 4th Division and assigned to the 8th Division [later redesignated as the 8th Infantry Division].) Inactivated 5 June 1940 at Fort Benning, Georgia. Activated 1 July 1940 at Camp Jackson, South Carolina. (34th Infantry relieved 12 June 1943 from assignment to the 8th Infantry Division and assigned to the 24th Infantry Division.)

Redesignated 5 June 1958 as Headquarters and Headquarters Company, 1st Battle Group, 34th Infantry and remained assigned to the 24th Infantry Division (organic elements concurrently constituted and activated 1 July 1958 in Germany). Reorganized and redesignated 1 February 1963 as the 1st Battalion, 34th Infantry. Inactivated 15 April 1970 at Fort Riley, Kansas.

CAMPAIGN PARTICIPATION CREDIT

World War I
  *Lorraine 1918

World War II
  *New Guinea
  *Leyte (with arrowhead)
  *Luzon

*Southern Philippines

Korean War
  *UN defensive
  *UN summer-fall offensive
  *Korea, summer 1953

DECORATIONS

*Presidential Unit Citation (Army), Streamer embroidered KILAY RIDGE (1st Battalion, 34th Infantry cited; WD GO 30, 1945)

*Presidential Unit Citation (Army), Streamer embroidered CORREGIDOR (Company A, 34th Infantry cited; WD GO 53, 1945)

*Presidential Unit Citation (Army), Streamer embroidered DEFENSE OF KOREA (24th Infantry Division cited; DA GO 45, 1950)

*Philippine Presidential Unit Citation, Streamer embroidered 17

OCTOBER 1944 TO 4 JULY 1945 (34th Infantry cited; DA GO 47, 1950)

*Republic of Korea Presidential Unit Citation, Streamer embroidered PYONGTAEK (34th Infantry cited; DA GO 35, 1951)

*Republic of Korea Presidential Unit Citation, Streamer embroidered KOREA (34th Infantry cited; DA GO 33, 1953, as amended by DA GO 41, 1955)

2d BATTALION, 34th INFANTRY

RA
(inactive)

LINEAGE

Constituted 1 July 1916 in the Regular Army as Company B, 34th Infantry. Organized 15 July 1916 at El Paso, Texas. (34th Infantry assigned 6 December 1917 to the 7th Division; relieved 24 March 1923 from assignment to the 7th Division and assigned to the 8th Division; relieved 15 August 1927 from assignment to the 8th Division and assigned to the 4th Division; relieved 1 October 1933 from assignment to the 4th Division and assigned to the 8th Division [later redesignated as the 8th Infantry Division].) Inactivated 5 June 1940 at Fort Benning, Georgia. Activated 1 July 1940 at Camp Jackson, South Carolina. (34th Infantry relieved 12 June 1943 from assignment to the 8th Infantry Division and assigned to the 24th Infantry Division.)

Reorganized and redesignated 1 July 1957 as Headquarters and Headquarters Company, 2d Battle Group, 34th Infantry, relieved from assignment to the 24th Infantry Division, and assigned to the 7th Infantry Division (organic elements concurrently constituted and activated). Reorganized and redesignated 1 February 1963 as the 2d Battalion, 34th Infantry; concurrently, relieved from assignment to the 7th Infantry Division and assigned to the 24th Infantry Division. Inactivated 15 April 1970 at Fort Riley, Kansas.

CAMPAIGN PARTICIPATION CREDIT

World War I
  *Lorraine 1918

World War II
  *New Guinea
  *Leyte (with arrowhead)
  *Luzon

*Southern Philippines

Korean War
  *UN defensive
  *UN summer-fall offensive
  *Korea, summer 1953

DECORATIONS

*Presidential Unit Citation (Army), Streamer embroidered KILAY RIDGE (1st Battalion, 34th Infantry cited; DA GO 30, 1945)

Presidential Unit Citation (Army), Streamer embroidered CORREGIDOR

*Presidential Unit Citation (Army), Streamer embroidered DEFENSE

579

OF KOREA (24th Infantry Division cited; DA GO 45, 1950)

*Philippine Presidential Unit Citation, Streamer embroidered 17 OCTOBER 1944 TO 4 JULY 1945 (34th Infantry cited; DA GO 47, 1950)

*Republic of Korea Presidential Unit Citation, Streamer embroidered PYONGTAEK (34th Infantry cited; DA GO 35, 1951)

*Republic of Korea Presidential Unit Citation, Streamer embroidered KOREA (34th Infantry cited; DA GO 33, 1953, as amended by DA GO 41, 1955)

3d BATTLE GROUP, 34th INFANTRY

AR
(inactive)

LINEAGE

Constituted 1 July 1916 in the Regular Army as Company C, 34th Infantry. Organized 15 July 1916 at El Paso, Texas. (34th Infantry assigned 6 December 1917 to the 7th Division; relieved 24 March 1923 from assignment to the 7th Division and assigned to the 8th Division; relieved 15 August 1927 from assignment to the 8th Division and assigned to the 4th Division; relieved 1 October 1933 from assignment to the 4th Division and assigned to the 8th Division [later redesignated as the 8th Infantry Division].) Inactivated 5 June 1940 at Fort Benning, Georgia. Activated 1 July 1940 at Camp Jackson, South Carolina. (34th Infantry relieved 12 June 1943 from assignment to the 8th Infantry Division and assigned to the 24th Infantry Division.)

Inactivated 5 June 1958 and relieved from assignment to the 24th Infantry Division; concurrently, redesignated as Headquarters and Headquarters Company, 3d Battle Group, 34th Infantry. Withdrawn 17 March 1959 from the Regular Army, allotted to the Army Reserve, and assigned to the 79th Infantry Division (organic elements concurrently constituted). Battle Group activated 23 March 1959 with Headquarters at Uniontown, Pennsylvania. Inactivated 28 March 1963 at Uniontown, Pennsylvania; concurrently, relieved from assignment to the 79th Infantry Division.

CAMPAIGN PARTICIPATION CREDIT

World War I
  *Lorraine 1918

World War II
  *New Guinea
  *Leyte (with arrowhead)

*Luzon
*Southern Philippines

Korean War
  *UN defensive
  *UN summer-fall offensive
  *Korea, summer 1953

DECORATIONS

*Presidential Unit Citation (Army), Streamer embroidered KILAY RIDGE (1st Battalion, 34th Infantry cited; WD GO 30, 1945)

Presidential Unit Citation (Army), Streamer embroidered CORREGIDOR

*Presidential Unit Citation (Army), Streamer embroidered DEFENSE OF KOREA (24th Infantry Division cited; DA GO 45, 1950)

*Philippine Presidential Unit Citation, Streamer embroidered 17 OCTOBER 1944 TO 4 JULY 1945 (34th Infantry cited; DA GO 47, 1950)

*Republic of Korea Presidential Unit Citation, Streamer embroidered PYONGTAEK (34th Infantry cited; DA GO 35, 1951)

*Republic of Korea Presidential Unit Citation, Streamer embroidered KOREA (34th Infantry cited; DA GO 33, 1953, as amended by DA GO 41, 1955)

34TH INFANTRY, BIBLIOGRAPHY

Appleman, Roy E. *South to the Naktong, North to the Yalu.* United States Army in the Korean War. Washington: Government Printing Office, 1961.

Belote, James H. and William M. *Corregidor: The Saga of a Fortress.* New York: Harper and Row, Publishers, 1967.

Cannon, M. Hamlin. *Leyte: The Return to the Philippines.* United States Army in World War II. Washington: Government Printing Office, 1954.

Carte, Merle, ed. *A Brief Illustrated History, 1916–1953: 34th Infantry Regiment.* n.p., 1953.

Falk, Stanley L. *Decision at Leyte.* New York: W. W. Norton and Company, Inc., 1966.

Hermes, Walter G. *Truce Tent and Fighting Front.* United States Army in the Korean War. Washington: Government Printing Office, 1966.

Smith, Robert Ross. *The Approach to the Philippines.* United States Army in World War II. Washington: Government Printing Office, 1953.

————. *Triumph in the Philippines.* United States Army in World War II. Washington: Government Printing Office, 1963.

The 34th Infantry: A Brief History. n.p., 1954.

35th INFANTRY
(The Cacti)

HERALDIC ITEMS

COAT OF ARMS

Shield: Argent, a giant cactus vert; on a canton embattled azure, a cross pattée of the field charged with an acorn gules.

Crest: On a wreath of the colors a walnut tree proper.

Motto: Take Arms.

Symbolism: This regiment was originally organized in Arizona with personnel from the 11th, 18th, and 22d Infantry. These organizations are shown on the canton. During the Civil War the predecessor of the 11th Infantry was in the 2d Division, V Corps, the badge of which was a white Maltese cross; the 18th Infantry was in the 1st Division, XIV Corps, with a red acorn as the badge. The 22d Infantry is represented by the embattled partition line of the canton. The cactus represents the original service of the 35th Infantry on the Mexican border.

The crest commemorates the regiment's baptism of fire at Nogales, the Spanish for walnut trees.

DISTINCTIVE INSIGNIA

The distinctive insignia is the shield of the coat of arms.

LINEAGE AND HONORS

LINEAGE

Constituted 1 July 1916 in the Regular Army as the 35th Infantry. Organized 8–19 July 1916 at Douglas, Arizona. Assigned 7 August 1918 to the 18th Division. Relieved 14 February 1919 from assignment to the 18th Division. Assigned 17 October 1922 to the Hawaiian Division. Relieved 26 August 1941 from assignment to the Hawaiian Division and assigned to the 25th Infantry Division.

Relieved 1 February 1957 from assignment to the 25th Infantry Division and reorganized as a parent regiment under the Combat Arms Regimental System.

Campaign Participation Credit

World War II
  Central Pacific
  Guadalcanal
  Northern Solomons (with arrowhead)
  Luzon

UN summer-fall offensive
Second Korean winter
Korea, summer-fall 1952
Third Korean winter
Korea, summer 1953

Korean War
  UN defensive
  UN offensive
  CCF intervention
  First UN counteroffensive
  CCF spring offensive

Vietnam
  Counteroffensive
  Counteroffensive, Phase II
  Counteroffensive, Phase III
  Tet Counteroffensive
  (other campaigns to be determined)

Decorations

Presidential Unit Citation (Army), Streamer embroidered GUADAL-CANAL (35th Infantry cited; DA GO 36, 1951)

Presidential Unit Citation (Army), Streamer embroidered NAM RIVER (35th Infantry [less 3d Battalion and Heavy Tank Company] cited; DA GO 49, 1951, as amended by DA GO 103, 1952)

Meritorious Unit Commendation, Streamer embroidered VIETNAM 1967–1968 (2d Battalion, 35th Infantry cited; DA GO 17, 1969)

Philippine Presidential Unit Citation, Streamer embroidered 17 OCTOBER 1944 TO 4 JULY 1945 (25th Infantry Division cited; DA GO 47, 1950)

Republic of Korea Presidential Unit Citation, Streamer embroidered MASAN-CHINJU (35th Infantry cited; DA GO 35, 1951)

Republic of Korea Presidential Unit Citation, Streamer embroidered MUNSAN-NI (35th Infantry cited; DA GO 19, 1955)

Republic of Korea Presidential Unit Citation, Streamer embroidered KOREA (35th Infantry cited; DA GO 24, 1954)

1st BATTALION, 35th INFANTRY

(The Cacti)

RA
(inactive)

LINEAGE

Constituted 1 July 1916 in the Regular Army as Company A, 35th Infantry. Organized 13 July 1916 at Douglas, Arizona. (35th Infantry assigned 7 August 1918 to the 18th Division; relieved 14 February 1919 from assignment to the 18th Division; assigned 17 October 1922 to the Hawaiian Division; relieved 26 August 1941 from assignment to the Hawaiian Division and assigned to the 25th Infantry Division.)

Reorganized and redesignated 1 February 1957 as Headquarters and Headquarters Company, 1st Battle Group, 35th Infantry and remained assigned to the 25th Infantry Division (organic elements concurrently constituted and activated). Reorganized and redesignated 12 August 1963 as the 1st Battalion, 35th Infantry. Relieved 1 August 1967 from assignment to the 25th Infantry Division and assigned to the 4th Infantry Division. Inactivated 10 April 1970 at Fort Lewis, Washington.

CAMPAIGN PARTICIPATION CREDIT

World War II
*Central Pacific
*Guadalcanal
*Northern Solomons (with arrowhead)
*Luzon

*UN summer-fall offensive
*Second Korean winter
*Korea, summer-fall 1952
*Third Korean winter
*Korea, summer 1953

Korean War
*UN defensive
*UN offensive
*CCF intervention
*First UN counteroffensive
*CCF spring offensive

Vietnam
*Counteroffensive
*Counteroffensive, Phase II
*Counteroffensive, Phase III
*Tet Counteroffensive
  (other campaigns to be determined)

DECORATIONS

*Presidential Unit Citation (Army), Streamer embroidered GUADALCANAL (35th Infantry cited; DA GO 36, 1951)

*Presidential Unit Citation (Army), Streamer embroidered NAM RIVER (35th Infantry [less 3d Battalion and Heavy Tank Company] cited; DA GO 49, 1951, as amended by DA GO 103, 1952)

*Philippine Presidential Unit Citation, Streamer embroidered 17 OCTOBER 1944 TO 4 JULY 1945 (25th Infantry Division cited; DA GO 47, 1950)

*Republic of Korea Presidential Unit Citation, Streamer embroidered MASAN-CHINJU (35th Infantry cited; DA GO 35, 1951)

*Republic of Korea Presidential Unit Citation, Streamer embroidered MUNSAN-NI (35th Infantry cited; DA GO 19, 1955)

*Republic of Korea Presidential Unit Citation, Streamer embroidered KOREA (35th Infantry cited; DA GO 24, 1954)

*Vietnamese Cross of Gallantry with Palm, Streamer embroidered VIETNAM 1966–1967 (1st Battalion, 35th Infantry cited; DA GO 48, 1971)

*Vietnamese Cross of Gallantry with Palm, Streamer embroidered VIETNAM 1967–1969 (1st Battalion, 35th Infantry cited; DA GO 3, 1970, as amended by DA GO 38, 1970)

*Vietnamese Civil Action Honor Medal, First Class, Streamer embroidered VIETNAM 1967–1969 (1st Battalion, 35th Infantry cited; DA GO 53, 1970)

Company A additionally entitled to: Presidential Unit Citation (Army), Streamer embroidered PLEIKU PROVINCE (Company A, 1st Battalion, 35th Infantry cited; DA GO 51, 1968); Valorous Unit Award, Streamer embroidered DARLAC PROVINCE (Company A, 1st Battalion, 35th Infantry cited; DA GO 17, 1968)

2d BATTALION, 35th INFANTRY

(The Cacti)

RA

(25th Infantry Division)

LINEAGE

Constituted 1 July 1916 in the Regular Army as Company B, 35th Infantry. Organized 13 July 1916 at Douglas, Arizona. (35th Infantry assigned 7 August 1918 to the 18th Division; relieved 14 February 1919 from assignment to the 18th Division; assigned 17 October 1922 to the Hawaiian Division; relieved 26 August 1941 from assignment to the Hawaiian Division and assigned to the 25th Infantry Division.)

Inactivated 1 February 1957 in Hawaii and relieved from assignment to the 25th Infantry Division; concurrently, redesignated as Headquarters and Headquarters Company, 2d Battle Group, 35th Infantry. Activated 19 February 1962 in Hawaii and assigned to the 25th Infantry Division (organic elements concurrently constituted and activated). Reorganized and redesignated 12 August 1963 as the 2d Battalion, 35th Infantry. Relieved 1 August 1967 from assignment to the 25th Infantry Division and assigned to the 4th Infantry Division. Relieved 15 December 1970 from assignment to the 4th Infantry Division and assigned to the 25th Infantry Division.

CAMPAIGN PARTICIPATION CREDIT

World War II
*Central Pacific
*Guadalcanal
*Northern Solomons (with arrowhead)
*Luzon

*UN summer-fall offensive
*Second Korean winter
*Korea, summer-fall 1952
*Third Korean winter
*Korea, summer 1953

Korean War
*UN defensive
*UN offensive
*CCF intervention
*First UN counteroffensive
*CCF spring offensive

Vietnam
*Counteroffensive
*Counteroffensive, Phase II
*Counteroffensive, Phase III
*Tet Counteroffensive
(other campaigns to be determined)

DECORATIONS

*Presidential Unit Citation (Army), Streamer embroidered GUADALCANAL (35th Infantry cited; DA GO 36, 1951)

*Presidential Unit Citation (Army), Streamer embroidered NAM RIVER (35th Infantry [less 3d Battalion and Heavy Tank Company] cited; DA GO 49, 1951, as amended by DA GO 103, 1952)

*Meritorious Unit Commendation, Streamer embroidered VIETNAM 1967–1968 (2d Battalion, 35th Infantry cited; DA GO 17, 1969)

*Philippine Presidential Unit Citation, Streamer embroidered 17 OCTOBER 1944 TO 4 JULY 1945 (25th Infantry Division cited; DA GO 47, 1950)

*Republic of Korea Presidential Unit Citation, Streamer embroidered MASAN-CHINJU (35th Infantry cited; DA GO 35, 1951)

*Republic of Korea Presidential Unit Citation, Streamer embroidered MUNSAN-NI (35th Infantry cited; DA GO 19, 1955)

*Republic of Korea Presidential Unit Citation, Streamer embroidered KOREA (35th Infantry cited; DA GO 24, 1954)

*Vietnamese Cross of Gallantry with Palm, Streamer embroidered VIETNAM 1966–1967 (2d Battalion, 35th Infantry cited; DA GO 48, 1971)

*Vietnamese Cross of Gallantry with Palm, Streamer embroidered VIETNAM 1967–1969 (2d Battalion, 35th Infantry cited; DA GO 3, 1970, as amended by DA GO 38, 1970)

*Vietnamese Civil Action Honor Medal, First Class, Streamer embroidered VIETNAM 1967–1969 (2d Battalion, 35th Infantry cited; DA GO 53, 1970)

Company A additionally entitled to: Valorous Unit Award, Streamer embroidered PLEIKU PROVINCE (Company A, 2d Battalion, 35th Infantry cited; DA GO 17, 1968)

Company B additionally entitled to: Presidential Unit Citation (Army), Streamer embroidered PLEIKU PROVINCE (Company B, 2d Battalion, 35th Infantry cited; DA GO 51, 1968)

3d BATTALION, 35th INFANTRY

(The Cacti)

AR
(187th Infantry Brigade)

LINEAGE

Constituted 1 July 1916 in the Regular Army as Company C, 35th Infantry. Organized 13 July 1916 at Douglas, Arizona. (35th Infantry assigned 7 August 1918 to the 18th Division; relieved 14 February 1919 from assignment to the 18th Division; assigned 17 October 1922 to the Hawaiian Division; relieved 26 August 1941 from assignment to the Hawaiian Division and assigned to the 25th Infantry Division.)

Inactivated 1 February 1957 in Hawaii and relieved from assignment to the 25th Infantry Division; concurrently, redesignated as Headquarters and Headquarters Company, 3d Battle Group, 35th Infantry. Withdrawn 6 April 1959 from the Regular Army, allotted to the Army Reserve, and assigned to the 94th Infantry Division (organic elements concurrently constituted). Battle Group activated 1 May 1959 with Headquarters at Springfield, Massachusetts (concurrently, Headquarters and Headquarters Company consolidated with Headquarters and Headquarters Company, 2d Battalion, 376th Infantry [see ANNEX] and consolidated unit designated as Headquarters and Headquarters Company, 3d Battle Group, 35th Infantry).

Reorganized and redesignated 5 November 1962 as the 3d Battalion, 35th Infantry. Relieved 7 January 1963 from assignment to the 94th Infantry Division and assigned to the 187th Infantry Brigade.

ANNEX

Constituted 24 June 1921 in the Organized Reserves as Headquarters and Headquarters Company, 2d Battalion, 376th Infantry, an element of the 94th Division (later redesignated as the 94th Infantry Division). Organized in November 1921 at Winchester, Massachusetts. Ordered into active military service 15 September 1942 and reorganized at Fort Custer, Michigan. Inactivated 1 February 1946 at Camp Kilmer, New Jersey.

Activated 13 February 1947 in the Organized Reserves at Springfield, Massachusetts. (Organized Reserves redesignated 25 March 1948 as the Organized Reserve Corps; redesignated 9 July 1952 as the Army Reserve.)

Consolidated 1 May 1959 with Headquarters and Headquarters Company, 3d Battle Group, 35th Infantry and consolidated unit designated as Headquarters and Headquarters Company, 3d Battle Group, 35th Infantry (remainder of 376th Infantry inactivated).

HOME AREA: First United States Army

CAMPAIGN PARTICIPATION CREDIT

World War II
  *Central Pacific
  *Guadalcanal
  *Northern Solomons (with arrowhead)
  *Luzon
  *Northern France
  *Rhineland
  *Ardennes-Alsace
  *Central Europe

Korean War
  *UN defensive
  *UN offensive
  *CCF intervention
  *First UN counteroffensive
  *CCF spring offensive
  *UN summer-fall offensive
  *Second Korean winter
  *Korea, summer-fall 1952
  *Third Korean winter
  *Korea, summer 1953

DECORATIONS

*Presidential Unit Citation (Army), Streamer embroidered GUADAL-CANAL (35th Infantry cited; DA GO 36, 1951)

*Presidential Unit Citation (Army), Streamer embroidered NAM RIVER (35th Infantry [less 3d Battalion and Heavy Tank Company] cited; DA GO 49, 1951, as amended by DA GO 103, 1952)

*Philippine Presidential Unit Citation, Streamer embroidered 17 OCTOBER 1944 TO 4 JULY 1945 (25th Infantry Division cited; DA GO 47, 1950)

*Republic of Korea Presidential Unit Citation, Streamer embroidered MASAN-CHINJU (35th Infantry cited; DA GO 35, 1951)

*Republic of Korea Presidential Unit Citation, Streamer embroidered MUNSAN-NI (35th Infantry cited; DA GO 19, 1955)

*Republic of Korea Presidential Unit Citation, Streamer embroidered KOREA (35th Infantry cited; DA GO 24, 1954)

35TH INFANTRY, BIBLIOGRAPHY

Appleman, Roy E. *South to the Naktong, North to the Yalu.* United States Army in the Korean War. Washington: Government Printing Office, 1961.

The Cacti. Newspaper of the 35th Infantry, c. 1935.

The Cacti, 1955–1956. Honolulu: Honolulu Star Bulletin, 1955.

The Cacti, 35th Infantry Regiment, Schofield Barracks, 1954–1955. Honolulu, 1954.

1st Battle Group, 35th Infantry, the Cacti. Schofield Barracks, 1957.

1st Battle Group, 35th Infantry, the Cacti. Schofield Barracks, 1958.

Gugeler, Russell A. *Combat Actions in Korea.* Washington: Combat Forces Press, 1954.

History of the 35th Infantry (The Cacti). n.p., 1953.

Marshall, S. L. A. *West to Cambodia.* New York: Cowles Education Corporation, 1968.

Miller, John, jr. *CARTWHEEL: The Reduction of Rabaul.* United States Army in World War II. Washington: Government Printing Office, 1959.

————. *Guadalcanal: The First Offensive.* United States Army in World War II. Washington: Government Printing Office, 1949.

"Organization Day, Thirty-fifth Infantry, August 22, 1941. Schofield Barracks, Oahu, T.H., 1941." n.p., 1941.

Smith, Robert Ross. *Triumph in the Philippines.* United States Army in World War II. Washington: Government Printing Office, 1963.

Welcome to the 35th Infantry. Printed by the I Corps Engineer Reproduction Plant, 1946?

36th INFANTRY

COAT OF ARMS

Shield: Azure, a sword bayonet in fess or within a bordure of the like; on a canton argent a cross of the field overall a cactus proper.

Crest: On a wreath of the colors a six-bastioned fort vert charged with a mullet argent.

Motto: Deeds Not Words.

Symbolism: The field of the shield is blue, the infantry color. The sword bayonet and bordure are taken from the unofficial insignia adopted by the 12th Division to which the 36th Infantry was assigned in 1918–1919. The regiment was originally organized at Brownsville, Texas, with personnel from the 4th, 26th, and 28th Infantry. These units are symbolized on the canton. The 4th and 28th Infantry both took part in the Vera Cruz expedition of 1914, the name suggesting the cross in blue for infantry. The cactus represents the Mexican border service of all three regiments.

The crest symbolizes the birthplace of the 36th Infantry. The origin of Brownsville was the fort built by General Zachary Taylor in 1846, known as Fort Texas. During the Mexican War the 4th Infantry participated in the battles of Palo Alto and Resaca de la Palma, which were fought for the defense of Fort Texas. This is shown by the six-bastioned fort in green, an allusion to the Mexican color, charged with the silver lone star of Texas.

DISTINCTIVE INSIGNIA

The distinctive insignia is the crest of the coat of arms.

LINEAGE AND HONORS

LINEAGE

Constituted 1 July 1916 in the Regular Army as the 36th Infantry.

Organized 27 July 1917 at Brownsville, Texas. Assigned 5 July 1918 to the 12th Division. Relieved 31 January 1919 from assignment to the 12th Division. Inactivated 13 October 1921 at Fort Jay, New York. Assigned 24 March 1923 to the 9th Division. Relieved 1 August 1940 from assignment to the 9th Division.

Activated 15 April 1941 at Camp Beauregard, Louisiana, as the 36th Infantry (Armored), an element of the 3d Armored Division. Redesignated 1 January 1942 as the 36th Armored Infantry. Inactivated 10 November 1945 in Germany. Regiment broken up 7 July 1947 and its elements redesignated as elements of the 3d Armored Division as follows: Headquarters as Headquarters, Reserve Command, 3d Armored Division; 1st Battalion as the 36th Armored Infantry Battalion; 2d Battalion as the 37th Armored Infantry Battalion; 3d Battalion as the 13th Armored Infantry Battalion. Battalions activated 15 July 1947 at Fort Knox, Kentucky.

36th, 37th, and 13th Armored Infantry Battalions relieved 1 October 1957 from assignment to the 3d Armored Division and consolidated to form the 36th Infantry, a parent regiment under the Combat Arms Regimental System; concurrently, former Headquarters, Reserve Command, 3d Armored Division expanded and redesignated as Headquarters, 36th Infantry and as Headquarters and Headquarters Company, Combat Command C, 3d Armored Division (Headquarters and Headquarters Company, Combat Command C, 3d Armored Division—hereafter separate lineage).

CAMPAIGN PARTICIPATION CREDIT

World War II
   Normandy
   Northern France
   Rhineland
   Ardennes-Alsace
   Central Europe

DECORATIONS

Presidential Unit Citation (Army), Streamer embroidered SIEGFRIED LINE (1st Battalion, 36th Armored Infantry cited; WD GO 54, 1945)

Belgian Fourragere 1940 (36th Armored Infantry cited; DA GO 43, 1950)

Cited in the Order of the Day of the Belgian Army for action in BELGIUM (36th Armored Infantry cited; DA GO 43, 1950)

Cited in the Order of the Day of the Belgian Army for action in the ARDENNES (36th Armored Infantry cited; DA GO 43, 1950)

1st BATTALION, 36th INFANTRY

RA

(3d Armored Division)

LINEAGE

Constituted 1 July 1916 in the Regular Army as Company A, 36th Infantry. Organized 27 July 1917 at Brownsville, Texas. (36th Infantry assigned 5 July 1918 to the 12th Division; relieved 31 January 1919 from assignment to the 12th Division.) Inactivated 13 October 1921 at Fort Jay, New York. (36th Infantry assigned 24 March 1923 to the 9th Division; relieved 1 August 1940 from assignment to the 9th Division.)

Activated 15 April 1941 at Camp Beauregard, Louisiana, as Company A, 36th Infantry (Armored), an element of the 3d Armored Division. Redesignated 1 January 1942 as Company A, 36th Armored Infantry. Inactivated 10 November 1945 in Germany. Redesignated 7 July 1947 as Company A, 36th Armored Infantry Battalion, an element of the 3d Armored Division. Activated 15 July 1947 at Fort Knox, Kentucky.

Reorganized and redesignated 15 February 1957 as Headquarters and Headquarters Company, 1st Armored Rifle Battalion, 36th Infantry, relieved from assignment to the 3d Armored Division, and assigned to the 1st Armored Division (organic elements concurrently constituted and activated). Inactivated 23 December 1957 at Fort Polk, Louisiana. Activated 3 February 1962 in Germany; concurrently, relieved from assignment to the 1st Armored Division and assigned to the 3d Armored Division. Reorganized and redesignated 1 September 1963 as the 1st Battalion, 36th Infantry.

CAMPAIGN PARTICIPATION CREDIT

World War II
  *Normandy
  *Northern France
  *Rhineland
  *Ardennes-Alsace
  *Central Europe

DECORATIONS

*Presidential Unit Citation (Army), Streamer embroidered SIEGFRIED LINE (1st Battalion, 36th Armored Infantry cited; WD GO 54, 1945)

*Presidential Unit Citation (Army), Streamer embroidered ECHTZ (Company A, 36th Armored Infantry cited; WD GO 24, 1945)

*Belgian Fourragere 1940 (36th Armored Infantry cited; DA GO 43, 1950)

*Cited in the Order of the Day of the Belgian Army for action in BELGIUM (36th Armored Infantry cited; DA GO 43, 1950)

*Cited in the Order of the Day of the Belgian Army for action in the ARDENNES (36th Armored Infantry cited; DA GO 43, 1950)

2d BATTALION, 36th INFANTRY

RA

(3d Armored Division)

LINEAGE

Constituted 1 July 1916 in the Regular Army as Company B, 36th Infantry. Organized 27 July 1917 at Brownsville, Texas. (36th Infantry assigned 5 July 1918 to the 12th Division; relieved 31 January 1919 from assignment to the 12th Division.) Inactivated 13 October 1921 at Fort Jay, New York. (36th Infantry assigned 24 March 1923 to the 9th Division; relieved 1 August 1940 from assignment to the 9th Division.)

Activated 15 April 1941 at Camp Beauregard, Louisiana, as Company B, 36th Infantry (Armored), an element of the 3d Armored Division. Redesignated 1 January 1942 as Company B, 36th Armored Infantry. Inactivated 10 November 1945 in Germany. Redesignated 7 July 1947 as Company B, 36th Armored Infantry Battalion, an element of the 3d Armored Division. Activated 15 July 1947 at Fort Knox, Kentucky.

Reorganized and redesignated 1 October 1957 as Headquarters and Headquarters Company, 2d Armored Rifle Battalion, 36th Infantry and remained assigned to the 3d Armored Division (organic elements concurrently constituted and activated). Reorganized and redesignated 1 September 1963 as the 2d Battalion, 36th Infantry.

CAMPAIGN PARTICIPATION CREDIT

World War II
* *Normandy
* *Northern France
* *Rhineland
* *Ardennes-Alsace
* *Central Europe

DECORATIONS

*Presidential Unit Citation (Army), Streamer embroidered SIEGFRIED LINE (1st Battalion, 36th Armored Infantry cited; WD GO 54, 1945)

*Belgian Fourragere 1940 (36th Armored Infantry cited; DA GO 43, 1950)

*Cited in the Order of the Day of the Belgian Army for action in BELGIUM (36th Armored Infantry cited; DA GO 43, 1950)

*Cited in the Order of the Day of the Belgian Army for action in the ARDENNES (36th Armored Infantry cited; DA GO 43, 1950)

3d BATTALION, 36th INFANTRY

RA
(3d Armored Division)

LINEAGE

Constituted 1 July 1916 in the Regular Army as Company C, 36th Infantry. Organized 27 July 1917 at Brownsville, Texas. (36th Infantry assigned 5 July 1918 to the 12th Division; relieved 31 January 1919 from assignment to the 12th Division.) Inactivated 13 October 1921 at Fort Jay, New York. (36th Infantry assigned 24 March 1923 to the 9th Division; relieved 1 August 1940 from assignments to the 9th Division.)

Activated 15 April 1941 at Camp Beauregard, Louisiana, as Company C, 36th Infantry (Armored), an element of the 3d Armored Division. Redesignated 1 January 1942 as Company C, 36th Armored Infantry. Inactivated 10 November 1945 in Germany. Redesignated 7 July 1947 as Company C, 36th Armored Infantry Battalion, an element of the 3d Armored Division. Activated 15 July 1947 at Fort Knox, Kentucky.

Inactivated 1 October 1957 in Germany and relieved from assignment to the 3d Armored Division; concurrently, redesignated as Headquarters and Headquarters Company, 3d Battle Group, 36th Infantry. Redesignated 3 February 1962 as Headquarters and Headquarters Company, 3d Armored Rifle Battalion, 36th Infantry, assigned to the 3d Armored Division, and activated in Germany (organic elements concurrently constituted and activated.) Reorganized and redesignated 1 September 1963 as the 3d Battalion, 36th Infantry.

CAMPAIGN PARTICIPATION CREDIT

World War II
* *Normandy
* *Northern France
* *Rhineland
* *Ardennes-Alsace
* *Central Europe

DECORATIONS

*Presidential Unit Citation (Army), Streamer embroidered SIEGFRIED LINE (1st Battalion, 36th Armored Infantry cited; WD GO 54, 1945)

*Presidential Unit Citation (Army), Streamer embroidered OBERGEICH-HOVEN (Company C, 36th Armored Infantry cited; WD GO 24, 1945)

600

*Belgian Fourragere 1940 (36th Armored Infantry cited; DA GO 43, 1950)

*Cited in the Order of the Day of the Belgian Army for action in BELGIUM (36th Armored Infantry cited; DA GO 43, 1950)

*Cited in the Order of the Day of the Belgian Army for action in the ARDENNES (36th Armored Infantry cited; DA GO 43, 1950)

36TH INFANTRY, BIBLIOGRAPHY

Blumenson, Martin. *Breakout and Pursuit.* United States Army in World War II. Washington: Government Printing Office, 1961.

Directory: 36th Armored Infantry Regiment. Gerabronn, Germany: M. Rueckert's Buchdruckerei, 1945.

Dreyer, D., compiler. *36th, 40th, 41st U.S. Infantry, Fort Snelling, Minnesota, 1917.* Iowa City: D. Dreyer, 1917.

Historical Section, War Department. *St-Lô.* American Forces in Action Series. Washington: Government Printing Office, 1946.

Regimental History, 36th U.S. Infantry. Camp Devens, Massachusetts, 1919.

"36th Armored Infantry Battalion," *Historical and Pictorial Review, Third Armored Division . . . Camp Polk, Louisiana, 1942.* Baton Rouge: Army and Navy Publishing Company, 1942.

38th INFANTRY
(Rock of the Marne)

HERALDIC ITEMS

COAT OF ARMS

Shield: Azure, in chief a chevron reversed rompu point enhanced argent, in base three bendlets sinister of the last. (And for informal use, pendant from the escutcheon a French Croix de Guerre with Palm proper.)

Crest: On a wreath of the colors a boulder proper.

Motto: The Rock of the Marne.

Symbolism: This regiment served in World War I as an element of the 3d Division. Its most remarkable feat was near Chateau Thierry on the Marne on 15 July 1918, where it broke the point of the German attack. This achievement is shown by the broken chevron, the rock, and the motto. The divisional insignia is suggested by the base of the shield.

DISTINCTIVE INSIGNIA

The distinctive insignia is the shield, crest, and motto of the coat of arms.

LINEAGE AND HONORS

LINEAGE

Constituted 15 May 1917 in the Regular Army as the 38th Infantry. Organized 1 June 1917 at Syracuse, New York. Assigned 1 October 1917 to the 3d Division. (1st Battalion inactivated 1 October 1933 at Fort Sill, Oklahoma; activated 1 May 1939 at Fort Sill, Oklahoma.) Relieved 16 October 1939 from assignment to the 3d Division and assigned to the 2d Division (later redesignated as the 2d Infantry Division).

Relieved 8 November 1957 from assignment to the 2d Infantry Division and reorganized as a parent regiment under the Combat Arms Regimental System.

603

Campaign Participation Credit

World War I
  Aisne
  Champagne-Marne
  Aisne-Marne
  St. Mihiel
  Meuse-Argonne
  Champagne 1918

World War II
  Normandy
  Northern France
  Rhineland
  Ardennes-Alsace
  Central Europe

Korean War
  UN defensive
  UN offensive
  CCF intervention
  First UN counteroffensive
  CCF spring offensive
  UN summer-fall offensive
  Second Korean winter
  Korea, summer-fall 1952
  Third Korean winter
  Korea, summer 1953

Decorations

Presidential Unit Citation (Army), Streamer embroidered KRINKELT (1st, 2d, and 3d Battalions, 38th Infantry cited; WD GO's 30 and 34, 1945, and WD GO 63, 1946)

Presidential Unit Citation (Army), Streamer embroidered HILL 154, BREST (3d Battalion, 38th Infantry cited; WD GO 15, 1945)

Presidential Unit Citation (Army), Streamer embroidered HONGCHON (2d Infantry Division cited; DA GO 72, 1951)

French Croix de Guerre with Palm, World War I, Streamer embroidered MARNE RIVER (38th Infantry cited; WD GO 11, 1924)

French Croix de Guerre with Silver-Gilt Star, World War II, Streamer embroidered BREST (38th Infantry cited; DA GO 43, 1950)

Republic of Korea Presidential Unit Citation, Streamer embroidered NAKTONG RIVER LINE (38th Infantry cited; DA GO 35, 1951)

Republic of Korea Presidential Unit Citation, Streamer embroidered KOREA 1950–1952 (38th Infantry cited; DA GO 33, 1953, as amended by DA GO 41, 1955)

Republic of Korea Presidential Unit Citation, Streamer embroidered KOREA 1950–1953 (38th Infantry cited; DA GO 10, 1954)

Belgian Fourragere 1940 (38th Infantry cited; DA GO 43, 1950)

Cited in the Order of the Day of the Belgian Army for action in the ARDENNES (38th Infantry cited; DA GO 43, 1950)

Cited in the Order of the Day of the Belgian Army for action at ELSENBORN CREST (38th Infantry cited; DA GO 43, 1950)

1st BATTALION, 38th INFANTRY

(Rock of the Marne)

RA
(2d Infantry Division)

LINEAGE

Constituted 15 May 1917 in the Regular Army as Company A, 38th Infantry. Organized 1 June 1917 at Syracuse, New York. (38th Infantry assigned 1 October 1917 to the 3d Division.) Inactivated 1 October 1933 at Fort Sill, Oklahoma. Activated 1 May 1939 at Fort Sill, Oklahoma. (38th Infantry relieved 16 October 1939 from assignment to the 3d Division and assigned to the 2d Division [later redesignated as the 2d Infantry Division].)

Redesignated 8 November 1957 as Headquarters and Headquarters Company, 1st Battle Group, 38th Infantry; concurrently, relieved from assignment to the 2d Infantry Division. Inactivated 4 March 1958. (Organic elements constituted 26 January 1962.) Battle Group activated 19 February 1962 at Fort Benning, Georgia, and assigned to the 2d Infantry Division. Reorganized and redesignated 10 May 1963 as the 1st Battalion, 38th Infantry.

CAMPAIGN PARTICIPATION CREDIT

World War I
  *Aisne
  *Champagne-Marne
  *Aisne-Marne
  *St. Mihiel
  *Meuse-Argonne
  *Champagne 1918

World War II
  *Normandy
  *Northern France
  *Rhineland
  *Ardennes-Alsace
  *Central Europe

Korean War
  *UN defensive
  *UN offensive
  *CCF intervention
  *First UN counteroffensive
  *CCF spring offensive
  *UN summer-fall offensive
  *Second Korean winter
  *Korea, summer-fall 1952
  *Third Korean winter
  *Korea, summer 1953

DECORATIONS

*Presidential Unit Citation (Army), Streamer embroidered KRINKELT (1st Battalion, 38th Infantry cited; WD GO 30, 1945)

Presidential Unit Citation (Army), Streamer embroidered HILL 154, BREST

*Presidential Unit Citation (Army), Streamer embroidered HONG-CHON (2d Infantry Division cited; DA GO 72, 1951)

*French Croix de Guerre with Palm, World War I, Streamer embroidered MARNE RIVER (38th Infantry cited; WD GO 11, 1924)

*French Croix de Guerre with Silver-Gilt Star, World War II, Streamer embroidered BREST (38th Infantry cited; DA GO 43, 1950)

*Republic of Korea Presidential Unit Citation, Streamer embroidered NAKTONG RIVER LINE (38th Infantry cited; DA GO 35, 1951)

*Republic of Korea Presidential Unit Citation, Streamer embroidered KOREA 1950–1952 (38th Infantry cited; DA GO 33, 1953, as amended by DA GO 41, 1955)

*Republic of Korea Presidential Unit Citation, Streamer embroidered KOREA 1950–1953 (38th Infantry cited; DA GO 10, 1954)

*Belgian Fourragere 1940 (38th Infantry cited; DA GO 43, 1950)

*Cited in the Order of the Day of the Belgian Army for action in the ARDENNES (38th Infantry cited; DA GO 43, 1950)

*Cited in the Order of the Day of the Belgian Army for action at ELSENBORN CREST (38th Infantry cited; DA GO 43, 1950)

2d BATTALION, 38th INFANTRY

(Rock of the Marne)

RA
(2d Infantry Division)

LINEAGE

Constituted 15 May 1917 in the Regular Army as Company B, 38th Infantry. Organized 1 June 1917 at Syracuse, New York. (38th Infantry assigned 1 October 1917 to the 3d Division.) Inactivated 1 October 1933 at Fort Sill, Oklahoma. Activated 1 May 1939 at Fort Sill Oklahoma. (38th Infantry relieved 16 October 1939 from assignment to the 3d Division and assigned to the 2d Division [later redesignated as the 2d Infantry Division].)

Reorganized and redesignated 1 July 1957 as Headquarters and Headquarters Company, 2d Battle Group, 38th Infantry, relieved from assignment to the 2d Infantry Division, and assigned to the 3d Infantry Division (organic elements concurrently constituted and activated). Reorganized and redesignated 1 April 1963 as the 2d Battalion, 38th Infantry; concurrently, relieved from assignment to the 3d Infantry Division and assigned to the 2d Infantry Division.

CAMPAIGN PARTICIPATION CREDIT

World War I
*Aisne
*Champagne-Marne
*Aisne-Marne
*St. Mihiel
*Meuse-Argonne
*Champagne 1918

World War II
*Normandy
*Northern France
*Rhineland
*Ardennes-Alsace
*Central Europe

Korean War
*UN defensive
*UN offensive
*CCF intervention
*First UN counteroffensive
*CCF spring offensive
*UN summer-fall offensive
*Second Korean winter
*Korea, summer-fall 1952
*Third Korean winter
*Korea, summer 1953

DECORATIONS

*Presidential Unit Citation (Army), Streamer embroidered KRINKELT (1st Battalion, 38th Infantry cited; WD GO 30, 1945)

607

Presidential Unit Citation (Army), Streamer embroidered HILL 154, BREST

*Presidential Unit Citation (Army), Streamer embroidered HONG-CHON (2d Infantry Division cited; DA GO 72, 1951)

*French Croix de Guerre with Palm, World War I, Streamer embroidered MARNE RIVER (38th Infantry cited; WD GO 11, 1924)

*French Croix de Guerre with Silver-Gilt Star, World War II, Streamer embroidered BREST (38th Infantry cited; DA GO 43, 1950)

*Republic of Korea Presidential Unit Citation, Streamer embroidered NAKTONG RIVER LINE (38th Infantry cited; DA GO 35, 1951)

*Republic of Korea Presidential Unit Citation, Streamer embroidered KOREA 1950–1952 (38th Infantry cited; DA GO 33, 1953, as amended by DA GO 41, 1955)

*Republic of Korea Presidential Unit Citation, Streamer embroidered KOREA 1950–1953 (38th Infantry cited; DA GO 10, 1954)

*Belgian Fourragere 1940 (38th Infantry cited; DA GO 43, 1950)

*Cited in the Order of the Day of the Belgian Army for action in the ARDENNES (38th Infantry cited; DA GO 43, 1950)

*Cited in the Order of the Day of the Belgian Army for action at ELSENBORN CREST (38th Infantry cited; DA GO 43, 1950)

3d BATTALION, 38th INFANTRY

(Rock of the Marne)

AR
(inactive)

LINEAGE

Constituted 15 May 1917 in the Regular Army as Company C, 38th Infantry. Organized 1 June 1917 at Syracuse, New York. (38th Infantry assigned 1 October 1917 to the 3d Division.) Inactivated 1 October 1933 at Fort Sill, Oklahoma. Activated 1 May 1939 at Fort Sill, Oklahoma. (38th Infantry relieved 16 October 1939 from assignment to the 3d Division and assigned to the 2d Division [later redesignated as the 2d Infantry Division].)

Redesignated 8 November 1957 as Headquarters and Headquarters Company, 3d Battle Group, 38th Infantry; concurrently, relieved from assignment to the 2d Infantry Division. Inactivated 4 March 1958. Withdrawn 29 April 1959 from the Regular Army, allotted to the Army Reserve, and assigned to the 96th Infantry Division (organic elements concurrently constituted). Battle Group activated 1 June 1959 with Headquarters at Provo, Utah.

Reorganized and redesignated 15 March 1963 as the 3d Battalion, 38th Infantry; concurrently, relieved from assignment to the 96th Infantry Division. Assigned 10 August 1963 to the 191st Infantry Brigade. Inactivated 29 February 1968 at Provo, Utah.

CAMPAIGN PARTICIPATION CREDIT

World War I
* *Aisne
* *Champagne-Marne
* *Aisne-Marne
* *St. Mihiel
* *Meuse-Argonne
* *Champagne 1918

World War II
* *Normandy
* *Northern France
* *Rhineland
* *Ardennes-Alsace
* *Central Europe

Korean War
* *UN defensive
* *UN offensive
* *CCF intervention
* *First UN counteroffensive
* *CCF spring offensive
* *UN summer-fall offensive
* *Second Korean winter
* *Korea, summer-fall 1952
* *Third Korean winter
* *Korea, summer 1953

DECORATIONS

*Presidential Unit Citation (Army), Streamer embroidered KRINKELT (1st Battalion, 38th Infantry cited; WD GO 30, 1945)

Presidential Unit Citation (Army), Streamer embroidered HILL 154, BREST

*Presidential Unit Citation (Army), Streamer embroidered HONG-CHON (2d Infantry Division cited; DA GO 72, 1951)

*French Croix de Guerre with Palm, World War I, Streamer embroidered MARNE RIVER (38th Infantry cited; WD GO 11, 1924)

*French Croix de Guerre with Silver-Gilt Star, World War II, Streamer embroidered BREST (38th Infantry cited; DA GO 43, 1950)

*Republic of Korea Presidential Unit Citation, Streamer embroidered NAKTONG RIVER LINE (38th Infantry cited; DA GO 35, 1951)

*Republic of Korea Presidential Unit Citation, Streamer embroidered KOREA 1950–1952 (38th Infantry cited; DA GO 33, 1953, as amended by DA GO 41, 1955)

*Republic of Korea Presidential Unit Citation, Streamer embroidered KOREA 1950–1953 (38th Infantry cited; DA GO 10, 1954)

*Belgian Fourragere 1940 (38th Infantry cited; DA GO 43, 1950)

*Cited in the Order of the Day of the Belgian Army for action in the ARDENNES (38th Infantry cited; DA GO 43, 1950)

*Cited in the Order of the Day of the Belgian Army for action at ELSENBORN CREST (38th Infantry cited; DA GO 43, 1950)

38TH INFANTRY, BIBLIOGRAPHY

Appleman, Roy E. *South to the Naktong, North to the Yalu.* United States Army in the Korean War. Washington: Government Printing Office, 1961.

Blumenson, Martin. *Breakout and Pursuit.* United States Army in World War II. Washington: Government Printing Office, 1961.

Cole, Hugh M. *The Ardennes: Battle of the Bulge.* United States Army in World War II. Washington: Government Printing Office, 1964.

Fretwell, Frank M. *The Rock of the Marne, A Narrative of the Military Exploits of General Ulysses Grant McAlexander at the Second Battle of the Marne.* Seattle, 1923.

'The German Offensive of July 15, 1918." (Marne Source Book.) Fort Leavenworth, Kansas: General Service Schools, 1923.

Gugeler, Russell A. *Combat Actions in Korea.* Washington: Combat Forces Press, 1954.

Harrison, Gordon A. *Cross-Channel Attack.* United States Army in World War II. Washington: Government Printing Office, 1951.

Hermes, Walter G. *Truce Tent and Fighting Front.* United States Army in the Korean War. Washington: Government Printing Office, 1966.

Historical Section, War Department. *Omaha Beachhead.* American Forces in Action Series. Washington: Government Printing Office, 1945.

————. *St. Lô.* American Forces in Action Series. Washington: Government Printing Office, 1946.

A History of the 38th U.S. Infantry. Schweinfurt, 1959.

The History of the 38th U.S. Infantry Regiment. n.p., 1956.

Lovejoy, Clarence Earle. *The Story of the Thirty-eighth.* Coblenz: Gorres-Druckerei, 1919.

MacDonald, Charles B. *The Siegfried Line Campaign.* United States Army in World War II. Washington: Government Printing Office, 1963.

MacHugh, Robert E., ed. *APHOREC (Army Photographic Record) 38th Regimental Combat Team Mountain and Winter Warfare Training Annual, 1947–1948.* Pueblo, Colorado: R. C. Pierre Bacque, O'Brien Printing and Stationery Company, 1947.

Marshall, S. L. A. *The River and the Gauntlet.* New York: William Morrow and Company, 1956.

Rock of the Marne (Weekly). Neidermendig, Germany, 1919.

38th Regimental Combat Team, Camp Carson, Colorado. Baton Rouge: Army and Navy Publishing Company, 1947.

38th United States Infantry. n.p., 1953.

Wooldridge, Jesse Walton. *The Giants of the Marne: A Story of Mc-Alexander and his Regiment.* Salt Lake City: Seagull Press, 1923.
———. *The Rock of the Marne: A Chronological Story of the 38th Regiment.* Columbia, South Carolina: University Press, 1920.

39th INFANTRY
(AAA–O)

Heraldic Items

Coat of Arms

Shield: Azure, a fleur-de-lis argent between two oak trees eradicated in fess or; on a canton of the second a boar's head erased sable. (And for informal use, pendant from the escutcheon a French Croix de Guerre with Gilt Star proper.)

Crest: On a wreath of the colors a falcon's head erased or, in the bill an ivy leaf vert.

Motto: *D'une Vaillance Admirable* (With a Military Courage Worthy of Admiration).

Symbolism: The shield is blue for infantry. The fleur-de-lis from the arms of Soissons and the two trees representing the Grove of Cresnes, the capture of which was the regiment's first success, are used to show service in the Aisne-Marne campaign. The boar's head on the canton is from the crest of the 30th Infantry and indicates that this regiment was organized with personnel from the 30th.

The crest is a falcon's head for Montfaucon in the Meuse-Argonne, holding in his bill an ivy leaf from the shoulder sleeve insignia of the 4th Division, to which the 39th was assigned during World War I. The motto is a quotation from the French citation awarding the Croix de Guerre with Gilt Star to the regiment for service in World War I.

Distinctive Insignia

The distinctive insignia is the shield, crest, and motto of the coat of arms.

LINEAGE AND HONORS

LINEAGE

Constituted 15 May 1917 in the Regular Army as the 39th Infantry. Organized 1 June 1917 at Syracuse, New York. Assigned 19 November 1917 to the 4th Division. Inactivated 21 September 1921 at Camp Lewis, Washington. Relieved 15 August 1927 from assignment to the 4th Division and assigned to the 7th Division. Relieved 1 October 1933 from assignment to the 7th Division and assigned to the 4th Division. Relieved 1 August 1940 from assignment to the 4th Division and assigned to the 9th Division (later redesignated as the 9th Infantry Division). Activated 9 August 1940 at Fort Bragg, North Carolina. Inactivated 30 November 1946 in Germany. Activated 15 July 1947 at Fort Dix, New Jersey.

Relieved 1 December 1957 from assignment to the 9th Infantry Division and reorganized as a parent regiment under the Combat Arms Regimental System.

CAMPAIGN PARTICIPATION CREDIT

World War I
  Aisne-Marne
  St. Mihiel
  Meuse-Argonne
  Champagne 1918
  Lorraine 1918

World War II
  Algeria-French Morocco
    (with arrowhead)
  Tunisia
  Sicily

  Normandy
  Northern France
  Rhineland
  Ardennes-Alsace
  Central Europe

Vietnam
  Counteroffensive, Phase II
  Counteroffensive, Phase III
  Tet Counteroffensive
    (other campaigns to be determined)

DECORATIONS

Presidential Unit Citation (Army), Streamer embroidered COTENTIN PENINSULA (1st Battalion, 39th Infantry cited; WD GO 10, 1945)

Presidential Unit Citation (Army), Streamer embroidered CHERENCE LE ROUSSEL (1st Battalion, 39th Infantry cited; WD GO 10, 1945)

Presidential Unit Citation (Army), Streamer embroidered LE DESERT (2d Battalion, 39th Infantry cited; WD GO 24, 1945)

Presidential Unit Citation (Army), Streamer embroidered DINH TUONG PROVINCE (2d Battalion, 39th Infantry cited; DA GO 60, 1969)

Valorous Unit Award, Streamer embroidered BEN TRE CITY (2d Battalion and 3d Battalion [less Companies A, D, and E], 39th Infantry cited; DA GO 42, 1969)

Valorous Unit Award, Streamer embroidered SAIGON (3d and 4th Battalions, 39th Infantry cited; DA GO 43, 1970)

French Croix de Guerre with Gilt Star, World War I, Streamer embroidered AISNE-MARNE (39th Infantry cited; WD GO 11, 1924)

Belgian Fourragere 1940 (39th Infantry cited; DA GO 43, 1950)

Cited in the Order of the Day of the Belgian Army for action on the MEUSE RIVER (39th Infantry cited; DA GO 43, 1950)

Cited in the Order of the Day of the Belgian Army for action in the ARDENNES (39th Infantry cited; DA GO 43, 1950)

1st BATTALION, 39th INFANTRY

(AAA–O)

RA
(8th Infantry Division)

LINEAGE

Constituted 15 May 1917 in the Regular Army as Company A, 39th Infantry. Organized 1 June 1917 at Syracuse, New York. (39th Infantry assigned 19 November 1917 to the 4th Division.) Inactivated 21 September 1921 at Camp Lewis, Washington. (39th Infantry relieved 15 August 1927 from assignment to the 4th Division and assigned to the 7th Division; relieved 1 October 1933 from assignment to the 7th Division and assigned to the 4th Division; relieved 1 August 1940 from assignment to the 4th Division and assigned to the 9th Division [later redesignated as the 9th Infantry Division].) Activated 9 August 1940 at Fort Bragg, North Carolina. Inactivated 30 November 1946 in Germany. Activated 15 July 1947 at Fort Dix, New Jersey.

Reorganized and redesignated 1 December 1957 as Headquarters and Headquarters Company, 1st Battle Group, 39th Infantry and remained assigned to the 9th Infantry Division (organic elements concurrently constituted and activated). Inactivated 31 January 1962 at Fort Carson, Colorado. Redesignated 20 September 1962 as the 1st Battalion, 39th Infantry; concurrently, relieved from assignment to the 9th Infantry Division and assigned to the 197th Infantry Brigade. Activated 24 September 1962 at Fort Benning, Georgia. Relieved 4 January 1963 from assignment to the 197th Infantry Brigade. Inactivated 1 February 1963 at Fort Benning, Georgia. Assigned 27 March 1963 to the 8th Infantry Division. Activated 1 April 1963 in Germany.

CAMPAIGN PARTICIPATION CREDIT

World War I
  *Aisne-Marne
  *St. Mihiel
  *Meuse-Argonne
  *Champagne 1918
  *Lorraine 1918

World War II
  *Algeria-French Morocco
    (with arrowhead)
  *Tunisia
  *Sicily
  *Normandy
  *Northern France
  *Rhineland
  *Ardennes-Alsace
  *Central Europe

Decorations

*Presidential Unit Citation (Army), Streamer embroidered COTENTIN PENINSULA (1st Battalion, 39th Infantry cited; WD GO 10, 1945)

*Presidential Unit Citation (Army), Streamer embroidered CHERENCE LE ROUSSEL (1st Battalion, 39th Infantry cited; WD GO 10, 1945)

Presidential Unit Citation (Army), Streamer embroidered LE DESERT

*French Croix de Guerre with Gilt Star, World War I, Streamer embroidered AISNE-MARNE (39th Infantry cited; WD GO 11, 1924)

*French Croix de Guerre with Palm, World War II, Streamer embroidered SAINT JACQUES DE NEHOU (1st Battalion, 39th Infantry cited; DA GO 43, 1950)

*French Croix de Guerre with Palm, World War II, Streamer embroidered CHERENCE LE ROUSSEL (1st Battalion, 39th Infantry cited; DA GO 43, 1950)

*French Croix de Guerre, World War II, Fourragere (1st Battalion, 39th Infantry cited; DA GO 37, 1961)

*Belgian Fourragere 1940 (39th Infantry cited; DA GO 43, 1950)

*Cited in the Order of the Day of the Belgian Army for action on the MEUSE RIVER (39th Infantry cited; DA GO 43, 1950)

*Cited in the Order of the Day of the Belgian Army for action in the ARDENNES (39th Infantry cited; DA GO 43, 1950)

2d BATTALION, 39th INFANTRY

(AAA-O)

RA
(inactive)

LINEAGE

Constituted 15 May 1917 in the Regular Army as Company B, 39th Infantry. Organized 1 June 1917 at Syracuse, New York. (39th Infantry assigned 19 November 1917 to the 4th Division.) Inactivated 21 September 1921 at Camp Lewis, Washington. (39th Infantry relieved 15 August 1927 from assignment to the 4th Division and assigned to the 7th Division; relieved 1 October 1933 from assignment to the 7th Division and assigned to the 4th Division; relieved 1 August 1940 from assignment to the 4th Division and assigned to the 9th Division [later redesignated as the 9th Infantry Division].) Activated 9 August 1940 at Fort Bragg, North Carolina. Inactivated 30 November 1946 in Germany. Activated 15 July 1947 at Fort Dix, New Jersey.

Reorganized and redesignated 1 April 1957 as Headquarters and Headquarters Company, 2d Battle Group, 39th Infantry, relieved from assignment to the 9th Infantry Division and assigned to the 4th Infantry Division (organic elements concurrently constituted and activated). Inactivated 1 October 1963 at Fort Lewis, Washington, and relieved from assignment to the 4th Infantry Division. Redesignated 1 February 1966 as the 2d Battalion, 39th Infantry; concurrently, assigned to the 9th Infantry Division and activated at Fort Riley, Kansas. Inactivated 25 September 1969 at Schofield Barracks, Hawaii.

CAMPAIGN PARTICIPATION CREDIT

World War I
 *Aisne-Marne
 *St. Mihiel
 *Meuse-Argonne
 *Champagne 1918
 *Lorraine 1918

World War II
 *Algeria-French Morocco
  (with arrowhead)
 *Tunisia
 *Sicily

*Normandy
*Northern France
*Rhineland
*Ardennes-Alsace
*Central Europe

Vietnam
 *Counteroffensive, Phase II
 *Counteroffensive, Phase III
 *Tet Counteroffensive
  (other campaigns to be determined)

DECORATIONS

*Presidential Unit Citation (Army), Streamer embroidered COTENTIN PENINSULA (1st Battalion, 39th Infantry cited; WD GO 10, 1945)

*Presidential Unit Citation (Army), Streamer embroidered CHERENCE LE ROUSSEL (1st Battalion, 39th Infantry cited; WD GO 10, 1945)

Presidential Unit Citation (Army), Streamer embroidered LE DESERT

*Presidential Unit Citation (Army), Streamer embroidered DINH TUONG PROVINCE (2d Battalion, 39th Infantry cited; DA GO 60, 1969)

*Valorous Unit Award, Streamer embroidered BEN TRE CITY (2d Battalion, 39th Infantry cited; DA GO 42, 1969)

*French Croix de Guerre with Gilt Star, World War I, Streamer embroidered AISNE-MARNE (39th Infantry cited; WD GO 11, 1924)

*French Croix de Guerre with Palm, World War II, Streamer embroidered SAINT JACQUES DE NEHOU (1st Battalion, 39th Infantry cited; DA GO 43, 1950)

*French Croix de Guerre with Palm, World War II, Streamer embroidered CHERENCE LE ROUSSEL (1st Battalion, 39th Infantry cited; DA GO 43, 1950)

*French Croix de Guerre, World War II, Fourragere (1st Battalion, 39th Infantry cited; DA GO 37, 1961)

*Belgian Fourragere 1940 (39th Infantry cited; DA GO 43, 1950)

*Cited in the Order of the Day of the Belgian Army for action on the MEUSE RIVER (39th Infantry cited; DA GO 43, 1950)

*Cited in the Order of the Day of the Belgian Army for action in the ARDENNES (39th Infantry cited; DA GO 43, 1950)

*Vietnamese Cross of Gallantry with Palm, Streamer embroidered VIETNAM 1967–1968 (2d Battalion, 39th Infantry cited; DA GO 31, 1969)

*Vietnamese Cross of Gallantry with Palm, Streamer embroidered VIETNAM 1968 (2d Battalion, 39th Infantry cited; DA GO 31, 1969)

*Vietnamese Cross of Gallantry with Palm, Streamer embroidered VIETNAM 1969 (2d Battalion, 39th Infantry cited; DA GO 59, 1969)

*Vietnamese Civil Action Honor Medal, First Class, Streamer embroidered VIETNAM 1967–1969 (2d Battalion, 39th Infantry cited; DA GO 59, 1969)

3d BATTALION, 39th INFANTRY

(AAA–O)

RA
(inactive)

LINEAGE

Constituted 15 May 1917 in the Regular Army as Company C, 39th Infantry. Organized 1 June 1917 at Syracuse, New York. (39th Infantry assigned 19 November 1917 to the 4th Division.) Inactivated 21 September 1921 at Camp Lewis, Washington. (39th Infantry relieved 15 August 1927 from assignment to the 4th Division and assigned to the 7th Division; relieved 1 October 1933 from assignment to the 7th Division and assigned to the 4th Division; relieved 1 August 1940 from assignment to the 4th Division and assigned to the 9th Division [later redesignated as the 9th Infantry Division].) Activated 9 August 1940 at Fort Bragg, North Carolina. Inactivated 30 November 1946 in Germany. Activated 15 July 1947 at Fort Dix, New Jersey.

Inactivated 1 December 1957 at Fort Carson, Colorado, and relieved from assignment to the 9th Infantry Division; concurrently, redesignated as Headquarters and Headquarters Company, 3d Battle Group, 39th Infantry. Redesignated 1 February 1966 as Headquarters and Headquarters Company, 3d Battalion, 39th Infantry, assigned to the 9th Infantry Division, and activated at Fort Riley, Kansas (organic elements concurrently constituted and activated). Inactivated 25 September 1969 at Schofield Barracks, Hawaii.

CAMPAIGN PARTICIPATION CREDIT

World War I
 *Aisne-Marne
 *St. Mihiel
 *Meuse-Argonne
 *Champagne 1918
 *Lorraine 1918

World War II
 *Algeria-French Morocco
  (with arrowhead)
 *Tunisia
 *Sicily

 *Normandy
 *Northern France
 *Rhineland
 *Ardennes-Alsace
 *Central Europe

Vietnam
 *Counteroffensive, Phase II
 *Counteroffensive, Phase III
 *Tet Counteroffensive
  (other campaigns to be determined)

Decorations

*Presidential Unit Citation (Army), Streamer embroidered COTENTIN PENINSULA (1st Battalion, 39th Infantry cited; WD GO 10, 1945)

*Presidential Unit Citation (Army), Streamer embroidered CHERENCE LE ROUSSEL (1st Battalion, 39th Infantry cited; WD GO 10, 1945)

Presidential Unit Citation (Army), Streamer embroidered LE DESERT

*Valorous Unit Award, Streamer embroidered BEN TRE CITY (3d Battalion [less Companies A, D, and E], 39th Infantry cited; DA GO 42, 1969)

*Valorous Unit Award, Streamer embroidered SAIGON (3d Battalion, 39th Infantry cited; DA GO 43, 1970)

*French Croix de Guerre with Gilt Star, World War I, Streamer embroidered AISNE-MARNE (39th Infantry cited; WD GO 11, 1924)

*French Croix de Guerre with Palm, World War II, Streamer embroidered SAINT JACQUES DE NEHOU (1st Battalion, 39th Infantry cited; DA GO 43, 1950)

*French Croix de Guerre with Palm, World War II, Streamer embroidered CHERENCE LE ROUSSEL (1st Battalion, 39th Infantry cited; DA GO 43, 1950)

*French Croix de Guerre, World War II, Fourragere (1st Battalion, 39th Infantry cited; DA GO 37, 1961)

*Belgian Fourragere 1940 (39th Infantry cited; DA GO 43, 1950)

*Cited in the Order of the Day of the Belgian Army for action on the MEUSE RIVER (39th Infantry cited; DA GO 43, 1950)

*Cited in the Order of the Day of the Belgian Army for action in the ARDENNES (39th Infantry cited; DA GO 43, 1950)

*Vietnamese Cross of Gallantry with Palm, Streamer embroidered VIETNAM 1967–1968 (3d Battalion, 39th Infantry cited; DA GO 31, 1969)

*Vietnamese Cross of Gallantry with Palm, Streamer embroidered VIETNAM 1968 (3d Battalion, 39th Infantry cited; DA GO 31, 1969)

*Vietnamese Cross of Gallantry with Palm, Streamer embroidered VIETNAM 1969 (3d Battalion, 39th Infantry cited; DA GO 59, 1969)

*Vietnamese Civil Action Honor Medal, First Class, Streamer embroidered VIETNAM 1967–1969 (3d Battalion, 39th Infantry cited; DA GO 59, 1969, as amended by DA GO 43, 1970)

4th BATTALION, 39th INFANTRY

(AAA–O)

RA
(inactive)

LINEAGE

Constituted 15 May 1917 in the Regular Army as Company D, 39th Infantry. Organized 1 June 1917 at Syracuse, New York. (39th Infantry assigned 19 November 1917 to the 4th Division.) Inactivated 21 September 1921 at Camp Lewis, Washington. (39th Infantry relieved 15 August 1927 from assignment to the 4th Division and assigned to the 7th Division; relieved 1 October 1933 from assignment to the 7th Division and assigned to the 4th Division; relieved 1 August 1940 from assignment to the 4th Division and assigned to the 9th Division [later redesignated as the 9th Infantry Division].) Activated 9 August 1940 at Fort Bragg, North Carolina. Inactivated 30 November 1946 in Germany. Activated 15 July 1947 at Fort Dix, New Jersey.

Inactivated 1 December 1957 at Fort Carson, Colorado, and relieved from assignment to the 9th Infantry Division; concurrently, redesignated as Headquarters and Headquarters Company, 4th Battle Group, 39th Infantry. Redesignated 1 February 1966 as Headquarters and Headquarters Company, 4th Battalion, 39th Infantry, assigned to the 9th Infantry Division, and activated at Fort Riley, Kansas (organic elements concurrently constituted and activated). Inactivated 25 September 1969 at Schofield Barracks, Hawaii.

CAMPAIGN PARTICIPATION CREDIT

World War I
  *Aisne-Marne
  *St. Mihiel
  *Meuse-Argonne
  *Champagne 1918
  *Lorraine 1918

World War II
  *Algeria-French Morocco
    (with arrowhead)
  *Tunisia
  *Sicily

  *Normandy
  *Northern France
  *Rhineland
  *Ardennes-Alsace
  *Central Europe

Vietnam
  *Counteroffensive, Phase II
  *Counteroffensive, Phase III
  *Tet Counteroffensive
    (other campaigns to be determined)

622

DECORATIONS

*Presidential Unit Citation (Army), Streamer embroidered COTENTIN PENINSULA (1st Battalion, 39th Infantry cited; WD GO 10, 1945)

*Presidential Unit Citation (Army), Streamer embroidered CHERENCE LE ROUSSEL (1st Battalion, 39th Infantry cited; WD GO 10, 1945)

Presidential Unit Citation (Army), Streamer embroidered LE DESERT

*Valorous Unit Award, Streamer embroidered SAIGON (4th Battalion, 39th Infantry cited; DA GO 43, 1970)

*French Croix de Guerre with Gilt Star, World War I, Streamer embroidered AISNE-MARNE (39th Infantry cited; WD GO 11, 1924)

*French Croix de Guerre with Palm, World War II, Streamer embroidered SAINT JACQUES DE NEHOU (1st Battalion, 39th Infantry cited; DA GO 43, 1950)

*French Croix de Guerre with Palm, World War II, Streamer embroidered CHERENCE LE ROUSSEL (1st Battalion, 39th Infantry cited; DA GO 43, 1950)

*French Croix de Guerre, World War II, Fourragere (1st Battalion, 39th Infantry cited; DA GO 37, 1961)

*Belgian Fourragere 1940 (39th Infantry cited; DA GO 43, 1950)

*Cited in the Order of the Day of the Belgian Army for action on the MEUSE RIVER (39th Infantry cited; DA GO 43, 1950)

*Cited in the Order of the Day of the Belgian Army for action in the ARDENNES (39th Infantry cited; DA GO 43, 1950)

*Vietnamese Cross of Gallantry with Palm, Streamer embroidered VIETNAM 1967–1968 (4th Battalion, 39th Infantry cited; DA GO 31, 1969)

*Vietnamese Cross of Gallantry with Palm, Streamer embroidered VIETNAM 1968 (4th Battalion, 39th Infantry cited; DA GO 31, 1969)

*Vietnamese Cross of Gallantry with Palm, Streamer embroidered VIETNAM 1969 (4th Battalion, 39th Infantry cited; DA GO 59, 1969)

*Vietnamese Civil Action Honor Medal, First Class, Streamer embroidered VIETNAM 1967–1969 (4th Battalion, 39th Infantry cited; DA GO 59, 1969)

Company B additionally entitled to: Valorous Unit Award, Streamer embroidered LONG BINH–BIEN HOA (Company B, 4th Battalion, 39th Infantry cited; DA GO 5, 1969)

39TH INFANTRY, BIBLIOGRAPHY

Blumenson, Martin. *Breakout and Pursuit.* United States Army in World War II. Washington: Government Printing Office, 1961.

Cole, Robert B. and Barnard Eberlin, eds. *The History of the 39th U.S. Infantry in the World War.* New York: Press of Joseph D. McGuire, 1919.

The Fighting Falcons—NATO's Best—39th Anniversary. n.p., 1956.

Garland, Albert N. and Howard McGaw Smyth. *Sicily and the Surrender of Italy.* United States Army in World War II. Washington: Government Printing Office, 1965.

Harrison, Gordon A. *Cross-Channel Attack.* United States Army in World War II. Washington: Government Printing Office, 1951.

Historical Section, War Department. *Anzio Beachhead.* American Forces in Action Series. Washington: Government Printing Office, 1947.

————. *To Bizerte with the II Corps.* American Forces in Action Series. Washington: Government Printing Office, 1943.

————. *St-Lô.* American Forces in Action Series. Washington: Government Printing Office, 1946.

————. *Utah Beach to Cherbourg.* American Forces in Action Series. Washington: Government Printing Office, 1947.

History of the 4th Infantry Division and Brief Histories of its Components. Fort Lewis, Washington, 1958.

Howe, George F. *Northwest Africa: Seizing the Initiative in the West.* United States Army in World War II. Washington: Government Printing Office, 1957.

Lavender, D. E. *Nudge Blue: A Chronicle of World War II Experience.* n.p., 1964.

MacDonald, Charles B. *The Battle of Huertgen Forest.* New York and Philadelphia: J. B. Lippincott Company, 1963.

————. *The Siegfried Line Campaign.* United States Army in World War II. Washington: Government Printing Office, 1963.

41st INFANTRY

HERALDIC ITEMS

COAT OF ARMS

Shield: Azure, within an annulet or a martello tower argent masoned sable; on a canton of the third a six-bastioned fort vert charged with a mullet of the third.

Crest: On a wreath or and azure, issuing from three waves barry wavy of three of the last and argent a tower with four battlements of the like masoned sable surmounted by a lion rampant party per fess of the third and gules armed and langued counterchanged charged on the shoulder with a decrescent of the second grasping and breaking a tilting spear of the first.

Motto: Straight and Stalwart.

Symbolism: The field is blue for infantry. The charges on the canton show that the regiment was originally organized with personnel from the 36th Infantry at Fort Snelling, Minnesota, represented by the tower. During World War I it was in the 10th Division; the annulet is taken from the unofficial insignia of that division.

The lion rampant is from the coat of arms of Belgium; it refers to the regiment's participation in the Battle of the Bulge in Belgium during World War II. The lion is red for valor; the upper part is white in reference to the snow-covered terrain of the battle. The broken spear refers to the breaking of the German salient or spearhead. The crescent stands for Algeria and alludes to the regiment's first combat service in World War II. The tower represents the fortress of Europe; its four battlements stand for the unit's four Presidential Unit Citations (Army). The waves refer to the regiment's assault landings in World War II.

DISTINCTIVE INSIGNIA

The distinctive insignia is the shield and motto of the coat of arms.

LINEAGE AND HONORS

LINEAGE

Constituted 15 May 1917 in the Regular Army as the 41st Infantry. Organized 20 June 1917 at Fort Snelling. Minnesota. Assigned 9 July 1918 to the 10th Division. Relieved 18 February 1919 from assignment to the 10th Division. Inactivated 22 September 1921 at Camp Meade, Maryland.

Activated 15 July 1940 at Fort Benning. Georgia. as the 41st Infantry (Armored) and assigned to the 2d Armored Division. Redesignated 1 January 1942 as the 41st Armored Infantry. Regiment broken up 25 March 1946 and its elements reorganized and redesignated as elements of the 2d Armored Division as follows: Headquarters as Headquarters. Reserve Command, 2d Armored Division: 1st Battalion as the 41st Armored Infantry Battalion: 2d Battalion as the 42d Armored Infantry Battalion: 3d Battalion as the 12th Armored Infantry Battalion.

41st, 42d, and 12th Armored Infantry Battalions relieved 1 July 1957 from assignment to the 2d Armored Division and consolidated to form the 41st Infantry, a parent regiment under the Combat Arms Regimental System: concurrently, former Headquarters, Reserve Command, 2d Armored Division expanded and redesignated as Headquarters, 41st Infantry and as Headquarters and Headquarters Company, Combat Command C, 2d Armored Division (Headquarters and Headquarters Company, Combat Command C, 2d Armored Division—hereafter separate lineage).

CAMPAIGN PARTICIPATION CREDIT

World War II
  Algeria-French Morocco
    (with arrowhead)
  Sicily (with arrowhead)
  Normandy

Northern France
Rhineland
Ardennes-Alsace
Central Europe

DECORATIONS

Presidential Unit Citation (Army), Streamer embroidered NORMANDY (1st and 3d Battalions, 41st Armored Infantry cited; DA GO 28, 1948)

Presidential Unit Citation (Army), Streamer embroidered CHERBOURG (Headquarters and Headquarters Company, 41st Armored Infantry cited; WD GO 108, 1945)

Presidential Unit Citation (Army), Streamer embroidered ARDENNES (1st Battalion, 41st Armored Infantry cited; WD GO 11, 1946)

Presidential Unit Citation (Army), Streamer embroidered PUFFENDORFROER (2d Battalion, 41st Armored Infantry cited; WD GO 108, 1945)

Belgian Fourragere 1940 (41st Armored Infantry cited; DA GO 43, 1950)

Cited in the Order of the Day of the Belgian Army for action in BELGIUM (41st Armored Infantry cited; DA GO 43, 1950)

Cited in the Order of the Day of the Belgian Army for action in the ARDENNES (41st Armored Infantry cited; DA GO 43, 1950)

1st BATTALION, 41st INFANTRY

RA
(2d Armored Division)

LINEAGE

Constituted 15 May 1917 in the Regular Army as Company A, 41st Infantry. Organized 20 June 1917 at Fort Snelling, Minnesota. (41st Infantry assigned 9 July 1918 to the 10th Division; relieved 18 February 1919 from assignment to the 10th Division.) Inactivated 22 September 1921 at Camp Meade, Maryland.

Activated 15 July 1940 at Fort Benning, Georgia, as Company A, 41st Infantry (Armored), an element of the 2d Armored Division. Redesignated 1 January 1942 as Company A, 41st Armored Infantry. Reorganized and redesignated 25 March 1946 as Company A, 41st Armored Infantry Battalion, an element of the 2d Armored Division.

Reorganized and redesignated 1 July 1957 as Headquarters and Headquarters Company, 1st Armored Rifle Battalion, 41st Infantry and remained assigned to the 2d Armored Division (organic elements concurrently constituted and activated). Reorganized and redesignated 1 July 1963 as the 1st Battalion, 41st Infantry.

CAMPAIGN PARTICIPATION CREDIT

World War II
*Algeria-French Morocco
  (with arrowhead)
*Sicily (with arrowhead)
*Normandy

*Northern France
*Rhineland
*Ardennes-Alsace
*Central Europe

DECORATIONS

*Presidential Unit Citation (Army), Streamer embroidered NORMANDY (1st Battalion, 41st Armored Infantry cited; DA GO 28, 1948)

Presidential Unit Citation (Army), Streamer embroidered CHERBOURG

*Presidential Unit Citation (Army), Streamer embroidered ARDENNES (1st Battalion, 41st Armored Infantry cited; WD GO 11, 1946)

Presidential Unit Citation (Army), Streamer embroidered PUFFENDORF-ROER

*Belgian Fourragere 1940 (41st Armored Infantry cited; DA GO 43, 1950)

628

*Cited in the Order of the Day of the Belgian Army for action in BELGIUM (41st Armored Infantry cited; DA GO 43, 1950)

*Cited in the Order of the Day of the Belgian Army for action in the ARDENNES (41st Armored Infantry cited; DA GO 43, 1950)

2d BATTALION, 41st INFANTRY

RA

(2d Armored Division)

Constituted 15 May 1917 in the Regular Army as Company B, 41st Infantry. Organized 20 June 1917 at Fort Snelling, Minnesota. (41st Infantry assigned 9 July 1918 to the 10th Division; relieved 18 February 1919 from assignment to the 10th Division.) Inactivated 22 September 1921 at Camp Meade, Maryland.

Activated 15 July 1940 at Fort Benning, Georgia, as Company B, 41st Infantry (Armored), an element of the 2d Armored Division. Redesignated 1 January 1942 as Company B, 41st Armored Infantry. Reorganized and redesignated 25 March 1946 as Company B, 41st Armored Infantry Battalion, an element of the 2d Armored Division.

Reorganized and redesignated 1 April 1957 as Headquarters and Headquarters Company, 2d Armored Rifle Battalion, 41st Infantry, relieved from assignment to the 2d Armored Division, and assigned to the 4th Armored Division (organic elements concurrently constituted and activated). Reorganized and redesignated 1 July 1963 as the 2d Battalion, 41st Infantry; concurrently, relieved from assignment to the 4th Armored Division and assigned to the 2d Armored Division.

CAMPAIGN PARTICIPATION CREDIT

World War II
*Algeria-French Morocco
  (with arrowhead)
*Sicily (with arrowhead)
*Normandy

*Northern France
*Rhineland
*Ardennes-Alsace
*Central Europe

DECORATIONS

*Presidential Unit Citation (Army), Streamer embroidered NORMANDY (1st Battalion, 41st Armored Infantry cited; DA GO 28, 1948)

Presidential Unit Citation (Army), Streamer embroidered CHERBOURG

*Presidential Unit Citation (Army), Streamer embroidered ARDENNES (1st Battalion, 41st Armored Infantry cited; WD GO 11, 1946)

Presidential Unit Citation (Army), Streamer embroidered PUFFENDORF-ROER

*Belgian Fourragere 1940 (41st Armored Infantry cited; DA GO 43, 1950)

*Cited in the Order of the Day of the Belgian Army for action in BELGIUM (41st Armored Infantry cited; DA GO 43, 1950)

*Cited in the Order of the Day of the Belgian Army for action in the ARDENNES (41st Armored Infantry cited; DA GO 43, 1950)

3d ARMORED RIFLE BATTALION, 41st INFANTRY

RA
(inactive)

LINEAGE

Constituted 15 May 1917 in the Regular Army as Company C, 41st Infantry. Organized 20 June 1917 at Fort Snelling, Minnesota. (41st Infantry assigned 9 July 1918 to the 10th Division; relieved 18 February 1919 from assignment to the 10th Division.) Inactivated 22 September 1921 at Camp Meade, Maryland.

Activated 15 July 1940 at Fort Benning, Georgia, as Company C, 41st Infantry (Armored), an element of the 2d Armored Division. Redesignated 1 January 1942 as Company C, 41st Armored Infantry. Reorganized and redesignated 25 March 1946 as Company C, 41st Armored Infantry Battalion, an element of the 2d Armored Division.

Inactivated 1 July 1957 in Germany and relieved from assignment to the 2d Armored Division; concurrently, redesignated as Headquarters and Headquarters Company, 3d Armored Rifle Battalion, 41st Infantry. (Organic elements constituted 17 April 1961.) Battalion activated 25 April 1961 at Fort Ord, California. Inactivated 21 December 1962 at Fort Ord, California.

CAMPAIGN PARTICIPATION CREDIT

World War II
  *Algeria-French Morocco
    (with arrowhead)
  *Sicily (with arrowhead)
  *Normandy

*Northern France
*Rhineland
*Ardennes-Alsace
*Central Europe

DECORATIONS

*Presidential Unit Citation (Army), Streamer embroidered NORMANDY (1st Battalion, 41st Armored Infantry cited; DA GO 28, 1948)

Presidential Unit Citation (Army), Streamer embroidered CHERBOURG

*Presidential Unit Citation (Army), Streamer embroidered ARDENNES (1st Battalion, 41st Armored Infantry cited; WD GO 11, 1946)

Presidential Unit Citation (Army), Streamer embroidered PUFFENDORF-ROER

*Belgian Fourragere 1940 (41st Armored Infantry cited; DA GO 43, 1950)

632

*Cited in the Order of the Day of the Belgian Army for action in
BELGIUM (41st Armored Infantry cited; DA GO 43, 1950)

*Cited in the Order of the Day of the Belgian Army for action in the
ARDENNES (41st Armored Infantry cited; DA GO 43, 1950)

COMPANY D, 41st INFANTRY

RA
(nondivisional)

Constituted 15 May 1917 in the Regular Army as Company D, 41st Infantry. Organized 20 June 1917 at Fort Snelling, Minnesota. (41st Infantry assigned 9 July 1918 to the 10th Division; relieved 18 February 1919 from assignment to the 10th Division.) Inactivated 22 September 1921 at Camp Meade, Maryland.

Activated 15 July 1940 at Fort Benning, Georgia, as Company D, 41st Infantry (Armored), an element of the 2d Armored Division. Redesignated 1 January 1942 as Company D, 41st Armored Infantry. Reorganized and redesignated 25 March 1946 as Company A, 42d Armored Infantry Battalion, an element of the 2d Armored Division.

Inactivated 1 July 1957 in Germany and relieved from assignment to the 2d Armored Division; concurrently, redesignated as Headquarters and Headquarters Company, 4th Armored Rifle Battalion, 41st Infantry. Redesignated 2 October 1962 as Headquarters and Headquarters Company, 4th Battalion, 41st Infantry and assigned to the 194th Armored Brigade (organic elements concurrently constituted). Battalion activated 21 December 1962 at Fort Ord, California.

Inactivated 4 January 1968 at Fort Ord, California, and relieved from assignment to the 194th Armored Brigade; concurrently, Headquarters and Headquarters Company, 4th Battalion, 41st Infantry redesignated as Company D, 41st Infantry and activated at Fort Ord, California.

CAMPAIGN PARTICIPATION CREDIT

World War II-EAME
  Sicily (with arrowhead)
  Normandy
  Northern France

Rhineland
Ardennes-Alsace
Central Europe

DECORATIONS

Presidential Unit Citation (Army), Streamer embroidered PUFFENDORF-ROER (2d Battalion, 41st Armored Infantry cited; WD GO 108, 1945)

French Croix de Guerre with Silver-Gilt Star, World War II, Streamer embroidered PUFFENDORF-ROER (2d Battalion, 41st Armored Infantry cited; DA GO 43, 1950)

634

Belgian Fourragere 1940 (41st Armored Infantry cited; DA GO 43, 1950)

Cited in the Order of the Day of the Belgian Army for action in BELGIUM (41st Armored Infantry cited; DA GO 43, 1950)

Cited in the Order of the Day of the Belgian Army for action in the ARDENNES (41st Armored Infantry cited; DA GO 43, 1950)

COMPANY E, 41st INFANTRY

RA
(nondivisional)

LINEAGE

Constituted 15 May 1917 in the Regular Army as Company E, 41st Infantry. Organized 20 June 1917 at Fort Snelling, Minnesota. (41st Infantry assigned 9 July 1918 to the 10th Division; relieved 18 February 1919 from assignment to the 10th Division.) Inactivated 22 September 1921 at Camp Meade, Maryland.

Activated 15 July 1940 at Fort Benning, Georgia, as Company E, 41st Infantry (Armored), an element of the 2d Armored Division. Redesignated 1 January 1942 as Company E, 41st Armored Infantry. Reorganized and redesignated 25 March 1946 as Company B, 42d Armored Infantry Battalion, an element of the 2d Armored Division.

Inactivated 1 July 1957 in Germany and relieved from assignment to the 2d Armored Division; concurrently, redesignated as Headquarters and Headquarters Company, 5th Armored Rifle Battalion, 41st Infantry. (Organic elements constituted 5 December 1962.) Battalion activated 18 December 1962 at Fort Chaffee, Arkansas. Inactivated 25 March 1963 at Fort Chaffee, Arkansas. Headquarters and Headquarters Company, 5th Armored Rifle Battalion, 41st Infantry redesignated 4 January 1968 as Company E, 41st Infantry and activated at Fort Ord, California.

CAMPAIGN PARTICIPATION CREDIT

World War II-EAME
    Sicily (with arrowhead)
    Normandy
    Northern France

Rhineland
Ardennes-Alsace
Central Europe

DECORATIONS

Presidential Unit Citation (Army), Streamer embroidered PUFFENDORF-ROER (2d Battalion, 41st Armored Infantry cited; WD GO 108, 1945)

French Croix de Guerre with Silver-Gilt Star, World War II, Streamer embroidered PUFFENDORF-ROER (2d Battalion, 41st Armored Infantry cited; DA GO 43, 1950)

Belgian Fourragere 1940 (41st Armored Infantry cited; DA GO 43, 1950)

636

Cited in the Order of the Day of the Belgian Army for action in BELGIUM (41st Armored Infantry cited; DA GO 43, 1950)

Cited in the Order of the Day of the Belgian Army for action in the ARDENNES (41st Armored Infantry cited; DA GO 43, 1950)

COMPANY F, 41st INFANTRY

RA
(nondivisional)

LINEAGE

Constituted 15 May 1917 in the Regular Army as Company F, 41st Infantry. Organized 20 June 1917 at Fort Snelling, Minnesota. (41st Infantry assigned 9 July 1918 to the 10th Division; relieved 18 February 1919 from assignment to the 10th Division.) Inactivated 22 September 1921 at Camp Meade, Maryland.

Activated 15 July 1940 at Fort Benning, Georgia, as Company F, 41st Infantry (Armored), an element of the 2d Armored Division. Redesignated 1 January 1942 as Company F, 41st Armored Infantry. Reorganized and redesignated 25 March 1946 as Company C, 42d Armored Infantry Battalion, an element of the 2d Armored Division.

Inactivated 1 July 1957 in Germany and relieved from assignment to the 2d Armored Division; concurrently, redesignated as Headquarters and Headquarters Company, 6th Armored Rifle Battalion, 41st Infantry. Redesignated 4 January 1968 as Company F, 41st Infantry and activated at Fort Ord, California.

CAMPAIGN PARTICIPATION CREDIT

World War II-EAME
  Sicily (with arrowhead)
  Normandy
  Northern France

Rhineland
Ardennes-Alsace
Central Europe

DECORATIONS

Presidential Unit Citation (Army), Streamer embroidered PUFFENDORF-ROER (2d Battalion, 41st Armored Infantry cited; WD GO 108, 1945)

French Croix de Guerre with Silver-Gilt Star, World War II, Streamer embroidered PUFFENDORF-ROER (2d Battalion, 41st Armored Infantry cited; DA GO 43, 1950)

Belgian Fourragere 1940 (41st Armored Infantry; DA GO 43, 1950)

Cited in the Order of the Day of the Belgian Army for action in BELGIUM (41st Armored Infantry cited; DA GO 43, 1950)

Cited in the Order of the Day of the Belgian Army for action in the ARDENNES (41st Armored Infantry cited; DA GO 43, 1950)

COMPANY G, 41st INFANTRY

RA
(inactive)

LINEAGE

Constituted 15 May 1917 in the Regular Army as Company G, 41st Infantry. Organized 20 June 1917 at Fort Snelling, Minnesota. (41st Infantry assigned 9 July 1918 to the 10th Division; relieved 18 February 1919 from assignment to the 10th Division.) Inactivated 22 September 1921 at Camp Meade, Maryland.

Activated 15 July 1940 at Fort Benning, Georgia, as Company G, 41st Infantry (Armored), an element of the 2d Armored Division. Redesignated 1 January 1942 as Company G, 41st Armored Infantry. Reorganized and redesignated 25 March 1946 as Company A, 12th Armored Infantry Battalion, an element of the 2d Armored Division.

Inactivated 1 July 1957 in Germany and relieved from assignment to the 2d Armored Division; concurrently, redesignated as Headquarters and Headquarters Company, 7th Armored Rifle Battalion, 41st Infantry. Redesignated 4 January 1968 as Company G, 41st Infantry and activated at Fort Ord, California. Inactivated 30 March 1970 at Fort Ord, California.

CAMPAIGN PARTICIPATION CREDIT

World War II-EAME
  Sicily (with arrowhead)
  Normandy
  Northern France

Rhineland
Ardennes-Alsace
Central Europe

DECORATIONS

Presidential Unit Citation (Army), Streamer embroidered NORMANDY (3d Battalion, 41st Armored Infantry cited; DA GO 28, 1948)

Belgian Fourragere 1940 (41st Armored Infantry cited; DA GO 43, 1950)

Cited in the Order of the Day of the Belgium Army for action in BELGIUM (41st Armored Infantry cited; DA GO 43, 1950)

Cited in the Order of the Day of the Belgian Army for action in the ARDENNES (41st Armored Infantry cited; DA GO 43, 1950)

639

COMPANY H, 41st INFANTRY

RA
(inactive)

Constituted 15 May 1917 in the Regular Army as Company H, 41st Infantry. Organized 20 June 1917 at Fort Snelling, Minnesota. (41st Infantry assigned 9 July 1918 to the 10th Division; relieved 18 February 1919 from assignment to the 10th Division.) Inactivated 22 September 1921 at Camp Meade, Maryland.

Activated 15 July 1940 at Fort Benning, Georgia, as Company H, 41st Infantry (Armored), an element of the 2d Armored Division. Redesignated 1 January 1942 as Company H, 41st Armored Infantry. Reorganized and redesignated 25 March 1946 as Company B, 12th Armored Infantry Battalion, an element of the 2d Armored Division.

Inactivated 1 July 1957 in Germany and relieved from assignment to the 2d Armored Division; concurrently, redesignated as Headquarters and Headquarters Company, 8th Armored Rifle Battalion, 41st Infantry. Redesignated 4 January 1968 as Company H, 41st Infantry and activated at Fort Ord, California. Inactivated 30 March 1970 at Fort Ord, California.

CAMPAIGN PARTICIPATION CREDIT

World War II-EAME
Sicily (with arrowhead)
Normandy
Northern France

Rhineland
Ardennes-Alsace
Central Europe

DECORATIONS

Presidential Unit Citation (Army), Streamer embroidered NORMANDY (3d Battalion, 41st Armored Infantry cited; DA GO 28, 1948)

Presidential Unit Citation (Army), Streamer embroidered BARENTON (Company H, 41st Armored Infantry cited; WD GO 30, 1945)

French Croix de Guerre with Silver Star, World War II, Streamer embroidered MORTAIN (Company H, 41st Armored Infantry cited; DA GO 43, 1950)

Belgian Fourragere 1940 (41st Armored Infantry cited; DA GO 43, 1950)

Cited in the Order of the Day of the Belgian Army for action in BELGIUM (41st Armored Infantry cited; DA GO 43, 1950)

640

Cited in the Order of the Day of the Belgian Army for action in the ARDENNES (41st Armored Infantry cited; DA GO 43, 1950)

41ST INFANTRY, BIBLIOGRAPHY

Dreyer, D., compiler. *36th, 40th, 41st U.S. Infantry, Fort Snelling, Minnesota, 1917*. Iowa City: D. Dreyer, 1917.

Garland, Albert N. and Howard McGaw Smyth. *Sicily and the Surrender of Italy*. United States Army in World War II. Washington: Government Printing Office, 1965.

Historical Section, War Department. *Omaha Beachhead*. American Forces in Action Series. Washington: Government Printing Office, 1945.

Howe, George F. *Northwest Africa: Seizing the Initiative in the West*. United States Army in World War II. Washington: Government Printing Office, 1957.

46th INFANTRY

(The Professionals)

COAT OF ARMS

Shield: Azure, in pale a mullet and a flaming torch or; on a canton argent a Roman numeral "X" of the first superimposed on a Roman sword in scabbard palewise point down or fimbriated of the field.

Crest: On a wreath or and azure between two pine trees eradicated gules a spear issuant from base of the first charged on the point with a fleur-de-lis of the second and enfiled by a castle tower sable masoned of the first charged with a lion rampant argent.

Motto: None.

Symbolism: This regiment was originally organized at Fort Benjamin Harrison, Indiana, with personnel from the 10th Infantry. The field is blue, the infantry color. The charge, a gold torch and star, is taken from the flag of the state of Indiana, while the badge of the 10th Infantry is shown on the canton.

The spearhead bearing a fleur-de-lis represents the unit's participation in the drive from the Normandy Peninsula through Northern France. The black castle signifies the penetration of the Siegfried Line. The operations in Luxembourg, for which the unit received the Croix de Guerre, are noted by the white lion rampant (adopted from the arms of the town of Diekirch). The red pine trees represent the bitter, arduous fighting in the area of the Hurtgen Forest of Germany.

DISTINCTIVE INSIGNIA

The distinctive insignia is the shield of the coat of arms.

LINEAGE AND HONORS

LINEAGE

Constituted 15 May 1917 in the Regular Army as the 46th Infantry. Organized 4 June 1917 at Fort Benjamin Harrison, Indiana. Assigned 5 July 1918 to the 9th Division. Relieved 15 February 1919 from assignment to the 9th Division. Inactivated 16 November 1921 at Camp Travis, Texas. Demobilized 31 July 1922.

Reconstituted 28 August 1941 in the Regular Army as the 46th Infantry (Armored), an element of the 5th Armored Division. Activated 1 October 1941 at Fort Knox, Kentucky. Redesignated 1 January 1942 as the 46th Armored Infantry. Regiment broken up 20 September 1943 and its elements reorganized and redesignated as elements of the 5th Armored Division as follows: 46th Armored Infantry (less 1st and 2d Battalions) as the 46th Armored Infantry Battalion; 1st Battalion as the 47th Armored Infantry Battalion; 2d Battalion as the 15th Armored Infantry Battalion. Battalions inactivated 8–13 October 1945 at Camp Myles Standish, Massachusetts; activated 6 July 1948 at Camp Chaffee, Arkansas; inactivated 1 February 1950 at Camp Chaffee, Arkansas; activated 1 September 1950 at Camp Chaffee, Arkansas; inactivated 16 March 1956 at Camp Chaffee, Arkansas; relieved 15 February 1957 from assignment to the 5th Armored Division.

46th, 47th, and 15th Armored Infantry Battalions consolidated 1 July 1959 to form the 46th Infantry, a parent regiment under the Combat Arms Regimental System.

CAMPAIGN PARTICIPATION CREDIT

World War II	*Vietnam*
Normandy	Counteroffensive, Phase III
Northern France	Tet Counteroffensive
Rhineland	(other campaigns to be determined)
Ardennes-Alsace	
Central Europe	

DECORATIONS

Presidential Unit Citation (Army), Streamer embroidered HURTGEN FOREST (47th Armored Infantry Battalion cited; WD GO 31, 1947)

Luxembourg Croix de Guerre, Streamer embroidered LUXEMBOURG (46th, 47th, and 15th Armored Infantry Battalions cited; DA GO 44, 1951)

1st BATTALION, 46th INFANTRY

(The Professionals)

RA
(23d Infantry Division)

LINEAGE

Constituted 15 May 1917 in the Regular Army as Company A, 46th Infantry. Organized 4 June 1917 at Fort Benjamin Harrison, Indiana. (46th Infantry assigned 5 July 1918 to the 9th Division; relieved 15 February 1919 from assignment to the 9th Division.) Inactivated 16 November 1921 at Camp Travis, Texas. Demobilized 31 July 1922.

Reconstituted 28 August 1941 in the Regular Army as Company A, 46th Infantry (Armored), an element of the 5th Armored Division. Activated 1 October 1941 at Fort Knox, Kentucky. Redesignated 1 January 1942 as Company A, 46th Armored Infantry. Reorganized and redesignated 20 September 1943 as Company A, 47th Armored Infantry Battalion, an element of the 5th Armored Division. Inactivated 8 October 1945 at Camp Myles Standish, Massachusetts. Activated 6 July 1948 at Camp Chaffee, Arkansas. Inactivated 1 February 1950 at Camp Chaffee, Arkansas. Activated 1 September 1950 at Camp Chaffee, Arkansas. Inactivated 16 March 1956 at Camp Chaffee, Arkansas.

Redesignated 15 February 1957 as Headquarters and Headquarters Company, 1st Armored Rifle Battalion, 46th Infantry, relieved from assignment to the 5th Armored Division, assigned to the 1st Armored Division, and activated at Fort Polk, Louisiana (organic elements concurrently constituted and activated). Inactivated 23 December 1957 at Fort Polk, Louisiana. Relieved 25 February 1958 from assignment to the 1st Armored Division. Activated 1 April 1958 in Germany.

Reorganized and redesignated 3 February 1962 as the 1st Battalion, 46th Infantry and assigned to the 1st Armored Division. Relieved 12 May 1967 from assignment to the 1st Armored Division and assigned to the 198th Infantry Brigade. Relieved 15 February 1969 from assignment to the 198th Infantry Brigade and assigned to the 23d Infantry Division.

645

Campaign Participation Credit

World War II
- *Normandy
- *Northern France
- *Rhineland
- *Ardennes-Alsace
- *Central Europe

Vietnam
- *Counteroffensive, Phase III
- *Tet Counteroffensive
- (other campaigns to be determined)

Decorations

*Presidential Unit Citation (Army), Streamer embroidered HURTGEN FOREST (47th Armored Infantry Battalion cited; WD GO 31, 1947)

*French Croix de Guerre with Silver Star, World War II, Streamer embroidered WALLENDORF (47th Armored Infantry Battalion cited; DA GO 43, 1950)

*Luxembourg Croix de Guerre, Streamer embroidered LUXEMBOURG (47th Armored Infantry Battalion cited; DA GO 44, 1951)

*Cited in the Order of the Day of the Belgian Army for action in the ARDENNES (Company A, 47th Armored Infantry Battalion cited; DA GO 43, 1950)

2d BATTALION, 46th INFANTRY

(The Professionals)

RA
(1st Armored Division)

LINEAGE

Constituted 15 May 1917 in the Regular Army as Company B, 46th Infantry. Organized 4 June 1917 at Fort Benjamin Harrison, Indiana. (46th Infantry assigned 5 July 1918 to the 9th Division; relieved 15 February 1919 from assignment to the 9th Division.) Inactivated 16 November 1921 at Camp Travis, Texas. Demobilized 31 July 1922.

Reconstituted 28 August 1941 in the Regular Army as Company B, 46th Infantry (Armored), an element of the 5th Armored Division. Activated 1 October 1941 at Fort Knox, Kentucky. Redesignated 1 January 1942 as Company B, 46th Armored Infantry. Reorganized and redesignated 20 September 1943 as Company B, 47th Armored Infantry Battalion, an element of the 5th Armored Division. Inactivated 8 October 1945 at Camp Myles Standish, Massachusetts. Activated 6 July 1948 at Camp Chaffee, Arkansas. Inactivated 1 February 1950 at Camp Chaffee, Arkansas. Activated 1 September 1950 at Camp Chaffee, Arkansas. Inactivated 16 March 1956 at Camp Chaffee, Arkansas. (47th Armored Infantry Battalion relieved 15 February 1957 from assignment to the 5th Armored Division.)

Redesignated 1 October 1957 as Headquarters and Headquarters Company, 2d Armored Rifle Battalion, 46th Infantry, assigned to the 3d Armored Division, and activated in Germany (organic elements concurrently constituted and activated). Reorganized and redesignated 3 February 1962 as the 2d Battalion, 46th Infantry; concurrently, relieved from assignment to the 3d Armored Division and assigned to the 1st Armored Division.

CAMPAIGN PARTICIPATION CREDIT

World War II
  *Normandy
  *Northern France

*Rhineland
*Ardennes-Alsace
*Central Europe

647

DECORATIONS

*Presidential Unit Citation (Army), Streamer embroidered HURTGEN FOREST (47th Armored Infantry Battalion cited; WD GO 31, 1947)

*Presidential Unit Citation (Army), Streamer embroidered MEUSE RIVER (Company B, 47th Armored Infantry Battalion cited; WD GO 45, 1945)

*French Croix de Guerre with Silver Star, World War II, Streamer embroidered WALLENDORF (47th Armored Infantry Battalion cited; DA GO 43, 1950)

*Luxembourg Croix de Guerre, Streamer embroidered LUXEMBOURG (47th Armored Infantry Battalion cited; DA GO 44, 1951)

3d ARMORED RIFLE BATTALION, 46th INFANTRY

(The Professionals)

RA
(inactive)

LINEAGE

Constituted 15 May 1917 in the Regular Army as Company C, 46th Infantry. Organized 4 June 1917 at Fort Benjamin Harrison, Indiana. (46th Infantry assigned 5 July 1918 to the 9th Division; relieved 15 February 1919 from assignment to the 9th Division.) Inactivated 16 November 1921 at Camp Travis, Texas. Demobilized 31 July 1922.

Reconstituted 28 August 1941 in the Regular Army as Company C, 46th Infantry (Armored), an element of the 5th Armored Division. Activated 1 October 1941 at Fort Knox, Kentucky. Redesignated 1 January 1942 as Company C, 46th Armored Infantry. Reorganized and redesignated 20 September 1943 as Company C, 47th Armored Infantry Battalion, an element of the 5th Armored Division. Inactivated 8 October 1945 at Camp Myles Standish, Massachusetts. Activated 6 July 1948 at Camp Chaffee, Arkansas. Inactivated 1 February 1950 at Camp Chaffee, Arkansas. Activated 1 September 1950 at Camp Chaffee, Arkansas. Inactivated 16 March 1956 at Camp Chaffee, Arkansas. (47th Armored Infantry Battalion relieved 15 February 1957 from assignment to the 5th Armored Division.)

Redesignated 1 July 1959 as Headquarters and Headquarters Company, 3d Battle Group, 46th Infantry. Redesignated 3 February 1962 as Headquarters and Headquarters Company, 3d Armored Rifle Battalion, 46th Infantry and activated in Germany (organic elements concurrently constituted and activated). Inactivated 1 February 1963 in Germany.

649

Campaign Participation Credit

World War II
  *Normandy
  *Northern France

*Rhineland
*Ardennes-Alsace
*Central Europe

Decorations

*Presidential Unit Citation (Army), Streamer embroidered HURTGEN FOREST (47th Armored Infantry Battalion cited; WD GO 31, 1947)

*Presidential Unit Citation (Army), Streamer embroidered MEUSE RIVER (Company C, 47th Armored Infantry Battalion cited; WD GO 38, 1945)

*French Croix de Guerre with Silver Star, World War II, Streamer embroidered WALLENDORF (47th Armored Infantry Battalion cited; DA GO 43, 1950)

*Luxembourg Croix de Guerre, Streamer embroidered LUXEMBOURG (47th Armored Infantry Battalion cited; DA GO 44, 1951)

4th BATTALION, 46th INFANTRY

(The Professionals)

RA
(1st Armored Division)

Constituted 15 May 1917 in the Regular Army as Company D, 46th Infantry. Organized 4 June 1917 at Fort Benjamin Harrison, Indiana. (46th Infantry assigned 5 July 1918 to the 9th Division; relieved 15 February 1919 from assignment to the 9th Division.) Inactivated 16 November 1921 at Camp Travis, Texas. Demobilized 31 July 1922.

Reconstituted 28 August 1941 in the Regular Army as Company D, 46th Infantry (Armored), an element of the 5th Armored Division. Activated 1 October 1941 at Fort Knox, Kentucky. Redesignated 1 January 1942 as Company D, 46th Armored Infantry. Reorganized and redesignated 20 September 1943 as Company A, 15th Armored Infantry Battalion, an element of the 5th Armored Division. Inactivated 8 October 1945 at Camp Myles Standish, Massachusetts. Activated 6 July 1948 at Camp Chaffee, Arkansas. Inactivated 1 February 1950 at Camp Chaffee, Arkansas. Activated 1 September 1950 at Camp Chaffee, Arkansas. Inactivated 16 March 1956 at Camp Chaffee, Arkansas. (15th Armored Infantry Battalion relieved 15 February 1957 from assignment to the 5th Armored Division.)

Redesignated 1 July 1959 as Headquarters and Headquarters Company, 4th Battle Group, 46th Infantry. Redesignated 9 May 1967 as Headquarters and Headquarters Company, 4th Battalion, 46th Infantry and assigned to the 1st Armored Division (organic elements concurrently constituted). Battalion activated 12 May 1967 at Fort Hood, Texas.

CAMPAIGN PARTICIPATION CREDIT

World War II
  *Normandy
  *Northern France

*Rhineland
*Ardennes-Alsace
*Central Europe

DECORATIONS

Presidential Unit Citation (Army), Streamer embroidered HURTGEN FOREST

*Luxembourg Croix de Guerre, Streamer embroidered LUXEMBOURG (15th Armored Infantry Battalion cited; DA GO 44, 1951)

5th BATTALION, 46th INFANTRY

(The Professionals)

RA
(23d Infantry Division)

LINEAGE

Constituted 15 May 1917 in the Regular Army as Company E, 46th Infantry. Organized 4 June 1917 at Fort Benjamin Harrison, Indiana. (46th Infantry assigned 5 July 1918 to the 9th Division; relieved 15 February 1919 from assignment to the 9th Division.) Inactivated 16 November 1921 at Camp Travis, Texas. Demobilized 31 July 1922.

Reconstituted 28 August 1941 in the Regular Army as Company E, 46th Infantry (Armored), an element of the 5th Armored Division. Activated 1 October 1941 at Fort Knox, Kentucky. Redesignated 1 January 1942 as Company E, 46th Armored Infantry. Reorganized and redesignated 20 September 1943 as Company B, 15th Armored Infantry Battalion, an element of the 5th Armored Division. Inactivated 8 October 1945 at Camp Myles Standish, Massachusetts. Activated 6 July 1948 at Camp Chaffee, Arkansas. Inactivated 1 February 1950 at Camp Chaffee, Arkansas. Activated 1 September 1950 at Camp Chaffee, Arkansas. Inactivated 16 March 1956 at Camp Chaffee, Arkansas. (15th Armored Infantry Battalion relieved 15 February 1957 from assignment to the 5th Armored Division.)

Redesignated 1 July 1959 as Headquarters and Headquarters Company, 5th Battle Group, 46th Infantry. Redesignated 2 October 1967 as Headquarters and Headquarters Company, 5th Battalion, 46th Infantry and activated at Fort Hood, Texas (organic elements concurrently constituted and activated). Assigned 31 March 1968 to the 198th Infantry Brigade. Relieved 15 February 1969 from assignment to the 198th Infantry Brigade and assigned to the 23d Infantry Division.

CAMPAIGN PARTICIPATION CREDIT

World War II
  *Normandy
  *Northern France
  *Rhineland
  *Ardennes-Alsace
  *Central Europe

Vietnam
  *Tet Counteroffensive
    (other campaigns to be determined)

DECORATIONS

Presidential Unit Citation (Army), Streamer embroidered HURTGEN FOREST

*Luxembourg Croix de Guerre, Streamer embroidered LUXEMBOURG (15th Armored Infantry Battalion cited; DA GO 44, 1951)

46TH INFANTRY, BIBLIOGRAPHY

Illustrated Review, Headquarters Company, 46th U.S. Infantry, 1918
. . . Montgomery, 1918.

MacDonald, Charles B. *The Siegfried Line Campaign.* United States
Army in World War II. Washington: Government Printing Office,
1963.

47th INFANTRY

HERALDIC ITEMS

COAT OF ARMS

Shield: Argent, the shoulder sleeve insignia of the 4th Division, vert; on a canton azure an imperial Chinese five-toed dragon affronté or scaled of the third.

Crest: On a wreath of the colors a water wheel azure encircling a fleur-de-lis or.

Motto: *Ex Virtute Honos* (Honor Comes From Virtue).

Symbolism: This regiment was originally organized with personnel from the 9th Infantry, as shown by the canton taken from its arms. Service of the 47th during World War I with the 4th Division is represented by the divisional insignia on the shield.

The water wheel and the fleur-de-lis symbolize engagements in France. The first important battle in which the unit participated was at Sergy on the Ourcq River. The water wheel represents the mill located at the approach to Sergy. Later the 47th also fought at Bazoches on the Vesle. Both Sergy and Bazoches were formerly included in the province of Ile de France, which bore the royal arms, three gold fleurs-de-lis on a blue field.

DISTINCTIVE INSIGNIA

The distinctive insignia is the shield of the coat of arms.

LINEAGE AND HONORS

LINEAGE

Constituted 15 May 1917 in the Regular Army as the 47th Infantry. Organized 1 June 1917 at Syracuse, New York. Assigned 19 November 1917 to the 4th Division. Inactivated 22 September 1921 at Camp Lewis, Washington. Relieved 15 August 1927 from assignment to the 4th Division and assigned to the 7th Division. Relieved 1 October 1933 from assignment to the 7th Division. Assigned 1 August 1940 to the 9th Division (later redesignated as the 9th Infantry Division). Activated 10

August 1940 at Fort Bragg, North Carolina. Inactivated 31 December 1946 in Germany. Activated 15 July 1947 at Fort Dix, New Jersey.

Relieved 1 December 1957 from assignment to the 9th Infantry Division and reorganized as a parent regiment under the Combat Arms Regimental System.

CAMPAIGN PARTICIPATION CREDIT

World War I
Aisne-Marne
St. Mihiel
Meuse-Argonne
Lorraine 1918
Champagne 1918

World War II
Algeria-French Morocco
(with arrowhead)
Tunisia
Sicily

Normandy
Northern France
Rhineland
Ardennes-Alsace
Central Europe

Vietnam
Counteroffensive, Phase II
Counteroffensive, Phase III
Tet Counteroffensive
(other campaigns to be determined)

DECORATIONS

Presidential Unit Citation (Army), Streamer embroidered CHERBOURG (2d Battalion, 47th Infantry cited; WD GO 86, 1944)

Presidential Unit Citation (Army), Streamer embroidered HAGUE PENINSULA (3d Battalion, 47th Infantry cited; WD GO 28, 1945)

Presidential Unit Citation (Army), Streamer embroidered ROETGEN, GERMANY (3d Battalion, 47th Infantry cited; WD GO 139, 1946)

Presidential Unit Citation (Army), Streamer embroidered NOTHBERG, GERMANY (1st Battalion, 47th Infantry cited; WD GO 123, 1945)

Presidential Unit Citation (Army), Streamer embroidered FREUZENBERG CASTLE (2d Battalion, 47th Infantry cited; DA GO 25, 1948)

Presidential Unit Citation (Army), Streamer embroidered REMAGEN, GERMANY (47th Infantry cited; WD GO 65, 1946)

Presidential Unit Citation (Army), Streamer embroidered OBERKIRCHEN, GERMANY (2d Battalion, 47th Infantry cited; WD GO 98, 1946)

Presidential Unit Citation (Army), Streamer embroidered MEKONG DELTA (3d Battalion, 47th Infantry cited; DA GO 45, 1969)

Valorous Unit Award, Streamer embroidered LONG BINH–BIEN HOA (2d Battalion, 47th Infantry cited; DA GO 5, 1969)

Valorous Unit Award, Streamer embroidered SAIGON (2d Battalion, 47th Infantry cited; DA GO 43, 1970)

Meritorious Unit Commendation, Streamer embroidered VIETNAM 1968 (3d Battalion, 47th Infantry cited; DA GO 36, 1970)

French Croix de Guerre with Palm, World War II, Streamer embroidered CHERBOURG (47th Infantry cited; DA GO 43, 1950)

Belgian Fourragere 1940 (47th Infantry cited; DA GO 43, 1950)

Cited in the Order of the Day of the Belgian Army for action at the MEUSE RIVER (47th Infantry cited; DA GO 43, 1950)

Cited in the Order of the Day of the Belgian Army for action in the ARDENNES (47th Infantry cited; DA GO 43, 1950)

1st BATTALION, 47th INFANTRY

RA
(171st Infantry Brigade)

LINEAGE

Constituted 15 May 1917 in the Regular Army as Company A, 47th Infantry. Organized 1 June 1917 at Syracuse, New York. (47th Infantry assigned 19 November 1917 to the 4th Division.) Inactivated 22 September 1921 at Camp Lewis, Washington. (47th Infantry relieved 15 August 1927 from assignment to the 4th Division and assigned to the 7th Division; relieved 1 October 1933 from assignment to the 7th Division; assigned 1 August 1940 to the 9th Division [later redesignated as the 9th Infantry Division].) Activated 10 August 1940 at Fort Bragg, North Carolina. Inactivated 31 December 1946 in Germany. Activated 15 July 1947 at Fort Dix, New Jersey.

Reorganized and redesignated 1 December 1957 as Headquarters and Headquarters Company, 1st Battle Group, 47th Infantry and remained assigned to the 9th Infantry Division (organic elements concurrently constituted and activated). Inactivated 31 January 1962 at Fort Carson, Colorado. Redesignated 20 May 1963 as the 1st Battalion, 47th Infantry; concurrently, relieved from assignment to the 9th Infantry Division and assigned to the 171st Infantry Brigade. Activated 1 July 1963 in Alaska.

CAMPAIGN PARTICIPATION CREDIT

World War I
*   *Aisne-Marne
*   *St. Mihiel
*   *Meuse-Argonne
*   *Lorraine 1918
*   *Champagne 1918

World War II
*   *Algeria-French Morocco
    (with arrowhead)

*   *Tunisia
*   *Sicily
*   *Normandy
*   *Northern France
*   *Rhineland
*   *Ardennes-Alsace
*   *Central Europe

DECORATIONS

Presidential Unit Citation (Army), Streamer embroidered CHER-
BOURG

Presidential Unit Citation (Army), Streamer embroidered HAGUE
PENINSULA

Presidential Unit Citation (Army), Streamer embroidered ROETGEN,
GERMANY

*Presidential Unit Citation (Army), Streamer embroidered NOTH-
BERG, GERMANY (1st Battalion, 47th Infantry cited; WD GO 123, 1945)

Presidential Unit Citation (Army), Streamer embroidered FREUZEN-
BERG CASTLE

*Presidential Unit Citation (Army), Streamer embroidered REMAGEN,
GERMANY (47th Infantry cited; WD GO 65, 1946)

Presidential Unit Citation (Army), Streamer embroidered OBER-
KIRCHEN, GERMANY

*French Croix de Guerre with Palm, World War II, Streamer em-
broidered CHERBOURG (47th Infantry cited; DA GO 43, 1950)

*Belgian Fourragere 1940 (47th Infantry cited; DA GO 43, 1950)

*Cited in the Order of the Day of the Belgian Army for action at the
MEUSE RIVER (47th Infantry cited; DA GO 43, 1950)

*Cited in the Order of the Day of the Belgian Army for action in the
ARDENNES (47th Infantry cited; DA GO 43, 1950)

2d BATTALION, 47th INFANTRY

RA
(inactive)

LINEAGE

Constituted 15 May 1917 in the Regular Army as Company B, 47th Infantry. Organized 1 June 1917 at Syracuse, New York. (47th Infantry assigned 19 November 1917 to the 4th Division.) Inactivated 22 September 1921 at Camp Lewis, Washington. (47th Infantry relieved 15 August 1927 from assignment to the 4th Division and assigned to the 7th Division; relieved 1 October 1933 from assignment to the 7th Division; assigned 1 August 1940 to the 9th Division [later redesignated as the 9th Infantry Division].) Activated 10 August 1940 at Fort Bragg, North Carolina. Inactivated 31 December 1946 in Germany. Activated 15 July 1947 at Fort Dix, New Jersey.

Reorganized and redesignated 1 April 1957 as Headquarters and Headquarters Company, 2d Battle Group, 47th Infantry, relieved from assignment to the 9th Infantry Division, and assigned to the 4th Infantry Division (organic elements concurrently constituted and activated). Inactivated 1 October 1963 at Fort Lewis, Washington, and relieved from assignment to the 4th Infantry Division. Redesignated 1 February 1966 as the 2d Battalion, 47th Infantry, assigned to the 9th Infantry Division, and activated at Fort Riley, Kansas. Inactivated 13 October 1970 at Fort Lewis, Washington.

CAMPAIGN PARTICIPATION CREDIT

World War I
*Aisne-Marne
*St. Mihiel
*Meuse-Argonne
*Lorraine 1918
*Champagne 1918

World War II
*Algeria-French Morocco
  (with arrowhead)
*Tunisia
*Sicily

*Normandy
*Northern France
*Rhineland
*Ardennes-Alsace
*Central Europe

Vietnam
*Counteroffensive, Phase II
*Counteroffensive, Phase III
*Tet Counteroffensive
  (other campaigns to be determined)

DECORATIONS

Presidential Unit Citation (Army), Streamer embroidered CHERBOURG

Presidential Unit Citation (Army), Streamer embroidered HAGUE PENINSULA

Presidential Unit Citation (Army), Streamer embroidered ROETGEN, GERMANY

*Presidential Unit Citation (Army), Streamer embroidered NOTH-BERG, GERMANY (1st Battalion, 47th Infantry cited; WD GO 123, 1945)

Presidential Unit Citation (Army), Streamer embroidered FREUZEN-BERG CASTLE

*Presidential Unit Citation (Army), Streamer embroidered REMAGEN, GERMANY (47th Infantry cited; WD GO 65, 1946)

Presidential Unit Citation (Army), Streamer embroidered OBER-KIRCHEN, GERMANY

*Valorous Unit Award, Streamer embroidered LONG BINH–BIEN HOA (2d Battalion, 47th Infantry cited; DA GO 5, 1969)

*Valorous Unit Award, Streamer embroidered SAIGON (2d Battalion, 47th Infantry cited; DA GO 43, 1970)

*French Croix de Guerre with Palm, World War II, Streamer embroidered CHERBOURG (47th Infantry cited; DA GO 43, 1950)

*Belgian Fourragere 1940 (47th Infantry cited; DA GO 43, 1950)

*Cited in the Order of the Day of the Belgian Army for action at the MEUSE RIVER (47th Infantry cited; DA GO 43, 1950)

*Cited in the Order of the Day of the Belgian Army for action in the ARDENNES (47th Infantry cited; DA GO 43, 1950)

*Vietnamese Cross of Gallantry with Palm, Streamer embroidered VIETNAM 1967–1968 (2d Battalion, 47th Infantry cited; DA GO 31, 1969)

*Vietnamese Cross of Gallantry with Palm, Streamer embroidered VIETNAM 1968 (2d Battalion, 47th Infantry cited; DA GO 31, 1969)

*Vietnamese Cross of Gallantry with Palm, Streamer embroidered VIETNAM 1969 (2d Battalion, 47th Infantry cited; DA GO 59, 1969)

*Vietnamese Civil Action Honor Medal, First Class, Streamer embroidered VIETNAM 1967–1969 (2d Battalion, 47th Infantry cited; DA GO 59, 1969)

3d BATTALION, 47th INFANTRY

RA
(inactive)

LINEAGE

Constituted 15 May 1917 in the Regular Army as Company C, 47th Infantry. Organized 1 June 1917 at Syracuse, New York. (47th Infantry assigned 19 November 1917 to the 4th Division.) Inactivated 22 September 1921 at Camp Lewis, Washington. (47th Infantry relieved 15 August 1927 from assignment to the 4th Division and assigned to the 7th Division; relieved 1 October 1933 from assignment to the 7th Division; assigned 1 August 1940 to the 9th Division [later redesignated as the 9th Infantry Division].) Activated 10 August 1940 at Fort Bragg, North Carolina. Inactivated 31 December 1946 in Germany. Activated 15 July 1947 at Fort Dix, New Jersey.

Inactivated 1 December 1957 at Fort Carson, Colorado, and relieved from assignment to the 9th Infantry Division; concurrently, redesignated as Headquarters and Headquarters Company, 3d Battle Group, 47th Infantry. Withdrawn 10 April 1959 from the Regular Army, allotted to the Army Reserve, and assigned to the 81st Infantry Division (organic elements concurrently constituted). Battle Group activated 1 May 1959 with Headquarters at Atlanta, Georgia. Inactivated 1 April 1963 at Atlanta, Georgia, and relieved from assignment to the 81st Infantry Division.

Redesignated 1 February 1966 as the 3d Battalion, 47th Infantry; concurrently, withdrawn from the Army Reserve, allotted to the Regular Army, assigned to the 9th Infantry Division, and activated at Fort Riley, Kansas. Inactivated 1 August 1969 at Fort Riley, Kansas.

662

CAMPAIGN PARTICIPATION CREDIT

World War I
*Aisne-Marne
*St. Mihiel
*Meuse-Argonne
*Lorraine 1918
*Champagne 1918

*Normandy
*Northern France
*Rhineland
*Ardennes-Alsace
*Central Europe

World War II
*Algeria-French Morocco
(with arrowhead)
*Tunisia
*Sicily

Vietnam
*Counteroffensive, Phase II
*Counteroffensive, Phase III
*Tet Counteroffensive
(other campaigns to be determined)

DECORATIONS

Presidential Unit Citation (Army), Streamer embroidered CHERBOURG

Presidential Unit Citation (Army), Streamer embroidered HAGUE PENINSULA

Presidential Unit Citation (Army), Streamer embroidered ROETGEN, GERMANY

*Presidential Unit Citation (Army), Streamer embroidered NOTHBERG, GERMANY (1st Battalion, 47th Infantry cited; WD GO 123, 1945)

Presidential Unit Citation (Army), Streamer embroidered FREUZENBERG CASTLE

*Presidential Unit Citation (Army), Streamer embroidered REMAGEN, GERMANY (47th Infantry cited; WD GO 65, 1946)

Presidential Unit Citation (Army), Streamer embroidered OBERKIRCHEN, GERMANY

*Presidential Unit Citation (Army), Streamer embroidered MEKONG DELTA (3d Battalion, 47th Infantry cited; DA GO 45, 1969)

*Meritorious Unit Commendation, Streamer embroidered VIETNAM 1968 (3d Battalion, 47th Infantry cited; DA GO 36, 1970)

*French Croix de Guerre with Palm, World War II, Streamer embroidered CHERBOURG (47th Infantry cited; DA GO 43, 1950)

*Belgian Fourragere 1940 (47th Infantry cited; DA GO 43, 1950)

*Cited in the Order of the Day of the Belgian Army for action at the MEUSE RIVER (47th Infantry cited; DA GO 43, 1950)

*Cited in the Order of the Day of the Belgian Army for action in the ARDENNES (47th Infantry cited; DA GO 43, 1950)

*Vietnamese Cross of Gallantry with Palm, Streamer embroidered VIETNAM 1967–1968 (3d Battalion, 47th Infantry cited; DA GO 31, 1969)

*Vietnamese Cross of Gallantry with Palm, Streamer embroidered VIETNAM 1969 (3d Battalion, 47th Infantry cited; DA GO 59, 1969)

*Vietnamese Civil Action Honor Medal, First Class, Streamer embroidered VIETNAM 1967–1969 (3d Battalion, 47th Infantry cited; DA GO 59, 1969)

4th BATTALION, 47th INFANTRY

RA
(inactive)

LINEAGE

Constituted 15 May 1917 in the Regular Army as Company D, 47th Infantry. Organized 1 June 1917 at Syracuse, New York. (47th Infantry assigned 19 November 1917 to the 4th Division.) Inactivated 22 September 1921 at Camp Lewis, Washington. (47th Infantry relieved 15 August 1927 from assignment to the 4th Division and assigned to the 7th Division; relieved 1 October 1933 from assignment to the 7th Division; assigned 1 August 1940 to the 9th Division [later redesignated as the 9th Infantry Division].) Activated 10 August 1940 at Fort Bragg, North Carolina. Inactivated 31 December 1946 in Germany. Activated 15 July 1947 at Fort Dix, New Jersey.

Inactivated 1 December 1957 at Fort Carson, Colorado, and relieved from assignment to the 9th Infantry Division; concurrently, redesignated as Headquarters and Headquarters Company, 4th Battle Group, 47th Infantry. Redesignated 1 February 1966 as Headquarters and Headquarters Company, 4th Battalion, 47th Infantry, assigned to the 9th Infantry Division, and activated at Fort Riley, Kansas (organic elements concurrently constituted and activated). Inactivated 1 August 1969 at Fort Riley, Kansas.

CAMPAIGN PARTICIPATION CREDIT

World War I
 *Aisne-Marne
 *St. Mihiel
 *Meuse-Argonne
 *Lorraine 1918
 *Champagne 1918

World War II
 *Algeria-French Morocco
  (with arrowhead)
 *Tunisia
 *Sicily

 *Normandy
 *Northern France
 *Rhineland
 *Ardennes-Alsace
 *Central Europe

Vietnam
 *Counteroffensive, Phase II
 *Counteroffensive, Phase III
 *Tet Counteroffensive
  (other campaigns to be determined)

DECORATIONS

Presidential Unit Citation (Army), Streamer embroidered CHERBOURG

Presidential Unit Citation (Army), Streamer embroidered HAGUE PENINSULA

Presidential Unit Citation (Army), Streamer embroidered ROETGEN, GERMANY

*Presidential Unit Citation (Army), Streamer embroidered NOTHBERG, GERMANY (1st Battalion, 47th Infantry cited; WD GO 123, 1945)

Presidential Unit Citation (Army), Streamer embroidered FREUZENBERG CASTLE

*Presidential Unit Citation (Army), Streamer embroidered REMAGEN, GERMANY (47th Infantry cited; WD GO 65, 1946)

Presidential Unit Citation (Army), Streamer embroidered OBERKIRCHEN, GERMANY

*French Croix de Guerre with Palm, World War II, Streamer embroidered CHERBOURG (47th Infantry cited; DA GO 43, 1950)

*Belgian Fourragere 1940 (47th Infantry cited; DA GO 43, 1950)

*Cited in the Order of the Day of the Belgian Army for action at the MEUSE RIVER (47th Infantry cited; DA GO 43, 1950)

*Cited in the Order of the Day of the Belgian Army for action in the ARDENNES (47th Infantry cited; DA GO 43, 1950)

*Vietnamese Cross of Gallantry with Palm, Streamer embroidered VIETNAM 1967–1968 (4th Battalion, 47th Infantry cited; DA GO 31, 1969)

*Vietnamese Cross of Gallantry with Palm, Streamer embroidered VIETNAM 1969 (4th Battalion, 47th Infantry cited; DA GO 59, 1969)

*Vietnamese Civil Action Honor Medal, First Class, Streamer embroidered VIETNAM 1967–1969 (4th Battalion, 47th Infantry cited; DA GO 59, 1969)

Company C additionally entitled to: Presidential Unit Citation (Army), Streamer embroidered MEKONG DELTA (Company C, 4th Battalion, 47th Infantry cited; DA GO 45, 1969)

47TH INFANTRY, BIBLIOGRAPHY

Albright, John, John A. Cash, and Allan W. Sandstrum. *Seven Firefights in Vietnam.* Washington: Government Printing Office, 1970.

Blumenson, Martin. *Breakout and Pursuit.* United States Army in World War II. Washington: Government Printing Office, 1961.

————. *The Duel for France.* Boston: Houghton Mifflin Company, 1963.

Garland, Albert N. and Howard McGaw Smyth. *Sicily and the Surrender of Italy.* United States Army in World War II. Washington: Government Printing Office, 1965.

Gillespie, David E. *History of the 47th Infantry Regiment.* Munich: F. Bruckmann KG, 1946.

Harrison, Gordon A. *Cross-Channel Attack.* United States Army in World War II. Washington: Government Printing Office, 1951.

Historical Section, War Department. *St-Lô.* American Forces in Action Series. Washington: Government Printing Office, 1946.

————. *To Bizerte with the II Corps.* American Forces in Action Series. Washington: Government Printing Office, 1946.

————. *Utah Beach to Cherbourg.* American Forces in Action Series. Washington: Government Printing Office, 1947.

History of the 4th Infantry Division and Brief Histories of its Components. Fort Lewis, Washington, 1958.

Larson, William B. "Hill 223," *Infantry Journal,* LV (September 1944), 23–27.

MacDonald, Charles B. *The Battle of Huertgen Forest.* Philadelphia and New York: J. B. Lippincott Company, 1963.

————. *The Siegfried Line Campaign.* United States Army in World War II. Washington: Government Printing Office, 1963.

Pollard, James. *The Forty-seventh Infantry, A History, 1917–1918–1919.* Saginaw, Michigan: Seeman and Peters, 1919.

Randle, Edwin Hubert. *Safi Adventure—The First Operation of a Famous Regimental Combat Team.* Clearwater, Florida: Eldnar Press, 1965.

48th INFANTRY

HERALDIC ITEMS

COAT OF ARMS

Shield: Per pale azure and sable, a lion rampant or; on a canton argent a chevron wavy of the first.

Crest: On a wreath or and azure two hunting horns in saltire or, inserts argent, mouthpieces gules and straps interlaced sable buckled of the first.

Motto: Dragoons.

Symbolism: The colors blue and white are the present and former infantry colors. Black and gold are the colors of the Belgian coat of arms from which the Belgian lion is adapted. The wavy chevron on the canton is for descent from personnel of the 9th Infantry. The Belgian lion represents the organization's actions in the Ardennes and at St. Vith, for which it was cited twice in the Order of the Day of the Belgian Army.

The crest, consisting of Teutonic hunting horns, alludes to the German battle honors of World War II.

DISTINCTIVE INSIGNIA

The distinctive insignia is the shield and motto of the coat of arms.

LINEAGE AND HONORS

LINEAGE

Constituted 15 May 1917 in the Regular Army as the 48th Infantry. Organized 1 June 1917 in Syracuse, New York, as an element of the 20th Division. Relieved 28 February 1919 from assignment to the 20th Division. Inactivated 14 October 1921 at Camp Travis, Texas. Demobilized 31 July 1922.

Reconstituted 27 February 1942 in the Regular Army as the 48th Armored Infantry, an element of the 7th Armored Division. Activated 2 March 1942 at Camp Polk, Louisiana. Regiment broken up 20 September 1943 and its elements reorganized and redesignated as elements of

669

the 7th Armored Division as follows: 48th Armored Infantry (less 1st and 2d Battalions) as the 48th Armored Infantry Battalion; 1st Battalion as the 38th Armored Infantry Battalion; 2d Battalion as the 23d Armored Infantry Battalion. Battalions inactivated 8–11 October 1945 at Camp Myles Standish, Massachusetts, Camp Shanks, New York, and Camp Kilmer, New Jersey; activated 24 November 1950 at Camp Roberts, California; inactivated 15 November 1953 at Camp Roberts, California.

48th, 38th, and 23d Armored Infantry Battalions relieved 15 February 1957 from assignment to the 7th Armored Division and consolidated to form the 48th Infantry, a parent regiment under the Combat Arms Regimental System.

CAMPAIGN PARTICIPATION CREDIT

World War II   Ardennes-Alsace
   Northern France   Central Europe
   Rhineland

DECORATIONS

Presidential Unit Citation (Army), Streamer embroidered ST. VITH (38th and 23d Armored Infantry Battalions cited; DA GO 48, 1948)

Belgian Fourragere 1940 (48th, 38th, and 23d Armored Infantry Battalions cited; DA GO 43, 1950)

Cited in the Order of the Day of the Belgian Army for action in the ARDENNES (48th, 38th, and 23d Armored Infantry Battalions cited; DA GO 43, 1950)

Cited in the Order of the Day of the Belgian Army for action at ST. VITH (48th, 38th, and 23d Armored Infantry Battalions cited; DA GO 43, 1950)

1st BATTALION, 48th INFANTRY

RA
(3d Armored Division)

LINEAGE

Constituted 15 May 1917 in the Regular Army as Company A, 48th Infantry. Organized 1 June 1917 at Syracuse, New York, as an element of the 20th Division. (48th Infantry relieved 28 February 1919 from assignment to the 20th Division.) Inactivated 14 October 1921 at Camp Travis, Texas. Demobilized 31 July 1922.

Reconstituted 27 February 1942 in the Regular Army as Company A, 48th Armored Infantry, an element of the 7th Armored Division. Activated 2 March 1942 at Camp Polk, Louisiana. Reorganized and redesignated 20 September 1943 as Company A, 38th Armored Infantry Battalion, an element of the 7th Armored Division. Inactivated 11 October 1945 at Camp Shanks, New York. Activated 24 November 1950 at Camp Roberts, California. Inactivated 15 November 1953 at Camp Roberts, California.

Redesignated 15 February 1957 as Headquarters and Headquarters Company, 1st Armored Rifle Battalion, 48th Infantry, relieved from assignment to the 7th Armored Division, assigned to the 1st Armored Division, and activated at Fort Polk, Louisiana (organic elements concurrently constituted and activated). Inactivated 23 December 1957 at Fort Polk, Louisiana. Relieved 25 February 1958 from assignment to the 1st Armored Division. Activated 1 April 1958 in Germany. Reorganized and redesignated 1 September 1963 as the 1st Battalion, 48th Infantry; concurrently, assigned to the 3d Armored Division.

CAMPAIGN PARTICIPATION CREDIT

World War II
* *Northern France
* *Rhineland
* *Ardennes-Alsace
* *Central Europe

DECORATIONS

*Presidential Unit Citation (Army), Streamer embroidered ST. VITH (38th Armored Infantry Battalion cited; DA GO 48, 1948)

*Belgian Fourragere 1940 (38th Armored Infantry Battalion cited; DA GO 43, 1950)

671

*Cited in the Order of the Day of the Belgian Army for action in the ARDENNES (38th Armored Infantry Battalion cited; DA GO 43, 1950)

*Cited in the Order of the Day of the Belgian Army for action at ST. VITH (38th Armored Infantry Battalion cited; DA GO 43, 1950)

2d BATTALION, 48th INFANTRY

RA

(3d Armored Division)

LINEAGE

Constituted 15 May 1917 in the Regular Army as Company B, 48th Infantry. Organized 1 June 1917 at Syracuse, New York, as an element of the 20th Division. (48th Infantry relieved 28 February 1919 from assignment to the 20th Division.) Inactivated 14 October 1921 at Camp Travis, Texas. Demobilized 31 July 1922.

Reconstituted 27 February 1942 in the Regular Army as Company B, 48th Armored Infantry, an element of the 7th Armored Division. Activated 2 March 1942 at Camp Polk, Louisiana. Reorganized and redesignated 20 September 1943 as Company B, 38th Armored Infantry Battalion, an element of the 7th Armored Division. Inactivated 11 October 1945 at Camp Shanks, New York. Activated 24 November 1950 at Camp Roberts, California. Inactivated 15 November 1953 at Camp Roberts, California. (38th Armored Infantry Battalion relieved 15 February 1957 from assignment to the 7th Armored Division.)

Redesignated 1 October 1957 as Headquarters and Headquarters Company, 2d Armored Rifle Battalion, 48th Infantry, assigned to the 3d Armored Division, and activated in Germany (organic elements concurrently constituted and activated). Reorganized and redesignated 1 September 1963 as the 2d Battalion, 48th Infantry.

CAMPAIGN PARTICIPATION CREDIT

World War II
* *Northern France
* *Rhineland

* *Ardennes-Alsace
* *Central Europe

DECORATIONS

*Presidential Unit Citation (Army), Streamer embroidered ST. VITH (38th Armored Infantry Battalion cited; DA GO 48, 1948)

*Belgian Fourragere 1940 (38th Armored Infantry Battalion cited; DA GO 43, 1950)

*Cited in the Order of the Day of the Belgian Army for action in the ARDENNES (38th Armored Infantry Battalion cited; DA GO 43, 1950)

*Cited in the Order of the Day of the Belgian Army for action at ST. VITH (38th Armored Infantry Battalion cited; DA GO 43, 1950)

48TH INFANTRY, BIBLIOGRAPHY

Cole, Hugh M. *The Ardennes: Battle of the Bulge.* United States Army in World War II. Washington: Government Printing Office, 1964.
———. *The Lorraine Campaign.* United States Army in World War II. Washington: Government Printing Office, 1950.
Jones, William Eugene and Irene. *"Buzzings of Company B,"* 23d Armored Infantry Battalion of the 7th Armored (Lucky Seventh) Division. Winston-Salem: Clay Printing Company, 1946.

50th INFANTRY

HERALDIC ITEMS

COAT OF ARMS

Shield: Argent, on a pale wavy azure a dolphin hauriant embowed of the field; on a canton of the second the totem pole of the 23d Infantry proper.

Crest: On a wreath of the colors an eagle's head erased sable, beaked and langued gules.

Motto: Play the Game.

Symbolism: The regiment was originally organized at Syracuse, New York, with personnel from the 23d Infantry. The shield is in the former and present colors of the infantry (white and blue). The dolphin is the device of Syracuse, and the totem pole in the canton is taken from the crest of the 23d Infantry. The pale with wavy edges indicates the regiment's occupation duty in the Rhine Province after World War I. At the time of the armistice on 11 November 1918 the 50th had been under orders for Silesia. The crest is the eagle's head of these two provinces.

DISTINCTIVE INSIGNIA

The distinctive insignia is the shield and motto of the coat of arms.

LINEAGE AND HONORS

LINEAGE

Constituted 15 May 1917 in the Regular Army as the 50th Infantry. Organized 1 June 1917 at Syracuse, New York. Assigned 31 July 1918 to the 20th Division. Relieved 28 February 1919 from assignment to the 20th Division. Inactivated 31 December 1921 in Germany. Demobilized 31 July 1922.

Reconstituted 8 January 1942 in the Regular Army as the 50th Armored Infantry and assigned to the 6th Armored Division. Activated 15 February 1942 at Fort Knox, Kentucky. Regiment broken up 20 September 1943 and its elements reorganized and redesignated as ele-

675

ments of the 6th Armored Division as follows: 50th Armored Infantry (less 1st and 2d Battalions) as the 50th Armored Infantry Battalion; 1st Battalion as the 44th Armored Infantry Battalion; 2d Battalion as the 9th Armored Infantry Battalion. Battalions inactivated 18–19 September 1945 at Camp Shanks, New York; activated 5 September 1950 at Fort Leonard Wood, Missouri; inactivated 16 March 1956 at Fort Leonard Wood, Missouri; relieved 1 July 1957 from assignment to the 6th Armored Division.

50th, 44th, and 9th Armored Infantry Battalions consolidated 1 July 1959 to form the 50th Infantry, a parent regiment under the Combat Arms Regimental System.

Campaign Participation Credit

World War II
   Normandy
   Northern France
   Rhineland
   Ardennes-Alsace
   Central Europe

Vietnam
   Counteroffensive, Phase III
   Tet Counteroffensive
   (other campaigns to be determined)

Decorations

Valorous Unit Award, Streamer embroidered BINH DUONG PROVINCE (Company F, 50th Infantry cited; DA GO 39, 1970, as amended by DA GO 2, 1971)

French Croix de Guerre with Palm, World War II, Streamer embroidered BREST (50th Armored Infantry Battalion cited; DA GO 43, 1950)

1st BATTALION, 50th INFANTRY

RA
(2d Armored Division)

LINEAGE

Constituted 15 May 1917 in the Regular Army as Company A, 50th Infantry. Organized 1 June 1917 at Syracuse, New York. (50th Infantry assigned 31 July 1918 to the 20th Division; relieved 28 February 1919 from assignment to the 20th Division.) Inactivated 31 December 1921 in Germany. Demobilized 31 July 1922.

Reconstituted 8 January 1942 in the Regular Army as Company A, 50th Armored Infantry, an element of the 6th Armored Division. Activated 15 February 1942 at Fort Knox, Kentucky. Reorganized and redesignated 20 September 1943 as Company A, 44th Armored Infantry Battalion, an element of the 6th Armored Division. Inactivated 19 September 1945 at Camp Shanks, New York. Activated 5 September 1950 at Fort Leonard Wood, Missouri. Inactivated 16 March 1956 at Fort Leonard Wood, Missouri.

Redesignated 1 July 1957 as Headquarters and Headquarters Company, 1st Armored Rifle Battalion, 50th Infantry, relieved from assignment to the 6th Armored Division, assigned to the 2d Armored Division, and activated in Germany (organic elements concurrently constituted and activated). Reorganized and redesignated 1 July 1963 as the 1st Battalion, 50th Infantry. Relieved 1 September 1967 from assignment to the 2d Armored Division. Assigned 16 December 1970 to the 2d Armored Division.

CAMPAIGN PARTICIPATION CREDIT

World War II
  *Normandy
  *Northern France
  *Rhineland
  *Ardennes-Alsace
  *Central Europe

Vietnam
  *Counteroffensive, Phase III
  *Tet Counteroffensive
    (other campaigns to be determined)

DECORATIONS

None.

2d BATTALION, 50th INFANTRY

RA
(2d Armored Division)

LINEAGE

Constituted 15 May 1917 in the Regular Army as Company B, 50th Infantry. Organized 1 June 1917 at Syracuse, New York. (50th Infantry assigned 31 July 1918 to the 20th Division; relieved 28 February 1919 from assignment to the 20th Division.) Inactivated 31 December 1921 in Germany. Demobilized 31 July 1922.

Reconstituted 8 January 1942 in the Regular Army as Company B, 50th Armored Infantry, an element of the 6th Armored Division. Activated 15 February 1942 at Fort Knox, Kentucky. Reorganized and redesignated 20 September 1943 as Company B, 44th Armored Infantry Battalion, an element of the 6th Armored Division. Inactivated 19 September 1945 at Camp Shanks, New York. Activated 5 September 1950 at Fort Leonard Wood, Missouri. Inactivated 16 March 1956 at Fort Leonard Wood, Missouri.

Redesignated 1 April 1957 as Headquarters and Headquarters Company, 2d Armored Rifle Battalion, 50th Infantry, relieved from assignment to the 6th Armored Division, assigned to the 4th Armored Division, and activated at Fort Hood, Texas (organic elements concurrently constituted and activated). Reorganized and redesignated 1 July 1963 as the 2d Battalion, 50th Infantry; concurrently, relieved from assignment to the 4th Armored Division and assigned to the 2d Armored Division.

CAMPAIGN PARTICIPATION CREDIT

World War II
  *Normandy
  *Northern France
  *Rhineland
  *Ardennes-Alsace
  *Central Europe

DECORATIONS

None.

678

3d ARMORED RIFLE BATTALION, 50th INFANTRY

RA
(inactive)

LINEAGE

Constituted 15 May 1917 in the Regular Army as Company C, 50th Infantry. Organized 1 June 1917 at Syracuse, New York. (50th Infantry assigned 31 July 1918 to the 20th Division; relieved 28 February 1919 from assignment to the 20th Division.) Inactivated 31 December 1921 in Germany. Demobilized 31 July 1922.

Reconstituted 8 January 1942 in the Regular Army as Company C, 50th Armored Infantry, an element of the 6th Armored Division. Activated 15 February 1942 at Fort Knox, Kentucky. Reorganized and redesignated 20 September 1943 as Company C, 44th Armored Infantry Battalion, an element of the 6th Armored Division. Inactivated 19 September 1945 at Camp Shanks, New York. Activated 5 September 1950 at Fort Leonard Wood, Missouri. Inactivated 16 March 1956 at Fort Leonard Wood, Missouri.

Redesignated 25 February 1958 as Headquarters and Headquarters Company, 3d Armored Rifle Battalion, 50th Infantry and relieved from assignment to the 6th Armored Division (organic elements concurrently constituted). Battalion activated 1 April 1958 in Germany. Inactivated 15 July 1963 in Germany.

CAMPAIGN PARTICIPATION CREDIT

World War II
* *Normandy
* *Northern France
* *Rhineland
* *Ardennes-Alsace
* *Central Europe

DECORATIONS

None.

COMPANY E, 50th INFANTRY

RA
(inactive)

LINEAGE

Constituted 15 May 1917 in the Regular Army as Company E, 50th Infantry. Organized 1 June 1917 at Syracuse, New York. (50th Infantry assigned 31 July 1918 to the 20th Division; relieved 28 February 1919 from assignment to the 20th Division.) Inactivated 31 December 1921 in Germany. Demobilized 31 July 1922.

Reconstituted 8 January 1942 in the Regular Army as Company E, 50th Armored Infantry, an element of the 6th Armored Division. Activated 15 February 1942 at Fort Knox, Kentucky. Reorganized and redesignated 20 September 1943 as Company B, 9th Armored Infantry Battalion, an element of the 6th Armored Division. Inactivated 18 September 1945 at Camp Shanks, New York. Activated 5 September 1950 at Fort Leonard Wood, Missouri. Inactivated 16 March 1956 at Fort Leonard Wood, Missouri. (9th Armored Infantry Battalion relieved 1 July 1957 from assignment to the 6th Armored Division.)

Redesignated 1 July 1959 as Headquarters and Headquarters Company, 5th Battle Group, 50th Infantry. Redesignated 20 December 1967 as Company E, 50th Infantry; concurrently, activated in Vietnam. Inactivated 1 February 1969 in Vietnam.

CAMPAIGN PARTICIPATION CREDIT

World War II-EAME
Normandy
Northern France
Rhineland
Ardennes-Alsace
Central Europe

Vietnam
Counteroffensive, Phase III
Tet Counteroffensive
(other campaigns to be determined)

DECORATIONS

French Croix de Guerre with Palm, World War II, Streamer embroidered CHAMBREY (9th Armored Infantry Battalion cited; DA GO 43, 1950)

Vietnamese Cross of Gallantry with Palm, Streamer embroidered VIETNAM 1967–1968 (Company E, 50th Infantry cited; DA GO 31, 1969)

Vietnamese Cross of Gallantry with Palm, Streamer embroidered

VIETNAM 1969 (Company E, 50th Infantry cited; DA GO 59, 1969, as amended by DA GO 53, 1970)

Vietnamese Civil Action Honor Medal, First Class, Streamer embroidered VIETNAM 1967–1969 (Company E, 50th Infantry cited; DA GO 59, 1969, as amended by DA GO 53, 1970)

COMPANY F, 50th INFANTRY

RA
(inactive)

LINEAGE

Constituted 15 May 1917 in the Regular Army as Company F, 50th Infantry. Organized 1 June 1917 at Syracuse, New York. (50th Infantry assigned 31 July 1918 to the 20th Division; relieved 28 February 1919 from assignment to the 20th Division.) Inactivated 31 December 1921 in Germany. Demobilized 31 July 1922.

Reconstituted 8 January 1942 in the Regular Army as Company F, 50th Armored Infantry, an element of the 6th Armored Division. Activated 15 February 1942 at Fort Knox, Kentucky. Reorganized and redesignated 20 September 1943 as Company C, 9th Armored Infantry Battalion, an element of the 6th Armored Division. Inactivated 18 September 1945 at Camp Shanks, New York. Activated 5 September 1950 at Fort Leonard Wood, Missouri. Inactivated 16 March 1956 at Fort Leonard Wood, Missouri. (9th Armored Infantry Battalion relieved 1 July 1957 from assignment to the 6th Armored Division.)

Redesignated 1 July 1959 as Headquarters and Headquarters Company, 6th Battle Group, 50th Infantry. Redesignated 20 December 1967 as Company F, 50th Infantry; concurrently, activated in Vietnam. Inactivated 1 February 1969 in Vietnam.

CAMPAIGN PARTICIPATION CREDIT

World War II-EAME
Normandy
Northern France
Rhineland
Ardennes-Alsace
Central Europe

Vietnam
Counteroffensive, Phase III
Tet Counteroffensive
(other campaigns to be determined)

DECORATIONS

Valorous Unit Award, Streamer embroidered BINH DUONG PROVINCE (Company F, 50th Infantry cited; DA GO 39, 1970, as amended by DA GO 2, 1971)

French Croix de Guerre with Palm, World War II, Streamer embroidered CHAMBREY (9th Armored Infantry Battalion cited; DA GO 43, 1950)

682

Vietnamese Cross of Gallantry with Palm, Streamer embroidered
VIETNAM 1967–1968 (Company F, 50th Infantry cited; DA GO 48, 1971)

Vietnamese Cross of Gallantry with Palm, Streamer embroidered
VIETNAM 1969 (Company F, 50th Infantry cited; DA GO 43, 1970, as
amended by DA GO 48, 1971)

50TH INFANTRY, BIBLIOGRAPHY

Buckley, Joseph D. *A History of the 50th Armored Infantry Battalion.* Frankfurt am Main: Baier and Wurm, 1945.

Cole, Hugh M. *The Ardennes: Battle of the Bulge.* United States Army in World War II. Washington: Government Printing Office, 1964.

————. *The Lorraine Campaign.* United States Army in World War II. Washington: Government Printing Office, 1950.

51st INFANTRY

HERALDIC ITEMS

COAT OF ARMS

Shield: Azure, a bend or.

Crest: On a wreath of the colors a ragged tree trunk eradicated proper.

Motto: I Serve.

Symbolism: The shield is blue for infantry, with the bend taken from the coat of arms of Alsace. The ragged tree trunk symbolizes the Meuse-Argonne campaign of World War I.

DISTINCTIVE INSIGNIA

The distinctive insignia is the shield and motto of the coat of arms.

LINEAGE AND HONORS

LINEAGE

Constituted 15 May 1917 in the Regular Army as the 51st Infantry. Organized 16 June 1917 at Chickamauga Park, Georgia. Assigned 16 November 1917 to the 6th Division. Inactivated 22 September 1921 at Camp Grant, Illinois. Relieved 15 August 1927 from assignment to the 6th Division and assigned to the 9th Division. Relieved 1 October 1933 from assignment to the 9th Division and assigned to the 6th Division. Relieved 16 December 1940 from assignment to the 6th Division.

Activated 15 April 1941 at Pine Camp, New York, as the 51st Infantry (Armored), an element of the 4th Armored Division. Redesignated 1 January 1942 as the 51st Armored Infantry. Regiment broken up 10 September 1943 and its elements reorganized and redesignated as elements of the 4th Armored Division as follows: 51st Armored Infantry (less 1st and 2d Battalions) as the 51st Armored Infantry Battalion; 1st Battalion as the 53d Armored Infantry Battalion; 2d Battalion as the 10th Armored Infantry Battalion.

51st Armored Infantry Battalion converted and redesignated 1 May 1946 as the 51st Constabulary Squadron; concurrently, relieved from assignment to the 4th Armored Division and assigned to the 11th Constabulary Regiment. Inactivated 20 December 1948 in Germany and relieved from assignment to the 11th Constabulary Regiment; concurrently, converted and redesignated as the 51st Armored Infantry Battalion and assigned to the 4th Armored Division. Activated 15 June 1954 at Fort Hood, Texas. Inactivated 1 April 1957 at Fort Hood, Texas, and relieved from assignment to the 4th Armored Division.

53d Armored Infantry Battalion converted and redesignated 1 May 1946 as the 53d Constabulary Squadron; concurrently, relieved from assignment to the 4th Armored Division and assigned to the 6th Constabulary Regiment. Relieved 16 November 1948 from the 6th Constabulary Regiment and assigned to the United States Constabulary. Inactivated 20 May 1949 in Germany and relieved from assignment to the United States Constabulary; concurrently, converted and redesignated as the 53d Armored Infantry Battalion and assigned to the 4th Armored Division. Redesignated 25 February 1953 as the 553d Armored Infantry Battalion. Activated 15 June 1954 at Fort Hood, Texas. Inactivated 1 April 1957 at Fort Hood, Texas, and relieved from assignment to the 4th Armored Division.

10th Armored Infantry Battalion converted and redesignated 1 May 1946 as the 10th Constabulary Squadron; concurrently, relieved from assignment to the 4th Armored Division and assigned to the 14th Constabulary Regiment. Inactivated 20 December 1948 in Germany and relieved from assignment to the 14th Constabulary Regiment; concurrently, converted and redesignated as the 10th Armored Infantry Battalion and assigned to the 4th Armored Division. Redesignated 25 February 1953 as the 510th Armored Infantry Battalion. Activated 15 June 1954 at Fort Hood, Texas. Inactivated 1 April 1957 at Fort Hood, Texas, and relieved from assignment to the 4th Armored Division.

51st, 553d, and 510th Armored Infantry Battalions consolidated 1 July 1959 to form the 51st Infantry, a parent regiment under the Combat Arms Regimental System.

CAMPAIGN PARTICIPATION CREDIT

World War I
  Meuse-Argonne
  Alsace 1918

World War II
  Normandy
  Northern France
  Rhineland

Ardennes-Alsace
Central Europe

Vietnam
  Counteroffensive, Phase II
  Counteroffensive, Phase III
  Tet Counteroffensive
  (other campaigns to be determined)

DECORATIONS

Presidential Unit Citation (Army), Streamer embroidered ARDENNES (4th Armored Division cited; WD GO 54, 1945)

Valorous Unit Award, Streamer embroidered SAIGON–LONG BINH (Company F, 51st Infantry cited; DA GO 48, 1968)

Meritorious Unit Commendation, Streamer embroidered VIETNAM 1967–1968 (Company D, 51st Infantry cited; DA GO 55, 1968)

Meritorious Unit Commendation, Streamer embroidered VIETNAM 1968–1969 (Company E, 51st Infantry cited; DA GO 53, 1970, as amended by DA GO 2, 1971)

French Croix de Guerre with Palm, World War II, Streamer embroidered NORMANDY (51st, 53d, and 10th Armored Infantry Battalions cited; DA GO 43, 1950)

French Croix de Guerre with Palm, World War II, Streamer embroidered MOSELLE RIVER (51st, 53d, and 10th Armored Infantry Battalions cited; DA GO 43, 1950)

French Croix de Guerre, World War II, Fourragere (51st, 53d, and 10th Armored Infantry Battalions cited; DA GO 43, 1950)

1st BATTALION, 51st INFANTRY

RA

(4th Armored Division)

Constituted 15 May 1917 in the Regular Army as Company A, 51st Infantry. Organized 16 June 1917 at Chickamauga Park, Georgia. (51st Infantry assigned 16 November 1917 to the 6th Division.) Inactivated 22 September 1921 at Camp Grant, Illinois. (51st Infantry relieved 15 August 1927 from assignment to the 6th Division and assigned to the 9th Division; relieved 1 October 1933 from assignment to the 9th Division and assigned to the 6th Division; relieved 16 December 1940 from assignment to the 6th Division.)

Activated 15 April 1941 at Pine Camp, New York, as Company A, 51st Infantry (Armored), an element of the 4th Armored Division. Redesignated 1 January 1942 as Company A, 51st Armored Infantry. Reorganized and redesignated 10 September 1943 as Company A, 53d Armored Infantry Battalion, an element of the 4th Armored Division.

Converted and redesignated 1 May 1946 as Troop A, 53d Constabulary Squadron, an element of the 6th Constabulary Regiment. (53d Constabulary Squadron relieved 16 November 1948 from assignment to the 6th Constabulary Regiment and assigned to the United States Constabulary.) Inactivated 20 May 1949 in Germany; concurrently, converted and redesignated as Company A, 53d Armored Infantry Battalion, an element of the 4th Armored Division. Redesignated 25 February 1953 as Company A, 553d Armored Infantry Battalion, an element of the 4th Armored Division. Activated 15 June 1954 at Fort Hood, Texas. Inactivated 1 April 1957 at Fort Hood, Texas (concurrently, 553d Armored Infantry Battalion relieved from assignment to the 4th Armored Division).

Redesignated 1 July 1957 as Headquarters and Headquarters Company, 1st Armored Rifle Battalion, 51st Infantry, assigned to the 2d Armored Division, and activated in Germany (organic elements concurrently constituted and activated). Reorganized and redesignated 1 July 1963 as the 1st Battalion, 51st Infantry; concurrently, relieved from assignment to the 2d Armored Division and assigned to the 4th Armored Division.

688

CAMPAIGN PARTICIPATION CREDIT

World War I
  * Meuse-Argonne
  * Alsace 1918

World War II
  * Normandy
  * Northern France
  * Rhineland
  * Ardennes-Alsace
  * Central Europe

DECORATIONS

*Presidential Unit Citation (Army), Streamer embroidered ARDENNES (4th Armored Division cited; WD GO 54, 1945)

*French Croix de Guerre with Palm, World War II, Streamer embroidered NORMANDY (53d Armored Infantry Battalion cited; DA GO 43, 1950)

*French Croix de Guerre with Palm, World War II, Streamer embroidered MOSELLE RIVER (53d Armored Infantry Battalion cited; DA GO 43, 1950)

*French Croix de Guerre, World War II, Fourragere (53d Armored Infantry Battalion cited; DA GO 43, 1950)

2d BATTALION, 51st INFANTRY

RA

(4th Armored Division)

Constituted 15 May 1917 in the Regular Army as Company B, 51st Infantry. Organized 16 June 1917 at Chickamauga Park, Georgia. (51st Infantry assigned 16 November 1917 to the 6th Division.) Inactivated 22 September 1921 at Camp Grant, Illinois. (51st Infantry relieved 15 August 1927 from assignment to the 6th Division and assigned to the 9th Division; relieved 1 October 1933 from assignment to the 9th Division and assigned to the 6th Division; relieved 16 December 1940 from assignment to the 6th Division.)

Activated 15 April 1941 at Pine Camp, New York, as Company B, 51st Infantry (Armored), an element of the 4th Armored Division. Redesignated 1 January 1942 as Company B, 51st Armored Infantry. Reorganized and redesignated 10 September 1943 as Company B, 53d Armored Infantry Battalion, an element of the 4th Armored Division.

Converted and redesignated 1 May 1946 as Troop B, 53d Constabulary Squadron, an element of the 6th Constabulary Regiment. (53d Constabulary Squadron relieved 16 November 1948 from assignment to the 6th Constabulary Regiment and assigned to the United States Constabulary.) Inactivated 20 May 1949 in Germany; concurrently, converted and redesignated as Company B, 53d Armored Infantry Battalion, an element of the 4th Armored Division. Redesignated 25 February 1953 as Company B, 553d Armored Infantry Battalion, an element of the 4th Armored Division. Activated 15 June 1954 at Fort Hood, Texas.

Reorganized and redesignated 1 April 1957 as Headquarters and Headquarters Company, 2d Armored Rifle Battalion, 51st Infantry and remained assigned to the 4th Armored Division (organic elements concurrently constituted and activated). Reorganized and redesignated 1 August 1963 as the 2d Battalion, 51st Infantry.

690

CAMPAIGN PARTICIPATION CREDIT

World War I
  *Meuse-Argonne
  *Alsace 1918

World War II
  *Normandy
  *Northern France
  *Rhineland
  *Ardennes-Alsace
  *Central Europe

DECORATIONS

*Presidential Unit Citation (Army), Streamer embroidered ARDENNES (4th Armored Division cited; WD GO 54, 1945)

*French Croix de Guerre with Palm, World War II, Streamer embroidered NORMANDY (53d Armored Infantry Battalion cited; DA GO 43, 1950)

*French Croix de Guerre with Palm, World War II, Streamer embroidered MOSELLE RIVER (53d Armored Infantry Battalion cited; DA GO 43, 1950)

*French Croix de Guerre, World War II, Fourragere (53d Armored Infantry Battalion cited; DA GO 43, 1950)

3d BATTALION, 51st INFANTRY

RA
(4th Armored Division)

LINEAGE

Constituted 15 May 1917 in the Regular Army as Company C, 51st Infantry. Organized 16 June 1917 at Chickamauga Park, Georgia. (51st Infantry assigned 16 November 1917 to the 6th Division.) Inactivated 22 September 1921 at Camp Grant, Illinois. (51st Infantry relieved 15 August 1927 from assignment to the 6th Division and assigned to the 9th Division; relieved 1 October 1933 from assignment to the 9th Division and assigned to the 6th Division; relieved 16 December 1940 from assignment to the 6th Division.)

Activated 15 April 1941 at Pine Camp, New York, as Company C, 51st Infantry (Armored), an element of the 4th Armored Division. Redesignated 1 January 1942 as Company C, 51st Armored Infantry. Reorganized and redesignated 10 September 1943 as Company C, 53d Armored Infantry Battalion, an element of the 4th Armored Division.

Converted and redesignated 1 May 1946 as Troop C, 53d Constabulary Squadron, an element of the 6th Constabulary Regiment. (53d Constabulary Squadron relieved 16 November 1948 from assignment to the 6th Constabulary Regiment and assigned to the United States Constabulary.) Inactivated 20 May 1949 in Germany; concurrently, converted and redesignated as Company C, 53d Armored Infantry Battalion, an element of the 4th Armored Division. Redesignated 25 February 1953 as Company C, 553d Armored Infantry Battalion, an element of the 4th Armored Division. Activated 15 June 1954 at Fort Hood, Texas. Inactivated 1 April 1957 at Fort Hood, Texas (concurrently 553d Armored Infantry Battalion relieved from assignment to the 4th Armored Division).

Redesignated 25 February 1958 as Headquarters and Headquarters Company, 3d Armored Rifle Battalion, 51st Infantry (organic elements concurrently constituted). Battalion activated 1 April 1958 in Germany. Assigned 1 April 1963 to the 4th Armored Division. Reorganized and redesignated 15 August 1963 as the 3d Battalion, 51st Infantry.

692

Campaign Participation Credit

World War I
  *Meuse-Argonne
  *Alsace 1918

World War II
  *Normandy
  *Northern France
  *Rhineland
  *Ardennes-Alsace
  *Central Europe

Decorations

*Presidential Unit Citation (Army), Streamer embroidered ARDENNES (4th Armored Division cited; WD GO 54, 1945)

*French Croix de Guerre with Palm, World War II, Streamer embroidered NORMANDY (53d Armored Infantry Battalion cited; DA GO 43, 1950)

*French Croix de Guerre with Palm, World War II, Streamer embroidered MOSELLE RIVER (53d Armored Infantry Battalion cited; DA GO 43, 1950)

*French Croix de Guerre, World War II, Fourragere (53d Armored Infantry Battalion cited; DA GO 43, 1950)

COMPANY D, 51st INFANTRY

RA
(nondivisional)

Constituted 15 May 1917 in the Regular Army as Company D, 51st Infantry. Organized 16 June 1917 at Chickamauga Park, Georgia. (51st Infantry assigned 16 November 1917 to the 6th Division.) Inactivated 22 September 1921 at Camp Grant, Illinois. (51st Infantry relieved 15 August 1927 from assignment to the 6th Division and assigned to the 9th Division; relieved 1 October 1933 from assignment to the 9th Division and assigned to the 6th Division; relieved 16 December 1940 from assignment to the 6th Division.)

Activated 15 April 1941 at Pine Camp, New York, as Company D, 51st Infantry (Armored), an element of the 4th Armored Division. Redesignated 1 January 1942 as Company D, 51st Armored Infantry. Reorganized and redesignated 10 September 1943 as Company A, 10th Armored Infantry Battalion, an element of the 4th Armored Division.

Converted and redesignated 1 May 1946 as Troop A, 10th Constabulary Squadron, an element of the 14th Constabulary Regiment. Inactivated 20 December 1948 in Germany; concurrently, converted and redesignated as Company A, 10th Armored Infantry Battalion, an element of the 4th Armored Division. Redesignated 25 February 1953 as Company A, 510th Armored Infantry Battalion, an element of the 4th Armored Division. Activated 15 June 1954 at Fort Hood, Texas. Inactivated 1 April 1957 at Fort Hood, Texas (concurrently, 510th Armored Infantry Battalion relieved from assignment to the 4th Armored Division).

Redesignated 1 July 1959 as Headquarters and Headquarters Company, 4th Battle Group, 51st Infantry. Redesignated 23 March 1966 as Company D, 51st Infantry. Activated 1 June 1966 at Fort Lewis, Washington.

CAMPAIGN PARTICIPATION CREDIT

World War I
Meuse-Argonne
Alsace 1918

Ardennes-Alsace
Central Europe

Vietnam
Counteroffensive, Phase II
World War II-EAME
Normandy
Northern France
Rhineland
Counteroffensive, Phase III
Tet Counteroffensive
(other campaigns to be determined)

DECORATIONS

Presidential Unit Citation (Army), Streamer embroidered ARDENNES (4th Armored Division cited; WD GO 54, 1945)

Meritorious Unit Commendation, Streamer embroidered VIETNAM 1967–1968 (Company D, 51st Infantry cited; DA GO 55, 1968)

French Croix de Guerre with Palm, World War II, Streamer embroidered NORMANDY (10th Armored Infantry Battalion cited; DA GO 43, 1950)

French Croix de Guerre with Palm, World War II, Streamer embroidered MOSELLE RIVER (10th Armored Infantry Battalion cited; DA GO 43, 1950)

French Croix de Guerre, World War II, Fourragere (10th Armored Infantry Battalion cited; DA GO 43, 1950)

COMPANY E, 51st INFANTRY

RA
(inactive)

Constituted 15 May 1917 in the Regular Army as Company E, 51st Infantry. Organized 16 June 1917 at Chickamauga Park, Georgia. (51st Infantry assigned 16 November 1917 to the 6th Division.) Inactivated 22 September 1921 at Camp Grant, Illinois. (51st Infantry relieved 15 August 1927 from assignment to the 6th Division and assigned to the 9th Division; relieved 1 October 1933 from assignment to the 9th Division and assigned to the 6th Division; relieved 16 December 1940 from assignment to the 6th Division.)

Activated 15 April 1941 at Pine Camp, New York, as Company E, 51st Infantry (Armored), an element of the 4th Armored Division. Redesignated 1 January 1942 as Company E, 51st Armored Infantry. Reorganized and redesignated 10 September 1943 as Company B, 10th Armored Infantry Battalion, an element of the 4th Armored Division.

Converted and redesignated 1 May 1946 as Troop B, 10th Constabulary Squadron, an element of the 14th Constabulary Regiment. Inactivated 20 December 1948 in Germany; concurrently, converted and redesignated as Company B, 10th Armored Infantry Battalion, an element of the 4th Armored Division. Redesignated 25 February 1953 as Company B, 510th Armored Infantry Battalion, an element of the 4th Armored Division. Activated 15 June 1954 at Fort Hood, Texas. Inactivated 1 April 1957 at Fort Hood, Texas (concurrently, 510th Armored Infantry Battalion relieved from assignment to the 4th Armored Division).

Redesignated 1 July 1959 as Headquarters and Headquarters Company, 5th Battle Group, 51st Infantry. Redesignated 20 December 1967 as Company E, 51st Infantry; concurrently, activated in Vietnam. Inactivated 1 February 1969 in Vietnam.

696

Campaign Participation Credit

World War I
  Meuse-Argonne
  Alsace 1918

Ardennes-Alsace
Central Europe

World War II-EAME
  Normandy
  Northern France
  Rhineland

Vietnam
  Counteroffensive, Phase III
  Tet Counteroffensive,
  (other campaigns to be determined)

Decorations

Presidential Unit Citation (Army), Streamer embroidered ARDENNES (4th Armored Division cited; WD GO 54, 1945)

Meritorious Unit Commendation, Streamer embroidered VIETNAM 1968–1969 (Company E, 51st Infantry cited; DA GO 53, 1970, as amended by DA GO 2, 1971)

French Croix de Guerre with Palm, World War II, Streamer embroidered NORMANDY (10th Armored Infantry Battalion cited; DA GO 43, 1950)

French Croix de Guerre with Palm, World War II, Streamer embroidered MOSELLE RIVER (10th Armored Infantry Battalion cited; DA GO 43, 1950)

French Croix de Guerre, World War II, Fourragere (10th Armored Infantry Battalion cited; DA GO 43, 1950)

COMPANY F, 51st INFANTRY

RA
(inactive)

LINEAGE

Constituted 15 May 1917 in the Regular Army as Company F, 51st Infantry. Organized 16 June 1917 at Chickamauga Park, Georgia. (51st Infantry assigned 16 November 1917 to the 6th Division.) Inactivated 22 September 1921 at Camp Grant, Illinois. (51st Infantry relieved 15 August 1927 from assignment to the 6th Division and assigned to the 9th Division; relieved 1 October 1933 from assignment to the 9th Division and assigned to the 6th Division; relieved 16 December 1940 from assignment to the 6th Division.)

Activated 15 April 1941 at Pine Camp, New York, as Company F, 51st Infantry (Armored), an element of the 4th Armored Division. Redesignated 1 January 1942 as Company F, 51st Armored Infantry. Reorganized and redesignated 10 September 1943 as Company C, 10th Armored Infantry Battalion, an element of the 4th Armored Division.

Converted and redesignated 1 May 1946 as Troop C, 10th Constabulary Squadron, an element of the 14th Constabulary Regiment. Inactivated 20 December 1948 in Germany; concurrently, converted and redesignated as Company C, 10th Armored Infantry Battalion, an element of the 4th Armored Division. Redesignated 25 February 1953 as Company C, 510th Armored Infantry Battalion, an element of the 4th Armored Division. Activated 15 June 1954 at Fort Hood, Texas. Inactivated 1 April 1957 at Fort Hood, Texas (concurrently, 510th Armored Infantry Battalion relieved from assignment to the 4th Armored Division).

Redesignated 1 July 1959 as Headquarters and Headquarters Company, 6th Battle Group, 51st Infantry. Redesignated 11 August 1967 as Company F, 51st Infantry. Activated 25 September 1967 in Vietnam. Inactivated 26 December 1968 in Vietnam.

CAMPAIGN PARTICIPATION CREDIT

World War I
Meuse-Argonne
Alsace 1918

Ardennes-Alsace
Central Europe

Vietnam
Counteroffensive, Phase III
Tet Counteroffensive
(other campaigns to be determined)

World War II-EAME
Normandy
Northern France
Rhineland

DECORATIONS

Presidential Unit Citation (Army), Streamer embroidered ARDENNES (4th Armored Division cited; WD GO 54, 1945)

Valorous Unit Award, Streamer embroidered SAIGON–LONG BINH (Company F, 51st Infantry cited; DA GO 48, 1968)

French Croix de Guerre with Palm, World War II, Streamer embroidered NORMANDY (10th Armored Infantry Battalion cited; DA GO 43, 1950)

French Croix de Guerre with Palm, World War II, Streamer embroidered MOSELLE RIVER (10th Armored Infantry Battalion cited; DA GO 43, 1950)

French Croix de Guerre, World War II, Fourragere (10th Armored Infantry Battalion cited; DA GO 43, 1950)

Vietnamese Cross of Gallantry with Palm, Streamer embroidered VIETNAM 1968 (Company F, 51st Infantry cited; DA GO 43, 1970)

51ST INFANTRY, BIBLIOGRAPHY

Cole, Hugh M. *The Ardennes: Battle of the Bulge.* United States Army in World War II. Washington: Government Printing Office, 1964.

————. *The Lorraine Campaign.* United States Army in World War II. Washington: Government Printing Office, 1950.

Historical and Pictorial Review, 51st Armored Infantry Regiment, Fourth Armored Division. Baton Rouge: Army and Navy Publishing Company, 1942.

Historical Section, War Department. "Singling," *Small Unit Actions.* American Forces in Action Series. Washington: Government Printing Office, 1946.

52d INFANTRY

(Ready Rifles)

HERALDIC ITEMS

COAT OF ARMS

Shield: Azure, on a bend or a six-pointed mullet gules; on a sinister canton argent a fusil of the third bearing a cross pattée argent charged with an acorn gules.

Crest: On a wreath of the colors a mace palewise or.

Motto: *Fortis et Certus* (Brave and True).

Symbolism: The shield is blue for infantry. The charges on the canton represent the 11th Infantry from whose personnel this regiment was organized. Its first combat service was in the Gérardmer Sector in the province of Alsace, a short distance west of Colmar; therefore, a mace taken from the arms of Colmar has been used for the crest. The bend from the arms of Alsace is charged with the 6th Division shoulder sleeve insignia to show that the regiment was with that division in France during World War I.

DISTINCTIVE INSIGNIA

The distinctive insignia is the shield and motto of the coat of arms.

LINEAGE AND HONORS

LINEAGE

Constituted 15 May 1917 in the Regular Army as the 52d Infantry. Organized 16 June 1917 at Chickamauga Park, Georgia. Assigned 16 November 1917 to the 6th Division. Inactivated 1 September 1921 at Camp Grant, Illinois. Relieved 15 August 1927 from assignment to the 6th Division and assigned to the 9th Division. Relieved 1 October 1933 from assignment to the 9th Division and assigned to the 6th Division. Relieved 1 October 1940 from assignment to the 6th Division.

Redesignated 15 July 1942 as the 52d Armored Infantry, assigned to the 9th Armored Division, and activated at Fort Riley, Kansas. Regiment broken up 9 October 1943 and its elements reorganized and redesignated as elements of the 9th Armored Division as follows: 52d Armored Infantry (less 1st, 2d, and 3d Battalions) as the 52d Armored Infantry Battalion; 1st Battalion as the 60th Armored Infantry Battalion; 2d Battalion as the 27th Armored Infantry Battalion; 3d Battalion disbanded. Battalions inactivated 13 October 1945 at Camp Patrick Henry, Virginia; relieved 14 September 1950 from assignment to the 9th Armored Division and concurrently consolidated to form the 52d Infantry, an element of the 71st Infantry Division.

52d Infantry relieved 25 February 1953 from assignment to the 71st Infantry Division; concurrently, regiment broken up and its elements redesignated as elements of the 9th Armored Division as follows: 52d Infantry (less 1st, 2d, and 3d Battalions) as the 52d Armored Infantry Battalion; 1st Battalion as the 560th Armored Infantry Battalion; 2d Battalion as the 527th Armored Infantry Battalion; former 3d Battalion reconstituted as the 528th Armored Infantry Battalion. 52d Armored Infantry Battalion relieved 23 July 1956 from assignment to the 9th Armored Division; activated 15 August 1956 at Vicenza, Italy; inactivated 24 June 1958 at Vicenza, Italy. 560th, 527th, and 528th Armored Infantry Battalions relieved 1 March 1957 from assignment to the 9th Armored Division.

52d, 560th, 527th, and 528th Armored Infantry Battalions consolidated 1 July 1959 to form the 52d Infantry, a parent regiment under the Combat Arms Regimental System.

CAMPAIGN PARTICIPATION CREDIT

World War I
  Meuse-Argonne
  Alsace 1918

World War II
  Rhineland
  Ardennes-Alsace
  Central Europe

Vietnam
  Counteroffensive, Phase II
  Counteroffensive, Phase III
  Tet Counteroffensive
  (other campaigns to be determined)

DECORATIONS

Presidential Unit Citation (Army), Streamer embroidered BASTOGNE (52d Armored Infantry Battalion cited; WD GO 17, 1945)

Presidential Unit Citation (Army), Streamer embroidered REMAGEN BRIDGEHEAD (52d and 27th Armored Infantry Battalions cited; WD GO 72, 1945)

Presidential Unit Citation (Army), Streamer embroidered SAIGON–TET OFFENSIVE (Company C, 52d Infantry cited; DA GO 17, 1969)

Meritorious Unit Commendation, Streamer embroidered VIETNAM

1967 (Company D, 52d Infantry cited; DA GO 54, 1968)

Meritorious Unit Commendation, Streamer embroidered VIETNAM 1968 (Company C and Company D, 52d Infantry cited; DA GO 48, 1969, and DA GO 39, 1970)

Meritorious Unit Commendation, Streamer embroidered VIETNAM 1968–1969 (Company C, 52d Infantry cited; DA GO 51, 1971)

Belgian Croix de Guerre 1940 with Palm, Streamer embroidered BASTOGNE; cited in the Order of the Day of the Belgian Army for action at BASTOGNE (52d Armored Infantry Battalion cited; DA GO 43, 1950, as amended by DA GO 27, 1959)

1st BATTALION, 52d INFANTRY

(Ready Rifles)

RA
(23d Infantry Division)

LINEAGE

Constituted 15 May 1917 in the Regular Army as Company A, 52d Infantry. Organized 16 June 1917 at Chickamauga Park, Georgia. (52d Infantry assigned 16 November 1917 to the 6th Division.) Inactivated 1 September 1921 at Camp Grant, Illinois. (52d Infantry relieved 15 August 1927 from assignment to the 6th Division and assigned to the 9th Division; relieved 1 October 1933 from assignment to the 9th Division and assigned to the 6th Division; relieved 1 October 1940 from assignment to the 6th Division.)

Redesignated 15 July 1942 as Company A, 52d Armored Infantry and activated at Fort Riley, Kansas, as an element of the 9th Armored Division. Reorganized and redesignated 9 October 1943 as Company A, 60th Armored Infantry Battalion, an element of the 9th Armored Division. Inactivated 13 October 1945 at Camp Patrick Henry, Virginia. Redesignated 14 September 1950 as Company A, 52d Infantry, an element of the 71st Infantry Division. Redesignated 25 February 1953 as Company A, 560th Armored Infantry Battalion, an element of the 9th Armored Division.

Redesignated 1 March 1957 as Headquarters and Headquarters Company, 1st Armored Rifle Battalion, 52d Infantry, relieved from assignment to the 9th Armored Division, and activated at Fort Hood, Texas (organic elements concurrently constituted and activated). Reorganized and redesignated 3 February 1962 as the 1st Battalion, 52d Infantry and assigned to the 1st Armored Division. Relieved 12 May 1967 from assignment to the 1st Armored Division and assigned to the 198th Infantry Brigade. Relieved 15 February 1969 from assignment to the 198th Infantry Brigade and assigned to the 23d Infantry Division.

704

CAMPAIGN PARTICIPATION CREDIT

World War I
* *Meuse-Argonne
* *Alsace 1918

World War II
* *Rhineland
* *Ardennes-Alsace
* *Central Europe

Vietnam
* *Counteroffensive, Phase III
* *Tet Counteroffensive
  (other campaigns to be determined)

DECORATIONS

Presidential Unit Citation (Army), Streamer embroidered BASTOGNE
Presidential Unit Citation (Army), Streamer embroidered REMAGEN
BRIDGEHEAD

2d BATTALION, 52d INFANTRY

(Ready Rifles)

RA
(1st Armored Division)

LINEAGE

Constituted 15 May 1917 in the Regular Army as Company B, 52d Infantry. Organized 16 June 1917 at Chickamauga Park, Georgia. (52d Infantry assigned 16 November 1917 to the 6th Division.) Inactivated 1 September 1921 at Camp Grant, Illinois. (52d Infantry relieved 15 August 1927 from assignment to the 6th Division and assigned to the 9th Division; relieved 1 October 1933 from assignment to the 9th Division and assigned to the 6th Division; relieved 1 October 1940 from assignment to the 6th Division.)

Redesignated 15 July 1942 as Company B, 52d Armored Infantry and activated at Fort Riley, Kansas, as an element of the 9th Armored Division. Reorganized and redesignated 9 October 1943 as Company B, 60th Armored Infantry Battalion, an element of the 9th Armored Division. Inactivated 13 October 1945 at Camp Patrick Henry, Virginia. Redesignated 14 September 1950 as Company B, 52d Infantry, an element of the 71st Infantry Division. Redesignated 25 February 1953 as Company B, 560th Armored Infantry Battalion, an element of the 9th Armored Division. (560th Armored Infantry Battalion relieved 1 March 1957 from assignment to the 9th Armored Division.)

Redesignated 30 August 1957 as Headquarters and Headquarters Company, 2d Armored Rifle Battalion, 52d Infantry (organic elements concurrently constituted). Battalion activated 1 October 1957 in Germany and assigned to the 3d Armored Division. Reorganized and redesignated 3 February 1962 as the 2d Battalion, 52d Infantry; concurrently, relieved from assignment to the 3d Armored Division and assigned to the 1st Armored Division. Inactivated 10 September 1963 at Fort Hood, Texas. Activated 12 May 1967 at Fort Hood, Texas.

706

Campaign Participation Credit

World War I
  *Meuse-Argonne
  *Alsace 1918

World War II
  *Rhineland
  *Ardennes-Alsace
  *Central Europe

Decorations

Presidential Unit Citation (Army), Streamer embroidered BASTOGNE
Presidential Unit Citation (Army), Streamer embroidered REMAGEN
BRIDGEHEAD

COMPANY C, 52d INFANTRY

(Ready Rifles)

RA
(nondivisional)

LINEAGE

Constituted 15 May 1917 in the Regular Army as Company C, 52d Infantry. Organized 16 June 1917 at Chickamauga Park, Georgia. (52d Infantry assigned 16 November 1917 to the 6th Division.) Inactivated 1 September 1921 at Camp Grant, Illinois. (52d Infantry relieved 15 August 1927 from assignment to the 6th Division and assigned to the 9th Division; relieved 1 October 1933 from assignment to the 9th Division and assigned to the 6th Division; relieved 1 October 1940 from assignment to the 6th Division.)

Redesignated 15 July 1942 as Company C, 52d Armored Infantry and activated at Fort Riley, Kansas, as an element of the 9th Armored Division. Reorganized and redesignated 9 October 1943 as Company C, 60th Armored Infantry Battalion, an element of the 9th Armored Division. Inactivated 13 October 1945 at Camp Patrick Henry, Virginia. Redesignated 14 September 1950 as Company C, 52d Infantry, an element of the 71st Infantry Division. Redesignated 25 February 1953 as Company C, 560th Armored Infantry Battalion, an element of the 9th Armored Division. (560th Armored Infantry Battalion relieved 1 March 1957 from assignment to the 9th Armored Division.)

Redesignated 1 July 1959 as Headquarters and Headquarters Company, 3d Battle Group, 52d Infantry. Redesignated 23 March 1966 as Company C, 52d Infantry. Activated 1 June 1966 at Fort Lewis, Washington.

CAMPAIGN PARTICIPATION CREDIT

World War I
 Meuse-Argonne
 Alsace 1918

World War II-EAME
 Rhineland
 Ardennes-Alsace
 Central Europe

Vietnam
 Counteroffensive, Phase II
 Counteroffensive, Phase III
 Tet Counteroffensive
 (other campaigns to be determined)

708

DECORATIONS

Presidential Unit Citation (Army), Streamer embroidered SAIGON–TET OFFENSIVE (Company C, 52d Infantry cited; DA GO 17, 1969)

Meritorious Unit Commendation, Streamer embroidered VIETNAM 1968 (Company C, 52d Infantry cited; DA GO 48, 1969)

Meritorious Unit Commendation, Streamer embroidered VIETNAM 1968–1969 (Company C, 52d Infantry cited; DA GO 51, 1971)

COMPANY D, 52d INFANTRY

(Ready Rifles)

RA
(inactive)

LINEAGE

Constituted 15 May 1917 in the Regular Army as Company D, 52d Infantry. Organized 16 June 1917 at Chickamauga Park, Georgia. (52d Infantry assigned 16 November 1917 to the 6th Division.) Inactivated 1 September 1921 at Camp Grant, Illinois. (52d Infantry relieved 15 August 1927 from assignment to the 6th Division and assigned to the 9th Division; relieved 1 October 1933 from assignment to the 9th Division and assigned to the 6th Division; relieved 1 October 1940 from assignment to the 6th Division.)

Redesignated 15 July 1942 as Company D, 52d Armored Infantry and activated at Fort Riley, Kansas, as an element of the 9th Armored Division. Reorganized and redesignated 9 October 1943 as Company A, 27th Armored Infantry Battalion, an element of the 9th Armored Division. Inactivated 13 October 1945 at Camp Patrick Henry, Virginia. Redesignated 14 September 1950 as Company E, 52d Infantry, an element of the 71st Infantry Division. Redesignated 25 February 1953 as Company A, 527th Armored Infantry Battalion, an element of the 9th Armored Division. (527th Armored Infantry Battalion relieved 1 March 1957 from assignment to the 9th Armored Division.)

Redesignated 1 July 1959 as Headquarters and Headquarters Company, 4th Battle Group, 52d Infantry. Redesignated 23 March 1966 as Company D, 52d Infantry. Activated 1 June 1966 at Fort Lewis, Washington. Inactivated 22 November 1969 in Vietnam.

CAMPAIGN PARTICIPATION CREDIT

World War I
Meuse-Argonne
Alsace 1918

World War II-EAME
Rhineland
Ardennes-Alsace
Central Europe

Vietnam
Counteroffensive, Phase II
Counteroffensive, Phase III
Tet Counteroffensive
(other campaigns to be determined)

710

DECORATIONS

Presidential Unit Citation (Army), Streamer embroidered REMAGEN BRIDGEHEAD (27th Armored Infantry Battalion cited; WD GO 72, 1945)

Meritorious Unit Commendation, Streamer embroidered VIETNAM 1967 (Company D, 52d Infantry cited; DA GO 54, 1968)

Meritorious Unit Commendation, Streamer embroidered VIETNAM 1968 (Company D, 52d Infantry cited; DA GO 39, 1970)

Cited in the Order of the Day of the Belgian Army for action in the ARDENNES (27th Armored Infantry Battalion cited; DA GO 43, 1950)

COMPANY E, 52d INFANTRY

(Ready Rifles)

RA
(inactive)

LINEAGE

Constituted 15 May 1917 in the Regular Army as Company E, 52d Infantry. Organized 16 June 1917 at Chickamauga Park, Georgia. (52d Infantry assigned 16 November 1917 to the 6th Division.) Inactivated 1 September 1921 at Camp Grant, Illinois. (52d Infantry relieved 15 August 1927 from assignment to the 6th Division and assigned to the 9th Division; relieved 1 October 1933 from assignment to the 9th Division and assigned to the 6th Division; relieved 1 October 1940 from assignment to the 6th Division.)

Redesignated 15 July 1942 as Company E, 52d Armored Infantry and activated at Fort Riley, Kansas, as an element of the 9th Armored Division. Reorganized and redesignated 9 October 1943 as Company B, 27th Armored Infantry Battalion, an element of the 9th Armored Division. Inactivated 13 October 1945 at Camp Patrick Henry, Virginia. Redesignated 14 September 1950 as Company F, 52d Infantry, an element of the 71st Infantry Division. Redesignated 25 February 1953 as Company B, 527th Armored Infantry Battalion, an element of the 9th Armored Division. (527th Armored Infantry Battalion relieved 1 March 1957 from assignment to the 9th Armored Division.)

Redesignated 1 July 1959 as Headquarters and Headquarters Company, 5th Battle Group, 52d Infantry. Redesignated 20 December 1967 as Company E, 52d Infantry; concurrently, activated in Vietnam. Inactivated 1 February 1969 in Vietnam.

CAMPAIGN PARTICIPATION CREDIT

World War I
  Meuse-Argonne
  Alsace 1918

World War II-EAME
  Rhineland
  Ardennes-Alsace
  Central Europe

Vietnam
  Counteroffensive, Phase III
  Tet Counteroffensive
  (other campaigns to be determined)

712

DECORATIONS

Presidential Unit Citation (Army), Streamer embroidered REMAGEN BRIDGEHEAD (27th Armored Infantry Battalion cited; WD GO 72, 1945)

Cited in the Order of the Day of the Belgian Army for action in the ARDENNES (27th Armored Infantry Battalion cited; DA GO 43, 1950)

Vietnamese Cross of Gallantry with Palm, Streamer embroidered VIETNAM 1967–1969 (Company E, 52d Infantry cited; DA GO 49, 1969, as amended by DA GO 53, 1970)

COMPANY F, 52d INFANTRY

(Ready Rifles)

RA
(inactive)

LINEAGE

Constituted 15 May 1917 in the Regular Army as Company F, 52d Infantry. Organized 16 June 1917 at Chickamauga Park, Georgia. (52d Infantry assigned 16 November 1917 to the 6th Division.) Inactivated 1 September 1921 at Camp Grant, Illinois. (52d Infantry relieved 15 August 1927 from assignment to the 6th Division and assigned to the 9th Division; relieved 1 October 1933 from assignment to the 9th Division and assigned to the 6th Division; relieved 1 October 1940 from assignment to the 6th Division.)

Redesignated 15 July 1942 as Company F, 52d Armored Infantry and activated at Fort Riley, Kansas, as an element of the 9th Armored Division. Reorganized and redesignated 9 October 1943 as Company C, 27th Armored Infantry Battalion, an element of the 9th Armored Division. Inactivated 13 October 1945 at Camp Patrick Henry, Virginia. Redesignated 14 September 1950 as Company G, 52d Infantry, an element of the 71st Infantry Division. Redesignated 25 February 1953 as Company C, 527th Armored Infantry Battalion, an element of the 9th Armored Division. (527th Armored Infantry Battalion relieved 1 March 1957 from assignment to the 9th Armored Division.)

Redesignated 1 July 1959 as Headquarters and Headquarters Company, 6th Battle Group, 52d Infantry. Redesignated 20 December 1967 as Company F, 52d Infantry; concurrently, activated in Vietnam. Inactivated 1 February 1969 in Vietnam.

CAMPAIGN PARTICIPATION CREDIT

World War I
Meuse-Argonne
Alsace 1918

World War II-EAME
Rhineland
Ardennes-Alsace
Central Europe

Vietnam
Counteroffensive, Phase III
Tet Counteroffensive
(other campaigns to be determined)

714

DECORATIONS

Presidential Unit Citation (Army), Streamer embroidered REMAGEN BRIDGEHEAD (27th Armored Infantry Battalion cited; WD GO 72, 1945)

Cited in the Order of the Day of the Belgian Army for action in the ARDENNES (27th Armored Infantry Battalion cited; DA GO 43, 1950)

Vietnamese Civil Action Honor Medal, First Class, Streamer embroidered VIETNAM 1967–1968 (Company F, 52d Infantry cited; DA GO 53, 1970, as amended by DA GO 48, 1971)

52D INFANTRY, BIBLIOGRAPHY

Cole, Hugh M. *The Ardennes: Battle of the Bulge.* United States Army in World War II. Washington: Government Printing Office, 1964.
Hechler, Ken. *The Bridge at Remagen.* New York: Ballantine Books, 1957.

54th INFANTRY

COAT OF ARMS

Shield: Azure, a bend or, in base a ragged tree trunk eradicated argent; on a sinister canton of the last a scaling ladder vert.

Crest: On a wreath of the colors a six-pointed star gules charged with a mailed foot argent.

Motto: I Will Cast My Shoe Over It.

Symbolism: This regiment was originally organized with personnel from the 6th Infantry, which is represented on the canton. The shield is blue for infantry with a gold bend taken from the arms of Alsace where the regiment saw its first combat service. The ragged tree trunk is for the Meuse-Argonne campaign.

The crest is the insignia of the 6th Division, with which the regiment served during World War I, charged with a mailed foot to commemorate the march from the Vosges to the Argonne and back to southern France.

DISTINCTIVE INSIGNIA

The distinctive insignia is the shield of the coat of arms.

LINEAGE AND HONORS

LINEAGE

Constituted 15 May 1917 in the Regular Army as the 54th Infantry. Organized 16 June 1917 at Chickamauga Park, Georgia. Assigned 16 November 1917 to the 6th Division. Inactivated 24 October 1922 at Fort Wayne, Michigan. Relieved 24 March 1923 from assignment to the 6th Division and assigned to the 7th Division. Relieved 1 October 1940 from assignment to the 7th Division.

Redesignated 14 June 1942 as the 54th Armored Infantry. Activated 15 July 1942 at Fort Benning, Georgia, as an element of the 10th Armored Division. Regiment broken up 20 September 1943 and its elements reorganized and redesignated as elements of the 10th Armored Division as follows: 54th Armored Infantry (less 1st, 2d, and 3d Battalions) as the 54th Armored Infantry Battalion; 1st Battalion as the 61st Armored Infantry Battalion; 2d Battalion as the 20th Armored Infantry Battalion; 3d Battalion disbanded. Battalions inactivated 13–23 October 1945 at Camp Patrick Henry, Virginia; relieved 14 September 1950 from assignment to the 10th Armored Division and concurrently consolidated to form the 54th Infantry, an element of the 71st Infantry Division.

54th Infantry relieved 25 February 1953 from assignment to the 71st Infantry Division; concurrently, regiment broken up and its elements redesignated as elements of the 10th Armored Division as follows: 54th Infantry (less 1st, 2d, and 3d Battalions) as the 54th Armored Infantry Battalion; 1st Battalion as the 561st Armored Infantry Battalion; 2d Battalion as the 520th Armored Infantry Battalion; former 3d Battalion reconstituted as the 554th Armored Infantry Battalion. Battalions relieved 1 April 1957 from assignment to the 10th Armored Division.

54th, 561st, 520th, and 554th Armored Infantry Battalions consolidated 1 July 1959 to form the 54th Infantry, a parent regiment under the Combat Arms Regimental System.

CAMPAIGN PARTICIPATION CREDIT

World War I
  Meuse-Argonne
  Alsace 1918

World War II
  Rhineland
  Ardennes-Alsace
  Central Europe

Vietnam
  Counteroffensive, Phase II
  Counteroffensive, Phase III
  Tet Counteroffensive
  (other campaigns to be determined)

DECORATIONS

Presidential Unit Citation (Army), Streamer embroidered BASTOGNE (54th Armored Infantry Battalion [less Companies A and C] and 20th Armored Infantry Battalion [less Company A] cited; WD GO 17, 1945)

Meritorious Unit Commendation, Streamer embroidered VIETNAM 1967–1968 (Company C, 54th Infantry cited; DA GO 55, 1968)

Belgian Croix de Guerre 1940 with Palm, Streamer embroidered BASTOGNE; cited in the Order of the Day of the Belgian Army for action at BASTOGNE (54th Armored Infantry Battalion [less Companies A and C] and 20th Armored Infantry Battalion [less Company A] cited; DA GO 43, 1950, as amended by DA GO 27, 1959)

1st BATTALION, 54th INFANTRY

LINEAGE

Constituted 15 May 1917 in the Regular Army as Company A, 54th Infantry. Organized 16 June 1917 at Chickamauga Park, Georgia. (54th Infantry assigned 16 November 1917 to the 6th Division.) Inactivated 24 October 1922 at Fort Wayne, Michigan. (54th Infantry relieved 24 March 1923 from assignment to the 6th Division and assigned to the 7th Division; relieved 1 October 1940 from assignment to the 7th Division.)

Redesignated 14 June 1942 as Company A, 54th Armored Infantry. Activated 15 July 1942 at Fort Benning, Georgia, as an element of the 10th Armored Division. Reorganized and redesignated 20 September 1943 as Company A, 61st Armored Infantry Battalion, an element of the 10th Armored Division. Inactivated 23 October 1945 at Camp Patrick Henry, Virginia. Redesignated 14 September 1950 as Company A, 54th Infantry, an element of the 71st Infantry Division. Redesignated 25 February 1953 as Company A, 561st Armored Infantry Battalion, an element of the 10th Armored Division.

Redesignated 1 April 1957 as Headquarters and Headquarters Company, 1st Armored Rifle Battalion, 54th Infantry, relieved from assignment to the 10th Armored Division, assigned to the 4th Armored Division, and activated at Fort Hood, Texas (organic elements concurrently constituted and activated). Reorganized and redesignated 5 June 1963 as the 1st Battalion, 54th Infantry.

CAMPAIGN PARTICIPATION CREDIT

World War I
*Meuse-Argonne
*Alsace 1918

World War II
*Rhineland
*Ardennes-Alsace
*Central Europe

DECORATIONS

Presidential Unit Citation (Army), Streamer embroidered BASTOGNE

2d BATTALION, 54th INFANTRY

RA

(4th Armored Division)

Constituted 15 May 1917 in the Regular Army as Company B, 54th Infantry. Organized 16 June 1917 at Chickamauga Park, Georgia. (54th Infantry assigned 16 November 1917 to the 6th Division.) Inactivated 24 October 1922 at Fort Wayne, Michigan. (54th Infantry relieved 24 March 1923 from assignment to the 6th Division and assigned to the 7th Division; relieved 1 October 1940 from assignment to the 7th Division.)

Redesignated 14 June 1942 as Company B, 54th Armored Infantry. Activated 15 July 1942 at Fort Benning, Georgia, as an element of the 10th Armored Division. Reorganized and redesignated 20 September 1943 as Company B, 61st Armored Infantry Battalion, an element of the 10th Armored Division. Inactivated 23 October 1945 as Camp Patrick Henry, Virginia. Redesignated 14 September 1950 as Company B, 54th Infantry, an element of the 71st Infantry Division. Redesignated 25 February 1953 as Company B, 561st Armored Infantry Battalion, an element of the 10th Armored Division. (561st Armored Infantry Battalion relieved 1 April 1957 from assignment to the 10th Armored Division.)

Redesignated 29 August 1957 as Headquarters and Headquarters Company, 2d Armored Rifle Battalion, 54th Infantry (organic elements concurrently constituted). Battalion activated 23 September 1957 at Fort Knox, Kentucky. Reorganized and redesignated 15 July 1963 as the 2d Battalion, 54th Infantry and assigned to the 4th Armored Division.

CAMPAIGN PARTICIPATION CREDIT

World War I
  *Meuse-Argonne
  *Alsace 1918

World War II
  *Rhineland
  *Ardennes-Alsace
  *Central Europe

DECORATIONS

Presidential Unit Citation (Army), Streamer embroidered BASTOGNE

COMPANY C, 54th INFANTRY

RA
(nondivisional)

LINEAGE

Constituted 15 May 1917 in the Regular Army as Company C, 54th Infantry. Organized 16 June 1917 at Chickamauga Park, Georgia. (54th Infantry assigned 16 November 1917 to the 6th Division.) Inactivated 24 October 1922 at Fort Wayne, Michigan. (54th Infantry relieved 24 March 1923 from assignment to the 6th Division and assigned to the 7th Division; relieved 1 October 1940 from assignment to the 7th Division.)

Redesignated 14 June 1942 as Company C, 54th Armored Infantry. Activated 15 July 1942 at Fort Benning, Georgia, as an element of the 10th Armored Division. Reorganized and redesignated 20 September 1943 as Company C, 61st Armored Infantry Battalion, an element of the 10th Armored Division. Inactivated 23 October 1945 at Camp Patrick Henry, Virginia. Redesignated 14 September 1950 as Company C, 54th Infantry, an element of the 71st Infantry Division. Redesignated 25 February 1953 as Company C, 561st Armored Infantry Battalion, an element of the 10th Armored Division. (561st Armored Infantry Battalion relieved 1 April 1957 from assignment to the 10th Armored Division.)

Redesignated 1 July 1959 as Headquarters and Headquarters Company, 3d Battle Group, 54th Infantry. Redesignated 23 March 1966 as Company C, 54th Infantry. Activated 1 June 1966 at Fort Lewis, Washington.

CAMPAIGN PARTICIPATION CREDIT

World War I
Meuse-Argonne
Alsace 1918

World War II-EAME
Rhineland
Ardennes-Alsace
Central Europe

Vietnam
Counteroffensive, Phase II
Counteroffensive, Phase III
Tet Counteroffensive
(other campaigns to be determined)

DECORATIONS

Meritorious Unit Commendation, Streamer embroidered VIETNAM 1967–1968 (Company C, 54th Infantry cited; DA GO 55, 1968)

4th BATTALION, 54th INFANTRY

RA

(194th Armored Brigade)

LINEAGE

Constituted 15 May 1917 in the Regular Army as Company D, 54th Infantry. Organized 16 June 1917 at Chickamauga Park, Georgia. (54th Infantry assigned 16 November 1917 to the 6th Division.) Inactivated 24 October 1922 at Fort Wayne, Michigan. (54th Infantry relieved 24 March 1923 from assignment to the 6th Division and assigned to the 7th Division; relieved 1 October 1940 from assignment to the 7th Division.)

Redesignated 14 June 1942 as Company D, 54th Armored Infantry. Activated 15 July 1942 at Fort Benning, Georgia, as an element of the 10th Armored Division. Reorganized and redesignated 20 September 1943 as Company A, 20th Armored Infantry Battalion, an element of the 10th Armored Division. Inactivated 13 October 1945 at Camp Patrick Henry, Virginia. Redesignated 14 September 1950 as Company E, 54th Infantry, an element of the 71st Infantry Division. Redesignated 25 February 1953 as Company A, 520th Armored Infantry Battalion, an element of the 10th Armored Division. (520th Armored Infantry Battalion relieved 1 April 1957 from assignment to the 10th Armored Division.)

Redesignated 1 July 1959 as Headquarters and Headquarters Company, 4th Battle Group, 54th Infantry. Redesignated 18 April 1963 as Headquarters and Headquarters Company, 4th Armored Rifle Battalion, 54th Infantry (organic elements concurrently constituted). Battalion activated 15 July 1963 at Fort Knox, Kentucky. Reorganized and redesignated 24 September 1963 as the 4th Battalion, 54th Infantry. Assigned 15 April 1968 to the 194th Armored Brigade.

CAMPAIGN PARTICIPATION CREDIT

World War I
  *Meuse-Argonne
  *Alsace 1918

World War II
  *Rhineland
  *Ardennes-Alsace
  *Central Europe

DECORATIONS

Presidential Unit Citation (Army), Streamer embroidered BASTOGNE

722

COMPANY E, 54th INFANTRY

RA
(nondivisional)

Constituted 15 May 1917 in the Regular Army as Company E, 54th Infantry. Organized 16 June 1917 at Chickamauga Park, Georgia. (54th Infantry assigned 16 November 1917 to the 6th Division.) Inactivated 24 October 1922 at Fort Sheridan, Illinois. (54th Infantry relieved 24 March 1923 from assignment to the 6th Division and assigned to the 7th Division; relieved 1 October 1940 from assignment to the 7th Division.)

Redesignated 14 June 1942 as Company E, 54th Armored Infantry. Activated 15 July 1942 at Fort Benning, Georgia, as an element of the 10th Armored Division. Reorganized and redesignated 20 September 1943 as Company B, 20th Armored Infantry Battalion, an element of the 10th Armored Division. Inactivated 13 October 1945 at Camp Patrick Henry, Virginia. Redesignated 14 September 1950 as Company F, 54th Infantry, an element of the 71st Infantry Division. Redesignated 25 February 1953 as Company B, 520th Armored Infantry Battalion, an element of the 10th Armored Division. (520th Armored Infantry Battalion relieved 1 April 1957 from assignment to the 10th Armored Division.)

Redesignated 1 July 1959 as Headquarters and Headquarters Company, 5th Battle Group, 54th Infantry. Redesignated 25 July 1967 as Company E, 54th Infantry; concurrently, activated at Fort Stewart, Georgia.

CAMPAIGN PARTICIPATION CREDIT

World War I
Meuse-Argonne
Alsace 1918

World War II-EAME
Rhineland
Ardennes-Alsace
Central Europe

DECORATIONS

Presidential Unit Citation (Army), Streamer embroidered BASTOGNE (20th Armored Infantry Battalion [less Company A] cited; WD GO 17, 1945)

723

Belgian Croix de Guerre 1940 with Palm, Streamer embroidered BASTOGNE; cited in the Order of the Day of the Belgian Army for action at BASTOGNE (20th Armored Infantry Battalion [less Company A] cited; DA GO 43, 1950, as amended by DA GO 27, 1959)

54TH INFANTRY, BIBLIOGRAPHY

Mabry, Gregory. *Recollections of a Recruit: An Official History of the Fifty-fourth U.S. Infantry.* New York: Schilling Press, Inc., 1919.

Pace, James W., ed. *Historical's History: Twentieth Armored Infantry Battalion, Tenth Armored Tiger Division.* Schongau: Karl Motz and Company, 1945.

58th INFANTRY
(The Patriots)

HERALDIC ITEMS

COAT OF ARMS

Shield: Azure, a chevron rompu point enhanced argent between in chief two fleurs-de-lis the dexter of the last the sinister or, and in base on an inescutcheon vert fimbriated of the second (argent) a cross pattée of the like.

Crest: On a wreath of the colors a torpedo argent charged with an ivy leaf vert.

Motto: Love of Country.

Symbolism: The field is blue for infantry. The regiment was originally organized with personnel from the 4th Infantry, as shown by the small shield. The broken chevron commemorates the piercing of the German line during World War I between Soissons and Rheims, which are represented by the silver and gold fleurs-de-lis taken from the arms of those cities, respectively.

The torpedo in the crest commemorates the first losses of the regiment on 23 May 1918, when the troop ship *Moldavia* carrying part of the unit was torpedoed by the Germans. World War I service in France as an element of the 4th Division is shown by the ivy leaf from the divisional shoulder sleeve insignia.

DISTINCTIVE INSIGNIA

The distinctive insignia is the shield and motto of the coat of arms.

LINEAGE AND HONORS

LINEAGE

Constituted 15 May 1917 in the Regular Army as the 58th Infantry. Organized 5 June 1917 at Gettysburg National Park, Pennsylvania. Assigned 19 November 1917 to the 4th Division. Inactivated 21 June 1922

727

at Fort George Wright, Washington. Demobilized 31 July 1922; concurrently, relieved from assignment to the 4th Division.

Reconstituted 8 April 1942 in the Regular Army as the 58th Infantry. Activated 24 April 1942 at Fort Lewis, Washington. Regiment broken up 26 January 1944 and its elements reorganized and redesignated as follows: Headquarters disbanded; 1st Battalion as the 203d Infantry Battalion; 2d Battalion as the 204th Infantry Battalion; 3d Battalion as the 205th Infantry Battalion.

Headquarters, 58th Infantry reconstituted 10 July 1951 in the Regular Army; concurrently, consolidated with the 203d Infantry Battalion (inactivated 2 March 1945 at Camp Shelby, Mississippi) and with the 58th Armored Infantry Battalion (see ANNEX) and consolidated unit designated as the 58th Armored Infantry Battalion, an element of the 8th Armored Division. Relieved 23 July 1956 from assignment to the 8th Armored Division. Activated 15 August 1956 in Germany. Inactivated 9 August 1957 in Germany.

204th Infantry Battalion inactivated 8 March 1945 at Camp Shelby, Mississippi. Redesignated 30 September 1948 as the 43d Armored Infantry Battalion. Activated 28 January 1949 at Fort Sill, Oklahoma, as an element of the 2d Armored Division. Inactivated 1 July 1957 in Germany and relieved from assignment to the 2d Armored Division.

205th Infantry Battalion inactivated 6 March 1945 at Camp Shelby, Mississippi. Redesignated 18 June 1948 as the 45th Armored Infantry Battalion. Activated 6 July 1948 at Camp Chaffee, Arkansas, as an element of the 5th Armored Division. Inactivated 1 February 1950 at Camp Chaffee, Arkansas. Activated 1 September 1950 at Camp Chaffee, Arkansas. Inactivated 16 March 1956 at Camp Chaffee, Arkansas. Relieved 15 February 1957 from assignment to the 5th Armored Division.

58th, 43d, and 45th Armored Infantry Battalions consolidated 1 July 1959 to form the 58th Infantry, a parent regiment under the Combat Arms Regimental System.

ANNEX

Constituted 15 May 1917 in the Regular Army as the 1st Battalion, 49th Infantry. Organized 1 June 1917 at Syracuse, New York. Inactivated 18 November 1921 at Fort Snelling, Minnesota. Demobilized 31 July 1922.

Reconstituted 1 April 1942 in the Regular Army as the 1st Battalion, 49th Armored Infantry; concurrently, activated at Fort Knox, Kentucky, as an element of the 8th Armored Division. Reorganized and redesignated 20 September 1943 as the 58th Armored Infantry Battalion, an element of the 8th Armored Division. Inactivated 11 November 1945 at Camp

Kilmer, New Jersey. Consolidated 10 July 1951 with Headquarters, 58th Infantry and with the 203d Infantry Battalion and consolidated unit designated as the 58th Armored Infantry Battalion, an element of the 8th Armored Division.

CAMPAIGN PARTICIPATION CREDIT

World War I
    Aisne-Marne
    St. Mihiel
    Meuse-Argonne
    Champagne 1918
    Lorraine 1918

World War II
    Aleutian Islands

Rhineland
Ardennes-Alsace
Central Europe

Vietnam
    Counteroffensive, Phase II
    Counteroffensive, Phase III
    Tet Counteroffensive
    (other campaigns to be determined)

DECORATIONS

Meritorious Unit Commendation, Streamer embroidered VIETNAM 1967–1968 (Company D, 58th Infantry cited; DA GO 72, 1968)

1st BATTALION, 58th INFANTRY

(The Patriots)

RA
(197th Infantry Brigade)

LINEAGE

Constituted 15 May 1917 in the Regular Army as Company A, 58th Infantry. Organized 5 June 1917 at Gettysburg National Park, Pennsylvania. (58th Infantry assigned 19 November 1917 to the 4th Division.) Inactivated 21 June 1922 at Fort George Wright, Washington. Demobilized 31 July 1922 (concurrently, 58th Infantry relieved from assignment to the 4th Division).

Reconstituted 8 April 1942 in the Regular Army as Company A, 58th Infantry. Activated 24 April 1942 at Fort Lewis, Washington. Reorganized and redesignated 26 January 1944 as Company A, 203d Infantry Battalion. Inactivated 2 March 1945 at Camp Shelby, Mississippi. Consolidated 10 July 1951 with Company A, 58th Armored Infantry Battalion (see ANNEX) and consolidated unit designated as Company A, 58th Armored Infantry Battalion, an element of the 8th Armored Division. (58th Armored Infantry Battalion relieved 23 July 1956 from assignment to the 8th Armored Division.) Activated 15 August 1956 in Germany. Inactivated 9 August 1957 in Germany.

Redesignated 1 July 1959 as Headquarters and Headquarters Company, 1st Battle Group, 58th Infantry. Redesignated 18 March 1960 as Headquarters and Headquarters Company, 1st Armored Rifle Battalion, 58th Infantry (organic elements concurrently constituted). Battalion activated 16 May 1960 at Fort Benning, Georgia, as an element of the 1st Infantry Brigade. Relieved 20 September 1962 from assignment to the 1st Infantry Brigade and assigned to the 197th Infantry Brigade. Reorganized and redesignated 24 September 1962 as the 1st Battalion, 58th Infantry.

ANNEX

Constituted 15 May 1917 in the Regular Army as Company A, 49th Infantry. Organized 1 June 1917 at Syracuse, New York. Inactivated 18 November 1921 at Fort Snelling, Minnesota. Demobilized 31 July 1922.

Reconstituted 1 April 1942 in the Regular Army as Company A, 49th

730

Armored Infantry; concurrently, activated at Fort Knox, Kentucky, as an element of the 8th Armored Division. Reorganized and redesignated 20 September 1943 as Company A, 58th Armored Infantry Battalion, an element of the 8th Armored Division. Inactivated 11 November 1945 at Camp Kilmer, New Jersey. Consolidated 10 July 1951 with Company A, 203d Infantry Battalion and consolidated unit designated as Company A, 58th Armored Infantry Battalion, an element of the 8th Armored Division.

CAMPAIGN PARTICIPATION CREDIT

World War I
   *Aisne-Marne
   *St. Mihiel
   *Meuse-Argonne
   *Champagne 1918
   *Lorraine 1918

World War II
   Aleutian Islands
   *Rhineland
   *Ardennes-Alsace
   *Central Europe

DECORATIONS
None.

2d ARMORED RIFLE BATTALION, 58th INFANTRY

(The Patriots)

RA
(inactive)

Constituted 15 May 1917 in the Regular Army as Company B, 58th Infantry. Organized 5 June 1917 at Gettysburg National Park, Pennsylvania. (58th Infantry assigned 19 November 1917 to the 4th Division.) Inactivated 21 June 1922 at Fort George Wright, Washington. Demobilized 31 July 1922 (concurrently, 58th Infantry relieved from assignment to the 4th Division).

Reconstituted 8 April 1942 in the Regular Army as Company B, 58th Infantry. Activated 24 April 1942 at Fort Lewis, Washington. Reorganized and redesignated 26 January 1944 as Company B, 203d Infantry Battalion. Inactivated 2 March 1945 at Camp Shelby, Mississippi. Consolidated 10 July 1951 with Company B, 58th Armored Infantry Battalion (see ANNEX) and consolidated unit designated as Company B, 58th Armored Infantry Battalion, an element of the 8th Armored Division. (58th Armored Infantry Battalion relieved 23 July 1956 from assignment to the 8th Armored Division.) Activated 15 August 1956 in Germany.

Reorganized and redesignated 1 July 1957 as Headquarters and Headquarters Company, 2d Armored Rifle Battalion, 58th Infantry and assigned to the 2d Armored Division (organic elements concurrently constituted and activated). Inactivated 1 July 1963 at Fort Hood, Texas, and relieved from assignment to the 2d Armored Division.

ANNEX

Constituted 15 May 1917 in the Regular Army as Company B, 49th Infantry. Organized 1 June 1917 at Syracuse, New York. Inactivated 18 November 1921 at Fort Snelling, Minnesota. Demobilized 31 July 1922.

Reconstituted 1 April 1942 in the Regular Army as Company B, 49th Armored Infantry; concurrently, activated at Fort Knox, Kentucky, as an element of the 8th Armored Division. Reorganized and redesignated 20 September 1943 as Company B, 58th Armored Infantry Battalion, an element of the 8th Armored Division. Inactivated 11 November 1945 at Camp Kilmer, New Jersey. Consolidated 10 July 1951 with Company B,

203d Infantry Battalion and consolidated unit designated as **Company B, 58th Armored Infantry Battalion, an element of the 8th Armored Division.**

CAMPAIGN PARTICIPATION CREDIT

World War I
* *Aisne-Marne
* *St. Mihiel
* *Meuse-Argonne
* *Champagne 1918
* *Lorraine 1918

World War II
Aleutian Islands
* *Rhineland
* *Ardennes-Alsace
* *Central Europe

DECORATIONS
None.

COMPANY C, 58th INFANTRY

(The Patriots)

RA
(inactive)

LINEAGE

Constituted 15 May 1917 in the Regular Army as Company C, 58th Infantry. Organized 5 June 1917 at Gettysburg National Park, Pennsylvania. (58th Infantry assigned 19 November 1917 to the 4th Division.) Inactivated 21 June 1922 at Fort George Wright, Washington. Demobilized 31 July 1922 (concurrently, 58th Infantry relieved from assignment to the 4th Division).

Reconstituted 8 April 1942 in the Regular Army as Company C, 58th Infantry. Activated 24 April 1942 at Fort Lewis, Washington. Reorganized and redesignated 26 January 1944 as Company C, 203d Infantry Battalion. Inactivated 2 March 1945 at Camp Shelby, Mississippi. Consolidated 10 July 1951 with Company C, 58th Armored Infantry Battalion (see ANNEX) and consolidated unit designated as Company C, 58th Armored Infantry Battalion, an element of the 8th Armored Division. (58th Armored Infantry Battalion relieved 23 July 1956 from assignment to the 8th Armored Division.) Activated 15 August 1956 in Germany. Inactivated 9 August 1957 in Germany.

Redesignated 1 July 1959 as Headquarters and Headquarters Company, 3d Battle Group, 58th Infantry. Redesignated 2 October 1962 as Company C, 58th Infantry and assigned to the 194th Armored Brigade. Activated 21 December 1962 at Fort Ord, California. Inactivated 15 May 1964 at Fort Ord, California, and relieved from assignment to the 194th Armored Brigade. Activated 15 May 1965 in Germany. Inactivated 10 February 1969 at Fort Carson, Colorado.

ANNEX

Constituted 15 May 1917 in the Regular Army as Company C, 49th Infantry. Organized 1 June 1917 at Syracuse, New York. Inactivated 18 November 1921 at Fort Snelling, Minnesota. Demobilized 31 July 1922.

Reconstituted 1 April 1942 in the Regular Army as Company C, 49th Armored Infantry; concurrently, activated at Fort Knox, Kentucky, as an element of the 8th Armored Division. Reorganized and redesignated 20 September 1943 as Company C, 58th Armored Infantry Battalion, an

734

element of the 8th Armored Division. Inactivated 11 November 1945 at Camp Kilmer, New Jersey. Consolidated 10 July 1951 with **Company C, 203d Infantry Battalion** and consolidated unit designated as **Company C, 58th Armored Infantry Battalion**, an element of the 8th Armored Division.

CAMPAIGN PARTICIPATION CREDIT

World War I
  Aisne-Marne
  St. Mihiel
  Meuse-Argonne
  Champagne 1918
  Lorraine 1918

World War II-EAME
  Rhineland
  Ardennes-Alsace
  Central Europe

DECORATIONS
  None.

COMPANY D, 58th INFANTRY

(The Patriots)

RA
(nondivisional)

LINEAGE

Constituted 15 May 1917 in the Regular Army as Company D, 58th Infantry. Organized 5 June 1917 at Gettysburg National Park, Pennsylvania. (58th Infantry assigned 19 November 1917 to the 4th Division.) Inactivated 21 June 1922 at Fort George Wright, Washington. Demobilized 31 July 1922 (concurrently, 58th Infantry relieved from assignment to the 4th Division).

Reconstituted 8 April 1942 in the Regular Army as Company D, 58th Infantry. Activated 24 April 1942 at Fort Lewis, Washington. Reorganized and redesignated 26 January 1944 as Company D, 203d Infantry Battalion. Inactivated 2 March 1945 at Camp Shelby, Mississippi. Consolidated 10 July 1951 with Service Company, 58th Armored Infantry Battalion (see ANNEX) and consolidated unit designated as Company D, 58th Armored Infantry Battalion, an element of the 8th Armored Division. (58th Armored Infantry Battalion relieved 23 July 1956 from assignment to the 8th Armored Division.) Activated 15 August 1956 in Germany. Inactivated 9 August 1957 in Germany.

Redesignated 1 July 1959 as Headquarters and Headquarters Company, 13th Battle Group, 58th Infantry. Redesignated 23 March 1966 as Company D, 58th Infantry. Activated 1 June 1966 at Fort Lewis, Washington.

ANNEX

Constituted 15 September 1943 in the Regular Army as Service Company, 58th Armored Infantry Battalion. Activated 20 September 1943 at Camp Polk, Louisiana, as an element of the 8th Armored Division. Inactivated 11 November 1945 at Camp Kilmer, New Jersey. Consolidated 10 July 1951 with Company D, 203d Infantry Battalion and consolidated unit designated as Company D, 58th Armored Infantry Battalion, an element of the 8th Armored Division.

736

CAMPAIGN PARTICIPATION CREDIT

World War I
Aisne-Marne
St. Mihiel
Meuse-Argonne
Champagne 1918
Lorraine 1918

World War II-EAME
Rhineland

Ardennes-Alsace
Central Europe

Vietnam
Counteroffensive, Phase II
Counteroffensive, Phase III
Tet Counteroffensive
(other campaigns to be determined)

DECORATIONS

Meritorious Unit Commendation, Streamer embroidered VIETNAM 1967–1968 (Company D, 58th Infantry cited; DA GO 72, 1968)

COMPANY E, 58th INFANTRY

(The Patriots)

RA
(inactive)

LINEAGE

Constituted 15 May 1917 in the Regular Army as Company E, 58th Infantry. Organized 5 June 1917 at Gettysburg National Park, Pennsylvania. (58th Infantry assigned 19 November 1917 to the 4th Division.) Inactivated 21 June 1922 at Fort George Wright, Washington. Demobilized 31 July 1922 (concurrently, 58th Infantry relieved from assignment to the 4th Division).

Reconstituted 8 April 1942 in the Regular Army as Company E, 58th Infantry. Activated 24 April 1942 at Fort Lewis, Washington. Reorganized and redesignated 26 January 1944 as Company A, 204th Infantry Battalion. Inactivated 8 March 1945 at Camp Shelby, Mississippi. Redesignated 30 September 1948 as Company A, 43d Armored Infantry Battalion. Activated 28 January 1949 at Fort Sill, Oklahoma, as an element of the 2d Armored Division. Inactivated 1 July 1957 in Germany (concurrently, 43d Armored Infantry Battalion relieved from assignment to the 2d Armored Division).

Redesignated 1 July 1959 as Headquarters and Headquarters Company, 4th Battle Group, 58th Infantry. Redesignated 20 December 1967 as Company E, 58th Infantry; concurrently, activated in Vietnam. Inactivated 1 February 1969 in Vietnam.

CAMPAIGN PARTICIPATION CREDIT

World War I
  Aisne-Marne
  St. Mihiel
  Meuse-Argonne
  Champagne 1918
  Lorraine 1918

World War II-AP
  Aleutian Islands

Vietnam
  Counteroffensive, Phase III
  Tet Counteroffensive
  (other campaigns to be determined)

DECORATIONS

Vietnamese Cross of Gallantry with Palm, Streamer embroidered VIETNAM 1967–1969 (Company E, 58th Infantry cited; DA GO 3, 1970)

Vietnamese Civil Action Honor Medal, First Class, Streamer embroidered VIETNAM 1967–1969 (Company E, 58th Infantry cited; DA GO 53, 1970)

COMPANY F, 58th INFANTRY

(The Patriots)

RA
(inactive)

LINEAGE

Constituted 15 May 1917 in the Regular Army as Company F, 58th Infantry. Organized 5 June 1917 at Gettysburg National Park, Pennsylvania. (58th Infantry assigned 19 November 1917 to the 4th Division.) Inactivated 21 June 1922 at Fort George Wright, Washington. Demobilized 31 July 1922 (concurrently, 58th Infantry relieved from assignment to the 4th Division).

Reconstituted 8 April 1942 in the Regular Army as Company F, 58th Infantry. Activated 24 April 1942 at Fort Lewis, Washington. Reorganized and redesignated 26 January 1944 as Company B, 204th Infantry Battalion. Inactivated 8 March 1945 at Camp Shelby, Mississippi. Redesignated 30 September 1948 as Company B, 43d Armored Infantry Battalion. Activated 28 January 1949 at Fort Sill, Oklahoma, as an element of the 2d Armored Division. Inactivated 1 July 1957 in Germany (concurrently, 43d Armored Infantry Battalion relieved from assignment to the 2d Armored Division).

Redesignated 1 July 1959 as Headquarters and Headquarters Company, 5th Battle Group, 58th Infantry. Redesignated 10 January 1968 as Company F, 58th Infantry; concurrently, activated in Vietnam. Inactivated 1 February 1969 in Vietnam.

CAMPAIGN PARTICIPATION CREDIT

World War I
  Aisne-Marne
  St. Mihiel
  Meuse-Argonne
  Champagne 1918
  Lorraine 1918

World War II-AP
  Aleutian Islands

Vietnam
  Counteroffensive, Phase III
  Tet Counteroffensive
  (other campaigns to be determined)

DECORATIONS

Vietnamese Cross of Gallantry with Palm, Streamer embroidered VIETNAM 1968–1969 (Company F, 58th Infantry cited; DA GO 43, 1970)

58TH INFANTRY, BIBLIOGRAPHY

Morrow, George L. *The Fifty-eighth Infantry in the World War, 1917–1918–1919*. 58th Infantry History Association, 1919.

"Unit Day, 24 June 1961. Love of Country. 2d Armored Rifle Battalion, 58th Infantry. Fort Hood, Texas." Fort Hood, 1961.

60th INFANTRY

HERALDIC ITEMS

COAT OF ARMS

Shield: Sable, a pale wavy argent charged with a fusil gules; on a canton embattled of the second a field gun of the third on a mount vert.

Crest: On a wreath of the colors a clenched dexter hand proper.

Motto: To the Utmost Extent of Our Power.

Symbolism: This regiment was originally organized with personnel from the 7th Infantry, which is represented on the canton. It participated in World War I as an element of the 5th Division, the insignia of which is carried on the shield. Black, white, and red show engagements against Germany, and the wavy pale is for the Meuse River, the crossing of which near Dun in November 1918 was an outstanding operation of the regiment.

The crest and motto symbolize the spirit of the regiment during the Meuse crossing and are guides for the future conduct of the organization.

DISTINCTIVE INSIGNIA

The distinctive insignia is the shield and motto of the coat of arms.

LINEAGE AND HONORS

LINEAGE

Constituted 15 May 1917 in the Regular Army as the 60th Infantry. Organized 10 June 1917 at Gettysburg National Park, Pennsylvania. Assigned 17 November 1917 to the 5th Division. Inactivated 2 September 1921 at Camp Jackson, South Carolina. Relieved 15 August 1927 from assignment to the 5th Division and assigned to the 8th Division. Relieved 1 October 1933 from assignment to the 8th Division and assigned to the 5th Division. Relieved 16 October 1939 from assignment to the 5th Division. Assigned 1 August 1940 to the 9th Division (later redesignated as the 9th Infantry Division). Activated 10 August 1940 at Fort Bragg,

North Carolina. Inactivated 30 November–28 December 1946 in Germany. Activated 15 July 1947 at Fort Dix, New Jersey.

Relieved 1 December 1957 from assignment to the 9th Infantry Division and reorganized as a parent regiment under the Combat Arms Regimental System.

CAMPAIGN PARTICIPATION CREDIT

World War I
  St. Mihiel
  Meuse-Argonne
  Alsace 1918
  Lorraine 1918

Normandy
Northern France
Rhineland
Ardennes-Alsace
Central Europe

World War II
  Algeria-French Morocco
    (with arrowhead)
  Tunisia
  Sicily

Vietnam
  Counteroffensive, Phase II
  Counteroffensive, Phase III
  Tet Counteroffensive
  (other campaigns to be determined)

DECORATIONS

Presidential Unit Citation (Army), Streamer embroidered STE. COLOMBE (2d Battalion, 60th Infantry cited; WD GO 90, 1944)

Presidential Unit Citation (Army), Streamer embroidered SCHWAMMANAUEL DAMS (2d Battalion, 60th Infantry cited; WD GO 68, 1945)

Presidential Unit Citation (Army), Streamer embroidered SEDJENANE VALLEY (2d Battalion, 60th Infantry cited; WD GO 1, 1944)

Presidential Unit Citation (Army), Streamer embroidered DINH TUONG PROVINCE (2d Battalion, 60th Infantry cited; DA GO 60, 1969)

Presidential Unit Citation (Army), Streamer embroidered MEKONG DELTA (3d Battalion, 60th Infantry cited; DA GO 45, 1969)

Valorous Unit Award, Streamer embroidered SAIGON (5th Battalion, 60th Infantry cited; DA GO 43, 1970)

French Croix de Guerre with Palm, World War II, Streamer embroidered COTENTIN PENINSULA (60th Infantry cited; DA GO 43, 1950)

Belgian Fourragere 1940 (60th Infantry cited; DA GO 43, 1950)

Cited in the Order of the Day of the Belgian Army for action at the MEUSE RIVER (60th Infantry cited; DA GO 43, 1950)

Cited in the Order of the Day of the Belgian Army for action in the ARDENNES (60th Infantry cited; DA GO 43, 1950)

1st BATTALION, 60th INFANTRY

RA

(172d Infantry Brigade)

LINEAGE

Constituted 15 May 1917 in the Regular Army as Company A, 60th Infantry. Organized 10 June 1917 at Gettysburg National Park, Pennsylvania. (60th Infantry assigned 17 November 1917 to the 5th Division.) Inactivated 2 September 1921 at Camp Jackson, South Carolina. (60th Infantry relieved 15 August 1927 from assignment to the 5th Division and assigned to the 8th Division; relieved 1 October 1933 from assignment to the 8th Division and assigned to the 5th Division; relieved 16 October 1939 from assignment to the 5th Division; assigned 1 August 1940 to the 9th Division [later redesignated as the 9th Infantry Division].) Activated 10 August 1940 at Fort Bragg, North Carolina. Inactivated 30 November 1946 in Germany. Activated 15 July 1947 at Fort Dix, New Jersey.

Reorganized and redesignated 1 December 1957 as Headquarters and Headquarters Company, 1st Battle Group, 60th Infantry and remained assigned to the 9th Infantry Division (organic elements concurrently constituted and activated). Inactivated 31 January 1962 at Fort Carson, Colorado. Redesignated 20 May 1963 as the 1st Battalion, 60th Infantry; concurrently, relieved from assignment to the 9th Infantry Division and assigned to the 172d Infantry Brigade. Activated 1 July 1963 in Alaska.

CAMPAIGN PARTICIPATION CREDIT

World War I
*St. Mihiel
*Meuse-Argonne
*Alsace 1918
*Lorraine 1918

World War II
*Algeria-French Morocco
(with arrowhead)

*Tunisia
*Sicily
*Normandy
*Northern France
*Rhineland
*Ardennes-Alsace
*Central Europe

DECORATIONS

Presidential Unit Citation (Army), Streamer embroidered STE. COLOMBE

745

Presidential Unit Citation (Army), Streamer embroidered SCHWAM-MANAUEL DAMS

Presidential Unit Citation (Army), Streamer embroidered SEDJENANE VALLEY

*French Croix de Guerre with Palm, World War II, Streamer embroidered COTENTIN PENINSULA (60th Infantry cited; DA GO 43, 1950)

*Belgian Fourragere 1940 (60th Infantry cited; DA GO 43, 1950)

*Cited in the Order of the Day of the Belgian Army for action at the MEUSE RIVER (60th Infantry cited; DA GO 43, 1950)

*Cited in the Order of the Day of the Belgian Army for action in the ARDENNES (60th Infantry cited; DA GO 43, 1950)

2d BATTALION, 60th INFANTRY

RA
(inactive)

LINEAGE

Constituted 15 May 1917 in the Regular Army as Company B, 60th Infantry. Organized 10 June 1917 at Gettysburg National Park, Pennsylvania. (60th Infantry assigned 17 November 1917 to the 5th Division.) Inactivated 2 September 1921 at Camp Jackson, South Carolina. (60th Infantry relieved 15 August 1927 from assignment to the 5th Division and assigned to the 8th Division; relieved 1 October 1933 from assignment to the 8th Division and assigned to the 5th Division; relieved 16 October 1939 from assignment to the 5th Division; assigned 1 August 1940 to the 9th Division [later redesignated as the 9th Infantry Division].) Activated 10 August 1940 at Fort Bragg, North Carolina. Inactivated 30 November 1946 in Germany. Activated 15 July 1947 at Fort Dix, New Jersey. Inactivated 1 December 1957 in Germany and relieved from assignment to the 9th Infantry Division.

Redesignated 12 February 1958 as Headquarters and Headquarters Company, 2d Battle Group, 60th Infantry (organic elements concurrently constituted). Battle Group activated 15 February 1958 at Fort Devens, Massachusetts, as an element of the 2d Infantry Brigade. Inactivated 19 February 1962 at Fort Devens, Massachusetts. Relieved 20 April 1962 from assignment to the 2d Infantry Brigade. Redesignated 1 February 1966 as the 2d Battalion, 60th Infantry; concurrently, assigned to the 9th Infantry Division and activated at Fort Riley, Kansas. Inactivated 13 October 1970 at Fort Lewis, Washington.

CAMPAIGN PARTICIPATION CREDIT

World War I
  *St. Mihiel
  *Meuse-Argonne
  *Alsace 1918
  *Lorraine 1918

World War II
  *Algeria-French Morocco
    (with arrowhead)
  *Tunisia
  *Sicily

*Normandy
*Northern France
*Rhineland
*Ardennes-Alsace
*Central Europe

Vietnam
  *Counteroffensive, Phase II
  *Counteroffensive, Phase III
  *Tet Counteroffensive
    (other campaigns to be determined)

747

DECORATIONS

Presidential Unit Citation (Army), Streamer embroidered STE. COLOMBE

Presidential Unit Citation (Army), Streamer embroidered SCHWAMMANAUEL DAMS

Presidential Unit Citation (Army), Streamer embroidered SEDJENANE VALLEY

*Presidential Unit Citation (Army), Streamer embroidered GERMANY (Company B, 60th Infantry cited; WD GO 55, 1945)

*Presidential Unit Citation (Army), Streamer embroidered DINH TUONG PROVINCE (2d Battalion, 60th Infantry cited; DA GO 60, 1969)

*French Croix de Guerre with Palm, World War II, Streamer embroidered COTENTIN PENINSULA (60th Infantry cited; DA GO 43, 1950)

*Belgian Fourragere 1940 (60th Infantry cited; DA GO 43, 1950)

*Cited in the Order of the Day of the Belgian Army for action at the MEUSE RIVER (60th Infantry cited; DA GO 43, 1950)

*Cited in the Order of the Day of the Belgian Army for action in the ARDENNES (60th Infantry cited; DA GO 43, 1950)

*Vietnamese Cross of Gallantry with Palm, Streamer embroidered VIETNAM 1966–1968 (2d Battalion, 60th Infantry cited; DA GO 31, 1969)

*Vietnamese Cross of Gallantry with Palm, Streamer embroidered VIETNAM 1968 (2d Battalion, 60th Infantry cited; DA GO 31, 1969)

*Vietnamese Cross of Gallantry with Palm, Streamer embroidered VIETNAM 1969 (2d Battalion, 60th Infantry cited; DA GO 59, 1969)

*Vietnamese Civil Action Honor Medal, First Class, Streamer embroidered VIETNAM 1966–1969 (2d Battalion, 60th Infantry cited; DA GO 59, 1969)

Company B additionally entitled to: Valorous Unit Award, Streamer embroidered BEN TRE CITY (Company B, 2d Battalion, 60th Infantry cited; DA GO 42, 1969)

3d BATTALION, 60th INFANTRY

LINEAGE

Constituted 15 May 1917 in the Regular Army as Company C, 60th Infantry. Organized 10 June 1917 at Gettysburg National Park, Pennsylvania. (60th Infantry assigned 17 November 1917 to the 5th Division.) Inactivated 2 September 1921 at Camp Jackson, South Carolina. (60th Infantry relieved 15 August 1927 from assignment to the 5th Division and assigned to the 8th Division; relieved 1 October 1933 from assignment to the 8th Division and assigned to the 5th Division; relieved 16 October 1939 from assignment to the 5th Division; assigned 1 August 1940 to the 9th Division [later redesignated as the 9th Infantry Division].) Activated 10 August 1940 at Fort Bragg, North Carolina. Inactivated 30 November 1946 in Germany. Activated 15 July 1947 at Fort Dix, New Jersey.

Inactivated 1 December 1957 in Germany and relieved from assignment to the 9th Infantry Division; concurrently, redesignated as Headquarters and Headquarters Company, 3d Battle Group, 60th Infantry. Redesignated 1 February 1966 as Headquarters and Headquarters Company, 3d Battalion, 60th Infantry, assigned to the 9th Infantry Division, and activated at Fort Riley, Kansas (organic elements concurrently constituted and activated). Inactivated 1 August 1969 at Fort Riley, Kansas.

CAMPAIGN PARTICIPATION CREDIT

World War I
  *St. Mihiel
  *Meuse-Argonne
  *Alsace 1918
  *Lorraine 1918

World War II
  *Algeria-French Morocco
    (with arrowhead)
  *Tunisia
  *Sicily

*Normandy
*Northern France
*Rhineland
*Ardennes-Alsace
*Central Europe

Vietnam
  *Counteroffensive, Phase II
  *Counteroffensive, Phase III
  *Tet Counteroffensive
    (other campaigns to be determined)

749

DECORATIONS

Presidential Unit Citation (Army), Streamer embroidered STE. COLOMBE

Presidential Unit Citation (Army), Streamer embroidered SCHWAM-MANAUEL DAMS

Presidential Unit Citation (Army), Streamer embroidered SEDJENANE VALLEY

*Presidential Unit Citation (Army), Streamer embroidered MEKONG DELTA (3d Battalion, 60th Infantry cited; DA GO 45, 1969)

*French Croix de Guerre with Palm, World War II, Streamer embroidered COTENTIN PENINSULA (60th Infantry cited; DA GO 43, 1950)

*Belgian Fourragere 1940 (60th Infantry cited; DA GO 43, 1950)

*Cited in the Order of the Day of the Belgian Army for action at the MEUSE RIVER (60th Infantry cited; DA GO 43, 1950)

*Cited in the Order of the Day of the Belgian Army for action in the ARDENNES (60th Infantry cited; DA GO 43, 1950)

*Vietnamese Cross of Gallantry with Palm, Streamer embroidered VIETNAM 1966–1968 (3d Battalion, 60th Infantry cited; DA GO 31, 1969)

*Vietnamese Cross of Gallantry with Palm, Streamer embroidered VIETNAM 1969 (3d Battalion, 6th Infantry cited; DA GO 59, 1969)

*Vietnamese Civil Action Honor Medal, First Class, Streamer embroidered VIETNAM 1966–1969 (3d Battalion, 60th Infantry cited; DA GO 59, 1969)

5th BATTALION, 60th INFANTRY

RA
(inactive)

LINEAGE

Constituted 15 May 1917 in the Regular Army as Company E, 60th Infantry. Organized 10 June 1917 at Gettysburg National Park, Pennsylvania. (60th Infantry assigned 17 November 1917 to the 5th Division.) Inactivated 2 September 1921 at Camp Jackson, South Carolina. (60th Infantry relieved 15 August 1927 from assignment to the 5th Division and assigned to the 8th Division; relieved 1 October 1933 from assignment to the 8th Division and assigned to the 5th Division; relieved 16 October 1939 from assignment to the 5th Division; assigned 1 August 1940 to the 9th Division [later redesignated as the 9th Infantry Division].) Activated 10 August 1940 at Fort Bragg, North Carolina. Inactivated 28 December 1946 in Germany. Activated 15 July 1947 at Fort Dix, New Jersey.

Inactivated 1 December 1957 in Germany and relieved from assignment to the 9th Infantry Division; concurrently, redesignated as Headquarters and Headquarters Company, 5th Battle Group, 60th Infantry. Redesignated 1 February 1966 as Headquarters and Headquarters Company, 5th Battalion, 60th Infantry, assigned to the 9th Infantry Division, and activated at Fort Riley, Kansas (organic elements concurrently constituted and activated). Inactivated 13 October 1970 at Fort Lewis, Washington.

CAMPAIGN PARTICIPATION CREDIT

World War I
*St. Mihiel
*Meuse-Argonne
*Alsace 1918
*Lorraine 1918

World War II
*Algeria-French Morocco
  (with arrowhead)
*Tunisia
*Sicily

*Normandy
*Northern France
*Rhineland
*Ardennes-Alsace
*Central Europe

Vietnam
*Counteroffensive, Phase II
*Counteroffensive, Phase III
*Tet Counteroffensive
  (other campaigns to be determined)

751

DECORATIONS

*Presidential Unit Citation (Army), Streamer embroidered STE. COLOMBE (2d Battalion, 60th Infantry cited; WD GO 90, 1944)

*Presidential Unit Citation (Army), Streamer embroidered SCHWAM-MANAUEL DAMS (2d Battalion, 60th Infantry cited; WD GO 68, 1945)

*Presidential Unit Citation (Army), Streamer embroidered SED-JENANE VALLEY (2d Battalion, 60th Infantry cited; WD GO 1, 1944)

*Valorous Unit Award, Streamer embroidered SAIGON (5th Battalion, 60th Infantry cited; DA GO 43, 1970)

*French Croix de Guerre with Palm, World War II, Streamer embroidered COTENTIN PENINSULA (60th Infantry cited; DA GO 43, 1950)

*Belgian Fourragere 1940 (60th Infantry cited; DA GO 43, 1950)

*Cited in the Order of the Day of the Belgian Army for action at the MEUSE RIVER (60th Infantry cited; DA GO 43, 1950)

*Cited in the Order of the Day of the Belgian Army for action in the ARDENNES (60th Infantry cited; DA GO 43, 1950)

*Vietnamese Cross of Gallantry with Palm, Streamer embroidered VIETNAM 1966–1968 (5th Battalion, 60th Infantry cited; DA GO 31, 1969, as amended by DA GO 46, 1969, and DA GO 43, 1970)

*Vietnamese Cross of Gallantry with Palm, Streamer embroidered VIETNAM 1968 (5th Battalion, 60th Infantry cited; DA GO 31, 1969, as amended by DA GO 46, 1969, and DA GO 43, 1970)

*Vietnamese Cross of Gallantry with Palm, Streamer embroidered VIETNAM 1969 (5th Battalion, 60th Infantry cited; DA GO 59, 1969)

*Vietnamese Civil Action Honor Medal, First Class, Streamer embroidered VIETNAM 1966–1969 (5th Battalion, 60th Infantry cited; DA GO 59, 1969)

Company B and Company C each additionally entitled to: Valorous Unit Award, Streamer embroidered CHOLON–SAIGON (Company B and Company C, 5th Battalion, 60th Infantry cited; DA GO 42, 1969)

60TH INFANTRY, BIBLIOGRAPHY

Albright, John, John A. Cash, and Allan W. Sandstrum. *Seven Firefights in Vietnam.* Washington: Government Printing Office, 1970.

Blumenson, Martin. *Breakout and Pursuit.* United States Army in World War II. Washington: Government Printing Office, 1961.

Garland, Albert N. and Howard McGaw Smyth. *Sicily and the Surrender of Italy.* United States Army in World War II. Washington: Government Printing Office, 1965.

Harrison, Gordon A. *Cross-Channel Attack.* United States Army in World War II. Washington: Government Printing Office, 1950.

Heldreth, Clyde, Capere Poston, and Clarence Kendall. *History of Company "D", 60th Infantry, U.S. Army.* Luxembourg, 1919.

Historical Section, War Department. *St-Lô.* American Forces in Action Series. Washington: Government Printing Office, 1946.

_____. *To Bizerte with the II Corps.* American Forces in Action Series. Washington: Government Printing Office, 1943.

_____. *Utah Beach to Cherbourg.* American Forces in Action Series. Washington: Government Printing Office, 1947.

Howe, George F. *Northwest Africa: Seizing the Initiative in the West.* United States Army in World War II. Washington: Government Printing Office, 1957.

MacDonald, Charles B. *The Battle of Huertgen Forest.* Philadelphia and New York: J. B. Lippincott Company, 1963.

_____. *The Siegfried Line Campaign.* United States Army in World War II. Washington: Government Printing Office, 1963.

Noble, Carl. *Jugheads Behind the Lines.* Edited by Grace Stone Coates. Caldwell, Idaho: Caxton Printers, 1938.

Stussman, Morton J. *Follow Thru.* Stuttgart: Chr. Scheuffle, 1945.

Wrentmore, Ernest L. *In Spite of Hell.* New York: Greenwich Book Publishers, 1958.

61st INFANTRY

HERALDIC ITEMS

COAT OF ARMS

Shield: Azure, a pale wavy argent charged with a fusil gules; on a canton embattled of the second a field gun of the third on a mount vert.

Crest: On a wreath of the colors a lion rampant sable grasping in his dexter paw the shoulder sleeve insignia of the 5th Division proper.

Motto: The Best Lead the Rest.

Symbolism: This regiment was originally organized with personnel from the 7th Infantry, which is represented on the canton. It participated in World War I as an element of the 5th Division, the insignia of which is carried on the shield and also in the crest. The wavy pale represents the Meuse River, the crossing of which near Dun in November 1918 was an outstanding operation of the regiment. The lion of the crest is taken from the arms of Montmédy, the nearest place to Dun having a coat of arms.

DISTINCTIVE INSIGNIA

The distinctive insignia is the shield of the coat of arms.

LINEAGE AND HONORS

LINEAGE

Constituted 15 May 1917 in the Regular Army as the 61st Infantry. Organized 10 June 1917 at Gettysburg National Park, Pennsylvania. Assigned 17 November 1917 to the 5th Division. Inactivated 2 September 1921 at Camp Jackson, South Carolina. Relieved 15 August 1927 from assignment to the 5th Division and assigned to the 8th Division. Relieved 1 October 1933 from assignment to the 8th Division and assigned to the 5th Division. Relieved 16 October 1939 from assignment to the 5th Division. Disbanded 11 November 1944.

Reconstituted 10 August 1950 in the Regular Army as an element of the 8th Infantry Division. Activated 17 August 1950 at Fort Jackson,

South Carolina. Inactivated 1 September 1956 at Fort Carson, Colorado, and relieved from assignment to the 8th Infantry Division.

Reorganized 17 January 1962 as a parent regiment under the Combat Arms Regimental System.

CAMPAIGN PARTICIPATION CREDIT

World War I
St. Mihiel
Meuse-Argonne
Alsace 1918
Lorraine 1918

Vietnam
(to be determined)

DECORATIONS

None.

1st BATTALION, 61st INFANTRY

RA
(5th Infantry Division)

LINEAGE

Constituted 15 May 1917 in the Regular Army as Company A, 61st Infantry. Organized 10 June 1917 at Gettysburg National Park, Pennsylvania. (61st Infantry assigned 17 November 1917 to the 5th Division.) Inactivated 2 September 1921 at Camp Jackson, South Carolina. (61st Infantry relieved 15 August 1927 from assignment to the 5th Division and assigned to the 8th Division; relieved 1 October 1933 from assignment to the 8th Division and assigned to the 5th Division; relieved 16 October 1939 from assignment to the 5th Division.) Disbanded 11 November 1944.

Reconstituted 10 August 1950 in the Regular Army as an element of the 8th Infantry Division. Activated 17 August 1950 at Fort Jackson, South Carolina. Inactivated 1 September 1956 at Fort Carson, Colorado (61st Infantry concurrently relieved from assignment to the 8th Infantry Division).

Redesignated 17 January 1962 as Headquarters and Headquarters Company, 1st Battalion, 61st Infantry. Activated 19 February 1962 at Fort Carson, Colorado, as an element of the 5th Infantry Division (organic elements concurrently constituted and activated).

CAMPAIGN PARTICIPATION CREDIT

World War I
*St. Mihiel
*Meuse-Argonne
*Alsace 1918
*Lorraine 1918

Vietnam
(to be determined)

DECORATIONS

*Vietnamese Cross of Gallantry with Palm, Streamer embroidered VIETNAM 1968 (1st Battalion, 61st Infantry cited; DA GO 43, 1970)

757

2d BATTALION, 61st INFANTRY

RA
(4th Infantry Division)

Constituted 15 May 1917 in the Regular Army as Company B, 61st Infantry. Organized 10 June 1917 at Gettysburg National Park, Pennsylvania. (61st Infantry assigned 17 November 1917 to the 5th Division.) Inactivated 2 September 1921 at Camp Jackson, South Carolina. (61st Infantry relieved 15 August 1927 from assignment to the 5th Division and assigned to the 8th Division; relieved 1 October 1933 from assignment to the 8th Division and assigned to the 5th Division; relieved 16 October 1939 from assignment to the 5th Division.) Disbanded 11 November 1944.

Reconstituted 10 August 1950 in the Regular Army as an element of the 8th Infantry Division. Activated 17 August 1950 at Fort Jackson, South Carolina. Inactivated 1 September 1956 at Fort Carson, Colorado (61st Infantry concurrently relieved from assignment to the 8th Infantry Division).

Redesignated 17 January 1962 as Headquarters and Headquarters Company, 2d Battalion, 61st Infantry. Activated 19 February 1962 at Fort Carson, Colorado, as an element of the 5th Infantry Division (organic elements concurrently constituted and activated). Relieved 15 December 1970 from assignment to the 5th Infantry Division and assigned to the 4th Infantry Division.

CAMPAIGN PARTICIPATION CREDIT

World War I
 *St. Mihiel
 *Meuse-Argonne
 *Alsace 1918
 *Lorraine 1918

DECORATIONS

None.

758

3d BATTALION, 61st INFANTRY

RA
(inactive)

LINEAGE

Constituted 15 May 1917 in the Regular Army as Company C, 61st Infantry. Organized 10 June 1917 at Gettysburg National Park, Pennsylvania. (61st Infantry assigned 17 November 1917 to the 5th Division.) Inactivated 2 September 1921 at Camp Jackson, South Carolina. (61st Infantry relieved 15 August 1927 from assignment to the 5th Division and assigned to the 8th Division; relieved 1 October 1933 from assignment to the 8th Division and assigned to the 5th Division; relieved 16 October 1939 from assignment to the 5th Division.) Disbanded 11 November 1944.

Reconstituted 10 August 1950 in the Regular Army as an element of the 8th Infantry Division. Activated 17 August 1950 at Fort Jackson, South Carolina. Inactivated 1 September 1956 at Fort Carson, Colorado (61st Infantry concurrently relieved from assignment to the 8th Infantry Division).

Redesignated 17 January 1962 as Headquarters and Headquarters Company, 3d Battalion, 61st Infantry. Activated 15 November 1969 at Fort Carson, Colorado, as an element of the 5th Infantry Division (organic elements concurrently constituted and activated). Inactivated 15 December 1970 at Fort Carson, Colorado.

CAMPAIGN PARTICIPATION CREDIT

World War I
  *St. Mihiel
  *Meuse-Argonne
  *Alsace 1918
  *Lorraine 1918

DECORATIONS

None.

61st Infantry, Bibliography

A History of the Sixty-First Infantry, World War, 1917–18–19. n.p., 1919.

75th INFANTRY
(Merrill's Marauders)

HERALDIC ITEMS

COAT OF ARMS

Shield: Quarterly azure and vert, between in the first and fourth quarters a radiant sun of twelve points and a mullet argent, a lightning flash couped bendsinisterwise gules fimbriated or.

Crest: None.

Motto: *Sua Sponte* (Of Their Own Accord).

Symbolism: The colors blue, white, red, and green represent four of the original six combat teams of the 5307th Composite Unit (Provisional), commonly referred to as "Merrill's Marauders," which were identified by color. (To avoid confusion, the other two colors, khaki and orange, were not represented in the design.) The unit's close co-operation with the Chinese forces in the China-Burma-India Theater is represented by the sun symbol from the Chinese flag. The white star represents the Star of Burma, the country in which the Marauders campaigned during World War II. The lightning bolt is symbolic of the strike characteristics of the Marauders' behind the line activities.

DISTINCTIVE INSIGNIA

The distinctive insignia is the shield of the coat of arms.

LINEAGE AND HONORS

LINEAGE

Organized 3 October 1943 in the Army of the United States in the China-Burma-India Theater of Operations as the 5307th Composite Unit (Provisional). Consolidated 10 August 1944 with the 475th Infantry (constituted 25 May 1944) and consolidated unit designated as the 475th Infantry. Inactivated 1 July 1945 in China.

Redesignated 21 June 1954 as the 75th Infantry. Allotted 26 October 1954 to the Regular Army. Activated 20 November 1954 on Okinawa. Inactivated 21 March 1956 on Okinawa.

Reorganized 1 January 1969 as a parent regiment under the Combat Arms Regimental System.

Company A activated 21 February 1969 at Fort Benning, Georgia. Company B activated 10 February 1969 at Fort Carson, Colorado. Company C activated 1 February 1969 in Vietnam. Company D activated 20 November 1969 in Vietnam; inactivated 10 April 1970 in Vietnam. Company E activated 1 February 1969 in Vietnam; inactivated 23 August 1969 at Fort Lewis, Washington; activated 1 October 1969 in Vietnam; inactivated 12 October 1970 in Vietnam. Company F activated 1 February 1969 in Vietnam. Company G activated 1 February 1969 in Vietnam.

Company H activated 1 February 1969 in Vietnam. Company I activated 1 February 1969 in Vietnam; inactivated 7 April 1970 in Vietnam. Company K activated 1 February 1969 in Vietnam; inactivated 10 December 1970 in Vietnam. Company L activated 1 February 1969 in Vietnam. Company M activated 1 February 1969 in Vietnam; inactivated 12 October 1970 in Vietnam. Company N activated 1 February 1969 in Vietnam. Company O activated 1 February 1969 in Vietnam; inactivated 20 November 1969 in Vietnam; activated 4 August 1970 in Alaska. Company P activated 1 February 1969 in Vietnam.

CAMPAIGN PARTICIPATION CREDIT

World War II
  India-Burma
  Central Burma

Vietnam
  (to be determined)

DECORATIONS

Presidential Unit Citation (Army), Streamer embroidered MYITKYINA (5307th Composite Unit cited; WD GO 54, 1944, as amended by WD GO 86, 1944)

Valorous Unit Award, Streamer embroidered BINH DUONG PROVINCE (Company F, 75th Infantry cited; DA GO 39, 1970, as amended by DA GO 2, 1971)

Valorous Unit Award, Streamer embroidered THUA THIEN–QUANG TRI (Company L, 75th Infantry cited; DA GO 48, 1971)

Meritorious Unit Commendation, Streamer embroidered VIETNAM 1969 (Company G, 75th Infantry cited; DA GO 53, 1970)

Meritorious Unit Commendation, Streamer embroidered VIETNAM 1969–1970 (Company M, 75th Infantry cited; DA GO 50, 1971)

Company E additionally entitled to: Vietnamese Cross of Gallantry with Palm, Streamer embroidered VIETNAM 1969 (Company F, 75th Infantry cited; DA GO 59, 1969, as amended by DA GO 53, 1970) ; Vietnamese Civil Action Honor Medal, First Class, Streamer embroidered VIETNAM 1969 (Company E, 75th Infantry cited; DA GO 59, 1969, as amended by DA GO 53, 1970)

Company F additionally entitled to: Vietnamese Cross of Gallantry with Palm, Streamer embroidered VIETNAM 1969 (Company F, 75th Infantry cited; DA GO 43, 1970, as amended by DA GO 48, 1971)

Company H additionally entitled to: Vietnamese Cross of Gallantry with Palm, Streamer embroidered VIETNAM 1969 (Company H, 75th Infantry cited; DA GO 59, 1969, as amended by DA GO 53, 1970)

Company I additionally entitled to: Vietnamese Civil Action Honor Medal, First Class, Streamer embroidered VIETNAM 1969–1970 (Company I, 75th Infantry cited; DA GO 53, 1970)

Company K additionally entitled to: Vietnamese Cross of Gallantry with Palm, Streamer embroidered VIETNAM 1969 (Company K, 75th Infantry cited; DA GO 3, 1970) ; Vietnamese Civil Action Honor Medal, First Class, Streamer embroidered VIETNAM 1969 (Company K, 75th Infantry cited; DA GO 53, 1970)

Company L additionally entitled to: Vietnamese Cross of Gallantry with Palm, Streamer embroidered VIETNAM 1969 (Company L, 75th Infantry cited; DA GO 43, 1970)

Company O additionally entitled to: Vietnamese Cross of Gallantry with Palm, Streamer embroidered VIETNAM 1969 (Company O, 75th Infantry cited; DA GO 43, 1970)

75TH INFANTRY, BIBLIOGRAPHY

Anders, Leslie. *The Ledo Road*. Norman: University of Oklahoma Press, 1965.

A Brief History of the 75th Infantry Regiment (Merrill's Marauders). Tokyo, 1954.

Connery, George. "The Inside Story of Merrill's Marauders in the Burma Jungle," *The Washington Post* (September 1944).

Eldridge, Fred. *Wrath in Burma*. Garden City: Doubleday and Company, 1946.

Historical Section, War Department. *Merrill's Marauders*. American Forces in Action Series. Washington: Government Printing Office, 1945.

Hunter, Charles N. *Galahad*. San Antonio, Texas: The Naylor Publishing Company, 1963.

Merrill, Frank D. "The War in the CBI," *Queen of Battles! Your Ground Forces in Action*, edited by Clary Thompson. New York: William H. Wise and Company, Inc., 1949.

Ogburn, Charlton, Jr. *The Marauders*. New York: Harper and Brothers, 1959.

————. "Merrill's Marauders," *Harper's Magazine*, CXCIV (January 1947), 29ff.

Randolph, John Hayward. *Marsmen in Burma*. Houston, Texas, 1946.

Romanus, Charles F. and Riley Sunderland. *Stilwell's Command Problems*. United States Army in World War II. Washington: Government Printing Office, 1956.

————. *Stilwell's Mission to China*. United States Army in World War II. Washington: Government Printing Office, 1953.

————. *Time Runs Out in CBI*. United States Army in World War II. Washington: Government Printing Office, 1960.

Stone, James H. "The Marauders and the Microbes," *Infantry Journal*, LXIV (March 1949), 4–11.

87th INFANTRY

Heraldic Items

Coat of Arms

Shield: Azure, on a mountain issuant from base argent, an ice axe and ski pole saltirewise points down proper, in base a horseshoe inverted gules.

Crest: On a wreath argent and azure rising from a castle tower of three battlements gules masoned or charged with a fountain, a demi-catamountain proper supporting a lance of the fourth with a split pennon parted fesswise of vert, of the first and of the third.

Motto: *Vires Montesque Vincimus* (We Conquer Power and Mountains).

Symbolism: The shield bears a snow capped mountain to represent both the region where the organization first received its specialized training and the normal home of mountain troops. The crossed ski pole and ice axe are symbolic of the tools used by mountain troops, while the horseshoe indicates the pack element of the organization. The fact that the 87th Infantry was the first organization of its kind is indicated by the single red horseshoe.

The red castle tower is reminiscent of the battle of Castel d'Aiano in Northern Italy, a bloody struggle against prepared positions, rough terrain, heavily mined areas, and enemy artillery fire; its three battlements stand for campaigns in the Aleutians, North Apennines, and Po Valley. The fountain (wavy white and blue-striped disc) represents the crossing of the Po River which brought the 87th to the foothills of the Alps. The catamountain or wildcat personifies the fighting spirit, cunning, and aggressiveness of the mountain infantry, and the lance and pennant allude to the arms of the province of Bologna where the unit emerged after fighting its way out of the Apennine Mountains.

425-618 O - 72 - 50

DISTINCTIVE INSIGNIA

The distinctive insignia is the shield and motto of the coat of arms.

LINEAGE AND HONORS

LINEAGE

Constituted 15 November 1941 in the Army of the United States as the 87th Infantry Mountain Regiment; concurrently, 1st Battalion activated at Fort Lewis, Washington. Redesignated 12 May 1942 as the 87th Mountain Infantry. Regiment (less 1st Battalion) activated 25 May 1942 at Fort Lewis, Washington. Reorganized and redesignated 22 February 1944 as the 87th Infantry and assigned to the 10th Light Division (later redesignated as the 10th Infantry Division). Reorganized and redesignated 6 November 1944 as the 87th Mountain Infantry. Inactivated 21 November 1945 at Camp Carson, Colorado. Redesignated 18 June 1948 as the 87th Infantry. Allotted 25 June 1948 to the Regular Army. Activated 1 July 1948 at Fort Riley, Kansas.

Relieved 1 July 1957 from assignment to the 10th Infantry Division and reorganized as a parent regiment under the Combat Arms Regimental System.

CAMPAIGN PARTICIPATION CREDIT

World War II	*Vietnam*
Aleutian Islands	Counteroffensive, Phase II
North Apennines	Counteroffensive, Phase III
Po Valley	Tet Counteroffensive
	(other campaigns to be determined)

DECORATIONS

Meritorious Unit Commendation, Streamer embroidered SAIGON AREA 1966–1967 (Company C, 87th Infantry cited; DA GO 17, 1968)

Meritorious Unit Commendation, Streamer embroidered VIETNAM 1967 (Company D, 87th Infantry cited; DA GO 54, 1968)

Meritorious Unit Commendation, Streamer embroidered VIETNAM 1967–1968 (Company C, 87th Infantry cited; DA GO 48, 1969)

Meritorious Unit Commendation, Streamer embroidered VIETNAM 1968 (Company D, 87th Infantry cited; DA GO 39, 1970)

1st BATTALION, 87th INFANTRY

RA
(8th Infantry Division)

LINEAGE

Constituted 15 November 1941 in the Army of the United States as Company A, 87th Infantry Mountain Regiment and activated at Fort Lewis, Washington. Redesignated 12 May 1942 as Company A, 87th Mountain Infantry. Reorganized and redesignated 22 February 1944 as Company A, 87th Infantry, an element of the 10th Light Division (later redesignated as the 10th Infantry Division). Reorganized and redesignated 6 November 1944 as Company A, 87th Mountain Infantry. Inactivated 21 November 1945 at Camp Carson, Colorado. Redesignated 18 June 1948 as Company A, 87th Infantry. Allotted 25 June 1948 to the Regular Army. Activated 1 July 1948 at Fort Riley, Kansas.

Reorganized and redesignated 1 July 1957 as Headquarters and Headquarters Company, 1st Battle Group, 87th Infantry and remained assigned to the 10th Infantry Division (organic elements concurrently constituted and activated). Relieved 14 June 1958 from assignment to the 10th Infantry Division and assigned to the 2d Infantry Division. Reorganized and redesignated 15 February 1963 as the 1st Battalion, 87th Infantry. Relieved 4 September 1963 from assignment to the 2d Infantry Division and assigned to the 8th Infantry Division.

CAMPAIGN PARTICIPATION CREDIT

World War II
 *Aleutian Islands
 *North Apennines
 *Po Valley

DECORATIONS

None.

2d BATTALION, 87th INFANTRY

RA
(inactive)

LINEAGE

Constituted 15 November 1941 in the Army of the United States as Company B, 87th Infantry Mountain Regiment and activated at Fort Lewis, Washington. Redesignated 12 May 1942 as Company B, 87th Mountain Infantry. Reorganized and redesignated 22 February 1944 as Company B, 87th Infantry, an element of the 10th Light Division (later redesignated as the 10th Infantry Division). Reorganized and redesignated 6 November 1944 as Company B, 87th Mountain Infantry. Inactivated 21 November 1945 at Camp Carson, Colorado. Redesignated 18 June 1948 as Company B, 87th Infantry. Allotted 25 June 1948 to the Regular Army. Activated 1 July 1948 at Fort Riley, Kansas.

Inactivated 1 July 1957 in Germany and relieved from assignment to the 10th Infantry Division; concurrently, redesignated as Headquarters and Headquarters Company, 2d Battle Group, 87th Infantry. Redesignated 25 January 1963 as Headquarters and Headquarters Company, 2d Battalion, 87th Infantry and assigned to the 2d Infantry Division (organic elements concurrently constituted). Battalion activated 15 February 1963 at Fort Benning, Georgia. Relieved 4 September 1963 from assignment to the 2d Infantry Division and assigned to the 8th Infantry Division. Inactivated 1 May 1966 in Germany.

CAMPAIGN PARTICIPATION CREDIT

World War II
  *Aleutian Islands
  *North Apennines
  *Po Valley

DECORATIONS
None.

768

COMPANY C, 87th INFANTRY

RA
(nondivisional)

LINEAGE

Constituted 15 November 1941 in the Army of the United States as Company C, 87th Infantry Mountain Regiment, and activated at Fort Lewis, Washington. Redesignated 12 May 1942 as Company C, 87th Mountain Infantry. Reorganized and redesignated 22 February 1944 as Company C, 87th Infantry, an element of the 10th Light Division (later redesignated as the 10th Infantry Division). Reorganized and redesignated 6 November 1944 as Company C, 87th Mountain Infantry. Inactivated 21 November 1945 at Camp Carson, Colorado. Redesignated 18 June 1948 as Company C, 87th Infantry. Allotted 25 June 1948 to the Regular Army. Activated 1 July 1948 at Fort Riley, Kansas.

Inactivated 1 July 1957 in Germany and relieved from assignment to the 10th Infantry Division; concurrently, redesignated as Headquarters and Headquarters Company, 3d Battle Group, 87th Infantry. Redesignated 23 March 1966 as Company C, 87th Infantry. Activated 1 June 1966 at Fort Lewis, Washington.

CAMPAIGN PARTICIPATION CREDIT

World War II-AP
 Aleutian Islands

World War II-EAME
 North Apennines
 Po Valley

Vietnam
 Counteroffensive, Phase II
 Counteroffensive, Phase III
 Tet Counteroffensive
 (other campaigns to be determined)

DECORATIONS

Meritorious Unit Commendation, Streamer embroidered SAIGON AREA 1966–1967 (Company C, 87th Infantry cited; DA GO 17, 1968)

Meritorious Unit Commendation, Streamer embroidered VIETNAM 1967–1968 (Company C, 87th Infantry cited; DA GO 48, 1969)

COMPANY D, 87th INFANTRY

RA
(inactive)

Constituted 15 November 1941 in the Army of the United States as Company D, 87th Infantry Mountain Regiment and activated at Fort Lewis, Washington. Redesignated 12 May 1942 as Company D, 87th Mountain Infantry. Absorbed 22 February 1944 by the regiment (87th Mountain Infantry concurrently reorganized and redesignated as the 87th Infantry and assigned to the 10th Light Division [later redesignated as the 10th Infantry Division]). Company D, 87th Mountain Infantry reorganized 6 November 1944 at Camp Swift, Texas (87th Infantry concurrently reorganized and redesignated as the 87th Mountain Infantry). Inactivated 21 November 1945 at Camp Carson, Colorado. Redesignated 18 June 1948 as Company D, 87th Infantry. Allotted 25 June 1948 to the Regular Army. Activated 1 July 1948 at Fort Riley, Kansas.

Inactivated 1 July 1957 in Germany and relieved from assignment to the 10th Infantry Division; concurrently, redesignated as Headquarters and Headquarters Company, 4th Battle Group, 87th Infantry. Redesignated 23 March 1966 as Company D, 87th Infantry. Activated 1 June 1966 at Fort Lewis, Washington. Inactivated 8 November 1969 in Vietnam.

CAMPAIGN PARTICIPATION CREDIT

World War II-AP
Aleutian Islands

World War II-EAME
North Apennines
Po Valley

Vietnam
Counteroffensive, Phase II
Counteroffensive, Phase III
Tet Counteroffensive,
(other campaigns to be determined)

DECORATIONS

Meritorious Unit Commendation, Streamer embroidered VIETNAM 1967 (Company D, 87th Infantry cited; DA GO 54, 1968)

Meritorious Unit Commendation, Streamer embroidered VIETNAM 1968 (Company D, 87th Infantry cited; DA GO 39, 1970)

770

87th Infantry, Bibliography

Earle, George F. *History of the 87th Mountain Infantry, Italy, 1945.* Denver: Bradford Robinson Printing Company, 1947?

Jay, John C. *History of the Mountain Training Center.* Army Ground Forces Study Number 24. Washington: Government Printing Office, 1948.

Jones, Alexander. *A Short History of Company "I", 87th Mountain Infantry, 10th Mountain Division.* Colorado Springs, 1945.

Lockwood, Theodore *et. al. Mountaineers.* Denver: Artcraft Press, 1945?

Rocker, Richard A. *This Was Italy, With the 87th Mountain Infantry, 10th Mountain Division.* Denver, 1946.

Templeton, Kenneth S. *America's Ski Troops.* Chicago, 1945.

187th INFANTRY

(Rakkasans)

HERALDIC ITEMS

COAT OF ARMS

Shield: Azure, on a pale nebuly argent a double handed sword erect gules.

Crest: On a wreath argent and azure between a Japanese city symbol gules and a mullet of seven points per fess wavy of the last and of the second, a sea lion or charged on the shoulder with a heart purpure and holding in his dexter paw a sword bendwise of the first with hilt and pommel of the fourth the blade notched three times to base of the third.

Motto: *Ne Desit Virtus* (Let Valor Not Fail).

Symbolism: The blue is for the infantry. The partition line of the pale representing clouds and the double handed sword, an ancient infantry weapon, symbolize the character of the organization as an airborne infantry unit.

The golden sea lion, adapted from the seal of the President of the Philippines, represents the award of the Philippine Presidential Unit Citation. The heart on the lion's shoulder points out the action on Purple Heart Hill. The winged sword with three notches in the blade signifies the unit's amphibious assault landing in the Philippines and its two combat jumps in Korea. The red diamond shape is the insignia of the city of Yokohama, Japan, where the 187th began four years of occupation duty. The seven-pointed star, divided in the manner of the Korean Tae-Guk, stands for the unit's participation in the Korean War.

DISTINCTIVE INSIGNIA

The distinctive insignia is the shield and motto of the coat of arms.

LINEAGE AND HONORS

LINEAGE

Constituted 12 November 1942 in the Army of the United States as the 187th Glider Infantry. Activated 25 February 1943 at Camp Mackall, North Carolina, as an element of the 11th Airborne Division. Allotted 15 November 1948 to the Regular Army. Reorganized and redesignated 30 June 1949 as the 187th Airborne Infantry. Relieved 1 February 1951 from assignment to the 11th Airborne Division. Assigned 1 July 1956 to the 101st Airborne Division.

Relieved 25 April 1957 from assignment to the 101st Airborne Division; concurrently, reorganized and redesignated as the 187th Infantry, a parent regiment under the Combat Arms Regimental System.

CAMPAIGN PARTICIPATION CREDIT

World War II
New Guinea
Leyte
Luzon (with arrowhead)

Korean War
UN offensive (with arrowhead)
CCF intervention
First UN counteroffensive
  (with arrowhead)

CCF spring offensive
Korea, summer-fall 1952
Korea, summer 1953

Vietnam
Counteroffensive, Phase III
Tet Counteroffensive
(other campaigns to be determined)

DECORATIONS

Presidential Unit Citation (Army), Streamer embroidered TAGAYTAY RIDGE (1st Battalion, 187th Glider Infantry cited; WD GO 68, 1945)

Presidential Unit Citation (Army), Streamer embroidered SUKCHON (3d Battalion, 187th Airborne Infantry and attached units cited; DA GO 36, 1951)

Presidential Unit Citation (Navy), Streamer embroidered INCHON (3d Battalion, 187th Airborne Infantry cited; DA GO 63, 1952)

Valorous Unit Award, Streamer embroidered THUA THIEN PROVINCE (3d Battalion, 187th Infantry cited; DA GO 2, 1971)

Philippine Presidential Unit Citation, Streamer embroidered 17 OCTOBER 1944 TO 4 JULY 1945 (187th Glider Infantry cited; DA GO 47, 1950)

Republic of Korea Presidential Unit Citation, Streamer embroidered KOREA 1950–1952 (187th Airborne Infantry cited; DA GO 33, 1953, as amended by DA GO 41, 1955)

Republic of Korea Presidential Unit Citation, Streamer embroidered KOREA 1952–1953 (187th Airborne Infantry cited; DA GO 23, 1954)

1st BATTALION, 187th INFANTRY

(Rakkasans)

RA
(inactive)

LINEAGE

Constituted 12 November 1942 in the Army of the United States as Company A, 187th Glider Infantry. Activated 25 February 1943 at Camp Mackall, North Carolina, as an element of the 11th Airborne Division. Allotted 15 November 1948 to the Regular Army. Reorganized and redesignated 30 June 1949 as Company A, 187th Airborne Infantry. (187th Airborne Infantry relieved 1 February 1951 from assignment to the 11th Airborne Division; assigned 1 July 1956 to the 101st Airborne Division.)

Reorganized and redesignated 1 March 1957 as Headquarters and Headquarters Company, 1st Airborne Battle Group, 187th Infantry, relieved from assignment to the 101st Airborne Division, and assigned to the 11th Airborne Division (organic elements concurrently constituted and activated). Relieved 1 July 1958 from assignment to the 11th Airborne Division and assigned to the 24th Infantry Division. Relieved 8 February 1959 from assignment to the 24th Infantry Division and assigned to the 82d Airborne Division. Relieved 6 March 1964 from assignment to the 82d Airborne Division.

Inactivated 25 May 1964 at Fort Bragg, North Carolina; concurrently, consolidated with the 1st Battalion, 187th Infantry (constituted and activated 1 February 1964 at Fort Benning, Georgia, as an element of the 11th Air Assault Division) and consolidated unit designated as the 1st Battalion, 187th Infantry, an element of the 11th Air Assault Division. Inactivated 30 June 1965 at Fort Benning, Georgia.

CAMPAIGN PARTICIPATION CREDIT

World War II
  *New Guinea
  *Leyte
  *Luzon (with arrowhead)

Korean War
  *UN offensive (with arrowhead)

*CCF intervention
*First UN counteroffensive
  (with arrowhead)
*CCF spring offensive
*Korea, summer-fall 1952
*Korea, summer 1953

DECORATIONS

*Presidential Unit Citation (Army), Streamer embroidered TAGAY-
TAY RIDGE (1st Battalion, 187th Glider Infantry cited; WD GO 68, 1945)

Presidential Unit Citation (Army), Streamer embroidered SUKCHON

Presidential Unit Citation (Navy), Streamer embroidered INCHON

*Philippine Presidential Unit Citation, Streamer embroidered 17
OCTOBER 1944 TO 4 JULY 1945 (187th Glider Infantry cited; DA GO 47,
1950)

*Republic of Korea Presidential Unit Citation, Streamer embroidered
KOREA 1950–1952 (187th Airborne Infantry cited; DA GO 33, 1953, as
amended by DA GO 41, 1955)

*Republic of Korea Presidential Unit Citation, Streamer embroidered
KOREA 1952–1953 (187th Airborne Infantry cited; DA GO 23, 1954)

2d AIRBORNE BATTLE GROUP, 187th INFANTRY

(Rakkasans)

RA
(inactive)

LINEAGE

Constituted 12 November 1942 in the Army of the United States as Company B, 187th Glider Infantry. Activated 25 February 1943 at Camp Mackall, North Carolina, as an element of the 11th Airborne Division. Allotted 15 November 1948 to the Regular Army. Reorganized and redesignated 30 June 1949 as Company B, 187th Airborne Infantry. (187th Airborne Infantry relieved 1 February 1951 from assignment to the 11th Airborne Division; assigned 1 July 1956 to the 101st Airborne Division.)

Reorganized and redesignated 25 April 1957 as Headquarters and Headquarters Company, 2d Airborne Battle Group, 187th Infantry and remained assigned to the 101st Airborne Division (organic elements concurrently constituted and activated). Relieved 1 February 1964 from assignment to the 101st Airborne Division. Inactivated 3 February 1964 at Fort Campbell, Kentucky.

CAMPAIGN PARTICIPATION CREDIT

World War II
  *New Guinea
  *Leyte
  *Luzon (with arrowhead)

Korean War
  *UN offensive (with arrowhead)

*CCF intervention
*First UN counteroffensive
  (with arrowhead)
*CCF spring offensive
*Korea, summer-fall 1952
*Korea, summer 1953

DECORATIONS

*Presidential Unit Citation (Army), Streamer embroidered TAGAY-TAY RIDGE (1st Battalion, 187th Glider Infantry cited; WD GO 68, 1945)

Presidential Unit Citation (Army), Streamer embroidered SUKCHON

Presidential Unit Citation (Navy), Streamer embroidered INCHON

*Philippine Presidential Unit Citation, Streamer embroidered 17 OCTOBER 1944 TO 4 JULY 1945 (187th Glider Infantry cited; DA GO 47, 1950)

*Republic of Korea Presidential Unit Citation, Streamer embroidered

KOREA 1950–1952 (187th Airborne Infantry cited; DA GO 33, 1953, as amended by DA GO 41, 1955)

*Republic of Korea Presidential Unit Citation, Streamer embroidered KOREA 1952–1953 (187th Airborne Infantry cited; DA GO 23, 1954)

3d BATTALION, 187th INFANTRY

(Rakkasans)

RA
(101st Airborne Division)

LINEAGE

Constituted 12 November 1942 in the Army of the United States as Company C, 187th Glider Infantry. Activated 25 February 1943 at Camp Mackall, North Carolina, as an element of the 11th Airborne Division. Allotted 15 November 1948 to the Regular Army. Reorganized and redesignated 30 June 1949 as Company C, 187th Airborne Infantry. (187th Airborne Infantry relieved 1 February 1951 from assignment to the 11th Airborne Division; assigned 1 July 1956 to the 101st Airborne Division.)

Inactivated 25 April 1957 at Fort Campbell, Kentucky, and relieved from assignment to the 101st Airborne Division; concurrently, redesignated as Headquarters and Headquarters Company, 3d Airborne Battle Group, 187th Infantry. Redesignated 1 February 1963 as Headquarters and Headquarters Company, 3d Battalion, 187th Infantry and assigned to the 11th Air Assault Division (organic elements concurrently constituted). Battalion activated 7 February 1963 at Fort Benning, Georgia. Relieved 1 February 1964 from assignment to the 11th Air Assault Division and assigned to the 101st Airborne Division.

CAMPAIGN PARTICIPATION CREDIT

World War II
  *New Guinea
  *Leyte
  *Luzon (with arrowhead)

Korean War
  *UN offensive (with arrowhead)
  *CCF intervention
  *First UN counteroffensive
    (with arrowhead)

*CCF spring offensive
*Korea, summer-fall 1952
*Korea, summer 1953

Vietnam
  *Counteroffensive, Phase III
  *Tet Counteroffensive
    (other campaigns to be determined)

DECORATIONS

*Presidential Unit Citation (Army), Streamer embroidered TAGAY-TAY RIDGE (1st Battalion, 187th Glider Infantry cited; WD GO 68, 1945)

779

Presidential Unit Citation (Army), Streamer embroidered SUKCHON
Presidential Unit Citation (Navy), Streamer embroidered INCHON
*Valorous Unit Award, Streamer embroidered THUA THIEN PROVINCE
(3d Battalion, 187th Infantry cited; DA GO 2, 1971)
*Philippine Presidential Unit Citation, Streamer embroidered 17
OCTOBER 1944 TO 4 JULY 1945 (187th Glider Infantry cited; DA GO 47,
1950)
*Republic of Korea Presidential Unit Citation, Streamer embroidered
KOREA 1950–1952 (187th Airborne Infantry cited; DA GO 33, 1953, as
amended by DA GO 41, 1955)
*Republic of Korea Presidential Unit Citation, Streamer embroidered
KOREA 1952–1953 (187th Airborne Infantry cited; DA GO 23, 1954)
*Vietnamese Cross of Gallantry with Palm, Streamer embroidered
VIETNAM 1968–1969 (3d Battalion, 187th Infantry cited; DA GO 43,
1970)

187TH INFANTRY, BIBLIOGRAPHY

"Airborne and Armor Linkup in Korea," *Life,* XXX (9 April 1951), 29–35.

Appleman, Roy E. *South to the Naktong, North to the Yalu.* United States Army in World War II. Washington: Government Printing Office, 1961.

Branch, Harlee. "Combat is Six," *Paraglide* (1 October 1954).

Cannon, M. Hamlin. *Leyte: The Return to the Philippines.* United States Army in World War II. Washington: Government Printing Office, 1954.

Deal, E. Lafayette. "Defense of the Low Ground," *Combat Forces Journal,* II (July 1952), 18–21.

Gugeler, Russell A. *Combat Actions in Korea.* Washington: Combat Forces Press, 1954.

Haggerty, James J. "Korea," *Pegasus,* XVII (November 1951).

Hermes, Walter G. *Truce Tent and Fighting Front.* United States Army in the Korean War. Washington: Government Printing Office, 1966.

Key, William G. "Combat Cargo—Korea '50–'51," *Pegasus,* XVII (November 1951).

"Koje Island in Perspective," *Combat Forces Journal,* III (August 1952), 24–25.

"Official Reports Describing the Day's Operations in Korea," *New York Times* (30 October 1950).

187th Airborne Infantry Regiment, 1950. Baton Rouge: Army and Navy Publishing Company, 1950.

187th Airborne Regimental Combat Team, 5th Anniversary Issue, 28 August 1954 to 27 August 1955. Beppu, Kyushu: Morizawa Printing Company, 1955.

187th Airborne RCT, The Year in Review, 1953–1954, Fourth Anniversary, Korea, Japan, Okinawa. Beppu, Kyushu: Morizawa Printing Company, Ltd., 1954.

Outline History of the 187th Airborne Regimental Combat Team. Korea, 1953.

"Rakkasans." n.p., 1956.

Smith, Robert Ross. *Triumph in the Philippines.* United States Army in World War II. Washington: Government Printing Office, 1963.

Sochurek, Howard. "Camera Records a Combat Jump," *Life,* XXIX (6 November 1950), 36–38.

Welcome to the 187th ABN RCT, Japan. Beppu, Kyushu: Morizawa Printing Company, Ltd., 1953.

188th INFANTRY

HERALDIC ITEMS

COAT OF ARMS

Shield: Azure, an eagle's wing displayed with armored sword hand argent grasping a short sword or point in dexter base severing a bendlet of chains debased of the second, and charged on the pinion with three torteaux, two and one.

Crest: On a wreath argent and azure a mount gules in base behind a sun of eight rays or surmounted in pale by an arrowhead of the second charged with an escallop of the first.

Motto: Winged Attack.

Symbolism: The principal colors of the shield are the present and old colors of infantry. The eagle's wing is symbolic of the method of vertical attack and striking power of the airborne forces. The golden sword of freedom severing the chain is symbolic of the organization's participation in the liberation of 2000 prisoners of war at the Los Baños prison camp in Luzon, Philippine Islands. The three red roundels (torteaux) on the wing represent the organization's three campaigns: New Guinea, Luzon, and Leyte.

The golden sun, adapted from the Philippine Presidential Seal, represents the award of the Philippine Presidential Unit Citation. The blue arrowhead bearing a scallop shell denotes the unit's participation in the amphibious assault landing on Nasugbu Point, Luzon. This unit's claim to the first landing in Japan (at Atsugi Airfield) is symbolized by the red mountain.

DISTINCTIVE INSIGNIA

The distinctive insignia is the shield and motto of the coat of arms.

783

Lineage and Honors

Lineage

Constituted 12 November 1942 in the Army of the United States as the 188th Glider Infantry. Activated 25 February 1943 at Camp Mackall, North Carolina, as an element of the 11th Airborne Division. Reorganized and redesignated 20 July 1945 as the 188th Parachute Infantry. Allotted 15 November 1948 to the Regular Army. Redesignated 30 June 1949 as the 188th Airborne Infantry; concurrently, inactivated at Camp Campbell, Kentucky. Activated 16 November 1950 at Fort Campbell, Kentucky. Inactivated 1 March 1957 in Germany and relieved from assignment to the 11th Airborne Division.

Reorganized and redesignated 15 May 1963 as the 188th Infantry, a parent regiment under the Combat Arms Regimental System.

Campaign Participation Credit

World War II
   New Guinea
   Leyte
   Luzon (with arrowhead)

Decorations

Presidential Unit Citation (Army), Streamer embroidered LUZON (Regimental Headquarters and Headquarters Company and 1st and 2d Battalions, 188th Infantry cited; WD GO 68, 1945)

Philippine Presidential Unit Citation, Streamer embroidered 17 OCTOBER 1944 TO 4 JULY 1945 (188th Glider Infantry cited; DA GO 47, 1950)

1st BATTALION, 188th INFANTRY

RA
(inactive)

LINEAGE

Constituted 12 November 1942 in the Army of the United States as Company A, 188th Glider Infantry. Activated 25 February 1943 at Camp Mackall, North Carolina, as an element of the 11th Airborne Division. Reorganized and redesignated 20 July 1945 as Company A, 188th Parachute Infantry. Allotted 15 November 1948 to the Regular Army. Redesignated 30 June 1949 as Company A, 188th Airborne Infantry; concurrently, inactivated at Camp Campbell, Kentucky. Activated 16 November 1950 at Fort Campbell, Kentucky. Inactivated 1 March 1957 in Germany (188th Airborne Infantry concurrently relieved from assignment to the 11th Airborne Division).

Redesignated 17 July 1963 as Headquarters and Headquarters Company, 1st Battalion, 188th Infantry and assigned to the 11th Air Assault Division (organic elements concurrently constituted). Battalion activated 18 July 1963 at Fort Benning, Georgia. Inactivated 30 June 1965 at Fort Benning, Georgia.

CAMPAIGN PARTICIPATION CREDIT

World War II
  *New Guinea
  *Leyte
  *Luzon (with arrowhead)

DECORATIONS

*Presidential Unit Citation (Army), Streamer embroidered LUZON (1st Battalion, 188th Glider Infantry cited; WD GO 68, 1945)

*Philippine Presidential Unit Citation, Streamer embroidered 17 OCTOBER 1944 TO 4 JULY 1945 (188th Glider Infantry cited; DA GO 47, 1950)

785

COMPANY E, 188th INFANTRY

RA
(inactive)

LINEAGE

Constituted 12 November 1942 in the Army of the United States as Company E, 188th Glider Infantry. Activated 25 February 1943 at Camp Mackall, North Carolina, as an element of the 11th Airborne Division. Reorganized and redesignated 20 July 1945 as Company E, 188th Parachute Infantry. Allotted 15 November 1948 to the Regular Army. Redesignated 30 June 1949 as Company E, 188th Airborne Infantry; concurrently, inactivated at Camp Campbell, Kentucky. Activated 16 November 1950 at Fort Campbell, Kentucky. Inactivated 1 March 1957 in Germany (188th Airborne Infantry concurrently relieved from assignment to the 11th Airborne Division).

Redesignated 15 May 1963 as Headquarters and Headquarters Company, 4th Battalion, 188th Infantry. Redesignated 25 August 1965 as Company E, 188th Infantry. Activated 2 November 1965 at Fort Benning, Georgia. Inactivated 16 November 1965 at Fort Benning, Georgia.

CAMPAIGN PARTICIPATION CREDIT

World War II
   New Guinea
   Leyte
   Luzon (with arrowhead)

DECORATIONS

Presidential Unit Citation (Army), Streamer embroidered LUZON (2d Battalion, 188th Glider Infantry cited; WD GO 68, 1945)

Philippine Presidential Unit Citation, Streamer embroidered 17 OCTOBER 1944 TO 4 JULY 1945 (188th Glider Infantry cited; DA GO 47, 1950)

786

188TH INFANTRY, BIBLIOGRAPHY

Smith, Robert Ross. *Triumph in the Philippines.* United States Army in World War II. Washington: Government Printing Office, 1963.

325th INFANTRY

HERALDIC ITEMS

COAT OF ARMS

Shield: Argent, a fess azure between in chief a hurt charged with the three-columned temple of Georgia of the first and in base a Lorraine cross of the second.

Crest: On a wreath of the colors a pair of wings conjoined in lure argent, the dexter charged with an estoile gules and the sinister with a lion rampant of the like, a trident palewise vert, the staff surmounted by a truncated pyramid of the first, charged with a linden leaf of the fourth.

Motto: Let's Go.

Symbolism: The shield is white with a blue fess, the old and present infantry colors. The blue disc is from the shoulder sleeve insignia of the 82d Division and the white temple is from the seal of the state of Georgia. The blue Lorraine cross indicates the service of the regiment in World War I in the province of that name.

As the 325th Infantry was a glider unit during World War II, the wings are an adaption of those used on the Glider Qualification Badge. The red six-pointed star (from the arms of Cherbourg) alludes to the glider landing on the Cherbourg Peninsula and, with the red erect lion, to the glider landing at Nijmegen in the Netherlands. The trident alludes to Operation NEPTUNE which launched the invasion of Normandy, and the three tines of the trident refer to North Africa and action in Sicily and Italy prior to the Normandy assault. The truncated pyramid simulates a type of tank obstacle (dragon's tooth) which protected the Siegfried Line, the linden leaf alluding to the fact that the regiment pierced and overran its defenses. (According to Teutonic mythology, Siegfried bathed in the blood of the dragon, Fafnir, and as a result was said to be invulnerable; only between the shoulders where a leaf had settled could

789

he be overcome and killed.) The linden leaf also refers to the subsequent occupation of Berlin.

DISTINCTIVE INSIGNIA

The distinctive insignia is the shield and motto of the coat of arms.

LINEAGE AND HONORS

LINEAGE

Constituted 5 August 1917 in the National Army as the 325th Infantry, an element of the 82d Division. Organized 1 September 1917 at Camp Gordon, Georgia. Demobilized 18–25 May 1919 at Camp Upton, New York. Reconstituted 24 June 1921 in the Organized Reserves as the 325th Infantry, an element of the 82d Division (later redesignated as the 82d Airborne Division). Organized in January 1922 with Headquarters at Albany, Georgia.

Ordered into active military service 25 March 1942 and reorganized at Camp Claiborne, Louisiana. Reorganized and redesignated 15 August 1942 as the 325th Glider Infantry. (3d Battalion consolidated 6 April 1945 with the 2d Battalion, 401st Glider Infantry [see ANNEX] and consolidated unit designated as the 3d Battalion, 325th Glider Infantry.) Reorganized and redesignated 15 December 1947 as the 325th Infantry. Allotted 15 November 1948 to the Regular Army. Reorganized and redesignated 15 December 1948 as the 325th Airborne Infantry.

Relieved 1 September 1957 from assignment to the 82d Airborne Division; concurrently, reorganized and redesignated as the 325th Infantry, a parent regiment under the Combat Arms Regimental System.

ANNEX

Constituted 12 March 1918 in the National Army as the 2d Battalion, 401st Infantry. Allotted 24 June 1921 to the Organized Reserves and assigned to the 101st Division (later redesignated as the 101st Airborne Division). Organized in November 1921 with Headquarters at Milwaukee, Wisconsin. Disbanded 15 August 1942; concurrently, reconstituted in the Army of the United States as the 2d Battalion, 401st Glider Infantry, an element of the 101st Airborne Division, and activated at Camp Claiborne, Louisiana. Disbanded 1 March 1945 in France and relieved from assignment to the 101st Airborne Division. Reconstituted 6 April 1945; concurrently, consolidated with the 3d Battalion, 325th Glider Infantry and consolidated unit designated as the 3d Battalion, 325th Glider Infantry.

CAMPAIGN PARTICIPATION CREDIT

World War I
St. Mihiel
Meuse-Argonne
Lorraine 1918

World War II
Sicily
Naples-Foggia
Normandy (with arrowhead)
Rhineland (with arrowhead)
Ardennes-Alsace
Central Europe

DECORATIONS

Presidential Unit Citation (Army), Streamer embroidered STE. MERE EGLISE (325th Glider Infantry cited; WD GO 14, 1945)

French Croix de Guerre with Palm, World War II, Streamer embroidered STE. MERE EGLISE (325th Glider Infantry cited; DA GO 43, 1950)

French Croix de Guerre with Palm, World War II, Streamer embroidered COTENTIN (325th Glider Infantry cited; DA GO 43, 1950)

French Croix de Guerre, World War II, Fourragere (325th Glider Infantry cited; DA GO 43, 1950)

Military Order of William (Degree of the Knight of the Fourth Class), Streamer embroidered NIJMEGEN 1944 (325th Glider Infantry cited; DA GO 43, 1950)

Netherlands Orange Lanyard (325th Glider Infantry cited; DA GO 43, 1950)

Belgian Fourragere 1940 (325th Glider Infantry cited; DA GO 43, 1950)

Cited in the Order of the Day of the Belgian Army for action in the ARDENNES (325th Glider Infantry cited; DA GO 43, 1950)

Cited in the Order of the Day of the Belgian Army for action in BELGIUM AND GERMANY (325th Glider Infantry cited; DA GO 43, 1950)

1st BATTALION, 325th INFANTRY

RA
(82d Airborne Division)

LINEAGE

Constituted 5 August 1917 in the National Army as Company A, 325th Infantry, an element of the 82d Division. Organized 1 September 1917 at Camp Gordon, Georgia. Demobilized 18 May 1919 at Camp Upton, New York. Reconstituted 24 June 1921 in the Organized Reserves as Company A, 325th Infantry, an element of the 82d Division (later redesignated as the 82d Airborne Division). Organized in January 1922 at Columbus, Georgia.

Ordered into active military service 25 March 1942 and reorganized at Camp Claiborne, Louisiana. Reorganized and redesignated 15 August 1942 as Company A, 325th Glider Infantry. Reorganized and redesignated 15 December 1947 as Company A, 325th Infantry. Allotted 15 November 1948 to the Regular Army. Reorganized and redesignated 15 December 1948 as Company A, 325th Airborne Infantry.

Reorganized and redesignated 1 September 1957 as Headquarters and Headquarters Company, 1st Airborne Battle Group, 325th Infantry and remained assigned to the 82d Airborne Division (organic elements concurrently constituted and activated). Reorganized and redesignated 25 May 1964 as the 1st Battalion, 325th Infantry.

CAMPAIGN PARTICIPATION CREDIT

World War I
* *St. Mihiel
* *Meuse-Argonne
* *Lorraine 1918

World War II
* *Sicily

* *Naples-Foggia
* *Normandy (with arrowhead)
* *Rhineland (with arrowhead)
* *Ardennes-Alsace
* *Central Europe

DECORATIONS

*Presidential Unit Citation (Army), Streamer embroidered STE. MERE EGLISE (325th Glider Infantry cited; WD GO 14, 1945)

*French Croix de Guerre with Palm, World War II, Streamer embroidered STE. MERE EGLISE (325th Glider Infantry cited; DA GO 43, 1950)

*French Croix de Guerre with Palm, World War II, Streamer embroidered COTENTIN (325th Glider Infantry cited; DA GO 43, 1950)

*French Croix de Guerre, World War II, Fourragere (325th Glider Infantry cited; DA GO 43, 1950)

*Military Order of William (Degree of the Knight of the Fourth Class), Streamer embroidered NIJMEGEN 1944 (325th Glider Infantry cited; DA GO 43, 1950)

*Netherlands Orange Lanyard (325th Glider Infantry cited; DA GO 43, 1950)

*Belgian Fourragere 1940 (325th Glider Infantry cited; DA GO 43, 1950)

*Cited in the Order of the Day of the Belgian Army for action in the ARDENNES (325th Glider Infantry cited; DA GO 43, 1950)

*Cited in the Order of the Day of the Belgian Army for action in BELGIUM AND GERMANY (325th Glider Infantry cited; DA GO 43, 1950)

2d BATTALION, 325th INFANTRY

RA

(82d Airborne Division)

LINEAGE

Constituted 5 August 1917 in the National Army as Company B, 325th Infantry, an element of the 82d Division. Organized 1 September 1917 at Camp Gordon, Georgia. Demobilized 18 May 1919 at Camp Upton, New York. Reconstituted 24 June 1921 in the Organized Reserves as Company B, 325th Infantry, an element of the 82d Division (later redesignated as the 82d Airborne Division). Organized in January 1922 at Columbus, Georgia.

Ordered into active military service 25 March 1942 and reorganized at Camp Claiborne, Louisiana. Reorganized and redesignated 15 August 1942 as Company B, 325th Glider Infantry. Reorganized and redesignated 15 December 1947 as Company B, 325th Infantry. Allotted 15 November 1948 to the Regular Army. Reorganized and redesignated 15 December 1948 as Company B, 325th Airborne Infantry.

Inactivated 1 September 1957 at Fort Bragg, North Carolina, and relieved from assignment to the 82d Airborne Division; concurrently, redesignated as Headquarters and Headquarters Company, 2d Airborne Battle Group, 325th Infantry. Redesignated 6 March 1964 as Headquarters and Headquarters Company, 2d Battalion, 325th Infantry and assigned to the 82d Airborne Division (organic elements concurrently constituted). Battalion activated 25 May 1964 at Fort Bragg, North Carolina.

CAMPAIGN PARTICIPATION CREDIT

<table>
<tr><td>

World War I
 *St. Mihiel
 *Meuse-Argonne
 *Lorraine 1918

</td><td>

World War II
 *Sicily
 *Naples-Foggia
 *Normandy (with arrowhead)
 *Rhineland (with arrowhead)
 *Ardennes-Alsace
 *Central Europe

</td></tr>
</table>

DECORATIONS

*Presidential Unit Citation (Army), Streamer embroidered STE. MERE EGLISE (325th Glider Infantry cited; WD GO 14, 1945)

*French Croix de Guerre with Palm, World War II, Streamer em-

broidered STE. MERE EGLISE (325th Glider Infantry cited; DA GO 43, 1950)

*French Croix de Guerre with Palm, World War II, Streamer embroidered COTENTIN (325th Glider Infantry cited; DA GO 43, 1950)

*French Croix de Guerre, World War II, Fourragere (325th Glider Infantry cited; DA GO 43, 1950)

*Military Order of William (Degree of the Knight of the Fourth Class), Streamer embroidered NIJMEGEN 1944 (325th Glider Infantry cited; DA GO 43, 1950)

*Netherlands Orange Lanyard (325th Glider Infantry cited; DA GO 43, 1950)

*Belgian Fourragere 1940 (325th Glider Infantry cited; DA GO 43, 1950)

*Cited in the Order of the Day of the Belgian Army for action in the ARDENNES (325th Glider Infantry cited; DA GO 43, 1950)

*Cited in the Order of the Day of the Belgian Army for action in BELGIUM AND GERMANY (325th Glider Infantry cited; DA GO 43, 1950)

3d BATTALION, 325th INFANTRY

LINEAGE

Constituted 5 August 1917 in the National Army as Company C, 325th Infantry, an element of the 82d Division. Organized 1 September 1917 at Camp Gordon, Georgia. Demobilized 18 May 1919 at Camp Upton, New York. Reconstituted 24 June 1921 in the Organized Reserves as Company C, 325th Infantry, an element of the 82d Division (later redesignated as the 82d Airborne Division). Organized in January 1922 at Columbus, Georgia.

Ordered into active military service 25 March 1942 and reorganized at Camp Claiborne, Louisiana. Reorganized and redesignated 15 August 1942 as Company C, 325th Glider Infantry. Reorganized and redesignated 15 December 1947 as Company C, 325th Infantry. Allotted 15 November 1948 to the Regular Army. Reorganized and redesignated 15 December 1948 as Company C, 325th Airborne Infantry.

Inactivated 1 September 1957 at Fort Bragg, North Carolina, and relieved from assignment to the 82d Airborne Division; concurrently, redesignated as Headquarters and Headquarters Company, 3d Airborne Battle Group, 325th Infantry. Redesignated 6 March 1964 as Headquarters and Headquarters Company, 3d Battalion, 325th Infantry, and assigned to the 82d Airborne Division (organic elements concurrently constituted). Battalion activated 25 May 1964 at Fort Bragg, North Carolina.

CAMPAIGN PARTICIPATION CREDIT

World War I
  *St. Mihiel
  *Meuse-Argonne
  *Lorraine 1918

World War II
  *Sicily
  *Naples-Foggia
  *Normandy (with arrowhead)
  *Rhineland (with arrowhead)
  *Ardennes-Alsace
  *Central Europe

DECORATIONS

*Presidential Unit Citation (Army), Streamer embroidered STE. MERE EGLISE (325th Glider Infantry cited; WD GO 14, 1945)

*French Croix de Guerre with Palm, World War II, Streamer em-

broidered STE. MERE EGLISE (325th Glider Infantry cited; DA GO 43, 1950)

*French Croix de Guerre with Palm, World War II, Streamer embroidered COTENTIN (325th Glider Infantry cited; DA GO 43, 1950)

*French Croix de Guerre, World War II, Fourragere (325th Glider Infantry cited; DA GO 43, 1950)

*Military Order of William (Degree of the Knight of the Fourth Class), Streamer embroidered NIJMEGEN 1944 (325th Glider Infantry cited; DA GO 43, 1950)

*Netherlands Orange Lanyard (325th Glider Infantry cited; DA GO 43, 1950)

*Belgian Fourragere 1940 (325th Glider Infantry cited; DA GO 43, 1950)

*Cited in the Order of the Day of the Belgian Army for action in the ARDENNES (325th Glider Infantry cited; DA GO 43, 1950)

*Cited in the Order of the Day of the Belgian Army for action in BELGIUM AND GERMANY (325th Glider Infantry cited; DA GO 43, 1950)

4th BATTALION, 325th INFANTRY

RA
(inactive)

LINEAGE

Constituted 5 August 1917 in the National Army as **Company D, 325th Infantry**, an element of the 82d Division. Organized 1 September 1917 at Camp Gordon, Georgia. Demobilized 18 May 1919 at Camp Upton, New York. Reconstituted 24 June 1921 in the Organized Reserves as Company D, 325th Infantry, an element of the 82d Division (later redesignated as the 82d Airborne Division). Organized in January 1922 at Columbus, Georgia.

Ordered into active military service 25 March 1942 and reorganized at Camp Claiborne, Louisiana. Absorbed 15 August 1942 by the regiment (325th Infantry concurrently reorganized and redesignated as the 325th Glider Infantry). Company D, 325th Glider Infantry reorganized 1 March 1945 in France (Company D shares the history and honors of the 325th Glider Infantry during the period 15 August 1942 to 1 March 1945). Reorganized and redesignated 15 December 1947 as Company D, 325th Infantry. Allotted 15 November 1948 to the Regular Army. Reorganized and redesignated 15 December 1948 as Company D, 325th Airborne Infantry.

Inactivated 1 September 1957 at Fort Bragg, North Carolina, and relieved from assignment to the 82d Airborne Division; concurrently, redesignated as Headquarters and Headquarters Company, 4th Airborne Battle Group, 325th Infantry. Redesignated 3 July 1968 as Headquarters and Headquarters Company, 4th Battalion, 325th Infantry (organic elements concurrently constituted). Battalion activated 15 July 1968 at Fort Bragg, North Carolina, and assigned to the 82d Airborne Division. Inactivated 15 December 1969 at Fort Bragg, North Carolina, and relieved from assignment to the 82d Airborne Division.

CAMPAIGN PARTICIPATION CREDIT

World War I
  *St. Mihiel
  *Meuse-Argonne
  *Lorraine 1918

World War II
  *Sicily
  *Naples-Foggia
  *Normandy (with arrowhead)
  *Rhineland (with arrowhead)
  *Ardennes-Alsace
  *Central Europe

DECORATIONS

*Presidential Unit Citation (Army) , Streamer embroidered STE. MERE EGLISE (325th Glider Infantry cited; WD GO 14, 1945)

*French Croix de Guerre with Palm, World War II, Streamer embroidered STE. MERE EGLISE (325th Glider Infantry cited; DA GO 43, 1950)

*French Croix de Guerre with Palm, World War II, Streamer embroidered COTENTIN (325th Glider Infantry cited; DA GO 43, 1950)

*French Croix de Guerre, World War II, Fourragere (325th Glider Infantry cited: DA GO 43, 1950)

*Military Order of William (Degree of the Knight of the Fourth Class) , Streamer embroidered NIJMEGEN 1944 (325th Glider Infantry cited; DA GO 43, 1950)

*Netherlands Orange Lanyard (325th Glider Infantry cited; DA GO 43, 1950)

*Belgian Fourragere 1940 (325th Glider Infantry cited; DA GO 43, 1950)

*Cited in the Order of the Day of the Belgian Army for action in the ARDENNES (325th Glider Infantry cited; DA GO 43, 1950)

*Cited in the Order of the Day of the Belgian Army for action in BELGIUM AND GERMANY (325th Glider Infantry cited; DA GO 43, 1950)

325TH INFANTRY, BIBLIOGRAPHY

Blumenson, Martin. *Breakout and Pursuit*. United States Army in World War II. Washington: Government Printing Office, 1961.

Exercise Snow Storm, January–March 1953, Camp Drum, New York. Fort Jay, New York, 1953.

Harrison, Gordon A. *Cross-Channel Attack*. United States Army in World War II. Washington: Government Printing Office, 1951.

Historical Section, War Department. *Utah Beach to Cherbourg*. American Forces in Action Series. Washington: Government Printing Office, 1947.

History Section, European Theater of Operations. *The Forcing of the Merderet Causeway at La Fiere, France, An Action by the 3d Battalion, 325th Glider Infantry and Other Elements*. (Regimental Unit Study Number 4.) n.p., 1945.

Story of the 325th. Bordeaux: A. Saugnac and E. Drouillard, 1919.

Vaughn, Robert E. *History of Company "B", 325th Infantry, 82d Division, A.E.F.* Porterville, New York, 1919.

327th INFANTRY

(Bastogne Bulldogs)

HERALDIC ITEMS

COAT OF ARMS

Shield: Azure, a palmetto tree eradicated argent, overall a bend gules fimbriated of the second charged with three fleurs-de-lis palewise of the like.

Crest: On a wreath argent and azure, in front of a plate nebuly and pierced, two spears saltirewise staffs sable spearheads gules, in base overall two sprigs of oak conjoined vert fructed of the fourth.

Motto: Honor and Country.

Symbolism: The shield is blue for infantry. Blue is also the color of the state flag of South Carolina, the location of the 327th Infantry between World Wars I and II. The palmetto tree also alludes to South Carolina. The red bend is taken from the arms of the ancient province of Lorraine, and the fleurs-de-lis indicate the regiment's three World War I campaigns.

The nebuly delineation, a heraldic simulation for clouds, represents the regiment's service as the 327th Glider Infantry in World War II. The two spearheads surmounting the nebuly pierced disc indicate the unit's combat glider landings and its aggressive action in Normandy and in the Rhineland. The oak leaves and acorn connote Bastogne in the Ardennes. The pierced white disc further alludes to the snow and to encircled Bastogne during the Battle of the Bulge, for which the organization was awarded the Presidential Unit Citation (Army). The colors red and green refer to the regiment's French and Belgian decorations.

DISTINCTIVE INSIGNIA

The distinctive insignia is the shield and motto of the coat of arms.

801

Lineage and Honors

Lineage

Constituted 5 August 1917 in the National Army as the 327th Infantry, an element of the 82d Division. Organized 17 September 1917 at Camp Gordon, Georgia. Demobilized 26 May 1919 at Camp Upton, New York. Reconstituted 24 June 1921 in the Organized Reserves as the 327th Infantry, an element of the 82d Division (later redesignated as the 82d Airborne Division). Organized in December 1921 with Headquarters at Greenville, South Carolina.

Ordered into active military service 25 March 1942 and reorganized at Camp Claiborne, Louisiana. Reorganized and redesignated 15 August 1942 as the 327th Glider Infantry; concurrently, relieved from assignment to the 82d Airborne Division and assigned to the 101st Airborne Division. (3d Battalion consolidated 6 April 1945 with the 1st Battalion, 401st Glider Infantry [see ANNEX] and consolidated unit designated as the 3d Battalion, 327th Glider Infantry.) Inactivated 30 November 1945 at Auxerre, France. Redesignated 18 June 1948 as the 516th Airborne Infantry. Allotted 25 June 1948 to the Regular Army.

Activated 6 July 1948 at Camp Breckinridge, Kentucky. (1st Battalion inactivated 1 April 1949 at Camp Breckinridge, Kentucky.) Regiment (less 1st Battalion) inactivated 22 April 1949 at Camp Breckinridge, Kentucky. Regiment activated 25 August 1950 at Camp Breckinridge, Kentucky. Inactivated 1 December 1953 at Camp Breckinridge, Kentucky. Relieved 27 April 1954 from assignment to the 101st Airborne Division. Activated 15 May 1954 at Fort Jackson, South Carolina. Reorganized and redesignated 1 July 1956 as the 327th Airborne Infantry and assigned to the 101st Airborne Division.

Relieved 25 April 1957 from assignment to the 101st Airborne Division; concurrently, reorganized and redesignated as the 327th Infantry, a parent regiment under the Combat Arms Regimental System.

ANNEX

Constituted 12 March 1918 in the National Army as the 1st Battalion, 401st Infantry. Allotted 24 June 1921 to the Organized Reserves and assigned to the 101st Division (later redesignated as the 101st Airborne Division). Organized in November 1921 with Headquarters at Milwaukee, Wisconsin. Disbanded 15 August 1942; concurrently, reconstituted in the Army of the United States as the 1st Battalion, 401st Glider Infantry, an element of the 101st Airborne Division, and activated at Camp Claiborne, Louisiana. Disbanded 1 March 1945 in France and relieved from assignment to the 101st Airborne Division. Reconstituted 6 April 1945; concurrently, consolidated with the 3d Battalion, 327th

Glider Infantry and consolidated unit designated as the 3d Battalion, 327th Glider Infantry.

CAMPAIGN PARTICIPATION CREDIT

World War I
St. Mihiel
Meuse-Argonne
Lorraine 1918

World War II
Normandy (with arrowhead)
Rhineland (with arrowhead)
Ardennes-Alsace
Central Europe

Vietnam
Defense
Counteroffensive
Counteroffensive, Phase II
Counteroffensive, Phase III
Tet Counteroffensive
(other campaigns to be determined)

DECORATIONS

Presidential Unit Citation (Army), Streamer embroidered BASTOGNE (101st Airborne Division cited; WD GO 17, 1945)

Presidential Unit Citation (Army), Streamer embroidered DAK TO, VIETNAM 1966 (1st Battalion and Company B, 2d Battalion, 327th Infantry cited; DA GO 59, 1968)

Presidential Unit Citation (Army), Streamer embroidered TRUNG LUONG (2d Battalion, 327th Infantry cited; DA GO 73, 1968)

Valorous Unit Award, Streamer embroidered TUY HOA (1st and 2d Battalions, 327th Infantry cited; DA GO 17, 1968, as amended by DA GO 1, 1969)

Meritorious Unit Commendation, Streamer embroidered VIETNAM 1965–1966 (1st and 2d Battalions, 327th Infantry cited; DA GO 17, 1968, as amended by DA GO 1, 1969)

French Croix de Guerre with Palm, World War II, Streamer embroidered NORMANDY (327th Glider Infantry cited; DA GO 43, 1950)

Netherlands Orange Lanyard (327th Glider Infantry cited; DA GO 43, 1950)

Belgian Croix de Guerre 1940 with Palm, Streamer embroidered BASTOGNE; cited in the Order of the Day of the Belgian Army for action at BASTOGNE (327th Glider Infantry cited; DA GO 43, 1950, as amended by DA GO 27, 1959)

Belgian Fourragere 1940 (327th Glider Infantry cited; DA GO 43, 1950)

Cited in the Order of the Day of the Belgian Army for action in FRANCE AND BELGIUM (327th Glider Infantry cited; DA GO 43, 1950)

1st BATTALION, 327th INFANTRY

(Bastogne Bulldogs)

RA
(101st Airborne Division)

LINEAGE

Constituted 5 August 1917 in the National Army as Company A, 327th Infantry, an element of the 82d Division. Organized 17 September 1917 at Camp Gordon, Georgia. Demobilized 26 May 1919 at Camp Upton, New York. Reconstituted 24 June 1921 in the Organized Reserves as Company A, 327th Infantry, an element of the 82d Division (later redesignated as the 82d Airborne Division). Organized in December 1921 in South Carolina.

Ordered into active military service 25 March 1942 and reorganized at Camp Claiborne, Louisiana. Reorganized and redesignated 15 August 1942 as Company A, 327th Glider Infantry, an element of the 101st Airborne Division. Inactivated 30 November 1945 at Auxerre, France. Redesignated 18 June 1948 as Company A, 516th Airborne Infantry, an element of the 101st Airborne Division. Allotted 25 June 1948 to the Regular Army.

Activated 6 July 1948 at Camp Breckinridge, Kentucky. Inactivated 1 April 1949 at Camp Breckinridge, Kentucky. Activated 25 August 1950 at Camp Breckinridge, Kentucky. Inactivated 1 December 1953 at Camp Breckinridge, Kentucky. (516th Airborne Infantry relieved 27 April 1954 from assignment to the 101st Airborne Division.) Activated 15 May 1954 at Fort Jackson, South Carolina. Reorganized and redesignated 1 July 1956 as Company A, 327th Airborne Infantry, an element of the 101st Airborne Division.

Reorganized and redesignated 25 April 1957 as Headquarters and Headquarters Company, 1st Airborne Battle Group, 327th Infantry and remained assigned to the 101st Airborne Division (organic elements concurrently constituted and activated). Reorganized and redesignated 3 February 1964 as the 1st Battalion, 327th Infantry.

CAMPAIGN PARTICIPATION CREDIT

World War I
*St. Mihiel
*Meuse-Argonne
*Lorraine 1918

World War II
*Normandy (with arrowhead)
*Rhineland (with arrowhead)
*Ardennes-Alsace
*Central Europe

Vietnam
*Defense
*Counteroffensive
*Counteroffensive, Phase II
*Counteroffensive, Phase III
*Tet Counteroffensive
(other campaigns to be determined)

DECORATIONS

*Presidential Unit Citation (Army), Streamer embroidered BASTOGNE (101st Airborne Division cited; WD GO 17, 1945)

*Presidential Unit Citation (Army), Streamer embroidered DAK TO, VIETNAM 1966 (1st Battalion, 327th Infantry cited; DA GO 59, 1968)

*Valorous Unit Award, Streamer embroidered TUY HOA (1st Battalion, 327th Infantry cited; DA GO 17, 1968, as amended by DA GO 1, 1969)

*Meritorious Unit Commendation, Streamer embroidered VIETNAM 1965–1966 (1st Battalion, 327th Infantry cited; DA GO 17, 1968, as amended by DA GO 1, 1969)

*French Croix de Guerre with Palm, World War II, Streamer embroidered NORMANDY (327th Glider Infantry cited; DA GO 43, 1950)

*Netherlands Orange Lanyard (327th Glider Infantry cited; DA GO 43, 1950)

*Belgian Croix de Guerre 1940 with Palm, Streamer embroidered BASTOGNE; cited in the Order of the Day of the Belgian Army for action at BASTOGNE (327th Glider Infantry cited; DA GO 43, 1950, as amended by DA GO 27, 1959)

*Belgian Fourragere 1940 (327th Glider Infantry cited; DA GO 43, 1950)

*Cited in the Order of the Day of the Belgian Army for action in FRANCE AND BELGIUM (327th Glider Infantry cited; DA GO 43, 1950)

*Vietnamese Cross of Gallantry with Palm, Streamer embroidered VIETNAM 1966–1967 (1st Battalion, 327th Infantry cited; DA GO 21, 1969)

*Vietnamese Cross of Gallantry with Palm, Streamer embroidered VIETNAM 1968–1969 (1st Battalion, 327th Infantry cited; DA GO 43, 1970)

2d BATTALION, 327th INFANTRY

(Bastogne Bulldogs)

RA
(101st Airborne Division)

LINEAGE

Constituted 5 August 1917 in the National Army as Company B, 327th Infantry, an element of the 82d Division. Organized 17 September 1917 at Camp Gordon, Georgia. Demobilized 26 May 1919 at Camp Upton, New York. Reconstituted 24 June 1921 in the Organized Reserves as Company B, 327th Infantry, an element of the 82d Division (later redesignated as the 82d Airborne Division). Organized in December 1921 in South Carolina.

Ordered into active military service 25 March 1942 and reorganized at Camp Claiborne, Louisiana. Reorganized and redesignated 15 August 1942 as Company B, 327th Glider Infantry, an element of the 101st Airborne Division. Inactivated 30 November 1945 at Auxerre, France. Redesignated 18 June 1948 as Company B, 516th Airborne Infantry, an element of the 101st Airborne Division. Allotted 25 June 1948 to the Regular Army.

Activated 6 July 1948 at Camp Breckinridge, Kentucky. Inactivated 1 April 1949 at Camp Breckinridge, Kentucky. Activated 25 August 1950 at Camp Breckinridge, Kentucky. Inactivated 1 December 1953 at Camp Breckinridge, Kentucky. (516th Airborne Infantry relieved 27 April 1954 from assignment to the 101st Airborne Division.) Activated 15 May 1954 at Fort Jackson, South Carolina. Reorganized and redesignated 1 July 1956 as Company B, 327th Airborne Infantry, an element of the 101st Airborne Division.

Inactivated 25 April 1957 at Fort Campbell, Kentucky, and relieved from assignment to the 101st Airborne Division; concurrently, redesignated as Headquarters and Headquarters Company, 2d Airborne Battle Group, 327th Infantry. Redesignated 21 January 1964 as Headquarters and Headquarters Company, 2d Battalion, 327th Infantry and assigned to the 101st Airborne Division (organic elements concurrently constituted). Battalion activated 3 February 1964 at Fort Campbell, Kentucky.

806

Campaign Participation Credit

World War I
*St. Mihiel
*Meuse-Argonne
*Lorraine 1918

Vietnam
*Defense
*Counteroffensive
*Counteroffensive, Phase II
*Counteroffensive, Phase III
*Tet Counteroffensive
 (other campaigns to be determined)

World War II
*Normandy (with arrowhead)
*Rhineland (with arrowhead)
*Ardennes-Alsace
*Central Europe

Decorations

*Presidential Unit Citation (Army), Streamer embroidered BASTOGNE (101st Airborne Division cited; WD GO 17, 1945)

*Presidential Unit Citation (Army), Streamer embroidered TRUNG LUONG (2d Battalion, 327th Infantry cited; DA GO 73, 1968)

*Valorous Unit Award, Streamer embroidered TUY HOA (2d Battalion, 327th Infantry cited; DA GO 17, 1968, as amended by DA GO 1, 1969)

*Meritorious Unit Commendation, Streamer embroidered VIETNAM 1965–1966 (2d Battalion, 327th Infantry cited; DA GO 17, 1968, as amended by DA GO 1, 1969)

*French Croix de Guerre with Palm, World War II, Streamer embroidered NORMANDY (327th Glider Infantry cited; DA GO 43, 1950)

*Netherlands Orange Lanyard (327th Glider Infantry cited; DA GO 43, 1950)

*Belgian Croix de Guerre 1940 with Palm, Streamer embroidered BASTOGNE; cited in the Order of the Day of the Belgian Army for action at BASTOGNE (327th Glider Infantry cited; DA GO 43, 1950, as amended by DA GO 27, 1959)

*Belgian Fourragere 1940 (327th Glider Infantry cited; DA GO 43, 1950)

*Cited in the Order of the Day of the Belgian Army for action in FRANCE AND BELGIUM (327th Glider Infantry cited; DA GO 43, 1950)

*Vietnamese Cross of Gallantry with Palm, Streamer embroidered VIETNAM 1966–1967 (2d Battalion, 327th Infantry cited; DA GO 21, 1969)

*Vietnamese Cross of Gallantry with Palm, Streamer embroidered VIETNAM 1968–1969 (2d Battalion, 327th Infantry cited; DA GO 43, 1970)

Company B additionally entitled to: Presidential Unit Citation (Army), Streamer embroidered DAK TO, VIETNAM 1966 (Company B, 2d Battalion, 327th Infantry cited; DA GO 59, 1968)

327TH INFANTRY, BIBLIOGRAPHY

Harrison, Gordon A. *Cross-Channel Attack*. United States Army in World War II. Washington: Government Printing Office, 1951.

Historical Section, War Department. *Omaha Beachhead*. American Forces in Action Series. Washington: Government Printing Office, 1945.

————. *Utah Beach to Cherbourg*. American Forces in Action Series. Washington: Government Printing Office, 1947.

Sparks, George McIntosh. *The 327th Under Fire, History of the 327th Infantry, 82d Division in the Great World War*. Fitzgerald, Georgia: B. E. Wilcox, 1919?

501st INFANTRY

Heraldic Items

Coat of Arms

Shield: Argent an Ojibway (Chippewa) thunderbird azure garnished gules.

Crest: On a wreath argent and azure a lion rampant or langued and armed gules charged on the shoulder with an escutcheon per pale of the like and of the second and holding in his right paw a staff bend sinisterwise of the third flying a standard per fess of the second and of the third, and in his left paw a key bendwise of the last.

Motto: Geronimo.

Symbolism: The colors blue and white indicate the infantry nature of the organization. The thunderbird is an appropriate symbol for a parachute unit. The motto has its origin in a cry uttered in the maiden jump of the unit's test platoon and is now tradition with the 501st Infantry.

The blue and yellow standard is the official standard of the town of Veghel, Holland. It was presented by the town to the 501st in honor of its efforts in liberating the town from the enemy. The lion refers to the Belgian Croix de Guerre and the Citation in the Order of the Day of the Belgian Army for the unit's action at Bastogne, whose arms are suggested by the red and blue shield on the lion's shoulder. The key refers to the position of Bastogne as a focal point of the German counterattack.

Distinctive Insignia

The distinctive insignia is the shield and motto of the coat of arms.

Lineage and Honors

Lineage

Constituted 24 February 1942 in the Army of the United States as the 501st Parachute Infantry (concurrently, 1st Battalion consolidated with the 501st Parachute Battalion [constituted 16 September 1940 and activated 1 October 1940 at Fort Benning, Georgia] and consolidated unit designated as the 1st Battalion, 501st Parachute Infantry). (1st Battalion inactivated 2 November 1942 in Australia.) Regiment activated 15 November 1942 at Camp Taccoa, Georgia. Disbanded 20 August 1945 in Germany.

Reconstituted 1 August 1946 in the Army of the United States as the 501st Parachute Infantry Battalion; concurrently, activated at Fort Benning, Georgia. Inactivated 23 November 1948 at Fort Benning, Georgia. Expanded and redesignated 21 April 1951 as the 501st Airborne Infantry and allotted to the Regular Army. Activated 10 May 1951 at Camp Breckinridge, Kentucky. Inactivated 1 December 1953 at Camp Breckinridge, Kentucky. Assigned 27 April 1954 to the 101st Airborne Division. Activated 15 May 1954 at Fort Jackson, South Carolina.

Relieved 25 April 1957 from assignment to the 101st Airborne Division; concurrently, reorganized and redesignated as the 501st Infantry, a parent regiment under the Combat Arms Regimental System.

CAMPAIGN PARTICIPATION CREDIT

World War II
   Normandy (with arrowhead)
   Rhineland (with arrowhead)
   Ardennes-Alsace
   Central Europe
   Asiatic-Pacific Theater without
     inscription

Vietnam
   Counteroffensive, Phase III
   Tet Counteroffensive
   (other campaigns to be determined)

DECORATIONS

Presidential Unit Citation (Army), Streamer embroidered BASTOGNE (501st Parachute Infantry cited; WD GO 17, 1945)

Presidential Unit Citation (Army), Streamer embroidered NORMANDY (501st Parachute Infantry cited; WD GO 4, 1945)

French Croix de Guerre with Palm, World War II, Streamer embroidered NORMANDY (501st Parachute Infantry cited; DA GO 43, 1950)

Netherlands Orange Lanyard (501st Parachute Infantry cited; DA GO 43, 1950)

Belgian Croix de Guerre 1940 with Palm, Streamer embroidered BASTOGNE; cited in the Order of the Day of the Belgian Army for action at BASTOGNE (501st Parachute Infantry cited; DA GO 43, 1950, as amended by DA GO 27, 1959)

Belgian Fourragere 1940 (501st Parachute Infantry cited; DA GO 43, 1950)

Cited in the Order of the Day of the Belgian Army for action in FRANCE AND BELGIUM (501st Parachute Infantry cited; DA GO 43, 1950)

1st BATTALION, 501st INFANTRY

LINEAGE

Constituted 16 September 1940 in the Army of the United States as Company A, 501st Parachute Battalion. Activated 1 October 1940 at Fort Benning, Georgia. Consolidated 24 February 1942 with Company A, 501st Parachute Infantry (concurrently constituted) and consolidated unit designated as Company A, 501st Parachute Infantry. Inactivated 2 November 1942 in Australia. Activated 15 November 1942 at Camp Taccoa, Georgia. Disbanded 20 August 1945 in Germany.

Reconstituted 1 August 1946 in the Army of the United States as Company A, 501st Parachute Infantry Battalion; concurrently, activated at Fort Benning, Georgia. Inactivated 23 November 1948 at Fort Benning, Georgia. Redesignated 21 April 1951 as Company A, 501st Airborne Infantry and allotted to the Regular Army. Activated 10 May 1951 at Camp Breckinridge, Kentucky. Inactivated 1 December 1953 at Camp Breckinridge, Kentucky. (501st Airborne Infantry assigned 27 April 1954 to the 101st Airborne Division.) Activated 15 May 1954 at Fort Jackson, South Carolina.

Reorganized and redesignated 25 April 1957 as Headquarters and Headquarters Company, 1st Airborne Battle Group, 501st Infantry and remained assigned to the 101st Airborne Division (organic elements concurrently constituted and activated). Reorganized and redesignated 3 February 1964 as the 1st Battalion, 501st Infantry.

CAMPAIGN PARTICIPATION CREDIT

World War II
  *Normandy (with arrowhead)
  *Rhineland (with arrowhead)
  *Ardennes-Alsace
  *Central Europe
  *Asiatic-Pacific Theater without
    inscription

Vietnam
  *Counteroffensive, Phase III
  *Tet Counteroffensive
    (other campaigns to be determined)

DECORATIONS

*Presidential Unit Citation (Army), Streamer embroidered BASTOGNE (501st Parachute Infantry cited; WD GO 17, 1945)

*Presidential Unit Citation (Army), Streamer embroidered NOR-
MANDY (501st Parachute Infantry cited; WD GO 4, 1945)

*French Croix de Guerre with Palm, World War II, Streamer em-
broidered NORMANDY (501st Parachute Infantry cited; DA GO 43, 1950)

*Netherlands Orange Lanyard (501st Parachute Infantry cited; DA
GO 43, 1950)

*Belgian Croix de Guerre 1940 with Palm, Streamer embroidered
BASTOGNE; cited in the Order of the Day of the Belgian Army for action
at BASTOGNE (501st Parachute Infantry cited; DA GO 43, 1950, as
amended by DA GO 27, 1959)

*Belgian Fourragere 1940 (501st Parachute Infantry cited; DA GO
43, 1950)

*Cited in the Order of the Day of the Belgian Army for action in
FRANCE AND BELGIUM (501st Parachute Infantry cited; DA GO 43, 1950)

*Vietnamese Cross of Gallantry with Palm, Streamer embroidered
VIETNAM 1968 (1st Battalion, 501st Infantry cited; DA GO 21, 1969)

*Vietnamese Cross of Gallantry with Palm, Streamer embroidered
VIETNAM 1968–1969 (1st Battalion, 501st Infantry cited; DA GO 43,
1970)

2d BATTALION, 501st INFANTRY

RA

(101st Airborne Division)

LINEAGE

Constituted 16 September 1940 in the Army of the United States as Company B, 501st Parachute Battalion. Activated 1 October 1940 at Fort Benning, Georgia. Consolidated 24 February 1942 with Company B, 501st Parachute Infantry (concurrently constituted) and consolidated unit designated as Company B, 501st Parachute Infantry. Inactivated 2 November 1942 in Australia. Activated 15 November 1942 at Camp Taccoa, Georgia. Disbanded 20 August 1945 in Germany.

Reconstituted 1 August 1946 in the Army of the United States as Company B, 501st Parachute Infantry Battalion; concurrently, activated at Fort Benning, Georgia. Inactivated 23 November 1948 at Fort Benning, Georgia. Redesignated 21 April 1951 as Company B, 501st Airborne Infantry and allotted to the Regular Army. Activated 10 May 1951 at Camp Breckinridge, Kentucky. Inactivated 1 December 1953 at Camp Breckinridge, Kentucky. (501st Airborne Infantry assigned 27 April 1954 to the 101st Airborne Division.) Activated 15 May 1954 at Fort Jackson, South Carolina. Inactivated 25 April 1957 at Fort Campbell, Kentucky, and relieved from assignment to the 101st Airborne Division.

Reorganized and redesignated 1 September 1957 as Headquarters and Headquarters Company, 2d Airborne Battle Group, 501st Infantry, assigned to the 82d Airborne Division, and activated at Fort Bragg, North Carolina (organic elements concurrently constituted and activated). Relieved 1 February 1964 from assignment to the 82d Airborne Division and assigned to the 101st Airborne Division. Reorganized and redesignated 3 February 1964 as the 2d Battalion, 501st Infantry.

CAMPAIGN PARTICIPATION CREDIT

World War II
  *Normandy (with arrowhead)
  *Rhineland (with arrowhead)
  *Ardennes-Alsace
  *Central Europe
  *Asiatic-Pacific Theater without
    inscription

Vietnam
  *Counteroffensive, Phase III
  *Tet Counteroffensive
    (other campaigns to be determined)

813

DECORATIONS

*Presidential Unit Citation (Army), Streamer embroidered BASTOGNE (501st Parachute Infantry cited; WD GO 17, 1945)

*Presidential Unit Citation (Army), Streamer embroidered NORMANDY (501st Parachute Infantry cited; WD GO 4, 1945)

*French Croix de Guerre with Palm, World War II, Streamer embroidered NORMANDY (501st Parachute Infantry cited; DA GO 43, 1950)

*Netherlands Orange Lanyard (501st Parachute Infantry cited; DA GO 43, 1950)

*Belgian Croix de Guerre 1940 with Palm, Streamer embroidered BASTOGNE; cited in the Order of the Day of the Belgian Army for action at BASTOGNE (501st Parachute Infantry cited; DA GO 43, 1950, as amended by DA GO 27, 1959)

*Belgian Fourragere 1940 (501st Parachute Infantry cited; DA GO 43, 1950)

*Cited in the Order of the Day of the Belgian Army for action in FRANCE AND BELGIUM (501st Parachute Infantry cited; DA GO 43, 1950)

*Vietnamese Cross of Gallantry with Palm, Streamer embroidered VIETNAM 1968 (2d Battalion, 501st Infantry cited; DA GO 21, 1969)

*Vietnamese Cross of Gallantry with Palm, Streamer embroidered VIETNAM 1968–1969 (2d Battalion, 501st Infantry cited; DA GO 43, 1970)

Company C additionally entitled to: Valorous Unit Award, Streamer embroidered THUA THIEN PROVINCE (Company C, 2d Battalion, 501st Infantry cited; DA GO 2, 1971)

501st Infantry, Bibliography

Critchell, Laurence. *Four Stars of Hell*. New York: Declan X. McMullen
    Company, 1947.

Harrison, Gordon A. *Cross-Channel Attack*. United States Army in
    World War II. Washington: Government Printing Office, 1951.

Historical Section, War Department. *Utah Beach to Cherbourg*. American Forces in Action Series. Washington: Government Printing
    Office, 1947.

History Section, European Theater of Operations. *The Fight at the
    Lock*. (Regimental Unit Study Number 2.) n.p., 1945.

————. *Three Day Attack by 501–1*. (Battalion and Small Unit Study
    Number 1.) n.p., 1945.

502d INFANTRY

HERALDIC ITEMS

COAT OF ARMS

Shield: Azure issuant from chief, an eagle's claw, talons extended or, armed sable.

Crest: On a wreath or and azure, an eagle's feather palewise tenné behind two bayonets saltirewise of the first hilted sable garnished gold surmounted by a gunstone bearing a four-bastioned fort argent charged with an ermine spot of the fourth.

Motto: Strike.

Symbolism: The blue of the shield is for infantry. The grasping eagle's claw is a representation of the airborne functions of the organization. The motto is expressive of the power of the organization.

The bayonets refer to the unit's bayonet charge at Carentan, Normandy. They are two in number in reference to the regiment's two Presidential Unit Citations (Army) and its two assault landings in World War II. The eagle's feather stands for the unit's airborne function; orange, the national color of the Netherlands, refers to the liberation of Best, Holland. The white four-bastioned fort encircled by a black background represents Bastogne, Belgium, surrounded by the German salient in the Battle of the Bulge. The ermine spot on the white fort refers to the snow which blanketed the battle's terrain.

DISTINCTIVE INSIGNIA

The distinctive insignia is the shield and motto of the coat of arms.

LINEAGE AND HONORS

LINEAGE

Constituted 24 February 1942 in the Army of the United States as the 502d Parachute Infantry (concurrently, 1st Battalion consolidated with the 502d Parachute Battalion [constituted 14 March 1941 and activated 1 July 1941 at Fort Benning, Georgia] and consolidated unit designated as the 1st Battalion, 502d Parachute Infantry). Regiment (less 1st Battalion) activated 2 March 1942 at Fort Benning, Georgia. Assigned 15 August 1942 to the 101st Airborne Division. Inactivated 30 November 1945 in France. Redesignated 18 June 1948 as the 502d Airborne Infantry. Allotted 25 June 1948 to the Regular Army.

Activated 6 July 1948 at Camp Breckinridge, Kentucky. Inactivated 1 April 1949 at Camp Breckinridge, Kentucky. Activated 25 August 1950 at Camp Breckinridge, Kentucky. Inactivated 1 December 1953 at Camp Breckinridge, Kentucky. Activated 15 May 1954 at Fort Jackson, South Carolina.

Relieved 25 April 1957 from assignment to the 101st Airborne Division; concurrently, reorganized and redesignated as the 502d Infantry, a parent regiment under the Combat Arms Regimental System.

CAMPAIGN PARTICIPATION CREDIT

World War II
    Normandy (with arrowhead)
    Rhineland (with arrowhead)
    Ardennes-Alsace
    Central Europe

Vietnam
    Defense
    Counteroffensive
    Counteroffensive, Phase II
    Counteroffensive, Phase III
    Tet Counteroffensive
    (other campaigns to be determined)

DECORATIONS

Presidential Unit Citation (Army), Streamer embroidered BASTOGNE (101st Airborne Division cited; WD GO 17, 1945)

Presidential Unit Citation (Army), Streamer embroidered NORMANDY (502d Parachute Infantry cited; WD GO 4, 1945)

Presidential Unit Citation (Army), Streamer embroidered AN KHE (2d Battalion, 502d Infantry cited; DA GO 20, 1967)

Presidential Unit Citation (Army), Streamer embroidered DAK TO, VIETNAM 1966 (2d Battalion, 502d Infantry cited; DA GO 59, 1968)

Valorous Unit Award, Streamer embroidered TUY HOA (2d Battalion, 502d Infantry cited; DA GO 17, 1968, as amended by DA GO 1, 1969)

Valorous Unit Award, Streamer embroidered QUANG THUONG DISTRICT (1st Battalion, 502d Infantry cited; DA GO 2, 1971)

Valorous Unit Award, Streamer embroidered NAM HOA DISTRICT (2d Battalion, 502d Infantry cited; DA GO 48, 1971)

Valorous Unit Award, Streamer embroidered BA LONG DISTRICT (2d Battalion, 502d Infantry cited; DA GO 50, 1971)

Meritorious Unit Commendation, Streamer embroidered VIETNAM

1965–1966 (2d Battalion, 502d Infantry cited; DA GO 17, 1968, as amended by DA GO 1, 1969)

French Croix de Guerre with Palm, World War II, Streamer embroidered NORMANDY (502d Parachute Infantry cited; DA GO 43, 1950)

Netherlands Orange Lanyard (502d Parachute Infantry cited; DA GO 43, 1950)

Belgian Croix de Guerre 1940 with Palm, Streamer embroidered BASTOGNE; cited in the Order of the Day of the Belgian Army for action at BASTOGNE (502d Parachute Infantry cited; DA GO 43, 1950, as amended by DA GO 27, 1959)

Belgian Fourragere 1940 (502d Parachute Infantry cited; DA GO 43, 1950)

Cited in the Order of the Day of the Belgian Army for action in FRANCE AND BELGIUM (502d Parachute Infantry cited; DA GO 43, 1950)

1st BATTALION, 502d INFANTRY

RA

(101st Airborne Division)

LINEAGE

Constituted 14 March 1941 in the Army of the United States as Company A, 502d Parachute Battalion. Activated 1 July 1941 at Fort Benning, Georgia. Consolidated 24 February 1942 with Company A, 502d Parachute Infantry (concurrently constituted) and consolidated unit designated as Company A, 502d Parachute Infantry. (502d Parachute Infantry assigned 15 August 1942 to the 101st Airborne Division.) Inactivated 30 November 1945 in France. Redesignated 18 June 1948 as Company A, 502d Airborne Infantry. Allotted 25 June 1948 to the Regular Army.

Activated 6 July 1948 at Camp Breckinridge, Kentucky. Inactivated 1 April 1949 at Camp Breckinridge, Kentucky. Activated 25 August 1950 at Camp Breckinridge, Kentucky. Inactivated 1 December 1953 at Camp Breckinridge, Kentucky. Activated 15 May 1954 at Fort Jackson, South Carolina.

Reorganized and redesignated 25 April 1957 as Headquarters and Headquarters Company, 1st Airborne Battle Group, 502d Infantry and remained assigned to the 101st Airborne Division (organic elements concurrently constituted and activated). Reorganized and redesignated 3 February 1964 as the 1st Battalion, 502d Infantry.

CAMPAIGN PARTICIPATION CREDIT

World War II
* *Normandy (with arrowhead)
* *Rhineland (with arrowhead)
* *Ardennes-Alsace
* *Central Europe

Vietnam
* *Counteroffensive, Phase III
* *Tet Counteroffensive
* (other campaigns to be determined)

DECORATIONS

*Presidential Unit Citation (Army), Streamer embroidered BASTOGNE (101st Airborne Division cited; WD GO 17, 1945)

*Presidential Unit Citation (Army), Streamer embroidered NORMANDY (502d Parachute Infantry cited; WD GO 4, 1945)

*Valorous Unit Award, Streamer embroidered QUANG THUONG DISTRICT (1st Battalion, 502d Infantry cited; DA GO 2, 1971)

*French Croix de Guerre with Palm, World War II, Streamer

820

embroidered NORMANDY (502d Parachute Infantry cited; DA GO 43, 1950)

*Netherlands Orange Lanyard (502d Parachute Infantry cited; DA GO 43, 1950)

*Belgian Croix de Guerre 1940 with Palm, Streamer embroidered BASTOGNE; cited in the Order of the Day of the Belgian Army for action at BASTOGNE (502d Parachute Infantry cited; DA GO 43, 1950, as amended by DA GO 27, 1959)

*Belgian Fourragere 1940 (502d Parachute Infantry cited; DA GO 43, 1950)

*Cited in the Order of the Day of the Belgian Army for action in FRANCE AND BELGIUM (502d Parachute Infantry cited; DA GO 43, 1950)

*Vietnamese Cross of Gallantry with Palm, Streamer embroidered VIETNAM 1968 (1st Battalion, 502d Infantry cited; DA GO 21, 1969)

*Vietnamese Cross of Gallantry with Palm, Streamer embroidered VIETNAM 1968–1969 (1st Battalion, 502d Infantry cited; DA GO 43, 1970)

2d BATTALION, 502d INFANTRY

RA
(101st Airborne Division)

LINEAGE

Constituted 14 March 1941 in the Army of the United States as Company B, 502d Parachute Battalion. Activated 1 July 1941 at Fort Benning, Georgia. Consolidated 24 February 1942 with Company B, 502d Parachute Infantry (concurrently constituted) and consolidated unit designated as Company B, 502d Parachute Infantry. (502d Parachute Infantry assigned 15 August 1942 to the 101st Airborne Division.) Inactivated 30 November 1945 in France. Redesignated 18 June 1948 as Company B, 502d Airborne Infantry. Allotted 25 June 1948 to the Regular Army.

Activated 6 July 1948 at Camp Breckinridge, Kentucky. Inactivated 1 April 1949 at Camp Breckinridge, Kentucky. Activated 25 August 1950 at Camp Breckinridge, Kentucky. Inactivated 1 December 1953 at Camp Breckinridge, Kentucky. Activated 15 May 1954 at Fort Jackson, South Carolina.

Reorganized and redesignated 1 March 1957 as Headquarters and Headquarters Company, 2d Airborne Battle Group, 502d Infantry, relieved from assignment to the 101st Airborne Division, and assigned to the 11th Airborne Division (organic elements concurrently constituted and activated). Inactivated 1 July 1958 in Germany. Redesignated 21 January 1964 as the 2d Battalion, 502d Infantry; concurrently, relieved from assignment to the 11th Airborne Division and assigned to the 101st Airborne Division. Activated 3 February 1964 at Fort Campbell, Kentucky.

CAMPAIGN PARTICIPATION CREDIT

World War II
*Normandy (with arrowhead)
*Rhineland (with arrowhead)
*Ardennes-Alsace
*Central Europe

Vietnam
*Defense
*Counteroffensive
*Counteroffensive, Phase II
*Counteroffensive, Phase III
*Tet Counteroffensive
(other campaigns to be determined)

DECORATIONS

*Presidential Unit Citation (Army), Streamer embroidered BASTOGNE (101st Airborne Division cited; WD GO 17, 1945)

*Presidential Unit Citation (Army), Streamer embroidered NOR-MANDY (502d Parachute Infantry cited; WD GO 4, 1945)

*Presidential Unit Citation (Army), Streamer embroidered AN KHE (2d Battalion, 502d Infantry cited; DA GO 20, 1967)

*Presidential Unit Citation (Army), Streamer embroidered DAK TO, VIETNAM 1966 (2d Battalion, 502d Infantry cited; DA GO 59, 1968)

*Valorous Unit Award, Streamer embroidered TUY HOA (2d Battalion, 502d Infantry cited; DA GO 17, 1968, as amended by DA GO 1, 1969)

*Valorous Unit Award, Streamer embroidered NAM HOA DISTRICT (2d Battalion, 502d Infantry cited; DA GO 48, 1971)

*Valorous Unit Award, Streamer embroidered BA LONG DISTRICT (2d Battalion, 502d Infantry cited; DA GO 50, 1971)

*Meritorious Unit Commendation, Streamer embroidered VIETNAM 1965–1966 (2d Battalion, 502d Infantry cited; DA GO 17, 1968, as amended by DA GO 1, 1969)

*French Croix de Guerre with Palm, World War II, Streamer embroidered NORMANDY (502d Parachute Infantry cited; DA GO 43, 1950)

*Netherlands Orange Lanyard (502d Parachute Infantry cited; DA GO 43, 1950)

*Belgian Croix de Guerre 1940 with Palm, Streamer embroidered BASTOGNE; cited in the Order of the Day of the Belgian Army for action at BASTOGNE (502d Parachute Infantry cited; DA GO 43, 1950, as amended by DA GO 27, 1959)

*Belgian Fourragere 1940 (502d Parachute Infantry cited; DA GO 43, 1950)

*Cited in the Order of the Day of the Belgian Army for action in FRANCE AND BELGIUM (502d Parachute Infantry cited; DA GO 43, 1950)

*Vietnamese Cross of Gallantry with Palm, Streamer embroidered VIETNAM 1966–1967 (2d Battalion, 502d Infantry cited; DA GO 21, 1969)

*Vietnamese Cross of Gallantry with Palm, Streamer embroidered VIETNAM 1968–1969 (2d Battalion, 502d Infantry cited; DA GO 43, 1970, as amended by DA GO 48, 1971)

502D INFANTRY, BIBLIOGRAPHY

Cole, Hugh M. *The Ardennes: Battle of the Bulge.* United States Army in World War II. Washington: Government Printing Office, 1964.

Harrison, Gordon A. *Cross-Channel Attack.* United States Army in World War II. Washington: Government Printing Office, 1951.

Historical Section, War Department. *Utah Beach to Cherbourg.* American Forces in Action Series. Washington: Government Printing Office, 1947.

History Section, European Theater of Operations. *The Caretan Causeway Fight.* (Regimental Unit Study Number 1.) n.p., 1945.

————. *Cassidy's Battalion.* (Battalion and Small Unit Study Number 9.) n.p., 1945.

————. *502d Regiment at Best, 17–19 September 1944.* (Battalion and Small Unit Study Number 6.) n.p., 1945.

MacDonald, Charles B. *The Siegfried Line Campaign.* United States Army in World War II. Washington: Government Printing Office, 1963.

Marshall, S. L. A. "The Fight at Best," *Marine Corps Gazette,* **XXXII** (October 1948), 10–17; **XXXII** (November 1948), 14–19; **XXXII** (December 1948), 27–31.

Sweetser, Warren E. "Dustpan and Broom," *Marine Corps Gazette,* **XXXI** (August 1947), 8–15.

503d INFANTRY

(The Rock Regiment)

HERALDIC ITEMS

COAT OF ARMS

Shield: Argent, a fort voided azure, pierced to the center by
a pile of the second counterchanged with the fort and
bearing three parachutes of the first, two and one.

Crest: None.

Motto: The Rock.

Symbolism: The colors, blue and white, are the current and old colors
of infantry. The inverted triangle terminating in the
broken fort symbolizes the drop on Corregidor during
the Luzon campaign, whereas the three parachutes represent the three other campaigns of the organization in
World War II.

DISTINCTIVE INSIGNIA

The distinctive insignia is the shield and motto of the coat of arms.

LINEAGE AND HONORS

LINEAGE

Constituted 24 February 1942 in the Army of the United States as the
503d Parachute Infantry (concurrently, 1st Battalion consolidated with
the 503d Parachute Battalion [constituted 14 March 1941 and activated
22 August 1941 at Fort Benning, Georgia] and 2d Battalion consolidated
with the 504th Parachute Battalion [constituted 14 March 1941 and
activated 5 October 1941 at Fort Benning, Georgia] and consolidated
units designated as the 1st and 2d Battalions, 503d Parachute Infantry).

Regiment (less 1st, 2d, and 3d Battalions) activated 2 March 1942 at
Fort Benning, Georgia. (3d Battalion activated 8 June 1942 at Fort
Bragg, North Carolina.) (2d Battalion reorganized and redesignated 2
November 1942 as the 2d Battalion, 509th Parachute Infantry—hereafter
separate lineage; concurrently, new 2d Battalion, 503d Infantry activated

in Australia.) Regiment inactivated 24 December 1945 at Camp Anza, California. Redesignated 1 February 1951 as the 503d Airborne Infantry; concurrently, allotted to the Regular Army and assigned to the 11th Airborne Division. Activated 2 March 1951 at Fort Campbell, Kentucky.

Relieved 1 March 1957 from assignment to the 11th Airborne Division; concurrently, reorganized and redesignated as the 503d Infantry, a parent regiment under the Combat Arms Regimental System.

CAMPAIGN PARTICIPATION CREDIT

World War II
  New Guinea
  Leyte
  Luzon (with arrowhead)
  Southern Philippines

Vietnam
  Defense
  Counteroffensive
  Counteroffensive, Phase II
    (with arrowhead)
  Counteroffensive, Phase III
  Tet Counteroffensive
  (other campaigns to be determined)

DECORATIONS

Presidential Unit Citation (Army), Streamer embroidered CORREGIDOR (503d Parachute Infantry cited; WD GO 53, 1945)

Presidential Unit Citation (Army), Streamer embroidered BIEN HOA (1st Battalion, 503d Infantry cited; DA GO 40, 1966)

Presidential Unit Citation (Army), Streamer embroidered PHOUC VINH (2d Battalion, 503d Infantry cited; DA GO 40, 1967)

Presidential Unit Citation (Army), Streamer embroidered DAK TO (173d Airborne Brigade [less 3d Battalion, 503d Infantry] cited; DA GO 42, 1969)

Meritorious Unit Commendation, Streamer embroidered VIETNAM 1965–1967 (1st, 2d, and 4th Battalions, 503d Infantry cited; DA GO 48, 1968)

Philippine Presidential Unit Citation, Streamer embroidered 17 OCTOBER 1944 TO 4 JULY 1945 (503d Parachute Infantry cited; DA GO 47, 1950)

1st BATTALION, 503d INFANTRY

(The Rock Regiment)

RA
(173d Airborne Brigade)

LINEAGE

Constituted 14 March 1941 in the Army of the United States as Company A, 503d Parachute Battalion. Activated 22 August 1941 at Fort Benning, Georgia. Consolidated 24 February 1942 with Company A, 503d Parachute Infantry (concurrently constituted) and consolidated unit designated as Company A, 503d Parachute Infantry. Inactivated 24 December 1945 at Camp Anza, California. Redesignated 1 February 1951 as Company A, 503d Airborne Infantry, an element of the 11th Airborne Division, and allotted to the Regular Army. Activated 2 March 1951 at Fort Campbell, Kentucky.

Reorganized and redesignated 1 March 1957 as Headquarters and Headquarters Company, 1st Airborne Battle Group, 503d Infantry and remained assigned to the 11th Airborne Division (organic elements concurrently constituted and activated). Relieved 1 July 1958 from assignment to the 11th Airborne Division and assigned to the 24th Infantry Division. Relieved 7 January 1959 from assignment to the 24th Infantry Division and assigned to the 82d Airborne Division. Relieved 26 March 1963 from assignment to the 82d Airborne Division and assigned to the 173d Airborne Brigade. Reorganized and redesignated 25 June 1963 as the 1st Battalion, 503d Infantry.

CAMPAIGN PARTICIPATION CREDIT

World War II	*Vietnam*
*New Guinea	*Defense
*Leyte	*Counteroffensive
*Luzon (with arrowhead)	*Counteroffensive, Phase II
*Southern Philippines	*Counteroffensive, Phase III
	*Tet Counteroffensive
	(other campaigns to be determined)

DECORATIONS

*Presidential Unit Citation (Army), Streamer embroidered CORREGIDOR (503d Parachute Infantry cited; WD GO 53, 1945)

*Presidential Unit Citation (Army), Streamer embroidered BIEN HOA (1st Battalion, 503d Infantry cited; DA GO 40, 1966)

*Presidential Unit Citation (Army), Streamer embroidered DAK TO (173d Airborne Brigade [less 3d Battalion, 503d Infantry] cited; DA GO 42, 1969)

*Meritorious Unit Commendation, Streamer embroidered VIETNAM 1965–1967 (1st Battalion, 503d Infantry cited; DA GO 48, 1968)

*Philippine Presidential Unit Citation, Streamer embroidered 17 OCTOBER 1944 TO 4 JULY 1945 (503d Parachute Infantry cited; DA GO 47, 1950)

2d BATTALION, 503d INFANTRY

(The Rock Regiment)

RA
(173d Airborne Brigade)

LINEAGE

Constituted 14 March 1941 in the Army of the United States as Company B, 503d Parachute Battalion. Activated 22 August 1941 at Fort Benning, Georgia. Consolidated 24 February 1942 with Company B, 503d Parachute Infantry (concurrently constituted) and consolidated unit designated as Company B, 503d Parachute Infantry. Inactivated 24 December 1945 at Camp Anza, California. Redesignated 1 February 1951 as Company B, 503d Airborne Infantry, an element of the 11th Airborne Division, and allotted to the Regular Army. Activated 2 March 1951 at Fort Campbell, Kentucky. Inactivated 1 March 1957 in Germany and relieved from assignment to the 11th Airborne Division.

Redesignated 1 September 1957 as Headquarters and Headquarters Company, 2d Airborne Battle Group, 503d Infantry, assigned to the 82d Airborne Division, and activated at Fort Bragg, North Carolina (organic elements concurrently constituted and activated). Relieved 24 June 1960 from assignment to the 82d Airborne Division and assigned to the 25th Infantry Division. Relieved 1 July 1961 from assignment to the 25th Infantry Division. Assigned 26 March 1963 to the 173d Airborne Brigade. Reorganized and redesignated 25 June 1963 as the 2d Battalion, 503d Infantry.

CAMPAIGN PARTICIPATION CREDIT

World War II	Vietnam
*New Guinea	*Defense
*Leyte	*Counteroffensive
*Luzon (with arrowhead)	*Counteroffensive, Phase II
*Southern Philippines	(with arrowhead)
	*Counteroffensive, Phase III
	*Tet Counteroffensive
	(other campaigns to be determined)

DECORATIONS

*Presidential Unit Citation (Army), Streamer embroidered CORREGIDOR (503d Parachute Infantry cited; WD GO 53, 1945)

*Presidential Unit Citation (Army), Streamer embroidered PHOUC VINH (2d Battalion, 503d Infantry cited; DA GO 40, 1967)

*Presidential Unit Citation (Army), Streamer embroidered DAK TO (173d Airborne Brigade [less 3d Battalion, 503d Infantry] cited; DA GO 42, 1969)

*Meritorious Unit Commendation, Streamer embroidered VIETNAM 1965–1967 (2d Battalion, 503d Infantry cited; DA GO 48, 1968)

*Philippine Presidential Unit Citation, Streamer embroidered 17 OCTOBER 1944 TO 4 JULY 1945 (503d Parachute Infantry cited; DA GO 47, 1950)

3d BATTALION, 503d INFANTRY

(The Rock Regiment)

RA
(173d Airborne Brigade)

LINEAGE

Constituted 14 March 1941 in the Army of the United States as Company C, 503d Parachute Battalion. Activated 22 August 1941 at Fort Benning, Georgia. Consolidated 24 February 1942 with Company C, 503d Parachute Infantry (concurrently constituted) and consolidated unit designated as Company C, 503d Parachute Infantry. Inactivated 24 December 1945 at Camp Anza, California. Redesignated 1 February 1951 as Company C, 503d Airborne Infantry, an element of the 11th Airborne Division, and allotted to the Regular Army. Activated 2 March 1951 at Fort Campbell, Kentucky.

Inactivated 1 March 1957 in Germany and relieved from assignment to the 11th Airborne Division; concurrently, redesignated as Headquarters and Headquarters Company, 3d Airborne Battle Group, 503d Infantry. Redesignated 6 February 1967 as Headquarters and Headquarters Company, 3d Battalion, 503d Infantry (organic elements concurrently constituted). Battalion activated 1 April 1967 at Fort Bragg, North Carolina, and assigned to the 173d Airborne Brigade.

CAMPAIGN PARTICIPATION CREDIT

World War II
 *New Guinea
 *Leyte
 *Luzon (with arrowhead)
 *Southern Philippines

Vietnam
 *Counteroffensive, Phase III
 *Tet Counteroffensive
 (other campaigns to be determined)

DECORATIONS

*Presidential Unit Citation (Army), Streamer embroidered CORREGIDOR (503d Parachute Infantry cited; WD GO 53, 1945)

*Philippine Presidential Unit Citation, Streamer embroidered 17 OCTOBER 1944 TO 4 JULY 1945 (503d Parachute Infantry cited; DA GO 47, 1950)

4th BATTALION, 503d INFANTRY

(The Rock Regiment)

RA
(173d Airborne Brigade)

LINEAGE

Activated 2 November 1942 in the Army of the United States in Australia as Company D, 503d Parachute Infantry. Inactivated 24 December 1945 at Camp Anza, California. Redesignated 1 February 1951 as Company D, 503d Airborne Infantry, an element of the 11th Airborne Division, and allotted to the Regular Army. Activated 2 March 1951 at Fort Campbell, Kentucky.

Inactivated 1 March 1957 in Germany and relieved from assignment to the 11th Airborne Division; concurrently, redesignated as Headquarters and Headquarters Company, 4th Airborne Battle Group, 503d Infantry. Redesignated 26 March 1966 as Headquarters and Headquarters Company, 4th Battalion, 503d Infantry and assigned to the 173d Airborne Brigade (organic elements concurrently constituted). Battalion activated 1 April 1966 at Fort Campbell, Kentucky.

CAMPAIGN PARTICIPATION CREDIT

World War II
  *New Guinea
  *Leyte
  *Luzon (with arrowhead)
  *Southern Philippines

Vietnam
  *Counteroffensive
  *Counteroffensive, Phase II
  *Counteroffensive, Phase III
  *Tet Counteroffensive
    (other campaigns to be determined)

DECORATIONS

*Presidential Unit Citation (Army), Streamer embroidered CORREGIDOR (503d Parachute Infantry cited; WD GO 53, 1945)

*Presidential Unit Citation (Army), Streamer embroidered DAK TO (173d Airborne Brigade [less 3d Battalion, 503d Infantry] cited; DA GO 42, 1969)

*Meritorious Unit Commendation, Streamer embroidered VIETNAM 1966–1967 (4th Battalion, 503d Infantry cited; DA GO 48, 1968)

*Philippine Presidential Unit Citation, Streamer embroidered 17 OCTOBER 1944 TO 4 JULY 1945 (503d Parachute Infantry cited; DA GO 47, 1950)

832

503D INFANTRY, BIBLIOGRAPHY

Albright, John, John A. Cash, and Allan W. Sandstrum. *Seven Firefights in Vietnam*. Washington: Government Printing Office, 1970.

Belote, James H. and William M. *Corregidor. The Saga of a Fortress*. New York: Harper and Row, Publishers, 1967.

"Brief History of the 503d Parachute Infantry Regiment," *Fort Campbell Courier* (3 March 1953).

Miller, John, jr. *CARTWHEEL: The Reduction of Rabaul*. United States Army in World War II. Washington: Government Printing Office, 1959.

"Parachute Attack—It Helps the Allies Capture Lae," *Life*, XV (25 October 1943).

Raff, Edson Duncan. *We Jumped to Fight*. New York: Eagle Books, 1944.

Smith, Robert Ross. *The Approach to the Philippines*. United States Army in World War II. Washington: Government Printing Office, 1953.

————. *Triumph in the Philippines*. United States Army in World War II. Washington: Government Printing Office, 1963.

Templeman, Harold. *The Return to Corregidor*. New York: Strand Press, 1945.

504th INFANTRY

Coat of Arms

Shield: Azure, a sword in bend argent, hilt and pommel or, fired proper.

Crest: On a wreath or and azure, a bridge embattled of three arches tenné masoned of the first each arch surmounted by a pheon argent; on the battlements thereof a wyvern sable winged of the fourth armed and garnished of the first; in base four waves transfluent barry wavy of three of the fourth and second.

Motto: Strike—Hold.

Symbolism: The blue is the color of the infantry whose functions are represented by the sword, flaming through the sky, the flames symbolizing the zeal of the personnel in the performance of their duties. The motto is expressive of the determination of the personnel to strike swiftly and hold their ground at any cost; therefore, it is appropriate for the organization.

The wyvern and the bridge stand for the regiment's combat service in World War II at Anzio, Italy, and at Nijmegen, Holland, for each of which actions the Presidential Unit Citation (Army) was awarded. The wyvern is black in reference to the nickname "black-hearted devils in baggy pants" given to paratroopers of the regiment at Anzio. The bridge, orange for the Netherlands, further alludes to the attack on the bridges at Nijmegen. The three pheons stand for the regiment's three assault landings, in Sicily, at Anzio, and in the Rhineland.

Distinctive Insignia

The distinctive insignia is the shield and motto of the coat of arms.

Lineage and Honors

Lineage

Constituted 24 February 1942 in the Army of the United States as the 504th Parachute Infantry. Activated 1 May 1942 at Fort Benning, Georgia. Assigned 15 August 1942 to the 82d Airborne Division. Reorganized and redesignated 15 December 1947 as the 504th Airborne Infantry. Allotted 15 November 1948 to the Regular Army.

Relieved 1 September 1957 from assignment to the 82d Airborne Division; concurrently, reorganized and redesignated as the 504th Infantry, a parent regiment under the Combat Arms Regimental System.

Campaign Participation Credit

World War II
  Sicily (with arrowhead)
  Naples-Foggia
  Anzio (with arrowhead)
  Rhineland (with arrowhead)
  Ardennes-Alsace
  Central Europe

Decorations

Presidential Unit Citation (Army), Streamer embroidered ANZIO BEACHHEAD (3d Battalion, 504th Parachute Infantry cited; WD GO 36, 1944)

Presidential Unit Citation (Army), Streamer embroidered NIJMEGEN, HOLLAND (1st and 3d Battalions, 504th Parachute Infantry cited; WD GO's 62 and 65, 1946)

Presidential Unit Citation (Army), Streamer embroidered CHENEUX, BELGIUM (1st Battalion [less Company A], 504th Parachute Infantry cited; WD GO 32, 1945)

Military Order of William (Degree of the Knight of the Fourth Class), Streamer embroidered NIJMEGEN 1944 (504th Parachute Infantry cited; DA GO 43, 1950)

Netherlands Orange Lanyard (504th Parachute Infantry cited; DA GO 43, 1950)

Belgian Fourragere 1940 (504th Parachute Infantry cited; DA GO 43, 1950)

Cited in the Order of the Day of the Belgian Army for action in the ARDENNES (504th Parachute Infantry cited; DA GO 43, 1950)

Cited in the Order of the Day of the Belgian Army for action in BELGIUM AND GERMANY (504th Parachute Infantry cited; DA GO 43, 1950)

1st BATTALION, 504th INFANTRY

RA

(82d Airborne Division)

LINEAGE

Constituted 24 February 1942 in the Army of the United States as Company A, 504th Parachute Infantry. Activated 1 May 1942 at Fort Benning, Georgia. (504th Parachute Infantry assigned 15 August 1942 to the 82d Airborne Division.) Reorganized and redesignated 15 December 1947 as Company A, 504th Airborne Infantry. Allotted 15 November 1948 to the Regular Army.

Reorganized and redesignated 1 September 1957 as Headquarters and Headquarters Company, 1st Airborne Battle Group, 504th Infantry and remained assigned to the 82d Airborne Division (organic elements concurrently constituted and activated). Relieved 11 December 1958 from assignment to the 82d Airborne Division and assigned to the 8th Infantry Division. Relieved 1 April 1963 from assignment to the 8th Infantry Division and assigned to the 82d Airborne Division. Reorganized and redesignated 25 May 1964 as the 1st Battalion, 504th Infantry.

CAMPAIGN PARTICIPATION CREDIT

World War II
  *Sicily (with arrowhead)
  *Naples-Foggia
  *Anzio (with arrowhead)

*Rhineland (with arrowhead)
*Ardennes-Alsace
*Central Europe

DECORATIONS

Presidential Unit Citation (Army), Streamer embroidered ANZIO BEACHHEAD

*Presidential Unit Citation (Army), Streamer embroidered NIJMEGEN, HOLLAND (1st Battalion, 504th Parachute Infantry cited; WD GO 62, 1946)

Presidential Unit Citation (Army), Streamer embroidered CHENEUX, BELGIUM

*Presidential Unit Citation (Army), Streamer embroidered RHINE RIVER (Company A, 504th Parachute Infantry cited; WD GO 66, 1945)

*Military Order of William (Degree of the Knight of the Fourth Class), Streamer embroidered NIJMEGEN 1944 (504th Parachute Infantry cited; DA GO 43, 1950)

837

*Netherlands Orange Lanyard (504th Parachute Infantry cited; DA GO 43, 1950)

*Belgian Fourragere 1940 (504th Parachute Infantry cited; DA GO 43, 1950)

*Cited in the Order of the Day of the Belgian Army for action in the ARDENNES (504th Parachute Infantry cited; DA GO 43, 1950)

*Cited in the Order of the Day of the Belgian Army for action in BELGIUM AND GERMANY (504th Parachute Infantry cited; DA GO 43, 1950)

2d BATTALION, 504th INFANTRY

RA
(82d Airborne Division)

LINEAGE

Constituted 24 February 1942 in the Army of the United States as Company B, 504th Parachute Infantry. Activated 1 May 1942 at Fort Benning, Georgia. (504th Parachute Infantry assigned 15 August 1942 to the 82d Airborne Division.) Reorganized and redesignated 15 December 1947 as Company B, 504th Airborne Infantry. Allotted 15 November 1948 to the Regular Army.

Reorganized and redesignated 1 March 1957 as Headquarters and Headquarters Company, 2d Airborne Battle Group, 504th Infantry, relieved from assignment to the 82d Airborne Division, and assigned to the 11th Airborne Division (organic elements concurrently constituted and activated). Inactivated 1 July 1958 in Germany. Relieved 9 May 1960 from assignment to the 11th Airborne Division and assigned to the 82d Airborne Division. Activated 1 July 1960 at Fort Bragg, North Carolina. Reorganized and redesignated 25 May 1964 as the 2d Battalion, 504th Infantry.

CAMPAIGN PARTICIPATION CREDIT

World War II
*Sicily (with arrowhead)
*Naples-Foggia
*Anzio (with arrowhead)

*Rhineland (with arrowhead)
*Ardennes-Alsace
*Central Europe

DECORATIONS

Presidential Unit Citation (Army), Streamer embroidered ANZIO BEACHHEAD

*Presidential Unit Citation (Army), Streamer embroidered NIJMEGEN, HOLLAND (1st Battalion, 504th Parachute Infantry cited; WD GO 62, 1946)

*Presidential Unit Citation (Army), Streamer embroidered CHENEUX, BELGIUM (1st Battalion [less Company A], 504th Parachute Infantry cited; WD GO 32, 1945)

*Military Order of William (Degree of the Knight of the Fourth Class), Streamer embroidered NIJMEGEN 1944 (504th Parachute Infantry cited; DA GO 43, 1950)

839

*Netherlands Orange Lanyard (504th Parachute Infantry cited; DA GO 43, 1950)

*Belgian Fourragere 1940 (504th Parachute Infantry cited; DA GO 43, 1950)

*Cited in the Order of the Day of the Belgian Army for action in the ARDENNES (504th Parachute Infantry cited; DA GO 43, 1950)

*Cited in the Order of the Day of the Belgian Army for action in BELGIUM AND GERMANY (504th Parachute Infantry cited; DA GO 43, 1950)

3d BATTALION, 504th INFANTRY

RA
(inactive)

LINEAGE

Constituted 24 February 1942 in the Army of the United States as Company C, 504th Parachute Infantry. Activated 1 May 1942 at Fort Benning, Georgia. (504th Parachute Infantry assigned 15 August 1942 to the 82d Airborne Division.) Reorganized and redesignated 15 December 1947 as Company C, 504th Airborne Infantry. Allotted 15 November 1948 to the Regular Army.

Inactivated 1 September 1957 at Fort Bragg, North Carolina, and relieved from assignment to the 82d Airborne Division; concurrently, redesignated as Headquarters and Headquarters Company, 3d Airborne Battle Group, 504th Infantry. Redesignated 3 July 1968 as Headquarters and Headquarters Company, 3d Battalion, 504th Infantry (organic elements concurrently constituted). Battalion activated 15 July 1968 at Fort Bragg, North Carolina, as an element of the 82d Airborne Division. Inactivated 15 December 1969 at Fort Bragg, North Carolina, and relieved from assignment to the 82d Airborne Division.

CAMPAIGN PARTICIPATION CREDIT

World War II
  *Sicily (with arrowhead)
  *Naples-Foggia
  *Anzio (with arrowhead)
*Rhineland (with arrowhead)
*Ardennes-Alsace
*Central Europe

DECORATIONS

Presidential Unit Citation (Army), Streamer embroidered ANZIO BEACHHEAD

*Presidential Unit Citation (Army), Streamer embroidered NIJMEGEN, HOLLAND (1st Battalion, 504th Parachute Infantry cited; WD GO 62, 1946)

*Presidential Unit Citation (Army), Streamer embroidered CHENEUX, BELGIUM (1st Battalion [less Company A], 504th Parachute Infantry cited; WD GO 32, 1945)

*Military Order of William (Degree of the Knight of the Fourth Class), Streamer embroidered NIJMEGEN 1944 (504th Parachute Infantry cited; DA GO 43, 1950)

*Netherlands Orange Lanyard (504th Parachute Infantry cited; DA GO 43, 1950)

*Belgian Fourragere 1940 (504th Parachute Infantry cited; DA GO 43, 1950)

*Cited in the Order of the Day of the Belgian Army for action in the ARDENNES (504th Parachute Infantry cited; DA GO 43, 1950)

*Cited in the Order of the Day of the Belgian Army for action in BELGIUM AND GERMANY (504th Parachute Infantry cited; DA GO 43, 1950)

504TH INFANTRY, BIBLIOGRAPHY

Carter, Ross S. *Those Devils in Baggy Pants.* New York: Appleton-Century-Crofts, Inc., 1951. (Also published in paperback in 1962 by Signet.)

Exercise Snow Storm, January–March 1953, Camp Drum, New York. Fort Jay, New York, 1952.

504th Airborne Infantry. Dayton: McGregor and Werner Midwest Corporation, 1956?

Garland, Albert N. and Howard McGaw Smyth. *Sicily and the Surrender of Italy.* United States Army in World War II. Washington: Government Printing Office, 1965.

Historical Section, War Department. *Anzio Beachhead.* American Forces in Action Series. Washington: Government Printing Office, 1947.

————. *Fifth Army at the Winter Line.* American Forces in Action Series. Washington: Government Printing Office, 1945.

————. *From the Volturno to the Winter Line.* American Forces in Action Series. Washington: Government Printing Office, 1945.

————. *Salerno: American Operations from the Beaches to the Volturno.* American Forces in Action Series. Washington: Government Printing Office, 1944.

Mandle, William and David Whittier, compilers. *Combat Record of the 504th Parachute Infantry Regiment, April 1943–June 1945.* Paris: Draeger Frères, 1945.

Pictorial History, 504th Parachute Infantry Regiment, 1947. n.p., 1947.

Sheehan, Fred. *Anzio.* Norman: University of Oklahoma Press, 1964.

505th INFANTRY
(Panthers)

HERALDIC ITEMS

COAT OF ARMS

Shield: Argent, four bendlets azure surmounted by a winged black panther salient inverted proper, that part on the bendlets fimbriated of the first.

Crest: On a wreath of the colors a winged arrowhead point down gules, in front of a cloud proper.

Motto: H-Minus.

Symbolism: Blue and white are the old and present colors of infantry. The black panther symbolizes stealth, speed, and courage, all characteristics of a good parachutist. The wings are added to represent entry into combat via air, and the bendlets symbolize the unit's parachute drops into combat.

The winged red arrowhead in the crest is used to represent the regiment's first combat attack in Sicily during World War II.

DISTINCTIVE INSIGNIA

The distinctive insignia is the shield, crest, and motto of the coat of arms.

LINEAGE AND HONORS

LINEAGE

Constituted 24 June 1942 in the Army of the United States as the 505th Parachute Infantry. Activated 6 July 1942 at Fort Benning, Georgia. Assigned 10 February 1943 to the 82d Airborne Division. Reorganized and redesignated 15 December 1947 as the 505th Airborne Infantry. Allotted 15 November 1948 to the Regular Army.

Relieved 1 September 1957 from assignment to the 82d Airborne Division; concurrently, reorganized and redesignated as the 505th Infantry, a parent regiment under the Combat Arms Regimental System.

CAMPAIGN PARTICIPATION CREDIT

World War II
Sicily (with arrowhead)
Naples-Foggia
Normandy (with arrowhead)
Rhineland (with arrowhead)
Ardennes-Alsace
Central Europe

Vietnam
Tet Counteroffensive
(other campaigns to be determined)

DECORATIONS

Presidential Unit Citation (Army), Streamer embroidered STE. MERE EGLISE (505th Parachute Infantry cited; WD GO 76, 1944)

Presidential Unit Citation (Army), Streamer embroidered NIJMEGEN (2d Battalion, 505th Parachute Infantry cited; WD GO 65, 1946)

French Croix de Guerre with Palm, World War II, Streamer embroidered STE. MERE EGLISE (505th Parachute Infantry cited; DA GO 43, 1950)

French Croix de Guerre with Palm, World War II, Streamer embroidered COTENTIN (505th Parachute Infantry cited; DA GO 43, 1950)

French Croix de Guerre, World War II, Fourragere (505th Parachute Infantry cited; DA GO 43, 1950)

Military Order of William (Degree of the Knight of the Fourth Class), Streamer embroidered NIJMEGEN 1944 (505th Parachute Infantry cited; DA GO 43, 1950)

Netherlands Orange Lanyard (505th Parachute Infantry cited; DA GO 43, 1950)

Belgian Fourragere 1940 (505th Parachute Infantry cited; DA GO 43, 1950)

Cited in the Order of the Day of the Belgian Army for action in the ARDENNES (505th Parachute Infantry cited; DA GO 43, 1950)

Cited in the Order of the Day of the Belgian Army for action in BELGIUM AND GERMANY (505th Parachute Infantry cited; DA GO 43, 1950)

1st BATTALION, 505th INFANTRY

(Panthers)

RA
(82d Airborne Division)

LINEAGE

Constituted 24 June 1942 in the Army of the United States as Company A, 505th Parachute Infantry. Activated 6 July 1942 at Fort Benning, Georgia. (505th Parachute Infantry assigned 10 February 1943 to the 82d Airborne Division.) Reorganized and redesignated 15 December 1947 as Company A, 505th Airborne Infantry. Allotted 15 November 1948 to the Regular Army.

Reorganized and redesignated 1 September 1957 as Headquarters and Headquarters Company, 1st Airborne Battle Group, 505th Infantry and remained assigned to the 82d Airborne Division (organic elements concurrently constituted and activated). Relieved 15 January 1959 from assignment to the 82d Airborne Division and assigned to the 8th Infantry Division. Relieved 1 April 1963 from assignment to the 8th Infantry Division and assigned to the 82d Airborne Division. Reorganized and redesignated 25 May 1964 as the 1st Battalion, 505th Infantry.

CAMPAIGN PARTICIPATION CREDIT

World War II
  *Sicily (with arrowhead)
  *Naples-Foggia
  *Normandy (with arrowhead)
  *Rhineland (with arrowhead)
  *Ardennes-Alsace
  *Central Europe

Vietnam
  *Tet Counteroffensive
  (other campaigns to be determined)

DECORATIONS

*Presidential Unit Citation (Army), Streamer embroidered STE. MERE EGLISE (505th Parachute Infantry cited; WD GO 76, 1944)

Presidential Unit Citation (Army), Streamer embroidered NIJMEGEN

*French Croix de Guerre with Palm, World War II, Streamer embroidered STE. MERE EGLISE (505th Parachute Infantry cited; DA GO 43, 1950)

*French Croix de Guerre with Palm, World War II, Streamer embroidered COTENTIN (505th Parachute Infantry cited; DA GO 43, 1950)

847

*French Croix de Guerre, World War II, Fourragere (505th Parachute Infantry cited; DA GO 43, 1950)

*Military Order of William (Degree of the Knight of the Fourth Class), Streamer embroidered NIJMEGEN 1944 (505th Parachute Infantry cited; DA GO 43, 1950)

*Netherlands Orange Lanyard (505th Parachute Infantry cited; DA GO 43, 1950)

*Belgian Fourragere 1940 (505th Parachute Infantry cited; DA GO 43, 1950)

*Cited in the Order of the Day of the Belgian Army for action in the ARDENNES (505th Parachute Infantry cited; DA GO 43, 1950)

*Cited in the Order of the Day of the Belgian Army for action in BELGIUM AND GERMANY (505th Parachute Infantry cited; DA GO 43, 1950)

*Vietnamese Cross of Gallantry with Palm, Streamer embroidered VIETNAM 1968–1969 (1st Battalion, 505th Infantry cited; DA GO 43, 1970)

2d BATTALION, 505th INFANTRY

(Panthers)

RA
(82d Airborne Division)

LINEAGE

Constituted 24 June 1942 in the Army of the United States as Company B, 505th Parachute Infantry. Activated 6 July 1942 at Fort Benning, Georgia. (505th Parachute Infantry assigned 10 February 1943 to the 82d Airborne Division.) Reorganized and redesignated 15 December 1947 as Company B, 505th Airborne Infantry. Allotted 15 November 1948 to the Regular Army.

Reorganized and redesignated 1 March 1957 as Headquarters and Headquarters Company, 2d Airborne Battle Group, 505th Infantry, relieved from assignment to the 82d Airborne Division, and assigned to the 11th Airborne Division (organic elements concurrently constituted and activated). Inactivated 1 July 1958 in Germany. Redesignated 6 March 1964 as the 2d Battalion, 505th Infantry; concurrently, relieved from assignment to the 11th Airborne Division and assigned to the 82d Airborne Division. Activated 25 May 1964 at Fort Bragg, North Carolina.

CAMPAIGN PARTICIPATION CREDIT

World War II
  *Sicily (with arrowhead)
  *Naples-Foggia
  *Normandy (with arrowhead)
  *Rhineland (with arrowhead)
  *Ardennes-Alsace
  *Central Europe

Vietnam
  *Tet Counteroffensive
  (other campaigns to be determined)

DECORATIONS

*Presidential Unit Citation (Army), Streamer embroidered STE. MERE EGLISE (505th Parachute Infantry cited; WD GO 76, 1944)

Presidential Unit Citation (Army), Streamer embroidered NIJMEGEN

*French Croix de Guerre with Palm, World War II, Streamer embroidered STE. MERE EGLISE (505th Parachute Infantry cited; DA GO 43, 1950)

*French Croix de Guerre with Palm, World War II, Streamer embroidered COTENTIN (505th Parachute Infantry cited; DA GO 43, 1950)

*French Croix de Guerre, World War II, Fourragere (505th Parachute Infantry cited; DA GO 43, 1950)

*Military Order of William (Degree of the Knight of the Fourth Class) , Streamer embroidered NIJMEGEN 1944 (505th Parachute Infantry cited; DA GO 43, 1950)

*Netherlands Orange Lanyard (505th Parachute Infantry cited; DA GO 43, 1950)

*Belgian Fourragere 1940 (505th Parachute Infantry cited; DA GO 43, 1950)

*Cited in the Order of the Day of the Belgian Army for action in the ARDENNES (505th Parachute Infantry cited; DA GO 43, 1950)

*Cited in the Order of the Day of the Belgian Army for action in BELGIUM AND GERMANY (505th Parachute Infantry cited; DA GO 43, 1950)

*Vietnamese Cross of Gallantry with Palm, Streamer embroidered VIETNAM 1968–1969 (2d Battalion, 505th Infantry cited; DA GO 43, 1970)

3d BATTALION, 505th INFANTRY

(Panthers)

RA
(inactive)

LINEAGE

Constituted 24 June 1942 in the Army of the United States as Company C, 505th Parachute Infantry. Activated 6 July 1942 at Fort Benning, Georgia. (505th Parachute Infantry assigned 10 February 1943 to the 82d Airborne Division.) Reorganized and redesignated 15 December 1947 as Company C, 505th Airborne Infantry. Allotted 15 November 1948 to the Regular Army.

Inactivated 1 September 1957 at Fort Bragg, North Carolina, and relieved from assignment to the 82d Airborne Division; concurrently, redesignated as Headquarters and Headquarters Company, 3d Airborne Battle Group, 505th Infantry. Redesignated 3 July 1968 as Headquarters and Headquarters Company, 3d Battalion, 505th Infantry (organic elements concurrently constituted). Battalion activated 15 July 1968 at Fort Bragg, North Carolina, as an element of the 82d Airborne Division. Inactivated 15 December 1969 at Fort Bragg, North Carolina, and relieved from assignment to the 82d Airborne Division.

CAMPAIGN PARTICIPATION CREDIT

World War II
  *Sicily (with arrowhead)
  *Naples-Foggia
  *Normandy (with arrowhead)

*Rhineland (with arrowhead)
*Ardennes-Alsace
*Central Europe

DECORATIONS

*Presidential Unit Citation (Army), Streamer embroidered STE. MERE EGLISE (505th Parachute Infantry cited; WD GO 76, 1944)

Presidential Unit Citation (Army), Streamer embroidered NIJMEGEN
*French Croix de Guerre with Palm, World War II, Streamer embroidered STE. MERE EGLISE (505th Parachute Infantry cited; DA GO 43, 1950)

*French Croix de Guerre with Palm, World War II, Streamer embroidered COTENTIN (505th Parachute Infantry cited; DA GO 43, 1950)

851

*French Croix de Guerre, World War II, Fourragere (505th Parachute Infantry cited; DA GO 43, 1950)

*Military Order of William (Degree of the Knight of the Fourth Class) , Streamer embroidered NIJMEGEN 1944 (505th Parachute Infantry cited; DA GO 43, 1950)

*Netherlands Orange Lanyard (505th Parachute Infantry cited; DA GO 43, 1950)

*Belgian Fourragere 1940 (505th Parachute Infantry cited; DA GO 43, 1950)

*Cited in the Order of the Day of the Belgian Army for action in the ARDENNES (505th Parachute Infantry cited; DA GO 43, 1950)

*Cited in the Order of the Day of the Belgian Army for action in BELGIUM AND GERMANY (505th Parachute Infantry cited; DA GO 43, 1950)

505TH INFANTRY, BIBLIOGRAPHY

Airborne Assault Operations. (505th Regimental Combat Team in the vicinity of city and province of Trapani, Sicily.) n.p., 1943.

Black Panther Regiment. Fort Bragg, North Carolina, 1954.

Blumenson, Martin. *Breakout and Pursuit.* United States Army in World War II. Washington: Government Printing Office, 1961.

Cole, Hugh M. *The Ardennes: Battle of the Bulge.* United States Army in World War II. Washington: Government Printing Office, 1964.

Exercise Snow Storm, January–March 1953, Camp Drum, New York. Fort Jay, New York, 1952.

Exercise Snowdrop, Pine Camp, New York, 1 November 1947 Through 8 February 1948. n.p., 1948.

Garland, Albert N. and Howard McGaw Smyth. *Sicily and the Surrender of Italy.* United States Army in World War II. Washington: Government Printing Office, 1965.

Gavin, James M. *War and Peace in the Space Age.* New York: Harper and Brothers, 1958. (Pages 52–78 describe General Gavin's account of his activities in the airborne assault of Sicily.)

Harrison, Gordon A. *Cross-Channel Attack.* United States Army in World War II. Washington: Government Printing Office, 1951.

Historical Section, War Department. *Salerno: American Operations from the Beaches to the Volturno.* American Forces in Action Series. Washington: Government Printing Office, 1944.

————. *Utah Beach to Cherbourg.* American Forces in Action Series. Washington: Government Printing Office, 1947.

History Section, European Theater of Operations. *The Capture of Ste. Mère Eglise, An Action by the 505th Infantry. . . 82d Airborne Division.* (Regimental Unit Study Number 6.) n.p., 1945.

Howe, George F. *Northwest Africa: Seizing the Initiative in the West.* United States Army in World War II. Washington: Government Printing Office, 1957.

MacDonald, Charles B. *The Siegfried Line Campaign.* United States Army in World War II. Washington: Government Printing Office, 1963.

506th INFANTRY

(Currahee)

HERALDIC ITEMS

COAT OF ARMS

Shield: Azure, a lightning flash in bend throughout argent, in chief, six parachutes, three, two and one of the last, in base a mountain issuant proper.

Crest: On a wreath argent and azure, in front of a demi-plate bearing a demi-torteau surmounted overall in pale by a winged sword-breaker point to base or wings elevated of the first, two caltraps conjoined gold that to the dexter bearing a fleur-de-lis of the second and that to the sinister a bugle horn of the like.

Motto: *Currahee* (Stands Alone).

Symbolism: The blue field of the shield is for the infantry. The thunderbolt indicates the regiment's particular threat and technique of attack: striking with speed, power, and surprise from the sky. Six parachutes represent the fact that the 506th was the sixth parachute regiment constituted in the U.S. Army. The green silhouette represents Currahee Mountain—the site of the regiment's activation (Camp Toccoa, Georgia)—and symbolizes the organization's strength, independence, and ability to stand alone for which paratroops are renowned. In fact *Currahee* is the American aboriginal Cherokee Indian equivalent for "Stands Alone."

The winged sword-breaker represents airborne troops. The conjoined caltraps stand for the enemy line of defense behind which paratroopers are dropped. They are two in number in reference to the unit's two air assault landings. The fleur-de-lis is for the Normandy invasion and the bugle horn, from the arms of Eindhoven, Holland, refers to the organization's capture of that objective. The spikes of the caltraps stand for the unit's World War

855

II decorations. The demi-roundel represents a section of the hub of a wheel. It stands for Bastogne, Belgium, strategic crossroads of highways and railways. The hub, surmounted by the winged sword-breaker, commemorates the organization's heroic defense of Bastogne in the Battle of the Bulge.

DISTINCTIVE INSIGNIA

The distinctive insignia is the shield and motto of the coat of arms.

LINEAGE AND HONORS

LINEAGE

Constituted 1 July 1942 in the Army of the United States as the 506th Parachute Infantry. Activated 20 July 1942 at Camp Toccoa, Georgia. Assigned 1 March 1945 to the 101st Airborne Division. Inactivated 30 November 1945 at Auxerre, France. Redesignated 18 June 1948 as the 506th Airborne Infantry. Allotted 25 June 1948 to the Regular Army.

Activated 6 July 1948 at Camp Breckinridge, Kentucky. Inactivated 1 April 1949 at Camp Breckinridge, Kentucky. Activated 25 August 1950 at Camp Breckinridge, Kentucky. Inactivated 1 December 1953 at Camp Breckinridge, Kentucky. Activated 15 May 1954 at Fort Jackson, South Carolina.

Relieved 25 April 1957 from assignment to the 101st Airborne Division; concurrently, reorganized and redesignated as the 506th Infantry, a parent regiment under the Combat Arms Regimental System.

CAMPAIGN PARTICIPATION CREDIT

World War II
    Normandy (with arrowhead)
    Rhineland (with arrowhead)
    Ardennes-Alsace
    Central Europe

Vietnam
    Counteroffensive, Phase III
    Tet Counteroffensive
    (other campaigns to be determined)

DECORATIONS

Presidential Unit Citation (Army), Streamer embroidered BASTOGNE (506th Parachute Infantry cited; WD GO 17, 1945)

Presidential Unit Citation (Army), Streamer embroidered NORMANDY (506th Parachute Infantry cited; WD GO 4, 1945)

Valorous Unit Award, Streamer embroidered PHAN THIET (3d Battalion, 506th Infantry cited; DA GO 43, 1970)

French Croix de Guerre with Palm, World War II, Streamer embroidered NORMANDY (506th Parachute Infantry cited; DA GO 43, 1950)

Netherlands Orange Lanyard (506th Parachute Infantry cited; DA GO 43, 1950)

Belgian Croix de Guerre 1940 with Palm, Streamer embroidered BASTOGNE; cited in the Order of the Day of the Belgian Army for action at BASTOGNE (506th Parachute Infantry cited; DA GO 43, 1950, as amended by DA GO 27, 1959)

Belgian Fourragere 1940 (506th Parachute Infantry cited; DA GO 43, 1950)

Cited in the Order of the Day of the Belgian Army for action in FRANCE AND BELGIUM (506th Parachute Infantry cited; DA GO 43, 1950)

1st BATTALION, 506th INFANTRY

(Currahee)

RA
(101st Airborne Division)

LINEAGE

Constituted 1 July 1942 in the Army of the United States as Company A, 506th Parachute Infantry. Activated 20 July 1942 at Camp Toccoa, Georgia. (506th Parachute Infantry assigned 1 March 1945 to the 101st Airborne Division.) Inactivated 30 November 1945 at Auxerre, France. Redesignated 18 June 1948 as Company A, 506th Airborne Infantry. Allotted 25 June 1948 to the Regular Army.

Activated 6 July 1948 at Camp Breckinridge, Kentucky. Inactivated 1 April 1949 at Camp Breckinridge, Kentucky. Activated 25 August 1950 at Camp Breckinridge, Kentucky. Inactivated 1 December 1953 at Camp Breckinridge, Kentucky. Activated 15 May 1954 at Fort Jackson, South Carolina.

Reorganized and redesignated 25 April 1957 as Headquarters and Headquarters Company, 1st Airborne Battle Group, 506th Infantry and remained assigned to the 101st Airborne Division (organic elements concurrently constituted and activated). Reorganized and redesignated 3 February 1964 as the 1st Battalion, 506th Infantry.

CAMPAIGN PARTICIPATION CREDIT

World War II
  *Normandy (with arrowhead)
  *Rhineland (with arrowhead)
  *Ardennes-Alsace
  *Central Europe

Vietnam
  *Counteroffensive, Phase III
  *Tet Counteroffensive
  (other campaigns to be determined)

DECORATIONS

*Presidential Unit Citation (Army), Streamer embroidered BASTOGNE (506th Parachute Infantry cited; WD GO 17, 1945)

*Presidential Unit Citation (Army), Streamer embroidered NORMANDY (506th Parachute Infantry cited; WD GO 4, 1945)

*French Croix de Guerre with Palm, World War II, Streamer embroidered NORMANDY (506th Parachute Infantry cited; DA GO 43, 1950)

*Netherlands Orange Lanyard (506th Parachute Infantry cited; DA GO 43, 1950)

*Belgian Croix de Guerre 1940 with Palm, Streamer embroidered BASTOGNE; cited in the Order of the Day of the Belgian Army for action at BASTOGNE (506th Parachute Infantry cited; DA GO 43, 1950, as amended by DA GO 27, 1959)

*Belgian Fourragere 1940 (506th Parachute Infantry cited; DA GO 43, 1950)

*Cited in the Order of the Day of the Belgian Army for action in FRANCE AND BELGIUM (506th Parachute Infantry cited; DA GO 43, 1950)

*Vietnamese Cross of Gallantry with Palm, Streamer embroidered VIETNAM 1968–1969 (1st Battalion, 506th Infantry cited; DA GO 43, 1970)

2d BATTALION, 506th INFANTRY

(Currahee)

RA
(101st Airborne Division)

Constituted 1 July 1942 in the Army of the United States as Company B, 506th Parachute Infantry. Activated 20 July 1942 at Camp Taccoa, Georgia. (506th Parachute Infantry assigned 1 March 1945 to the 101st Airborne Division.) Inactivated 30 November 1945 at Auxerre, France. Redesignated 18 June 1948 as Company B, 506th Airborne Infantry. Allotted 25 June 1948 to the Regular Army.

Activated 6 July 1948 at Camp Breckinridge, Kentucky. Inactivated 1 April 1949 at Camp Breckinridge, Kentucky. Activated 25 August 1950 at Camp Breckinridge, Kentucky. Inactivated 1 December 1953 at Camp Breckinridge, Kentucky. Activated 15 May 1954 at Fort Jackson, South Carolina.

Inactivated 25 April 1957 at Fort Campbell, Kentucky, and relieved from assignment to the 101st Airborne Division; concurrently, redesignated Headquarters and Headquarters Company, 2d Airborne Battle Group, 506th Infantry. Redesignated 21 January 1964 as Headquarters and Headquarters Company, 2d Battalion, 506th Infantry and assigned to the 101st Airborne Division (organic elements concurrently constituted). Battalion activated 3 February 1964 at Fort Campbell, Kentucky.

CAMPAIGN PARTICIPATION CREDIT

World War II
- *Normandy (with arrowhead)
- *Rhineland (with arrowhead)
- *Ardennes-Alsace
- *Central Europe

Vietnam
- *Counteroffensive, Phase III
- *Tet Counteroffensive
- (other campaigns to be determined)

DECORATIONS

*Presidential Unit Citation (Army), Streamer embroidered BASTOGNE (506th Parachute Infantry cited; WD GO 17, 1945)

*Presidential Unit Citation (Army), Streamer embroidered NORMANDY (506th Parachute Infantry cited; WD GO 4, 1945)

*French Croix de Guerre with Palm, World War II, Streamer embroidered NORMANDY (506th Parachute Infantry cited; DA GO 43, 1950)

*Netherlands Orange Lanyard (506th Parachute Infantry cited; DA GO 43, 1950)

*Belgian Croix de Guerre 1940 with Palm, Streamer embroidered BASTOGNE; cited in the Order of the Day of the Belgian Army for action at BASTOGNE (506th Parachute Infantry cited; DA GO 43, 1950, as amended by DA GO 27, 1959)

*Belgian Fourragere 1940 (506th Parachute Infantry cited; DA GO 43, 1950)

*Cited in the Order of the Day of the Belgian Army for action in FRANCE AND BELGIUM (506th Parachute Infantry cited; DA GO 43, 1950)

*Vietnamese Cross of Gallantry with Palm, Streamer embroidered VIETNAM 1968–1969 (2d Battalion, 506th Infantry cited; DA GO 43, 1970)

3d BATTALION, 506th INFANTRY

(Currahee)

RA
(101st Airborne Division)

LINEAGE

Constituted 1 July 1942 in the Army of the United States as Company C, 506th Parachute Infantry. Activated 20 July 1942 at Camp Toccoa, Georgia. (506th Parachute Infantry assigned 1 March 1945 to the 101st Airborne Division.) Inactivated 30 November 1945 at Auxerre, France. Redesignated 18 June 1948 as Company C, 506th Airborne Infantry. Allotted 25 June 1948 to the Regular Army.

Activated 6 July 1948 at Camp Breckinridge, Kentucky. Inactivated 1 April 1949 at Camp Breckinridge, Kentucky. Activated 25 August 1950 at Camp Breckinridge, Kentucky. Inactivated 1 December 1953 at Camp Breckinridge, Kentucky. Activated 15 May 1954 at Fort Jackson, South Carolina.

Inactivated 25 April 1957 at Fort Campbell, Kentucky, and relieved from assignment to the 101st Airborne Division; concurrently, redesignated as Headquarters and Headquarters Company, 3d Airborne Battle Group, 506th Infantry. Redesignated 6 February 1967 as Headquarters and Headquarters Company, 3d Battalion, 506th Infantry (organic elements concurrently constituted). Battalion activated 1 April 1967 at Fort Campbell, Kentucky, and assigned to the 101st Airborne Division.

CAMPAIGN PARTICIPATION CREDIT

World War II
  *Normandy (with arrowhead)
  *Rhineland (with arrowhead)
  *Ardennes-Alsace
  *Central Europe

Vietnam
  *Counteroffensive, Phase III
  *Tet Counteroffensive
  (other campaigns to be determined)

DECORATIONS

*Presidential Unit Citation (Army), Streamer embroidered BASTOGNE (506th Parachute Infantry cited; WD GO 17, 1945)

*Presidential Unit Citation (Army), Streamer embroidered NORMANDY (506th Parachute Infantry cited; WD GO 4, 1945)

*Valorous Unit Award, Streamer embroidered PHAN THIET (3d Battalion, 506th Infantry cited; DA GO 43, 1970)

*French Croix de Guerre with Palm, World War II, Streamer embroidered NORMANDY (506th Parachute Infantry cited; DA GO 43, 1950)

*Netherlands Orange Lanyard (506th Parachute Infantry cited; DA GO 43, 1950)

*Belgian Croix de Guerre 1940 with Palm, Streamer embroidered BASTOGNE; cited in the Order of the Day of the Belgian Army for action at BASTOGNE (506th Parachute Infantry cited; DA GO 43, 1950, as amended by DA GO 27, 1959)

*Belgian Fourragere 1940 (506th Parachute Infantry cited; DA GO 43, 1950)

*Cited in the Order of the Day of the Belgian Army for action in FRANCE AND BELGIUM (506th Parachute Infantry cited; DA GO 43, 1950)

*Vietnamese Cross of Gallantry with Palm, Streamer embroidered VIETNAM 1968–1969 (3d Battalion, 506th Infantry cited; DA GO 43, 1970)

506TH INFANTRY, BIBLIOGRAPHY

Burgett, Donald Robert. *Currahee*. Boston: Houghton Mifflin Company, 1967.

Cole, Hugh M. *The Ardennes: Battle of the Bulge*. United States Army in World War II. Washington: Government Printing Office, 1964.

Harrison, Gordon A. *Cross-Channel Attack*. United States Army in World War II. Washington: Government Printing Office, 1951.

Historical Section, War Department. *Utah Beach to Cherbourg*. American Forces in Action Series. Washington: Government Printing Office, 1947.

History Section, European Theater of Operations. *506th Parachute Infantry Regiment in Normandy Drop*. (Regimental Unit Study Number 3.) n.p., 1945.

MacDonald, Charles B. *The Siegfried Line Campaign*. United States Army in World War II. Washington: Government Printing Office, 1963.

Scrapbook: 506th Parachute Infantry Regiment, 20 July 1942–4 July 1945. Munich: F. Bruckmann KG, 1945.

Webster, David Kenyon. "We Drank Hitler's Champagne," *Saturday Evening Post*, CXXIV (3 May 1952), 25ff.

508th INFANTRY

HERALDIC ITEMS

COAT OF ARMS

Shield: Azure, on a bend argent a lion passant guardant gules, armed and langued of the first.

Crest: On a wreath argent and azure a pheon with fourteen barbs, divided per pale or and sable in front of a wyvern statant gules.

Motto: Fury From the Sky.

Symbolism: The two principal colors of the shield (blue and white) are the current and old colors of infantry. The lion on the coat of arms is the same as the French leopard used in the arms of Normandy, and commemorates the organization's landing and campaign in that province. The silver bar, called a bend, is in honor of the organization's service in the Rhineland.

The wyvern in the crest is taken from the shoulder sleeve insignia of the 508th Airborne Regimental Combat Team in which the regiment was the primary element in the 1950's. The color red alludes to the unit's unofficial nickname, "Red Devils." The arrowhead divided in two colors, yellow and black, refers to the two assault landings made by the 508th in Normandy and in the Rhineland. The fourteen notches of the arrowhead allude to the regiment's overall honors in World War II—four campaigns and ten decorations.

DISTINCTIVE INSIGNIA

The distinctive insignia is the shield and motto of the coat of arms.

LINEAGE AND HONORS

LINEAGE

Constituted 6 October 1942 in the Army of the United States as the 508th Parachute Infantry. Activated 20 October 1942 at Camp Blanding,

Florida. Inactivated 25 November 1946 at Camp Kilmer, New Jersey. Redesignated 16 April 1951 as the 508th Airborne Infantry; concurrently, allotted to the Regular Army and activated at Fort Bragg, North Carolina. Inactivated 22 March 1957 at Fort Campbell, Kentucky.

Reorganized and redesignated 15 July 1962 as the 508th Infantry, a parent regiment under the Combat Arms Regimental System.

CAMPAIGN PARTICIPATION CREDIT

World War II
    Normandy (with arrowhead)
    Rhineland (with arrowhead)
    Ardennes-Alsace
    Central Europe

Vietnam
    Tet Counteroffensive
    (other campaigns to be determined)

DECORATIONS

Presidential Unit Citation (Army), Streamer embroidered COTENTIN PENINSULA (508th Parachute Infantry cited; WD GO 76, 1944)

Valorous Unit Award, Streamer embroidered HUE AND SAIGON (1st Battalion, 508th Infantry cited; DA GO 43, 1970)

French Croix de Guerre with Palm, World War II, Streamer embroidered STE. MERE EGLISE (508th Parachute Infantry cited; DA GO 43, 1950)

French Croix de Guerre with Palm, World War II, Streamer embroidered COTENTIN (508th Parachute Infantry cited; DA GO 43, 1950)

French Croix de Guerre, World War II, Fourragere (508th Parachute Infantry cited; DA GO 43, 1950)

Military Order of William (Degree of the Knight of the Fourth Class), Streamer embroidered NIJMEGEN 1944 (508th Parachute Infantry cited; DA GO 43, 1950)

Netherlands Orange Lanyard (508th Parachute Infantry cited; DA GO 43, 1950)

Belgian Fourragere 1940 (508th Parachute Infantry cited; DA GO 43, 1950)

Cited in the Order of the Day of the Belgian Army for action in the ARDENNES (508th Parachute Infantry cited; DA GO 43, 1950)

Cited in the Order of the Day of the Belgian Army for action in BELGIUM AND GERMANY (508th Parachute Infantry cited; DA GO 43, 1950)

Cited in the Order of the Day of the Belgian Army for action at ST. VITH (508th Parachute Infantry cited; DA GO 43, 1950)

1st BATTALION, 508th INFANTRY

RA
(82d Airborne Division)

LINEAGE

Constituted 6 October 1942 in the Army of the United States as Company A, 508th Parachute Infantry. Activated 20 October 1942 at Camp Blanding, Florida. Inactivated 25 November 1946 at Camp Kilmer, New Jersey. Redesignated 16 April 1951 as Company A, 508th Airborne Infantry; concurrently, allotted to the Regular Army and activated at Fort Bragg, North Carolina. Inactivated 22 March 1957 at Fort Campbell, Kentucky.

Redesignated 15 July 1962 as Headquarters and Headquarters Company, 1st Battalion, 508th Infantry. Assigned 6 March 1964 to the 82d Airborne Division (organic elements concurrently constituted). Battalion activated 25 May 1964 at Fort Bragg, North Carolina.

CAMPAIGN PARTICIPATION CREDIT

World War II
  *Normandy (with arrowhead)
  *Rhineland (with arrowhead)
  *Ardennes-Alsace
  *Central Europe

Vietnam
  *Tet Counteroffensive
  (other campaigns to be determined)

DECORATIONS

*Presidential Unit Citation (Army), Streamer embroidered COTENTIN PENINSULA (508th Parachute Infantry cited; WD GO 76, 1944)

*Valorous Unit Award, Streamer embroidered HUE AND SAIGON (1st Battalion, 508th Infantry cited; DA GO 43, 1970)

*French Croix de Guerre with Palm, World War II, Streamer embroidered STE. MERE EGLISE (508th Parachute Infantry cited; DA GO 43, 1950)

*French Croix de Guerre with Palm, World War II, Streamer embroidered COTENTIN (508th Parachute Infantry cited; DA GO 43, 1950)

*French Croix de Guerre, World War II, Fourragere (508th Parachute Infantry cited; DA GO 43, 1950)

*Military Order of William (Degree of the Knight of the Fourth Class), Streamer embroidered NIJMEGEN 1944 (508th Parachute Infantry cited; DA GO 43, 1950)

*Netherlands Orange Lanyard (508th Parachute Infantry cited; DA GO 43, 1950)

*Belgian Fourragere 1940 (508th Parachute Infantry cited; DA GO 43, 1950)

*Cited in the Order of the Day of the Belgian Army for action in the ARDENNES (508th Parachute Infantry cited; DA GO 43, 1950)

*Cited in the Order of the Day of the Belgian Army for action in BELGIUM AND GERMANY (508th Parachute Infantry cited; DA GO 43, 1950)

*Cited in the Order of the Day of the Belgian Army for action at ST. VITH (508th Parachute Infantry cited; DA GO 43, 1950)

*Vietnamese Cross of Gallantry with Palm, Streamer embroidered VIETNAM 1968–1969 (1st Battalion, 508th Infantry cited; DA GO 43, 1970)

2d BATTALION, 508th INFANTRY

RA

(82d Airborne Division)

LINEAGE

Constituted 6 October 1942 in the Army of the United States as Company B, 508th Parachute Infantry. Activated 20 October 1942 at Camp Blanding, Florida. Inactivated 25 November 1946 at Camp Kilmer, New Jersey. Redesignated 16 April 1951 as Company B, 508th Airborne Infantry; concurrently, allotted to the Regular Army and activated at Fort Bragg, North Carolina. Inactivated 22 March 1957 at Fort Campbell, Kentucky.

Redesignated 15 July 1962 as Headquarters and Headquarters Company, 2d Battalion, 508th Infantry. Assigned 6 March 1964 to the 82d Airborne Division (organic elements concurrently constituted). Battalion activated 25 May 1964 at Fort Bragg, North Carolina.

CAMPAIGN PARTICIPATION CREDIT

World War II
  *Normandy (with arrowhead)
  *Rhineland (with arrowhead)

*Ardennes-Alsace
*Central Europe

DECORATIONS

*Presidential Unit Citation (Army), Streamer embroidered COTENTIN PENINSULA (508th Parachute Infantry cited; WD GO 76, 1944)

*French Croix de Guerre with Palm, World War II, Streamer embroidered STE. MERE EGLISE (508th Parachute Infantry cited; DA GO 43, 1950)

*French Croix de Guerre with Palm, World War II, Streamer embroidered COTENTIN (508th Parachute Infantry cited; DA GO 43, 1950)

*French Croix de Guerre, World War II, Fourragere (508th Parachute Infantry cited; DA GO 43, 1950)

*Military Order of William (Degree of the Knight of the Fourth Class), Streamer embroidered NIJMEGEN 1944 (508th Parachute Infantry cited; DA GO 43, 1950)

*Netherlands Orange Lanyard (508th Parachute Infantry cited; DA GO 43, 1950)

*Belgian Fourragere 1940 (508th Parachute Infantry cited; DA GO 43, 1950)

869

*Cited in the Order of the Day of the Belgian Army for action in the ARDENNES (508th Parachute Infantry cited; DA GO 43, 1950)

*Cited in the Order of the Day of the Belgian Army for action in BELGIUM AND GERMANY (508th Parachute Infantry cited; DA GO 43, 1950)

*Cited in the Order of the Day of the Belgian Army for action at ST. VITH (508th Parachute Infantry cited; DA GO 43, 1950)

3d BATTALION, 508th INFANTRY

RA
(inactive)

LINEAGE

Constituted 6 October 1942 in the Army of the United States as Company C, 508th Parachute Infantry. Activated 20 October 1942 at Camp Blanding, Florida. Inactivated 25 November 1946 at Camp Kilmer, New Jersey. Redesignated 16 April 1951 as Company C, 508th Airborne Infantry; concurrently, allotted to the Regular Army and activated at Fort Bragg, North Carolina. Inactivated 22 March 1957 at Fort Campbell, Kentucky.

Redesignated 15 July 1962 as Headquarters and Headquarters Company, 3d Battalion, 508th Infantry. Assigned 3 August 1962 to the 193d Infantry Brigade (organic elements concurrently constituted). Battalion activated 8 August 1962 at Fort Kobbe, Canal Zone. Inactivated 26 June 1968 at Fort Kobbe, Canal Zone.

CAMPAIGN PARTICIPATION CREDIT

World War II
 *Normandy (with arrowhead)
 *Rhineland (with arrowhead)
*Ardennes-Alsace
*Central Europe

DECORATIONS

*Presidential Unit Citation (Army), Streamer embroidered COTENTIN PENINSULA (508th Parachute Infantry cited; WD GO 76, 1944)

*French Croix de Guerre with Palm, World War II, Streamer embroidered STE. MERE EGLISE (508th Parachute Infantry cited; DA GO 43, 1950)

*French Croix de Guerre with Palm, World War II, Streamer embroidered COTENTIN (508th Parachute Infantry cited; DA GO 43, 1950)

*French Croix de Guerre, World War II, Fourragere (508th Parachute Infantry cited; DA GO 43, 1950)

*Military Order of William (Degree of the Knight of the Fourth Class), Streamer embroidered NIJMEGEN 1944 (508th Parachute Infantry cited; DA GO 43, 1950)

*Netherlands Orange Lanyard (508th Parachute Infantry cited; DA GO 43, 1950)

*Belgian Fourragere 1940 (508th Parachute Infantry cited; DA GO 43, 1950)

*Cited in the Order of the Day of the Belgian Army for action in the ARDENNES (508th Parachute Infantry cited; DA GO 43, 1950)

*Cited in the Order of the Day of the Belgian Army for action in BELGIUM AND GERMANY (508th Parachute Infantry cited; DA GO 43, 1950)

*Cited in the Order of the Day of the Belgian Army for action at ST. VITH (508th Parachute Infantry cited; DA GO 43, 1950)

508TH INFANTRY, BIBLIOGRAPHY

Blumenson, Martin. *Breakout and Pursuit*. United States Army in World War II. Washington: Government Printing Office, 1961.

Cole, Hugh M. *The Ardennes: Battle of the Bulge*. United States Army in World War II. Washington: Government Printing Office, 1964.

Harrison, Gordon A. *Cross-Channel Attack*. United States Army in World War II. Washington: Government Printing Office, 1951.

Historical Section, War Department. *Utah Beach to Cherbourg*. American Forces in Action Series. Washington: Government Printing Office, 1947.

Lord, William G. *History of the 508th Parachute Infantry*. Washington: Infantry Journal Press, 1948.

MacDonald, Charles B. *The Siegfried Line Campaign*. United States Army in World War II. Washington: Government Printing Office, 1963.

Marshall, S. L. A. "Affair at Hill 30," *Marine Corps Gazette*, XXXII (February 1948), 8 14; XXXII (March 1948), 20–25.

"Red Devils From Heaven," *Pegasus*, II (August 1943), 6–7ff.

Wolf, Joe. *508th Airborne Regimental Combat Team, June 1951–August 1952, Fort Benning, Georgia*. Baton Rouge: Army and Navy Publishing Company, 1952.

509th INFANTRY

HERALDIC ITEMS

COAT OF ARMS

Shield: Gules, a fess nebuly counter wavy argent a barrulet wavy azure, on a pile sable fimbriated of the second, between in base four arrowheads points down palewise of the same, another of the like below a stylized figure of a parachutist or.

Crest: On a wreath argent and gules, a rock proper (gray) charged with a crescent or, a prowling desert jackal (as depicted on the regimental badge of the French 3d Zouaves Regiment) of the like.

Motto: All the Way.

Symbolism: The stylized yellow (gold) figure of a parachutist on a black ground is adapted from the device worn by the regiment during World War II and by which it was known throughout the Mediterranean Theater. The red field alludes to the red berets worn by the British 1st Airborne Division and the close association between it and the regiment during World War II in England and North Africa. The nebuly (heraldic delineation for water) white and blue bars (the colors blue and white are used for infantry) refer to the record breaking flight from England parachuting into North Africa on 8 November 1942. The two segments of the wavy blue bar simulate the streamers of the Presidential Unit Citations (Army) awarded for the gallant actions at Carano, Italy, and Liege, Belgium, and in being a heraldic symbol of water refer to the amphibious landing on the Anzio-Nettuno beachhead on 22 January 1944. The black pile simulates a parachute jump and in also being a heraldic symbol used frequently for engineers (i.e., pile driving), the two sides refer to the ground defense the organization participated in during the Anzio and Ardennes-Alsace (Battle of the Bulge) campaigns. The five arrowheads are for the five assault landings made by the regiment in World War II.

The jackal and crescent are taken from the regimental badge of the French 3d Zouaves Regiment, and symbolize the parachute jump and seizure of the airfield at Youks-les-Bains near the border of Tunisia. One of the results of this hazardous operation on 15 November 1942 was the authority granted by the French Commander in Chief for personnel of the 509th Infantry to wear the badge of the 3d Zouaves Regiment. The rock and crescent allude to the subsequent successful action at Faid Pass in Tunisia.

DISTINCTIVE INSIGNIA

The distinctive insignia is the shield and motto of the coat of arms.

LINEAGE AND HONORS

LINEAGE

Constituted 14 March 1941 in the Army of the United States as the 504th Parachute Battalion. Activated 5 October 1941 at Fort Benning, Georgia. Reorganized and redesignated 24 February 1942 as the 2d Battalion, 503d Parachute Infantry. Reorganized and redesignated 2 November 1942 as the 2d Battalion, 509th Parachute Infantry. Reorganized and redesignated 10 December 1943 as the 509th Parachute Infantry Battalion. Disbanded 1 March 1945 in France. Reconstituted 12 May 1947 in the Regular Army as the 509th Parachute Infantry Battalion.

Reorganized and redesignated 1 April 1963 as the 509th Infantry, a parent regiment under the Combat Arms Regimental System.

CAMPAIGN PARTICIPATION CREDIT

World War II	Anzio (with arrowhead)
Algeria-French Morocco	Rome-Arno
(with arrowhead)	Southern France (with arrowhead)
Tunisia (with arrowhead)	Rhineland
Naples-Foggia (with arrowhead)	Ardennes-Alsace

DECORATIONS

Presidential Unit Citation (Army), Streamer embroidered LIEGE, BELGIUM (509th Parachute Infantry Battalion cited; WD GO 30, 1945)

Presidential Unit Citation (Army), Streamer embroidered CARANO, ITALY (509th Parachute Infantry Battalion cited; WD GO 53, 1944)

French Croix de Guerre with Silver Star, World War II, Streamer embroidered MUY EN PROVENCE (509th Parachute Infantry Battalion cited; DA GO 43, 1950)

Cited in the Order of the Day of the Belgian Army for action in the ARDENNES (509th Parachute Infantry Battalion cited; DA GO 43, 1950)

Cited in the Order of the Day of the Belgian Army for action at ST. VITH (509th Parachute Infantry Battalion cited; DA GO 43, 1950)

Personnel authorized to wear the insignia of the French 3d Zouaves Regiment (2d Battalion, 503d Parachute Infantry cited; Letter Order 969, French Commander in Chief, 6 February 1944, and DF, Comment 1, WD, G-1, 27 December 1944)

1st BATTALION, 509th INFANTRY

RA
(8th Infantry Division)

LINEAGE

Constituted 14 March 1941 in the Army of the United States as Company A, 504th Parachute Battalion. Activated 5 October 1941 at Fort Benning, Georgia. Reorganized and redesignated 24 February 1942 as Company D, 503d Parachute Infantry. Reorganized and redesignated 2 November 1942 as Company D, 509th Parachute Infantry. Reorganized and redesignated 10 December 1943 as Company A, 509th Parachute Infantry Battalion. Disbanded 1 March 1945 in France. Reconstituted 12 May 1947 in the Regular Army as Company A, 509th Parachute Infantry Battalion.

Redesignated 27 March 1963 as Headquarters and Headquarters Company, 1st Battalion, 509th Infantry and assigned to the 8th Infantry Division (organic elements concurrently constituted) . Battalion activated 1 April 1963 in Germany.

CAMPAIGN PARTICIPATION CREDIT

World War II
*Algeria-French Morocco
(with arrowhead)
*Tunisia (with arrowhead)
*Naples-Foggia (with arrowhead)

*Anzio (with arrowhead)
*Rome-Arno
*Southern France (with arrowhead)
*Rhineland
*Ardennes-Alsace

DECORATIONS

*Presidential Unit Citation (Army), Streamer embroidered LIEGE, BELGIUM (509th Parachute Infantry Battalion cited; WD GO 30, 1945)

*Presidential Unit Citation (Army), Streamer embroidered CARANO, ITALY (509th Parachute Infantry Battalion cited; WD GO 53, 1944)

*French Croix de Guerre with Silver Star, World War II, Streamer embroidered MUY EN PROVENCE (509th Parachute Infantry Battalion cited; DA GO 43, 1950)

*Cited in the Order of the Day of the Belgian Army for action in the ARDENNES (509th Parachute Infantry Battalion cited; DA GO 43, 1950)

*Cited in the Order of the Day of the Belgian Army for action at ST. VITH (509th Parachute Infantry Battalion cited; DA GO 43, 1950)

*Personnel authorized to wear the insignia of the French 3d Zouaves Regiment (2d Battalion, 503d Parachute Infantry cited; Letter Order 969, French Commander in Chief, 6 February 1944, and DF, Comment 1, WD, G-1, 27 December 1944)

2d BATTALION, 509th INFANTRY

RA
(8th Infantry Division)

LINEAGE

Constituted 14 March 1941 in the Army of the United States as Company B, 504th Parachute Battalion. Activated 5 October 1941 at Fort Benning, Georgia. Reorganized and redesignated 24 February 1942 as Company E, 503d Parachute Infantry. Reorganized and redesignated 2 November 1942 as Company E, 509th Parachute Infantry. Reorganized and redesignated 10 December 1943 as Company B, 509th Parachute Infantry Battalion. Disbanded 1 March 1945 in France. Reconstituted 12 May 1947 in the Regular Army as Company B, 509th Parachute Infantry Battalion.

Redesignated 27 March 1963 as Headquarters and Headquarters Company, 2d Battalion, 509th Infantry, and assigned to the 8th Infantry Division (organic elements concurrently constituted). Battalion activated 1 April 1963 in Germany.

CAMPAIGN PARTICIPATION CREDIT

World War II
  *Algeria-French Morocco
    (with arrowhead)
  *Tunisia (with arrowhead)
  *Naples-Foggia (with arrowhead)

*Anzio (with arrowhead)
*Rome-Arno
*Southern France (with arrowhead)
*Rhineland
*Ardennes-Alsace

DECORATIONS

*Presidential Unit Citation (Army), Streamer embroidered LIEGE, BELGIUM (509th Parachute Infantry Battalion cited; WD GO 30, 1945)

*Presidential Unit Citation (Army), Streamer embroidered CARANO, ITALY (509th Parachute Infantry Battalion cited; WD GO 53, 1944)

*French Croix de Guerre with Silver Star, World War II, Streamer embroidered MUY EN PROVENCE (509th Parachute Infantry Battalion cited; DA GO 43, 1950)

*Cited in the Order of the Day of the Belgian Army for action in the ARDENNES (509th Parachute Infantry Battalion cited; DA GO 43, 1950)

*Cited in the Order of the Day of the Belgian Army for action at ST. VITH (509th Parachute Infantry Battalion cited; DA GO 43, 1950)

*Personnel authorized to wear the insignia of the French 3d Zouaves

Regiment (2d Battalion, 503d Parachute Infantry cited; Letter Order 969, French Commander in Chief, 6 February 1944, and DF, Comment 1, WD, G-1, 27 December 1944)

509TH INFANTRY, BIBLIOGRAPHY

Bennett, Lowell. *Assignment to Nowhere (The Battle for Tunisia)*. New York: Vanguard Press, 1953, pp. 48–53, 63–66, ch.5.

Blumenson, Martin. *Salerno to Cassino*. United States Army in World War II. Washington: Government Printing Office, 1969.

Carvey, James B. "Faid Pass," *Infantry Journal*, LV (September 1944), 8–13.

Historical Section, War Department. *Anzio Beachhead*. American Forces in Action Series. Washington: Government Printing Office, 1947.

––––––. *From the Volturno to the Winter Line*. American Forces in Action Series. Washington: Government Printing Office, 1944.

––––––. *Salerno: American Operations from the Beaches to the Volturno*. American Forces in Action Series. Washington: Government Printing Office, 1945.

Howe, George F. *Northwest Africa: Seizing the Initiative in the West*. United States Army in World War II. Washington: Government Printing Office, 1957.

Hutton, Bud. "Nice Kids, Our Daredevils," *The New York Times Magazine* (3 January 1943), 4.

Life, XV (18 January 1943), 30–31. (Photographs.)

Parachute Battalion. Baton Rouge: Army and Navy Publishing Company, 1942.

Raff, Edson Duncan. *We Jumped to Fight*. New York: Eagle Books, 1944.

Sheehan, Fred. *Anzio*. Norman: University of Oklahoma Press, 1964.

Wharton, Don. "Dan DeLeo: Paratrooper in Tunisia," *Look*, VII (9 July 1943), 42.

––––––. "Paratroop Doctor Saves Lives in Desert Hell," *Look*, VII (13 July 1943), 52.

Yarborough, William P. "House Party in Jerryland," *The Infantry Journal*, LV (July 1944), 8–15.

511th INFANTRY

HERALDIC ITEMS

COAT OF ARMS

Shield: Per fess nebuly abased azure and vert, on a wedge arched in chief argent, between in base a kris and a Polynesian war club saltirewise and a sun with rays (as depicted on the national flag of the Philippines) all or, a torii gules.

Crest: None.

Motto: Strength From Above.

Symbolism: Blue is the infantry color, and the blue and green signify the sky and the earth—the nebuly dividing line being the heraldic symbol for clouds. The white, wedge-shaped figure represents a parachute (for airborne infantry) and is also indicative of a wedge being driven from sky to earth, thus alluding to the regimental motto, "Strength From Above." The sun with rays is for service in the Philippines; the crossed kris and war club represent service in New Guinea; and the torii symbolizes service in Japan.

DISTINCTIVE INSIGNIA

The distinctive insignia is the shield and motto of the coat of arms.

LINEAGE AND HONORS

LINEAGE

Constituted 12 November 1942 in the Army of the United States as the 511th Parachute Infantry. Activated 5 January 1943 at Camp Toccoa, Georgia. Assigned 25 February 1943 to the 11th Airborne Division. Allotted 15 November 1948 to the Regular Army. Reorganized and redesignated 30 June 1949 as the 511th Airborne Infantry. Inactivated 1 March 1957 in Germany and relieved from assignment to the 11th Airborne Division.

Reorganized and redesignated 15 May 1963 as the 511th Infantry, a parent regiment under the Combat Arms Regimental System.

Campaign Participation Credit

World War II
  New Guinea
  Leyte
  Luzon (with arrowhead)

Decorations

Presidential Unit Citation (Army), Streamer embroidered MANILA (Regimental Headquarters and Headquarters Company and 1st, 2d, and 3d Battalions, 511th Parachute Infantry cited; WD GO's 71 and 68, 1945)

Philippine Presidential Unit Citation, Streamer embroidered 17 OCTOBER 1944 TO 4 JULY 1945 (511th Parachute Infantry cited; DA GO 47, 1950)

1st BATTALION, 511th INFANTRY

RA
(inactive)

LINEAGE

Constituted 12 November 1942 in the Army of the United States as Company A, 511th Parachute Infantry. Activated 5 January 1943 at Camp Toccoa, Georgia. (511th Parachute Infantry assigned 25 February 1943 to the 11th Airborne Division.) Allotted 15 November 1948 to the Regular Army. Reorganized and redesignated 30 June 1949 as Company A, 511th Airborne Infantry. Inactivated 1 March 1957 in Germany (511th Airborne Infantry concurrently relieved from assignment to the 11th Airborne Division).

Redesignated 17 July 1963 as Headquarters and Headquarters Company, 1st Battalion, 511th Infantry and assigned to the 11th Air Assault Division (organic elements concurrently constituted). Battalion activated 18 July 1963 at Fort Benning, Georgia. Inactivated 30 June 1965 at Fort Benning, Georgia, and relieved from assignment to the 11th Air Assault Division. (Headquarters and Headquarters Company activated 2 November 1965 at Fort Benning, Georgia; inactivated 16 November 1965 at Fort Benning, Georgia.)

CAMPAIGN PARTICIPATION CREDIT

World War II
  *New Guinea
  *Leyte
  *Luzon (with arrowhead)

DECORATIONS

*Presidential Unit Citation (Army), Streamer embroidered MANILA (1st Battalion, 511th Parachute Infantry cited; WD GO 68, 1945)

*Philippine Presidential Unit Citation, Streamer embroidered 17 OCTOBER 1944 TO 4 JULY 1945 (511th Parachute Infantry cited; DA GO 47, 1950)

511TH INFANTRY, BIBLIOGRAPHY

"Brief History of the 511th Airborne Infantry Regiment," *Fort Campbell Courier* (13 January 1953).

Faulkner, Lyman Sanders. *The Operations of the 511th Parachute Infantry Regiment (11th Airborne Division) in the Mount Malepunyo Mountain Pass, East of Lipa, Luzon, Philippine Islands, 12 April–2 May 1945.* Fort Riley, Kansas: U.S. Army Ground General School, 1949.

511th Airborne Infantry Regiment, 1950. Baton Rouge: Army and Navy Publishing Company, 1950.

511th Parachute Infantry: Regimental History, Leyte Campaign, 18 November–27 December 1944. Washington: The Adjutant General's Office, n.d.

Smith, Robert Ross. *Triumph in the Philippines.* United States Army in World War II. Washington: Government Printing Office, 1963.

1st SPECIAL FORCES

HERALDIC ITEMS

COAT OF ARMS

Shield: Argent, a fighting knife in bend hilt to base sable.

Crest: On a wreath of the colors two arrows saltirewise argent.

Motto: *De Oppresso Liber* (Liberate From Oppression).

Symbolism: The shield was originally approved for the 1st Special Service Force of World War II on 26 February 1943. The knife is of a distinctive shape and pattern and was issued only to the 1st Special Service Force.

The crest is the crossed arrow collar (branch) insignia of the 1st Special Service Force, World War II, changed from gold to silver for harmony with the shield and to make a difference from collar insignia. The motto more fully translated means "from oppression we will liberate them."

DISTINCTIVE INSIGNIA

The distinctive insignia is the crest and motto of the coat of arms combined with the fighting knife from the shield in the form of a badge.

LINEAGE AND HONORS

LINEAGE

Constituted 5 July 1942 in the Army of the United States as the 1st Special Service Force, a joint Canadian-American organization to consist of the First, Second, and Third Regiments and Service Battalion. Activated 9 July 1942 at Fort William Henry Harrison, Montana. Disbanded 6 January 1945 in France.

Reconstituted (less Service Battalion) 15 April 1960 in the Regular Army; concurrently, consolidated with the 1st, 3d, 4th, 5th, and 6th Ranger Infantry Battalions and the 2d Infantry Battalion (see ANNEXES 1–6) to form the 1st Special Forces, a parent regiment under the Combat Arms Regimental System.

ANNEX 1

Constituted 27 May 1942 in the Army of the United States as the 1st Ranger Battalion. Activated 19 June 1942 at Carrickfergus, Northern Ireland. Redesignated 1 August 1943 as the 1st Ranger Infantry Battalion. Disbanded 15 August 1944 in the United States.

Reconstituted 1 September 1948 in the Army of the United States and redesignated (less Companies E and F) as the 1st Infantry Battalion; concurrently, activated at Fort Gulick, Canal Zone (Company E redesignated as the 559th Infantry Company—hereafter separate lineage; Company F redesignated as the 560th Infantry Company). Battalion inactivated 4 January 1950 at Fort Gulick, Canal Zone.

Company A redesignated 25 October 1950 as the 1st Ranger Infantry Company and allotted to the Regular Army; activated 28 October 1950 at Fort Benning, Georgia; inactivated 1 August 1951 in Korea. Company B redesignated 2 November 1950 as the 5th Ranger Infantry Company and allotted to the Regular Army; activated 20 November 1950 at Fort Benning, Georgia; inactivated 1 August 1951 in Korea. Battalion redesignated 24 November 1952 as the 1st Ranger Infantry Battalion and allotted to the Regular Army (concurrently, former companies [less Company E] restored to unit by redesignation).

Consolidated 15 April 1960 with the 1st Battalion, First Regiment, 1st Special Service Force to form Headquarters and Headquarters Companies of the 1st, 7th, 8th, and 9th Special Forces Groups, 1st Special Forces.

ANNEX 2

Organized 21 May 1943 in North Africa as the 3d Ranger Battalion (Provisional). (Constituted 21 July 1943 in the Army of the United States as the 3d Ranger Battalion.) Redesignated 1 August 1943 as the 3d Ranger Infantry Battalion. Disbanded 15 August 1944 in the United States.

Company A reconstituted 25 October 1950 in the Regular Army as the 3d Ranger Infantry Company; activated 28 October 1950 at Fort Benning, Georgia; inactivated 1 August 1951 in Korea. Company B reconstituted 2 November 1950 in the Regular Army as the 7th Ranger Infantry Company; activated 20 November 1950 at Fort Benning, Georgia; inactivated 5 November 1951 at Fort Benning, Georgia. Company C reconstituted 15 December 1950 in the Regular Army as the 11th Ranger Infantry Company; activated 5 January 1951 at Fort Benning, Georgia; inactivated 21 September 1951 in Japan. Company D reconstituted 15 December 1950 in the Regular Army as the 12th Ranger Infantry Company; activated 1 February 1951 at Fort Benning, Georgia; inactivated 27 October 1951 at Camp Atterbury, Indiana. Company E reconstituted 15 December 1950 in the Regular Army as the 13th **Ranger** Infantry Company; activated 1 February 1951 at Fort Benning, Georgia; inactivated 15 October 1951 at Camp Pickett, Virginia. Battalion reconstituted 24 November 1952 in the Regular Army (concurrently, former companies restored to unit by redesignation).

Consolidated 15 April 1960 with the 1st Battalion, Second Regiment, 1st Special Service Force to form Headquarters and Headquarters Companies of the 3d, 13th, 14th, and 15th Special Forces Groups, 1st Special Forces.

ANNEX 3

Organized 29 May 1943 in North Africa as the 4th Ranger Battalion (Provisional). (Constituted 21 July 1943 in the Army of the United States as the 4th Ranger Battalion.) Redesignated 1 August 1943 as the 4th Ranger Infantry Battalion. Disbanded 24 October 1944 at Camp Butner, North Carolina.

Company A reconstituted 25 October 1950 in the Regular Army as the 4th Ranger Infantry Company; activated 28 October 1950 at Fort Benning, Georgia; inactivated 1 August 1951 in Korea. Company B reconstituted 2 November 1950 in the Regular Army as the 8th Ranger Infantry Company; activated 20 November 1950 at Fort Benning, Georgia; inactivated 1 August 1951 in Korea. Battalion reconstituted 24 November 1952 in the Regular Army (concurrently, former companies restored to unit by redesignation).

Consolidated 15 April 1960 with the 2d Battalion, Second Regiment, 1st Special Service Force to form Headquarters and Headquarters Companies of the 4th, 16th, 17th, and 18th Special Forces Groups, 1st Special Forces.

ANNEX 4

Constituted 21 July 1943 in the Army of the United States as the 5th Ranger Battalion. Redesignated 1 August 1943 as the 5th Ranger Infantry Battalion. Activated 1 September 1943 at Camp Forrest, Tennessee. Inactivated 22 October 1945 at Camp Myles Standish, Massachusetts.

Consolidated 15 April 1960 with the 1st Battalion, Third Regiment, 1st Special Service Force to form Headquarters and Headquarters Companies of the 5th, 19th, 20th, and 21st Special Forces Groups, 1st Special Forces.

ANNEX 5

Constituted 16 December 1940 in the Regular Army as the 98th Field Artillery Battalion. Activated 20 January 1941 at Fort Lewis, Washington. Converted and redesignated 25 September 1944 as the 6th Ranger Infantry Battalion. Inactivated 30 December 1945 in Japan.

Consolidated 15 April 1960 with the 2d Battalion, Third Regiment, 1st Special Service Force to form Headquarters and Headquarters Companies of the 6th, 22d, 23d, and 24th Special Forces Groups, 1st Special Forces.

ANNEX 6

Constituted 11 March 1943 in the Army of the United States as the 2d Ranger Battalion. Activated 1 April 1943 at Camp Forrest, Tennessee. Redesignated 1 August 1943 as the 2d Ranger Infantry Battalion. Inactivated 23 October 1945 at Camp Patrick Henry, Virginia. Redesignated 29 July 1949 as the 2d Infantry Battalion (concurrently, Companies E and F disbanded). Activated 15 September 1949 at Fort Gulick, Canal Zone. Inactivated 4 January 1950 at Fort Gulick, Canal Zone.

Company A redesignated 25 October 1950 as the 2d Ranger Infantry Company and allotted to the Regular Army; activated 28 October 1950 at Fort Benning, Georgia; inactivated 1 August 1951 in Korea. Company B redesignated 2 November 1950 as the 6th Ranger Infantry Company and allotted to the Regular Army; activated 20 November 1950 at Fort Benning, Georgia; inactivated 1 December 1951 in Germany. Company C redesignated 27 February 1951 as the 14th Ranger Infantry Company and allotted to the Regular Army; concurrently, activated at Fort Benning, Georgia; inactivated 27 October 1951 at Camp Carson, Colorado. Company D redesignated 27 February 1951 as the 15th Ranger Infantry Company and allotted to the Regular Army; concurrently, activated at Fort Benning, Georgia; inactivated 5 November 1951 at Fort Benning, Georgia. Company E reconstituted 15 December 1950 in the Regular Army as the 9th Ranger Infantry Company; activated 5 January 1951 at Fort Benning, Georgia; inactivated 5 November 1951 at Fort Benning, Georgia. Company F reconstituted 15 December 1950 in the Regular Army as the 10th Ranger Infantry Company; activated 5 January 1951 at Fort Benning, Georgia; inactivated 15 September 1951 in Japan.

Battalion redesignated 24 November 1952 as the 2d Ranger Infantry Battalion and allotted to the Regular Army (concurrently, former companies restored to unit by redesignation). Redesignated 14 June 1955 as the 2d Infantry Battalion (concurrently, Companies E and F absorbed by battalion). Activated 1 July 1955 in Iceland. Inactivated 11 March 1960 at Fort Hamilton, New York.

Consolidated 15 April 1960 with the 2d Battalion, First Regiment, 1st Special Service Force to form Headquarters and Headquarters Companies of the 2d, 10th, 11th, and 12th Special Forces Groups, 1st Special Forces.

Campaign Participation Credit

World War II
    Algeria-French Morocco
      (with arrowhead)
    Tunisia
    Sicily (with arrowhead)
    Naples-Foggia (with arrowhead)
    Anzio (with arrowhead)
    Rome-Arno
    Normandy (with arrowhead)
    Northern France
    Southern France (with arrowhead)
    Rhineland
    Ardennes-Alsace
    Central Europe

    Aleutian Islands
    New Guinea
    Leyte (with arrowhead)
    Luzon

Vietnam
    Advisory
    Defense
    Counteroffensive
    Counteroffensive, Phase II
    Counteroffensive, Phase III
    Tet Counteroffensive
    (other campaigns to be determined)

Decorations

Presidential Unit Citation (Army), Streamer embroidered EL GUET-TAR (1st Ranger Battalion cited; WD GO 56, 1944)

Presidential Unit Citation (Army), Streamer embroidered SALERNO (1st and 3d Ranger Battalions cited; WD GO 41, 1947)

Presidential Unit Citation (Army), Streamer embroidered POINTE DU HOE (2d and 5th Ranger Infantry Battalions cited; WD GO 10, 1945, and WD GO 73, 1944)

Presidential Unit Citation (Army), Streamer embroidered SAAR RIVER AREA (5th Ranger Infantry Battalion cited; WD GO 23, 1947)

Presidential Unit Citation (Army), Streamer embroidered VIETNAM 1966–1968 (5th Special Forces Group, 1st Special Forces cited; **DA GO** 45, 1969)

Meritorious Unit Commendation, Streamer embroidered VIETNAM 1968 (5th Special Forces Group, 1st Special Forces cited; DA GO 70, 1969)

1st SPECIAL FORCES GROUP, 1st SPECIAL FORCES

RA
(active)

LINEAGE

Constituted 5 July 1942 in the Army of the United States as the 2d Company, 1st Battalion, First Regiment, 1st Special Service Force, a joint Canadian-American organization. Activated 9 July 1942 at Fort William Henry Harrison, Montana. Disbanded 6 January 1945 in France.

Reconstituted 15 April 1960 in the Regular Army; concurrently, consolidated with Company B, 1st Ranger Infantry Battalion (see ANNEX) and consolidated unit designated as Headquarters and Headquarters Company, 1st Special Forces Group, 1st Special Forces. Consolidated 30 September 1960 with Headquarters and Headquarters Company, 1st Special Forces Group (constituted 14 June 1957 and activated 24 June 1957 in Japan) and consolidated unit designated as Headquarters and Headquarters Company, 1st Special Forces Group, 1st Special Forces (organic elements concurrently constituted and activated 4 October 1960 on Okinawa).

ANNEX

Constituted 27 May 1942 in the Army of the United States as Company B, 1st Ranger Battalion. Activated 19 June 1942 at Carrickfergus, Northern Ireland. Redesignated 1 August 1943 as Company B, 1st Ranger Infantry Battalion. Disbanded 15 August 1944 in the United States.

Reconstituted 1 September 1948 in the Army of the United States as Company B, 1st Infantry Battalion; concurrently, activated at Fort Gulick, Canal Zone. Inactivated 4 January 1950 at Fort Gulick, Canal Zone. Redesignated 2 November 1950 as the 5th Ranger Infantry Company and allotted to the Regular Army. Activated 20 November 1950 at Fort Benning, Georgia. Inactivated 1 August 1951 in Korea. Redesignated 24 November 1952 as Company B, 1st Ranger Infantry Battalion.

CAMPAIGN PARTICIPATION CREDIT

World War II
  *Algeria-French Morocco
    (with arrowhead)
  *Tunisia
  *Sicily (with arrowhead)
  *Naples-Foggia (with arrowhead)
  *Anzio (with arrowhead)
  *Rome-Arno
   Normandy (with arrowhead)
   Northern France
  *Southern France (with arrowhead)
  *Rhineland

   Ardennes-Alsace
   Central Europe
  *Aleutian Islands
   New Guinea
   Leyte (with arrowhead)
   Luzon

Korean War
  *First UN counteroffensive
  *CCF spring offensive
  *UN summer-fall offensive

DECORATIONS

*Presidential Unit Citation (Army), Streamer embroidered EL GUET-TAR (1st Ranger Battalion cited; WD GO 56, 1944)

*Presidential Unit Citation (Army), Streamer embroidered SALERNO (1st Ranger Battalion cited; WD GO 41, 1947)

Presidential Unit Citation (Army), Streamer embroidered POINTE DU HOE

Presidential Unit Citation (Army), Streamer embroidered SAAR RIVER AREA

*Republic of Korea Presidential Unit Citation, Streamer embroidered KOREA (5th Ranger Infantry Company cited; DA GO 33, 1953, as amended by DA GO 41, 1955)

425-618 O - 72 - 58

2d SPECIAL FORCES GROUP, 1st SPECIAL FORCES

AR
(inactive)

LINEAGE

Constituted 5 July 1942 in the Army of the United States as Headquarters and Headquarters Detachment, 2d Battalion, First Regiment, 1st Special Service Force, a joint Canadian-American organization. Activated 9 July 1942 at Fort William Henry Harrison, Montana. Disbanded 6 January 1945 in France.

Reconstituted 15 April 1960 in the Regular Army; concurrently, consolidated with Headquarters, Headquarters and Service Company, 2d Infantry Battalion (see ANNEX) and consolidated unit designated as Headquarters and Headquarters Company, 2d Special Forces Group, 1st Special Forces. Withdrawn 14 December 1960 from the Regular Army and allotted to the Army Reserve (organic elements concurrently constituted). Group activated 15 March 1961 with Headquarters at Columbus, Ohio. Inactivated 31 January 1966 at Columbus, Ohio.

ANNEX

Constituted 11 March 1943 in the Army of the United States as Headquarters and Headquarters Company, 2d Ranger Battalion. Activated 1 April 1943 at Camp Forrest, Tennessee. Redesignated 1 August 1943 as Headquarters and Headquarters Company, 2d Ranger Infantry Battalion. Inactivated 23 October 1945 at Camp Patrick Henry, Virginia. Redesignated 29 July 1949 as Headquarters and Headquarters Company, 2d Infantry Battalion. Activated 15 September 1949 at Fort Gulick, Canal Zone. Inactivated 4 January 1950 at Fort Gulick, Canal Zone.

Redesignated 24 November 1952 as Headquarters and Headquarters Company, 2d Ranger Infantry Battalion and allotted to the Regular Army. Redesignated 14 June 1955 as Headquarters, Headquarters and Service Company, 2d Infantry Battalion. Activated 1 July 1955 in Iceland. Inactivated 11 March 1960 at Fort Hamilton, New York.

894

CAMPAIGN PARTICIPATION CREDIT

World War II
    Algeria-French Morocco
       (with arrowhead)
    Tunisia
    Sicily (with arrowhead)
    *Naples-Foggia (with arrowhead)
    *Anzio (with arrowhead)
    *Rome-Arno
    *Normandy (with arrowhead)

    *Northern France
    *Southern France (with arrowhead)
    *Rhineland
    *Ardennes-Alsace
    *Central Europe
    *Aleutian Islands
    New Guinea
    Leyte (with arrowhead)
    Luzon

DECORATIONS

Presidential Unit Citation (Army), Streamer embroidered EL GUETTAR

Presidential Unit Citation (Army), Streamer embroidered SALERNO

*Presidential Unit Citation (Army), Streamer embroidered POINTE DU HOE (2d Ranger Infantry Battalion cited; WD GO 10, 1945)

Presidential Unit Citation (Army), Streamer embroidered SAAR RIVER AREA

*French Croix de Guerre with Silver-Gilt Star, World War II, Streamer embroidered POINTE DU HOE (2d Ranger Infantry Battalion cited; DA GO 43, 1950)

3d SPECIAL FORCES GROUP, 1st SPECIAL FORCES

RA
(inactive)

LINEAGE

Constituted 5 July 1942 in the Army of the United States as Headquarters and Headquarters Detachment, 1st Battalion, Second Regiment, 1st Special Service Force, a joint Canadian-American organization. Activated 9 July 1942 at Fort William Henry Harrison, Montana. Disbanded 6 January 1945 in France.

Reconstituted 15 April 1960 in the Regular Army; concurrently, consolidated with Headquarters and Headquarters Company, 3d Ranger Infantry Battalion (see ANNEX) and consolidated unit designated as Headquarters and Headquarters Company, 3d Special Forces Group, 1st Special Forces. Activated 5 December 1963 at Fort Bragg, North Carolina. (Organic elements constituted 18 February 1964 and activated 10 March 1964 at Fort Bragg, North Carolina.) Group inactivated 1 December 1969 at Fort Bragg, North Carolina.

ANNEX

Organized 21 May 1943 in North Africa as Headquarters and Headquarters Company, 3d Ranger Battalion (Provisional). (Constituted 21 July 1943 in the Army of the United States as Headquarters and Headquarters Company, 3d Ranger Battalion.) Redesignated 1 August 1943 as Headquarters and Headquarters Company, 3d Ranger Infantry Battalion. Disbanded 15 August 1944 in the United States. Reconstituted 24 November 1952 in the Regular Army as Headquarters and Headquarters Company, 3d Ranger Infantry Battalion.

CAMPAIGN PARTICIPATION CREDIT

World War II
  Algeria-French Morocco
    (with arrowhead)
  Tunisia
  *Sicily (with arrowhead)
  *Naples-Foggia (with arrowhead)
  *Anzio (with arrowhead)
  *Rome-Arno
  Normandy (with arrowhead)
Northern France
*Southern France (with arrowhead)
*Rhineland
Ardennes-Alsace
Central Europe
*Aleutian Islands
New Guinea
Leyte (with arrowhead)
Luzon

896

DECORATIONS

Presidential Unit Citation (Army), Streamer embroidered EL GUET-TAR

*Presidential Unit Citation (Army), Streamer embroidered SALERNO (3d Ranger Battalion cited; WD GO 41, 1947)

Presidential Unit Citation (Army), Streamer embroidered POINTE DU HOE

Presidential Unit Citation (Army), Streamer embroidered SAAR RIVER AREA

5th SPECIAL FORCES GROUP, 1st SPECIAL FORCES

RA

(active)

LINEAGE

Constituted 5 July 1942 in the Army of the United States as Headquarters and Headquarters Detachment, 1st Battalion, Third Regiment, 1st Special Service Force, a joint Canadian-American organization. Activated 9 July 1942 at Fort William Henry Harrison, Montana. Disbanded 6 January 1945 in France.

Reconstituted 15 April 1960 in the Regular Army; concurrently, consolidated with Headquarters and Headquarters Company, 5th Ranger Infantry Battalion (see ANNEX) and consolidated unit designated as Headquarters and Headquarters Company, 5th Special Forces Group, 1st Special Forces. (Organic elements constituted 8 September 1961.) Group activated 21 September 1961 at Fort Bragg, North Carolina.

ANNEX

Constituted 21 July 1943 in the Army of the United States as Headquarters and Headquarters Company, 5th Ranger Battalion. Redesignated 1 August 1943 as Headquarters and Headquarters Company, 5th Ranger Infantry Battalion. Activated 1 September 1943 at Camp Forrest, Tennessee. Inactivated 22 October 1945 at Camp Myles Standish, Massachusetts.

CAMPAIGN PARTICIPATION CREDIT

World War II
  Algeria-French Morocco
    (with arrowhead)
  Tunisia
  Sicily (with arrowhead)
  *Naples-Foggia (with arrowhead)
  *Anzio (with arrowhead)
  *Rome-Arno
  *Normandy (with arrowhead)
  *Northern France
  *Southern France (with arrowhead)
  *Rhineland
  *Ardennes-Alsace
  *Central Europe

  *Aleutian Islands
  New Guinea
  Leyte (with arrowhead)
  Luzon

Vietnam
  *Advisory
  *Defense
  *Counteroffensive
  *Counteroffensive, Phase II
  *Counteroffensive, Phase III
  *Tet Counteroffensive
    (other campaigns to be determined)

DECORATIONS

Presidential Unit Citation (Army), Streamer embroidered EL GUET-TAR

Presidential Unit Citation (Army), Streamer embroidered SALERNO

*Presidential Unit Citation (Army), Streamer embroidered POINTE DU HOE (5th Ranger Infantry Battalion cited; WD GO 73, 1944)

*Presidential Unit Citation (Army), Streamer embroidered SAAR RIVER AREA (5th Ranger Infantry Battalion cited; WD GO 23, 1947)

*Presidential Unit Citation (Army), Streamer embroidered VIETNAM 1966–1968 (5th Special Forces Group, 1st Special Forces cited; DA GO 45, 1969)

*Meritorious Unit Commendation, Streamer embroidered VIETNAM 1968 (5th Special Forces Group, 1st Special Forces cited; DA GO 70, 1969)

*French Croix de Guerre with Silver-Gilt Star, World War II, Streamer embroidered POINTE DU HOE (5th Ranger Infantry Battalion cited; DA GO 43, 1950)

*Vietnamese Cross of Gallantry with Palm, Streamer embroidered VIETNAM 1964–1969 (5th Special Forces Group, 1st Special Forces cited; DA GO 59, 1969)

6th SPECIAL FORCES GROUP, 1st SPECIAL FORCES

RA
(active)

LINEAGE

Constituted 5 July 1942 in the Army of the United States as Headquarters and Headquarters Detachment, 2d Battalion, Third Regiment, 1st Special Service Force, a joint Canadian-American organization. Activated 9 July 1942 at Fort William Henry Harrison, Montana. Disbanded 6 January 1945 in France.

Reconstituted 15 April 1960 in the Regular Army; concurrently, consolidated with Headquarters and Headquarters Company, 6th Ranger Infantry Battalion (see ANNEX) and consolidated unit designated as Headquarters and Headquarters Company, 6th Special Forces Group, 1st Special Forces. Activated 1 May 1963 at Fort Bragg, North Carolina. (Organic elements constituted 30 October 1963 and activated in December 1963 at Fort Bragg, North Carolina.)

ANNEX

Constituted 16 December 1940 in the Regular Army as Headquarters and Headquarters Battery, 98th Field Artillery Battalion. Activated 20 January 1941 at Fort Lewis, Washington. Converted and redesignated 25 September 1944 as Headquarters and Headquarters Company, 6th Ranger Infantry Battalion. Inactivated 30 December 1945 in Japan.

CAMPAIGN PARTICIPATION CREDIT

World War II
Algeria-French Morocco
(with arrowhead)
Tunisia
Sicily (with arrowhead)
*Naples-Foggia (with arrowhead)
*Anzio (with arrowhead)
*Rome-Arno
Normandy (with arrowhead)
Northern France
*Southern France (with arrowhead)
*Rhineland
Ardennes-Alsace
Central Europe
*Aleutian Islands
*New Guinea
*Leyte (with arrowhead)
*Luzon

DECORATIONS

Presidential Unit Citation (Army), Streamer embroidered EL GUETTAR

Presidential Unit Citation (Army), Streamer embroidered SALERNO

900

Presidential Unit Citation (Army), Streamer embroidered POINTE DU HOE

Presidential Unit Citation (Army), Streamer embroidered SAAR RIVER AREA

*Philippine Presidential Unit Citation, Streamer embroidered 17 OCTOBER 1944 TO 4 JULY 1945 (6th Ranger Infantry Battalion cited; DA GO 47, 1950)

7th SPECIAL FORCES GROUP, 1st SPECIAL FORCES

RA
(active)

LINEAGE

Constituted 5 July 1942 in the Army of the United States as the 1st Company, 1st Battalion, First Regiment, 1st Special Service Force, a joint Canadian-American organization. Activated 9 July 1942 at Fort William Henry Harrison, Montana. Disbanded 6 January 1945 in France.

Reconstituted 15 April 1960 in the Regular Army; concurrently, consolidated with Company A, 1st Ranger Infantry Battalion (see ANNEX) and consolidated unit designated as Headquarters and Headquarters Company, 7th Special Forces Group, 1st Special Forces. Consolidated 6 June 1960 with Headquarters and Headquarters Company, 77th Special Forces Group (constituted 16 September 1953 and activated 25 September 1953 at Fort Bragg, North Carolina) and consolidated unit designated as Headquarters and Headquarters Company, 7th Special Forces Group, 1st Special Forces (organic elements [constituted 20 May 1960] concurrently activated at Fort Bragg, North Carolina).

ANNEX

Constituted 27 May 1942 in the Army of the United States as Company A, 1st Ranger Battalion. Activated 19 June 1942 at Carrickfergus, Northern Ireland. Redesignated 1 August 1943 as Company A, 1st Ranger Infantry Battalion. Disbanded 15 August 1944 in the United States.

Reconstituted 1 September 1948 in the Army of the United States as Company A, 1st Infantry Battalion; concurrently, activated at Fort Gulick, Canal Zone. Inactivated 4 January 1950 at Fort Gulick, Canal Zone. Redesignated 25 October 1950 as the 1st Ranger Infantry Company and allotted to the Regular Army. Activated 28 October 1950 at Fort Benning, Georgia. Inactivated 1 August 1951 in Korea. Redesignated 24 November 1952 as Company A, 1st Ranger Infantry Battalion.

CAMPAIGN PARTICIPATION CREDIT

World War II
- *Algeria-French Morocco
  (with arrowhead)
- *Tunisia
- *Sicily (with arrowhead)
- *Naples-Foggia (with arrowhead)
- *Anzio (with arrowhead)
- *Rome-Arno
- Normandy (with arrowhead)
- Northern France
- *Southern France (with arrowhead)
- *Rhineland
- Ardennes-Alsace

- Central Europe
- *Aleutian Islands
- New Guinea
- Leyte (with arrowhead)
- Luzon

Korean War
- *CCF intervention
- *First UN counteroffensive
- *CCF spring offensive
- *UN summer-fall offensive

DECORATIONS

*Presidential Unit Citation (Army), Streamer embroidered EL GUETTAR (1st Ranger Battalion cited; WD GO 56, 1944)

*Presidential Unit Citation (Army), Streamer embroidered SALERNO (1st Ranger Battalion cited; WD GO 41, 1947)

Presidential Unit Citation (Army), Streamer embroidered POINTE DU HOE

Presidential Unit Citation (Army), Streamer embroidered SAAR RIVER AREA

*Presidential Unit Citation (Army), Streamer embroidered HONG-CHON (1st Ranger Infantry Company cited; DA GO 72, 1951)

*Presidential Unit Citation (Army), Streamer embroidered CHIPYONG-NI (1st Ranger Infantry Company cited; DA GO 49, 1951)

8th SPECIAL FORCES GROUP, 1st SPECIAL FORCES

RA
(active)

LINEAGE

Constituted 5 July 1942 in the Army of the United States as Headquarters and Headquarters Detachment, 1st Battalion, First Regiment, 1st Special Service Force, a joint Canadian-American organization. Activated 9 July 1942 at Fort William Henry Harrison, Montana. Disbanded 6 January 1945 in France.

Reconstituted 15 April 1960 in the Regular Army; concurrently, consolidated with Headquarters and Headquarters Company, 1st Ranger Infantry Battalion (see ANNEX) and consolidated unit designated as Headquarters and Headquarters Company, 8th Special Forces Group, 1st Special Forces. Activated 1 April 1963 at Fort Gulick, Canal Zone (organic elements concurrently constituted and activated).

ANNEX

Constituted 27 May 1942 in the Army of the United States as Headquarters and Headquarters Company, 1st Ranger Battalion. Activated 19 June 1942 at Carrickfergus, Northern Ireland. Redesignated 1 August 1943 as Headquarters and Headquarters Company, 1st Ranger Infantry Battalion. Disbanded 15 August 1944 in the United States.

Reconstituted 1 September 1948 in the Army of the United States as Headquarters and Headquarters Company, 1st Infantry Battalion; concurrently, activated at Fort Gulick, Canal Zone. Inactivated 4 January 1950 at Fort Gulick, Canal Zone. Redesignated 24 November 1952 as Headquarters and Headquarters Company, 1st Ranger Infantry Battalion and allotted to the Regular Army.

904

CAMPAIGN PARTICIPATION CREDIT

World War II
- *Algeria-French Morocco (with arrowhead)
- *Tunisia
- *Sicily (with arrowhead)
- *Naples-Foggia (with arrowhead)
- *Anzio (with arrowhead)
- *Rome-Arno
- Normandy (with arrowhead)
- Northern France
- *Southern France (with arrowhead)
- *Rhineland
- Ardennes-Alsace
- Central Europe
- *Aleutian Islands
- New Guinea
- Leyte (with arrowhead)
- Luzon

DECORATIONS

*Presidential Unit Citation (Army), Streamer embroidered EL GUETTAR (1st Ranger Battalion cited; WD GO 56, 1944)

*Presidential Unit Citation (Army), Streamer embroidered SALERNO (1st Ranger Battalion cited; WD GO 41, 1947)

Presidential Unit Citation (Army), Streamer embroidered POINTE DU HOE

Presidential Unit Citation (Army), Streamer embroidered SAAR RIVER AREA

9th SPECIAL FORCES GROUP, 1st SPECIAL FORCES

AR
(inactive)

LINEAGE

Constituted 5 July 1942 in the Army of the United States as the 3d Company, 1st Battalion, First Regiment, 1st Special Service Force, a joint Canadian-American organization. Activated 9 July 1942 at Fort William Henry Harrison, Montana. Disbanded 6 January 1945 in France.

Reconstituted 15 April 1960 in the Regular Army; concurrently, consolidated with Company C, 1st Ranger Infantry Battalion (see ANNEX) and consolidated unit designated as Headquarters and Headquarters Company, 9th Special Forces Group, 1st Special Forces. Withdrawn 14 December 1960 from the Regular Army and allotted to the Army Reserve (organic elements concurrently constituted). Group activated 1 February 1961 with Headquarters at Little Rock, Arkansas. Inactivated 31 January 1966 at Little Rock, Arkansas.

ANNEX

Constituted 27 May 1942 in the Army of the United States as Company C, 1st Ranger Battalion. Activated 19 June 1942 at Carrickfergus, Northern Ireland. Redesignated 1 August 1943 as Company C, 1st Ranger Infantry Battalion. Disbanded 15 August 1944 in the United States.

Reconstituted 1 September 1948 in the Army of the United States as Company C, 1st Infantry Battalion; concurrently, activated at Fort Gulick, Canal Zone. Inactivated 4 January 1950 at Fort Gulick, Canal Zone. Redesignated 24 November 1952 as Company C, 1st Ranger Infantry Battalion and allotted to the Regular Army.

CAMPAIGN PARTICIPATION CREDIT

World War II
*Algeria-French Morocco
 (with arrowhead)
*Tunisia
*Sicily (with arrowhead)
*Naples-Foggia (with arrowhead)
*Anzio (with arrowhead)
*Rome-Arno
 Normandy (with arrowhead)

Northern France
*Southern France (with arrowhead)
*Rhineland
 Ardennes-Alsace
 Central Europe
*Aleutian Islands
 New Guinea
 Leyte (with arrowhead)
 Luzon

906

Decorations

*Presidential Unit Citation (Army), Streamer embroidered EL GUET-
TAR (1st Ranger Battalion cited; WD GO 56, 1944)

*Presidential Unit Citation (Army), Streamer embroidered SALERNO
(1st Ranger Battalion cited; WD GO 41, 1947)

Presidential Unit Citation (Army), Streamer embroidered POINTE
DU HOE

Presidential Unit Citation (Army), Streamer embroidered SAAR RIVER
AREA

10th SPECIAL FORCES GROUP, 1st SPECIAL FORCES

RA

(active)

Constituted 5 July 1942 in the Army of the United States as the 4th Company, 2d Battalion, First Regiment, 1st Special Service Force, a joint Canadian-American organization. Activated 9 July 1942 at Fort William Henry Harrison, Montana. Disbanded 6 January 1945 in France.

Reconstituted 15 April 1960 in the Regular Army; concurrently, consolidated with Company A, 2d Infantry Battalion (see ANNEX) and consolidated unit designated as Headquarters and Headquarters Company, 10th Special Forces Group, 1st Special Forces. Consolidated 30 September 1960 with Headquarters and Headquarters Company, 10th Special Forces Group (constituted 19 May 1952 and activated 11 June 1952 at Fort Bragg, North Carolina) and consolidated unit designated as Headquarters and Headquarters Company, 10th Special Forces Group, 1st Special Forces (organic elements concurrently constituted and activated 20 March 1961 in Germany).

ANNEX

Constituted 11 March 1943 in the Army of the United States as Company A, 2d Ranger Battalion. Activated 1 April 1943 at Camp Forrest, Tennessee. Redesignated 1 August 1943 as Company A, 2d Ranger Infantry Battalion. Inactivated 23 October 1945 at Camp Patrick Henry, Virginia. Redesignated 29 July 1949 as Company A, 2d Infantry Battalion. Activated 15 September 1949 at Fort Gulick, Canal Zone. Inactivated 4 January 1950 at Fort Gulick, Canal Zone.

Redesignated 25 October 1950 as the 2d Ranger Infantry Company and allotted to the Regular Army. Activated 28 October 1950 at Fort Benning, Georgia. Inactivated 1 August 1951 in Korea. Redesignated 24 November 1952 as Company A, 2d Ranger Infantry Battalion. Redesignated 14 June 1955 as Company A, 2d Infantry Battalion. Activated 1 July 1955 in Iceland. Inactivated 11 March 1960 at Fort Hamilton, New York.

CAMPAIGN PARTICIPATION CREDIT

World War II
  Algeria-French Morocco
    (with arrowhead)
  Tunisia
  Sicily (with arrowhead)
  *Naples-Foggia (with arrowhead)
  *Anzio (with arrowhead)
  *Rome-Arno
  *Normandy (with arrowhead)
  *Northern France
  *Southern France (with arrowhead)
  *Rhineland
  *Ardennes-Alsace

  *Central Europe
  *Aleutian Islands
  New Guinea
  Leyte (with arrowhead)
  Luzon

Korean War
  *CCF intervention
  *First UN counteroffensive
    (with arrowhead)
  *CCF spring offensive
  *UN summer-fall offensive

DECORATIONS

Presidential Unit Citation (Army), Streamer embroidered EL GUET-TAR

Presidential Unit Citation (Army), Streamer embroidered SALERNO

*Presidential Unit Citation (Army), Streamer embroidered POINTE DU HOE (2d Ranger Infantry Battalion cited; WD GO 10, 1945)

Presidential Unit Citation (Army), Streamer embroidered SAAR RIVER AREA

*French Croix de Guerre with Silver-Gilt Star, World War II, Streamer embroidered POINTE DU HOE (2d Ranger Infantry Battalion cited; DA GO 43, 1950)

11th SPECIAL FORCES GROUP, 1st SPECIAL FORCES

AR
(active)

Constituted 5 July 1942 in the Army of the United States as the 5th Company, 2d Battalion, First Regiment, 1st Special Service Force, a joint Canadian-American organization. Activated 9 July 1942 at Fort William Henry Harrison, Montana. Disbanded 6 January 1945 in France.

Reconstituted 15 April 1960 in the Regular Army; concurrently, consolidated with Company B, 2d Infantry Battalion (see ANNEX) and consolidated unit designated as Headquarters and Headquarters Company, 11th Special Forces Group, 1st Special Forces. Withdrawn 14 December 1960 from the Regular Army and allotted to the Army Reserve (organic elements concurrently constituted). Group activated 1 March 1961 with Headquarters at Boston, Massachusetts. (Location of Headquarters changed 22 March 1963 to Staten Island, New York.)

ANNEX

Constituted 11 March 1943 in the Army of the United States as Company B, 2d Ranger Battalion. Activated 1 April 1943 at Camp Forrest, Tennessee. Redesignated 1 August 1943 as Company B, 2d Ranger Infantry Battalion. Inactivated 23 October 1945 at Camp Patrick Henry, Virginia. Redesignated 29 July 1949 as Company B, 2d Infantry Battalion. Activated 15 September 1949 at Fort Gulick, Canal Zone. Inactivated 4 January 1950 at Fort Gulick, Canal Zone.

Redesignated 2 November 1950 as the 6th Ranger Infantry Company and allotted to the Regular Army. Activated 20 November 1950 at Fort Benning, Georgia. Inactivated 1 December 1951 in Germany. Redesignated 24 November 1952 as Company B, 2d Ranger Infantry Battalion. Redesignated 14 June 1955 as Company B, 2d Infantry Battalion. Activated 1 July 1955 in Iceland. Inactivated 11 March 1960 at Fort Hamilton, New York.

HOME AREA: First and Third United States Armies

910

Campaign Participation Credit

World War II
  Algeria-French Morocco
    (with arrowhead)
  Tunisia
  Sicily (with arrowhead)
  *Naples-Foggia (with arrowhead)
  *Anzio (with arrowhead)
  *Rome-Arno
  *Normandy (with arrowhead)

*Northern France
*Southern France (with arrowhead)
*Rhineland
*Ardennes-Alsace
*Central Europe
*Aleutian Islands
  New Guinea
  Leyte (with arrowhead)
  Luzon

Decorations

Presidential Unit Citation (Army), Streamer embroidered EL GUET-TAR

Presidential Unit Citation (Army), Streamer embroidered SALERNO

*Presidential Unit Citation (Army), Streamer embroidered POINTE DU HOE (2d Ranger Infantry Battalion cited; WD GO 10, 1945)

Presidential Unit Citation (Army), Streamer embroidered SAAR RIVER AREA

*French Croix de Guerre with Silver-Gilt Star, World War II, Streamer embroidered POINTE DU HOE (2d Ranger Infantry Battalion cited; DA GO 43, 1950)

12th SPECIAL FORCES GROUP, 1st SPECIAL FORCES

AR
(active)

LINEAGE

Constituted 5 July 1942 in the Army of the United States as the 6th Company, 2d Battalion, First Regiment, 1st Special Service Force, a joint Canadian-American organization. Activated 9 July 1942 at Fort William Henry Harrison, Montana. Disbanded 6 January 1945 in France.

Reconstituted 15 April 1960 in the Regular Army; concurrently, consolidated with Company C, 2d Infantry Battalion (see ANNEX) and consolidated unit designated as Headquarters and Headquarters Company, 12th Special Forces Group, 1st Special Forces. Withdrawn 14 December 1960 from the Regular Army and allotted to the Army Reserve (organic elements concurrently constituted). Group activated 24 March 1961 with Headquarters at Chicago, Illinois. (Location of Headquarters changed 19 January 1964 to Oak Park, Illinois.)

ANNEX

Constituted 11 March 1943 in the Army of the United States as Company C, 2d Ranger Battalion. Activated 1 April 1943 at Camp Forrest, Tennessee. Redesignated 1 August 1943 as Company C, 2d Ranger Infantry Battalion. Inactivated 23 October 1945 at Camp Patrick Henry, Virginia. Redesignated 29 July 1949 as Company C, 2d Infantry Battalion. Activated 15 September 1949 at Fort Gulick, Canal Zone. Inactivated 4 January 1950 at Fort Gulick, Canal Zone.

Redesignated 27 February 1951 as the 14th Ranger Infantry Company and allotted to the Regular Army; concurrently, activated at Fort Benning, Georgia. Inactivated 27 October 1951 at Camp Carson, Colorado. Redesignated 24 November 1952 as Company C, 2d Ranger Infantry Battalion. Redesignated 14 June 1955 as Company C, 2d Infantry Battalion. Activated 1 July 1955 in Iceland. Inactivated 11 March 1960 at Fort Hamilton, New York.

HOME AREA: Fifth and Sixth United States Armies

912

CAMPAIGN PARTICIPATION CREDIT

World War II
  Algeria-French Morocco
    (with arrowhead)
  Tunisia
  Sicily (with arrowhead)
  *Naples-Foggia (with arrowhead)
  *Anzio (with arrowhead)
  *Rome-Arno
  *Normandy (with arrowhead)

  *Northern France
  *Southern France (with arrowhead)
  *Rhineland
  *Ardennes-Alsace
  *Central Europe
  *Aleutian Islands
  New Guinea
  Leyte (with arrowhead)
  Luzon

DECORATIONS

Presidential Unit Citation (Army), Streamer embroidered EL GUETTAR

Presidential Unit Citation (Army), Streamer embroidered SALERNO

*Presidential Unit Citation (Army), Streamer embroidered POINTE DU HOE (2d Ranger Infantry Battalion cited; WD GO 10, 1945)

Presidential Unit Citation (Army), Streamer embroidered SAAR RIVER AREA

*French Croix de Guerre with Silver-Gilt Star, World War II, Streamer embroidered POINTE DU HOE (2d Ranger Infantry Battalion cited; DA GO 43, 1950)

13th SPECIAL FORCES GROUP, 1st SPECIAL FORCES

AR
(inactive)

LINEAGE

Constituted 5 July 1942 in the Army of the United States as the 1st Company, 1st Battalion, Second Regiment, 1st Special Service Force, a joint Canadian-American organization. Activated 9 July 1942 at Fort William Henry Harrison, Montana. Disbanded 6 January 1945 in France.

Reconstituted 15 April 1960 in the Regular Army; concurrently, consolidated with Company A, 3d Ranger Infantry Battalion (see ANNEX) and consolidated unit designated as Headquarters and Headquarters Company, 13th Special Forces Group, 1st Special Forces. Withdrawn 14 December 1960 from the Regular Army and allotted to the Army Reserve (organic elements concurrently constituted). Group activated 1 March 1961 with Headquarters at Jacksonville, Florida. Headquarters and Headquarters Company inactivated 15 April 1963 at Jacksonville, Florida; organic elements inactivated 21 January 1966.

ANNEX

Organized 21 May 1943 in North Africa as Company A, 3d Ranger Battalion (Provisional). (Constituted 21 July 1943 in the Army of the United States as Company A, 3d Ranger Battalion.) Redesignated 1 August 1943 as Company A, 3d Ranger Infantry Battalion. Disbanded 15 August 1944 in the United States.

Reconstituted 25 October 1950 in the Regular Army as the 3d Ranger Infantry Company. Activated 28 October 1950 at Fort Benning, Georgia. Inactivated 1 August 1951 in Korea. Redesignated 24 November 1952 as Company A, 3d Ranger Infantry Battalion.

914

CAMPAIGN PARTICIPATION CREDIT

World War II
  Algeria-French Morocco
    (with arrowhead)
  Tunisia
  *Sicily (with arrowhead)
  *Naples-Foggia (with arrowhead)
  *Anzio (with arrowhead)
  *Rome-Arno
  Normandy (with arrowhead)
  Northern France
  *Southern France (with arrowhead)
  *Rhineland

Ardennes-Alsace
Central Europe
*Aleutian Islands
New Guinea
Leyte (with arrowhead)
Luzon

Korean War
  *First UN counteroffensive
  *CCF spring offensive
  *UN summer-fall offensive

DECORATIONS

Presidential Unit Citation (Army), Streamer embroidered EL GUET-TAR

*Presidential Unit Citation (Army), Streamer embroidered SALERNO (3d Ranger Battalion cited; WD GO 41, 1947)

Presidential Unit Citation (Army), Streamer embroidered POINTE DU HOE

Presidential Unit Citation (Army), Streamer embroidered SAAR RIVER AREA

*Republic of Korea Presidential Unit Citation, Streamer embroidered UIJONGBU CORRIDOR (3d Ranger Infantry Company cited; DA GO 20, 1953)

*Republic of Korea Presidential Unit Citation, Streamer embroidered KOREA (3d Ranger Infantry Company cited; DA GO 33, 1953, as amended by DA GO 41, 1955)

17th SPECIAL FORCES GROUP, 1st SPECIAL FORCES

AR

(inactive)

LINEAGE

Constituted 5 July 1942 in the Army of the United States as the 5th Company, 2d Battalion, Second Regiment, 1st Special Service Force, a joint Canadian-American organization. Activated 9 July 1942 at Fort William Henry Harrison, Montana. Disbanded 6 January 1945 in France.

Reconstituted 15 April 1960 in the Regular Army; concurrently, consolidated with Company B, 4th Ranger Infantry Battalion (see ANNEX) and consolidated unit designated as Headquarters and Headquarters Company, 17th Special Forces Group, 1st Special Forces. Withdrawn 14 December 1960 from the Regular Army and allotted to the Army Reserve (organic elements concurrently constituted). Group activated 3 April 1961 with Headquarters at Boise, Idaho. (Location of Headquarters changed 1 September 1961 to Seattle, Washington.) Inactivated 31 January 1966 at Seattle, Washington.

ANNEX

Organized 29 May 1943 in North Africa as Company B, 4th Ranger Battalion (Provisional). (Constituted 21 July 1943 in the Army of the United States as Company B, 4th Ranger Battalion.) Redesignated 1 August 1943 as Company B, 4th Ranger Infantry Battalion. Disbanded 24 October 1944 at Camp Butner, North Carolina.

Reconstituted 2 November 1950 in the Regular Army as the 8th Ranger Infantry Company. Activated 20 November 1950 at Fort Benning, Georgia. Inactivated 1 August 1951 in Korea. Redesignated 24 November 1952 as Company B, 4th Ranger Infantry Battalion.

Campaign Participation Credit

World War II
   Algeria-French Morocco
     (with arrowhead)
   Tunisia
   *Sicily (with arrowhead)
   *Naples-Foggia (with arrowhead)
   *Anzio (with arrowhead)
   *Rome-Arno
   Normandy (with arrowhead)
   Northern France
   *Southern France (with arrowhead)
   *Rhineland

   Ardennes-Alsace
   Central Europe
   *Aleutian Islands
   New Guinea
   Leyte (with arrowhead)
   Luzon

Korean War
   *First UN counteroffensive
   *CCF spring offensive
   *UN summer-fall offensive

Decorations

Presidential Unit Citation (Army), Streamer embroidered EL GUETTAR

Presidential Unit Citation (Army), Streamer embroidered SALERNO

Presidential Unit Citation (Army), Streamer embroidered POINTE DU HOE

Presidential Unit Citation (Army), Streamer embroidered SAAR RIVER AREA

*Republic of Korea Presidential Unit Citation, Streamer embroidered KOREA (8th Ranger Infantry Company cited; DA GO 33, 1953, as amended by DA GO 41, 1955)

24th SPECIAL FORCES GROUP, 1st SPECIAL FORCES

AR
(inactive)

Constituted 5 July 1942 in the Army of the United States as the 6th Company, 2d Battalion, Third Regiment, 1st Special Service Force, a joint Canadian-American organization. Activated 9 July 1942 at Fort William Henry Harrison, Montana. Disbanded 6 January 1945 in France.

Reconstituted 15 April 1960 in the Regular Army; concurrently, consolidated with Company C, 6th Ranger Infantry Battalion (see ANNEX) and consolidated unit designated as Headquarters and Headquarters Company, 24th Special Forces Group, 1st Special Forces. Withdrawn 14 December 1960 from the Regular Army and allotted to the Army Reserve (organic elements concurrently constituted). Group activated 6 January 1961 at Fort DeRussy, Hawaii. Inactivated 31 January 1966 at Fort DeRussy, Hawaii.

ANNEX

Constituted 16 December 1940 in the Regular Army as Battery C, 98th Field Artillery Battalion. Activated 20 January 1941 at Fort Lewis, Washington. Converted and redesignated 25 September 1944 as Company C, 6th Ranger Infantry Battalion. Inactivated 30 December 1945 in Japan.

CAMPAIGN PARTICIPATION CREDIT

World War II
Algeria-French Morocco
 (with arrowhead)
Tunisia
Sicily (with arrowhead)
*Naples-Foggia (with arrowhead)
*Anzio (with arrowhead)
*Rome-Arno
Normandy (with arrowhead)
Northern France
*Southern France (with arrowhead)
*Rhineland
Ardennes-Alsace
Central Europe
*Aleutian Islands
*New Guinea
*Leyte (with arrowhead)
*Luzon

DECORATIONS

Presidential Unit Citation (Army), Streamer embroidered EL GUETTAR

Presidential Unit Citation (Army), Streamer embroidered SALERNO

918

Presidential Unit Citation (Army), Streamer embroidered POINTE DU HOE

Presidential Unit Citation (Army), Streamer embroidered SAAR RIVER AREA

*Presidential Unit Citation (Army), Streamer embroidered CABU, LUZON (Company C, 6th Ranger Infantry Battalion cited; WD GO 26, 1945)

*Philippine Presidential Unit Citation, Streamer embroidered 17 OCTOBER 1944 TO 4 JULY 1945 (6th Ranger Infantry Battalion cited; DA GO 47, 1950)

1st Special Forces, Bibliography

Adams, Raymond E. "Special Forces Aidman," *Army Information Digest,* XVIII (October 1963) , 57–59.

Ahern, Neal J. "What It Is That's So Special About Special Forces," *The Army Reservist,* IX (November 1963) , 5–7.

Albright, John, John A. Cash, and Allan W. Sandstrum. *Seven Firefights in Vietnam.* Washington: Government Printing Office, 1970.

Altieri, James J. *Darby's Rangers.* Durham: The Seaman Printery, 1945.

————. *The Spearheaders.* Indianapolis: Bobbs-Merrill Company, 1960.

Baer, Alfred E., Jr. *D-for-Dog: The Story of a Ranger Company.* Memphis, 1946.

Blumenson, Martin. *Anzio: The Gamble That Failed.* New York: J. B. Lippincott Company, 1963.

————. *Breakout and Pursuit.* United States Army in World War II. Washington: Government Printing Office, 1961.

————. *Kasserine Pass.* Boston: Houghton Mifflin Company, 1967.

"Building Blocks of Unconventional Warfare," *Armed Forces Management,* XII (May 1966) , 59.

Burhans, Robert D. *The First Special Service Force: A War History of the North Americans, 1942–1944.* Washington: Infantry Journal Press, 1947.

Cannon, M. Hamlin. *Leyte: The Return to the Philippines.* United States Army in World War II. Washington: Government Printing Office, 1954.

Dodson, Charles A. "Special Forces," *Army,* XI (June 1961) , 44–52.

Easterbrook, Ernest F. "Realism in Counterinsurgency Training," *Army Information Digest,* XVII (October 1962) , 12–21.

"Flair for Adventure, Disregard for Danger," *The Army Reservist,* VI (July–August 1960) , 3–4.

Garland, Albert N. and Howard McGaw Smyth. *Sicily and the Surrender of Italy.* United States Army in World War II. Washington: Government Printing Office, 1965.

Glassman, Harry S. *Lead the Way, Rangers: A History of the Fifth Ranger Battalion.* Munich, Germany: F. Bruckmann KG, 1945.

Green Beret. (Authorized monthly publication for personnel of the 5th Special Forces Group, 1st Special Forces in Vietnam.)

Gugeler, Russell A. *Combat Actions in Korea.* Washington: Combat Forces Press, 1954.

Hamlett, Barksdale. "Special Forces: Training for Peace and War," *Army Information Digest,* XVI (June 1961) , 2–9.

Harkins, Paul D. and Philip. *The Army Officer's Guide*. New York: McGraw-Hill Book Company, 1951.

Harrison, Gordon A. *Cross-Channel Attack*. United States Army in World War II. Washington: Government Printing Office, 1951.

Historical Section, War Department. *Anzio Beachhead*. American Forces in Action Series. Washington: Government Printing Office, 1947.

─────. *Fifth Army at the Winter Line*. American Forces in Action Series. Washington: Government Printing Office, 1945.

─────. *From the Volturno to the Winter Line*. American Forces in Action Series. Washington: Government Printing Office, 1943.

─────. *Omaha Beachhead*. American Forces in Action Series. Washington: Government Printing Office, 1945.

─────. *Salerno: American Operations from the Beaches to the Volturno*. American Forces in Action Series. Washington: Government Printing Office, 1944.

─────. *Small Unit Actions*. American Forces in Action Series. Washington: Government Printing Office, 1946.

Howe, George F. *Northwest Africa: Seizing the Initiative in the West*. United States Army in World War II. Washington: Government Printing Office, 1957.

Kinard, William H. "This is Special Warfare—U.S. Army Style," *Army Information Digest*, XV (June 1960), 2–11.

MacDonald, Charles B. *The Siegfried Line Campaign*. United States Army in World War II. Washington: Government Printing Office, 1963.

McGlasson, W. D. "Have Guts, Will Travel," *The National Guardsman*, XIV (April 1960), 2–3ff.

Minter, Jim and Paul Price. "Rangers Ready," *Army Information Digest*, VIII (January 1953), 13–20.

Prince, Morris. *Company A, 2d Ranger Battalion, Overseas and Then—Over the Top*. Washington, 1946.

Ranger. Fort Benning, Georgia: United States Army Infantry School, 1959.

"The Rangers Have a Long History," *Army Times* (11 March 1964).

Reports of General MacArthur. Washington: Government Printing Office, 1966.

Sage, Jerry M. "10th Special Forces," *Army Information Digest*, XIX (June 1964), 4–10.

Schweitz, Robert E. "U.S. Making Guerrilla Warfare Experts," *Army-Navy-Air Force Register*, LCIX (10 March 1962), 11–14.

"SF Beret," *Army Times* (4 November 1961).

Sharp, U. S. G. and W. G. Westmoreland. *Report on the War in Viet-*

nam. Washington: Government Printing Office, 1968.

Sheehan, Fred. *Anzio.* Norman: University of Oklahoma Press, 1964.

Smith, Robert Ross. *Triumph in the Philippines.* United States Army in World War II. Washington: Government Printing Office, 1963.

Special Warfare, U.S. Army: An Army Specialty. Washington: Government Printing Office, 1962.

Stacey, C. P. *Official History of the Canadian Army in the Second World War.* Volume I. Ottawa: Queen's Printer, 1955.

Starr, Chester G., ed. *Salerno to the Alps—A History of the Fifth Army, 1943–1945.* Washington: Infantry Journal Press, 1948.

"United States Army Special Warfare," Fort Bragg, North Carolina: United States Army Special Warfare Center, 1962.

Van Houten, John V. "The Rangers are Back," *Army Information Digest,* VI (August 1951), 35–41.

"Vietnam Returnees Advising Reserve Component SF Units," *Army Times* (European edition) (21 August 1963).

Wagner, Joe. "Army Special Forces—Step Child or Child Prodigy?" *Armed Forces Management,* XII (May 1966), 54–59.

Whitmire, Chuck. "Ready to Respond," *Army Digest,* XXV (February 1970), 20–26.

Windsor, Joseph. "Rugged and Ready," *The Infantry School Quarterly,* XLII (January 1953), 94–103.

Winkler, Melvin L. "The Army's Special Forces," *Army Information Digest,* XXI (October 1966), 26–31.

Glossary of Lineage Terms

ACTIVATE. To bring into being or establish a unit that has been constituted. Usually personnel and equipment are assigned at this time; however, a unit may be active at zero strength, that is, without personnel or equipment. This term was not used before 1921. It is never used when referring to Army National Guard units, and only since World War II has it been used in connection with Army Reserve units. (See also ORGANIZE.)

ALLOT. To assign a unit to one of the components of the United States Army. The present components of the Army are the Regular Army (RA), the Army National Guard (ARNG), and the Army Reserve (AR), which was formerly known as the Organized Reserves and the Organized Reserve Corps. During World War I units were also allotted to the National Army, and during World War II to the Army of the United States. A unit may be withdrawn from any component except the Army National Guard and allotted to another. The new allotment, however, does not change the history, lineage, and honors of the unit.

ASSIGN. To make a unit part of a larger organization and place it under that organization's command and control until it is relieved from the assignment. As a rule, only divisional and separate brigade assignments are shown in unit lineages.

CONSOLIDATE. To merge or combine two or more units into one new unit. The new unit may retain the designation of one of the original units or it may have a new designation, but it inherits the history, lineage, and honors of all of the units affected by the merger. In the nineteenth century, consolidation was frequently a merger of several understrength units to form one full-strength unit. At the present time, in the Regular Army and the Army Reserve, units are usually consolidated when they are inactive or when only one of the units is active; therefore, personnel and equipment are seldom involved. In the Army National Guard, on the other hand, active units are often consolidated, and their personnel are combined in the new unit.

CONSTITUTE. To place the designation of a new unit on the official rolls of the Army.

CONVERT. To transfer a unit from one branch of the Army to another, for example, from infantry to armor. Such a move always requires a redesignation, with the unit adopting the name of its new branch; however, there is no break in the historical continuity of the unit. If the unit is active, it must also be reorganized under a new table of organization and equipment (TOE).

DEMOBILIZE. To remove the designation of a unit from the official rolls of the Army. If the unit is active, it must also be inactivated. This term is used in unit lineages only when referring to the period during and immediately after World War I. (For other periods, see DISBAND.)

DESIGNATION. The official title of a unit, consisting usually of a number and a name.

DISBAND. To remove the designation of a unit from the official rolls of the Army. If the unit is active, it must also be inactivated.

ELEMENT. A unit that is assigned to or part of a larger organization. (See also ORGANIC ELEMENT.)

INACTIVATE. To place a unit that is not currently needed in an inoperative status without assigned personnel or equipment. The unit's designation, however, is retained on the rolls of the Army, and it can be reactivated whenever needed. Its personnel and equipment are reassigned to one or more active units, but its organizational properties and trophies are put in storage. When the unit is activated again, it is assigned new personnel and equipment, but it keeps its old history, honors, and organizational properties and trophies. This term has been used only since 1921. Before that time, units either remained active or were removed from the rolls of the Army.

ORDER INTO ACTIVE MILITARY SERVICE. To place an Army Reserve unit on full-time active duty usually during a war or a major crisis, such as the Berlin crisis of 1961–62. After completing its active duty, the unit may be inactivated or it may be released from active military service, reverting to reserve status. This phrase does not apply to Army Reserve units on annual active duty training.

ORGANIC ELEMENT. A unit that is an integral part of a larger organization, for example, a lettered company of a battalion or regiment.

ORGANIZE. To assign personnel and equipment to a unit and make it operative, that is, capable of performing its mission.

RECONSTITUTE. To restore to the official rolls of the Army a unit that has been disbanded or demobilized. The reconstituted unit may have a new designation, but it retains its former history, lineage, and honors.

REDESIGNATE. To change a unit's official name or number or both. Redesignation is a change of title only; the unit's history, lineage, and honors remain the same. Active as well as inactive units can be redesignated, but personnel and equipment of an active unit are not changed unless it is reorganized at the same time.

REORGANIZE. To change the structure of a unit in accordance with a new table of organization and equipment (TOE), or to change from one type of unit to another within the same branch of the Army, for example, from mechanized to airborne infantry. (For reorganizations involving a new branch, see CONVERT.) When referring to the Army National Guard, however, this term also means to organize an active unit again.

TRANSFER LESS PERSONNEL AND EQUIPMENT. To move a unit from one place to another without its personnel and equipment. The transfer is, therefore, merely a move on paper. The unit is usually reorganized at its new location with newly assigned personnel and equipment, but it retains its own lineage, honors, and organizational properties and trophies. The original personnel and equipment are reassigned to one or more units.

ARMY LINEAGE SERIES

Published Volumes
Armor-Cavalry, Part I: Regular Army and Army Reserve
Infantry, Part I: Regular Army

Tentative List of Future Volumes
Air Defense Artillery
Armies and Corps
Armor-Cavalry, Part II: Army National Guard
Aviation
Divisions and Separate Brigades
Engineers
Field Artillery
Infantry, Part II: Army Reserve and Army National Guard
Medical
Service and Support Organizations
Signal and Military Police

425-618 O - 72 - 60

Unit Index